Thomas Grant QC is a practising barrister and author. His first book, *Jeremy Hutchi~~~ ~'s C ~istories* was a *Sunday Times* bestseller.

Praise for Thomas Grant

'Grant is a master at conveying the cut-and-thrust of cross-examination . . . His style is drily witty, but just when you start to think he is a bit too detached . . . he soars into a rhetorical flight'   *Sunday Telegraph*

'Grant brings out the essence of each case . . . with clarity and wit'
Ben Macintyre, *The Times*

'Grant brilliantly recaptures the tensions and drama of some of the most seminal Old Bailey criminal trials'   *Evening Standard*

'First rate . . . Grant doesn't put a foot wrong'   *Standpoint*

'Grant writes with . . . style and fluency . . . He makes judicious use of his rich material'   *Times Literary Supplement*

'Grant's book is clearly and elegantly written'
Dominic Sandbrook, *Literary Review*

'Grant recounts these trials in limpid prose which clarifies obscurities'
Richard Davenport-Hines, *Guardian*

Court Number One, The Old Bailey

The Trials and Scandals that Shocked Modern Britain

THOMAS GRANT

JOHN MURRAY

In memory of Jeremy Hutchinson QC
Never to be forgotten

And to my brother, Alex Grant

First published in Great Britain in 2019 by John Murray (Publishers)
An Hachette UK company

This paperback edition published in 2020

1

Part-title illustrations by Martin Millard

A CIP catalogue record for this title is available from the British Library

Paperback ISBN 978-1-47365-163-0
eBook ISBN 978-1-47365-162-3

Typeset in Bembo by Palimpsest Book Production Limited, Falkirk, Stirlingshire
Printed and bound in Great Britain by Clays Ltd, Elcograf S.p.A.

John Murray policy is to use papers that are natural,
renewable and recyclable products and made from wood grown in
sustainable forests. The logging and manufacturing processes are expected to
conform to the environmental regulations of the country of origin.

John Murray (Publishers)
Carmelite House
50 Victoria Embankment
London EC4Y 0DZ

www.johnmurraypress.co.uk

Contents

Court Number One, The Old Bailey   1

PART I: Spectacle

1. The Camden Town Murder: *R v Wood (1907)*   23
2. 'The Cult of the Clitoris': *R v Billing (1918)*   60

PART II: Glamour

3. Unnatural Practices*: R v Fahmy (1923)*   95
4. Poor Little Rich Girl: *R v Barney (1932)*   123

PART III: War

5. Haw-Haw: *R v Joyce (1945)*   143

PART IV: Gloom

6. 'Christie done it': *R v Evans (1950)*   177
7. 'It is obvious that when I shot him I intended to kill him': *R v Ellis (1955)*   210

PART V: Politics

8. 'Equipment for a spy': *R v Martelli (1963)*   247
9. 'Trial of the Century': *R v Thorpe (1979)*   268
10. 'No apologies and no regrets': *R v Randle and Pottle (1991)*   313

PART VI: Grief

11. 'There is no greater task for the criminal justice
    system than to protect the vulnerable':
    R v Huntley and Carr (2003)   345

*Appendix I: The Old Bailey – A Brief History from
1907*   377
*Appendix II: The Criminal Trial by His Honour Judge
Edward Bindloss*   389

Acknowledgements   403
Illustration Credits   405
Notes   407
Select Bibliography   417
Index   425

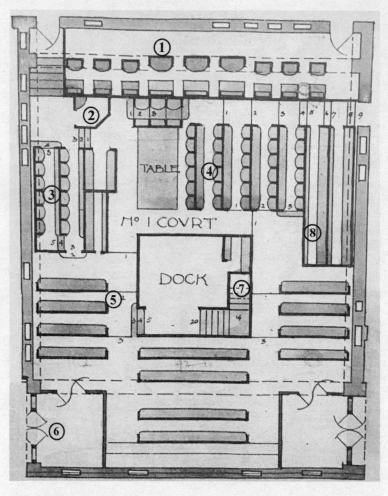

Plan of Court Number One from an architectural drawing created during the construction of the new Old Bailey.

1. Judge's chair
2. Witness box
3. Jury box
4. Counsel's rows
5. Press benches
6. Main entrance
7. Staircase from cells below
8. Benches of the former City Lands Committee

Court Number One, The Old Bailey

IT IS SEPTEMBER 2018 at the Central Criminal Court in the City of London, known to all as the Old Bailey. Court Number One, the largest of the four courts that give off from the marble Grand Hall of the original Edwardian building, is softly humming with the sound of multiple computer monitors, oblong monoliths that populate the room in front of the various teams of lawyers. Two larger screens look down from the judge's bench for the benefit of the press and the public. They all flicker simultaneously into life to reveal a new document, summoned up by a woman sitting with a look of concentration at the vast table in the well of the courtroom. It is day seven of the Westminster Terror Inquests, an exhaustive examination of the circumstances in which four civilians and one police officer were all fatally injured in the space of eighty-two seconds on 22 March 2017. Khalid Masood, a convert to jihadist Islamism, drove a car along Westminster Bridge, mounting the pavement and indiscriminately targeting pedestrians. Having crashed the car into railings on the north side of the river, close by the iconic Elizabeth Tower that houses Big Ben, Masood ran through the gates leading into New Palace Yard, where he stabbed to death PC Keith Palmer. Shortly afterwards he was shot dead by another policeman.

Jonathan Hough QC, counsel to the coroner, stands in the front row examining a police officer in the witness box. Hough, a veteran of many public enquiries, is businesslike and undramatic. His job is not to score points or put a case, but to lead out evidence efficiently and fairly. His Honour Judge Mark Lucraft QC, the Chief Coroner, sits at his desk making careful notes. The police officer gives his evidence confidently and precisely. Counsel's benches are filled with lawyers, each representing interested parties: the Metropolitan Police, the families of victims, the security services. For a courtroom built to try criminal cases this is a new departure. In the jury box sit some of the relatives of those who died. The dock is occupied, perhaps uniquely in the long history of Court Number One, not by defendants on trial, but by journalists – there must be ten today – intently following the proceedings. There are some 45,000 documents gathered together on the court computer system, each uniquely numbered. The atmosphere is one of a profoundly serious joint endeavour to arrive at an understanding of precisely what happened, why it happened, and what lessons can be learned to prevent such a thing happening again. Sitting as a spectator in a corner I am overwhelmed by the majesty of the law and of the courtroom in which its processes are being practised.

The wooden dock where the journalists are seated is largely unchanged from when the 'new' Old Bailey was opened in 1907. Looking at that dock it is hard not to think of the disparate people it has temporarily housed over the preceding decades. In that space have sat Ian Huntley and Maxine Carr, Barry George, Colin Stagg, Dennis Nilsen, Peter Sutcliffe, Jeremy Thorpe, John Stonehouse, members of the so-called Angry Brigade, Jonathan Aitken, the Kray Twins, Stephen Ward, Dr John Bodkin Adams, Ruth Ellis, John Christie, Timothy Evans, Neville Heath, William Joyce, Edith Thompson, George 'Brides in the Bath' Smith, Frederick Seddon and Dr Crippen, to name just a few of the more or less famous or infamous people – some guilty, some not – who have faced trial there over the last hundred and more years.

The proceedings taking place in Court Number One now, in 2018, hold an unforgiving mirror up to our age, just as dozens of earlier trials have done before. This is a book about this courtroom, about some of the people who have appeared in it, whether as defendant, counsel or judge, and about the practice of criminal law. It is also intended to be about British sensibilities and preoccupations over the last hundred years. It is one of the contentions of this book that through the criminal trials that have occurred in Britain's foremost court there can be traced at least one version of the history of social and moral change over the last century.

In one sense a court is simply a space bordered by four walls and laid out with internal fixtures. In the case of Court Number One the faintly ecclesiastical furnishings can be, to those who have come to watch justice being done, intrusive. The author Sybille Bedford, writing in 1957, thought that as 'an auditorium it boasts some drawbacks. For one thing it is cramful of woodwork. Stained oak obstructs foot and eye. Boxes, desks, tables, benches fitted ingeniously enough, jut at all angles.' Three years later Bedford sat through the *Lady Chatterley's Lover* trial. Like many journalists before and after her she again struggled to hear what was being said or to see the action. 'Number One is the largest courtroom in the building, which does not mean it is not fairly cramped and small. It uncomfortably holds two hundred people.' Sylvia Plath was also at the *Chatterley* trial and she too thought the 'famous' Court Number One (as she put it) was small and jammed (though she reported in a letter that she had enjoyed her day out 'immensely'). But for all its archaic inconveniences Court Number One is magnificent and its configuration is heavy with meaning and symbolism.

We start at the centre, the dock, which dominates the courtroom. Bulky and vast, it is like an impregnable fortress, a room within a room, measuring some sixteen feet by fourteen feet. It interferes with sightlines; it tells all present that the business of the court is inexorably directed at the person or persons it contains, referred to for much of the twentieth century as 'the prisoner', now known more neutrally as 'the defendant'. It also seems to set the defendant at an initial disadvantage; the presumption of innocence that the person accused of a crime enjoys seems at odds with the grandeur of this palladium that pens them in. Defendants can take a rather more jaundiced view of their enclosure. To Jonathan Aitken, tried (and acquitted) in Court Number One in 1971 in the so-called *Sunday Telegraph* secrets case, it looked and felt like 'a rather run-down municipal swimming-baths'. It can easily accommodate ten or more occupants (in one case a plan identifying the position in the dock of each of the defendants had to be pinned to its panelled wall to assist the jury). A single defendant can look lost. This is John Vassall, the Soviet spy, recalling his trial in 1962:

> When I was called up the steps to the Number 1 Court at the Old Bailey, I found a hushed court room; the only sound was the hum of the central heating. My little corner was so small I hardly felt that I appeared on the stage of life at all . . . The atmosphere was so quiet that one might have been in the Athenaeum Club. There was only Lord Parker sitting on the bench, and he gave no sign of what he was thinking. I felt absolutely insignificant.

Sybille Bedford noted a similar ambience a year later when she attended the trial of Dr Stephen Ward:

> The day began in the atmosphere peculiar to sensational trials in England: queues, excitement, gaping crowds, police outside; coolness and almost humdrum calm in court. Applications argued and dismissed in low legal mutter. A jury called, sworn in, eleven men and one woman, two rows

of uncommitted faces, the product of some unobtrusive mills of fate. Dr Ward is suddenly perceived in the enormous dock. One sees that he looks young, slight, with a vulnerable face . . . He looks classless, displaced, and uncomfortably human . . . he strikes one as the only lay-figure.

The defendant accesses the dock, always after the court is assembled and the judge is in place, via hidden steps that emerge out of the bowels of the Old Bailey, which contain a warren of cells holding defendants who that morning will have been brought from nearby prisons to attend their trial or some other hearing. It is a shock to those defendants to come up into the light and find themselves almost the last arrived component of a trial. Here is Jonathan Aitken again:

> The scene that greeted the three defendants as we walked up into the dock from the cells was strangely theatrical. The judge Mr Justice Caulfield was being bowed into his judicial throne by an escort consisting of the Lord Mayor of London in full regalia and two City Aldermen wearing gold chains and fur robes. This procession was led by a sword bearer holding aloft the sword of Justice . . . The judge, who was carrying the black cap and a nosegay of flowers, then took his seat, after exchanging bows with the twelve bewigged barristers in the case.

The defendant must then sit on the seat at the front of the dock facing the judge's bench, almost at eye level with the judge some twenty-five feet away, across the well of the court. Defendant and judge are raised above the other participants in the court process. On three sides of the dock there is a reinforced glass surround, the low panel at the front more recently installed; but a sufficiently determined person could easily vault over it (and some have, in one celebrated example rushing to attack the prosecutor rather than the judge). This lack of security has limited Court Number One's utility in more recent decades as the fare of the Old Bailey has shifted from the traditional criminal motivations to offences of ideology. Most Irish republican, and more recently Islamist and extreme right-wing terrorism cases are tried in nearby Court Number Two, or the newer courts added in the 1970s, whose docks are entirely enclosed by toughened glass.

To the judge's left and the defendant's right are counsel's rows, running perpendicular to the dock and the judge's bench. The advocates position themselves in rows of green leather seats built into the bench behind. Like the chairs in a theatre stall, they can be flipped up; like misericords in a cathedral they can be leaned against. The barristers have a narrow wooden desk on which to place their papers and lectern. Prosecution and defence counsel occupy the same row; the prosecutor closest to the judge, the defence closest to the dock, where counsel can easily consult with their client. Behind counsel there are rows of benches raking up to the outer wall, reserved for what used to be known as the City Lands Committee of the Corporation of London. What this means in practice is that in big trials they are allocated to City dignitaries, those with connections, or underemployed members of the Bar, interested in viewing the proceedings at close hand, segregated from hoi polloi like the privileged in the Royal Enclosure at Ascot. In especially sensational cases of the past these benches – the stalls of Court Number One as it were – were often crowded with the prurient or the merely curious. The courtroom could seem like part of the London social season. When Frederick Bywaters and Edith Thompson went on trial in December 1922 for the murder of Edith's husband one spectator thought that the atmosphere resembled the opening night of a West End play. As we will see, the metaphor of the theatre is constantly employed in accounts of trials in the twentieth century.

When counsel stand to address the judge they must crane their heads round to their right. If they look straight ahead they see the fourth side of the internal square that makes up the dramatic vortex of the courtroom: the so-called jury box, in fact two enclosed rows, one behind the other, accommodating six jurors each. The reason for this priority of communication is clear: for counsel the members of the jury are the most significant people in the criminal courtroom. All the business of this court is directed ultimately to the task of persuasion. The judge, up on a dais to the right of counsel, acts as umpire. But the final arbiters of fact and guilt are the twelve randomly selected men and women sitting ringside. Judges sometimes complain to counsel that when they are making a submission notionally addressed to the bench they are actually looking straight ahead, eyes heavy with implication, at the jury. This is not for fear of a cricked neck.

The raised bench runs the full width of the courtroom. Behind it the woodwork becomes elaborate and imposing: there is a large Palladian broken pediment flanked by double Corinthian pilasters, as if classical grandeur were synonymous with the doing of justice. It has a number of high-backed chairs – they are more like thrones – arrayed in a row with desks in front of each. The chairs sit on runners to ease the accommodation of the judicial posterior: the art for the court usher is to push it forward on its tram tracks, like a practised *maître d'hôte*, just as the judge bends the knee. The chair in the very centre, dignified by Edward VII's coat of arms and, at least in the past, the Sword of Justice on the wall behind, generally lies empty.[1] It is a peculiarity of Court Number One that the judge must sit off-centre, for the middle chair is reserved for the Lord Mayor, who will generally only exercise his ancient prerogative at the formal opening of the Old Bailey session. The other chairs are for the sheriff and City aldermen who in the past, when judicial dignity was set at a high premium, would process into the courtroom with the judge, like attendant lords swelling the scene. Occasionally in the past, other judges used to come to watch the proceedings from the bench. It was even known for judicial wives (and of course it was then only wives, not husbands) to sit on the bench. Jeremy Hutchinson, junior counsel for Penguin Books in the *Lady Chatterley's Lover* trial, was surprised to see Lady Byrne sitting beside her husband, Mr Justice Byrne, glaring disapprovingly throughout the trial, as if willing the jury to convict.

The judge's arrival is presaged by three heavy raps at a door at the far corner of the bench. The words 'Be upstanding in Court!' ring out, followed by a rhetorical formulation that changes every so often in a forlorn effort to keep up with the times. (It is now 'All persons who have anything to do before my Lords and Ladies the Queen's Justices at the Central Criminal Court draw near and give your attendance. God Save the Queen.') The words 'and Ladies' are a recent and well-made addition. Today of the thirteen full-time Bailey judges six are women. Sybille Bedford describes what happens next: 'The Judge came on swiftly. Out of the side-door, an ermined puppet progressing weightless along the bench, head held at an angle, an arm swinging, the other crooked under cloth and gloves, trailing a wake of subtlety, of secret powers, age; an Elizabethan shadow gliding across the arras.'

In a corner of this internal square, between the jury box and the bench, is the witness box. To approach it a witness has to walk into the well of the court, the jury to the left, the large 'Treasury Table' which divides jurors from counsel to the right (where in the past the exhibits were kept), and then up a short flight of steps. The witness stands – they may even be invited to sit – at conversational distance from the judge and facing counsel. It is one of the peculiarities of the configuration of Court Number One that the jury cannot see the witness distinctly. From the jury box the witness is visible only in profile.

Some writers have been surprised at Court Number One's supposed smallness. It is as if they half expected the most important courtroom of the Old Bailey to be akin to an auditorium. But there is an intimacy in the interplay between the various participants in an English criminal trial which size would tend to undermine. Cross-examination cannot be conducted by megaphone. Witnesses should not have to raise their voice. Ludovic Kennedy, who sat through the trial of Stephen Ward in 1963, observed the tight circle created by the players. Yet he also complained about the exclusion of those outside that circle. Journalists can sit on rows to either side of the dock. Even from here sightlines are interrupted by all the stage scenery. A theatre might call them 'restricted view seats'. And when there is a big show many have to sit on benches directly behind the dock, severed entirely from the epicentre of the court. From this place of ostracism Kennedy struggled to hear and see the action. And what action it was! The evidence of Christine Keeler and Mandy Rice-Davies at Stephen Ward's trial on charges of living off (their) immoral earnings, was given with an insouciance which was unlike anything ever heard in an English criminal court. It was as if a new register was being forged in Court Number One:

> MERVYN GRIFFITHS-JONES [prosecuting counsel]: Did you have intercourse with other men at the flat?
>
> MANDY RICE-DAVIES [nonchalant]: With Peter Rachman.
>
> GRIFFITHS-JONES: With anyone else?
>
> RICE-DAVIES: Douglas Fairbanks.
>
> GRIFFITHS-JONES: Anyone else?
>
> RICE-DAVIES: A boyfriend of mine.
>
> GRIFFITHS-JONES: Were you paid by anyone?
>
> RICE-DAVIES: No. Except Rachman. He kept me. I had a weekly allowance . . .
>
> RICE-DAVIES: Stephen said he had friends everywhere . . .
>
> GRIFFITHS-JONES: What were the friends going to do for you?
>
> RICE-DAVIES [grinning]: They're always useful, aren't they? They could be financially useful . . .
>
> JUDGE: If you were to receive financial help from such people, what was to be the quid pro quo? [Rice-Davies leaning forward smiling but not fully understanding the question.] Do you understand what I mean?
>
> RICE-DAVIES: No.
>
> JUDGE: What were you going to give for what you were getting financially?
>
> RICE-DAVIES: Oh. Sex I suppose.

As the eye looks up, patinated woodwork gives way to white walls. Four arches then support a huge circular skylight. In the past this allowed in daylight; now, sadly, the multiple panes of glass making up the circle are translucent rather than transparent and also admit electric light from fittings concealed above. Just below this is the public gallery, accessed by an entirely separate entrance, jutting out over part of the courtroom, and cut off from the drama beneath. Here, in the upper circle as it were, thirty or so members of the public can come to get a glimpse of justice at work. In most of the trials considered in this book that glimpse was hard-won. Over the last century newspapers have unerringly reported the patient (and sometimes not so patient) queues that formed outside the side door of the Bailey, on Newgate Street, which leads to the public galleries of the original courts in the Edwardian building. It is as if their length and the timing of their formation serve as a barometer to the significance of what is shortly to take place within. Sometimes the queue starts at four o'clock in the morning, sometimes as early as two. Sometimes it forms the evening before, as if it were made up of hardy bargain-hunters bivouacked outside a department store for the first day of the sales. 'I got here at one. It was a lovely night. I had a nice four hours' kip on the pavement. Bar accidents I'm in,' Ludovic Kennedy was told on the day Christine Keeler was due to give evidence in the Stephen Ward trial. Below privilege, above democracy, he thought. During the early part of the twentieth century it was not unknown for individuals to take up their place in the queue with a view to selling it on; the going rate in the Bywaters and Thompson trial was £5, then a princely sum.

Throughout much of the twentieth century cases tried in Court Number One held a mesmeric attraction for the public. The principal courtroom of the Old Bailey, itself the most important criminal court in England, invariably hosted the most significant trials. It was to Court Number One that red-robed High Court judges would come down from the Royal Courts of Justice in the Strand at the beginning of each session to try the heaviest fare. George Orwell noted in his essay 'Decline of the English Murder', the English are very good at crime, and murder in particular.[2] He might have added that the English are also very good at trials. As John Mortimer once put it, his tongue only partially in his cheek: 'High among the great British contributions to world civilisation, the plays of Shakespeare, the full breakfast, the herbaceous border and the presumption of innocence, must rank our considerable achievement in having produced most of the best murder trials in the long history of crime.'

Putting aside the question of its fairness or otherwise, the English adversarial trial is the perfect platform for ritualising and dramatising the quotidian. Throughout much of the twentieth century a major criminal trial was a public event. It would fill the newspapers (in his memoirs the great advocate Sir Patrick Hastings – whom I write about in Chapter 4 – noted that 'when the courts were closed, the papers were half-empty, and people knew that the silly season had arrived: something was missing from their daily lives. And how right they were'). It would dominate saloon-bar and drawing-room conversation alike. When the public gallery was full to bursting, a big case would often attract huge crowds that would form and mill on the street outside the Bailey. The photograph on the front cover of this book shows the scene when, having given evidence in the Ward trial, Christine Keeler and Mandy Rice-Davies left the Old Bailey, in festive air, on 22 July 1963, jostled by the rubber-neckers and the press photographers. It is a paradigm image of the Old Bailey's centrality to the public consciousness. There might be nothing to see, other than the hope perhaps of a momentary glimpse of an acquitted defendant, or some glamorous witness, emerging from court, yet somehow proximity to where something significant was occurring, or had occurred, was its own justification and its own reward. 'Well, mister, it's life, ain't it?' one member of the crowd told a journalist to explain his presence outside the Bailey at one trial. But this was not quite right. A criminal trial could transfigure the ordinary into the extraordinary. The defendants in the dock were objects of fascination. Their supposed crimes had set them apart from the common run of humanity; they were now participating in a great drama. A kind of enhanced reality was being enacted. And once it was over the trial and its participants would pass into the great repository of collective memory we might call the national consciousness. Momentous and tragic stories of humanity *in extremis* were written at the Old Bailey. They became part of a modern folklore.

The weight of history suffuses Court Number One. When Jonathan Aitken sat in the dock in 1971 he thought of the 'roll call of dishonour' of those who had preceded him: 'Dr Crippen, Lord Haw-Haw, Christie, Blake, Haigh, the Kray Brothers and the Hoseins'.[3] Many such lists can be made. Ludovic Kennedy, at the trial of Stephen Ward in 1963, also thought atavis-tically of the past: 'Thompson and Bywaters, Hatry[4] and Bottomley,[5] Evans and Christie, Birkett, Hastings and Marshall Hall are amongst its ghosts.' That Kennedy referred to barristers as well as those who had been in the dock reflects the fact that the mythology of the Old Bailey includes its celebrated counsel as well as those who have gone on trial. The later decades have added further names, both famous and infamous.

I doubt there is any court anywhere in the world that has a name that is more than a mere designation. Court Number One has its own identity. When a trial takes place here reportage is invariably prefaced with the words 'in the historic' or 'in the famous' Court Number One. It is no coincidence that the first published Rumpole story was set in Court Number One. When Billy Wilder filmed *Witness for the Prosecution* in 1957 he had an exact replica of Court Number One constructed, at huge cost, in Hollywood. It is not just a backdrop; it seems to invest significance and dignity to the proceedings. No other courtroom can claim such a monopoly on the key moments of a nation's recent history. This is not simply to say that − as is the case − the most celebrated trials of the last hundred and more years took place in this courtroom. The English have the knack of confecting cases that seem to involve more than the mere determination of guilt or absence of guilt (an acquitted defendant is not found 'innocent', simply 'not guilty'). The trial of William Joyce in 1945 had a quality of atonement to it; the quietness and outward fairness of the proceedings were a rebuke to the philosophy he espoused. The trial of Ruth Ellis in 1955, and her subsequent execution, profoundly affected the public consciousness and played its part in altering its view on the death penalty. The prosecution of Penguin Books in the *Lady Chatterley's Lover* trial in 1960 is credited, with some justification, with ushering in a moral and social revolution. The 1971 *Sunday Telegraph* secrets case resulted in the reform of Britain's secrecy laws. The fact that in 1979 Jeremy Thorpe was found not guilty here seems irrelevant now; the trial, not the verdict, signalled his destruction.

And for those, like me, who are thrilled to know that Mary Queen of Scots once slept in *this* particular room, or that Charles Dickens wrote *Great Expectations* in *this* particular house, who believe in the transporting power of place, Court Number One is a magical space. One looks around the courtroom: it is there in that witness box that in the *Lady Chatterley* trial Richard Hoggart spoke of the cleansing power of D.H. Lawrence's use of the word 'fuck'; it is just there in counsel's row that Richard Muir stood up to open the prosecution of Crippen; it is a little further along where Jeremy Hutchinson performed his extraordinary thumb gesture when cross-examining Mary Whitehouse's myopic solicitor in the *Romans in Britain* trial and where Marshall Hall made his 'scales of justice' speech on behalf of Seddon; it is there in that dock that Stephen Ward listened to the judge's summing-up and concluded that he would rather die by his own hand that night than await an unjust verdict; it was on that staircase leading down to the cells that Edith Thompson desperately screamed out her innocence after sentence of death had been pronounced upon her.

When a particular place links the present with the past then the sense of the passage of time can be suspended. Even more so when that place remains largely unaltered. Before courtroom photography was banned in 1925 a number of photographs of Court Number One were taken from the public gallery. There are surviving photographs from the trials of Robert Wood, Frederick Seddon and Dr Crippen. Looking at them now and comparing them with the present courtroom is a giddy experience. Over a period of more than a century, while the world at large has undergone a scale of transformation unparalleled in human history, virtually nothing has changed. Even the inkwells on the little plinth at the front of the dock, visible in the photographs, look now exactly as they did. Counsel's wigs and gowns are as they were; the judicial robe is virtually as it was. All that seems to have changed is the introduction of some discreet computer screens and less formality in jurors' clothing. (Here is Brian Masters at the start of the trial of the serial murderer Dennis Nilsen in 1983: 'There were eight men and four women, dressed unspectacularly in jeans and shirt-sleeves, crumpled suits or skirts and jumpers, collectively an eloquent demonstration that the ultimate decision rests in law with twelve ordinary men and women of the world. They might have walked off the street, their very incongruity in the awesome surroundings of Court Number 1 acting as a kind of reassurance.') This sense of continuity is an apt metaphor for the majesty of the law and its processes. Yet it is also deceptive. The practice of law in Court Number One, as in every other criminal courtroom in England has, over the same span of years, undergone a revolution. A criminal trial now is a lot fairer and more humane than it was in 1907, or even in 1983.

Court Number One's status as a kind of national cockpit began to wane towards the end of the twentieth century as its inconveniences in a paper-heavy, computerised, security-conscious age drove judges to other courts at the Old Bailey to try the biggest cases. (I discuss this in Chapter 11.) Its years of ascendancy coincided with what might be described as the golden age of English crime. Perversely, the excitement of a criminal trial can be inversely proportionate to its fairness, both as to ensuring the acquittal of the innocent and the conviction of the guilty. Elderly barristers sometimes look back with a degree of nostalgia to a time before DNA profiling, ubiquitous CCTV, and taped police interviews. These advances have to some extent removed the potential for uncertainty and curtailed the rhetorical deployment of doubt, the defending criminal barrister's stock-in-trade. I do not mean to be flippant when I say that while scientific advances and increases in legal protections have enhanced the integrity of the criminal trial as a mechanism to achieve a just result, they have diminished its aesthetic or narrative appeal.

Two other factors also combined to bring to an end that golden age of courtroom dramatics. First, the abolition of the death penalty in 1965 removed, at a stroke, much of the tension in murder trials. A historian of the Old Bailey wrote, with distasteful accuracy, that 'Once the black cap became a museum piece and the prospect of a hanging had finally gone, spectators in the public gallery and newspaper readers had a distinct sense of *coitus interruptus*, like a bull fight without the kill.' Second, the liberalisation of the divorce laws removed much of the motivation to middle-class homicide. So many of the great murders of the twentieth century, and before, occurred because there was seen to be no other realistic way of ending a miserable marriage or starting a new life with a lover. Yet it is possible to celebrate an era while welcoming the changes that brought it to an end. There is a third factor which has diminished the importance of not only Court Number One but of the Old Bailey generally as a public crucible. Fifty years ago there were seven Press Association reporters at the Old Bailey and all the major newspapers had their own journalists semi-permanently there. That presence is now almost gone. Trials are simply not reported in the way they used to be. Most of the Old Bailey's proceedings are no longer relayed to the public.[6]

When he was writing his memoirs in the late 1940s Patrick Hastings remembered the Old Bailey as a place of undiluted melancholy. 'The whole atmosphere reeks of misery and squalor; it almost seems as though no human feeling could possibly exist within its walls, no hope, sympathy, nothing but indifference . . . England has been a civilised country for many centuries; to anyone who spends a day in the Central Criminal Courts, a reflection must arise as to whether civilisation has very much advanced.' While its Edwardian architecture is outwardly unchanged the Old Bailey of the twenty-first century is a very different place. There is enormous camaraderie among the barristers who practise here. One told me how he found a real sense of community at the modern Bailey, with Court Number One as its formal epicentre. The testy and acidic judges, many of whom feature in the chapters that follow, are now largely things of the past. Sentencing policy, which once was almost entirely arbitrary, has been rationalised and made more consistent. Whereas the victims of crimes, or their relatives, used to be largely ignored by the criminal justice system, they are now treated with tenderness and respect. Similarly witnesses, for whom giving evidence at the Bailey can be a traumatic experience, are provided support before and after their time in court by the Witness Service. As a court building the Bailey is also much more welcoming. The former Recorder of London, His Honour Judge Nicholas Hilliard QC, went out of his way to encourage visits from school and university students and community groups. He frequently held events in Court Number One for young people potentially at risk of getting caught up in knife or gang crime. The fathers of two boys who were stabbed to death in London often spoke; their words were as powerful as anything said by the advocates and judges of the past. A former sheriff founded a school debating challenge which took place in the courtroom. And every year *Trial and Error,* a medley of legal vignettes and songs, is put on in Court Number One, produced by a former Bailey judge, His Honour Peter Rook QC; it runs for four nights to packed houses and raises tens of thousands of pounds for the Old Bailey's own prisoner rehabilitation charity, the Sheriffs' and Recorder's Fund and Pan Intercultural Arts, a charity that assists formerly trafficked women. It is impossible to imagine this happening a hundred or even fifty years ago.

Still, the Old Bailey cannot escape the fact that its function is to try and sentence people who have committed sometimes appalling crimes and who are often both mentally vulnerable and very distressed by their ordeal. For all the excitement and drama of the trials I describe in the chapters that follow, it should not be forgotten that the Old Bailey remains – it cannot avoid being – a place of tragedy and trauma, for witnesses, victims and defendants alike. A guilty verdict or an acquittal can lead to terrible fights in the public galleries as supporters of the victim and the defendant clash. There can even be scraps in the dock as the recriminations start. In January 2020, after guilty verdicts were brought in on a gang-related murder, some of the five defendants were seen to be brawling in the dock. Their supporters started throwing seats from the public gallery and one even jumped down into the court below, only to be restrained by the athletic prosecutor, Oliver Glasgow QC.

Jonathan Aitken may hold a unique place in legal history for having been perhaps the only person ever to be tried twice in Court Number One for different offences (and certainly to have written books, published over thirty years apart, about each appearance). His first experience, as noted earlier, ended in triumphant acquittal. His second, when he was sentenced to eighteen months' imprisonment for perjury in 1999, saw the last act in the destruction of a glittering career. The book he wrote after his release, *Porridge and Passion*, recounts the day of his sentencing in painful detail, devoid of self-pity or any attempt at self-justification. It is as good an insight as any of the experience of being sentenced at the Old Bailey. Yet the most haunting passage relates to the time, after the hearing was over and Aitken had been taken down the steps of the dock, that he spent in the 'cage', the pen where defendants congregate before being returned to whichever prison awaits them. I quote from it at length, because it serves as a powerful counterweight to the 'upstairs' view of the Old Bailey that predominates in this book.

> For the best part of an hour I was in the cage. As its name suggests, this is an animalistic iron-barred enclosure, which holds the day's convicted and sentenced criminals from the courtrooms of the Old Bailey while they wait to be transported to their designated jails. I do not think I will ever forget the scene in the cage on that afternoon of 8 June 1999. It was a panorama of anger and despair. One young black prisoner was in such a fury that he kept charging the bars of the cage like a wild bull, battering himself over and over again until his head cut open and started to bleed. Elsewhere in the cage, three members of a gang were repeatedly kicking their fourth associate, apparently putting the blame on him for all their convictions as they were shouting, 'You got the script wrong! You effed up the effing script' . . . These scenes of aggression, furious though they were, somehow seemed sideshows in comparison with the overall atmosphere of the cage, which was one of catatonic gloom. Several heavily tattooed young men had their heads sunk into their hands. One or two of them were weeping. All seemed to be totally devastated . . . I thought it was the saddest environment I had ever been in during my life.

*

The literature of Court Number One is rich. The twentieth century saw the development of a discernible genre of trial writing, much of it spawned from cases tried there. Its leading literary exponents are Rebecca West, who wrote predominantly about the treason and spy cases of the 1940s to the 1960s in the original and revised versions of her classic *The Meaning of Treason* (the trials of Joyce, John Amery, Klaus Fuchs, the Krugers, George Blake and John Vassall all took place here), and Sybille Bedford, whose book about the trial in 1957 of Dr Bodkin Adams, *The Best We Can Do*, is generally regarded as the finest single-volume account of a criminal trial ever written. Bedford followed it up with a wonderful essay, *The Trial of Lady Chatterley's Lover*. Sadly, her essay on the Stephen Ward trial remains unpublished and she never wrote her planned account of Jeremy Thorpe's trial. (Fortunately Auberon Waugh produced his own richly ironic account, a classic that deserves resurrection: *The Last Word*.) Ludovic Kennedy's *10 Rillington Place* and *The Trial of Stephen Ward* also remain superbly readable, mixing close observation with tempered rage against the injustices of the court process. Very different writers they may be, but West, Bedford and Kennedy were all fascinated by the trial process not simply as the resolution of prior events, but as a subject in itself. This is the essence of trial writing.

Apart from overtly literary works, during the twentieth century there was an intermittent industry devoted to the publication of single-volume transcripts of famous trials, generally prefaced by a long introduction, mostly relating to trials that took place in Court Number One. The Notable British Trials series ran from 1905 to 1959 and produced eighty-three titles, including volumes on the trials of Robert Wood, William Joyce, and Evans and Christie, which have been invaluable sources for this book. Other similar ventures were attempted: there was a short-lived Old Bailey Trials series edited by C.E. Bechhofer Roberts, which ran in the 1940s, and a Celebrated Trials series edited by Jonathan Goodman had a brief flourishing in the 1970s. For a number of decades Penguin produced its own series of Famous Trials, drawing on the introductions to the earlier Notable British Trials. The Penguin editions sold in the hundreds of thousands. All these ventures were testament to the continuing fascination of the criminal trial to the reading public. This is to say nothing of the scores of books written about particular crimes, or alleged crimes, the investigations into which have eventually achieved a conclusion in Court Number One.

Writing in 1936 Basil Hogarth referred to the Camden Town murder case as the classic British criminal trial of the century (I write about it in Chapter 1). How, it may be asked, can a trial be 'classic'? And what is special about the English criminal trial? I have attempted an answer to the first question in the chapters that follow. As to the second, the answer is many-stranded. Courtroom ritual plays a significant part. The English trial was (and to an extent still is) marked by the flummery that attends its conventions: the stage business that sees the arrival into court of the judge, the eighteenth-century garb, the formality of address, the arraignment of the defendant. Yet the ritual extends beyond the antiquarian trappings. The trial itself is conducted according to strict rules;

things happen in accordance with procedures that may seem arcane to the uninitiated spectator. The sense of mystery is fortified by the highly regimented layout of the courtroom. As I have described earlier, the internal geography of Court Number One is, like all courtrooms from the same period, laden with symbolic significance. The nearest parallel is to a medieval church (the same royal arms adorn Church of England places of worship and courts). The overall impression on the spectator is of something out of the ordinary, something having an element of the sacred about it. This is not accidental.

Yet juxtaposed with the ritual elements of the courtroom and its processes are the human drama and sheer excitement of the trial. Here again there are many confluent elements. Any criminal trial involves the determination of the guilt or lack of it of the defendant. There are various ways of deciding guilt; the English criminal trial delegates that task to a lay jury of twelve men and women, randomly chosen, who deliver their unreasoned verdict after the trial has ended. The existence of the jury affects the trial itself. Counsel do not have to persuade a professional tribunal, and advocacy directed to a jury is a very different thing to advocacy to a judge. It is more emotive, more pointed, less stodgy; it is necessarily unburdened by dry and technical submissions of law. Great jury advocates must understand human motivations and be able to harness the power of language. The result is that overlaying the ritual is the demotic. Great jury speeches can be overwhelming; they have on occasion caused spectators and jurors to faint with emotion. One recent Old Bailey silk received a love letter accompanying a bottle of champagne from a juror in a trial in which he appeared. The premium set on advocacy pitched at a human level means that the advocate is a central figure in any trial. In the twentieth century some barristers acquired celebrity, even cult, status because of their courtroom performances and no account of the Old Bailey can exclude them as significant figures in their own right. In the chapters that follow I refer to many of the great counsel of the past.

There may well be a long delay as the jurors confer privately in the jury room. But everyone knows that, except when there is a hung jury, the trial will have a definite conclusion, and the sense of expectancy during the wait for the jurors' return to the courtroom to deliver their verdict can be stomach-churning, and not only for the defendant. Patrick Hastings described his feelings waiting for the return of the jury in capital cases:

I have never been able to free myself from the sense of horror which persists during the period in which a jury is considering its verdict. The prisoner has been taken down into the cells; the door through which the jury have passed is closed; until it opens, no one can ever guess what the result will be. At that moment there is a test which is almost infallible. If the jury look at the prisoner the verdict is NOT GUILTY; if they do not, the sentence is DEATH.

This is merely the last stage in the process. An English trial has an inexorable flow about it; step follows step within the court day, leading towards the inevitable conclusion of a verdict.

There is a further element. The English system places the burden of proof upon the prosecution. The prosecutor sets out to prove the defendant's guilt, the defence to controvert that proof. The result is a contest; two sides struggling against each other, albeit in accordance with strict rules. And at the heart of that struggle is perhaps the greatest contribution of the common law to justice, as well as to the aesthetics of a trial: the cross-examination. A well-constructed cross-examination can capsize a seemingly impregnable case. It can destroy an attractive defence. It can also be an extraordinary experience to watch. The frisson that must have rippled through Court Number One when Richard Muir asked the following questions of Dr Crippen in 1910 is still detectable on the page, more than a century on. Crippen's case was that he had last seen his wife alive in the morning of 1 February 1910, that he had not buried her body in the cellar, but that she had in fact left the house and travelled to America. He was undone by a series of short, simple questions.

MUIR: On the early morning of 1 February you were left alone in your house with your wife?
CRIPPEN: Yes.
MUIR: She was alive?
CRIPPEN: Yes.
MUIR: And well?
CRIPPEN: Yes.
MUIR: Do you know any person who has seen her alive since?
CRIPPEN: I do not.
MUIR: Do you know of any person in the world who has had a letter from her since?
CRIPPEN: I do not.

MUIR: Do you know of any person who can prove any fact showing that she ever left your house alive?

CRIPPEN: Absolutely not.

In the chapters that follow I have tried to bring to life some other cross-examinations that have occurred in Court Number One. I have also tried to identify the dangers of cross-examination as a vehicle of achieving justice: Timothy Evans was not the first, nor the last, vulnerable person to be destroyed by a clever lawyer. The result was that he was hanged for a crime of which he was not just 'not guilty', but indubitably innocent.

Most books about the Old Bailey involve a kind of whistle-stop tour of every great case tried there over the last 100 or 500 years (depending on whether one starts from the beginning or the building of the new court). A couple of breathless paragraphs will sketch the facts of the case; there will be an anecdote or two from the trial; perhaps a thumbnail sketch of the (to a greater or lesser extent monstrous) judge who presided; and then one is on to the next case.

I have never found this approach particularly satisfactory and have settled instead on a different one in this book. This is not a detailed account of the Old Bailey (though Appendix I contains a brief history for those who are interested). Nor is it an account of all the great legal personalities who have come to the Old Bailey (though a number are mentioned). I have instead chosen eleven trials that took place in Court Number One over the span of about a hundred years, from 1907, the year the current Old Bailey opened its doors, to the beginning of the twenty-first century. My selection is roughly evenly spread over the decades, the gaps getting wider as Court Number One's predominance gradually waned towards the end of the century. My selection is not intended to be representative of the usual run of cases that the Old Bailey tries, most of which, even in Court Number One, are workaday, of interest only to those involved in them. In each chapter I have started outside the courtroom and traced the events and influences that have led to the doors of Court Number One. A trial is not hermetically sealed. It is the culmination of a chain of human actions and choices, some less freely made than others, that have occurred in real life. I have also tried to recreate some of the tension and excitement of the trials themselves, conscious always that the words spoken in a trial are not part of a disembodied colloquium. I have sought to ensure that the physicality of the courtroom itself is always in view. Although each chapter is centred on a particular trial, it is not confined to it.

The subtitle to this book is 'The Trials and Scandals that Shocked Modern Britain'. I have taken an expansive view of the word 'modern', treating its reach as coterminous with the age of the courtroom. Some of the trials I have written about remain very well known; others have faded from public memory. My criteria for inclusion are various. Each of the cases seems to me to embody some distinctive aspect of the age from which it emerged, whether because of its subject matter, because of the public response to the trial, or because of its consequences. Each imprinted itself on the psyche of the period. They are all enthralling. Some are horrifying, whether on account of the crime that was being tried or because of the injustice that was perpetrated by the trial process; others have elements of humour or absurdity. At times the grotesque shades uncomfortably into the comic. Not all the cases tried in Court Number One were (or are now) murder trials; and likewise many of the chapters that follow consider other crimes. I have attempted to show that the courtroom is not always a place of order or calm; sometimes pandemonium reigns. Nor is the courtroom always a place of rational and dispassionate thinking; often it is overborne by shameless rhetoric. I have also tried to show how the practice of criminal law does not exist in some parallel universe, detached from its surroundings. The language and values of the courtroom are conditioned, sometimes to a shocking extent and to the detriment of justice, by the world around it.

Of course this approach necessarily involves leaving much out. My putative chapter on the Bodkin Adams case had to be abandoned for lack of space. I longed to write about the Stephen Ward trial in greater depth (it is mentioned in Chapter 8), but ultimately decided that it had been covered sufficiently in other recent books. I have not included the *Lady Chatterley* or *Romans in Britain* trials largely because I have already written about them at length in an earlier book.

I have made a policy decision to omit cases notable principally for their ghoulishness. This is not intended to be a book about 'true crime'; hence there is no discussion of the trials of Neville Heath, Peter Sutcliffe (the 'Yorkshire Ripper') or Dennis Nilsen. I have also settled on a policy of omitting any cases that were tried in the next-door courts in the Bailey. This is a book entitled, and about, Court Number One. This has been a painful discipline: planned chapters on Helen Duncan, the last person tried for witchcraft; the Balcombe Street siege and other IRA trials; the *Oz* and *Last Exit to Brooklyn* obscenity trials; the *Gay News* blasphemy case; and the Clive Ponting case all had to be abandoned when I discovered that they were tried in neighbouring courts, even if they were only a few yards away. I felt that the integrity of the title had to be maintained.

There are two appendices at the end of the book. The first, as I have mentioned, is a thumbnail history of the Old Bailey. The second, written by His Honour Judge Edward Bindloss, is a short survey of the legal and procedural underpinnings of the criminal trial. The non-lawyer does not need to read it to understand the preceding chapters but will find it, I think, illuminating.

Thomas Grant
February 2020

PART I

Spectacle

Martin Millard

I

The Camden Town Murder

R v Robert Wood (1907)

THE SO-CALLED 'Camden Town murder' case, the first of any significance held in Court Number One of the newly rebuilt Old Bailey,
stands out not because of the identity of its victim, or of the defendant,
but because of the intricacy of the evidence presented by the prosecution,
the excitement of the trial and the personality of the barrister who
conducted the defence.[1] Writing in 1936, in his introduction to the Notable
British Trials volume on the case, Basil Hogarth described the Camden
Town murder as 'the classic British crime of this century'. The fact that
the crime involved the near-decapitation of a young woman as she slept
in her bed could be said to make this claim particularly distasteful. But
the British have always been able to savour a case without too much
concern for the horror of the underlying crime. A criminal trial can
acquire the characteristics of a novel or a play; the victim serves as the
anchor, their death reduced almost to a plot device; the characters
are introduced; they are placed in conflict and jeopardy; crucial facts are
introduced to create surprise or undermine assumptions; and there is a
resolution. Seen as a work of fiction or a theatrical performance the trial
of Robert Wood remains a masterpiece.

Yet the material from which this 'classic' was moulded was wretched.
The victim was a twenty-three-year-old part-time prostitute, murdered
in the early hours of 12 September 1907 in her bedroom in a quiet road
running through a then notoriously seedy part of London. She was
forgotten almost as soon as the case ended. The witnesses at the trial
were working-class men and women who spent their evenings in London's
public houses or music halls, whose lodgings were typically rented rooms
in boarding houses, and whose existence was as precarious as it was
transient. They emerge out of obscurity to have their words, uttered in
the witness box or taken down and read out by police officers, transcribed
for posterity before disappearing back into the fog of the past.

The most vivid figure who shines out from the transcript and who dominated the trial from beginning to end was the leading counsel for the defence, Edward Marshall Hall KC. In an age that lionised barristers he would go on to become its dominant legal personality. Blessed with a tall, athletic frame, good looks and a sonorous voice, Marshall Hall was 'not merely counsel', his later biographer enthused, but also 'detective, showman, rhapsodist, actor, friend and even father confessor'. Edward Marjoribanks's starry-eyed *Life of Sir Edward Marshall Hall* is itself the most famous legal biography ever written, and boyhood readings of it spurred many legal careers.[2] Yet Marshall Hall's style of advocacy was very different from that of most barristers, either then or now. While the courtroom technique of more conventional barristers was that of an 'interested observer . . . altogether aloof and apart from the tragedy', Marjoribanks explained, Marshall Hall succeeded by 'identifying himself with the central figure of the case, speaking as if the prisoner's thoughts, actions and impulses were his own'. 'When a client briefed him, he did not merely buy the lawyer or even the advocate in Marshall Hall, but the whole man. He had the gift of throwing his whole personality into the case: by the fire of his rhetoric he threw a cloak of romance and drama round the sorry figures in the dock, convincing the jury that he believed passionately in every word he said – and for the time being he did.' Sometimes he went further, physically re-enacting from counsel's row the circumstances in which his client had – in self-defence, of course – apparently struck the fatal blow or fired the deadly bullets.

'Become one of them. Get into the jury box with them. Make yourself the thirteenth juror,' was one of Marshall Hall's adages. Others included: 'I have to create an atmosphere' and 'Facts, not principles, for me. I don't know much law, but I can learn what there is to be known about men and women.'

Having been called to the Bar in the early 1880s the first turning point in his career occurred in 1894 when, on a ten-guinea brief fee, he used his closing speech at the Old Bailey trial of a middle-aged prostitute named Marie Hermann – the first murder case at which Marshall Hall led for the defence – to launch into a blistering attack on the building's squalor and inadequacy.[3] Marshall Hall's famous peroration – 'Look at her, gentlemen of the jury. Look at her. God never gave her a chance – won't you?' – possibly extemporised, apparently provoked a round of applause in the courtroom and got her acquitted of murder: Hermann only served six years for the manslaughter of her seventy-two-year-old client. In those days an acquittal obtained in the face of overwhelming evidence could alter the course of a barrister's career. Marshall Hall had arrived and his future fame seemed assured. In June 1898 he took silk at the tender age of thirty-nine.

In days when judges were generally feared for their acidity or ill-temper, Marshall Hall became notorious early on for showing them sarcasm or even 'naked insolence', several examples of which have entered legal folklore. 'Is your client [an Irish labourer] not familiar with the maxim *res ipsa loquitur*?'[4] Marshall Hall was once asked by a pompous judge. 'My lord, on the remote hillside in County Donegal where my client comes from, they talk of little else,' was his unimprovable reply. Armed with a knack for taking on colourful cases that were bound to attract press interest – including fraudulent palmists, bogus bankers and a doctor who allegedly used hypnosis to procure a widow to leave him her fortune in her will – Marshall Hall could also be a 'cynical self-publicist and a consummate manipulator'.[5] He did not always prevail of course, and he often exaggerated the strength of the prosecution case to increase the drama of an acquittal, or lessen the humiliation of defeat.

Yet despite his fame Marshall Hall was known above all as the 'Great Defender', who would courageously stand up for the poor, and save blameless men and women from the gallows. (After its introduction by the former Lord Chancellor, Lord Birkenhead, Marjoribanks's biography carries the dedication *Perditae* – to the lost ones.)[6] Able to command very high fees, he would still take low-paying briefs: he defended the 'Brides in the Bath' murderer for the miserable sum of 17 guineas. According to his most recent biographer, Marshall Hall 'almost single-handedly introduced compassion into the Edwardian legal system'. 'Those who heard him in action were transported: observers reported unbearable tension, muffled sobs, breathless attention, hysterics and ecstatic applause.'

The year 1907 is a curiously overlooked moment in British history. Sir Henry Campbell-Bannerman, Prime Minister from 1905 to 1908, must rank as the most obscure of twentieth-century premiers even though the Liberal Party he led achieved the biggest landslide in British political history in 1906. It was a time of national self-confidence and success; modernism, Irish Home Rule and the most militant elements of suffragism were some way off. The Labour Party had yet to become a serious force. The storm clouds of impending European conflict were still over the horizon. The British Empire was at its zenith and its capital, London, was the greatest city on earth. But for Marshall Hall the first months of

1907 were a low point in his career. A Conservative, he had lost his seat in Parliament to the Liberals the year before (for a good part of the century the Bar and politics were close bedfellows, with days spent in court followed by evenings in the Palace of Westminster). He had recently been heavily admonished by the Court of Appeal for his overly strident conduct of two trials; the bad publicity had led to a collapse both in his practice and his income. The forty-nine-year-old Marshall Hall, who had flown so high and was now sunk so low, badly needed a big, high-profile case to get his career back on track. In November 1907 that brief came, to defend at the Old Bailey a man charged with murder. The world of this murder could not have been further removed from his own.

The victim of what had almost instantaneously been dubbed the 'Camden Town murder' was called Emily Dimmock. A couple of years earlier she had met her common-law husband, Bertram Shaw, at the Rising Sun, a great Victorian drinking palace and one of Emily's regular haunts, situated on the Euston Road, midway between Euston and St Pancras stations, an area long notorious for prostitution. She had lived with Shaw since January 1907 and, after several moves, they had settled in two-room lodgings on the ground floor of 29 St Paul's Road in July.

Emily was then twenty-three, tall, slim and handsome. The one distinctive photograph of her that survives shows her skittishly dressed in a sailor suit. One can imagine her a character playing charades in an E.M. Forster novel. In fact she was firmly excluded from that world; the sailor suit had not been pulled from a dressing-up box but belonged to a former lover serving on HMS *Prince of Wales*. She had graduated from working in a straw-hat factory, to domestic service, to becoming a 'butterfly of the streets', to use one of the euphemisms so beloved of early twentieth-century writers.

Emily wore a ring on her fourth finger and to the world at large she and Bert (as Shaw was universally known) appeared to be married: otherwise no self-respecting landlady would have allowed them lodgings. Emily told her landlords, Mr and Mrs Stocks, that she was a dressmaker and that she and Bert had left their last lodgings because of noisy children nearby. In fact they had been thrown out because of Emily's work as a prostitute, for which the designation 'dressmaker' was a common cover.

Before starting to live with Bert, Emily had lived at a host of dreary lodgings around King's Cross and Camden Town, most of them known brothels. Yet she had promised Bert to renounce her former life after they started living as man and wife. Bert earned only 27 shillings a week as a dining-car attendant on the Midland Railway, but his overnight absences in Sheffield (he would go up on the evening train from St Pancras and return on the morning express) allowed Emily opportunities to carry on her old habits. Soon, under the more exotic *nom de guerre* of Phyllis, she was a regular once again in the public houses on and off Euston Road, allowing men to buy her a port and lemon and give her a penny or two to slot into the automatic gramophone, before taking them back to St Paul's Road after Mr and Mrs Stocks, who lived in the basement, were safely asleep. The money was good – Emily could take in a night more than half what Bert earned in a week – and provided a welcome supplement to his wage.

Emily's alleged murderer, Robert Wood, was described by Marjoribanks as 'a weedy little artist'. A contemporary drawing shows a man with a thin face and sunken, sensitive eyes. He had been born in Edinburgh in 1887, the son of a *Scotsman* compositor. His mother died soon afterwards and the family moved to London. Thanks to Robert's artistic talent he landed a job at the London Sand and Blast Manufacturing Company, whose name belied the delicacy of the art nouveau glassware it produced. There he rose steadily to the position of 'artistic designer'. To his friends, colleagues and family Robert Wood was universally known as gentle and good-natured, and he lived in apparent domestic harmony with his father and stepbrother at 12 Frederick Street, just off the Gray's Inn Road.

Yet beneath the veneer of respectability that Wood was careful to maintain, some form of *nostalgie de la boue* drew him in the evenings to the dives of the Euston Road. On one such evening, Friday, 6 September 1907, Wood went into the Rising Sun. According to Wood's later account Emily approached him and asked for a drink. A young boy entered the bar selling postcards, and Emily told Wood she wanted to buy one. Emily was taken up by the worldwide postcard craze, which was then at its height, and was an avid collector. Wood liked to pose as a high-minded aesthete and he dismissed the cards on sale as 'common and inartistic'. Instead he produced from his pocket a postcard of his own, a Mother and Child depiction he had bought on a recent holiday in Bruges. When Emily flirtatiously asked him to write her a message on it, Wood obliged, drawing a cartoon of a rising sun with a smiling face and writing around it, 'Phillis [*sic*] Darling, If it pleases you meet me 8.15pm at the [there followed the sketch of a rising sun]. Yours to a cinder, Alice.' Emily had apparently cautioned Wood against using his real name, for fear that Bert would see it.

According to Wood, they met again on the Saturday night by chance at the Eagle tavern on what is now Royal College Street, opposite Camden Town station.[7] Emily coquettishly chided him for not sending the postcard. Wood eventually put it into a letter box outside the British Museum late on Sunday evening and it was delivered on the Monday morning (such was the efficiency of the Edwardian postal service). When Wood walked into the Rising Sun at about 8.30 p.m. on the Monday Emily was there again; perhaps keeping the assignment requested by the postcard? She and Wood were later seen leaving at 8.45 p.m. and returning at about eleven: enough time, perhaps, for a visit to St Paul's Road. At around midnight Wood went home, leaving Emily to the company of another man, Robert Roberts, a ship's cook who was happily liquidating his savings from a recent voyage and had stayed over with Emily the previous night. He was apparently sufficiently satisfied with their encounter that he repeated the experience on both the Monday and Tuesday nights.

While Roberts was still in Emily's rooms at eight o'clock on the morning of Wednesday, 11 September another lodger, a widow called Alice Lancaster, pushed two letters under her door: an advertising circular from a ladies' tailor and a letter from one of Emily's many admirers. For some reason Emily showed the letter to Roberts, along with the 'rising sun' postcard she had received two days earlier. They bore the same handwriting. The letter she then burned in her grate. It had read in part, so Roberts later claimed, something along the lines of 'Dear Phyllis, Will you meet me at the bar of the Eagle at Camden Town 8.30 tonight Wednesday – Bert', words that broadly tallied with what was later deciphered by police from the charred remains.

That Wednesday afternoon, so Emily's landlady Mrs Stocks later claimed, she washed and ironed linen. Bert left for St Pancras at about 5 p.m. and, her domestic tasks completed, in the evening Emily went out, her hair still in curling pins. It was not the look of someone seeking a new customer. At about a quarter to nine she arrived at the Eagle, some 700 yards from her home but not a pub she frequented. A friend of Wood's, a bookseller's assistant called Joseph Lambert, by chance called into the Eagle shortly after. He saw Wood, who introduced him to Emily as a 'merry girlfriend', who in turn apologised for looking 'untidy'. A barmaid at the Eagle, Lillian Raven, later said that she had seen Wood and Emily in each other's company until at least half past nine.

In the late morning of Thursday, 12 September Bert Shaw's mother arrived at 29 St Paul's Road, having come down by train from Northampton to visit the young couple. Mrs Stocks, the landlady, told her that Emily was still in bed so she waited quietly. A few minutes later Bert himself arrived home, returning from his night shift. The door to their rooms was found locked. Having obtained a spare key Bert discovered that the parlour had been ransacked. All the drawers had been pulled from the chest and some of the postcards from Emily's prized album were strewn on the floor as if there had been a frenzied search for something. Bert frantically rapped at the bedroom door, which led off from the parlour and was also locked. There was no reply and eventually he forced it. Bert found Emily lying naked, face half-down on the bed, the curling pins still in her hair. He must have thought she was sleeping, she looked so peaceful, until he noticed that blood had soaked through the mattress and formed a large pool on the floor. Now he appreciated the full horror of the scene. Emily's throat had been cut so deeply that her head was only attached to the torso by a few muscles. There was bloody water in the washstand basin; somebody appeared to have dried their hands on Emily's flannel petticoat. Four empty stout bottles and two plates, knives and forks were found, suggesting that Emily had dined the evening before with someone she knew. Some trinkets were missing, yet Emily's two gold rings remained untouched. This did not look like a murder for robbery.

When the police surgeon, seventy-two-year-old Dr John Thompson, arrived he found no trace of blood on Bert's two razors. The absence of any other weapon seemed to rule out suicide. His opinion was that Emily Dimmock had been murdered by a swift cut from a sharp blade, administered with great force from behind. There was no sign of any struggle; Emily seemed likely to have been asleep when attacked. The dreadful image conjured up was of Emily lying in bed with a man behind, cutting her throat with his arm stretched round her. There was, Dr Thompson said, some evidence 'that a man had had connection with her before her death'. Death had been almost instantaneous and was put at between four and six in the morning.

The police found that most of the obvious suspects had solid alibis for the night of the murder. Bert Shaw had been in Sheffield before returning to London on the early morning train. Emily's former pimp, John William Crabtree, had stalked her over an unpaid debt in the summer of 1907 but was now in prison. On the Wednesday evening Robert Roberts, the ship's cook, had been with a friend, Frank Clarke, waiting in vain for Emily at the Rising Sun, not the Eagle. They had returned after midnight to a temperance hotel on Euston Road, where their arrival had been noted by its proprietress.

Emily's double life was swiftly uncovered by the police investigation. Dozens of her fellow prostitutes, clientele and pub acquaintances were interviewed. Some clients reported that they had contracted syphilis from her. It was said that in the days before the murder Emily had been seen with a man of 'shabby genteel' appearance, aged about thirty, some five feet eight inches in height, with sunken eyes, and wearing a blue serge suit. But the police had no idea who he was: the description fitted thousands of men in London. Under the glare of the gas mantles of London's drinking establishments people rarely gave their full names.

The first genuine breakthrough came on 25 September when Bert Shaw, who was clearing out the rooms he had shared with Emily, discovered the postcard that Wood had sent to Emily in the days before her death, hidden between sheets of newspapers lining a drawer, and gave it to the police. Realising this could be crucial evidence − Roberts had mentioned in his police interviews both the letter and the card that Emily had shown him on the Wednesday morning before her death − the Assistant Metropolitan Police Commissioner authorised the postcard's reproduction in several newspapers on 28 and 29 September. The question that screamed out in the headlines was simple: who wrote this postcard?

As she read her copy of the *News of the World* − which offered a £100 reward for the identification of the writer of the 'rising sun' postcard − one person immediately recognised its handwriting. Three years earlier Robert Wood's nocturnal ramblings had brought him into contact with an attractive 'artist's model', Ruby Young. The two had become sweethearts after a fashion, although her move from King's Cross to Earl's Court in early 1907, and Wood's wandering eye, had led to a breach between them. Yet Wood had recently contacted Ruby and asked her to say, if ever she were questioned, that they always spent Monday and Wednesday evenings together. She now knew why. When Ruby confronted him she found Wood in an agony of anxiety. 'Ruby, I am in trouble.' Yes, he confessed, he had written the card that had appeared in the newspapers; but, he insisted, it was during a chance encounter with Emily Dimmock on the Friday night. Yes, he had met Emily again on the Monday evening, but he had not seen her since. Where had he been on the all-important Wednesday evening? demanded Ruby. Wood could provide no definite answer: 'I was just wandering about.' Yet he somehow managed to persuade his discarded lover to agree to provide a false alibi for him for that Wednesday evening: they had met outside a Southampton Row bootshop called Phit-Eesi's at six thirty, had tea at a Lyons café and then walked to Brompton Oratory, outside which they had parted at ten thirty; he had then travelled home alone, reaching Frederick Street by midnight.

There was also of course his friend Lambert, who had actually seen Wood in Emily's company at the Eagle on the Wednesday evening. Citing the 'gouty eczema' of his seventy-year-old father – any scandal would surely kill him, Wood warned – he also managed to prevail upon Lambert to keep silent and 'leave the girl out of it' if asked anything about their chance meeting on 11 September.

Although these actions were hardly proof of innocence, Wood's anxieties were now partially allayed. His connection to Emily Dimmock would surely bring him shame if known to his employer and family, regardless of whether he had killed her, but he comforted himself that he had managed to bury it. The Dr Jekyll in Robert Wood had a fetish for respectability. Mr Hyde had to be kept hidden. Inevitably, it was not to be. Ruby, riddled with her own anxiety at her complicity in Wood's falsehood, confided in a friend. That friend spoke to a *Weekly Despatch* reporter, who in turn went to the police.

On 4 October Ruby met Inspector Arthur Neil at Piccadilly Circus Underground station. Torn between loyalty to Wood and an impulse to tell the truth, she recounted the full story. That evening Ruby approached Wood as he left work, before Neil stepped forward to make the arrest. 'If England wants me, she must have me. Be true,' was Wood's histrionic response as he was bundled into a cab bound for Highgate Police Station. Poor Ruby was left in tears: she had betrayed the man she still loved.[8] Wood readily admitted to the police that he was the author of the postcard and that he had been in Emily's company at the Rising Sun on the Friday and the Monday evenings. But he also insisted that he and Emily had never met before that Friday or after that Monday. As to the evening of Wednesday, 11 September, unaware that Ruby had broken her covenant with him, Wood spun out their concocted alibi.

At a sequence of identity parades several witnesses – Roberts, a former prostitute called Emily Lawrence and a barman at the Rising Sun – identified Wood as the man seen on the Monday with Emily at the Rising Sun, leaving the pub with her at about 9 p.m. and then returning with her at around 11 p.m.[9] Both John Crabtree and a woman called Gladys Warren, with whom Emily had lodged at various addresses in 1906, confirmed that Wood had been a frequent visitor. It was now obvious to the police that Wood was a regular user of prostitutes.

Most seriously of all, Robert MacCowan, an unemployed carman,[10] picked out Wood as the man 'who walked with a peculiar jerk of the shoulders' he had seen leaving 29 St Paul's Road at about 5 a.m. on the morning of Thursday, 12 September. Worse still, Ruby Young had also referred to her former lover's strange gait. If that evidence was believed it placed Wood at the scene of the crime at the exact time of its commission. 'If it comes to a crisis I shall have to open out,' said Wood ambiguously to a constable between two parades.

The prosecution case was later described as a 'web of circumstance . . . spun with gossamer lightness'. It seemed to rest largely on eliminating all other suspects until only Wood was left. Yet it is of the essence of a case founded on circumstantial evidence that the whole is stronger than its individual parts. It can become an enveloping net from which there is no escape. In one criminal appeal it was said by the House of Lords that 'Circumstantial evidence . . . works by cumulatively, in geometrical progression, eliminating other possibilities.' And the net here was strong enough for a coroner's jury to conclude that 'the evidence we have received is sufficient to commit the accused for murder.' Ruby Young, who attended St Pancras Coroner's Court wearing black, fainted at this verdict. On 7 October Wood was charged with murder and appeared before Clerkenwell Police Court,[11] where he was refused bail and committed for trial at the Old Bailey.

By the time that the trial started on 12 December the case had attracted an extraordinary amount of press interest. Hogarth describes a 'colossal wave of mass hysteria' enveloping the country. The image of Emily's body, discovered lying beautiful and naked in what should have been the privacy and security of the bedroom, tepid sunlight streaming in through half-open shutters, was a powerful one. It was also a frightening one: the sheer precision and brutality of the crime revived memories of the terrible Jack the Ripper murders in Whitechapel twenty years earlier. The crime, and the world it exposed, seemed to challenge Britain's imperial self-assurance ('How terrible are the sidelights which this case throws on life in London,' the *Daily Chronicle* lamented). Baser feelings were also excited: morbid sightseers soon thronged the Rising Sun.

Wood's employers, anxious to avoid any more adverse publicity and apparently convinced of the innocence of their gentle designer, put £1,000 – then a huge amount of money – into his defence fund. Without this benevolence Wood would never have been able to secure the services of solicitor Arthur Newton (the most noted criminal defence solicitor of the period) and Marshall Hall, assisted by no fewer than three junior counsel. Ranged against him was one of Marshall's old adversaries, Senior Treasury Counsel Charles Mathews, who had prosecuted in the Hermann trial and had been recently knighted during the 'new' Old Bailey's opening ceremony in February 1907.

When he received the brief Marshall Hall proclaimed, 'This is the greatest case I have ever had.' It was a view shared by many others. A photograph taken on the trial's first day shows a scrum of umbrellas on the pavement outside the Bailey as Londoners battled to secure a seat in the public gallery. Court Number One itself was packed with journalists and spectating literary and theatrical celebrities. As we will see, a common feature of the great trials of the first decades of the twentieth century was the presence of writers and actors intently observing the proceedings, as if ringside at a boxing match. They flocked to the Bailey because they believed that the trial process could provide tantalising insights into the human condition. Where else could one view close-up such a gallery of personalities than in the witness box? Where else could one study so minutely the extremes of human character than in the dock? Trial writing of the early twentieth century has an element of prurience that harks back to the ghoulish fascination exerted by the lunatic asylums of the eighteenth century. On the benches behind counsel could be seen some of the biggest names in the Edwardian cultural firmament: A.E.W. Mason (author of the 1902 bestseller *The Four Feathers*); Sir Hall Caine (now almost forgotten, but a leading turn-of-the-century writer whose 1897 novel about prostitution, *The Christian*, was the first British novel to sell more than a million copies); the playwright Sir Arthur Wing Pinero; the producer and actor George Alexander, who had appeared in the first production of *The Importance of Being Earnest*; all were safely installed to see the show begin.

Counsel slouched into court, gowns tatty and wigs yellowing, the marks of long forensic experience. The Bar was a far smaller profession in those days, and barristers' paths would cross much more frequently. Marshall Hall and Mathews were not only adversaries, but also old friends; they were heard reminiscing about the Marie Hermann case. Into the courtroom processed the ageing Mr Justice Grantham, a shires Tory who had given up his seat in Parliament to become a judge twenty years earlier. He had not since then graced the bench with his wisdom, though was known to have handed down thirty death sentences. After Grantham's own death the *Dictionary of National Biography* delicately noted that 'he lacked the breadth of mind and the grasp of intellect necessary for trying great and complicated issues, and he was a very unsatisfactory judge in commercial cases. Among his failings was an inability to refrain from perpetual comment . . .' Still, he was devoted to all 'out-of-door sports' and was 'a notable critic of horseflesh'. One suspects that he had not often found himself at a loose end in the streets of Camden Town. Needless to say, Marshall Hall already had a history with Grantham. 'I will not sit down until you withdraw what you said,' he had told the judge during one heated encounter. Marshall Hall's reputation for obstreperousness did not deter other judges (it probably encouraged them) from joining Grantham on the bench for a look-in throughout the Camden Town murder trial.

The Clerk of Arraigns, bewigged and sitting below the judge, addressed Wood: 'You are indicted for and stand charged on the coroner's inquisition with the wilful murder of Emily Elizabeth Dimmock. Are you guilty or not guilty?'

Wood, standing, returned with 'I am not guilty.' What were his thoughts at that moment? Defendants facing capital charges rarely left coherent accounts of the experience of being on trial for their life, and Wood was no exception. Aside from a few broadly delineated characteristics – his vanity, his craving for respectability, his anxiety to preserve the good name he had built up – he is a void and we can only project our own thoughts on to the blank sheet that is Robert Wood. Extraordinarily, a photograph survives of the trial, taken from the public gallery (and at a time when, although discouraged, it was not illegal to take photographs in a courtroom).[12] We see the backs of the wigs of counsel in the front row; we see a bearded man in the witness box; we see the jurymen, each striking elaborate poses of concentration; we see journalists scribbling away on the benches below them, heavily coated to ward off the insidious cold in that December courtroom; we see an array of top hats placed on the table in the well of the court; we see Wood sitting alone in the dock, his legs crossed, his right hand hovering over his cheek. It is fitting that his face is smudged and out of focus.

From a pool of potential jurors who sat at the very back of the court a jury was empanelled. Marshall Hall, as he was entitled to do, challenged two without giving reasons. The final twelve took their seats in the jury box. The clerk to the court stood again and this time addressed the jurors: 'Gentlemen of the jury, Robert William Thomas George Cavers Wood is indicted for, and also stands charged on the coroner's inquisition with, the wilful murder of Emily Elizabeth Dimmock. To this indictment and inquisition he has pleaded not guilty, and it is your duty to inquire whether he is guilty or not.'

These twelve men, who were to be sequestered each night in a hotel for the duration of the trial, kept from the potential taint of contact with the world outside the courtroom, were the people who mattered most to Marshall Hall. Everything he did was directed to one purpose: to instil doubt in their collective mind as to whether his client had murdered Emily Dimmock.

Sir Charles Mathews stood up to make the opening speech for the prosecution. Photographs of him show a rather feline demeanour yet his voice was described as 'exceedingly grating and unpleasant to listen to for a number of hours consecutively', not an attribute one would expect in the Senior Treasury Counsel. The facts were delineated in careful, precise language. Reading the transcript one learns how fastidiously the Edwardians euphemised prostitution: 'With regards to the deceased young woman, she belonged to the "unfortunate" class and to the lowest class of unfortunates.'

There were a handful of forensic points that Mathews emphasised: first, that Wood had known Emily for much longer than he had admitted, since at least the spring of 1906. Wood had been emphatic that his first meeting with her was on the Friday before the murder. If a longer association could be proved it would be very damaging; or as Mathews put it with prosecutorial understatement: 'If you, gentlemen of the jury, should find in this material particular that the accused has not spoken the truth, it will become a matter for your most serious consideration.' The next matter of emphasis was Wood's attempts to persuade Ruby Young into a false alibi for the Wednesday evening. Third, Mathews drew the jury's attention to the postcard and the burned letter. If the jury were to conclude that they were both written by Wood then that would expose another falsehood in his statement. It would also point to Wood making a second assignation in a week with Emily.

Mathews then came to the fatal night. He suggested that when Emily left home early on the Wednesday evening she was going to meet Wood in accordance with his letter of assignation, at a place where she was not well-known. He placed significance on the dishevelment of her hair; did that not mean she was going to meet someone she knew well? What was more, two witnesses had seen Wood with Emily at the Eagle that evening. 'What became of them when they left?' Mathews explained the evidence of MacCowan, and that Ruby Young had herself corroborated Wood's jerky walk. Finally he dwelt on the postcards that had been found strewn on the floor in the 'death chamber', as he put it, with a dose of melodrama. 'The murderer evidently searched for a card which might be there.'

Marshall Hall had decided on a blanket strategy of attack, regardless of the identity of the witness. Bertram Shaw had an ironclad alibi; what is more, having made the terrible discovery of the body of his common-law wife, he was a figure of pity. Surely no benefit would be obtained in picking fights with him? Yet Marshall bounded in full-throttle.

'Did you know that Dimmock was leading an immoral life?' (the use of Emily's surname seems now perversely heartless).

'No.'

We might pause to consider the pain with which that answer is pregnant. Marshall Hall didn't. He blundered on.

> MARSHALL HALL: Did you know that she was in the habit of getting letters from people?
> SHAW: No.
> MARSHALL HALL: Was she frightened of you?
> SHAW: No.

Still the questions rained down. Had he written to Emily that week? Did he sign his letters 'Bert'? Why had he not found the 'rising sun' postcard until two weeks after Emily's death? Would he swear that he had not written the letter that was found in the grate? After all it had, according to Roberts, been signed 'Bert'. Had he ever been unkind to Emily? On the page these questions seem extraordinarily ill-judged. Yet there was a deeper strategy at work. It was not to show that Shaw had committed the murder, but to show that Shaw may well have felt sufficiently concerned about an accusation being made against him that he might try to cast suspicion on someone else.

In re-examination Mathews obtained clear confirmation from Shaw that he had not written the letter that Emily had received, and burned, on the Wednesday morning. Then this extraordinary intervention from Marshall Hall: 'It might save time if I admit there is no question that the handwriting on the fragment produced is the accused's handwriting. I never suggested the witness Shaw wrote the letter.'

Mathews and the judge looked at each in bemusement. This was precisely what Marshall had intimated. Mathews went further: 'Does my learned friend accept that Shaw was in Sheffield that night, or does he desire the alibi of the witness to be proved?'

Marshall Hall's questions had insinuated in the most veiled terms that

Shaw might have committed the crime. Mathews was determined to flush him out. Marshall backed away: 'I accept at once the statement that he was at Sheffield on this particular night. My object in asking the questions I did will be seen later.' Here was a classic form of retreat through bluster. Marshall never did explain why he had asked those questions. In fact what he was doing was indiscriminately sowing doubt wherever he could.

The landlady Mrs Stocks testified to Emily's activities on the last day of her life. A 'butterfly of the street' she may have been, but Emily still had her domestic tasks to discharge. Mrs Stocks was emphatic that she knew nothing of Emily's nocturnal visitors: 'I always went to bed early.' Can we believe that Emily was able, night after night, to smuggle in her clients in the evening and out again in the morning without Mrs Stocks, sleeping immediately below, knowing? Could her landlady really have been ignorant of Emily's true calling? Was this a case of economic necessity trumping outward propriety? The matter was not probed.

She was followed by Dr Thompson, who presented the terrible details of Emily's death to the court and recreated her final moments. 'I should say that her assailant was at her back in the bed between her and the wall. I should say the assailant placed his hand lightly on her forehead and grasped her hair in order to raise her head . . . Once the head was raised sufficiently it was a simple matter of a moment.' Yet, he remembered, her face had seemed calm and peaceful. Marshall Hall was interested in two issues: when was the time of death? Between about four and six in the morning: no earlier than four o'clock. Could either of Bert Shaw's razors have been used as the murder weapon? Dr Thompson thought not. A microscopic examination had revealed no trace of blood on them. The matter was left hanging but Marshall Hall's implication was clear: whoever killed Emily had come equipped. This was a crime of premeditation.

Robert Roberts now entered the witness box. It must have been horrible for him to have to admit, in front of a score of journalists noting down his every syllable, his three bought nights with Emily. He recalled the Monday evening when Wood had come to the Rising Sun and Emily had left his company to go to talk to the artist, before they left together for a while. Of course their meeting coincided precisely with the assignation suggested in the 'rising sun' postcard. The judge made it clear which way his thoughts were tending:

JUDGE: Dimmock and the accused were out long enough to enable them
    to go to St Paul's Road, stay some time, and then return?
ROBERTS: Yes.

Roberts presented real difficulty for Wood. He claimed to have seen the
two letters being pushed under the door on the Wednesday morning,
one of which proposed an appointment that evening at the Eagle. For
whatever reason Emily had compared the letter with the 'rising sun'
postcard. The handwriting had been identical.

Marshall Hall's imperious demeanour was known to terrorise witnesses
even before he had put a question. With a series of short sharp jabs he
managed to demonstrate that, when Roberts heard of the murder, he had
been terrified that he would be implicated. The witness admitted that he
had spoken with other regulars at the Rising Sun about Wood. The
implication was clear: Roberts had been coached by a friend to identify
Wood as the man in the Rising Sun on the Monday night and so deflect
the finger of blame away from himself. When questioned as to why Emily
had asked him to compare handwriting on the Wednesday morning the
wretched Roberts started studying his boots. How he longed to leave
the witness box! This allowed Marshall Hall to try one of his favourite
displays of courtroom sanctimony; utterly unfair, but completely effective:
'Look up, man. We are in a court of justice. Don't hang your head!'

If Wood had indeed written to Emily a second time seeking a rendezvous for the Wednesday night then that placed him in very grave danger.
Wood had denied it (while admitting that he may have doodled on a
notebook with Emily and given her some of the pages) and Marshall
Hall had to sow doubt on Roberts's bona fides. He did this very cleverly,
not by seeking to implicate Roberts in the murder (his alibi was unimpeachable), but by suggesting that Roberts – frantic with worry as the
man who had spent three successive nights with Emily immediately
before her death – had made up the letter to place the blame on poor
Bert Shaw.

MARSHALL HALL: I put it to you that this fragment was never part of such
    a letter. I put it to you that the story of this long letter is an invention.
ROBERTS: It is not so.
MARSHALL HALL: It was signed 'Bert'?
ROBERTS: Yes.
MARSHALL HALL: Are you quite certain about the contents of this letter?
    Repeat it again!

ROBERTS: 'Dear Phyllis, Will you meet me at the bar of the Eagle at
Camden Town 8.30 tonight, Wednesday, Bert.'

MARSHALL HALL: How could anybody writing that on the Tuesday write
'tonight' for Wednesday?

ROBERTS: You generally write that way to a person you know.

MARSHALL HALL: Do you usually, when writing on a Tuesday to make an
appointment for a Wednesday night, write 'Meet me tonight'?

ROBERTS: I do not.

MARSHALL HALL: I put it to you that that piece of burned paper is a
fragment which might have come from anywhere and which never
came through the post?

ROBERTS: It did.

MARSHALL HALL: Where did the name 'Bert' come from?

ROBERTS: I tell you it was written.

MARSHALL HALL: If the object had been to put suspicion on Shaw, the
suggestion would have been very useful?

ROBERTS: [No answer.]

The cross-examination ended on an even more extraordinary note: 'Are
you positive,' thundered Marshall Hall, 'that you were not in the neigh-
bourhood of Camden Town that Wednesday night, or are you prepared
to say that you were not in her company at all that night?' Roberts
looked astonished; was this not an allegation that he was implicated
in the murder? Mathews was seen to be whispering urgently with his
opponent on counsel's row. Marshall Hall spoke again: 'Most certainly I
do not accuse Roberts of the murder.'

In which case what was the point of that last question? It had been
gratuitous prejudice.

At the end of the trial's first day, Wood wrote a letter from Brixton
prison to his brother Charles in which he said he felt 'quite peaceful'
and was gratified by the 'whispers of good cheer' he had received in
court. 'Even the orderly who tends my room moved silently and with
some reverence this morning,' Wood noted. As for the Bailey, 'Little did
I think that one day I should appear on the capital charge under that
beautiful figure of Justice (by Frampton, RA) that towers over the Old
Bailey.' Wood added that he had had supper with Frampton 'on more
than one occasion'.[13] 'Be of good cheer,' he concludes, 'for I have done
no *grievous* wrong.'

When the second day started Mathews stood up to explain that,
prompted by Marshall Hall's line of questioning the day before, he was

introducing a new witness. Into the box came Emily's fellow lodger at St Paul's Road Alice Lancaster. She confirmed one curious fact: on the morning of Wednesday, 11 September she had pushed two letters under Emily's door. If Marshall Hall was flummoxed by this obviously honest witness he gave no sign of it (it is a cardinal rule for the advocate never to show the slightest hint of surprise at an unexpected development). But he established that when Mrs Lancaster had given a statement to the police on the day of the murder she had made no mention of the delivery of the letters. Mathews also called a witness who could testify that Roberts was safely back at the temperance hotel on Wednesday night. This provoked another outburst from Marshall Hall: 'I do not know why this witness is being called. I do not suggest that Roberts committed the murder and therefore it is unnecessary to prove an alibi. I am not saying anything against Roberts.'

This was too much for the judge, who testily responded: 'After the cross-examination yesterday, I think the prosecution are quite justified in calling these witnesses.' True to form, Marshall Hall was succeeding in antagonising the court.

Later that morning the next point of extreme danger for Wood came. Robert MacCowan gave evidence that he had been walking down St Paul's Road in the early morning of Thursday – according to the medical evidence at about the time the murder was committed – and had seen a man leaving number 29 and walking in the opposite direction. He described the jerky shoulder movement that had led him to pick out Wood from an identity parade at which fifteen men, fourteen of them pulled randomly off the street, were instructed to walk. If MacCowan's evidence held up, surely Wood would find his way to the gallows? This was to be the supreme test for Marshall Hall's skills as an advocate. He decided to apply the bludgeon, not the stiletto.

MacCowan's evidence, in answer to Mathews's questions, was that he had heard a man behind him leaving the gate of a house and going down the road. He had turned round and seen the man's back and his distinctive gait. But the statement he had made to the police was subtly different. It had read: 'I looked round and saw a man coming down the steps of No. 29.' Marshall challenged him on the discrepancy. MacCowan became flustered. 'When we got to make a statement [sic] we are not so fly as when we come to be cross-examined. I was not so particular – I did not listen particularly to what was read over to me.'

This was Marshall's cue to explode into a volcanic eruption of manufactured outrage. The following words must be read very loudly to understand their full effect.

MARSHALL HALL: You were 'not so fly'? Do you mean to say that knowing
that a man's life might depend on your description, you did not take
particular notice of what Sergeant Ball read over to you?

MACCOWAN: My description was that I saw the man's back.

. . .

MARSHALL HALL: Have you no regard for human life?

It was also a fact that in his first statement to the police MacCowan had
not mentioned the twitch of the shoulders. Instead he had described the
mystery man as 'stiffly built with broad-shoulders'. Marshall demanded that
Wood now stand up in the dock, put on his overcoat and turn his back
to the court. 'Now would you describe that man as broad-shouldered?' he
shouted. 'He has broader shoulders than I have,' came the answer.

The trap had been laid. The next minute was as close to Marshall
Hall gold as it is possible to get.

MARSHALL HALL: Would you describe a bluebottle as an elephant because
it is bigger than a fly?

MACCOWAN: I described him as broader than I.

MARSHALL HALL: Now, MacCowan, look again and think. Will you now
describe that man as of broad shoulders?

MACCOWAN: He is broader than me.

MARSHALL HALL: I ask you again, as an honest man, where a man's life
may be hanging on your words, would you describe him as a
broad-shouldered man?

MACCOWAN: I would describe him as broader than me.

MacCowan was a transparently honest man who knew none of the other
protagonists. He had no reason to lie and his evidence was in all probability truthful – though whether the man he saw was Wood is open to
question. He had been undone by a cross-examination that had successfully created a wedge out of the minor differences between his statement
to the police and his oral evidence.

Detective Inspector Neil, the chief investigating officer in the case,
then read out the statement Wood had made after his arrest. The pendulum
continued to swing back and forth. Yes, Neil accepted that nothing
belonging to Wood had been found at St Paul's Road; nor was there
anything to show he had ever set foot in the house. Nor had any of the
trinkets that were missing from Emily's rooms been traced to Wood. On
the other hand, assuming he was the murderer, surely Wood would have

seen to it that all clues were removed. He had time enough. And Inspector Neil had also noted Wood's distinctive shoulder movement when walking. Marshall Hall's response was typically histrionic: 'Do you know that not a single man in the firm where Wood was employed, sixty-five in all, had ever noticed this peculiarity? I will call the whole sixty-five if necessary.'

The next day was a Saturday. In 1907 the concept of the weekend was narrower than it is now and the court sat as usual. The prosecution called first William Moss, Wood's boss, to confirm that when they had discussed in passing the 'rising sun' postcard after its publication in the newspapers Wood had not confessed his authorship. The question of whether to call a particular witness is often a delicate one, both for the prosecution and defence. That witness may be able to slot in a piece of proof to build the picture. But, once thrown open to cross-examination, will he reveal weaknesses elsewhere? As Marshall Hall stood up to cross-examine, Mathews must have inwardly groaned. Moss's presence as a prosecution witness allowed Marshall Hall now to milk the affection he felt for his good-natured employee. Had he ever noticed anything peculiar about his walk? No. Was he an exceptionally amiable young man and kind to animals? Yes. The unspoken next question hung in the air. Could such a lover of the animal kingdom really be capable of slitting a woman's throat as she slept?

But Marshall Hall again overstepped the mark. Grantham was perhaps repelled by this display of admiration for the man in the dock. He intervened to ask Moss whether he knew that Wood was living an 'immoral life': after all Wood admitted a relationship with a prostitute and consorting with the denizens of Camden Town. Before Moss could answer, Marshall Hall intervened: looking studiedly at the jury he drawled, 'I do not understand Your Lordship's question.' It is an old trick, requiring courage. It is a way of saying to the jury: 'You and I understand each other quite well – please do not be distracted by the idiocy of that old man on the bench.' The judge could not contain his fury. 'Are you addressing me or the jury? If you are speaking to me, I wish you would not look at the jury.'

Joseph Lambert now gave evidence confirming his recollections of meeting Wood and Emily at the Eagle on the Wednesday evening and later being sworn to secrecy. When Marshall Hall got up to question him he indicated that Wood would not dispute that he was with Emily on the final evening of her life, tacitly accepting that his client had lied to the police in denying having seen Emily again after the Monday evening. But in this trial witnesses seemed to take with one hand yet give with the other. Lambert recalled Emily describing Wood as 'a nice boy' that evening. Lambert was clear: Emily had not seemed in any way afraid of Wood. Nor was he wearing or carrying an overcoat. Yet the man MacCowan had seen walking down the road the next morning was apparently wrapped in a heavy coat.

The flood of prosecution witnesses continued. Lillian Raven, the barmaid at the Eagle, had her five minutes in the spotlight. The one thing she could recollect was, on that Wednesday evening, Emily saying to Lambert, 'Please excuse me for coming out untidy, but I had to come and meet him.' It is a striking snippet of conversation, casting a subtly different slant on the atmosphere of that last evening. Did it have any significance?

The most important witness on that Saturday was Ruby Young, Wood's former sweetheart. How reluctantly she must have walked into the witness box. Not only was she having to give evidence against a man she still loved, she was going to have to reveal the facts of her life as an 'artist's model'. She started by explaining how she had first met Wood: on the Euston Road, followed by a flirtatious drink at the Rising Sun. It was almost exactly the same way Wood said he had encountered Emily Dimmock. The jurors must have realised by now – if they did not already know – that the Rising Sun was not a high-class establishment. Yes, she had been 'intimate' with Wood, but had broken off their relationship in July when she learned that Wood had been with another woman. Ruby now came to Wood's behaviour after Emily's death. After several weeks of silence since the summer her former lover was now all solicitude. Ruby told of a man doing his best to work on her residual affections to provide him with the all-important alibi. 'If your name gets besmirched in any way I will marry you if I get free,' he had vowed. Wood had reminded her about their concocted alibi so many times that she had once snapped at him, 'Yes, I'll be true! Don't bother me. It's getting on my nerves.'

Marshall Hall contested none of this evidence. Ruby spent much of her time in the witness box in tears and Wood's counsel needed to proceed with caution and delicacy. He concentrated on one big point:

> With regard to the arrangement which you say you had come to that you should say that the accused was in your company on the night of Wednesday, 11 September from six thirty to ten thirty, have you ever thought that, having regard to Dr Thompson's evidence [as to the time of death], that would be useless as an alibi for the murder, but a perfect alibi for the meeting of the girl?

Marshall Hall's point was obvious: if Wood was the murderer it was odd that he had not asked Ruby for an alibi for the small hours of 12 September, when Dr Thompson placed the time of the murder. Ruby, anxious to take any lifeline thrown to her, could only agree. So an apparent weakness was turned into what would become a cornerstone of the defence.

Sunday brought a brief respite. The jury remained cooped up in their hotel, permitted to go out to the Temple church only as a group and if husbanded by the jury bailiff. As for Marshall Hall, cross-examination is a tiring business and in the course of three days twenty-four witnesses had come into the witness box. He had questioned each one of them. He could now rest and prepare for the next wave.

On the trial's fourth day, Monday, 16 December, a number of 'disreputable women', as Marshall Hall's biographer Marjoribanks called them, were called to testify that Wood's connection with Emily was in fact a long-term acquaintance. Emily Lawrence, who presented herself as a respectable printer's wife, said she had first seen Emily with Wood at a pub on Gray's Inn Road, the Pindar of Wakefield, in the summer of 1906; at the Rising Sun on Monday, 9 September she and another former prostitute, Florence Smith (who testified later), had light-heartedly said to Wood, 'Don't tell Phyllis we've had a drink with you, or she might be jealous.' After her arrival, Emily had nervously 'passed some uncomplimentary remarks' about Wood, and then reluctantly headed off with him, apparently to the Holborn Empire, a nearby music hall. This was dangerous for the defence: not only had Emily known Wood very well, she was also evidently wary of him.

Marshall Hall's approach to Mrs Lawrence was one of sheer nastiness. He gratuitously put to her that she herself had been a prostitute, knowing that her quavering answer – 'Before I was married, five or six years ago' – would be broadcast across the next morning's newspapers. Then an attack on Emily herself – 'Was she not the lowest type of prostitute?' – which was met with a spirited defence of her dead friend – 'She was a very nice, respectable, clean and tidy girl' – followed by sneering contempt:

> MARSHALL HALL: As good as any in Euston Road?
> MRS LAWRENCE: Yes.
> MARSHALL HALL: I suppose there are classes of prostitutes even in the Euston Road?

'You are trying to make me a bad character,' Mrs Lawrence protested, with justification.

'God forbid that I should make you one!' Marshall Hall retorted –
presumably with insidious emphasis on the 'I'. Then another trick. What,
he asked her, was the origin of her ill-feeling against Wood? Mrs Lawrence
was taken aback – she barely knew Wood. She was simply in court to
speak the truth. 'Then why have you been looking at the prisoner as
you have done while giving your evidence?'

'Good gracious, aren't my eyes my own to look round with?'

One has to admire Emily Lawrence.

'I am using my eyes, too. Now, what is it you have got against him?'
Marshall Hall replied, his voice rising in a crescendo. This was all stage
business, purely for the benefit of the jury.

Later came Crabtree, who identified himself as the landlord of 1
Bidborough Street, just south of the Euston Road, where Emily had
lodged in 1906. 'Were the people who lived there respectable?' Mathews
asked him hopefully.

'Well, one was a railway porter,' Crabtree replied.

The reality was obvious: Crabtree had been a brothel-keeper and
Emily was one of his girls. Yet his evidence was dangerous: he testified
that Wood visited Emily often in her first-floor room; he referred to an
altercation during which Wood had called Emily 'bad names'; he recalled
being summoned up to Emily's room, and finding the two of them in
bed, Emily wrapped only in a sheet, asking him to pawn a silver cigarette
case belonging to Wood, presumably so that she could be paid for her
services. Again Marshall Hall decided on a policy of aggression. He
wasted no time in getting Crabtree to admit that he had served two
sentences of imprisonment for 'keeping a disorderly house', that he had
only been released from prison ten days before, and that he had served at
least two earlier sentences for 'street-stealing'.[14] 'Do you ever tell the truth?'
'Do you ever try to lead an honest life?' 'Has anyone ever enquired into
your medical condition?' 'Are you sober now?' The abuse rained down.

The prosecution case was now over. During the first four days of the
trial Marshall Hall had assumed the mask of studied outrage. His opening
speech for the defence was another two hours of derision and hyperbole.
This was the work of a sexual maniac, intoned Marshall Hall, calling to
mind the Whitechapel murders of twenty years earlier, supposedly the
work of Jack the Ripper. 'The murderer was a madman. Is this man in
the dock mad? Does he look mad?'

MacCowan's identification of Wood as the man who was lolloping
down St Paul's Road early on the morning of 12 September was dismissed
as 'the flimsiest and most unsatisfactory evidence ever put before a jury

in any court of justice in the world'. Really? As to Crabtree: 'No word can express the horror and contempt I feel for a man like him.' 'What do you think of a charge of murder that can rely for one of its bits of evidence upon the evidence of a thing like that we saw in the witness box just now?' The jury might have smiled inwardly at this particular flourish. If a defendant frequents brothels, can the prosecution be blamed for calling brothel-keepers as witnesses to testify to that fact? Still, it was a bravura performance and behind the oratorical flights Marshall Hall slipped in some crucial admissions, designed to blunt the sting of Mathews's cross-examination. Wood's alibi was false, yet it was created not to hide his guilt of murder but his association 'with a woman of the deceased's class, to prevent his being inculpated in associating with a woman who was a low harlot'; he had indeed met Emily on the Wednesday night at the Eagle; the burned fragments had been written by him. A spectator recalled that 'after twenty minutes of this passionate and pulverising rhetoric, the jury were in a state of pulp.' As Marshall Hall sat down, spontaneous applause broke out from the gallery. In the public mind the tide was turning in favour of Robert Wood.

The next day Marshall Hall began calling his witnesses. The first was Wood's elderly father George. When originally interviewed by Inspector Neil he had been unable to account for his son's movements on the crucial Wednesday night. Now he told an elaborate story which, so he said, meant that he could pinpoint Robert as having come home that evening at about midnight. Robert's stepbrother James corroborated the father. Both had seen Robert the next morning, the Thursday, as cheery and composed as ever. A lodger at Frederick Street, Joseph Rogers, testified that he had been in the front garden the previous night, collecting worms for a forthcoming fishing expedition, and had seen Wood come home at just before midnight. (In a rare moment of levity Marshall Hall asked him, 'Although a fisherman, your stories are not necessarily untrue, I hope?')

The collective force of this evidence was clear. The time of the murder was placed in the early morning of the Thursday. Yet three people had seen Robert Wood arriving home at Frederick Street at around midnight. Had he established his own impregnable alibi? There was also MacCowan's identification to demolish. Marshall Hall now made good on his earlier promise to call each of Wood's work colleagues to testify to the ordinariness of his gait. After two of these had come into the witness box Mathews surrendered. To save another sixty-three witnesses in the same vein he conceded that they would all speak to the unremarkable way that Wood walked.

Until the passing of the Criminal Evidence Act 1898 the law had prevented defendants charged with a criminal offence giving sworn evidence in their own defence. Although the intention of the Act was to bestow a benefit on defendants, its consequences had been far less clear-cut. The right to testify, if exercised, carried with it the obligation to submit to cross-examination. It was thought that since the Act was passed a searching cross-examination of the defendant by Crown counsel had brought convictions in trials that might have ended in acquittals in the old days, when defence counsel were free to tell the jury how difficult it was for the defendant, unable to explain the truth by enforced silence. The facts corroborated this: almost every defendant who had availed themselves of the right to give evidence in a murder case at the Old Bailey had been found guilty.

The 1898 Act of course did not oblige the defendant to enter the witness box; that remained entirely their own choice. Yet a failure to give evidence brought its own dangers: the judge might well invite an adverse inference and the jury might come to its own conclusion that the defendant was seeking to hide his guilt, regardless of any comment from the bench. Surely an innocent man would seize the chance to tell the jury his side of the story? Was a failure to take that opportunity consistent with innocence? The result was that the decision whether to call one's own client as a witness was a classic Hobson's choice, one of the most problematic judgements that counsel had to make. It weighed especially heavily on Marshall Hall: in the notorious Yarmouth murder case, tried at the (old) Old Bailey six years earlier, he had made the decision not to call the defendant Bennett, of whose innocence he was convinced. Bennett was convicted and hanged. Marshall Hall insisted thereafter that his clients sign a document stating whether they wished to give evidence or not (the one signed by the Brides in the Bath murderer, George Smith, still exists).

In the run-up to the trial Marshall's mind had wavered. He had met Wood in prison and reached a firm conclusion. Wood was, he told his chambers devil,[15] 'raving mad' and must be kept out of the witness box at all costs. Yet in fraught consultations with his legal team he had finally been convinced that Wood would surely hang if he did not explain his innocence to the jury. By 1907 it had already become customary for the defence to call the defendant to testify first, if they were to testify at all, but again Marshall Hall defied precedent. He called his client last of all.

For the previous four days Robert Wood had worn a look of supreme composure in the dock, alone apart from a warder. Now, on the afternoon of 17 December, he pushed his chair back and walked through the door of the dock into the well of the court. In the eight yards between dock and witness box every pair of eyes in court tried to discern whether Wood had the halting walk ascribed to him by MacCowan and Ruby Young. He made sure he gave them no grounds for doubt, whispering, 'Well, Dad, cheer up,' as he passed his father. The defence was having a good run.

Marshall Hall's initial question was to the point. Speaking in a clear, slow voice he asked, 'Did you kill Emily Dimmock?'

For several agonising moments Wood said nothing at all; Marshall Hall 'lean[t] forward with a look of eager expectation', one journalist noted, and he had to repeat the question. The reporter captured the moment that followed. 'It is only an instant, but seems an hour. One notices strange little details in a quaint, inconsequent fashion – the loose ends of the man's tie, the trembling beard of his old grey father huddled in a shrunken attitude on the steps of the jury box, the twist and turn of the judge's pen, and the constant rise and fall and flicker of the curiously modulated lights.'

Then the silence was broken by a petulant outburst. 'I mean it's ridiculous.'

Every barrister knows the experience of being let down by their witness. Marshall Hall must have been inwardly furious: this was not an answer that would endear Wood to the jury, and the hideous murder of a young woman was anything but 'ridiculous'. 'You must answer straight. I will only ask you straight questions. Did you kill her?'

Finally, a proper answer. 'No, I did not.' Wood found his feet again. He insisted that he had first met Emily on the Friday, 6 September. If that was true then a handful of prosecution witnesses had lied. Marshall Hall confronted him with Crabtree's evidence. Was it true? Wood's response showed that he had been infected by his own counsel's rhetoric. 'I hope God will destroy me this moment if I have ever entered a house of his or ever knew him.' When asked how he had met Emily, the aesthete in him, the artist in search of sensations, reasserted itself. 'Under the glare of the lights. I will leave that to the jury. No doubt many of the jury will know what goes on in public houses.'

Wood now admitted seeing Emily at the Eagle on the fatal night of

11 September. But it had been by chance – there was no assignation – and he insisted that he had left her there at about 11 p.m. and headed straight home. 'A certain amount of disgrace' had prompted him to ask Ruby for a false alibi, he admitted; 'knowing that the woman had been associated with a certain kind of public house I did not wish to be associated with it or the girls that went there.' He conceded that the charred letter 'has the appearance of a copy' of his handwriting, before later admitting that it was indeed his. Reading the trial transcript one can sense Marshall Hall bristling as Wood answered questions so piously, so priggishly, so casually. The barrister later said it was the hardest examination-in-chief he had ever carried out, so unbiddable was his client.

Wednesday, 18 December, the trial's sixth and final day, started with Mathews's cross-examination of Wood. 'Short, casual and harmless' was how Wood described his connection with Emily; 'she had some intelligence to appeal to,' he remarked in his superior way, although 'the association was low.' All the testimony that he had known her before 6 September was 'mistaken evidence, incorrect or concocted'. Mathews went through the burden of that evidence in detail. It was petulantly brushed aside. The judge butted in: if he had never met Emily before how could he explain addressing her as 'Phillis darling' in the 'rising sun' postcard, allegedly written on the very first night of their acquaintance? 'It was written to please her, I suppose. The Rising Sun company is friendly in a short time.' It was an inadequate answer.

Next Mathews set out the Crown's case as to what had really happened. He suggested that the 'rising sun' postcard had in fact been written on the Sunday – the night it was posted – for an assignation on the Monday, which Emily had duly kept. Mathews put it to Wood that he had called again at the Rising Sun on the Tuesday, only to see Emily in conversation with Roberts. Mrs Lawrence had said she had glimpsed Wood's head at the window and seen him gesturing at Emily. Wood had that night written another assignation letter to Emily – the one that was pushed under the door by Mrs Lancaster on the Wednesday morning – but had suggested the Eagle as a rendezvous, where Emily was unknown. The fragments of charred paper found in the grate were shown to Wood, on which were words he admitted were in his hand, though he denied that they were part of a letter, just bits of paper on which he had written 'amusing sketches and phrases' which Emily had taken from him when they had first met at the Rising Sun. What was legible read as follows: 'ill . . . you . . . ar . . . of . . . the . . . e . . . Town . . . S . . . ill . . . Wednes . . . if . . . rest . . . excuse . . . good . . . fond . . . Mon . . .

from.' Mathews went through each word with Wood, who took refuge in a blank memory and said he could offer no explanation: 'It is all a jumble and a surprise.' Mathews methodically did the work for him; did not the words read: 'Will you meet me at the bar of the Eagle near Camden Town station on Wednesday 8.15 . . . goodbye . . . Fondest love . . . From'? Did not the 'Mon' refer to 'Money'? The fragments were entirely consistent with this reconstruction. Wood said he did not even know the name of the Eagle on that Tuesday, when the letter had supposedly been written: yet he had already admitted having gone there with Emily on the Saturday. Wood was floundering.

Wood could not shake off the pompous tone that had marred his evidence throughout. He said he hadn't noticed what Emily was wearing as 'her personality was in my mind, not her dress'. When asked by Mathews if he had had 'sexual intercourse' with Emily (after so much circumlocution during the trial it comes as a mild shock to see the phrase used), his ludicrous reply was, 'It is only to you, Sir Charles, that I would answer that at all. I should be indignant with the average man.' His protestations that he had wanted to avoid 'association with low characters' seemed like shallow hypocrisy, not high-mindedness, given that he admitted an intimate relationship with Ruby Young, whom he knew to be a prostitute, for many months. And yet, and yet. It was curious that Mathews took Wood to the bedroom at St Paul's Road, so to speak, but did not put the murder itself to him. Nor was there one word about motive. When Mathews sat down the jury remained unenlightened as to the prosecution's theory as to *why* he almost severed the head of Emily Dimmock from her body. And the very oddity of his demeanour in the witness box may, paradoxically, have benefited him: could anyone believe that such a *poseur* could ever have the determination or will to murder anyone? 'His very badness as a witness began to tell in his favour,' wrote Marjoribanks.

According to the peculiar rules then prevailing, if the defence called any evidence then it forfeited the right to have the final word.[16] So it was for Marshall Hall to make his closing speech before that for the prosecution. One of the features that makes the English criminal trial so exciting for the onlooker is its seamlessness. After a particular climacteric the parties do not go away to regroup and consider. Everyone must be ready to carry on to the next preordained step. Scene follows scene without interruption. There are no intervals in the show. Immediately after Wood left the witness box his counsel stood up to make his final submission to the jury.

Leaning on his lectern towards the jury, Marshall Hall produced a peroration that even on the foxed page of the transcript is electric. The courtroom faded from his view. All that remained were the twelve men in heavy black suits sitting directly opposite him.

In this case I want to claim something more than a verdict tantamount to not proven; I claim a verdict of not guilty, which will, in effect, utterly kill this cruel charge in such a way that it can never afterwards be revived by the lying tongues of men or women and can never be galvanised into any semblance of life. I am confident as an advocate, and I hope I am confident in judging of your natures, that there is not one of you, least of all twelve of you, who dares to say: 'That man in the dock murdered Emily Dimmock.'

Flummery this may have been, but it was magnificently put and it was easy to be caught in the slipstream. Yet Marshall Hall had more concrete points with which to shore up his case. First, he rightly emphasised, and emphasised again, the absence of a suggested motive in a murder said to have been premeditated. 'I have searched in vain amidst the clouds of the evidence for some motive, some weapon, something which would nail Robert Wood to the fateful facts.'

Then there was the issue of timings. If Emily had been killed in the early morning, as the Crown contended, then the false alibi so carefully constructed by Wood was perfectly useless. MacCowan's testimony was 'not sufficient upon which to destroy a poor suffering animal, let alone a human being'. Yet Ruby Young – a 'poor, unfortunate, wretched woman', Marshall Hall reminded jurors again – had belatedly confirmed that Wood walked with the same peculiar gait that MacCowan had identified. This was castigated as a 'gross and vindictive lie'; a suggestion not put to her in cross-examination, as it should properly have been, but now hurled out at the jurors. In fact, said Marshall Hall, at the time MacCowan had supposedly seen him careering down St Paul's Road Wood was safely asleep at home. Fisherman Rogers, the lodger who had witnessed Wood returning home, was 'one of the most honest witnesses ever called before a jury'. Then the conclusion:

If you are satisfied beyond all reasonable doubt that the man standing there, on the night of 11 September murdered Emily Dimmock, although it breaks your heart to do so, find him guilty and send him to the scaffold. But if under the guidance of a Greater Power than any earthly power, making up your own mind for yourselves on the evidence, if you feel you cannot honestly and conscientiously say you are satisfied that the prosecution have proved this man to be guilty – if after giving effect to everything said by counsel for the prosecution and by the learned judge, you feel, on the evidence led before you, that you could not honestly and conscientiously say beyond all reasonable doubt that the prosecution have proved their case, then I say it will be your duty, as well as your pleasure, to say, as you are bound to say, that Robert Wood is not guilty of the murder of Emily Elizabeth Dimmock.

As Marshall laid down the trowel of rhetoric, a juror fainted. The oratorical techniques deployed at Marie Hermann's trial at a different Old Bailey thirteen years before were now perfected.

By contrast, Mathews's short closing speech that followed 'would hardly recommend itself to the present school of Treasury prosecutors', wrote Marjoribanks tactfully twenty years later. Marshall Hall's thunderous broadside had put Mathews on the defensive: he spent much of the time justifying the prosecution's tactics rather than articulating a coherent case against Wood. There was an air of surrender in Mathews's tone.

Afternoon gave way to evening, but the proceedings continued. The atmosphere of the courtroom became ever more sepulchral. All seemed to be black or permutations of grey. The cold had become so intolerable that several of the jurymen complained. Everyone now was seated to hear the judge's summing-up, the final act in the drama. His words percolated through the settling gloom. They began badly for the defence. 'You have been engaged in one of the most remarkable trials that is to be found in the annals of the Criminal Courts of England for many years – certainly the most remarkable in my time, which has not been a short one,' Grantham told the jury. The absence of a motive was not a 'safe test' of the prisoner's guilt or otherwise, he suggested. 'The whole of the evidence seems to me to point to the fact that the accused had been leading a double life.' A hundred years ago judges were less constrained in expressing their own views to a jury and Grantham told them that he thought the evidence demonstrated clearly that Wood had known Emily well before the Friday and that he had not properly explained the Eagle letter, the fragments of which had been found in her grate. The result was that Wood had lied at the very beginning and at the very end.

As the judge proceeded spectators in the public gallery could be heard rumbling with dissatisfaction. Somewhere someone muttered, 'Grossly unfair!' Marshall Hall, his work not over, sitting ramrod straight in counsel's row, began 'talking to the jury with his eyes'. But then old Grantham, who had throughout the trial seemed to question so much of Wood's case, suddenly changed tack. 'In this case there is not an atom of direct evidence against the prisoner.' He warned the jury that they must not find against Wood 'unless no loophole is left by which he can escape'. 'In my judgment, strong as the suspicion in this case undoubtedly is, I do not think that the prosecution has brought the case home near enough to the accused,' said Grantham, to applause that Court Number One's ushers failed to stifle with futile cries of 'Silence!' An extraordinary event had occurred: at the eleventh hour the crusty judge had virtually directed an acquittal.[17]

The jury retired at 7.43 p.m. It had been a very long day; nowadays a court would adjourn sometime after four but then, once the evidence was over, judges were anxious to obtain a verdict, even if that meant sitting into the night. 'While the jury deliberated he never turned a hair or moved a muscle,' the *News of the World* later reported of Wood. It was this extraordinary composure that mesmerised the gathered journalists. Wood had passed the time in court in continual sketching: even drawing Grantham during his summing-up, until a warder stopped him. In the anxious minutes after the jury's return into court Wood completed the portrait, titling it *The Last Moment*.

The trial had itself been a sensation, covered by every newspaper in the minutest detail. The horrifying circumstances of the murder; the twists and turns of the police investigation that led to Wood's arrest; the puzzle of the evidence; the vivid insight into the lower strata of London life that had been presented: many things had combined together to fascinate the public. And, for whatever reason, feeling had moved very strongly in favour of Robert Wood. That afternoon, from about three o'clock onwards, a huge crowd of onlookers – stretching all the way down from the Old Bailey to Ludgate Circus – had started to gather to await the verdict, seemingly indifferent to the midwinter weather. Many likened the crowds to those that had formed outside Newgate prison during the Gordon riots of 1780, or the jubilant throng that filled London to celebrate the relief of Mafeking in 1900. By six o'clock it was estimated as 10,000-strong. Such a response to a trial now is virtually inconceivable. In 1907, in an age before the advent of television and radio, and when cinema was still in its infancy, the criminal courts provided part of the entertainment that lightened the burden and grind of daily life. A policeman whispered to Wood's solicitor, Arthur Newton: 'If there's a conviction I don't know what will happen.'

Despite the judge's clear indications, the jury was expected to be out for hours, and many thought no verdict would come until the following morning. But at eight o'clock word got out that a verdict had been reached. There was a scramble to get back into court to witness the denouement. Counsel returned from the robing room. The jury filed back into court, dimly lit under its newly installed electric lights, after just seventeen minutes of deliberation. Finally the judge made his entrance. Only Robert Wood had remained in his seat throughout the anxious minutes: the cruel practice then was for the defendant to have to await the jury's verdict in the dock, their demeanour open to inspection at the time of their greatest crisis, like some exotic creature caged in a zoo. One newspaper, caught up in the melodrama of the moment, reported how he 'sat on like a man deeply interested in a new phase of life; like a child absorbed in a new plaything. Only in this case his plaything was death. Faces were glued to the glass screen of the dock, wherein sat Wood.'

The clerk stood and addressed the jury again:

CLERK: Gentlemen of the jury, have you agreed upon your verdict?
FOREMAN: We have.
CLERK: Do you find the prisoner at the bar guilty or not guilty of the wilful murder of Emily Elizabeth Dimmock?
FOREMAN: We find him not guilty.
CLERK: You say he is not guilty. Is that the verdict of you all?
FOREMAN: It is.

There was uproar in court; amid the upheaval Marshall Hall was unable to reach his client in the dock to congratulate him. Almost immediately, the crowd outside the Old Bailey reacted with collective joy, singing 'Auld Lang Syne' and 'For He's a Jolly Good Fellow' as news of Wood's acquittal spread among them. Fifty mounted police struggled to control them; according to one spectator their 'muffled roar' could be heard inside Court Number One itself. What is remarkable is that there was nothing for these 10,000 to see or hear: no big screen or loudspeakers to relay the verdict, and no balcony appearance by Wood or Marshall Hall. Wood was instead bundled out of the Bailey by Newton, virtually unnoticed, and driven in a car to dinner at a hotel on the Strand, where a newspaper boy, failing to recognise the hero of the hour, tried to sell him news of his own acquittal.

Across London shows were stopped mid-performance for the verdict to be announced; from one stage the announcement was made by the renowned actress Mrs Beerbohm Tree, who had dashed straight from

Court Number One, where she had been a spectator until the end. Her voice quivering with emotion, she told the audience the glad tidings: 'While the jury were out, we seemed to hold our breath, and we hoped, but we feared, perhaps the jury would after all . . . I was one of those who burst into tears.'

Above all else, the trial had been a triumph for Edward Marshall Hall KC. His client proved to be a nine-day wonder; after an ill-fated attempt to cash in on his momentary notoriety, he changed his name and slipped back into obscurity, to reconstruct the respectability that the trial had stripped from him. But obscurity was the last thing on his counsel's mind. Marshall Hall had, through his strenuous defence, completed the professional resurrection he had been striving for. Henceforth he was the undisputed star of the English Bar; a position he maintained almost to his death two decades later. The next years would see a succession of extraordinary murder trials that have become landmarks of the criminal history of England: the poisoner Frederick Seddon; the 'Brides in the Bath' murderer George Smith; the solicitor Harold Greenwood, acquitted of poisoning his wife with arsenic; the Eastbourne murderers Field and Gray. Seddon and Smith were both tried in Court Number One and it was during his closing speech on behalf of Seddon in 1912 that Marshall Hall perfected his so-called 'scales of justice' peroration, which he would thereafter regularly wheel out in criminal trials:

> Gentlemen, I often think, when I look at the great figure of Justice which towers over all our judicial proceedings, when I see the blind figure holding the scales I often think that possibly the bandage over the eyes of Justice has a twofold meaning. Not only is it put there so that the course of justice should not be warped by prejudice or undue influence one way or the other; but sometimes I think it is put there so that those who gaze should not see the look of infinite pity which is in the eyes of Justice behind that bandage,[18] the look of infinite mercy which must always temper justice in a just man.

The jury in Seddon was rather more impervious to this kind of shameless rhetoric than had been the jurors in Wood: they convicted. Similarly George Smith went to the gallows. We encounter Marshall Hall again in Chapter 3 in perhaps his most remarkable triumph.

★

It is very difficult now to understand the great swell of feeling in favour of Robert Wood. The crime for which he was charged was appalling and, once he knew that he was in danger, Wood had sought to manipulate Ruby Young into giving a false alibi in a way that was frankly nauseating. Even if Mathews's cross-examination had not revealed a killer it had exposed a man marred by profoundly unattractive characteristics: hypocrisy, petulance and vanity. (It did not stop at the court's door: after his acquittal Wood described Emily to a journalist, in revolting ersatz Baudelairean prose, as 'a crushed rose that had not lost all its fragrance . . . who appealed in some way to my sense of the artistic'.) Yet it was poor Ruby Young who had to be smuggled from court, to chants of 'Ruby, Ruby, won't you come out tonight', because the police felt that her safety was in danger from a mob that stigmatised her as a Judas. The cab she fled in had its windows smashed regardless. It was Gladys Warren who lost her job in domestic service because she had given evidence on behalf of the prosecution. Several prosecution witnesses spoke of the abuse and threats that they had received in the lead-up to the trial. Robert MacCowan told the judge that he had received letters threatening to cut his throat and that the words 'blood-money' had been chalked on his door. His evidence had ended on this poignant note: 'In future even if I actually saw with my own eyes a man getting his throat cut in the street I do not think I would give evidence again.'

Marshall Hall told reporters straight after the verdict that he had always been convinced of Wood's innocence. This was of course part of his stock-in-trade; it was what his clients paid for. Yet later in life he confided to his daughter that he had come to think that Wood was probably guilty after all. This is the conclusion that most writers about the case have also arrived at.

The portrait that Edward Marjoribanks painted of his hero in his life of Marshall Hall was of the solitary struggle for justice of an intuitive genius. A close reading of the transcript of the trial of Robert Wood[19] presents a rather different picture. Often Marshall Hall's points misfire or strike a discordant tone. He sometimes gets the facts wrong and makes bad judgement calls. In short, he behaves like any other fallible barrister. It is also obvious that the cross-examinations he undertakes and the speeches he makes are not, as Marjoribanks intimates, the product of some form of semi-divine inspiration. They are the fruits of hours and hours of out-of-court work by him and a large team of unsung junior barristers. A cross-examination is not just a series of questions: it is a plan of attack. For each of the thirty-five witnesses called by the Crown that plan had to be devised. Although the transcript does not of course record them, we can be confident that the case was punctuated by frantic tugs of the gown and urgent whispers in the ear from the juniors sitting in the row behind Marshall Hall as he started to veer off-piste.

There is undoubted brilliance; but there is also cynical manipulation of the jury's prejudices and limitations. In 1963 a juror's daughter wrote to the BBC alleging that her father had told her that 'Marshall Hall was a bully, intimidating witnesses by shouting at them and confusing them.' (Yet still he voted to acquit.) Marshall Hall had a heavy responsibility to his client, who stood in peril of his life, but time and again one sees in the trial an entirely calculated legerdemain with the truth. The trial became a game that Marshall Hall won not because the facts turned out as they did, but because Robert Wood was lucky enough to have him, in all his glorious ability to create 'an atmosphere', as his advocate. Marshall Hall exemplifies the proposition that in an adversarial system lawyers are not seekers after truth.

In a prim leader published the day after the verdict *The Times* sniffed that the 'case in all its aspects and bearings is a peculiarly squalid one, and it is difficult to find in it anything except its extreme squalidity to account for the exceptional interest and even excitement that it has aroused'. Squalid or not, the case has exercised a powerful grip on the artistic imagination ever since. Walter Sickert, whose studio was then located in Mornington Crescent, half a mile from St Paul's Road, had in 1906 started a series of paintings in which the central figure was a naked woman, her face obscured, lying on an iron bedstead in a dreary London room. Sickert continued the series after Emily's murder and Wood's trial, and started titling the canvases after the case. He now introduced into the paintings a mysterious male figure, sitting by or standing over the woman. The body of paintings, known as the *Camden Town Murders* and first exhibited in 1911, is very difficult to read. Does the man suggest threat or solicitude? Is the woman dead or asleep? Is she vulnerable or at peace?

Emily's body had been formally identified by her brother Henry, a plasterer's labourer from Tamworth. After his brief appearance as a witness on the first day the Dimmock family vanishes without trace. Emily herself ended up as anonymous as the faceless women in Sickert's paintings. Her individuality was effaced by the trial process just as it is by the artist's brush. Having looked at Sickert's paintings it is impossible to think about Emily except as mediated through his unsettling iconography of a dismal urban *anomie*.

The case also spawned a 1932 play, *Somebody Knows* by John Van Druten, several novels of the 1930s and 1940s (*Twenty Thousand Streets Under the Sky* by Patrick Hamilton and *For Them That Trespass* by Ernest Raymond among them), and even a modern Royal Opera House ballet. It featured in an episode of the 1989 BBC series *The Shadow of the Noose* (effectively a biopic of Marshall Hall, played by Jonathan Hyde), in which a young Peter Capaldi played Wood as an oleaginous womaniser who is clearly guilty as hell. Through the decades the central image of a young woman, beautiful, naked and dead, the victim of male desire and male violence, has exerted its baleful power on our culture.

A few days after the end of the trial the *Daily Mail* published an essay by the novelist Sir Hall Caine entitled 'The Law and the Man: A psychological study of the great trial'. Caine had sat fascinated in Court Number One throughout and was still in something approaching a state of post-orgasmic rapture (he told his readers that he was writing 'with all the physical exhaustion and emotional strain of a thrilling experience still upon me'). The piece offers some clues about why the case had so overwhelmed the public imagination. Caine refers to the 'hot interest of a human being on trial for his life. That the life which was in peril in this case should be saved, if possible, against the awful avenging power which was waiting to destroy it, this was all, or nearly all, the public heart was conscious of.'

Yet the frenzy of enthusiasm that inspired the crowds when the verdict of not guilty was brought in was not for Wood himself. 'Wood, the individual man, was never for one moment in mind,' Caine admitted. 'What was there instead was a very simple thing – the thought of a man who had lain three months under suspicion of murder, had stood six days in imminent danger of death, and was now declared innocent and permitted to go free.' The acquittal of Wood was the acquittal of everyman, with all his flaws, and so the acquittal of everyone in the surging crowd that had awaited the verdict outside the Old Bailey.

In the ecstatic aftermath of the trial experience Caine was generous in his appraisal of the English criminal system. He contrasted the Old Bailey favourably with the 'measureless and merciless delay' of the American courts. Grantham had shown 'obvious impartiality'; the police had been diligent and efficient; Sir Charles Mathews had 'no trace of bloodthirstiness, no straining for a conviction, no disposition to take even a momentary advantage of the prisoner's confusion of thought'; Marshall Hall's defence had been 'conducted with a strenuous and impetuous power that I have never seen excelled'. So pure was Old Bailey justice, Caine declared, that 'the life of an innocent man is safe.' Wood himself was the only participant in the drama whom Caine could not find room to praise. 'The prisoner would have been more convincing and immeasurably more sympathetic' if he hadn't entered the witness box. With his 'long delicate hands and tapering fingers . . . deep-set cavernous eyes and glistening eyeballs' Wood was, Caine thought, 'a human phenomenon'. Treading delicately, the novelist wondered if he might 'lack some necessary quality on the moral side of [his] nature'. Finally Caine recalled 'with shame' that it was only after the trial, as he drove away through the 'delirious crowds' celebrating Wood's acquittal, that he remembered that the murder of poor Emily Dimmock, 'a pitiful thing out of the puddle of civilised society', was the only reason that the trial had taken place at all. His lapse of memory is sadly telling: this murder trial had become pure entertainment, and its star was not the victim, or even the defendant, but only his box-office barrister.

2

'The Cult of the Clitoris'

R v Noel Pemberton Billing (1918)

OUR CONCEPTION OF the past can be obscured by received notions of it, accumulating like yellowing layers of old varnish on a painting. Particular themes can become dominant in modern thinking about historical events, pushing aside other currents. Against the fixed narrative, a criminal trial can provide an underground route into an understanding of the past that the standard histories do not offer. It can furnish a piece of micro-history which, by harnessing the voices of litigants, witnesses, judges and advocates, reveals the preoccupations and prejudices of a particular historical moment. The Noel Pemberton Billing case is a classic example of the power of a criminal trial to capsize our sense of a period. It is a story of egotism, hysteria, sexual terror and xenophobia that sits uneasily with one view of the British 'home front' during the First World War as being characterised by unity and common purpose. It also offers a corrective to the notion of the courtroom as a place of order, governed by prescriptive rules of behaviour, its participants engaged upon a quest for truth and justice. For six days in the early summer of 1918 Court Number One became what one newspaper described as a Mad Hatter's Tea Party ('Bedlam', 'a madhouse', were other descriptions), a platform for the propagation of outrageous lies and smears, and ultimately a brazen attempt to whip up popular frenzy and so alter government policy.

The story starts, almost thirty years before the trial, with Oscar Wilde's decision to create a decidedly modern version of the biblical narrative of a young dancer and John the Baptist. Originally written in French in 1891, *Salome* took as its starting point the brief accounts in the Gospels of the unnamed stepdaughter of Herod, who asks for the head of John the Baptist as a reward for a dance she performs for the king's guests. The sensuous and, as it was then thought, 'decadent' spin that Wilde gave to the story – he invented her 'dance of the seven veils' – was to make Salome the ur-femme fatale, her thwarted desire for the Baptist (dubbed Jokanaan in the play) the central driver of her actions. *Salome* is now seen as an innocuous if rather overwrought part of Wilde's oeuvre. But at the time its mixture of decapitation, overt female sexuality and perceived blasphemy was considered scandalous: in 1892 a proposed London production was banned by the Lord Chamberlain on the startling grounds that it depicted biblical characters on stage.

The play premiered instead in Paris in 1896, while Wilde was in Reading Gaol after his conviction at the Old Bailey for gross indecency the previous year. During the decades that followed to escape the censor's remit *Salome* could only be performed privately in England. So tainted was Wilde's name that even the great operatic version by Richard Strauss was also initially banned by the Lord Chamberlain. In the meantime a dance version of the play, entitled *The Vision of Salome*, was put on at the Palace Theatre in 1908, its producers somehow managing to evade the Lord Chamberlain's restrictions by arguing that it was only very loosely based on Wilde's original. Robbie Ross, a close friend of Wilde's and his literary executor, was appalled that audiences could observe Salome's 'burlesque dance of the seven veils [and] her strange gyrations to erotic music' without hearing the words of the original 'beautiful and reverential play'.

In this dance version Salome was played by Maud Allan, a leading dancer of the day, already in her thirties but making her British debut. Maud had been born in Toronto in 1873. Her family had moved from Canada to San Francisco, where in 1895 her older brother Theodore was convicted of, and later hanged for, the ritualistic murder of two young women whose mutilated bodies had been found in the Baptist church the family attended. By then Maud was in Europe and on her way to becoming an accomplished dancer. She had debuted her version of *Salome* in Vienna in December 1906 and had then taken the show across Europe, arriving, finally, in London in 1908.

Long-limbed, with wide-apart eyes, red-gold hair and high cheekbones, dancing in a sheer skirt with her stomach bare and her breasts covered by strategically placed strings of pearls, Maud was an Edwardian sex symbol who had a mesmerising effect on her London audiences. A contemporary account sums up her allure: 'one moment she is the vampire . . . next she is the lynx . . . Her slender and lissom body writhes in an ecstasy of fear, quivers at the exquisite touch of pain, laughs and sighs, shrinks and vaults, is swayed by passion . . . London has never seen such graceful and artistic dancing.'

Although Maud broke box-office records she was nonetheless subsidised by Margot Asquith, wife of the Liberal Prime Minister H.H. Asquith. Margot paid the rent on Maud's London apartments, situated in a wing of a grand mansion in Regent's Park, and was rumoured to be Maud's lesbian lover. Despite the extravagance of her performances she danced in front of Queen Alexandra and King Edward VII, whose mistress she was also whispered to be. But she was also a serious and internationally celebrated artist, a pioneer of modern dance, who once commissioned Debussy to compose her accompaniment.

Maud's success in 1908 had already led to her first brush with Wilde's former lover, Lord Alfred Douglas, who had by now metamorphosed from the Ganymede of the 1890s to strident Edwardian moralist. Douglas's magazine the *Academy* carried a negative review which accused Allan of not being a 'genuine dancer' at all. Douglas printed an apology after Maud threatened a libel action, but when they later ran into one another Douglas jeered, 'But your brother was a murderer!', prompting Maud to strike him in the face with her fan. Battle was now joined, although the denouement would take a decade to arrive.

Maud Allan had, inadvertently, been caught in the crossfire of a decades-long vendetta between two of Wilde's lovers, Alfred Douglas and Robbie Ross, who, it was rumoured, had seduced Wilde when Ross was only seventeen. It was a feud that highlighted the charged feelings that Wilde continued to inspire years after his death. Whereas Douglas had publicly renounced his former lover, Ross, by contrast, had spent the years after Wilde's death as the writer's executor seeking to restore his personal and literary reputation. In 1913 Douglas launched a libel action against the young Arthur Ransome (later of *Swallows and Amazons* fame), whose new biography of Wilde, which Ross had assisted in, carried previously unpublished sections of Wilde's *De Profundis*, the famous prison letter addressed to Douglas (but never delivered to him). This made it plain that the two had been lovers, as well as painfully recounting Douglas's insidious influence on Wilde.

At the trial for criminal libel before Mr Justice Darling (we shall meet him again), Douglas tried to turn the tables on Ross, whom he described as 'the High priest of all the Sodomites in London'. The libel action failed and, although Douglas was financially ruined, he was not finished.[1] In retaliation Douglas started accusing Ross and his secretary of being homosexual lovers. They may well have been, but in the days when homosexuality was a criminal offence, to say as much was potentially a gross libel. In January 1914 Douglas got T.W.H. Crosland, a journalist on the *Academy*, to write deliberately defamatory letters to Ross, accusing him of being a 'filthy bugger' and a 'notorious sodomite'. Rather than ignore Douglas, Ross rose to the bait and launched his own ill-advised criminal libel action, which began at the Old Bailey on 19 November 1914. Just like Wilde's libel action against Douglas's father, the Marquess of Queensberry, nineteen years earlier, the proceedings backfired spectacularly on Ross. Testimony was given of Ross 'painting and powdering' a youth's face. The court also heard of a party in 1911, attended by Ross, at which twenty or thirty men had danced together. Ross abandoned the libel action before the end of the trial and, himself financially ruined, had to pay Douglas's costs.

Still Douglas continued his vendetta, demanding that the Prime Minister, a close friend of Ross's, publicly denounce him. Instead the Asquiths signed a letter in his support, alongside 300 well-known figures. This only provoked Douglas into ever greater rage. He now started writing reams of doggerel polemic verse denouncing 'Lust unashamed and Filthiness Condoned/And crowned and comforted. This whited wall!' He even penned a philippic in the manner (albeit at some distance) of Alexander Pope entitled the *Rossiad*, lamenting that 'the country's rife/With people of progressive views/Nor are they "mostly German Jews"'. 'Two filthy fogs blot out thy light/The German, and the Sodomite', Douglas concluded his dubious tetrameter. The muddled elision in Douglas's mind between homosexuality, Jewishness and Germany was one that would come to the fore during the war that had just commenced.

Once it became clear that the war would not, after all, be over by Christmas, fear of invasion began to loom large. German bombing was of course far less extensive than the Luftwaffe's Blitz twenty-five years later. Nevertheless the German naval bombardment of several coastal towns, followed from May 1915 onwards by air raids over London by Zeppelin airships, had a huge impact on the British psyche. Tales of unspeakable atrocities committed by German troops – almost all apocryphal – began to circulate, and Prussian brutality was oddly equated with homosexuality. Many muttered about the close links that members of the upper classes had to Germany. Asquith had had a German governess; his wife was known to take gifts to German POWs; the society beauty Diana Manners had – horror of horrors – once been photographed with the Counsellor to the German Embassy in London. In July 1917 even the royal family felt obliged to adopt the suitably English-sounding dynastic name Windsor to replace the German Saxe-Coburg and Gotha.

This proved to be a wise decision when, a month later, Germany started dispatching its new Gotha planes to bomb London.

It is especially strange, given subsequent events, to find that German militarism and Jewry were also seen by some as bedfellows during the First World War. Many German Jews had emigrated to Britain in the nineteenth century; by the start of the war most had become fully anglicised, and a number held important positions in banking, business and politics. An attempt was made to force the merchant banker Sir Ernest Cassel, who had lived in Britain from the age of seventeen and converted to Catholicism, to resign from the Privy Council. In 1915 Sir Edgar Speyer, a financier and artistic philanthropist, who had been honorary treasurer of the fund raised to support Robert Falcon Scott's 1910 Antarctic expedition, emigrated to America after furious mobs, provoked by his German-Jewish roots, had besieged his home.

One common side effect of war is a general loosening of sexual *mores* on the home front. Illegitimate births in Britain rose by 30 per cent in the First World War. With husbands and sweethearts away on active service, there was a marked increase in the incidence not only of extra-marital sex, but also (if contemporary accounts are to be believed) of lesbianism and transvestism. There was widespread paranoia that a homosexual fifth column threatened to sap the nation's moral fibre and drain its martial spirit.

The fall of Asquith in 1916, amid rumours that he was about to accept a German peace offer, did little to satisfy those in the press and Parliament who saw the conflict in Manichean terms as a struggle between wholesome British values and German decadence. The supposed mantra of Asquith's successor David Lloyd George was simple: 'Win the War.' But that war only got bloodier and then seemed to be locked in stalemate. The outbreak of the Russian Revolution in March 1917, followed by the Bolshevik seizure of power in November, gave Germany a major boost. The German-Russian armistice in December 1917 allowed Germany to redirect men and materiel to the western front, and the signing of the Treaty of Brest-Litovsk in March 1918 brought a formal end to the war in the east. By now there were serious fears in London that the war might be lost. On 18 March 1918 Germany launched the so-called Ludendorff Offensive, breaking through Allied lines and surging southwards towards Paris. In London, secret contingency plans were laid to evacuate British forces and sue for peace.

Lloyd George's handling of the war had by early 1918 become the subject of heavy criticism both in Parliament and in the army. A loose right-wing grouping detected in government policy defeatism and lack of ardour in the relentless pursuit of total victory over the German war machine. If these 'Die-hards' had a leader by April 1918, it was arguably a thirty-seven-year-old independent MP called Noel Pemberton Billing.

Billing's life story reads like that of a real-life, if cranky, Richard Hannay. Born the son of a wealthy owner of iron foundries in London and Birmingham, Billing did not shine at school and left his first job, in the City of London, after assaulting, as he put it, 'a peculiarly offensive German clerk'. He then went to South Africa and fought in the Second Boer War. Billing returned to England with a passionate interest in gadgetry, and in the early 1900s he patented several more or less improbable inventions: a glider (whose inaugural flight almost cost him his life), a typewriter that could be operated by the index finger only, and a petrol-driven automatic gun. He also found time to start a magazine called the *British South-African Motor Car*, to work briefly as the manager of Richmond Theatre, and to build an aerodrome where he constructed the first British powered mono-plane aircraft to make it off the ground – albeit for only sixty feet.

Billing's was a life of relentless activity in which he seemed to race from one enthusiasm to another. He dabbled in property development in Sussex; he gambled at Monte Carlo; he even trained as a barrister at the Middle Temple and took chambers in Essex Court. Tall, dashing and sporting chiselled cheekbones, Billing was, according to one historian, 'fascinated by fast aircraft, fast speed-boats, fast cars and fast women'. His fleet of cars included a lemon-yellow Rolls-Royce and a strange hybrid Austro-Daimler which resembled a torpedo on wheels and which inev-itably landed him in court on multiple speeding charges. He then bought a disused coal wharf on the Solent where he developed a flying boat called the Supermarine, which he showed off at the Aero Show in Olympia in March 1914.[2] Although it refused to take off he secured an Admiralty order for twelve seaplanes of a different design, and an order from Germany for two flying boats.

At the outbreak of war Britain had only 100 military aircraft at its disposal. Partly out of derring-do and partly out of commercial self-interest, Billing joined the Royal Naval Air Service, while publicly campaigning for Britain to ramp up the manufacture of planes. He now wanted to make his mark on the political scene. In March 1916, standing as an independent, he was elected at a by-election in Hertford, winning by more than 1,000 votes on a ticket of 'purity in public life' and viru-lent anti-Germanism.

Throughout his parliamentary career, Billing saw his great task as campaigning for a new aviation policy, a role that saw him dubbed as the 'Member for the Air'. He quickly filled the parliamentary vacuum created by the resignation due to bankruptcy of the right-wing populist Horatio Bottomley in 1912. Billing argued that British planes were poorly built 'Fokker fodder', whose pilots had not been simply killed by the Germans but 'murdered' by British incompetence. His agitation led indirectly to the creation of a dedicated Air Ministry in 1917 and the birth of the RAF a year later. Yet he had a fractious relationship with the wartime coalition. He was resented for the outrageous parliamentary attacks he launched on ministers, and the government retaliated by exposing holes in Billing's exaggerated account of his own wartime activities, in which he claimed to have 'led the first British bombing raid on Germany'. He was little troubled by reality: in fact he had held the rank of squadron commander for only one day before resigning his commission in January 1916.

Billing's own increasingly extreme opinions were broadcast in his self-promoting weekly paper, the *Imperialist*. At the same time Billing set up his own political party, the Vigilantes Society, whose policies were given mouth in the *Imperialist*: militaristic, violently xenophobic, calling for an all-out strategy to win the war. In its pages Billing and his acolytes advocated the internment of all enemy aliens and the bombing of German cities, while denouncing British 'Teutophiles' and moral degeneracy on the home front which was, they raged, hobbling the war effort.

Like most proto-fascist movements the Vigilantes nursed many contradictory beliefs. They criticised the Jews both for being crypto-communists on the one hand, and for being gangster capitalists on the other. They were quick to condemn pacifists or anyone they thought was undermining the British war effort, but also sometimes argued that Germany was Britain's natural ally against its more pernicious foes: international communism and Jewish big business. And, needless to say, homosexuality also fell within the beam of the Billing moral spotlight. British homosexuals were seen both as unreliable traitors, 'citizens of nowhere' belonging to an international camaraderie that acknowledged no national allegiances, and as susceptible to blackmail by foreign spies who could coerce them to work on Germany's behalf. 'Londoner urnings [homosexuals] have more in common with Teuton urnings than with their own countrymen . . . Failure to intern all Germans is due to the invisible hand that protects urnings of enemy race,' seethed the *Imperialist*.

So when Billing was introduced in January 1918 to an invalided British

secret service officer called Harold Sherwood Spencer, who claimed to
have seen a certain 'Black Book', supposedly 1,000 pages thick and
containing the names of 47,000 sexually deviant Britons who were being
blackmailed by a 'hidden hand' of German conspirators in Britain, it was
manna from heaven. Spencer had in fact been discharged from the army
for 'delusional insanity'; nonetheless, or perhaps as a result, he was immediately engaged as Billing's assistant editor. In the 26 January issue of the
Imperialist and under the title 'The First 47,000' Billing thundered that:

> There exists in the *Cabinet noir* of a certain German Prince a book compiled
> by the Secret Service from the reports of German agents who have infested
> this country for the past twenty years, agents so vile and spreading
> debauchery of such lasciviousness as only German minds could conceive
> and only German bodies execute . . . It is a most Catholic miscellany.
> The names of privy councillors, youths of the chorus, wives of Cabinet
> Ministers, dancing girls, even Cabinet Ministers themselves, while diplo-
> mats, poets, bankers, editors, newspaper proprietors, and members of His
> Majesty's household follow each other with no order of precedence.

Billing became more confidential:

> The officer who discovered this book while on special service briefly
> outlined for me its stupefying contents . . . In the beginning of the book
> is a précis of general instructions regarding the propagation of evils which
> all decent men thought had perished in Sodom and Lesbia . . . In this
> black book of sin details were given of the unnatural defloration of chil-
> dren who were drawn to the parks by the summer evening concerts . . .
> Wives of men in supreme positions were entangled. In Lesbian ecstasy the
> most sacred secrets of state were betrayed.

On 9 February the *Imperialist* was reborn as the *Vigilante* and became even
more scurrilous. Billing had now started giving a string of hysterical speeches
calling for a 'poll tax' on all aliens living in Britain, and claiming that
German spies were busy both poisoning British confectionery and infecting
British soldiers with venereal disease. The government had by now had
enough of Billing's antics. But before further steps could be taken an
extraordinary sequence of events unfolded that looked likely to destroy
Billing without the government being seen to make a martyr of him.

★

By 1918 Maud Allan was forty-five and her career in decline. When offered the lead role in a new London production of Wilde's play by the drama critic and promoter of modern theatre J.T. Grein, she jumped at the chance. Grein was Dutch by birth and a Germanophile who had before the war taken a number of productions to Berlin. *Salome* was a provocative choice of play: amid the paranoia and hysteria that were at large in Britain in the fourth year of the war Oscar Wilde was to many the high priest of the moral degeneracy which that war was supposedly being fought to expunge. Sensitive to the furore that his production of *Salome* could cause, and knowing that the Lord Chamberlain would be unlikely to grant a licence for public presentation, Grein proposed just two private performances at the Prince of Wales Theatre on Coventry Street on consecutive Sundays, 7 and 14 April 1918. On 10 February the *Vigilante* was sent an advertisement that had been published in the *Sunday Times* about the upcoming performances by the novelist Marie Corelli, now justly forgotten but then one of the most famous writers in the country and a firm supporter of Billing's causes. While Billing lay ill in bed, Spencer received the letter. To his fevered mind everything fitted into place: a sadistic play written by a decadent homosexual, staged by a Dutchman of Jewish ancestry and German sympathies, starring a woman rumoured to be carrying on a lesbian affair with Margot Asquith. Everything that Billing's vigilantes detested seemed to have converged into one writhing mass of abomination. Spencer swung into venomous action. An article in the 16 February edition of *Vigilante*, bizarrely head-lined 'The Cult of the Clitoris', read: 'To be a member of Maud Allan's private performances in Oscar Wilde's *Salomé* one has to apply to a Miss Valetta of 9, Duke Street, Adelphi, W.C. If Scotland Yard were to seize the list of these members I have no doubt they would secure the names of several of the first 47,000.' Although this odd notice did not directly state that Maud was a German conspirator or a lesbian, the implication was clear.

On 5 March Grein saw the *Vigilante* article and showed it to Maud, whose predictable response was outrage. Robbie Ross was consulted and urged caution. Undeterred, Grein and Maud immediately commenced proceedings for criminal and obscene libel. The offence of criminal libel, finally to be abolished in 2010, was a curious legal hybrid. An action was brought by a plaintiff (normally a person who claimed that they had been grievously defamed by a publication) but prosecuted not in a civil court but in a criminal one: the maximum sentence was two years' imprisonment. It differed from a civil proceeding for libel in that it had to be shown that not only did the words published defame the plaintiff, but also tended to a breach of the peace.

The word 'clitoris' may never before have appeared in print other than in a medical or pornographic publication. Had no prosecution been brought then the libel would in all probability have withered on the vine, lost in the obscurity of yellowing newsprint. It would seem that few *Vigilante* readers, let alone members of the general public, even knew the meaning of the word. During the trial that followed Lord Albemarle reportedly asked fellow members of the Turf Club who 'this Greek chap Clitoris they were all talking about' was, while Spencer later claimed that in order to find a suitable title to the piece he had telephoned a local doctor to ask him the medical term for a female sex organ. (Though times were changing: Marie Stopes's *Married Love* was published in March 1918 and contained a detailed description of its importance to female sexuality; it rapidly became a bestseller.)

Billing seemed unperturbed by the summons, announcing that he had 'expected this . . . I wonder why it was left so long. When is the hearing? I see it is on the 6 April, that is significant as the *Salome* dance is to take place on Sunday 7th.' If anything, he was delighted by the attention. A public trial would suit his purity campaign very well.

In fact, after the Lord Chamberlain – solicitous to protect the Sabbath from Wildean sullying – objected to Sunday performances, the play had by now been rescheduled to a single invitation-only performance at the Kennington Theatre, south of the river, on 9 April. As if to insulate the play from further charges of depravity Grein proposed a double bill with Ibsen's *The Lady from the Sea* and the recitation of a patriotic poem, *A Tribute to Britain*, by the delightfully named Miss May Haystack, with all proceeds going to the Red Cross and YMCA. But the Kennington Theatre then took fright and disowned Grein's company. The itinerant production was forced to move yet again, now to the Royal Court Theatre in Sloane Square, later to become famous for its radical productions, where a single matinee performance was fixed for the afternoon of 12 April.

The initial hearing at Bow Street Magistrates Court on 6 April, at which the magistrate would decide whether there was sufficient evidence to commit the case for trial at the Old Bailey, provided a welcome distraction for the war-weary British public. The *World* reported that 'in a downpour of rain a queue some fifty yards long formed outside.' Maud Allan added a touch of glamour, arriving 'wearing a black fur cape with spangles on her bodice'. The prosecution was led by Travers Humphreys, who had a Wildean connection of his own: his father had acted as Wilde's solicitor in his own disastrous libel suit against Queensberry in 1895, which had commenced in the very same Bow Street courtroom, while Travers had acted as junior counsel for Wilde himself at the trial. Billing, who (perhaps predictably) had chosen to represent himself, concentrated on Grein rather than Maud in his cross-examination, highlighting the play's 'presentation of the physical orgasm' and claiming that this would attract sexual perverts who were controlled by the German authorities. Billing asked Grein, 'Are you of [the] opinion that this play is of a type calculated to raise the opinion of neutrals as to British morals and arts?' 'It has already done so,' Grein replied, to laughter.

Despite Billing's spirited defence, he was committed to stand trial at the Old Bailey. In fact, nothing could have suited his purposes better. He ended the hearing on a flourish: 'But, sir, so great is this issue, so wide and so significant are the powers for evil which this cult possesses, that I welcome the opportunity you have given me ['Hear, hear', could be heard from the public gallery] to present at a criminal court, before a jury of *my* countrymen ['Hear, hear'], the facts.'

After all the fuss the solitary matinee performance of *Salome* on 12 April 1918 was reportedly something of an anticlimax. Reviews were not glowing. *Variety* magazine ungallantly observed that 'Maud Allan, as Salome, would be well advised to stick to dancing, her nudity proving more attractive than her abilities as an actress.' The *Morning Post*, edited by H.A. Gwynne, a rabid anti-Semite, who was supportive of Billing's campaign, went further: '. . . a bizarre melodrama of disease . . . One may admit its atmosphere though it is an atmosphere people who are healthy and desire to remain so would do well to keep out of . . . One is reminded of some richly jewelled watch that does not go.'

Before the Old Bailey trial could begin there were yet more extraordinary twists to the tale. As Maud Allan was performing at the Royal Court the situation on the western front was becoming critical. On 11 April Field Marshal Haig issued his famous 'Backs to the Wall' order to British forces, urging them to fight on for 'the safety of our homes and the Freedom of mankind'. A clique of generals, appalled at Lloyd George's handling of the war effort and the current crisis, and fearful of rumours that the British government was entertaining thoughts of brokering a humiliating peace, started to plot the deposition of the Prime Minister. One of the plotters was a die-hard ally of Billing's, Lieutenant Colonel Charles A'Court Repington, the dashing former war correspondent of

The Times, now attached to the *Morning Post*. By 1918 Repington was being eagerly courted by generals wanting to undermine Lloyd George through the press. It has been suggested that in April 1918 Repington invited Billing to join his conspiracy against Lloyd George; Billing's part would be to create such anti-German sentiment at his trial that it would go some way to sabotaging peace talks being proposed – under the pretext of prisoner-exchange negotiations – to take place at The Hague. If Repington did make such a proposal it seems certain that Billing agreed. To maximise his ability to cause havoc at the Old Bailey Billing sought and obtained an adjournment of the trial to May. The year before the Attorney General had prosecuted at the Old Bailey a woman socialist accused of plotting to poison Lloyd George; now a case would be tried where the defendant was seeking to use the court process to assassinate the Prime Minister politically.

Just as the die-hards were hatching their plan the British government decided to use dirty-tricks tactics of its own against Billing. On 6 May he received a fan letter from a Mrs Eileen Villiers-Stuart:

Dear Mr Billing,

Please forgive the gross impertinence of an entire stranger writing to you. But altho' I'll admit until a few weeks I'd really never heard your name (I've not long returned to England), you've touched upon a subject very near to my heart . . . I am so *glad* you inserted that paragraph in the *Vigilante*. Of course you were sued for libel because when you wrote it you apparently 'hit home', and I consider always that a libel action is merely a cloak of pretended innocence for the apparently guilty. Also, I will say that I do not consider you were nearly severe enough when you said the 'first 47,000' – I should have written the 'first 470,000'. There are places around here not a hundred miles from my hotel [the Grosvenor Court Hotel, Mayfair], where the disgusting devices adopted by the late Oscar Wilde are hourly carried on, and considering the main people concerned in these places, or to put it plainer, the principal habitués, are men high up in naval and military circles, then one wonders how many of our state secrets and army positions are exposed under these conditions . . . One cannot write everything on paper, it would take too long, but if you'd care to take luncheon with me any day this week or next, I may be able to tell you many things that may interest and help you.

Eileen Villiers-Stuart was not what she seemed. Despite her surface Mayfair *grandeur* she had been born Eileen Graves, the daughter of a toothpaste salesman from the Wirral. In 1912 she had become the mistress of Neil Primrose, second son of the former Prime Minister Lord Rosebery, Liberal MP and a government whip, and had started working in some loose way for British intelligence. In 1913 she had married a bus driver, Percival Bray, possibly as a marriage of convenience to provide cover for Primrose's child. After Bray's apparent death on the western front in 1914, and Primrose's own departure to Palestine in 1917 (where he himself later was killed in action), she had married a Captain Percival Villiers-Stuart, who had been promptly posted to India.

Mrs Villiers-Stuart was an agent provocateur seeking to set what would now be described as a honey trap. She had been instructed at arm's length by the government, possibly with Lloyd George's knowledge, to lure Billing to a male brothel in Duke Street, Mayfair (where a photographer would be on hand), so as to ruin his reputation and put an end to his pernicious influence both in and out of Parliament. But her meeting with Billing did not go according to plan. She was so impressed by Billing's seeming sincerity and so overwhelmed by his magnetism, that she instantly switched her allegiance. The double agent became a triple agent. She disclosed to Billing her secret mission, agreeing to help his defence in any way she could, and promptly started an affair with the married purity-campaigner. Billing must have been a quick worker: the trial was due to start in late May 1918. (It was a crowded month for Billing; at about the same time he was apparently approached by a female member of the Christian Scientists, who had decided that he was 'The Saviour, Christ the King, come to redeem them in this moment of national peril'. In order to propagate his work into the next generation this woman, 'a senior lady in the movement – reputedly extremely plain', was deputed to offer herself up to him. It is said that a child was conceived days before the trial began. Unfortunately for the Christian Scientists when the boy was later presented to his father Billing refused to acknowledge him.)

On 21 May a confident Billing entered a 'plea of justification', pleading not guilty to criminal libel on the basis that 'all the defamatory matters alleged in the indictment are true' and that it had been in the public interest to publish them. The stage was set.

On 29 May 1918 *The Times* reported, in clinical sentences, huge German gains along the western front; Paris was now coming under artillery bombardment from long-range heavy guns. In the same edition, and under the heading 'Hope for Prisoners', it was stated that the government was about to open negotiations with Germany in neutral Holland for the repatriation of prisoners – negotiations it was widely assumed would range into deeper questions. On the same day Billing's trial in Court Number One of the Old Bailey began. It would prove to be one of the most absurd spectacles ever seen at the Central Criminal Court, a source of cynical amusement for war-weary soldiers, outraged indignation for those who had been inflamed by Billing's rhetoric, and horror to the establishment. Queues for the public gallery stretched down the street, swollen by ardent Billing supporters (many of them wounded soldiers in blue hospital uniforms), and, in fewer numbers, the idly curious. One young officer, recently returned from Flanders, later commented: 'I went to the Pemberton Billing trial for a little healthy excitement. Pantomime, circus, farce: that unique Court performance contained elements of all three . . . The excited gallery-audience cheered like spectators at a football match.'[3]

On the bench was the sixty-eight-year-old acting Lord Chief Justice[4] Charles Darling, who had two years earlier presided at a failed libel trial brought by Billing himself and before then at Alfred Douglas's disastrous action against Ransome. Darling – like so many High Court judges at the time – had been a Conservative MP, and had both a ready wit, too ready many thought, and, according to one contemporary, a 'daintiness and a finesse in his manner and in his physical "make-up" never associated with the average Britisher-born'. Nicknamed 'Little Darling', he was a frustrated writer who often quoted Shakespeare, Dickens and Tennyson in court. 'Who is this Mr Chaplin?' he once asked during a trial in which the name of Charlie Chaplin was invoked, thus perhaps starting a tradition of judicial obtuseness which continues to this day. 'My Lord, he is the Darling of the Halls,' replied counsel, to the judge's delight. Appointed to the bench in 1897, in 1911 he had tried Steinie Morrison, convicted in Court Number One for the notorious murder of a fellow Russian, Leon Beron, on Clapham Common. Darling had recently sat in the Court of Criminal Appeal to dismiss both Roger Casement's and Dr Crippen's appeals.

Travers Humphreys was now junior counsel to the fifty-five-year-old Ellis Hume-Williams KC, a Conservative MP and a 'fashionable divorce man rather out of his depth', according to one trial spectator (ominously, in his memoirs Hume-Williams refers to his 'rare appearances at the Old Bailey'). Because this was a criminal prosecution the choice of counsel had devolved to the Crown and an establishment man loyal to the government had been picked, tasked with preventing Billing prejudicing the peace talks or broadcasting too loudly the so-called fact of the 'first 47,000'. Although it was rumoured that he was receiving advice from a

KC behind the scenes, and despite having access to plenty of money, Billing continued to represent himself in court. It was a shrewd step; as an unrepresented defendant Billing had licence to misbehave in court in a way that no barrister could even dream of. (In Chapter 10 we shall see how, in the same courtroom seventy years later, Michael Randle and Pat Pottle took similar advantage of the latitude accorded to the defendant appearing 'in person'.) It also meant that he was liberated from the dock; instead Billing was permitted to sit in the well of the court at the table in front of counsel's row. From that solitary vantage point, directly facing the jury, he could paint himself as the individual battling the state in a lone quest to expose the truth.

Billing's first act of mischief-making was to object to Darling's presence on the bench. He complained it was unfair, because of Darling's notorious courtroom 'levity', which Billing had publicly criticised in the past, and the fact that they had crossed paths in court before. Darling gave him short shrift, saying that 'by the same process you might exhaust every judge upon the Bench'. Billing then asked for police protection for his two principal defence witnesses, none other than Eileen Villiers-Stuart and Harold Spencer, the insinuation being that they were at risk from nefarious forces. Again the judge brushed the request aside. Yet Billing knew precisely what he was doing and it had been a skilful start. The jury had to be schooled with the message that this was a case where not only the establishment was ranged against the defendant, so was the judge.

As she came into court that day, dressed in a red feather hat and a black cloak, did Maud Allan realise that the trial she had herself instigated would prove to have almost no connection with her actual complaint? Never has a court proceeding so completely detached itself from its original moorings. This would become a trial not about Maud's supposed lesbianism or lewdness; somehow Billing succeeded in turning it into an indictment of the government's war policy, the moral state of Britain and the scourge of supposed German perversion.

Hume-Williams outlined the case against Billing. The only charge that was being proceeded with at this trial was that of criminal libel against Maud. (Much to Billing's agitation the hearing of the charge brought by Grein – an easy target for the MP – was to be postponed to a later date.) Counsel for the prosecution explained the meaning of the words complained of. The mental pain of having to negotiate the word 'clitoris' in a public court was almost unbearable for him. 'Gentlemen, I am afraid once and for all, unpleasant as the task is – more particularly as I see there are some women in Court, I must describe to you (if these ladies *will* stay) what the meaning of the phrase is.' Having got through that terrible ordeal (which was shirked by the reporter from *The Times*, who merely reported that the heading of the article in question was 'unprintable') Hume-Williams explained that the words suggested that Maud Allan was a 'lewd, unchaste and immoral woman' whose performances were 'so designed as to foster and encourage obscene and unnatural practices among women'.

The *Daily Mirror* reported that 'there was a murmur of excitement when Miss Maud Allan entered the witness-box.' After listening to her examination-in-chief under the gentle questioning of Travers Humphreys, who would perform a kind of double act with his leader Hume-Williams throughout the trial, Billing rose to ride in for the kill. From under his desk he flourished a book entitled *Celebrated Criminal Cases of America*. He turned to a marked page and the book was handed to Maud in the witness box.

> BILLING: Is that a photograph of your brother? [A look of horror came
>   over Maud.]
> MAUD ALLAN: I ask if this has anything to do with the case?

It was obvious where Billing was travelling. Hume-Williams shot up to object to this outrageous question. Billing answered: 'I deeply regret it, My Lord, but I shall have to bring evidence to prove that that case and the vices referred to in that book are hereditary.'

So Billing was going to suggest that Theodore's murder of two girls twenty years earlier in San Francisco now explained Maud's decision to play the part of the sadistic Salome at a single-performance charity matinee in 1918. Darling's answer was equally disgraceful: 'I am bound to say I cannot exclude the evidence on any legal ground . . . You may put the question if you desire, Mr Billing.' Out came the whole awful story about the murders, apparently because Billing was going to prove that sadism was hereditary. Maud Allan looked desolate – the look of someone on whom was dawning the realisation that she had made a terrible mistake from which there was no return. She was now at Billing's mercy. He veered off on a new tangent. Had she understood the meaning of the term 'clitoris' in the heading of the *Vigilante* article? Maud replied that she had. 'Are you aware, Miss Allan, that out of twenty-four people who were shown that libel, including many professional men, only one of them, who happened to be a barrister, understood what it meant?' Billing looked meaningfully at the jury. Here was a woman who knew the meaning of the word clitoris without having to consult a medical dictionary.

Billing now turned to Maud's connections with Germany. He quoted from her autobiography, *My Life and Dancing*: 'It was decided that I should go to Berlin to take up my studies there.' 'This type of dancing is a German art? You had your instructions or training in Germany, did you not?' asked Billing, at a time when anything remotely associated with that country was anathema in Britain. Denial was futile: the point had been made and Billing turned his attention to Maud's society connections. 'Did you ever go to 10 Downing Street?'

'I had that honour.'

'Did you meet Mrs Asquith there?'

'Most naturally when I was her guest.'

Another meaningful look at the jury. Then a canter through the text of *Salome*. Billing asked Maud to read various passages; again it was an inspired rhetorical device. Maud was becoming Salome again in the witness box of Court Number One at the Old Bailey, lasciviously apostrophising the severed head of John the Baptist that seemed to hover invisibly before her:

MAUD ALLAN: Thy body is white like the lilies of a field that the mower hath never mowed . . . It is thy mouth that I desire Jokanaan. Thy mouth is like a band of scarlet on a tower of ivory. It is like a pomegranate cut with a knife of ivory. The pomegranate's flowers that blossom in the gardens of Tyre, and are redder than roses, are not so red . . . Thy mouth is redder than the feet of those who tread the wine in the wine-press . . . It is redder than the feet of him who cometh from a forest where he hath slain a lion, and seen gilded tigers.

JUDGE [perturbed; this prose was nothing like his beloved Dickens]: Gilded tigers?

MAUD ALLAN: Gilded tigers.

JUDGE: Go on.

MAUD ALLAN [miserably continuing to read]: Ah! I have kissed thy mouth Jokanaan, I have kissed thy mouth. There was a bitter taste on thy lips. Was it the taste of blood? But perchance it is the taste of love. They say that love hath a bitter taste.

BILLING: A taste of blood. Presumably that comes from the taste of the lips?

MAUD ALLAN: When you kiss people you do not bite people; at least I do not.

BILLING: You know biting of the lips is an act of sadism . . . When you were toying with what the play portrays as the bleeding head of John the Baptist, you were committing an act of sadism in pantomime, do you understand that?

The prosecution case finished with its first witness. That very evening Maud was dancing at the London Palladium.

The next day Billing opened his case to the jury.

You may find that it passes your understanding to believe that in this country, where we are today in the midst of a great war, this sort of thing should go on . . . It does go on. It is necessary in the public interest that it should be ventilated. The prosecution has thought fit to call no evidence in support of this play *Salome*. The prosecution could not find one member of the Church of England or the medical profession who had the courage to go into the witness box and to say one word in support of the play or of the foisting of it on the country at such a time as this by private performance on Sunday afternoons at five guineas a seat. I say that this type of play must be stopped.

What this had to do with Maud Allan was not stated; but no one pulled the moral crusader up. He started to call his own witnesses. They would prove to be a selection of the mendacious, the manic and the deranged. Even on its first day the trial had teetered on the edge of absurdity; it now descended into bedlam. The first step of the descent was taken by Billing's recently acquired lover, Eileen Villiers-Stuart. It was her task to tell the court that she had actually seen the so-called Black Book and that the allegations made in Billing's article in the *Imperialist* headed 'The First 47,000' were all true. But how had this woman seen a book that, if it existed, was surely a closely guarded secret of the German intelligence services? The objective observer might not have found her response entirely satisfactory. She had, so she told the court, been shown the book by her 'friend' Captain Neil Primrose and an associate of his, Major Evelyn Rothschild, while taking tea in a hotel near the Surrey village of Ripley. The image of the three of them leafing through a Prussian catalogue of perversion while sipping cups of Earl Grey was a striking one. Why the two officers had shown Mrs Villiers-Stuart such a book there (or anywhere) was unclear; how Primrose and Rothschild had come to have it in their hands in England in 1916 was equally opaque; what was clear was that the book was now unavailable ('Have you any idea where it is?' 'I have not. I suspect it to be in Germany, but I cannot say'). It was also convenient that both soldiers were now dead, killed in action in Palestine a few months earlier.

BILLING: Has *your* life ever been threatened in this connection?

MRS VILLIERS-STUART [dramatically]: It has.

HUME-WILLIAMS [intervening in agitation]: What has this got to do with the question in this case?

JUDGE: Nothing at all. You know, Mr Billing, I have allowed you a good deal of latitude, but you are putting questions which I should not allow any counsel to come near putting. If you undertake to conduct your own case, you must conduct it according to the ordinary rules of evidence.

Billing now lost his temper. Arms flailing, he started shouting at Darling:

BILLING: I know nothing about evidence, and I know nothing about the law [this was a lie: Billing had been called to the Bar]. I come to this court in the public interest to prove what I propose to prove.

JUDGE: Very well, then you must prove it according to the ordinary rules of evidence.

Billing banged the table with his fist. His face white with anger, he pointed at the judge.

BILLING: Is Mr Justice Darling's name in that book?

MRS VILLIERS-STUART [waving her hands wildly at the judge and shouting]: It is, and that book can be produced. Mr Justice Darling, we have got to win this war, and while you sit there, we will never win it. My men are fighting, other people's men are fighting—

BILLING: Is Mrs Asquith's name in the book?

MRS VILLIERS-STUART: It is.

BILLING: Is Mr Asquith's name in the book?

MRS VILLIERS-STUART: It is.

At this stage in the proceedings *The Times* report recorded 'excitement' in court. The judge was lost for words; he had also lost control of his court. He had been accused of being one of the 47,000 and yet he did nothing other than gape. There was cheering in the public gallery.

The next witness was Billing's deputy editor at the *Vigilante*, Harold

Spencer. He explained his military record and a posting to Albania just before the start of the war where he had somehow become aide-de-camp to the German Prince William of Wied, who had in March 1914 become the short-lived King of Albania. It was while he was in the king's service, so Spencer told the court, that he had also seen the Black Book, apparently shown to him by the monarch himself. Through some feat of arithmetic Spencer had been able to calculate that it contained approximately 47,000 names of British degenerates; that list included Mrs Asquith and the former Lord Chancellor Lord Haldane, though strangely Spencer could not swear that the former Prime Minister's name was in it. Spencer explained that he had immediately told the Admiralty of this crucial intelligence. Why? asked Billing. Spencer replied in stout tones: 'This was a German prince, and I knew Germany was planning to declare war on us. Everybody in the army and navy knew it, and I thought it was my duty to get all the information home that I could.' This rousing answer was accompanied by a further outburst of cheering from the public gallery.

Instead of suppressing these ravings the judge seemed to have become deeply interested in Spencer's evidence. The witness now told Billing that he had been warned that if he published his knowledge of the Black Book he stood at risk of assassination by a circle of plotters who were bent on restoring Asquith as Prime Minister and forging a peace with Germany. Ignoring Hume-Williams's attempts to stop him, Spencer blurted out that the principal go-between in these clandestine negotiations was none other than Alice Keppel, Edward VII's long-term mistress. The crowded court was agog. Even the fact that Spencer had been diagnosed as suffering from delusional hallucinations was turned to his advantage. He explained that this was a false diagnosis that provided cover for his incarceration by British authorities who wished to shut him up. Apparently this was a common practice: inconvenient truth-tellers would be marooned on Greek islands (presumably other than Lesbos).

> HUME-WILLIAMS: So the people who are able to get secret service agents marooned by the orders of the British government are in the German service?
>
> SPENCER [triumphantly]: Yes, I think I told you that privately . . . Do you never remember meeting me at dinner and my talking to you?
>
> HUME-WILLIAMS: I? Never! . . . I never met you before in my life!
>
> SPENCER: I quite expected you to say that . . . You were never at the Clitheroes?
>
> JUDGE [humorously]: I expect one or both of you will get marooned.

79

Spencer was suggesting that he had met leading counsel for the prosecution at a private dinner and had told him all about German infiltration of the British secret service. Laughter rang through the courtroom; even the judge was smiling. Counsel struggled to maintain his composure.

> HUME-WILLIAMS: Just let us be serious. Do you mean to tell the jury that at the present time there are Germans in England . . . holding such important positions that they are able to get secret service agents marooned who are in the English service?
>
> SPENCER: Admiral Troubridge can tell you of five on one island.

More laughter.

Spencer finally turned to his 'Cult of the Clitoris' article. He explained the choice of the word clitoris. 'In consulting with a physician I had been informed it was a superficial organ that, when unduly excited or over-developed, possessed the most dreadful influence on any woman . . . An exaggerated clitoris might even drive a woman to an elephant.' Manfully, the (all-male) jury took this revelation in their stride. It was Spencer's apparent view that Salome's feelings for Jokanaan were 'the mutterings of a child suffering from an enlarged and diseased clitoris', and this justified his heading. This interjection elicited some barely suppressed laughter from prosecution counsel.

> BILLING [all sanctimony]: I beg to call Your Lordship's attention to the humour that that arouses in counsel.

It is very difficult to cross-examine a madman. Certainly Hume-Williams was not up to the job. Bizarrely, he decided to embark upon a textual analysis of *Salome* with Captain Spencer, whose credentials as a literary critic or moralist were far from clear:

> HUME-WILLIAMS: You give it as your considered opinion that the kisses on the lips which had been refused to Salome during Jokanaan's lifetime were sadism?
>
> SPENCER: And produced an orgasm.
>
> HUME-WILLIAMS [all perturbation]: What?
>
> JUDGE: What is the word you used?
>
> SPENCER: I am quoting from Bloch [a German psychiatrist, who had rediscovered and published the manuscript of the Marquis de Sade's '120 Days of Sodom'].

JUDGE: Repeat the word you used.
SPENCER: Orgasm.
HUME-WILLIAMS: Is that some unnatural vice?
SPENCER: No, it is a function of the body.

Neither prosecution counsel nor the judge knew what an orgasm was. This was not an exchange reported in the newspapers.

In the transcript of the trial page upon page is devoted to Hume-Williams's attempts to pin down precisely how Spencer had seen the Black Book and what steps he had taken to inform the authorities about it. The application of cold reason to the witness's make-believe world, in which there was a ready and uncorroboratable answer to every point, was always going to be a futile enterprise. The cross-examination was a disaster. It was as if the reality of the courtroom was gradually being distorted by Spencer's infectious delusions. Even the judge appeared to be mesmerised. Maud Allan had now been forgotten; she had been replaced as the subject matter of the proceedings by protracted digressions on the supposed fact that a degenerate British establishment was in thrall to a camarilla of German agents. If that was right, might it explain the current critical position on the western front? And yet Hume-Williams fanned the flames of this insinuation:

HUME-WILLIAMS: Are the present government of this country and the various office-holders appointed by those in German pay?
SPENCER: The present Prime Minister is having a very hard time to get rid of these pro-Germans.

This prompted further cheering.

By the third day of the trial the reign of lunacy was complete. Spencer left the witness box to be replaced by a certain Dr Serrell Cooke, a specialist in the treatment of tuberculosis, who now purported to offer expert evidence on the psychopathology of sadism.

BILLING: Is there any evidence in *Salome* that Oscar Wilde had a close and intimate knowledge of sexual perverts?
COOKE: It would have been impossible for him to have written the book without that knowledge. The probability is that he had Krafft-Ebing's book *Psychopathia Sexualis* in front of him at the time.

Needless to say, Richard von Krafft-Ebing, the famous psychiatrist and authority on sexual deviancy, was a German. The court was told by the learned doctor that a healthy-minded person watching *Salome* would find it tiresome. By contrast a person of perverted instincts would take 'extreme delight in the whole play; it would appeal to them immensely, they would probably have sexual excitation, even orgasm, watching the play'. Two further doctors – one of whom was no less a figure than Sir Alfred Fripp, personal surgeon to King George V – who were allied with Billing presented themselves in court to speak to the perversion and sadism of *Salome*. Perhaps the 'medical' evidence now seemed overwhelming to the befuddled jury.

The fourth day brought Lord Alfred Douglas to court. He was intimately acquainted with the Old Bailey, albeit as serial litigant rather than mere witness. His entire life was now consumed by resentment against his former lover, a campaign of bile that had involved him in a stream of libel claims, both as plaintiff and defendant, and had forced him into bankruptcy.[5] Twenty-five years earlier Douglas had translated *Salome* into English from Wilde's original French and, from this vantage point, was now able to use the platform of the witness box to denounce both the play and its author. But constant immersion in the processes of the law had, as with so many others before and since, destabilised him mentally. The scowling figure giving evidence now was far removed from the ethereal youth of the famous photographs of the 1890s:

LORD ALFRED DOUGLAS: I think [Wilde] had a diabolical influence on everyone he met. I think he is the greatest force for evil that has appeared in Europe during the last 350 years . . . He was the agent of the devil in every possible way.

BILLING: Do you regard his works as classics . . . to be cherished by the nation?

LORD ALFRED DOUGLAS: I think most of them ought to be destroyed. I do not think he ever wrote a thing in his life that had not an evil intention.

Soon Douglas was raving at the judge, accusing Darling of having caused him to lose his case against Arthur Ransome a few years earlier. In cross-examination Hume-Williams decided to engage in some witness-baiting:

HUME-WILLIAMS: When did you cease to approve of sodomy?

LORD ALFRED DOUGLAS: When did I cease to approve of sodomy? . . . I do not think that is a fair question. That is like asking: When did you leave off beating your wife?

But the question allowed Douglas to revert to a favourite hobby-horse of his: that homosexuals were everywhere promoted and protected by the establishment. 'If I were still on Oscar Wilde's side, I should be getting praise from judges and Prime Ministers . . . and from greasy advocates.' This was of course music to the ears of Billing. Meanwhile Maud Allan sat quietly in the courtroom, lost in wonder that her case had derailed into an uncharted hinterland thick with crazed conspiracy-theorists.

Billing's parade of cranks trooped in and out of the witness box: theatre critics, a Jesuit priest, more dubious doctors; all well-schooled in the almanac of paranoia; all speaking of the dominion of Prussianism, homo-sexuality and depravity over the British ruling classes. And somehow this torrent of nonsense related to a play – 'a perfect museum of sexual pathology', according to the testimony of one of Billing's acolytes – written by a man almost twenty years dead about semi-mythical events in Judea two millennia earlier. Yet it was all (or almost all – the references to orgasms and clitorises were of course expurgated) lovingly taken down by the journalists and printed in column after column of the next day's papers, to be derisively chortled over at the front in the periods when the British soldiery were not trying to hold the line against the German onslaught.

And yet by the fifth day of the trial, Monday, 3 June, the newspapers were reporting that the German advance had been halted. In retrospect this would prove the decisive moment, the pivot that sealed the outcome of the war. But on that Monday morning there was no sense of optimism. The war still hung in the balance and Billing was going to do his best to use his platform in Court Number One to provide backbone to crumbling British resolve. He announced that Mrs Villiers-Stuart had been warned that if she went back into the witness box, as was proposed, she would be shot from the public gallery. Certainly any would-be assassin would have had a very good sightline. Darling retorted that perhaps it would be better if the gallery were cleared – an invitation that strangely Billing did not take up. Mrs Villiers-Stuart courageously returned, seem-ingly indifferent to her personal safety. She continued her narrative of the revelations of sexual degeneracy at the tea party in Ripley.

BILLING: Did you take any step to put this knowledge before any public person in this country, any public man?
MRS VILLIERS-STUART [confidentially]: May I answer, My Lord?
JUDGE: Yes.

MRS VILLIERS-STUART: I did.

BILLING: Was he a prominent public man?

JUDGE: You may ask his name . . . instead of beating about the bush.

MRS VILLIERS-STUART [with deliberation]: Mr Hume-Williams . . . at flat
7K The Albany, Piccadilly . . . at tea.

So the 'public person' with whom Mrs Villiers-Stuart had apparently shared the information about the Black Book was in fact a Conservative MP and the very prosecuting counsel now sitting a few feet away from her. Poor Hume-Williams was having a hard time of it: this was the second defence witness with whom he had supposedly hobnobbed outside court. And Mrs Villiers-Stuart's tea parties were certainly filled with incident. *The Times* recorded further 'laughter' in the courtroom. Hume-Williams looked discombobulated; his junior, Travers Humphreys, cross-examined in his stead, all sarcasm:

MRS VILLIERS-STUART: Mr Neil Primrose took me down to Ripley to
show me the Black Book.

HUMPHREYS: Because it is a nice public place?

MRS VILLIERS-STUART: No, quite the reverse, because it is quiet.

HUMPHREYS: Do you really suggest that it would have been difficult for
this book to have been shown to you in a quiet place in London?

MRS VILLIERS-STUART: I do not know any quiet place in London.

JUDGE [attempting another witty sally]: After all, there is this court.

MRS VILLIERS-STUART: It is hardly quiet, My Lord.

HUMPHREYS [irritated by the judge's levity]: I do not know whether this
court could always be described as a quiet place. It is quiet at this
moment.

For a fantasist Eileen Villiers-Stuart certainly had instant answers to all of counsel's questions. Previously vague on the question of the Black Book's current location, she was now more definite: it was in Berlin in the custody of a Prussian Guardsman. Both Primrose and Rothschild were now dead, shot in the back – two patriotic British officers murdered because of their knowledge of the incendiary cyclopedia. In any normal world Humphreys' deadpan questions would have exposed this 'evidence' as scurrilous nonsense. But Britain in June 1918 was not a normal world. Paranoia had trumped rationality; truth was in retreat. The jury looked on with sombre faces. Even the judge seemed to be enthralled by Mrs Villiers-Stuart's extraordinary story. And the fact that this story was being recounted in Court Number One somehow gave it an imprimatur of both authenticity and profound importance at this moment of national crisis.

As he rose to re-examine his witness and lover Billing was determined to capitalise on the ascendancy she had gained over the courtroom. He took Mrs Villiers-Stuart back to the tea party in Piccadilly with Mr Hume-Williams, the hapless prosecuting counsel.

BILLING: When you met Mr Hume-Williams at the flat in The Albany, did you give him details of this book? Did he ask for details, or did you tell him?

MRS VILLIERS-STUART: He asked for details.

BILLING: Did Mr Hume-Williams take you seriously?

MRS VILLIERS-STUART: Quite seriously. I mentioned the name of Mr Justice Darling as one of those who appeared in the book. Mr Hume-Williams said he knew Mr Justice Darling.

BILLING: And did you give serious answers; it was a serious discussion?

MRS VILLIERS-STUART: Yes, it was a most serious discussion.

BILLING: And did you tell him about the agents?

MRS VILLIERS-STUART: I did.

BILLING: Did you give him the names?

MRS VILLIERS-STUART: I gave him one name, yes.

BILLING: Which name did you give him?

MRS VILLIERS-STUART: Jack Thomas Grein.

BILLING: As an agent, or as one of the 47,000?

MRS VILLIERS-STUART: As an agent.

BILLING: As an agent for whom?

MRS VILLIERS-STUART: For Germany.

BILLING: What did Mr Hume-Williams say to that?

MRS VILLIERS-STUART: He did not seem surprised.

So the circle was complete: Grein a bringer of the prosecution, Darling the judge, Hume-Williams the counsel, all of them in it together, depraved illuminati of a vast conspiracy to corrupt and destroy Britain.

One of Billing's final bizarre acts was to call as a witness J.T. Grein himself, a co-prosecutor alongside Maud Allan, albeit the prosecution had wisely decided that his own charge of libel should be heard at a later date. Billing could not understand (or rather decided to ignore) that it is a cardinal rule of evidence that a party cannot cross-examine his own witness, but must confine himself to open questions that do not tend to suggest the answer. Of course the only thing Billing wanted to do was cross-examine Grein, and in the strongest terms: about his decision to stage *Salome* in a time of war, about his status as an alleged German agent, about his foreignness. In those dark days even birth in the Netherlands, a neutral state, carried its own stigma. Each time the judge stopped the impermissible question, and eventually Billing gave up: 'As I cannot ask this witness any questions, My Lord, I will sit down . . . The laws of evidence are beyond me.'

Again, Billing was playing a shrewd game. He well knew the laws of evidence and had intentionally sought to flout them. All that mattered was what the jury saw: a solitary truth-seeker trying to elicit evidence from a witness and being thwarted by a judge who, along with the witness himself, was one of the perverts catalogued in the Black Book. Here was the conspiracy of silence in action, even in Court Number One. Still, Grein's brief sojourn in the witness box allowed for perhaps the only moment of poignancy in an otherwise sordid trial. Because Grein had been called by Billing, Hume-Williams was permitted to cross-examine his own client. In answer to his gentle questioning Grein admitted to having been born in Holland to Dutch parents. He had lived in England for thirty-three years; he had been naturalised twenty-three years earlier.

HUME-WILLIAMS: Naturalised as an Englishman, and you look like one?
GREIN: I *feel* an Englishman.

That last answer has a striking contemporaneity. But it is doubtful it impressed the jury.

The flow of witnesses now ceased. Rarely had so many lies been told in a courtroom under the veil of apparent sincerity. And although the judge had repeatedly clashed with Billing, his last decision concerning the evidence was very much in the defendant's favour. Hume-Williams wished to call Admiral Hall, the Director of Naval Intelligence, to give testimony rebutting what Spencer had said in the witness box about his connections with the British secret service and his provision of information about the Black Book. No doubt Admiral Hall would be able to tell the court that Spencer was a fantasist who had been discharged because he was insane. But Hall was a busy man and had not been kicking his heels outside court waiting to be called as a witness; the journey from Admiralty House on Whitehall to the Old Bailey would take at least half an hour. Darling refused to adjourn the trial to allow the prosecution to call him. It may be that his private reasoning was that the case in fact had nothing to do with the Black Book and the so-called 47,000. As he later said, the only issue in the case was whether Billing could prove that Maud Allan was a 'lewd and unchaste' lesbian. Yet half the trial had been taken up with this mysterious directory and its mind-boggling contents and it was that which the world was now interested in. The evidence of its existence would go unrebutted.

The courtroom had provided Billing with precisely what he craved: the ears and eyes of Britain captivated by his every word. His closing speech, which now followed, was a bravura performance. For two hours Billing railed against the 'mysterious influence' that was undermining the British war effort and which seemed to prevent a trueborn Britisher – as opposed to a 'German Jew' – from getting 'a square job or a square deal'. And it was a masterclass in rhetoric: 'I expect there are people in this country today who think I am mad. I *am* mad . . . I am obsessed with one subject. And that is bringing our Empire out of this war a little cleaner than it was when it went in. That is my obsession; and I plead guilty to it . . .'

Billing finished with *Salome*. Quite erroneously, but very effectively, he told the jury that a verdict of not guilty should follow if they found that the play was 'wrong and rotten'. 'Oscar Wilde founded a cult of sodomy in this country, and travelled from end to end of it perverting youth wherever he could; he left behind his work, so that his crimes may be perpetrated even after he was dead. And I tried to stop that.'

Yet it is likely that the jury did not fully appreciate that Billing slipped into the last minutes of his peroration the concession that he positively acquitted Maud Allan of the charge of lesbianism. This was nothing less than an admission of the libel of which he was charged, but it was lost in the thunderous applause from the public gallery that broke out as Billing sat down. Maud was seen to be crying as she left court that day.

On the sixth and final day of the trial Billing was no longer sitting in the well of the court. For Hume-Williams's closing speech and the judge's summing-up he had theatrically put himself back in the dock from which Darling had released him at the beginning of the trial, to allow him to conduct his defence from the solicitors' table. It was a masterstroke of self-martyrdom. 'My Lord, I wish no further privilege from the bench,' he nobly declared. Prosecuting counsel's speech was perfectly reasonable, but it was hobbled by his inability – since counsel may not give evidence – to respond to the extraordinary allegations made about the tea party he had supposedly attended at the Albany. However much Hume-Williams sought to bring the case back to the narrow question of a libel on Maud Allan, the issue had been crowded out by a host of lurid irrelevancies. And Billing had no compunction in constantly interrupting the prosecutor in his closing submissions, shouting from the dock, knowing that the judge, intimidated and befuddled, would never dare eject him from the courtroom. As he wound up, Hume-Williams finally demonstrated that he had some fire in his belly, fiercely denouncing Billing's appalling tactics throughout the trial and his attacks on Maud. But he botched the point by then alluding to Billing's constant insults of the judge. 'For over twenty years His Lordship has been a judge in our land. It has recently pleased the King to make him a member of the Privy Council and to add the title of Right Honourable to his other distinctions as a mark of appreciation.'

This paean sounded altogether too unctuous, not least given Billing's allegations that the trial was an establishment stitch-up. It also allowed the judge again to strike precisely the wrong note with yet another ill-advised attempt at levity: 'I wish you would not allude to that, because Privy Counsellors are particularly mentioned in the 47,000.' It was a clubbish quip that won Darling few friends in the courtroom. As he summed up, both Captain Spencer and Lord Alfred Douglas, still in court, joined in with Billing in screaming abuse at the bench. Both were ejected from court (Douglas later had to slink ignominiously back in to fetch his hat and stick, left behind in the ruckus).

During the hour and a half of the jury's deliberation Billing sat, as Robert Wood had before him, stock-still in the dock, an object of fascination. The jury returned and its verdict was given by the foreman, later described by Travers Humphreys as 'a dour-looking Scot, with a beard and side-whiskers'. The words 'not guilty', appalling but inevitable, elicited even wilder cheering than Wood's acquittal had a decade earlier. *The Times* reported that a 'more remarkable demonstration has, perhaps, never been seen in the Central Criminal Court'. Nor has it in the century since. In a belated reassertion of control, Darling ordered that the court be cleared, assisted by policemen who were on hand.

Much can be read into the verdict. Was it a judgement on poor Maud Allan and her suggestive dancing? Was it a reaction to the continuing influence of Oscar Wilde and his supposedly sadistic play? Was it a response to the state of the war effort and the degeneracy of the ruling classes? Or was this simply a case of jury intimidation? Each of those jurors knew that the court was packed with Billing's supporters, who had whooped and stamped their feet at the more extravagant reaches of their hero's invective and hissed whenever Darling had tried to curb it. Did they reason that self-preservation dictated an acquittal? We shall never know. What is certain is that those six days in Court Number One of the Old Bailey were an object lesson in how the virus of populism can so quickly spawn hysteria and lies, which the forces of reason are power-less to check.

The press response to the outcome was almost universal distaste at Billing's tactics. The *Daily Mail* wrote that Billing had 'brought forward . . . a vast deal of hearsay testimony more appropriate to Bedlam or to a Drury Lane melodrama than to a British court of justice . . . The proceedings in court constituted in this respect nothing less than a libel on the nation . . . Scenes were enacted of such grotesque unseemliness that the court resembled a madhouse.' Darling was widely criticised for his failure to control the trial and his predilection for introducing inapt jokes into the proceedings. In fact the lawyers seemed altogether ashamed of their involvement in the case. Ellis Hume-Williams would go on to write a particularly unrevealing memoir, *The World, the House and the Bar*. The Billing prosecution was undoubtedly the most famous of all his cases, but it merited not a mention. In 1929 Evelyn Graham wrote, in collaboration with Lord Darling, as he had by then become, *Lord Darling and his Famous Trials: An Authentic Biography*. Yet its authenticity did not extend to even mentioning Billing in the index. Instead Travers Humphreys, writing many years later, lamented that the case had been a 'nightmare' and concluded: 'Poor Miss Allan; she had little cause to love the law, or should I say, the administration of it.'

The crowd that had gathered outside the Bailey to await the verdict had no such compunction; it read into Billing's acquittal an unequivocal vindication of his campaign. Billing descended the great staircase from Court Number One as if re-enacting a Roman Triumph. The hero of the hour, flanked by the faithful Captain Spencer and Mrs Villiers-Stuart, he emerged into the daylight to rapturous applause. A week later Billing addressed a packed rally of his Vigilantes in the Royal Albert Hall. He promised to fight for a 'cleaner Britain' and the 10,000 present resolved to call upon the government to intern immediately all enemy-born subjects and require all aliens, even if from friendly countries, to 'exhibit on the lapel of their coats the emblem of their nationality'.

But even at the hour of his triumph, Billing's moment was passing. The Ludendorff Offensive had run out of steam and fears of impending German victory had subsided. The sinking on 27 June of the hospital ship *Llandovery Castle* by a German U-boat off the Irish coast, with great loss of life, had anyway put paid to any peace talks. Billing's parliamentary antics continued but by 1 July the House of Commons authorities had had enough. After he refused to obey an order of the Speaker to give way Billing was forcibly removed from the chamber by four attendants, directed by the Sergeant at Arms. Shouting, 'Intern the aliens,' as he was hauled out, Billing was unceremoniously dumped in the lobby amid laughs and cheers. A long period of suspension from Parliament followed and with it Billing lost his most prominent public platform. Vigilante candidates lost two by-elections shortly afterwards: on 16 July at East Finsbury Captain Spencer's Old Bailey fame, and fresh boasts about his supposedly heroic defence of the Bank of Ireland during the Easter Rising, failed to carry him home. The Vigilante Society put up no further candidates and a few months later was wound up after doubts were raised over Billing's cavalier use of its funds. Having been heavily censored throughout the summer and autumn, the *Vigilante* also ceased publication.

Meanwhile the government was determined to neutralise whatever remaining threat Billing might pose. Shortly after the trial had ended Eileen Villiers-Stuart was arrested for bigamy, after it emerged that her first husband Percival Bray was not dead after all, but had been fighting in France for the past four years. In an attempt to curry favour with the authorities she swore an affidavit in which she asserted that Spencer had perjured himself at the Old Bailey in collusion with Billing. (About her own evidence she was coyly silent.) It was not enough to save her. She was tried on the bigamy charge at the Old Bailey in September 1918, where she was represented by Sir Edward Marshall Hall KC, presumably paid for by Billing. Even the Great Defender could not work his magic on such unpromising material. After she was taxed by the prosecutor with an account she had supposedly given to her current husband's family of her previous spouse, poor old Bray, having been supposedly mauled to death by a lion while hunting in Africa, and his body conveniently eaten, she decided to throw in the towel and plead guilty. The Recorder of London, sitting in Court Number Two, sentenced her to nine months' imprisonment. A few months later *The Times* reported divorce proceedings instituted by Bray (whose career as a bus driver had not brought him into much contact with big game) against his wife in which Billing was cited as co-respondent. Mrs Villiers-Stuart's fall from grace was replicated in the following years by Billing's other two principal witnesses. Both Spencer and Douglas were convicted in the early 1920s of criminal libel – in each case for peddling further unhinged conspiracy theories – and received prison sentences.

Meanwhile it was gleefully put about in the newspapers that Billing's own wife had in fact been born of a German father. She angrily denied it and wrote to the Home Secretary pledging that if any proof were forthcoming of her supposedly German blood she would insist on being interned. Sure enough, irrefutable evidence turned up, but Mr and Mrs Billing thereafter remained strangely quiet. Billing had become a figure of fun; one might even say an object of *schadenfreude*.

The copious diaries and memoirs of the period contain frequent mention of the Billing trial. The universal theme is of derision and disgust at Billing. A typical response is Siegfried Sassoon's, who noted in his diary that 'The papers are full of this foul "Billing case". Makes one glad to be away from "normal conditions". And the Germans are on the Marne and claim 4,500 more prisoners. The world is stark staring mad and I don't regret the prospect of leaving it, as long as I am with my friends.' But, as has been said, history is not written by the victors, it is written by the writers. Billing's populist targets included the literary as well as the upper classes. Not for the last time, a charismatic self-declared patriot persuaded many that a privileged metropolitan elite was rotten with 'enemies of the people'. A substantial section of the population, whose thoughts were not recorded for posterity, probably agreed with Billing's thesis that the present government comprised 'some of the biggest crooks in history' (again the hyperbolic language has a contemporary ring), and privately applauded the discomfiture of the ruling classes during those six days of misrule in May and June 1918. The trial, sealed with the imprimatur of a not guilty verdict, succeeded in shifting the register of acceptable thought and word towards overt intolerance. Just as after Wilde's conviction in 1895, public sentiment hardened against the unconventional and the supposedly deviant. It would take many years for it to soften.

Billing continued as an MP for three more years. But he had lost interest in politics by the 1920s, which he spent engaged on various business schemes, sailing his yacht, and writing a futuristic play, inspired by Fritz Lang's *Metropolis*, called *High Treason*, which imagined Britain in 1950 during a conflict between the 'United States of Europe' and the 'Empire of the Atlantic States', the last act of which was set at the Old Bailey. It closed after a two-week run at the Strand Theatre in November 1928, but a film version was released the following year, featuring one of

Billing's own helicopters. He spent the 1930s trying to run a casino in Mexico and then managed (of all places) the Royal Court Theatre, where the performance of *Salome* in 1918 had played such a crucial part in his life, as a cinema. He died in 1948.

In an article that Billing wrote immediately after his triumph he proclaimed that 'in this fight against a foul and bestial foe, we can be no respecter of persons – we are out to make a sure victory and a hard peace. Anything or anyone that stands in the way must be firmly, yes, even ruthlessly, removed.' He might have added that neither could he be a respecter of the truth. Billing's biographer claims that the idea for the '47,000' was hatched from his telephone number – Hertford 47 – with a few noughts thrown in for good measure. The Billing juggernaut certainly had a terrible effect on the two people who had been the initial victims of his ruthlessness. After the trial Maud Allan was left desolate, her reputation in ruins. Her career went downhill; after a series of performances at the London Coliseum in 1921, which were critically mauled, she gave up dancing. Living on to 1956 she drifted between California and Holford House in Regent's Park, which became an increasingly sorry sight after a pyromaniac maid tried to burn it down and subsequent bomb damage in the Blitz. Although Billing had, in his closing speech at the Old Bailey in June 1918, denied that he had made any imputation against Maud's sexuality, he had in fact been right: her later years involved a succession of lesbian love affairs. As for Maud's co-prosecutor, J.T. Grein's own charge of libel was hastily dropped after Billing's acquittal. Dismissed by the *Sunday Times* as its theatre critic, Grein reportedly had a nervous breakdown shortly afterwards. He died in 1935.

That afternoon in early June 1918, as he strode out of court to meet his fervent supporters, Billing must have thought that he had finally succeeded in destroying the so-called 'cult' of Oscar Wilde. Yet, however viciously Billing's cadre of mountebanks had engaged in 'kicking Oscar's corpse'[6] in Court Number One, a century on it is Wilde, a modern cultural icon whose plays still captivate theatre-going audiences the world over, who has triumphed.

PART II
Glamour

3

Unnatural Practices

R v Marguerite Fahmy (1923)

A FABULOUSLY WEALTHY Egyptian prince; a sophisticated French wife
almost ten years his senior, former mistress to royalty; extravagant
rooms at the Savoy Hotel; a blazing row on the dance floor; three bullets
fired into the neck and back while London cowered under the most
tremendous thunderstorm anyone could remember; revelations of 'Oriental'
sexual practices; an Old Bailey trial with Marshall Hall leading for the
defence – the case of *R v Fahmy* now seems so luridly fictional that it is
difficult to believe that all its constituent elements are actually true.

Monday, 9 July 1923 had been a hot, sullen day. The evening continued
close, punctuated by the rumbling of distant thunder. Just before midnight,
the weather broke and London was engulfed by a cataclysmic storm
accompanied by some of the most prolonged and vivid lightning strikes
ever observed in England. Many buildings were struck and some set afire.
There was torrential rain. In the midst of this meteorological drama, a
killing took place at the Savoy, the most fashionable hotel in London,
favoured by the rich and the exotic.

Staying in a nine guinea-a-night suite were an Egyptian playboy in
his early twenties, known as 'Prince' Ali Fahmy Bey, his thirty-two-
year-old French wife, Marguerite, and his private secretary and close
companion, Said Enani. They were accompanied by Fahmy's Sudanese
valet and his wife's maid. Not classically beautiful, Marguerite had large
eyes, a sensuous mouth and was possessed of great seductive power. Born
into the Parisian working class, she had worked her way up to the status
of a leading courtesan, acquiring considerable wealth along the way.
She seems to have boasted various specialisms, including playing the role
of dominatrix (complete with masculine outfit and riding crop) and
demonstrations of lesbian lovemaking for the delectation of her wealthy
clientele. During the First World War she had even managed to attract

the attentions of the then Prince of Wales (later Edward VIII), with whom she had arranged sporadic liaisons during the final two years of the conflict, when the prince was posted in France.[1]

Ali Fahmy had been an appealing prospect for Marguerite. His vast personal wealth derived from his father's holdings in the Egyptian cotton industry, which had soared in value during the war, in the early months of which Britain had imposed a military occupation of the former Ottoman province and declared it a British protectorate. Having met Marguerite in Cairo in July 1922, Fahmy had been instantly infatuated. During that summer and autumn the pair began spending time together in the fashionable restaurants and nightclubs of Paris and the smart coastal resorts of Deauville and Biarritz. By November of the same year, the romance seemed to become more serious; Marguerite travelled to Egypt to live with Fahmy as he moved between his various opulent residences. In December 1922 the couple were married in a civil ceremony, followed by an Islamic wedding in February 1923.

The marriage proved to be unhappy. For all his flamboyance, Fahmy had an immature and unstable character, and expected obedience from his new wife. He was distressed when he was quickly disabused of this expectation. Marguerite was a hard-nosed adventuress, who seems to have been planning a lucrative separation and divorce from her disposable spouse from an early stage. Even by the time of the Islamic ceremony, the ill-suited husband and wife were already quarrelling violently. As the heat of Egypt became overwhelming they sailed to Venice in May 1923. Over the following weeks public shouting matches and physical tussles were a frequent occurrence, as the couple threaded a meandering progress around the finer cities of Europe. Finally, at the beginning of July 1923 they arrived in London.

At about half past two on the morning of Tuesday, 10 July, as the storm reached its zenith, a hotel porter, John Paul Beattie, emerged from the lift, near to the suite where the Fahmys were staying. Fahmy Bey, wrapped in his silk dressing gown, came hurrying out, followed by Marguerite. It was clear that the pair were only part way through a no-holds-barred row. Catching sight of Beattie, Fahmy demanded that the porter look at his face, indicating his left cheek, on which could be seen a couple of faint red marks. 'Look what she's done!' he whined. The porter politely asked the guests, who had been troublesome throughout the course of their stay, to return to their rooms and to stop making a commotion in the corridor. Fahmy, however, demanded that the night manager be summoned. Beattie passed on the message to a lift attendant and then continued wheeling luggage along the corridor towards the room of some other recently arrived guests.

As he was about to turn the corner, Beattie heard a low whistle and looked back to see Fahmy stooping down, apparently calling to Marguerite's lapdog, which had wandered off when the door to the suite was opened. The porter continued on his way. Immediately afterwards he heard, above the thunder, three pistol shots fired in quick succession. He ran back and saw Marguerite throwing a handgun to the ground. Some twenty feet along the corridor from his suite, Fahmy lay on the floor, collapsed against the wall and bleeding heavily from a head wound. The scene was one of horror amid the decorous surroundings. Fragments of bone and brain tissue protruded from Fahmy's temple; around his head spread a rapidly expanding halo of blood.

Ignoring Marguerite's hysterical screams Beattie called the receptionist and asked for a doctor and ambulance. The night manager ensured that the police were also summoned. It was immediately apparent that Fahmy had been gravely wounded by three shots: one through the left temple, one at the nape of the neck and one in the back; and that he was very likely to die. Marguerite was repeatedly crying out in French, 'What am I going to do? I've shot him,' and 'I lost my head.' Ali's secretary, Said Enani, was telephoned and rushed to the scene. Dr Edward Gordon, the hotel doctor, who had been attending Marguerite over the past few days for an ailment, was also called. Fahmy was collected by ambulance quickly and discreetly. Just before 3.30 a.m. he died in Charing Cross Hospital.

Marguerite was taken to the nearby Bow Street Police Station. At about eleven in the morning, fewer than nine hours after the shots were fired, she was charged with her husband's murder. At the suggestion of Dr Gordon, she instructed the leading criminal solicitor Frederick Freke Palmer. Money being no object, Sir Edward Marshall Hall KC (he had been knighted in 1917) was in turn retained to act as leading counsel for the defence. Now sixty-five years old, the Great Defender had in recent years shifted his practice to civil litigation, where he could command very substantial fees. His last murder trial had been in 1921 and a frequent refrain to his clerk had been his disinclination, at this stage of his life, to endure the stress and anxiety of representing clients in capital cases. But the magnetism of Madame Fahmy, not to mention the sum of 652 guineas marked on his brief, was sufficient to lure him back to Court Number One of the Old Bailey.

There seemed at first sight very little to say in answer to the charge.

Marguerite's position was particularly precarious because as the law stood in 1923 the usual requirement in criminal cases that the prosecution prove the charge 'beyond reasonable doubt' was displaced in cases of homicide by an ancient principle that was stated by one judge in the following terms: 'the killing of a human being is homicide, however he may be killed, and all homicide is presumed to be malicious and murder, unless the contrary appears from circumstances of alleviation, excuse, or justification.' So, it would be for Marguerite to disprove a presumption of murder.

Marshall Hall's biographer summed up the prevailing view: "'The lady forgot she was not in Paris," many people said. "There, no doubt, she would have been acquitted – *crime passionel*, you know – but one cannot behave like that in London."' This would be a case where the participants would be viewed through fixed cultural stereotypes. Yet, whereas one kind of foreignness – Marguerite being a French woman – was a source of mildly disapproving amusement veering into sympathy for her misfortune in not being born British, the other kind, which was depicted on a spectrum from 'Oriental' to 'Black', denoted something far more 'primitive' and sinister.

Predictably enough, the press reported the case with an unedifying mixture of thrilled excitement and unabashed xenophobia. Egypt was certainly in fashion. In November the previous year, 1922, Howard Carter had made the sensational discovery of the tomb of Tutankhamun. He had subsequently been toasted aboard the Fahmys' steam-powered *dahabeeyah* at Luxor, where Carter's patron Lord Carnarvon was also a lunch guest. 'Tut-mania' gripped the world. Ancient Egyptian motifs, such as animal-headed gods, vultures and winged scarab beetles, began appearing on everything from clothing, jewellery and furniture to the gaudy architecture of cinemas. The sober account in *The Times*, on the day following the shooting, that 'relations between the Prince and his wife had appeared perfectly normal,' soon gave way to more colourful reporting. Many papers focused on the exotic opulence of the couple's itinerant lifestyle: 'From Luxor to Cairo, from Cairo to London, living all the time with the magnificence of a prince and princess in a fairy tale,' according to the *Sunday Express*. And it did not take long for the press to start taking a more hostile approach, with one newspaper accusing Fahmy of a 'voluptuousness truly Eastern' and another alluding to the supposed 'Secret life of boy "prince"' and darkly suggesting that the forthcoming trial was 'destined to rank among the most amazing dramas in the country', due to 'its romance, its association with the beautiful and the bestial'. If the fairy tale was supposed to be Beauty and the Beast, this did not bode well for the posthumous reputation of Ali Fahmy. Meanwhile, Marguerite's fragile and passive femininity was consistently emphasised: an odd inversion of her *demi-mondaine* past and the fact that it was, after all, she who had fired the gun.

Marguerite's lawyers swiftly fastened upon this narrative of the vulnerable woman imprisoned and mistreated by her beast of a husband as the basis for her answer to the charge of murder. How that might translate into any kind of legally recognisable defence was hard to see. It was not at that time a defence to murder to have been treated badly and finally to have lost one's temper, unless the trigger for the loss of control immediately preceded it so as to found the defence of provocation (a defence which in due course the judge would rule out). But this would be another case where legal principle would give way to Marshall Hall's rhetorical juggernaut.

The lawyers discovered that the immediate backdrop to the shooting was at odds with the superficial glamour of the Fahmys' lives. The ailment for which Marguerite had consulted Dr Gordon at the Savoy was an acute case of haemorrhoids, which had flared up in the heavy heat of July. Rather more significant was the alleged cause of her discomfort. Marguerite had told Dr Gordon, as she now revealed to her lawyers, that her husband had 'torn her by unnatural intercourse'; indeed that he was addicted to such practices. Then, on 9 July, on the afternoon before Fahmy's death, a further consultation had taken place, now attended also by a consultant surgeon, who had recommended a minor operation which could be carried out in London two days hence. Marguerite had seized on the need for an operation to justify an immediate return to Paris, her home city. Arrangements were swiftly made and tickets booked.

The last argument between the couple had started on a trip that evening to the theatre (to see a presciently titled operetta, Franz Lehár's *The Merry Widow* at Leicester Square) during which Marguerite had informed her husband of her planned journey to Paris the next day. Fahmy seems to have interpreted the trip as the prelude to a final breach. After the evening's entertainment, the argument continued over a late supper back at the hotel, Fahmy telling Marguerite that as his wife she should not be travelling to Paris alone. Marguerite's response was to point to the bottle of wine and threaten her husband: 'You shut up or I'll smash this over your head.' Eventually, well after midnight, Marguerite went to her room leaving Fahmy to head off to Piccadilly, perhaps in pursuit of more compliant company.

Marguerite, however, did not sleep. Instead she wrote a letter to Dr Gordon, recording that matters had reached crisis point between her and her husband and that he had 'refused to take responsibility for my operation'. She claimed to be heading to Paris to rejoin her family to have the operation there. This was a distinctly odd letter for Marguerite to have written. The false implication seems to have been that Fahmy was refusing to pay for the procedure to be carried out in London, which had left Marguerite in the embarrassing position of having to seek support in Paris in order to get the necessary medical help. Yet the reality – that Marguerite was already independently wealthy before she met her husband and that he was perfectly willing to pay for the operation in London – was not something that would ever be alluded to.

For all its peculiarities, this grisly story of sodomy and inflamed piles, so potently symbolic of perverted male cruelty and female subjugation, must have seemed to Marshall Hall like forensic manna from heaven. This would be the keystone of his defence; so appalling to a London jury that, in the right hands, it could trump all the factual and legal difficulties that lay in his way.

A crowd began forming outside the public entrance to the Central Criminal Court in the early morning of Monday, 10 September 1923. As it filled with spectators and participants there was an oddly festive air to Court Number One. Excitement mounted as five counsel strode in and took their seats, the first stage in the ritual that preceded the start of every criminal trial.

The prosecution was led by the experienced if dour Treasury Counsel, Percival Clarke, son of the great advocate Sir Edward Clarke, who had represented Oscar Wilde both in his calamitous action for libel against the Marquess of Queensberry and in the subsequent criminal prosecution. Sitting behind Clarke was his junior, Eustace Fulton, son of the former Recorder of London. Along the bench from Clarke sat the tall and charismatic Marshall Hall, now a martyr to various ailments (a cushion would be ceremoniously placed on his seat by his senior clerk before he took his place so even while standing he could gain some support)[2] but still vigorous, and his rather more rotund co-leader (and fellow knight) Sir Henry Curtis-Bennett KC. Behind sat the third member of the defence counsel team, Roland Oliver, eventually to become a notoriously crusty High Court judge. The Bar was a small place in 1923. Both Curtis-Bennett and Oliver had appeared in the same courtroom the year before in the notorious trial of *R v Bywaters and Thompson*, although on that occasion they were on opposing sides, Oliver acting as junior counsel for the Crown and Curtis-Bennett leading the defence of Mrs Thompson, who had sat in the dock alongside her lover and co-defendant.

The next stage in the ritual was marked by three sharp knocks at the door behind the bench, silencing the hubbub. Mr Justice Rigby Swift entered court with the sheriff. In the tradition of the time, only discontinued in the mid-1950s and traceable back to an age when they were deployed to ward off noxious smells, he and the sheriff carried posies of English garden flowers. 'All persons who have anything to do before my Lords the King's Justices of Oyer and Terminer,[3] and general gaol delivery for the jurisdiction of the Central Criminal Court draw near and give your attendance. God Save the King and my Lords the King's Justices,' intoned the usher. Then forty-nine years old, Swift was young for a High Court judge, but he had many years' experience of practice at the Bar, first in Liverpool and later in London. Plump and red-faced, Swift spoke in an emphatic Lancashire accent and saw himself as a plain-dealing representative of decent, middle-class society. The world that would be unfolded before him over the next few days would be far removed from his own.

The judge bowed to counsel and then sat down before the name 'Marie Marguerite Fahmy' was called out and the assembled throng could take their first look at the defendant. So commenced the third stage of the ritual, as Marguerite was processionally led up the stairs into the dock. According to the *Daily Mirror*, which failed to note the irony of the situation, the neophyte widow appeared 'in deep mourning, which emphasised the pallor of her complexion'. The indictment was read to her by the Clerk of Arraigns, all wig, gown and formality, from his desk immediately below the judge. There was a theatrical silence. The indictment was read a second time and now elicited a clear response. '*Non coupable.*' Finally the four sides of the square were completed as the jurors were sworn in and took their seats in the jury box. It is a surprise to discover that two of the jurors were women. Although the law had changed four years earlier to allow women – provided that they were over thirty and met certain property qualifications[4] – to sit as jurors, judges still habitually ensured men-only juries on cases that were thought might offend female sensibilities. One newspaper described them as 'matronly-looking, wearing gold-rimmed spectacles and dressed in black'. Perhaps Swift thought them sufficiently robust to cope with the sodomitical narrative they were about to hear.

Clarke's opening speech set the tone for what was to be a generally uninspiring performance by Treasury Counsel. The case against Marguerite was articulated in a dry and surprisingly brief fashion. 'Madame Fahmy was married to her husband in December last. Her husband was in the diplomatic service and was a man of wealth and position.' This book speaks in places about the effect of great advocacy on the fortunes of an accused. What is less often remarked on, but equally important in practice, are the effects of bad advocacy. Any barrister will have had the experience of watching his or her opposing counsel doing a poor job, whether due to inexperience, lack of preparation, or simply because they are having the proverbial bad day. When this happens it is remarkable how what appears on paper to be the most compelling case can have its life-blood leached out of it. This matters because there are rarely second chances in a courtroom. Although there will be a closing speech in which prosecuting counsel can in theory resuscitate their case, the purpose of the opening address – to set the scene and subtly focus the minds of the jurors on the narrative of the case that the prosecutor wishes them to absorb – will have passed by for ever.

Clarke did, inevitably, home in on the crucial evidence in support of the prosecution case: 'Just as the porter was going away he heard a slight whistle behind him and, looking back, saw the deceased man stooping down, whistling and snapping his fingers at a little dog which had come out of the suite. In that position this man was last seen before he was killed.' It was these simple facts – a man in his pyjamas shot in the back as he stooped to encourage his dog back to his room – that would convict Marguerite Fahmy if they remained firmly lodged in the jury's mind. It would be Marshall Hall's task to obliterate that central image by summoning up an altogether more vivid picture of the abominations and cruelty of the Orient and the plight of a Western woman caught in its maw.

Clarke's first witness was Fahmy's secretary, the suave and well-dressed Said Enani. Just as his examination by the prosecutor was beginning, Marshall Hall pounced. It is illustrative of the gulf that separates the present from 1923 that no copy of the Koran was available in Court Number One for Enani to swear upon. Marshall Hall chose to intervene at this moment, asking with faux-naivety which book the witness had been sworn on. When the usher confirmed that the New Testament had been used, Marshall, looking directly at the jury, cut across Percival Clarke to ask Enani, 'Does the oath on the Bible bind you?' It was an outrageous yet adroit piece of dog-whistle advocacy, which had the virtue of acting out, rather than articulating, the cultural, religious (and, implicitly, moral) divide that the defence would conjure up between Levantine equivocation and the sound British values of the court in which the trial was being heard.

However, it being 1923, there was no need for Marshall Hall to remain coy about the racial prejudices he wished to stir up in the courtroom. In examination-in-chief Enani gave evidence of a marriage in which the real Marguerite was far removed from the image of the abused wife that the defence wished to paint. During cross-examination, Marshall Hall returned to the question of Enani's oath. Conveniently, a male juror also expressed concern about whether an oath sworn on the New Testament was in fact binding on a Muslim. Enani responded by saying, 'We do not swear in our country on books. We swear on the name of Almighty God only.' It was the moment for Marshall Hall to go back on the attack: 'I suggest your oath does not bind you and you know it does not' – and then a gratuitous flourish and a sweep of the arm in the direction of the benches behind him – 'and there are Egyptian lawyers here who will say so.' Those lawyers were in fact acting for Fahmy's family, rightly anticipating a claim by Marguerite on her dead husband's estate if she were to be acquitted, and were very unlikely to offer support for Marshall Hall's thesis. But he knew perfectly well that they would never be called upon to do so, or given the opportunity to debunk it. The sly point had been made and he moved on.

What is clear throughout the cross-examination of Enani is that Marshall Hall was using the secretary as a springboard from which to do as much damage as possible to the reputation of the victim.

MARSHALL HALL: How long had you known Ali Fahmy?
ENANI: About seven years.
MARSHALL HALL: Before he came into his money, you lived together?
ENANI: No.

Fahmy had been only twenty-two when he died, and Said Enani was several years his senior. The implication behind Marshall Hall's question was plain: Fahmy had been involved from adolescence in a homosexual relationship with Enani. So was introduced another Western trope about the Orient and its supposed deviant practices. Marshall Hall secured Enani's agreement to the propositions, superficially innocuous but loaded with innuendo, that Ali was 'an Oriental and rather passionate' and that he, Enani, was 'very much attached to him'. But the loyal secretary baulked at Marshall's more overt suggestion that Fahmy was a man of 'vicious and eccentric sexual appetite'. It is likely that the cross-examination became rather more explicit at this stage but no full transcript survives and the newspapers all drew a veil over the head-on suggestion that Fahmy had required his wife to participate in unnatural intercourse. Marshall Hall showed the court a satirical cartoon published in Egypt that referred to Fahmy as 'the light', Enani as the 'shadow of the light' and Enani's own factotum (the secretary had his own secretary!) as the 'shadow of the shadow'.

'Was not the relationship between you and Fahmy *bey* notorious in Egypt?'

The character assassination did not end there. Marshall Hall directly accused Enani of having colluded with his master to lure Marguerite to Egypt by sending messages designed to deceive her into believing that, after a summer of dalliance, Fahmy was dangerously ill and could not live without her. The central idea, with a pedigree going as far back as the *Iliad*, was of a defenceless Western woman being lured from the safety of Europe to the peril of the Orient. This version of the worldly Marguerite, who had in fact travelled to Cairo intent on making her fortune, was risible. However, it did not stop Marshall Hall from intoning, 'I am putting it to you that you and Fahmy conspired together to make false statements in order to induce this woman to go to Egypt.' And once there Fahmy had sought to 'tame' his bride. A letter was produced in which the young husband had stated his philosophy: 'With women one must act with energy and be severe.' Had Fahmy not beaten his wife? Enani could not say, though he conceded his master had been 'unkind'. Had Fahmy not had other lovers? Yes.

> MARSHALL HALL: Do you know he treated them brutally, one and all?
> ENANI: No, sir, I cannot say brutally.
> MARSHALL HALL: He was entitled by law to have four wives, was he not?
> ENANI: Yes, sir.

A frisson of horror and excitement swept the public gallery, populated predominantly – so the newspapers noted – by fur-clad women. The overall theme was clear. Marguerite's spirit had been crushed by the experience of living under the despotic, 'Oriental' rule of her husband.

> MARSHALL HALL: Was not the Madame Fahmy of 1923 totally different from the Madame Laurent of 1922?
> ENANI: Perhaps.

MARSHALL HALL: From being a gay, cheerful, entertaining and fascinating
   woman, was she not sad and broken, miserable and wretched?
ENANI: They were always quarrelling.

This exchange is an example of how skilful cross-examination can paint a picture with which the witness appears largely to agree, when in fact there remains a gulf between the witness's account and the case the advocate is advancing.

After Enani, the key witness for the prosecution was, or ought to have been, John Beattie, the night porter. As a disinterested witness to events immediately prior to the shooting his testimony was potentially devastating to the defence. The fact that Beattie had seen Fahmy calling for Marguerite's lapdog just moments before she re-emerged from the suite and shot him three times from behind seemed to demolish any case of self-defence or provocation. How would Marshall Hall deal with this apparently insuperable impediment to his client's acquittal? His solution was a simple one: he would not engage with it. The less time Beattie spent in the witness box the better. Marshall Hall asked him the bare minimum of questions, only gently suggesting that it must have been difficult to hear Fahmy whistling for the dog over the sound of the storm that was raging outside. Beyond that, he left Beattie's testimony more or less where it stood and moved on.

On the second day of the trial, various Savoy employees completed the picture of events immediately following the shooting. Robert Churchill, the country's leading firearms expert, a man so famous in his day that he would eventually be the subject of a biography grandiloquently entitled *The Other Mr Churchill*, now went into the witness box. In a society awash with firearms, death by shooting was in the first half of the twentieth century very much more common than it is now, and Churchill was kept a busy man. He turns up in many of the causes célèbres of the period, almost as ubiquitous as the legendary pathologist Bernard Spilsbury. The prosecution had called Churchill to testify to the pull that was required to be exerted on the trigger of the pistol that had killed Fahmy. In the immediate aftermath Marguerite had said that she did not know how the pistol worked and had believed its chamber to be empty, having immediately before the fatal shots fired one shot out of the window of her suite. She had insisted that she had not intended to fire any subsequent shots but merely to frighten her husband. The problem with all this was that, as Churchill pointed out to the courtroom, the pull of the trigger was heavy – eight and a quarter pounds – so a person could not fire the pistol without the application of deliberate force for each shot. The gun had a threefold safety mechanism which meant that this was not a weapon that would go off accidentally. The notion that Marguerite was unfamiliar with the gun's operation appeared very difficult to credit.

Marshall Hall prided himself on his own expertise when it came to firearms. Two .32 Brownings, borrowed from a friendly gunsmith, and similar to the alleged murder weapon, were produced: one dismantled on the exhibit table and another brandished by Marshall Hall himself during the course of his cross-examination. A series of technical questions were put to Churchill to begin with, so that Marshall Hall's own credentials as someone who understood the working of firearms were clearly established before the jury. In the midst of the to and fro that ensued, Marshall Hall succeeded in neutralising the danger that Churchill posed. 'Is it not the case that when the pistol is tightly gripped a very small pressure on the trigger would discharge several shots?'

The *Manchester Guardian*'s report noted that the witness (perhaps nonplussed by this technically nonsensical question, since the Browning was not a machine pistol) 'hesitated'. For the prosecution, it was a fatal hesitation. Marshall Hall seized his advantage. 'Might an inexperienced person reload the weapon thinking in fact that he might be emptying it?' For some reason the normally robust Churchill had become docile. He meekly agreed. The danger was over.

The final witness for the prosecution was Dr Gordon. It was an odd decision to call so obviously friendly a witness and it allowed Marshall Hall to ask the doctor leading questions knowing precisely where they would lead. He gave evidence about the haemorrhoids, about which Marguerite had consulted him prior to the shooting. This led to the emergence of the letter Marguerite had written to the doctor and the supposed dispute between the couple about her intended trip to Paris for an operation. Dr Gordon recounted that Marguerite had told him, immediately following her arrest, that, just before the shooting, her husband had 'brutally handled and pestered her' in their suite and had advanced on her threateningly in her bedroom. He made reference to a scratch on Marguerite's neck, which she had had the foresight to show him. Marshall Hall asked if this was consistent with 'a hand clutching her throat'. Yes it was, said Dr Gordon. This led to cross-examination on the delicate question of Fahmy's sexual demands, tactfully reported in the sanitised press of the time as 'passionate . . . conduct on the part of her husband that made her ill'. This would not be the last time that the subject of anal sex was broached in the trial.

Marshall Hall opened the case for Marguerite Fahmy at the end of the second day. Her defence to the charge of murder was an uneasy combination of accident and self-defence: she had pulled the trigger fearing a final murderous assault by her husband in the corridor at the Savoy, yet believing the pistol was unloaded. But Marshall Hall understood only too well that to stand any chance of success, the thread of such a defence had to start long before that fatal night in London. He began by referring to the 'Eastern cunning' of Fahmy, who, with a fanfare of false tenderness, had lured a vulnerable woman to Egypt. What had in reality no doubt appeared as an extraordinary conquest for the courtesan was re-framed for the jury as an entrapment. 'But this man was what is known as a sadist, a man who enjoys the sufferings of women. He was abnormal [one of the many circumlocutions deployed throughout the trial for a sodomite] and brutal.' A stranger in a strange land, once she arrived the wretched Marguerite found herself at the mercy of her husband and 'his entourage of black servants . . . She could not go anywhere without these black things watching her.' Warming to his theme Marshall Hall explained that Fahmy 'demanded a slave-like obedience from her' before enumerating various baroque acts of brutality Marguerite had had to endure. The rhetoric reached new depths, told to a silent court, its spectators a-quiver with a mixture of horror and titillation:

> She discovered for the first time that he not only had the vilest of vile tempers, but was vile himself, with a filthy perverted taste.[5] From that day onwards to the very night, within a few moments of the time when a bullet sent that man to eternity, he was pestering her [every juror knew what for] . . . she will tell you that Fahmy kept a black valet to watch over this white woman's suite of rooms, conditions that really make me shudder, [placing her] in that state of obedience which a black man wants from a woman who is his chattel.

Needless to say the 'black valet' – who had actually witnessed the shooting! – did not give evidence. He is never even named in any of the accounts of the trial. He was just a 'thing'.

On the following morning Marshall Hall was to call Marguerite as a witness. We have seen in Chapter 1 how he (like all other advocates) agonised over whether to call his clients as witnesses in their own defence.

The decision a decade earlier to call Seddon into the witness box, and so expose him to the deadly cross-examination of the Attorney General, had probably sent him to the gallows. Yet here there could be no doubt: it was necessary for the person who admitted having pulled the trigger of the pistol that killed her husband to explain herself.

But before Marguerite went into the witness box, and in the absence of the jury, the judge had to decide a vital question. Anxious to reveal the true Marguerite to the jury, as opposed to the chimera presented by Marshall Hall, Percival Clarke had informed Marshall Hall that he intended to cross-examine Marguerite 'as to whether she had lived an immoral life, and was therefore a woman of the world, well able to take care of herself'. Section 1(f) of the Criminal Evidence Act 1898 allowed a defendant giving evidence to be questioned about their alleged bad character if defence counsel had made imputations on the character of any prosecution witnesses.[6] In this case Marshall Hall had launched an outrageous attack on Said Enani and the prosecutor wished to bring some balance back to the trial, to show that Marguerite was not the innocent the defence had set upon a pedestal before the jury. This was a significant moment, because if the way had been opened for questions about Marguerite's dubious and mercenary past, her position on that pedestal would have become very precarious indeed. Rigby Swift came to an immediate if perverse conclusion: ignoring Marshall Hall's barely concealed suggestions to Enani that he had made Fahmy his catamite, and that he had conspired with his friend and employer to deceive Marguerite into travelling to Egypt, the judge ruled that Clarke could only ask about her relations with her husband – with whom she admitted she had lived before they were married – but with no other men. As far as the twelve men and women of the jury would ever know, Marguerite was a broadly respectable, albeit adventurous, French woman whose only crime was loving not wisely but too well.

It was now up to Marguerite to give the performance of her lifetime. She started very well. Having been called to give evidence, she unsteadily left the dock via the side door that led into the well of the courtroom and, the very epitome of vulnerability, made the short walk on the guiding arm of a wardress. The judge, half in love already with what one newspaper described as the 'dark haired and lustrous eyed' figure who now entered the witness box, gallantly indicated that she could give her evidence seated. There she sat, immaculate in her mourning garb, the grieving widow all the way to her black-gloved fingers dabbing those lustrous eyes with a grey silk handkerchief. The impression of frailty only deepened as Marguerite was guided by her counsel through the narrative of her disastrous marriage.

And what a pathetic story it was, the pathos only made more vivid by the fact that she told it in French, before it was relayed to the courtroom through an interpreter. Punctuated by tears, swoons and shrugs, Marguerite's testimony covered what Marshall Hall had made sure was now familiar ground. Constant repetition of the salient facts would leave its mark on the collective consciousness of the jury. Marguerite relived the moment in Cairo earlier in the year when her husband had taken up the Holy Book in his hand and, apparently looking her straight in the eyes, told his wife, 'I swear on the Koran that I will kill you and that you shall die by my hand.' She described the occasion at Luxor when he had supposedly fired several shots over her head. She explained the unequal marriage contract she had entered which apparently prevented her divorcing her husband but allowed him to repudiate her at will. She told of being imprisoned for days on Fahmy's yacht, where she was kept 'alone on board surrounded by black men'. The *Manchester Guardian* delicately reported that Marguerite said that 'marital relations were never natural or normal', while the *Evening Standard* noted disapprovingly that at this stage of the evidence 'only' three women got up and left the public gallery. The rest were no doubt glued to their seats. 'Rows of fashionably-dressed young women sat with flushed cheeks and glittering eyes as Hall detailed monstrosity after monstrosity,' in the words of a contemporary account. There were further accounts of assaults with fists and horsewhips; of strangling hands at her throat; of threats that she would be disfigured with acid at the hands of a faithful factotum known as La Costa, who owed his 'liberty and life' to Fahmy (quite how the court never discovered); of a journey to the outskirts of Paris in the company of Fahmy and Enani apparently for the purpose of finding a house in which to imprison Marguerite (quite why, or for how long, and under whose guard, again remained questions that hung unanswered in the turbid air).

Marguerite's story was so encrusted with exotic detail and ornate malice that it seems to have a literary quality to it; derived perhaps from an amalgam of the Marquis de Sade and the Bluebeard story. From the point of view of making good a defence to a charge of murder it was perhaps too good to be true; in fact all the better because Bluebeard was now dead. Even Marshall Hall seems to have been aware that an obvious riposte to this tale of Oriental cruelty was, why not run away? He pre-empted the question. Marguerite's answer was not entirely convincing:

'I always hoped he would change. Every time I threatened to leave him he cried and promised to alter.'

And so they arrived finally in London in July 1923, where Marguerite's narrative continued at full pelt. There was an incident at a club by the Thames. 'I will throw you in there. I am tired of you,' was Fahmy's threat. When Marguerite had to endure another bout of 'unnatural' intercourse she told her husband she would rather die than go on living like this. In response Fahmy pointed to the open window of her room. 'It is quite easy. There are four floors.'

The day before the shooting a characteristic incident had occurred during lunch at the Savoy. The *chef d'orchestre* had asked Marguerite if she would like anything to be played. She had replied, 'Thank you very much. My husband is going to kill me in twenty-four hours, and I am not very anxious for music.' The conductor had responded, with admirable composure, 'I hope you will still be here tomorrow, madame.' Marguerite told the court that, before the trip to the theatre, she had become alarmed by her husband's threats and had taken the pistol from the drawer. She knew that it was loaded. 'He had told me so and I had not touched it since the day he left [to travel to Stuttgart, a few weeks earlier].' She then supposedly tried to eject the round from the chamber by pulling the breech cover, but lacked the strength to do so. (At this moment she was handed by Marshall Hall the very weapon that had killed her husband and demonstrated that lack of strength.) In the end she said she had shaken the gun in front of the open window when a shot went off unexpectedly. After this initial mishap, she claimed that she believed that the pistol was no longer dangerous. Her timing of events shifted in her oral evidence from what she had said in the immediate aftermath of the shooting. She now claimed that the shot through the open window took place much earlier in the day. She then moved on to a version of the row between husband and wife that was very difficult to reconcile with the night porter Beattie's testimony. After the initial altercation in the corridor she had returned to her room. As Fahmy banged his fist on the door she saw the pistol.

He advanced and had a very threatening expression. He said, 'I will revenge myself.' I had taken the pistol in my hand and he said, 'I will say that you have threatened me.' I went out into the corridor in front of the lift. He seized me suddenly and brutally by the throat with his left hand. His thumb was on my windpipe and his fingers were pressing on my neck. Then he crouched to spring on to me and said, 'I will kill you.' I now lifted my arm in front of me and without looking pulled the trigger.

The *Guardian* reported that 'Madame Fahmy practically relapsed into unconsciousness as she was relating this last scene.' But was this an uncontrollable surge of emotion or the realisation that too close a dissection of events would not ultimately help her case? What the porter had witnessed was Fahmy emerging from the suite, *followed* by his wife. He had seen Fahmy crouching not to launch a final murderous attack, but to call to the lapdog which had scampered down the corridor. And how was this evidence consistent with shots in the back?

Still, Percival Clarke had a delicate task. The protracted tale of marital brutality was difficult to contradict. Early twentieth-century sensibilities made controverting the tale of serial sodomy especially problematic. But Marguerite's account of the shooting was incoherent; she said that once she had fired the pistol out of the window she thought it was safe. Yet she had owned a gun since before the war and had kept it with her ever since; if she thought it was unloaded why had she pointed it at Fahmy and pulled the trigger three times? It is difficult to see why, in the face of these contradictions, Clarke chose to open with these questions.

CLARKE: Were you afraid he was going to kill you on that night?
FAHMY: Yes, I was very frightened.
CLARKE: When the pistol went off killing your husband, had you any idea that it was in a condition to be fired?
FAHMY: None. I thought there was no cartridge when you pulled the trigger, and that it could not be used.
CLARKE: When you threw your arm out, when the pistol was fired, what were you afraid of?
FAHMY: That he was going to jump on me. It was terrible. I had escaped once. He said, 'I will kill you, I will kill you.' It was so terrible.

It is impossible to see why prosecuting counsel should have thought it a good idea to commence with a series of leading questions that led in the wrong direction. Things did not get much better. Despite the judge's ruling, Clarke did try to make some tentative forays into Marguerite's status as a 'woman of the world'. Yet the answers that he received were impressively composed and did not come close to giving any sense of the reality of Marguerite's past career. Instead of emerging as a grasping gold-digger Marguerite was able to strike an inauthentic posture of noble world-weariness. 'I have had experience of life.'

We can imagine the slow, melancholic words, creeping over the courtroom, comprehensible to everyone even before they were rendered into English. Percival Clarke, a captive of his narrow Anglo-Saxon world-view, seemed to become smaller and smaller before Marguerite's tragic grandeur.

CLARKE: Madame, were you not very ambitious to become his wife?
FAHMY: Ambitious? No. I loved him so very much and wished to be with him . . .
CLARKE: What did you do while he was being so cruel – sit down quietly?
FAHMY: Once only I boxed his ears when he had beaten me very much.
CLARKE: Were you not often doing that?
FAHMY: No, he beat me so much when I did box his ears that I never dared do it again.

. . .

CLARKE: I take it that from the time of his first objectionable suggestion you hated your husband bitterly?
FAHMY: I loved my husband and, when he had been so bad, I despaired and I told him I hated him. I did not hate him, but only what he wanted me to do.

After a day and a half in the witness box Madame Fahmy returned to the dock. It was mid-afternoon on Thursday, the fourth day.

Marshall Hall now rose to give his closing speech for the defence. The oration would become an instant classic, its initial fame shifting towards notoriety as the decades have passed.[7] As we have seen in Chapter 1, one of Marshall Hall's sayings was that he strived always to 'create an atmosphere'; now, in search of that atmosphere, he would depart from the world of fact and lure the jurors into an alternative realm of pure unhinged feeling.

First a rhetorical sleight of hand, beloved of defence counsel. Marshall solemnly – and entirely dishonestly – asked the jurors not to allow their sympathy for this 'poor woman' to interfere with returning a 'proper verdict'. It was as if the Great Defender were seeking a pre-emptive exoneration from any suggestion that what he was about to say was in fact entirely aimed at eliciting sympathy for the outraged wife; and for good measure exciting loathing for the dead husband. An assurance to the jury that their emotions would not be taken advantage of allowed him to do with impunity precisely what he had forsworn. Next he asked the jurors not to 'descend to little minor and petty details, but to take a great, broad view of the situation'. Well he might! This was a defence that could not trouble itself with such trivialities as the order and actuality of events.

Now to the meat.

> Madame Fahmy made one mistake, possibly the greatest mistake any woman can make: a woman of the West married to an Oriental. I dare say the Egyptian civilisation is and may be one of the oldest and most wonderful civilisations in the world. I don't say that among the Egyptians there are not many magnificent and splendid men, but if you strip off the external civilisation of the Oriental, you get the real Oriental underneath . . .

In discussing Said Enani, whose character the judge had confirmed had not been impugned by the defence, Marshall asked the jury:

> Do you believe anything said by Said Enani that was hostile to this unfortunate woman? I suggest that it is a part of Eastern duplicity that is so well known . . . One almost smiled when my friend [i.e. Percival Clarke] asked yesterday, 'Why did you not get Said Enani to protect you?' You have seen Said Enani and have heard something about him. Is he the kind of man whom you would have as the sole buffer between yourselves and a man like Fahmy? . . . Do not forget La Costa, that great black Hercules, who came day after day for orders, and who was ready to do anything. Don't you think she had ground for fear of this great black blackguard who owed his life to Fahmy?

He returned to the beginnings.

> Picture this woman, inveigled into Egypt by false pretences, by a letter which for adulatory expression could hardly be equalled and which makes one feel sick . . . At first everything is honey and roses. He shows his beautiful palace, his costly motor cars, his wonderful motor-boat, his retinue of servants, his lavish luxuries, and cries, 'I am Fahmy Bey, I am a Prince.' This European woman became more fascinated and more attracted to all the Oriental extravagance . . .

Of course this exercise in miscegenation could not end well. 'The curse of this case is the Eastern feeling of possession of the woman, the Turk in his harem, this man who was entitled to have four wives if he liked – for chattels, which to we Western people, with our ideas of women, is almost unintelligible . . .'

Marshall now moved on to what he described as the 'sex question'. It was at this stage that the newspapers drew the familiar veil over their reporting and resorted to their favoured euphemisms. Fahmy had 'developed abnormal tendencies and he never treated Madame normally'. But they did report another favoured conceit of defence counsel: the sanctimonious chastisement of the gawpers in the public gallery. It was always women, not men, who stood condemned for their prurience. 'If women choose to come here to hear this case they must take the consequences. It is a matter of public duty that I must perform.'

Perhaps the ladies of fashion shifted uncomfortably in their seats. None was seen to leave. And so to the fatal night.

> You know the effect of such a storm when your nerves are normal. Imagine its effect on a woman of nervous temperament who had lived such a life as she had lived for the past six months − outraged, abused, beaten, degraded − a human wreck . . . Imagine the incessant flashes of lightning, almost hissing, as you remember, it seemed so close . . . She saw her husband outlined by a vivid flash in the doorway [this was pure invention] and there to her hand on the valise she saw the pistol − harmless, she thought . . .

He now came to the shooting: 'They struggle in the corridor. She kicks him and he takes her by the throat. Do you doubt it? The marks are spoken of in the prison doctor's report.'

Note the shift to the present tense and to quick, staccato sentences. A prelude to the final act, where Marshall Hall's advocacy now combined bodily and verbal expression. 'In sheer desperation − as he crouched for the last time, crouched like an animal, like an Oriental, retired for the last time to get a bound forward − she turned the pistol and put it to his face and to her horror the thing went off.'

And, unbelievably, at this moment Marshall imitated (or rather invented) that final crouch. The ecstatic Marjoribanks apostrophised it thus: 'he performed the most wonderful physical demonstration of his forensic career; he imitated the crouch of the stealthily advancing Oriental.' Marshall Hall bent down in his row as if he were about to spring out and attack the jurors. By this stage he had the pistol that had killed Fahmy in his hand. He had waved it at the jury and the judge as he addressed them. As he described the shooting he gave three loud raps on the wooden shelf in front of him and allowed the pistol to fall clattering to the floor, breaking the stunned silence of Court Number One.[8]

It is a wonder the court did not burst into applause. But there was more. 'To use the words of my learned friend's great father many years ago at the Old Bailey in the Bartlett case, "I do not ask you for a verdict. I demand a verdict at your hands."'[9]

The message was clear and drew on the logic of the American lynch-mob. Fahmy had brutalised and desecrated a Western woman and had accordingly forfeited his right to live. Surely Marshall Hall would choose to end his speech on this note? No, there was one final trick to be deployed:

> You will remember, all of you, that great work of fiction, written by Robert Hichens, *Bella Donna*. Some of you may have seen the masterly performance given of it at one of our theatres. If you have you will remember the influence of Mahmoud over the English woman, who, under his inspiration, poisons her English husband. You will remember the final scene, where this woman goes out of the gates of the garden into the dark night of the desert. Members of the jury, I want you to open the gates where the Western woman can go out, not into the dark night of the desert, but back to her friends, who love her in spite of her weakness, back to her friends, who will be glad to receive her, back to her child, who will be waiting for her with open arms. You will open the gate and let this Western woman go back into the light of God's great Western sun.

It is said that a shaft of sunlight penetrated the skylight of Court Number One and illuminated the proceedings at the very moment that Marshall Hall, exhausted, sank down.

How to respond to such an oration? All the newspapers noted the discrepancy between Marshall Hall's supercharged emotionalism and Clarke's cool and rational analysis of the evidence. Clarke attempted a change of tempo: 'I shall try and take you from the theatrical atmosphere which has prevailed in this court for three or four days. I shall not propose to endeavour to follow Sir Edward Marshall Hall in a form of advocacy which, although so well suited to the defence of a prisoner, would ill become those who represent the Crown.'

But who was listening? Facts did not matter any more. 'God's great Western sun', now a metaphor as much as a heavenly body, hung high above the proceedings, radiant with meaning, its light filtering down through the glass ceiling of Court Number One.

Even the judge seems to have become caught up in Marshall Hall's call for a violated Europa to be embraced by her kin. In his summing-up he seemed overborne by the evidence he had heard. 'Shocking, sickening and disgusting' were words he could barely leave alone. Under a veneer of even-handedness it was obvious in which direction he was tending. It was now Saturday, the sixth day of the trial. The jury was sent away just after noon. It is perhaps unsurprising that it only took an hour to reach its not guilty verdict (either of murder or manslaughter). Upon the foreman pronouncing these words there was a shriek from the public gallery and the whole of Court Number One broke into thunderous stamping and applause. One of the female jurors was seen to be in tears. The mayhem continued for a full five minutes before the judge was able to regain control of his courtroom. The vast crowd that had congregated outside the Old Bailey – the Greek chorus to all of Marshall Hall's tragedies – erupted into raucous cheers.

Not one newspaper commented adversely on the closing speech for the defence. (Indeed it precipitated a series of ruminations on the ill-advisability of mixed marriages which extended over the whole gamut of the press.) The judge had himself described the speech in his summing-up as 'brilliantly eloquent'. The days that followed Madame Fahmy's acquittal were Marshall Hall's apotheosis. The only note of dissent came from the *Bâtonnier* of the Egyptian Bar, who sent a telegram to the Attorney General expressing disquiet at the slurs made against the Egyptian people. Marshall Hall contented himself with a hollow apology: 'If by any chance, in the heat of advocacy, I was betrayed into saying anything that might be construed as an attack on the Egyptians as a nation, I shall be the first to disclaim any such intention.'

Almost a century on, the tone and content of Marshall Hall's defence of his client are astonishing. It need hardly be said that it would be impossible now to say anything even remotely comparable in a criminal court; to do so would risk professional disgrace and disbarment. Yet that defence squarely raises the ethical conundrum of how far an advocate should go in defence of their client. Madame Fahmy was on trial for her life and it cannot be doubted that Marshall Hall's denunciation of the supposed sins of the Orient was instrumental in her salvation. For Marshall Hall, single-mindedly devoted to one end, the fact of her acquittal would have been answer enough to any criticism of his conduct.

Putting aside the sensibilities of the twenty-first century, the defence of Madame Fahmy and the fact that Marshall Hall felt confident in saying what he did without fear of judicial reprimand or, more importantly, alienating his jury, tells us much about early twentieth-century attitudes. It also shows that, for all its formality, the court is not a hermetically sealed space, divorced from the values and prejudices of the world outside. The language of the courtroom is as much saturated in ideology as any other medium.

The defence of Marguerite Fahmy had been a carefully constructed piece of rhetoric that avowedly drew on prevalent literary and cultural motifs. England (and Western society generally) in the 1920s viewed 'Oriental' civilisation with the same mixture of fascination and horror that had overcome the public gallery in the Old Bailey during that intoxicating week in September 1923. The image of the Eastern man, cruel and sexually masterful, provided rich material for the fiction and cinema of the period. The novel that Marshall Hall referred to in his closing speech, Robert Hichens's *Bella Donna*, had been published in 1909 and was an international sensation. It told of an older English woman who travels with her honourable but dull husband to Egypt. There she starts an affair with an Egyptian businessman ('she felt cruelty in him and it attracted her, it lured her') and together they plot to poison her husband. *Bella Donna* was one of the first examples of the 'desert romance' genre which reached its high point in 1919 with E.M. Hull's bestseller *The Sheik*, in which Diana Mayo, an adventurous and independent-minded English woman, is captured in the Algerian desert by the eponymous sheik and, after being repeatedly raped, falls in love with him. One early passage describes Diana's outlook before her subjugation and seems to have been lifted wholesale by Marshall Hall:

> That women could submit to the degrading intimacy and fettered existence of married life filled her with scornful wonder. To be bound irrevocably to the will and pleasure of a man who would have the right to demand obedience in all that constituted marriage and the strength to enforce those claims revolted her. For a Western woman it was bad enough, but for the women of the East, mere slaves of the passions of the men who owned them, unconsidered, disregarded, reduced to the level of animals, the bare idea made her quiver.

The ghost of Fahmy Bey conjured into existence in Court Number One drew its inspiration from these novels, and was filled out by the fatal attraction of Rudolph Valentino, who had played the Sheik in a silent film version released in 1921. Marshall Hall was only able to summon up such a fully realised monster before the jury because they had seen him at the pictures and read about him in novels. In acquitting Marguerite the jurors were setting her free from the clutches of a fictional version of the Orient. They were, perhaps, also giving vent to a sense of resentment at Egypt's recent rejection of British colonialism. A mass uprising there against British rule had forced Britain to grant Egypt nominal independence in February 1922. Was Marshall Hall's ruthless characterisation of it as 'Oriental', utterly alien and antithetical to British values of decency – in a way that would then have been unthinkable in relation to (say) India – licensed by Egypt's having spurned the blessings of Empire?

Marshall Hall also drew on another strand of contemporary moral panic. In 1918 the actress Billie Carleton had died of a cocaine overdose in, of all places, the Savoy Hotel. The subsequent trial of those said to have supplied the drug, which took place in Court Number One in 1919, was perhaps the first prosecution in England under the 1916 Act that had proscribed the supply of narcotics (and so possibly the first 'drugs case' in English legal history). It was revealed that an English woman and her Chinese husband living in Limehouse (then London's 'China-Town') had been a source of opium which the twenty-two-year-old actress had regularly smoked. As the drug epidemic in fashionable society continued into the 1920s, the spectre was raised of a Chinese syndicate saturating London with opium and cocaine. This might explain Marshall Hall's mysterious reference during his final speech to the abuses of drugs, alcohol and sex, which caused 'all the dreadful trouble in the world'. 'Nature gave us the power to get morphia from the seed of the poppy, gave us alcohol, and cocaine from the seed of the coca plant in Peru . . . Just as they are the greatest boon to men and women, so probably these things taken together are three of the greatest curses that are in the world at the present moment.' There was nothing whatsoever in the evidence to indicate that Fahmy took drugs or had a drink problem; but he was, like the Chinese dope-dealers in their Limehouse opium dens, a foreigner at a time when foreignness was the unfortunate condition of all those born beyond the shores of the United Kingdom.

The Fahmy case may have been Marshall Hall's apogee, but it was also a watershed. Already an ill man, he died in January 1927 and with him died a style of advocacy. The new criminal advocates who followed, chief among whom were Norman Birkett and Patrick Hastings, adopted an altogether different courtroom manner. Hastings described the change in his memoirs, *Cases in Court*:

No one will ever know what is the real value of a speech for the defence in a murder case. There was a time when no defending counsel was worth his salt unless he could be relied upon for an exhibition of rhetorical emotion. Those days are past. A City of London jury has seen too many comic advocates upon the films to be greatly impressed by waving arms and streaming eyes. At one time it was thought effective to refer at repeated intervals to the blind Goddess of Justice sitting above the Central Criminal Court, and no advocate of any value was not fully equipped with a heart-breaking and totally irrelevant peroration . . . Those days of flatulent oratory are gone.

I cannot help thinking that Hastings had the Fahmy case in mind when he wrote these words. Yet I wonder whether the approach of 'pure logic, with a careful examination of the facts', which Hastings went on to advocate, would have seen Madame Fahmy acquitted.

In the space of nine months Sir Henry Curtis-Bennett KC had defended two women on charges of murder in Court Number One. In the first trial, which ran over five days in December 1922, Edith Thompson had been charged alongside her lover with the murder of her husband Percy. Edith had been born into the lower middle classes and, through talent and hard work, had acquired a well-paid and responsible job in a mill-inery firm in the City of London. Unhappily married to a dullard, she had started an affair with a much younger merchant seaman, Frederick Bywaters, while he lodged in the Thompsons' home. After he had moved out Edith carried on writing letters to her lover, which Bywaters unwisely kept. One evening in early October 1922, Mrs Thompson and her husband were walking back to their terraced house in Ilford after an evening in the West End, seeing a Ben Travers play at the Criterion, just a few hundred yards away from the theatre where the Fahmys would spend their own last evening together. The distracted Bywaters, on shore leave after a long voyage, sprang out from the shadows and, after a confrontation, stabbed Thompson to death. When the police discovered her letters to Bywaters, Mrs Thompson was charged as an accomplice to the murder, despite her lover's protests that he had acted alone and without her knowledge.

Those letters – so passionate, desperate, full of life – stand now as one of the most vivid insights into the interior life of an (at least outwardly) ordinary woman in the early part of the last century. But in Court Number One, as they were laboriously read out by Travers Humphreys, the junior prosecution counsel, they served to condemn her. One phrase particularly outraged the judge. Of her husband's unwelcome sexual advances Edith had written: 'He has the right by law to all that you have the right to by nature and love.' In his summing-up Mr Justice Shearman had sermonised: 'If that nonsense means anything, it means that the love of a husband for his wife means nothing because marriage is acknowledged by law. I have no doubt that the jury and every proper-minded person is filled with disgust by such expressions.' But there was worse. Imprisoned in her loveless marriage, Edith's letters had fantasised about poisoning her husband, just as she was writing to Bywaters about the novel she was then reading, *Bella Donna*. The book that later furnished the material for Marshall Hall's peroration on behalf of Madame Fahmy seemed to provide a blueprint and inspiration for Edith's murderous intent. It did not matter that the great pathologist Dr Spilsbury was constrained to accept in the witness box that no trace of any poison had been found in Percy Thompson's body.

Whereas it had been obvious to her counsel that Marguerite Fahmy should – had to – give evidence, Curtis-Bennett's advice to Edith had been that she remain in the dock and not submit to cross-examination. This was sound wisdom but Edith overrode it, determined to explain herself to the courtroom, as if her voice would make everything right. Her walk to the witness box fascinated the public just as much as Marguerite's would a few months later. But while Marguerite's performance had been a masterpiece of pathos Edith was snared in her own imaginary life. Fantasy is not a mode that fits well within the walls of a courtroom. Cross-examination on those letters must have been as professionally satisfying as anything ever done by prosecuting counsel. To him it was merely a question of driving home the proof. How to deploy the letters to best advantage to destroy the witness: an interesting, if not particularly difficult, forensic challenge. Whatever the case, the issues are the same for the advocate: how am I going to go about cross-examining this witness; how can I shake their credibility; how can I extract the admissions I need? Sentiment doesn't come into it. But to the reader of the transcript of that cross-examination, the destruction of Edith's hope of acquittal, and so of survival, is an unbearable process.

So Marguerite Fahmy left court free and fêted; while Edith Thompson, reviled, was taken down to the cells, futilely proclaiming her innocence. The one had pulled the trigger that killed her husband; the other had witnessed her husband stabbed to death before her eyes. Marguerite had managed to play down her sexuality by donning the mantle of victimhood in the way that the prevailing culture expected of her; Edith, the older seductress, was viewed in the dock and witness box in almost entirely erotic terms. 'A thrill passed through the court as Mrs Thompson walked slowly down the steps of the dock,' slavered the *Daily Express*. An observer at the trial later wrote that 'the first thing I noticed in that packed court at the Old Bailey was her physical attraction and her lovely neck. She exuded sex.' This was dangerous, as Ruth Ellis would later discover. The childless Edith was the villainess, the 'Messalina of Ilford' as the press characterised her. It was she who had cuckolded her husband with a lover eight years her junior; it was she who had committed to paper in singing, ecstatic sentences the joy of sexual love (all 'gush', as the judge put it); it was she who had shamelessly broken the compact of marriage; it was she, almost everyone agreed, who had lured and corrupted young Bywaters, so manly and fresh-faced, to the act of murder. Curtis-Bennett, well-known at the time as a convivial bon-viveur, took his client's conviction badly. He later said that Edith had been 'hanged for immorality'.

Few cases reveal the narrowness and mercilessness of the processes of the law more starkly than that of Bywaters and Thompson. Yet in this lawyers and judges did not stand apart from the world at large. The *Daily Sketch* promoted a petition for Bywaters's reprieve, which garnered more than a million signatures and was premised on the idea that he was an impressionable youth who had been coerced into the crime; no petition was raised for Edith. When reviewing Filson Young's edition of the case for the Notable British Trials series (so great was the interest it had come out before the end of 1923, less than a year after the defendants had been hanged) *The Times* noted: 'When all is said and done, nourishing hate in the heart is an evil process, and unfaithfulness in marriage is a grossly antisocial act . . . The woman sought to live in a dream world of freedom from all moral rules, where she dallied with the thought of murder and sunk herself in passion. Reality broke rudely in, and the end of that matter was the rope.'

Both trials were described at the time using theatrical metaphors, a common conceit. One reporter described how 'the diffused electric lights around the oak-panelled room and the presence of hatless but well-dressed women, chatting and munching chocolates, were reminiscent of a theatre scene between the acts.' But it is Edith Thompson who penetrated and lingered in the public and literary consciousness. Madame Fahmy exists now as another phantom alongside her husband, both equally caricatures drawn by the great enchanter Marshall Hall. Edith is flesh and blood; she is all feeling; as fully realised in those fatal letters as Mrs Dalloway or Molly Bloom. Her life and death have spawned novels, films and plays over the span of a century. Two days before Edith's hanging Virginia Woolf recorded in her diary a sleepless night. 'Then a woman cried, as if in anguish, in the street and I thought of Mrs Thompson waiting to be executed.' There are said to be almost fifty references to her love letters in James Joyce's novel *Finnegans Wake*, begun in the year of the trial and published seventeen years later. The siren of the early 1920s would over the decades metamorphose into a victim of injustice as well as an exemplar of female autonomy and self-fashioning. Her terrible scream as she was led by John Ellis, the hangman, to the execution shed at Holloway prison would come to haunt the conscience of the twentieth century.

4

Poor Little Rich Girl

R v Elvira Barney (1932)

THIRTEEN YEARS AFTER her unsuccessful prosecution of Noel Pemberton Billing, Maud Allan[1] was living in baroque retirement at Holford House, her crumbling mansion in Regent's Park.[2] It was here on 21 November 1931, in the depths of the Depression and just as the National Government headed by Ramsay MacDonald was being formed with the declared purpose of averting national catastrophe, that there was thrown what would subsequently be seen as one of the final hurrahs of the post-war movement of youthful exuberance and dandyism whose avatars became known as the 'Bright Young People' – the 'BYP'.

Arthur Jeffress, later to become a well-known art dealer, was then a prominent bright young person. Having arrived at an arrangement with Maud Allan, he hosted at her wing what was billed as the 'Red and White Party'. Amid decorations of red velvet and white silk Jeffress was seen to be welcoming guests dressed in angel-skin coloured pyjamas and adorned with elbow-length kid gloves, ruby and diamond bracelets and a ruff of white narcissi. The dress code was, needless to say, strictly red and white. The food presented to guests followed a similar scheme: lobster, red caviar and strawberries were on the menu, to be washed down with champagne and gin. Brenda Dean Paul, the most notorious drug addict of the period, was duly arrested after an unprovoked assault on a fellow guest and found to be in possession of morphine and cocaine. Late in the night the musician and composer Hugh Wade, dressed as Queen Elizabeth I, started playing 'Abide with Me' on the organ in the huge hall. Meanwhile the sleep-deprived Maud Allan had retreated to her upstairs rooms. No doubt repenting her agreement with Jeffress she sent down angry remonstrances concerning the dissipations below, which were duly ignored. The dancing was still going strong even at seven the next morning.

★

One of the guests that night was Elvira Barney. Then twenty-seven years old, Elvira was the daughter of Sir John Mullens, who had been the chief government stockbroker and lived in stately refinement in Belgrave Square. A minor theatrical career seems to have been abandoned almost before it could get started. Unhindered by the necessity to earn a living, Elvira devoted herself with increasing dedication to the cause of pleasure in the congeries of bohemian London. She married an American singer, who, after only a few months of marital discord and cruelty, swiftly retreated to the United States, never to return. Instead of returning to the security of the parental home Elvira then took up residence in a converted garage at William Mews, just off Lowndes Square in Knightsbridge. By the end of 1931 she was involved with an epicene youth known as Michael Scott Stephen, whose own brush with productive activity – he at one point styled himself as a 'dress-designer' – had been rendered otiose by Elvira's financial independence.

Relations between Elvira and Stephen were rackety; frequent late-night arguments punctured the respectable quiet of the chauffeurs' residences in the mews. But jealous recrimination would be swiftly followed by sentimental rapprochement. A surviving letter from Elvira to Stephen captures the pattern of their ups and downs:

> My darling baby, I nearly had heart failure reading your letter, it was so divine. I have never been thrilled over reading anything before . . . You hand me the biggest thrills I have ever had, my sweet, and all I hope is we can go on being thrilled endlessly. I adore it when you are sweet and kind to me . . . So you see it means a great deal and I feel like suicide when you are angry. Sometimes when you are feeling furious do try to think of the hell I had to endure with J.B. [her husband] and then you will relent, I think. Don't be jealous with me either, Baby, please as I suffered so much from that with him and if you trust me you won't need to be jealous. It absolutely ruined my marriage before and it leads to all kinds of misery, so do be a bit broadminded . . .
>
> All my love, really all, Elvira.

The 'thrills' referred to here appear to have been of a sado-masochist variety, fuelled by copious usage of cocaine. Someone who knew Elvira and many of her friends would later write that 'much of the fighting and screaming that went on between them was produced to whet the appetite of each partner in what was a perverse sexual relationship.' And it was also reported that at William Mews 'over the cocktail bar in the corner of the sitting-room was a wall painting which would have been a sensation in a brothel in Pompeii. The library was furnished with publications that could never have passed through His Majesty's Customs. The place was equipped with the impedimenta of fetishism and perversion.'

On Monday, 30 May 1932 Elvira threw one of her frequent cocktail parties at the mews. A low-key affair, some thirty guests floated in and out of her 'cottage', as she described it, during the early evening, arriving in large cars, which roared and groaned and annoyed the neighbours. Stephen stood behind the bar mixing gin and vermouth cocktails as the conversation hummed and the guests danced to new jazz numbers from a large gramophone. The guests, so far as they can be identified, tell us much about the milieu Elvira inhabited. Both Arthur Jeffress and Hugh Wade, impresarios of the Red and White Party, were present, as were the acknowledged senior royalty of the smart set, Brian Howard and Eddie Gathorne-Hardy. A number of well-known lesbians of the demi-monde were also in attendance, suggesting the bisexual aspect of Elvira's modus vivendi. The party wound up at about nine and Elvira, Stephen and Jeffress took a cab to the Café de Paris in Coventry Street, a favourite BYP haunt. There they had supper and danced – getting along well according to Jeffress's later account. The three of them then moved at about eleven to the Blue Angel, a nightclub in Dean Street where Wade was the resident pianist. Very drunk, Elvira and Stephen returned to William Mews at about two in the morning. Sometime later raised voices were heard. Then a shot. Then a woman's screams.

Inside, Michael Stephen, fully dressed and with a bullet lodged in his lung, was dying. In the immediate aftermath of the shot he does not appear to have understood the enormity of what had happened. He walked gingerly to the bathroom and called to Elvira that he thought she should phone a doctor. As the blood flooded his lungs he came out, now staggering. At the top of the stair he stopped and sat. He leaned his head against the wall and died, within ten minutes of the firing of the revolver. A doctor, known to Elvira and awoken by her frantic telephone calls, eventually came. Incoherent, Elvira could only moan to him, 'I love him so . . . He can't be dead . . . He wanted to see you to tell you it was only an accident . . . Let me die, I will kill myself.' These utterances were interspersed with impassioned kisses on the dead man's lips. When the police came dawn was breaking. It was difficult to obtain a clear story of what had happened. But the account that emerged, through sobs and howls, was of the two going to bed; a quarrel; Stephen getting up, dressing, and threatening to leave. Elvira in turn threatens to kill herself if he goes. Stephen picks up a revolver, which is conveniently hidden under a cushion on a chair in the bedroom, fearful that she will carry out her threat. Elvira tries to wrest the revolver from his hand. A struggle. Both hands on the weapon. A shot at point-blank range.

It is an insight into upper-class attitudes of the time that when the police suggested that Elvira should accompany them to the station to provide a full statement her response was to slap their faces and pull rank in imperious tones: 'You foul swine! When you know who my mother is you will be more careful what you say and do to me.' Nonetheless eventually she went, gave a statement that confirmed her earlier account, and, remarkably, was released unconditionally into the protective hands of her parents.

When the house was searched the remnants of the previous evening were discovered and meticulously listed: thirty glasses, four siphons, a cocktail shaker and numerous empty gin and vermouth bottles.

There are, occasionally, cases that epitomise a historical moment so perfectly that it can seem in retrospect that, far from emerging from a maelstrom of human contingency, they involve some element of collusion between the participants, as if all were engaged on a collective endeavour to hold a mirror to their age. The trial of Elvira Barney in 1932 comes close to the supreme example of this: the participants feel like minor characters in an early Evelyn Waugh novel; the fatal shooting took place after a party in a Knightsbridge mews at which jazz records were played while sexually ambiguous guests drank exotic cocktails; the subsequent trial itself featured some of the greatest names in the legal constellation and involved one of the most celebrated forensic displays of that or any age. The world that the trial uncovered was, at least in the eyes of many, one of moral vacuity and debasement. It is said that Elvira Barney's trial did for the jazz age what Oscar Wilde's, some forty years earlier, had done for the nascent English decadence. Moral outrage at the defendant's, and her victim's, way of life sparked a public reaction against the excesses of the BYP. In sum, on every level Elvira Barney's trial substantiates the thesis that the criminal trial can act as a metaphor for its time.

There is only one flaw in an otherwise perfect mise en scène. When one turns to look at a photograph of Elvira one expects to find a portrait of sylph-like, metallic languor. It is surprising instead to see the face of a puffed-up matron. By 1932 Elvira's way of living had taken its physical toll: images from her early twenties show a face both enigmatic and androgynous. Just five years had destroyed that.

On 4 June 1932 Elvira Barney was charged with the murder of Michael Stephen. What had changed the minds of the police? They had started interviewing the other residents of William Mews, chauffeurs and their wives, people to whom it is doubtful Elvira had ever given a moment's thought. One, Mrs Dorothy Hall, who lived opposite, told the police that 'at twenty-five past four, my little girl woke me up and I heard quarrelling. I went to the window and heard her screaming, "Get out of my house at once, I hate you. Get out, get out, I'll shoot you." I heard him mumbling something like "I'm going" and then I heard a shot, she screamed immediately in a hysterical manner and I heard him shout as if in pain, "Oh Good God what have you done."' Other residents also told of earlier incidents which would loom large in the trial.

The news that Elvira had been charged with murder must have hit the respectable Mullens household hard. We know nothing of Elvira's response, but the desperation of the family is revealed by the fact that counsel briefed for the trial was the most famous and glamorous barrister of the day. Then in his early fifties, Sir Patrick Hastings was the very quintessence of modernity. Elected a Labour MP in 1922, he had been the Attorney General during the first short-lived administration of Ramsay MacDonald in 1924. While maintaining a vast practice that covered the full compass of the law, he also pursued a parallel career as a playwright. A number of his plays were staged in the West End during the twenties, one of which had Tallulah Bankhead playing the lead.[3] So Hastings was no stranger to the BYP. He was described by a contemporary as

> the supreme example of a forensic master precisely attuned to the require-
> ments of the time. In any generation his exceptional talents would have
> won acknowledgement: his extraordinary acuteness as a cross-examiner;
> his agility and resourcefulness in argument; the vigour of his quick and
> lucid mind, keenly intelligent rather than deeply intellectual, which made
> him more at home – as befits a jury advocate – with people and affairs
> than with theories and ideas. But to these was added a decisive factor that
> served to set the lasting seal on his success and fame: a worldly knowledge
> that was rooted in the moment . . . That approach can be defined in a
> single word . . . More than any advocate of his comparable eminence,
> Hastings was a *sophisticated* advocate.

The sophistication of Hastings was displayed in understatement and a measure of detachment; the very obverse of Marshall Hall's grandiloquence and passion. And if the Fahmy[4] and Barney cases are connected by multiple similarities, there is one fundamental dissimilarity that reveals the chasm between the tone of the early twenties and that of the early thirties: the approach of counsel for the defendant to the task of securing an acquittal.

A consummate jury advocate, Hastings nonetheless had an aversion to capital trials. Early in his practice he had defended in the so-called 'Hooded Man' case; his client had been convicted and hanged, and the memory haunted him for the rest of his life. He later wrote that 'to a lawyer, a trial for murder must stand in a class by itself; to defend a man for his life, knowing full well that one indiscreet question, one momentary lack of concentration, may perhaps cause his death, places upon any counsel a responsibility which he must undertake with dread.' Yet Hastings agreed to take this brief, persuaded, so it is said, by his wife's feelings of sympathy for Elvira's parents.

The sensation the prosecution caused is very difficult to comprehend now in an age when sensations come from so many sources. Here was the first 'society' murder case since Madame Fahmy's almost ten years earlier, and it was treated with equal fascination by a people hungry for distraction from the economic crisis engulfing the nation. Slated to start on the morning of Monday, 4 July 1932 – barely a month after the killing – on the Sunday afternoon a queue started to form outside the Old Bailey. By midnight it snaked its way round the corner. The mood of the crowd was fractious and the police decided that it should be broken up; there was much protest, but instead of dispersing home, the would-be occupants of the public gallery formed into bands, plotting how they could effect an entry into Court Number One. At one point there was a full-scale assault on the police cordon. By the time the court proceedings commenced the gallery was full, not of the night marauders, but of elegantly dressed women, who had applied in advance for tickets, and now took their places as if, it was remarked, for the opening night of a West End play. It was a sight that nauseated Hastings as he came to take his place in counsel's row. He sat down quietly, without show or ostentation. And yet his presence seemed to dominate the entire court, just as much as Marshall Hall's had done in the preceding decade. All eyes seemed to be drawn to his composed figure, the still centre of a vortex of activity and hubbub that disordered the courtroom. The heavy weight of responsibility bore down on him.

The other figure who of course attracted attention was that of Elvira Barney. It is undoubtedly the case that a woman on trial for the murder of her husband or lover is more likely to receive a favourable hearing if she can combine beauty and vulnerability in her demeanour in the dock. Madame Fahmy achieved that combination. Elvira could not. Hastings remembered that her 'appearance was not calculated to move the hearts of a jury: indeed she was a melancholy and somewhat depressing figure as she stood in the dock with a wardress upon each side of her.'

Counsel for the prosecution was, suitably enough, Sir Percival Clarke, veteran of the Fahmy case and recently knighted. He opened the case high. He appeared to entertain no doubts of the justness of the charge and the inevitability of a conviction. He told the jury that

> The medical evidence can definitely establish the direction in which the revolver was held when fired. You will learn from that that it is practically impossible for the man to have caused this injury to himself. If he did not, who did? There was only one other person there. If you are forced to the conclusion that she shot him, you will have to consider whether she did so by accident or design. In that connection you will bear in mind that she had fired the gun during another quarrel on a previous occasion. Members of the jury, is there any explanation consistent with common sense which will enable you to understand how that man met his death unless this woman deliberately fired?

The one piece of evidence that Clarke laid heavy emphasis upon was that of Mrs Hall, one of the chauffeur's wives, whose nights over the preceding months had been disturbed by Elvira's altercations with her lover. As we have seen Mrs Hall had told the police, shortly after the fatal shooting, that she had heard Elvira screaming during the commotion in the early morning of 31 May: 'Get out, I'll shoot you.' Now that evidence, if accepted, was enough to convict Elvira. And it was to be interpreted in the light of an incident that had occurred just a couple of weeks earlier, when Elvira had been seen at the window of the mews house looking down on Stephen in the street below screaming, 'Laugh, baby; laugh for the last time,' before a shot was fired.

Mrs Hall was duly called by Clarke. She recited the events of two weeks before the fatal night. Arriving at the early morning of 31 May itself, Clarke picked up the narrative: 'So you heard the sounds of their quarrelling? Were there any words – any *important words* – you could pick out?'

The phrase 'important words' was laden with emphasis. Although the jury did not then know it, this was intended to be one of the climacterics of the trial. However minutely counsel prepare their cases, they face one contingency that they are virtually powerless to influence: witnesses. In civil claims witness training is permissible, if frowned upon. In criminal cases it is a cardinal rule that prosecution witnesses cannot be coached; and prosecution counsel are not permitted to discuss with them their evidence in advance. So there is the ever present anxiety that the witness will go 'rogue', will not conform to the case theory so carefully laid out before the jury in the opening speech. There is another cardinal rule of criminal trials that prevents counsel from righting the 'errors' of the witness. He cannot ask of his own witness a leading question; that is a question that tends to suggest the answer. The question Clarke did ask was permissible. Impermissible would have been to ask, 'Did you hear a female voice shouting, "I'll shoot you," that night?'

What Clarke heard next must have caused a minor explosion of annoyance and agitation in his brain. Every barrister has experienced it, though generally on less momentous occasions.

'Yes. Just before the shot I heard Mrs Barney say, "Get out, I'll shoot, I'll shoot."'

There was one crucial word missing from this account: 'you'. The words the witness said she had heard were as consistent with a threat to commit suicide as to commit murder. What could Clarke do? What he could *not* do was remind the witness that in her police statement, and at the earlier committal proceedings, she had included in her account of the events of the fracas the crucial word. Instead he tried the only strategy available to him: 'You heard her say "I'll shoot"?' It is easy to project oneself into Clarke's mind at that moment. He asked this subsidiary question very slowly, very deliberately, trying to give the witness the gentlest of tacit nudges; trying to get her to concentrate on that crucial moment of her recollection.

'Yes.'

Counsel in a criminal trial do not simply communicate verbally. Every aspect of their demeanour, whether they are on their feet or simply sitting in their row, may be studied by the jury. The identification of the defendant and their counsel is such that anxiety or confidence displayed in the lawyer's physiognomy may be carried over on to the client. During this crucial moment of the trial a less experienced advocate might have turned around to stare studiedly at Clarke, just a few feet away in the same row, waiting to pounce on the first hint of a leading question. Hastings did nothing of the sort. The observant juror, sitting directly opposite counsel's benches, across the well of Court Number One, might have detected, and wondered at, the concern that such a pose betrayed. Instead, arms crossed in a show of nonchalant indifference, his wig slightly tilted forward, Sir Patrick Hastings stared straight ahead. Clarke's attempt to reawaken in Mrs Hall her full recollection of the fatal argument had failed. He moved on.

Hastings got up to cross-examine Mrs Hall. Again, the inexperienced advocate might have been lured into returning to those crucial words 'I'll shoot', seeking to press the advantage, seeking to imprint on the jury's mind the disjunction between the way Clarke had opened the case ('There was distinctly heard the words "I'll shoot you"') and what the witness had actually said. Hastings knew better. The risk of Mrs Hall inserting that crucial word – 'you' – back into her testimony was too great. Had she done so the case might have been irretrievably lost. So he kept well away. The events of the fatal night were simply ignored. Hastings turned straight to the earlier incident in William Mews, relied upon by the prosecution as evidence of Elvira's murderous inclination.

HASTINGS: This incident in the mews – it happened late one night?
MRS HALL: Yes.
HASTINGS: About eleven o'clock next morning did you see the young man again?
MRS HALL: Yes.
HASTINGS: Was he then leaving the cottage?
MRS HALL: Yes.
HASTINGS: Was Mrs Barney with him?
MRS HALL: Yes.
HASTINGS: Did they seem friendly?
MRS HALL: Yes.
HASTINGS: On the best possible terms?
MRS HALL: Yes.

On the page this looks simple, almost banal. In fact this short exchange is an example of highly polished cross-examination. Short, closed questions, fired in quick succession, that demanded a yes or no answer. Questions that did not allow for expatiation or digression. A set of forced affirmatives that defused the latent danger that the previous incident in the mews presented to the defence. If Elvira had indeed fired a shot from the first-floor window, then it had hardly been treated by Stephen as an attempt on his life. Now straight to the actual earlier incident, on the face of it so pregnant with difficulty for Elvira's defence.

HASTINGS: After the shot was fired did you and Stephen speak?

MRS HALL: I told him to clear off, as he was a perfect nuisance in the mews.

HASTINGS: Did he reply?

MRS HALL: He said he didn't want to leave Mrs Barney because he was afraid she might kill herself.

This was of course a vital stepping-stone. Propensity to murder was now converted to propensity to self-harm. One final series of questions concerning the earlier incident was necessary to fully neutralise this witness.

HASTINGS: Did I rightly understand you to say that when the shot was fired you saw a puff of smoke?

MRS HALL: Yes.

HASTINGS: How big was it? As big as that? [Hastings placed his hands out so that they were about a foot apart.]

MRS HALL: Oh no; not as big as that.

HASTINGS: How big, then? [The question was put in a friendly, encouraging, tone.]

MRS HALL: Well not very big, just ordinary. [The witness replicated Hastings's hand gesture, but describing a rather smaller 'puff'.]

HASTINGS: I suppose you didn't know that Mrs Barney's revolver contained cordite cartridges? [In one sense this was a ridiculous question; how could the witness have known one way or the other?]

MRS HALL: No [indifferently].

HASTINGS: And I suppose you don't know either, that cordite cartridges don't make any smoke?

Hastings left it at that. He did not pick any sort of fight with the witness. (As he later wrote, prosecution witnesses in capital cases 'always intend to tell the truth. It is indeed rare for a person to swear away the life of an accused person, and it is therefore practically impossible to cross-examine any witness for the Crown with a suggestion that they are lying. Stupid, yes, or perhaps mistaken; even unconsciously exaggerating; but beyond that it is more than dangerous to go.') He merely placed a thought in the jury's mind and moved on.

A number of other residents of William Mews gave similar accounts of the night of 30/31 May and the lovers' argument a week or two earlier. One, carried away by the majesty of the occasion, and her small part in it, was soon testifying that she had heard more than one shot on the fatal night. Indeed by the time her evidence was over she was positive that at least five bullets had been fired. 'A regular fusillade,' Hastings noted sardonically. He did nothing to seek to put the witness right: in fact the uncontradicted evidence was that the revolver had only been fired twice. Better to leave the jury with the impression that the chauffeurs' wives, whose sleep had been so disrupted by Elvira's dissipations, were prepared to arrive at the wildest conclusions. Better not to be seen to be sparring with witnesses who had no interest in the outcome of the case.

Then came the moment that many had been waiting for. Sir Bernard Spilsbury, the Home Office pathologist whose name features in virtually every great murder trial of the early part of the twentieth century, whose evidence had helped to hang Dr Crippen and the 'Brides in the Bath' murderer, George Smith, stepped into the witness box. Spilsbury had by the early 1930s acquired a reputation of Olympian infallibility which brought with it an obstinacy and self-belief that had begun to occlude the possibility of doubt or a divergent opinion. Public adulation had puffed him up and encouraged a forensic method that no longer considered dispassionately the range of possible opinion but alighted on the first instinctive conclusion and refused thereafter to depart from it. If the great Spilsbury's initial view was X, then no amount of countervailing evidence would make him depart from X.

In the witness box Spilsbury explained that he had examined Stephen's body the day after the shooting and had ascertained that the gun was discharged horizontally some three inches from the body. Suicide was ruled out. The trouble for somebody in Hastings's position was that all the jurors no doubt knew of Spilsbury's reputation; his word was treated as near-conclusive. Yet, in fact, Spilsbury had not positively opined on the issue of whether the shot could have been fired by accident. Again, the inclination of the more inexperienced advocate might have been to probe the pathologist to seek his imprimatur to the theory of accident. But who could tell what Spilsbury might say? Hastings had no forensic evidence to rebut any damaging statements. Again discretion was required. Spectators who had anticipated a deadly struggle between two titans of the criminal courts were disappointed. Some desultory questions were posed; some desultory answers procured, and Hastings was sitting back down.

Spilsbury was followed by the Crown's other expert witness, an authority on firearms, himself also a colossus in the public mind and, as we have seen, a man who formed a sort of double act with Spilsbury.[5] Robert Churchill had first come to public prominence in the Hooded Man case as long ago as 1912. On that occasion Hastings, then a young man, had cross-examined Churchill on behalf of the defendant, again on trial for murder. That defence had failed and Hastings's client had been hanged. Hastings now had twenty years' forensic experience behind him and his next meeting with Robert Churchill would be on equal terms. In the rather breathless prose of an early account of the Barney trial: 'Level-headed, matter-of-fact, savant in his sphere, Churchill shared with Spilsbury an enviable legend of impregnability in cross-examination. Upon that legend a chill wind was now about to blow.'

The gravamen of Churchill's evidence was that the weapon that had killed Stephen, a .32 hammerless Smith and Wesson, was 'one of the safest revolvers ever made'. In order to be fired significant exertion was required on the trigger. An accidental firing was highly unlikely. Churchill considered the muzzle of the revolver to have been some three inches from Stephen's body when fired. Yet anyone could prevent it being fired by placing a finger on the cylinder.

This was evidence that could not be ignored or brushed away. It suggested in the clearest terms that this was no accident. Hastings had to set to.

HASTINGS: Do you seriously say, that this is one of the safest weapons made?

CHURCHILL: I do.

HASTINGS: Where is the safety device?

CHURCHILL: There isn't one.

HASTINGS: Isn't there one on most good hammerless revolvers?

CHURCHILL: Yes. What I mean was that it's safer than a revolver with a hammer, safer than an automatic pistol.

HASTINGS: I see. It does not require any terrific muscular development to fire it?

CHURCHILL: It would require more pulling if the weapon were held loosely. The weapon has a 14lb pull.

Hastings then allowed himself some theatre. He picked up the revolver, which was on the desk in front of him, swung round, and started pulling the trigger in the direction of the various junior counsel sitting behind him. They instinctively ducked down. The languor with which he pulled the trigger, making all the time an incessant clicking noise that filled the silent court, made its mark on the jury. (In fact it was later said that Hastings nursed a stiff and swollen finger for some time afterwards.) Churchill looked on in increasing discomfort.

> HASTINGS: Suppose a person had got the revolver and another person came and there was a struggle, it is extremely likely that if they continued to struggle and the revolver was loaded, it would go off. [This was a dangerous question to ask; but perhaps Hastings felt confident in the light of his display with the revolver.]
> CHURCHILL: Yes.
> HASTINGS: And it is quite impossible for anyone who was not there to know exactly how the revolver in these circumstances would go off?
> CHURCHILL: Yes.
> HASTINGS: And if the revolver were between three to six inches from one of them, and one person had it in his hand and the other person seized it, and the revolver was pointing towards him, it is certain that it would go off if it were pressed hard enough.
> CHURCHILL: Yes.
> HASTINGS: And if he happened to be there, opposite the revolver, he would be certain to be killed.
> CHURCHILL: Yes.

The questions shot out with the same remorselessness as Hastings had pulled the trigger on the now safe revolver. Churchill's evidence had been neutered.

As we have seen in Chapter 1, it is always a heavy question in a murder trial whether or not the defendant should be called to give evidence. Sometimes silence is preferable to exposure to questions to which there is no sensible answer or which will reveal the defendant's character too clearly before the jury. But this was a case in which Elvira had to explain herself. In the event, having mastered her emotions, she gave evidence that stood up and conformed to what she had said from the very beginning. Guided by Hastings's gentle questioning, she painted a picture of life with a man who leeched upon and beat her and yet whom she loved and could not bear to be without. Her cross-examination by Clarke inflicted no real blows upon that story.

Hastings stood up to re-examine. He had decided to perform, or rather let Elvira perform, a final piece of theatre with the revolver. He asked for it to be placed on the ledge of the witness box. He looked away. Seconds passed. He looked up towards the judge. Expectation mounted. He swung round. 'Pick up that revolver, Mrs Barney!' The words were harsh and peremptory.

Startled, Elvira instinctively responded to her counsel's demand. Her right hand darted forward. The gun was instantly in it. Mrs Hall, the chauffeur's wife, had distinctly said she had seen Elvira shooting out of the window down at her lover, holding the gun in her *left* hand.

The third day of the trial started with Sir Patrick Hastings's closing speech. There is a full account of it that can be pieced together from the assiduous newspaper reporters. It was a speech that has gone down in legal history as one of the most rigorous dismantlings of a prosecution case ever heard. Hastings eschewed bombast or rhetoric. There were to be no pleas to blind justice or God's 'great Western sun'. Instead he proceeded meticulously through each piece of evidence placed before the jury by the prosecution and exploded it. This was prefaced by a reminder to the jury of the intense seriousness of their task.

> Having regard to the terrible position of the lady I represent, I know you will not begrudge me a little time to put forward the other side of the case. I shall not indulge in flights of oratory or dramatic surprises, supposed to be the attributes of an advocate. They may be amusing, but we are not in this court to be amused. We leave that to the people who have been here the last two or three days, no doubt enjoying and gloating over every expression of agony; the distinguished authors here to see that people outside not sufficiently fortunate to join in the amusement should not miss the slightest sign of the things these distinguished gentlemen can show them. We rather despise some of the people here and loathe these things. If they expect to find amusement here, they will not find it from me.

And he ended:

> I am not going to ask you for the benefit of the doubt. I am not going to beg you for mercy and a lenient view of what has happened. I stand here and I claim of you that on the evidence that has been put before

The entrance to Court Number One from the Grand Hall of the Old Bailey.

Crowds form outside the Old Bailey during the trial of Dr Crippen, 1910.

The interior of Court Number One, shortly after the opening of the 'new' Old Bailey. The public gallery is above the clock; the dock just in view on the right.

The Camden Town murder: Robert Wood in the dock, December 1907. A photograph taken from the public gallery. Note the jurors' concentration despite the intense cold.

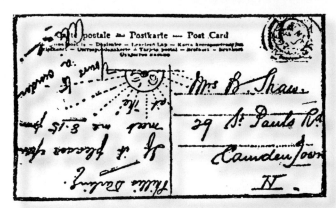

The 'rising sun' postcard received
by Emily Dimmock on Monday,
9 September 1907.

Emily Dimmock, skittishly
dressed in a sailor suit.

*The Camden Town Murder or What Shall We
Do about the Rent*, Walter Sickert, *c.* 1908.

Edwardian sex symbol:
Maud Allan as Salome
contemplates the head of
John the Baptist.

The Royal Albert Hall hosts
the Vigilantes, June 1918.
Early arrivals benefited from
an organ recital.

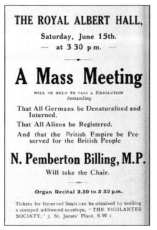

THE ROYAL ALBERT HALL,

Saturday, June 15th.
— at 3 30 p.m. —

A Mass Meeting

WILL BE HELD TO PASS A RESOLUTION
demanding

That All Germans be Denaturalised and
Interned.

That All Aliens be Registered.

And that the British Empire be Pre-
served for the British People

N. Pemberton Billing, M.P.

Will take the Chair.

Organ Recital 2.30 to 3 30 p.m.

Tickets for Reserved Seats can be obtained by sending
a stamped addressed envelope, "THE VIGILANTES
SOCIETY," 5. St. James' Place, S.W.1.

Noel Pemberton Billing
contemplates a morally
pure — and technologically
advanced — future.

Sir Edward Marshall Hall KC and Sir Henry Curtis-Bennett KC leave the Old Bailey after Madame Fahmy's acquittal, September 1923.

Mistress to royalty and others: the soon-to-be Marguerite Fahmy strikes a domineering pose, late 1910s.

'She felt cruelty in him and it attracted her, it lured her': Rudolph Valentino as *The Sheik*, 1921.

'The Messalina of Ilford': Edith Thompson, *c.*1921.

Elvira Barney as a gamine member of the 'Bright Young People', 1920s.

The party is over: Michael Scott Stephen's body is manhandled out of William Mews, Knightsbridge, May 1932.

A less gamine Elvira Barney in jaunty mood immediately after her acquittal, July 1932.

'The supreme example of a forensic master precisely attuned to the requirements of the time': Sir Patrick Hastings KC.

The Old Bailey at war:
bomb damage in May 1941.

A queue forms outside the
bricked-up courthouse, for
the 'Cleft Chin Murder'
trial, January 1945.

you, Mrs Barney is entitled as a right to a verdict in her favour. She is a young woman with the whole of her life before her. I beg you to remember that, and I ask of you as a matter of justice and as of right that you should set her free.

Even the judge, the then sixty-five-year-old Travers Humphreys, whom we met while he was a barrister in Chapter 2, was impressed by it. In his summing-up he said something that is almost unprecedented: 'You have listened to a remarkable forensic effort this morning. I am not paying compliments when I say that it is certainly one of the finest speeches I myself have ever heard at the Bar in the course of a somewhat protracted experience.' Certainly the view of one spectator was that, had the jury been asked to give its verdict before Hastings stood up to make his client's case, it would have surely convicted. He described a speech where the jury seemed to become wholly absorbed in what Hastings was telling them. And this is what he was doing: leading the jury by the hand down the path towards a single, inexorable conclusion.

As it was the jury retired at three o'clock on the third day of the trial. At a quarter to five it returned. The verdict visibly shocked Sir Percival Clarke as much as it surprised Sir Patrick Hastings. 'Not guilty', not only of murder but also of the lesser charge of manslaughter. For the crowds in the street, who had been awaiting a verdict for three days, the mood had, inexplicably, turned in favour of Elvira. Perhaps it was something to do with Hastings's speech. As he quietly slipped out of the Old Bailey he heard them singing 'Three Cheers for Mrs Barney' and 'For She's a Jolly Fellow'. On being told of the public sentiment, the judge, who had certainly formed no favourable impression of the defendant, was heard to say to his clerk: 'Most extraordinary! Apparently we should give her a pat on the back.'

The policeman-turned-writer C.H. Rolph was present at many murder trials at the Old Bailey in the pre-war period, including Elvira Barney's. Writing in his memoirs years later, after the abolition of capital punishment, he recalled the unhealthy atmosphere at the Bailey when 'word got round the building that the jury in some well-publicized murder trial was coming back into court with its verdict . . . every seat was quickly filled and the rear of the courtroom was crammed with standing onlookers – some of them officers of the court to whom the death sentence must have been a commonplace'. The prurience of the crowd had previously been satisfied by a public hanging. Now it had to make do with the tantalising moment when a person's fate was decided. Rolph noted that the effect of abolition had been to change the atmosphere of murder trials. 'The drama is much reduced, the morbidity has been extracted, justice seems to have edged a little nearer to civilisation.' All true; but he might have added that the other consequence was that much of the excitement of the murder trial was thereby lost.

Elvira Barney had been on trial for her life; and she had every reason to fear that she would be convicted. (It was less than ten years since Edith Thompson had been hanged.) Fifty years after the abolition of the death penalty, it is now difficult to fully comprehend the anxiety of a defendant on trial for a capital offence. One might think that having heard the words 'not guilty' the defendant to a capital charge would undergo some form of rebirth. It has been said that it is only those who have cheated death who fully appreciate the value of life.

Records of Elvira's life after the trial are limited, but suggest that her escape from the gallows did not set her upon any new path to self-aware-ness. On the very night of her acquittal, she was encountered in a seedy shebeen in Gerrard Street swaying drunkenly to a solitary jazz pianist while trying, unsuccessfully, to pick up a young actor. The next day she was photographed about to step into what seems to modern eyes an abnormally large motor car, holding a bouquet of irises and smiling broadly, as if on her way to a jolly day at the races. And on the Sunday after the trial ended the *Sunday Dispatch* (the sister paper to the *Daily Mail*) published what was said to be the beginning of a series of confes-sional articles. The first established that if not guilty of murder Elvira was at least culpable of crimes against decorum and literary style. 'I write in tears. People think of me as an exotic woman who was on trial for her life. They forget that my greater tragedy is with me yet. The man I loved more than anything else in the world is dead.'

The image she portrayed of her and Stephen's domestic life was perhaps not likely to garner credence from her readers: 'I did my own cooking at William Mews, and prepared meals for him. We often stayed in to listen to the wireless. He would read aloud, while I sewed.' Nothing was, of course, said about the implements of 'fetishism and perversion' discov-ered by the police.

It was this article that seems to have changed the public mood against Elvira and against the faction in society with which she was, perhaps unfairly, identified. The newspapers rose in unison in denunciation of the moral degeneracy embodied by Elvira's lifestyle and her decision to publish her 'story'. The feeling was captured in the *Spectator*: 'Every sentiment any person of normal decency would consider sacred and enshrouded with the reticence it demands, is ignored and paraded with every elaboration of naivety and ostentatious self-pity. For a woman to expose herself physically would be far less repellent than a deliberate parade of the secrets of what she would no doubt call her soul.' Others launched an attack against the wider movement of the BYP. Hannen Swaffer, in the *Daily Herald*, thundered: 'Bright Young Things are a danger not only to their own class, but to all the calluses in the land. They hate law and order. The Judge [who had referred to the 'useless lives' led by Stephen and Elvira] could see, with his wise old eyes, further than the dock. He could see the whole social order being undermined by a gang of pinheads who, because of the publicity they obtain, really think their importance merits it.' Sensing a shift in public mood the *Sunday Dispatch* hastily cancelled Elvira's contract, citing a convenient doctor's injunction to complete rest, and nothing further emerged from her pen to titillate, or bore, the nation.

The reverberations of the trial were more widely felt. The trial had opened the door to a manner of living that, in the midst of the Depression, was nauseating to many. The pranks and parties of the 1920s now seemed out of step with the times. In his memoirs Osbert Lancaster wrote of the revulsion that the acquittal had sparked off. Whereas previously when he attended parties there would be a throng of admirers hoping to catch a glimpse of the smart set, now, at a party in Chelsea in the summer of 1932, he was met with 'solicitous but ironic enquiries about the health of Mrs Barney and pious expressions of hope that the lady had not forgotten her gun'. (In fact the revolver was, wisely, confiscated and is now part of the collection in Scotland Yard's 'Black Museum'.)

Elvira's name cropped up again some weeks later in *The Times*, covering the inquest into the death of a heroin addict called Gertrude Gamble, who had thrown herself out of a hotel window in Half Moon Street. It was reported that her suicide note had asserted that Elvira Barney was 'responsible for this'. It appears that after Elvira's acquittal Gamble had been tasked by Lady Mullens with chaperoning her to France, out of the way of both harm and publicity. From a letter later written by Gamble, it is clear that the tears that flowed from Elvira's eyes in the aftermath of her acquittal soon dried up. Immediately they arrived in St Raphael Elvira took part in a cocaine-fuelled 'Chelsea Sandwich' with two theatrical siblings, Audrey and Kenneth Carten. It may be that Gertrude nursed a passion for Elvira and the events of that summer had involved some form of rejection. We shall never know.

Elvira's next appearance in the newspapers would be her last. On 27 December 1936 *The Times*'s Paris correspondent reported the death of Mrs Elvira Barney. Her body had been found on Christmas Day on her bed in her hotel in Paris, fully dressed in evening gown and fur coat. After a 'gay tour of Park night-spots' she had returned to her hotel. 'I am so cold,' she complained to the porter. The cause of death was reported as 'congested lungs due to cold and excessive drinking alcohol'. The gift of a second life that the jury had handed to her had been flung aside.

Barristers seldom meditate deeply on their cases after they have reached their conclusion. The hunger for the new is overwhelming and pushes them relentlessly on to their next brief. Hastings's own professional diary at the time of the Barney case is remarkable: he had finished a large probate trial on the Thursday before the Barney trial started on the Monday. The day after the case ended (on the Wednesday) he went straight into an appeal in a fraud case, which lasted another two weeks. This means he had essentially the weekend to prepare Elvira's defence. This is not an unusual schedule for barristers of the period.

When Hastings came to write his memoirs towards the end of his life, he devoted some pages to the case. The account is slightly disappointing for the absence of any great revelations or psychological aperçus about Elvira's character. But it ends with one striking memory. Hastings recounted how, a few weeks after the trial, at the end of the legal term, he was being driven out of Boulogne on the road to Paris. A long, low car, driven by a woman, dashed round the corner on the wrong side, almost killing him and his chauffeur. 'As he indignantly picked up his cap he said: "Did you know who was driving that car, sir? It was Mrs Barney!"'

PART III

War

5

Haw-Haw

R v William Joyce (1945)

ALMOST EIGHTY YEARS on, we now look back at the Second World War as a time of unprecedented national unity. Greed and self-interest were forgotten as Britain, and her allies, pulled together to defeat the enemy. Although the British were conscripted, rationed, forcibly evacuated and blitzed as never before, these discomforts applied to everyone: rich and poor huddled together in bomb shelters, and even Buckingham Palace suffered a direct hit. Adversity brought out the best in the British: neighbours helped each other, scarce resources were shared and few dared to cheat or steal.

Paradoxically, as memories of the war grow ever more distant, the more sanitised they become. But at the time things seemed very different. Overall crime in Britain rose by more than 60 per cent during the war, from 300,000 recorded crimes in 1939 to 475,000 in 1945. For many Britons the war was not a time to 'Keep Calm and Carry On' but a period of fear, panic and paranoia. Looters would often send bogus removal vans to pick up valuables from bomb sites; 'shelter gangs' stole from those seeking refuge in underground stations. There was the 'billeting lark' (landlords claiming allowances for phantom lodgers) and the 'bomb lark' (fraudsters who would falsely claim National Assistance payments; the Old Bailey often heard several such cases each day, including one man who had claimed to have been bombed out nineteen times in just five months). There were even several cases of fraudsters selling subscriptions for non-existent bomb shelters. In November 1940 six auxiliary firemen were sentenced at the Old Bailey to five years each for looting.

The ready availability of firearms, an influx of foreign servicemen and the cover of darkness lent by the blackout meant that violent crime also rose. In March 1940 London even saw a political assassination unconnected to the war: a Sikh extremist, Udham Singh, shot dead Sir Michael

O'Dwyer, a former Lieutenant Governor of the Punjab, at a public meeting in Caxton Hall. Singh, who was motivated to revenge the Amritsar massacre of 1919, was sentenced to death in Court Number One in June 1940, screaming abuse and spitting as he was dragged from the dock.[1] It turned out that the pistol used for the killing had been bought from a soldier in a pub. Although the murder rate only increased slightly, murders seemed to grow more brutal, cruel and motiveless. Throughout the early 1940s the Old Bailey heard a succession of grisly murder trials, the most notorious of which was that of the so-called 'Blackout Ripper'. An airman called Gordon Cummins was found guilty of the murder and mutilation of four women and the attempted murder of two others, in and around Marylebone.

The war had a direct physical impact on the Old Bailey: on the night of 10 May 1941 a large explosive bomb and several incendiaries killed two firewatchers on the roof and completely destroyed Court Number Two. Although the Bailey reopened just three weeks later with a temporary courtroom on the ground floor, the building was not fully repaired until the early 1950s. Juries were reduced in size from twelve to seven to reduce the risk of jurors being lost to air raids or military service. Increasingly, judges would vent their spleen from the Old Bailey bench about the ever-rising tide of crime. Much of the blame for Britain's supposed moral collapse was placed on American cultural influences. There had been much concern in the 1930s about American-style 'motor bandits', smash-and-grab robbers who would often target cinemas and evade capture by fast driving, and the unduly lenient sentences some received; many felt that the rising tide of American gangster films and paperback novels glamourised such crimes.[2] The 'White Slave Murders' of three prostitutes by the transatlantic gang that had pimped them on the streets of London only heightened fears of the American crime menace.

During the war some three million American servicemen passed through Britain. Just before D-Day 1.6 million Americans were based on British soil. This influx is now recalled fondly: it led to thousands of transatlantic friendships, 70,000 'GI bride' marriages, and a 'special relationship' that lasts to this day. But the Americans' arrival did not seem so welcome at the time. 'Have you heard about the new utility knickers? One yank and they're off', was one common joke about US servicemen's success with British women. American servicemen were mostly bored, single and with disposable income and easy access to firearms. By the end of the war eighteen American servicemen had been hanged or shot by firing squad for rape or murder, most of them at Shepton Mallet prison in Somerset, which was handed over to the Americans for the duration of the war.

Only one of these American murderers was tried at the Old Bailey. In October 1944 a twenty-two-year-old US army deserter, Private Karl Hulten, and his 'moll', an eighteen-year-old Welsh girl called Elizabeth Jones, went on a Bonnie-and-Clyde-style rampage in which a taxi driver was robbed and murdered with a stolen automatic pistol, and a woman hitch-hiker beaten and left for dead. Because Hulten had a British accomplice he was tried not at an American court martial but in Court Number One, where both he and Jones were found guilty of murder. Although Jones was reprieved, Hulten was hanged by Albert Pierrepoint at Pentonville on 8 March 1945. The case shocked the nation: it seemed that a new element of nihilism had entered the lexicon of crime. Here was 'murder for kicks': two ordinary, dislocated youths brought together by chance in unfamiliar surroundings who, because of some inexplicable interconnection, embarked on a concentrated murder spree. Eleven months later the Hulten and Jones case inspired George Orwell's famous essay 'Decline of the English Murder', in which Orwell juxtaposed the case with the classic English murder of the past as the basis for a sardonic meditation on nostalgia and moral decline. Orwell reminisced fondly about the pleasures of pre-war Sunday afternoons on the sofa, with a good pipe and a cup of 'mahogany-brown' tea, immersed in *News of the World* accounts of suburban murders. Most of these classic real murder cases, much like Agatha Christie's fictional ones, involved elaborate planning by the murderer, lengthy investigations, plot twists and dramatic coincidences. Orwell contrasted this world favourably with the sordid banality of the 'principal cause célèbre of the war years' – the Hulten and Jones case. 'The background was not domesticity, but the anonymous life of the dance halls and the false values of the American film . . . Jones and Hulten committed their murder to the tune of V1, and were convicted to the tune of V2.'

The Old Bailey also dealt with numerous espionage cases. Fifteen people were hanged at Wandsworth and Pentonville as spies during the war, many of them after Old Bailey trials. The first were a German and two Dutchmen who had come over to Britain in a dinghy in 1940 pretending to be refugees, secretly equipped with radio transmitters with which to send back intelligence to Nazi Germany. In 1941 the Old Bailey convicted Karel Richter, a German spy of Czech heritage who had been parachuted into Hertfordshire and was arrested after a suspicious lorry driver, who had asked him for directions and got no sensible reply, alerted the police. When hanged by Albert Pierrepoint at Wandsworth on 10 December 1941 – three days after Pearl Harbor – Richter had to be held down by five guards. Most of these espionage cases are forgotten today. The trial of William Joyce, better known as 'Lord Haw-Haw', held a month after the war ended, was very different: as someone who had broadcast propaganda throughout the war he could hardly be regarded as a covert spy.

Some trials perform a function that goes beyond the simple ascertainment of guilt or its absence. They can involve a form of reckoning, a ritual in which the perceived public desire for justice is satisfied. Of course in one sense every crime engages the public interest because it involves a breach of the rules that have been prescribed to preserve the civil peace. However much it is committed in a private sphere and directed against a particular victim or set of victims a crime is deemed to injure everyone, which is why it is prosecuted in the name of the monarch, as the embodiment of the state and its people. Still, some crimes involve more directly an affront to the public at large, and it is in trials of such offences that questions of proof seem to become secondary to a larger goal.

The trial of William Joyce was conducted in the knowledge of all its participants, Joyce included, that it engaged interests that touched upon the nation as a whole. It began on an overcast Monday morning, on 17 September 1945. After six years of war the Old Bailey had a battered majesty about it. The gash in its Portland stone façade, caused by the bombing in 1941, had been crudely patched up with bricks. Four months after the cessation of hostilities in Europe the blackout tarring that had been painted on to the Bailey's windows in 1939 remained (there being no one yet available, or at least inclined, to remove it), so that its halls, passages and stairs seemed to be in perpetual dusk. In Court Number One a new timber ceiling had been placed under the shattered glass skylight, occluding all natural light. Trials were now conducted under the harsh glare of electric bulbs. The courthouse stood amid the ruins of the City of London, a 'beautiful desert of charred stone', yellow ragwort growing unchecked through the surrounding rubble.

An unprecedented number of lawyers, guards and uniformed army officers crowded into Court Number One. Such was the vast press interest that a row of the public gallery was given over to reporters, one of whom was Rebecca West, at the time one of the starriest authors in the world. The articles she wrote for the *New Yorker* later formed the opening chapters of her book *The Meaning of Treason*, published in 1949. Written in a luxuriant Edwardian style, its tone of aristocratic hauteur sits uncomfortably with the stark modernity of its subject matter.

Queues started forming at two in the morning for the twenty public places that remained. Joyce's disembodied voice, rasping yet rich, peculiarly fascinating even as it gleefully predicted the imminent defeat of Britain in the face of the Nazi war machine, had been listened to by virtually every British adult at some point during the course of the war. Now the voice was made flesh and people wanted to see this oddity for themselves.

In the courtroom were six barristers, some on their way to becoming giants of the post-war English Bar, others to the High Court bench. Leading for the prosecution was Sir Hartley Shawcross KC MP, the Labour government's new Attorney General (the results of the recent general election, at which Shawcross had first been elected an MP, had been announced on 26 July 1945). A legal prodigy who had taken silk in 1939, aged just thirty-seven, Shawcross was glamorous and undoubtedly brilliant. But he was an unknown quantity as a government law officer: his success or failure at this trial – his first ever at the Old Bailey, at a time when law officers regularly prosecuted serious crimes[3] – would help determine the future of his career. Assisting him were two Treasury Counsel, Lawrence Byrne and Gerald Howard, who had both prosecuted in the Hulten and Jones trial some eight months earlier. Both were considerably older than Shawcross and had vastly more expertise in criminal prosecution. Byrne would become a High Court judge before the year was out, as would Howard a few years later. But this was a treason case, the first contested trial for the most serious offence known to English law since Sir Roger Casement's prosecution in 1916, and as such was deemed to require the attendance of the senior government law officer. Many men would have felt daunted by having two counsel of such standing sitting behind them and by the significance of the occasion; but Shawcross, still only forty-three years old, had a supreme – and justified – confidence in his own ability.

Acting for the defendant were Gerald Slade KC, a veteran silk eleven years older than Shawcross, leading Derek Curtis-Bennett KC (who would go on to defend Klaus Fuchs and John Christie in Court Number One and become the foremost criminal silk of the early 1950s), and a younger barrister called James Burge (who in 1963 would defend Stephen Ward and would be one of the models for John Mortimer's creation Horace Rumpole). Later chairman of the Bar Council and a fastidious teetotaller (Shawcross would recall that 'his proud boast was that no drop of alcohol had ever passed his lips'), Slade seemed to Rebecca West a man of Wordsworthian simplicity.

Were these three distressed to find themselves defending the most notorious 'traitor' of the war? The judge would in his summing-up express sympathy for their 'very uncongenial task'. In fact barristers generally delight in a 'big case', however notorious or repellent their client. One suspects that, despite the threats of death he received were his client to be acquitted, Slade was proud to be instructed on behalf of William Joyce. Still, whatever his private views, professional obligation meant that he could not refuse the brief. The 'cab-rank' rule – which in essence obliges a barrister to represent a litigant however much he may disapprove of them – prevailed in 1945 just as much as it prevails today (the next year Slade would appear for someone at the other end of the political spectrum from Joyce, the chairman of the National Executive Committee of the Labour Party, Harold Laski, in his calamitous libel trial against the *Newark Advertiser*). Yet the rule was easily evaded by the unscrupulous; when Roger Casement was charged in 1916 with treason his solicitor had been unable to find an English KC who would take the case. In the end he had to look to the Irish Bar for Casement's representation, the legendary Serjeant Sullivan.

'The men and women in the jury-box were all middle-aged, since the armies had not yet come home, and like everybody else in England at that date, they were puffy and haggard,' noted West. Once the court had assembled there were three raps on the door at the back of the court before the judge, Mr Justice Frederick Tucker, walked in accompanied by the Lord Mayor of London and two City aldermen. Ominously, Tucker carried a black cap as well as his silk gloves in his hands; although he hid the cap behind a row of books Joyce must have seen it as the judge entered.

The man in the dock bowed deeply to the dignitaries. It was the bow of a man whose entire political philosophy was founded on reverence for authority. As he emerged from the cells up the steps into the dock many had imagined a tall, Bertie Wooster-ish type, possibly sporting a monocle. Joyce was a man who was known to most only by his voice and during the war there had been much debate about its origins. Some suggested that it had an Oxford drawl about it, though J.W. Hall, an Oxonian barrister who edited the Notable British Trial volume on Joyce's case in 1946, would protest that it was 'such as Balliol never conceived, nor Magdalen heard'. To Rebecca West's disdainful ears, Joyce's voice was obviously the 'rasping' Irish brogue of a 'queer little bog trotter'; others detected traces of a Manchester, or even a Chicago, accent.

It was his phoney aristocratic delivery that had inspired the journalist Jonah Barrington to nickname Joyce 'Lord Haw-Haw', a moniker that has stuck ever since. Joyce stood just five feet six, and looked even shorter when flanked by two tall warders. There was a ghastly pallor about him made all the more livid by the deep scar that described a crescent moon from the bottom of his ear to the corner of his mouth. West noted with distaste his mousey hair, his misshapen nose – 'joined to his face at an odd angle' – and his lack of handsomeness. His eyes were 'hard and shiny', his shoulders dismissed as 'narrow and sloping', his arms 'very short and thick'. Whatever his physical shortcomings (and a Movietone film shot just after Joyce's arrest confirms West's perception of Joyce as 'a little knuckleduster of a man'), the road that had finally brought him to Court Number One of the Old Bailey was a remarkable one.

Joyce had in fact never been near Oxford. He had been brought up in Ireland by an Irish father and a British mother. Although Catholic the family was also staunchly loyalist: Joyce would later claim that his distinctive nasal voice resulted from being punched in the nose by a schoolmate who'd called him an 'Orangeman'. He was a precocious child who started giving schoolyard speeches about the dangers of Bolshevism at an early age. 'That boy will either do something very great in the world, or he will hang by the end of a rope,' one school report noted. He was soon doing much more than speechifying: he would later claim that during the Irish War of Independence of 1919–21 he acted as a teenage informer for the Royal Irish Constabulary's notorious 'Special Reserve' paramilitary units known as the Black and Tans. Several of the family's properties were torched by Nationalists; Joyce would have it that the IRA had tried to assassinate him. Two days after the Irish Free State was declared in 1921 Joyce sailed to Liverpool, followed by his parents and four younger siblings.

William soon gravitated to London. After taking his Higher School Certificate at the Battersea Polytechnic he started an English degree at the University of London's Birkbeck College, graduating in 1927 with a First – and a growing interest in Fascism. Joyce started a Master's degree in philology, writing a thesis on 'unrounded vowels in English', but quickly realised that he preferred practice to theory. After a short spell in the university's Conservative Association he gravitated rightwards, joining the British Fascisti, a Mussolini fan club formed following the

Duce's assumption of power in Italy in 1922, which later changed its name to the more Anglo-Saxon 'British Fascists'. He soon became one of the British far right's most gifted orators. Joyce also proved a doughty street-fighter. In 1924, on his way home from an election meeting in Lambeth, he was set upon and slashed across the right cheek by unknown assailants ('Jewish-communists!' Joyce claimed from his hospital bed). The scar stayed with him for life. His passion for brawling was undiminished, though he would seek to contain it for the future.

A self-fashioned patriot, Joyce met his first wife at a Cenotaph wreath-laying three weeks later, for which he had discharged himself from hospital against doctors' advice. They married in 1927, a week after Joyce's twenty-first birthday. After being rejected by the Foreign Office ('A little oily, don't you think?' a civil servant noted in the margins of Joyce's application form), Joyce started working as a tutor in a crammer. After a falling-out with British Fascists in 1928 Joyce rejoined the Tories – serving briefly as President of the Conservative Association in Chelsea, whose MP he dreamed of becoming – until rumours of an affair with a sixteen-year-old pupil forced him to resign in disgrace. In 1930 Joyce joined Oswald Mosley's New Party – later renamed the British Union of Fascists – forming a close attachment to a fellow-traveller, the MI5 officer Maxwell Knight, as well as Mosley himself.[4] MI5 saw the BUF's 'Clear out the Reds' campaign as a useful means for containing, and monitoring, trade union and communist insurgents and Knight probably recruited Joyce, albeit more as a channel of communication between MI5 and the British Fascist movement than as a spy.

Joyce was swiftly appointed the BUF's 'West London Area Administration Officer'. He had the relentless ambition of the outsider seeking to prove his worth, and threw himself into his work. He was promoted to Director of Propaganda, on a salary of £300 a year, often deputising for Mosley at rallies across the country, where he demonstrated his oratory to large crowds. In its early days the BUF placed as much emphasis on loyalty to King and Country, full employment, the abolition of private education and the curtailment of big business, as it did on anti-communism and anti-Semitism: the National Anthem was always sung at the end of its meetings. Until Hitler became German chancellor in 1933 many British politicians viewed the BUF as a boisterous, counter-cultural youth movement rather than a racist one. Many respectable figures from both left and right – among them John Strachey, Aneurin Bevan, Randolph Churchill, George Bernard Shaw, Lloyd George, Lord Rothermere (proprietor of the *Daily Mail*, which published his infamous

article entitled 'Hurrah for the Blackshirts!' in 1934), and Harold Nicolson
– expressed admiration for Mosley, with little or no qualification, at
some stage in the 1930s.

By 1934 the BUF had 50,000 members. Galvanised by Hitler's success
the previous year Mosley began to entertain wild thoughts about power.
In 1936 he fantasised that Edward VIII would react to the controversy
over his relationship with Wallis Simpson not by abdicating but by
dissolving Parliament and asking Mosley to form a government (notwithstanding the fact that his party had no MPs in Parliament). He even
pondered appointing Joyce as Viceroy of India.

In an attempt to clean up the BUF's image Joyce was put in charge
of I Squad, a black-shirted cadre trained in martial arts but drilled to
leave it to the police to restore order at rallies. In 1934 Joyce found
himself charged, alongside Mosley, with a public order offence arising
from a rally in Worthing; the police testified to his 'discipline under
provocation' and, thanks to some shrewd advocacy by Sir Patrick Hastings
KC, after a two-day trial at Lewes Assizes the charges were dismissed. It
was a good example of retaining counsel who can clothe his client with
his own respectability: as we have seen in Chapter 4, Hastings, a titan
of the Bar, had been a Labour MP between 1922 and 1926 and had
briefly served as Attorney General in 1924.

But the BUF's fortunes had already started to turn sour. A string of
riots at BUF parades at White City and Hyde Park, in which communist
counter-demonstrators were knocked unconscious, turned public opinion
against them. At the so-called battle of Cable Street in 1936 – where
7,000 BUF marchers were seen off by 100,000 counter-demonstrators
– Joyce's speech had to be cancelled. He had started to regard Mosley
as a weak leader (or 'Bleeder' as he said behind his back); MI5 later
intercepted a letter in which he described Mosley as 'little more than a
conceited popinjay'.[5] On New Year's Day 1937 a new Public Order Act
outlawed political uniforms. Joyce discarded his blackshirt and started
sporting a Nazi-style trenchcoat of the type made fashionable by Hitler,
and a toothbrush moustache. Hitler, not Mussolini, had now become
Joyce's hero. His anti-Semitism came to the fore; unlike Mosley he argued
that Britain should become an active ally of Hitler, not a neutral bystander
on the stage of European politics.

By now his wife, disenchanted by Joyce's political monomania, had
started an affair with another BUF member. In turn Joyce eloped with
Margaret White, a failed cabaret artiste turned secretary and head of the
BUF's women's section in Carlisle, who had devotedly attended Joyce's

speaking appearances during a tour of the Scottish Borders. Five days after Joyce's decree absolute arrived he and Margaret married. In lieu of a honeymoon they went door-knocking in Shoreditch, where Joyce was a BUF candidate in the council elections, coming a distant second behind Labour. A political split from Mosley followed soon afterwards. In April 1937 Mussolini stopped funding the BUF. Forced to cut 80 per cent of the BUF's staff, Mosley 'bore no rival near the throne', and Joyce was among those shown the door.

Joyce and his new wife – now living in a bizarre *ménage à trois* with fellow Fascist and mystic Angus MacNab – were forced to move to less salubrious rooms. He had to return to tutoring to make ends meet (his skill as a teacher, perhaps born of his own fervent auto-didacticism, was noted by many), before setting up the avowedly pro-Nazi National Socialist League with another BUF outcast (and, like Mosley, former Labour MP), John Beckett. But the League had to compete with several other Fascist splinter groups and the 'National Socialism Now' pamphlet they co-authored failed to attract more than a few dozen members, many of them Special Branch infiltrators.

Just as appeasement gave the BUF a new lease of life – its slogan 'Mind Britain's Business' could be seen daubed on walls across the country – Joyce retreated further into the shadows, sending abusive letters to those who campaigned on behalf of Jewish refugees. In 1939 he was twice tried for assault, and twice acquitted. After Joyce's student numbers dwindled the *ménage* moved again to a basement flat not far from the Earl's Court exhibition hall in which Mosley addressed 20,000 people in July 1939, said to be the largest indoor political rally in British history. Joyce's political career in England looked as if it had hit the buffers.

The impending war put Joyce in a real quandary. He had acquired a British passport in 1933. That passport lapsed after five years and in 1938 Joyce renewed it for a further year with a view to fleeing with Margaret to neutral Ireland. Joyce changed his mind when Chamberlain returned from Munich, having agreed to Hitler's dismemberment of Czechoslovakia. Along with many others in Britain Joyce regarded the prospect of war between Britain and Germany with horror: he considered the two countries as natural allies and vital bulwarks against communist Russia.

'Bloody well go and live in Germany if you like it so much,' a heckler once told Joyce; in 1939, as Chamberlain's promise of 'Peace in Our Time' began to ring more hollow, he started laying plans to do just that. He had a number of reasons to get out of England. Although Joyce was well-read and had a photographic memory – he could recite huge chunks of Dryden, Shelley and Tennyson – he was also a misfit who often used his own private dialect (Christmas was always called 'Christ-tide'). He could be arrogant and felt he was looked down upon by the upper-class leaders of the BUF (Rebecca West, who regarded Joyce as 'at best a street-corner speaker better known than most', says that the wife of a senior BUF member once described him as one of 'those dreadful common people we had had to use to get power' who would have been quickly purged had Mosley ever become a national leader).

In early August 1939, as war began to seem imminent, Joyce received assurances from Berlin that he and Margaret would be granted German citizenship if they fled to Germany. Warned by Maxwell Knight that they faced imminent arrest and internment if they stayed in London, Joyce renewed his passport again, extending its validity to July 1940, and he and Margaret obtained a German travel visa. Leaving Victoria station on 26 August, they caught the boat train to Ostend ('Berlin! That's a rum place to be going right now,' said a porter after inspecting their tickets).

There was no fanfare to greet them in Berlin. Ominously, they were now warned that in the event of war they would be interned, the very fate they had left London to avoid. Shamefacedly, on 30 August they started laying plans to return to London, but staff at the British Embassy, packing up ahead of the expected declaration of war, were too busy to help and suggested they go to the British Consulate in Cologne instead. The Joyces were stuck.

As their savings dwindled Joyce took poorly paid work translating Hitler's speeches into English. Although the German foreign ministry found the Joyces a flat to rent it was reluctant to avail itself of Joyce's proffered propaganda services: Admiral Canaris, head of the German military intelligence (the Abwehr), suspected he might be a British plant. But two weeks after the outbreak of war the feared internment hadn't transpired. Joyce then got a lucky break: after being invited to audition at Nazi Germany's state broadcasting organisation, the Reichs-Rundfunk-Gesellschaft (known as the Rundfunk for short) he was offered a job as an 'Editor and Speaker'. Margaret soon joined him, presenting *Weekly Talks for Women* and *End of the Weekend*, in which she goaded British housewives about the absence of food shortages in Berlin in a clipped, Celia Johnson voice that belied her Lancashire roots.

The Rundfunk was a huge operation: 500 people worked on its foreign services alone. It was under the direct control of the Third Reich's master propagandist, Joseph Goebbels. By the end of September 1939 Joyce moved from merely reading the news to making it; a five-and-a-half-year string of propaganda broadcasts, written and presented by Joyce, had begun. Joyce's nightly two-hour programme, *Germany Calling*, broadcast at 9 p.m. British time, soon became required listening: aimed squarely at British listeners, it was the only German radio programme to carry jazz, a musical form considered degenerate by the Nazis.

At first no one knew who its well-spoken presenter was. In early broadcasts Joyce often alternated with other propagandists who all spoke perfect English and may well have been confused with Joyce. He was first named in British newspapers in December 1939, though the first broadcast that the BBC would definitely say was by Joyce – a talk entitled 'Britain's Cowardice in War' – wasn't made until August 1940. Joyce relished his celebrity: in May 1940 he started introducing himself on-air as Lord Haw-Haw, the mock title Barrington had accorded him. By then *Germany Calling* had nine million listeners a week, more than the number listening to British news bulletins; BBC research found that by mid-1940 two-thirds of the British adult population were either occasional or regular listeners. Although contrary to myth Joyce rarely ranted or shouted, and some found his voice seductive, many others listened to his denunciations of Churchill and ludicrously overblown accounts of the war out of sceptical curiosity, amusement or even disgust.

Haw-Haw was soon lampooned by Max Miller, Arthur Askey and the Western Brothers, a then famous music-hall double act, who composed a popular song, 'Lord Haw-Haw, the Humbug of Hamburg'.[6] Joyce soon started playing up to these parodies, devising a clunking double act routine on *Germany Calling*, in which a German called Schmidt converses with an Englishman called Smith at a hotel bar in neutral Switzerland (and – of course – persuades Smith of the folly of the British government's war policy). The BBC Home Service sometimes scheduled talks by J.B. Priestley to clash with Joyce's broadcasts, but few switched over. Satire hadn't yet been properly invented in Britain: the nearest thing was *It's That Man Again*, in which the comedian Tommy Handley played the Minister of Aggravation in the Office of Twerps. Unintentionally Joyce became one of the funniest things on wartime radio ('You're much funnier than Handley,' a piece of fan mail read).

Others tuned in because *Germany Calling* was the only programme that regularly read out lists of newly captured prisoners of war – essential listening for those worried about missing sons, brothers and husbands – or to hear breaking news. Because of the BBC's quaint convention of delaying official announcements for several hours, Joyce was the first to announce the news of Leslie Hore-Belisha's dismissal as War Minister in January 1940.

Among both listeners and non-listeners alike, Joyce's own broadcasts soon acquired a prophetic quality. Apocryphal stories quickly spread that Joyce had correctly noted how many minutes town hall clocks were fast or slow by, or correctly forecast which town or village was due to be blitzed the following night (in the summer of 1940 'a hotbed of Haw-Haw rumours' swept the tiny Devon village of Newton Poppleford, which the Luftwaffe never deigned to bomb). But overall Haw-Haw may have helped boost British morale rather than dented it: his claims that the royal family were about to flee to Canada made it all the more certain that they would stay in London.

After Dunkirk and the Germans' failure to defeat the RAF in the Battle of Britain, Joyce's tone hardened, though research showed that British listeners were increasingly reacting to his broadcasts with disdain rather than anxiety. When Joyce described the British Eighth Army in North Africa as 'desert rats' they adopted the term as a badge of pride. Nonetheless, his German employers were delighted with Joyce's work. He and Margaret soon became celebrities in Berlin, regularly seen at the Foreign Club Press, the Kroll Opera House and the Hotel Adlon, where they drank heavily. During a holiday in Norway Joyce was warned, 'You'll be hanged if they get you.' 'I know. It doesn't matter,' Joyce calmly replied.

Joyce was a workaholic who refused to go to the Rundfunk's shelters during air raids and willingly toured prisoner-of-war camps in largely futile efforts to recruit British POWs as announcers. His marriage came under strain and in August 1941 the Joyces secretly divorced. But they remarried just six months later, after Margaret's German lover had been dispatched to the eastern front. Joyce's broadcasts became just as dysfunctional as his marriage. When Allied day and night bombing raids on Berlin reached their height in 1943, Joyce had to be temporarily evacuated to Luxemburg to carry on his broadcasts, which were increasingly aimed at stirring up tensions between the British and their Soviet allies rather than predicting German victory. But when the German invasion of the Soviet Union started to founder there was another reason for Britons to tune in to *Germany Calling*: *Schadenfreude*. Joyce made increasingly ludicrous attempts to put a positive spin on German defeats. After the Battle of Stalingrad Joyce claimed 'the main objectives of the enemy offensives have been frustrated' just as hundreds of thousands of German soldiers surrendered. After D-Day the Rundfunk added the noise of gunfire to news reports in a desperate attempt to convince listeners that its reporters were on the ground, covering a triumphant German fight-back, rather than in the relative safety of a studio in Berlin.

By then Berlin was a hellish place to live. Mass raids by hundreds of Allied bombers at a time were now common and Joyce narrowly escaped death several times. After scuffling with a guard in a communal bomb shelter, Joyce was charged with 'sub-treason', a crime that technically carried the death sentence. Only the death of a witness in another air raid, which also heavily damaged the courthouse in which the case was due to be heard, led to the charges being dropped. Joyce was lucky: in the first few months of 1945 at least 5,000 Berliners were executed for cowardice or desertion, in many cases just for trying to flee the city. In March, as Soviet forces began to close in, all Rundfunk employees were evacuated westwards to the town of Apen, twenty miles from the Dutch border, where the Joyces carried on broadcasting from a makeshift studio. By now Joyce knew that Germany faced certain defeat. 'Sad but true, we have made a complete balls of it,' he noted in his diary, alongside nostalgic recollections of his early life in England ('That magic evening in Princes' Risboro', one entry reads, improbably). Driven to distraction by shortages, Margaret made a perilous journey back to Berlin to retrieve a stash of tobacco and alcohol, as Apen's residents began to burn pictures of Hitler and erase swastikas from the town's walls ahead of the Allies' arrival.

'The Joyces are at all costs to be kept out of Allied hands,' Goebbels ordered in April 1945. They were moved again, this time eastwards to Hamburg, which like Berlin was in ruins and almost encircled by Allied forces: it was too late to escape by U-boat as planned. On 30 April Joyce went to Hamburg's Funkhaus (along with the Hotel Atlantik he was staying in, one of the few buildings untouched by Allied bombing) and made his final broadcast. Clearly drunk, with his slurring voice alternating between a shout and a whisper ('Lord Haw-Hic-Haw!' the *Daily Telegraph* gloated), Joyce nonetheless delivered an uncannily accur-ate forecast of the Cold War to come, ending with 'Heil Hitler . . . and farewell!' even though he knew his Führer had committed suicide just hours before.

At 3 a.m. the following day the SS drove Joyce northwards to Flensburg, a town by the Danish border and seat of the short-lived Dönitz govern-ment that was formed following Hitler's death. A handful of senior Nazis made their way there: Heinrich Himmler, head of the SS, committed suicide by swallowing hidden cyanide capsules after capture by the British.

But Joyce had no cyanide, and was unable to escape into neutral Sweden via Denmark; he had refused the offer of a forged foreign passport that might have saved his life.

After a couple of weeks moving from one guest house to another and several nights sleeping rough, Joyce all but gave himself up. On the evening of 28 May two British officers were gathering firewood in a forest just outside Flensburg. Joyce approached them and spoke to them in French, and then English, guiding them to where more branches could be found. Immediately recognising his voice, the officers asked him if he was William Joyce. As Joyce reached into his pocket for a false German passport, one of them thought he was about to draw a gun and shot him in the buttocks with his pistol. Taken to hospital in Lüneburg, Joyce ran the gauntlet of 'Jairmanny calling' jeers from British soldiers. 'In civilised countries wounded men are not used for peepshows,' he complained, to no avail. Interviewed in his hospital bed by Captain William (Jim) Skardon of MI5 (who would later become well known as the interrogator of Klaus Fuchs and other Soviet spies (see Chapter 8)), Joyce dictated a remarkably lucid statement which showed him entirely unrepentant about his conduct over the previous six years. He said that his 'vigorous political activities' in the 1920s and 1930s had been a natural reaction to British government policies, which he had feared would lead to the 'eventual disruption' of the Empire, and that his broadcasts had been inspired not by a hatred of Britain but by a desire to end war with Germany, which he considered a natural ally rather than a foe. After he had realised that Germany's defeat was inevitable, he said he had been motivated by 'hope of Anglo-German understanding' against the threats of the Soviet Union. 'I resent the accusation [of treachery] as I conceive myself to have been guilty of no underhand or deceitful act against Britain,' Joyce added blithely.

Margaret was arrested soon afterwards. Put in the same cell in Flensburg that had housed Himmler just days before, she was offered water intentionally laced with typhoid[7] and gawped at by guards, one of whom explained, 'I just wanted to see what a traitress looks like.' At least her cell had a mattress; after his discharge from hospital her husband had to sleep on bare boards.

On 16 June Joyce was flown from Brussels to an airfield at Odiham, Hampshire. As he looked down over First World War cemeteries in Flanders Joyce was heard to mutter, 'England and Germany at war with each other . . . madness, I tell you.' After almost six years in Germany he returned to England more like a returning celebrity than a prisoner facing a capital charge. 'We are about to pass over the white chalk cliffs, England's bulwark. It is a sacred moment in my life – and I can only say, whatever my fate be, God Bless Old England on the lee,' he wrote in a guard's autograph book.

After Joyce's capture Sir Theobald Mathew, the newly appointed Director of Public Prosecutions (DPP), had favoured a charge of treason. But Sir Donald Somervell, Attorney General until the dissolution of the wartime coalition and then Home Secretary in the caretaker administration that ran until the general election in July, was 'incredulous' at Mathew's suggestion, arguing instead for a prosecution under wartime Defence Regulations, for which the maximum sentence was a prison term of fourteen years. This was too short to satisfy what was perceived as a vengeful British public, egged on by its newspapers, which were openly demanding that Joyce be hanged. As soon as he landed in England Joyce was charged with treason.

Nonetheless this did not seem to cast a pall over Joyce. He positively enjoyed his incarceration at Brixton prison, working as a voluntary window cleaner and reading voraciously. Sprinkling his letters to Margaret with all sorts of affectionate nicknames, he would often sign off as 'Old Ram' or 'Brixton Bill', and played up to his faux Wodehousian image by describing his arrest as an 'indecorous event', his alleged crimes as 'Nazi caddishness'. In Brussels, Margaret's conditions also improved: in return for doing darning for her guards she obtained black-market goods. Offered 'female oddments' for her 'Mrs Thing' (the term the Joyces used for menstruation), she was extended courtesies few prisoners of the Nazis would ever have received. She wrote carefree letters to Joyce's younger brother Quentin, describing William as a 'Dismal Desmond', and to William himself, asking about the fate of Vidkun Quisling, the puppet the Nazis had installed in Norway, with all the insouciance of a middle-class housewife enquiring about a long-lost bridge partner.[8] Still committed to the Nazi ideology, she seemed to regard their arrest as a terrible misunderstanding, and assumed that she and William would soon be released and allowed to emigrate to South America.

Why were the Joyces so cheerful? At first glance they both seemed patently guilty of treason. Joyce, who had spent his life proclaiming himself a British national, had readily admitted broadcasting propaganda on behalf of the enemy during wartime, and doing so voluntarily. This seemed to put him well within the Treason Act 1351, an ancient statute in which the crime of treason was still codified and included being 'adherent to the King's Enemies in his Realm, giving to them Aid and Comfort in the Realm, or elsewhere'.

But was Joyce actually British, and if not, could he be guilty of treason? Initial doubts about what crime to charge Joyce with were soon replaced by a more serious worry: that Joyce might not be triable in an English courtroom at all. Joyce had always told everyone – including the Nazi authorities – that he was born in 1906 at Rutledge Terrace, Galway, and was thus a British citizen.[9] But it turned out that in an application letter to the Officer Training Corps in 1922 he had said he was born in the United States. And although Joyce had told Skardon during his interrogation that he was born in the US he had added that his family 'were generally counted as British subjects' after their arrival in Ireland in 1909, only adding to the confusion.

On 18 June Joyce was remanded in custody by the magistrate at Bow Street and assigned a competent solicitor – C.B.V. Head of Ludlow & Co. – who first raised the question of Joyce's nationality at a second hearing at Bow Street a week later. In early July 1945, on the eve of the general election, Mr Justice Charles agreed to postpone Joyce's Old Bailey trial – scheduled to begin just three days later – until September, giving the prosecution and defence two months to gather evidence.

The English authorities asked the FBI to make urgent enquiries – overseen by J. Edgar Hoover himself – to locate Joyce's birth certificate and confirm whether or not he was an American citizen. It was discovered that Joyce's father had emigrated from Ireland to the US in about 1888 and gained American citizenship in October 1894, thereby revoking his British citizenship more than a decade before William was born. In 1904 or 1905 he had visited Britain, meeting Joyce's mother in Lancashire and bringing her back to New York, where they married in May 1905, eleven months before William's birth. William had in fact been born at 1377 Herkimer Street, Brooklyn, and hadn't reached Ireland until after his third birthday. Joyce was thus incontrovertibly an American citizen, not a British one. His passport application in 1933, and his successive applications to renew it in 1938 and 1939, had been fraudulent because in all three he had falsely claimed to have been a 'British subject by birth', born in Ireland, not America.

Faced with this difficulty, it was hoped at first that if Joyce fell beyond the reach of English law, he could still be prosecuted in the United States. But it was then discovered that Joyce had become a German citizen not in 1943 as first thought, but in July 1940, almost eighteen months before America had entered the war. At the time a US law provided that any

American who obtained foreign citizenship automatically lost their US nationality. The chances of Joyce being found guilty by an American court were effectively nil.

While Joyce was held on remand at Brixton prison all his correspondence was illegally intercepted, and it has been claimed that all his meetings with his lawyers eavesdropped, in a desperate bid to amass any evidence that might assist the prosecution. It was soon agreed that the best chance of convicting him of treason lay not in establishing his British nationality – that now seemed almost impossible to prove – but on the novel basis that his possession of a British passport imposed a duty of allegiance on him, at least until its expiry in July 1940. A further problem presented itself. 'Lord Haw-Haw' had not admitted his true identity on air until 1941; if Joyce denied making any broadcasts before that date it might be difficult to prove that he had.

A witness had been found: a Detective Inspector Albert Hunt, who had kept the peace at various meetings at which Joyce gave speeches in his pre-war blackshirt days, said he would testify that he had heard the same voice on the Rundfunk in 1939, gloating that Dover and Folkestone had been destroyed by air raids. A Treason Act dating from 1695 required at least *two* witnesses to any act of treason. Anticipating this problem of proof (apparently the prosecution could find no other witness who could positively identify Joyce's voice from that period), in the two weeks between Joyce's arrest and charge a new Treason Act was specially enacted (it received royal assent just a day before Joyce's arrival in England)[10] to remove this requirement.

Joyce was a pathetic sight in the run-up to the trial. His false teeth (later stolen by souvenir-hunters) had been confiscated (they might contain a cyanide capsule), as had his suit buttons lest he try to choke himself on them; to his scalp he had applied a green ointment to treat his scurf. Predictably, he was jeered by other prisoners in the exercise yard at Brixton. But he was protected from physical assault and allowed a daily ration of a pint of beer, ten cigarettes and two sheets of paper for letters. And inwardly he was full of confidence.

Despite all the behind-the-scenes anxieties about the question of Joyce's nationality an observer sitting in the public gallery would have detected not a hint of doubt in Shawcross's courtroom demeanour. For all its historical moment, the three-day trial was a low-key affair. Joyce himself uttered just two words: 'Not guilty'. Joyce's counsel, Gerald Slade, explained to the jury sardonically that his client would not himself give evidence for the simple reason that he had no memory of when or where he was born. The reality of course was rather different: putting Joyce in the witness box would expose him to a wide-ranging and damaging cross-examination about his adherence to the Nazi cause – how Shawcross must have relished that prospect! – and more specifically to the danger that if asked (as he inevitably would be) when his broadcasting career had commenced, he would be unable credibly to deny that it had started in 1939, well before the expiry of his passport.

Keeping Joyce out of the witness box made sense, but it deprived the trial of the crackle of melodrama many had hoped for. The person everyone had come to hear remained silent. Instead the trial took on the tone of a civilised university tutorial, the lawyers and the judge all striving to outdo each other in punctilious effusions of legal politeness and courtesy, as if seeking to cleanse the courtroom of the taint of Joyce's misshapen oddity; or perhaps to ward off accusations that the proceedings were an exercise in victor's justice parodying a fair trial.

After Joyce had entered his plea and the jury had been empanelled, the bewigged clerk of the court rose and addressed the jurors:

> Members of the Jury, the prisoner at the bar, William Joyce, is charged in an indictment containing three counts: each of those counts is a charge of high treason. In the first count the particulars are that on the 18th September 1939 [the day Joyce commenced employment with Rundfunk], and on other days between that day and the 29th May 1945, he, being a person owing allegiance to the King, while a war was being carried on by the German Realm against the King, did traitorously adhere to the King's enemies by broadcasting propaganda. In the second count it is charged that he, on the 26th September 1940, being a person owing allegiance as before, did traitorously adhere to the enemies of the King by purporting to become naturalised as a subject of Germany, and in the third count, the particulars are the same as those in the first count, that is to say it is another charge of broadcasting propaganda on the 18th September 1939 and on other days between that day and the 2nd July 1940 [the date of expiry of his passport]. To this indictment he has pleaded not guilty, and it is your charge to say, having heard the evidence, whether he is guilty or not.

The obscurity of these words hid the distinction between counts one and two on the one hand and count three on the other. The first two counts were squarely founded on the supposed British nationality of

Joyce and the allegiance to the King which such nationality brought with it: to broadcast propaganda and ostensibly to become a German citizen during time of war being acts of 'adherence' to the King's enemies. The third count, however, was founded solely on the broadcasting of propaganda during the period of the validity of Joyce's British passport and engaged the untested legal question of whether the mere holding of a passport exposed the holder to a charge of treason. A man could only be found guilty of treason if he owed a duty of loyalty and faithfulness to the Crown: but did possession of a passport – especially one obtained by false means – carry with it such a duty?

Shawcross now rose to give his opening speech. It was a brilliant exercise in rhetorical dissembling. While the Attorney General sought to instil an atmosphere of rigorous objectivity into the proceedings he intruded into the minds of the jury the historical importance of their task:

> It would be idle to shut our eyes to the fact that some of us may know, or think we know, something about this case. We may in times past have read about this man in the newspapers; we may have discussed his activities – and indeed his activities were notorious enough – it may be even perhaps in those dark days of 1940 when this country was standing alone against the whole force and might of Nazi Germany, that some of us may have heard, or thought we heard, his voice on the wireless, attempting as we may have thought to undermine the morale of our people, and perhaps at that time some of us may have formed feelings of dislike or detestation at what he was doing, and perhaps later on some of us heard with a not altogether unnatural satisfaction that he had been apprehended and was to be brought to trial.
>
> If any of you had feelings of that kind about this man I ask you, as I know you will, to cast them entirely from your minds. You are sworn, you know, to try this man according to our law and upon the evidence alone. I dare say that in the years to come in the pages of history it will count for nothing what happens to William Joyce in the course of this trial. He will leave no mark upon those pages. But, it may count for a great deal that we, who in our various capacities are concerned in this trial, should act and comport ourselves in accordance with the best traditions of English law.

Sometimes a trial can meander down paths that seem far removed from the alleged crimes of the man in the dock. The business of legal proof, at times electrifying, can also be laborious and wearisome. Every part of a case must be formally proved: virtually nothing can be assumed, however obvious it may be. The next two days must have disappointed the sensation-seekers. A clutch of witnesses was called by the prosecution who gave unobtrusive evidence concerning Joyce's nationality and connection with Britain. Passport applications and birth certificates were studied; geneal-ogies were unpicked; inconsequential correspondence dating back to the 1920s was read out.

Then Albert Hunt was sworn to give the only direct evidence relied upon by the prosecution of Joyce's treachery. Hunt was not an impressive witness, admitting that before the war he had only ever heard Joyce giving speeches: they had never spoken. Worse, he could not recall precisely when he had heard Joyce's alleged 'Dover and Folkestone' broadcast – only that it was some time in the first month of the war. As to the contents of the broadcast itself Hunt's memory was vague. Slade cross-examined him:

SLADE: Of course the statement that Dover and Folkestone had been destroyed in September or up to 3rd October 1939 would have been fantastic?

HUNT: Not necessarily. It could have been destroyed.

SLADE: The statement was between 3rd September and 3rd October; that statement was fantastic?

HUNT: Well it was really.

SLADE: No bomb of any description was dropped in this country until about September 1940?

HUNT: I do not know.

. . .

SLADE: To what station did you tune in?

HUNT: I do not know, I was just tuning in my receiver round the wave-lengths when I heard the voice.

SLADE: Just twiddling it round you heard the voice. Was that all you heard, the words 'Folkestone and Dover have been destroyed'?

HUNT: No, I heard something else, but I cannot recall it.

Hunt claimed to have heard Joyce 'on sundry occasions' later in the autumn of 1939. Yet he had no memory of what Joyce had actually said and had only starting writing down transcripts of Joyce's broadcasts in 1943 and 1944. Hunt read them to the court and once again the bile and invective was given voice: 'The Prime Minister . . . is the servant not of the British public, or of the British Empire, but of international Jewish finance.' Of an allied air raid on Antwerp Joyce intoned: 'Such an act of malicious spite is not in my opinion typically British. It bears instead the hallmark of Jewish policy which has always been directed towards eradication of Gentiles who could not be made to serve the interests of Hebrew domination.' In August 1944, after Paris had fallen to the Allies, Hunt had noted Joyce's ravings, ever more unhinged from reality: 'I can assure you that the German people have never been so active in their determination to shape the course of events. Our enemies may indulge in short-lived jubilation. There is no need for discouragement. This premature celebration will be transmitted into bitterness and colossal disappointment.'

Slade did not challenge the accuracy of Hunt's notes. He knew he did not need to: as he was shortly to demonstrate, in 1943 and 1944 Joyce owed no duty of allegiance to the British Crown. However nauseating his words they could not constitute treason. Before the first day was out Shawcross closed the prosecution case, ending with the testimony of a Captain Lickorish, who had arrested Joyce, and Jim Skardon, his interrogator.

The evidence that the prosecution had been able to muster against Joyce was thin, and Shawcross knew it. Back in his room in the Royal Courts of Justice he mulled over the day's proceedings with Professor J.H. Morgan, the constitutional law expert who was assisting the Crown's case. 'Have we any chance?' Shawcross asked him. Morgan replied: 'No, I don't think you have, not unless the judge is prepared to make new law.'

Joyce returned to Brixton after that first day buoyed up. He shot off an update to Margaret: despite some 'grocery store brilliance' from Shawcross (whom Joyce now delighted in nicknaming 'Hotcross Buns') he felt that his counsel had made headway. One particular sentence must have pleased him: Slade had, as the day drew to its close, said, 'My submission to Your Lordship really comes to this, that if I am a Chinese, by screaming from the house tops fifty thousand times that I am a British subject, I do not become one; by making fifty thousand declarations that I am a British subject I do not become one.' True, Slade's submission of no case to answer, which he had made that afternoon, had been rejected by Tucker. But Slade had known that was inevitable: it was still a show of strength even to advance the proposition, in that courtroom stuffed with government lawyers, that the prosecution case should be dismissed there and then. Others had the same sense of a case that was looking shaky. That evening, sitting in his chambers surrounded by law reports and textbooks, preparing for the next day, Slade received a letter. It warned him that he would be killed if Joyce was acquitted – the perils of the cab-rank rule.

The threat of death did not prevent Slade returning to the Old Bailey and calling a host of witnesses – family members and friends – who all confirmed the obvious truth: Joyce was an American citizen, born in Brooklyn to a father who had himself acquired American citizenship years before. One of them was Quentin, William's younger brother and political follower, who had been interned for four years during the war because of his brother's broadcasts. Yet West noted that as he went into the box there passed between him and his brother 'a nod and a smile of pure love'. Shawcross did not cross-examine Quentin, nor any of the other witnesses whom Slade called, and by the afternoon the defence case was closed.

The judge now intervened to suggest to Shawcross that the evidence that Joyce was an American national was 'really overwhelming', so that the only effective matter was the third count that Joyce faced. Shawcross readily agreed. In fact he agreed so readily that one wonders whether the first two counts were included on the indictment solely so that evidence of the later broadcasts, made after the expiry of the passport and which Hunt had taken down near-verbatim, could be introduced into the minds of the jury to remind them of the poison that Lord Haw-Haw had spread. But these counts were now dead in the water; Joyce could only be found guilty of acts in the months up to the expiry of his passport in July 1940. False rumours abounded that Joyce had been acquitted; an angry crowd was seen to gather outside the Old Bailey. It dispersed when it was discovered that the prosecution was still continuing.

The trial now moved to the murky question that, however hidden from view it may have been when Shawcross opened the case, in fact lay at its heart. Did mere possession of a British passport create the bond of allegiance that could put its holder at risk of a treason charge? The judge treated this as a point of pure law for him, not the jury, to decide. Many hours passed as counsel on each side picked up the heavy dark volumes of law reports and the ancient textbooks lined up on their benches and cited passages dating back to the fifteenth century which supposedly bore on the question. Shorn to its essentials Shawcross's argument was that the holder of a British passport, whether or not that passport was obtained by illegal means and whether or not the holder was of British nationality, was entitled during its currency to the protection of the Crown when abroad. If a person was entitled to that protection, then – whether or not he actually sought it (and it is hard to imagine that Joyce made much use of his passport once he arrived in Germany in late August 1939) – he had a reciprocal obligation of allegiance to the Crown. If a person was subject to a duty of allegiance to the Crown, then, wherever he was physically, if he adhered to the Crown's enemies in time of war he was guilty of treason.

This argument was novel because previous learning, laid down at a time when the passport system had not developed, had confined itself to aliens actually resident within the kingdom and the temporary allegiance owed during that period of residence. Slade took his stand on the proposition that an alien 'only owes allegiance to His Majesty the King so long as he is resident within the King's dominions'. So, the argument ran, once Joyce left for Germany such allegiance as he owed because of his residence in Britain ceased. The argument wound on through to the end of the second day. 'People with legal minds were entranced, and others slept,' wrote Rebecca West. Slade cited case after case from the old books, like a walker gingerly negotiating stepping stones across a fast-flowing stream. Rebecca West was impressed: 'Now it seemed as impossible to convict William Joyce as it had been, when the prosecution was opening its case, to imagine him being acquitted.' And Joyce continued cheerful that second night, writing to Margaret that she could boast that her husband 'was something in the City', for a few days at least.

The third day would provide the denouement. It was for the judge to rule whether the holding of a passport did indeed impose a duty of allegiance on the holder. The point might have seemed abstruse, but it would in all likelihood decide whether Joyce lived or died. At two o'clock that afternoon Tucker decided in favour of the Crown.

Mr Attorney and Mr Slade, I shall direct the jury on count three that on 24th August 1939, when the passport was applied for, the prisoner, beyond a shadow of doubt, owed allegiance to the Crown of this country and that on the evidence given, if they accept it, nothing happened at the material time to put an end to the allegiance that he then owed. It will remain for the jury, and for the jury alone, as to whether or not at the relevant dates he adhered to the King's enemies with intent to assist the King's enemies.

All then that was left was for the jury to decide whether the voice Detective Inspector Hunt heard at the dawn of the war was that of William Joyce and whether such a broadcast constituted 'adherence to the enemy'. There was a forlorn tone to Slade's closing speech to the jury:

I can well understand a person saying: 'Don't try him at all; shoot him without trial.' You may think that that would be one of the best things to do. But what I do say is if you are going to try him, try him, and do not make a mockery of the trial. You, members of the jury, have of course a most difficult task. Joyce has been branded as 'Lord Haw-Haw'; he has been branded as a traitor. Everyone talks of him as though he were already condemned and convicted, but you are here to try whether he is guilty or not.

Unlike virtually every other criminal trial, here the defendant was well-known to each and every juror before they came to the jury box. His voice had haunted them for over five years. Yet it was now accepted by the prosecution that after July 1940 nothing he did could be criminal; his treason – if treason it was – was confined to that sliver of time when his passport, probably lying unwanted in some drawer, if not thrown away, was still technically valid. And there the evidence against Joyce was thin. Hunt's only memory of the September 1939 broadcast was that Joyce had said that Dover and Folkestone had been destroyed by German bombs. Slade rightly asked how likely it was that Joyce would have made a statement so easily falsifiable.

I should think that it would be the worst possible thing from the Germans' point of view, and the worst possible thing from Joyce's point of view, to start his broadcasts to the British nation, not merely with a lie – because a lie might be given a semblance of truth – but to start his career with a lie which was demonstrably and palpably false and which everyone must know to be false within forty-eight hours.

This was a strong point. If the jury were to confine themselves solely to the evidence before them – as they had sworn to do – could they real-istically convict? Shawcross's response – forensically wise – was to address the jury for only ten minutes in the broadest of brushes.

In his summing-up the judge explained to the jury why he had ruled that the holding of a passport created a duty of allegiance.

I think it is the law that if a man who owes allegiance by having made his home here, having come to live here permanently, thereby acquiring allegiance as he undoubtedly does, then steps out of this realm armed with the protection which is normally afforded to a British subject [of a passport] – improperly obtained maybe but none the less obtained – if he leaves the realm, as the Attorney General called it, wrapped up in the Union Jack, that is to say, using and availing himself of the protection of the Crown in an executive capacity which covers him while he is abroad, he does not thereby divest himself of the allegiance which he already owes.

Tucker seemed sensitive to suggestions that the trial was a sham and ended on an encomium to the integrity of the proceedings. He commended Slade and his fellow counsel for taking the case at all ('How can justice be administered if people charged with these offences are not defended, and are not defended by able and responsible counsel?'); he urged the jurors to put aside prejudice ('As you have already been told . . . William Joyce would play a very small part in the world's history, but our demeanour, the way we comport ourselves in this case, is of greater importance to us than is William Joyce'); he reminded jurors that, in fairness to Joyce, the trial had been delayed from July to September to allow time for the 'quiet and unhurried collection' of evidence that had helped the defence. In fact by modern standards Joyce's prosecution had moved at lightning speed: his trial was ending less than four months after he had been captured.

Throughout the trial Joyce had carried an air of curiosity, sometimes elevated to faint amusement. Rebecca West thought that he watched his lawyers with a 'cynical brightness, as if he were interested in seeing whether they could get away with all this nonsense, but had no warmer concern with the proceedings'. He would occasionally write notes to his counsel in an octavo notebook in a manuscript so grotesquely large that it was visible from the public gallery. Smiles would creep across his face when a point landed home, either for or against him. That sense of detachment infected others in court. After the jury retired, at 3.37 in the afternoon of the third day, the spectators got up from their seats and, so West noted, 'strolled about and chattered as if they were at a theatre between the acts'. Just twenty-three minutes later the jury returned – it was exactly 4 p.m. – 'looking as if they had been out for a cup of tea'. They had clearly not had any difficulty arriving at their verdict of guilty.

Every defendant found guilty of a capital crime had the right to speak before sentence was passed. The traditional wording ran as follows:

'Prisoner at the Bar, you stand convicted of high treason [or whatever crime it was]. Have you anything to say why the Court should not give you judgement according to law?' By the twentieth century these words were, in an age of legal representation, otiose. If the right was exercised at all it was usually to make a further plea of innocence for the benefit of family and friends. In 1912 the poisoner Seddon had used the occasion to assert, with bogus articulacy, that he was not guilty. After his conviction in 1916 Roger Casement had delivered a speech from the dock justifying his actions and pledging his life to the cause of Irish freedom. Not one person in the courtroom tried to stop him and the words he spoke, with great courage before a hostile bench of three judges, have since been celebrated as one of the great political statements of the twentieth century. Yet when given the same opportunity now, in Court Number One, Joyce, who had likewise done suicidal things for his political creed, said nothing.

Everyone who has written about the experience of hearing the pronouncement of a sentence of death has noted the awfulness and solemnity of that moment. John Mathew QC, one of the most formidable barristers of the second half of the twentieth century, and who prosecuted in many murder trials before the death penalty was abolished, recalls that he always left court beforehand, so unbearable did he find the event. So it was notable that now, when sentence was passed on Joyce, there was no discernible awe at what had been said. People were indifferent to William Joyce.

There was a small exception to this general mood. Even in September 1945 Joyce still had his supporters, young men with intense, unhappy expressions, whose faith had not been dimmed by the news from Bergen-Belsen and Auschwitz. They had sat miserably through the trial in comradeship with their hero in the dock. When sentence was passed Joyce's old friend Angus MacNab sobbed loudly. Quentin's eyes, 'soft and brown like a cow's', were wet with tears. Joyce gave another of his stiff bows to Tucker, waved to his brother, and then calmly descended the stairs down to the cells. Joyce's solicitor was heard to whisper to Quentin, as they descended the main staircase to the lobby, 'This is just what he expected, you know,' before adding, 'It's the appeal that matters.' At the cloakroom below, two jurors said goodbye as they collected their hats and coats like 'people parting at the end of a cruise', oblivious to the odd band of Fascists who stood behind them in the queue. Outside a large crowd had gathered; before their eyes the Fascists slipped away.

★

Joyce's appeal began on 30 October at the Royal Courts of Justice. Slade argued that the conviction was unsafe on four grounds: first, an English court had no jurisdiction to try an alien for crimes allegedly committed abroad; second, the judge had been wrong to direct the jury that Joyce owed allegiance to the Crown during the validity of the passport which had been issued in 1939; third, there was no evidence that Joyce had sought any protection from his ownership of the passport; and fourth, the question of whether Joyce owed allegiance during the life of that passport was a question for a jury, not a judge. But he was cut off before he could expand on the third and fourth grounds; early on in his submission the Lord Chief Justice interrupted to ask sarcastically whether 'an alien can go backwards and forwards across the Channel, owing allegiance when he arrives at Dover and no longer owing it when he lands at Calais'. Gently mocked by Shawcross, who said 'the slavish search for exact precedent was always a somewhat sterile pursuit', Slade was getting nowhere. Judgement was read out. The court ruled that Slade's contention that an alien could not commit treason 'without the realm' was a 'startling proposition, and one which after mature consideration this court is quite unable to accept'. Slade had seemed to equate Joyce with a 'foreigner who had once in his life paid a visit to the country of a few hours' duration'.

Joyce's hanging, originally scheduled for 23 November, was postponed to allow for a further appeal to the House of Lords' judicial subcommittee, which began on 10 December.[11] It was only here that the barristers' rhetoric really rose to the occasion. Shawcross said that it would be 'an unthinkable outrage if the crime of treason was held not to be committed' and Slade countered that 'of all the cases which have disfigured our legal history, trials for treason are the worst'. Compared to the 'rough-hewn' Old Bailey trial the House of Lords proceedings were as 'good an entertainment as first-class tennis', Rebecca West later wrote. Although everyone seemed to have visibly aged since the trial just twelve weeks before, Joyce now had a 'dignity and refinement' he had hitherto lacked. The setting may have helped. Joyce's final appeal was heard in the Palace of Westminster's Robing Room, in which the monarch puts on the Imperial State Crown and ceremonial robes before the annual state opening (the huge Royal Gallery next door, with its vast paintings of the battles of Trafalgar and Waterloo, was used as an anteroom).

At the start of each day's proceedings the Lord Chancellor, the newly appointed Lord Jowitt, processed in wearing a full-bottomed wig and carrying a black cap, preceded by the Sergeant at Arms (carrying the

Lords' mace, and followed by four other Law Lords wearing lounge suits. In the Robing Room the sons of peers exercised their right to sit on the steps of the throne; all the other benches were crowded with counsel, solicitors, MPs and peers, as well as Quentin, MacNab and the ever faithful Fascists.

Yet post-war austerity was omnipresent. One peer was seen to run his fingers up and down his lapel while listening to the legal arguments and discover, to his undisguised horror, a moth-hole (even lords were subject to clothes rationing). The unheated Robing Room was so cold that the Law Lords were given steamer rugs to put on their laps; every mid-morning they would be brought a 'very common little tea-tray'.

The argument continued for four days. When counsel had said all they had to say Lord Jowitt announced that judgement would be postponed until the following Tuesday, 18 December. On that day four of the five Law Lords said they would dismiss the appeal, with only Lord Porter against (their reasons would be given later). For Joyce this was the end of the road. After the announcement a Scottish supporter of Joyce, a 'young man with hollow eyes', shouted out that Joyce was innocent. It was the only moment of express dissent throughout all the legal proceedings. Attendants swiftly formed a wall around the forlorn protester as the Robing Room emptied before the Lords' next business (a debate on the post-war American Loan). 'William Joyce didna' betray his country. He had a fine position waiting for him in Germany and he just took it,' he told reporters.

Joyce is said to have received fifty-eight letters in the run-up to his appeals, many of them supportive (one letter contained a £50 contribution towards his legal costs, though another enclosed rat poison). Several of Joyce's old Birkbeck tutors wrote to say they 'wished him well', though they stopped short of asking for a reprieve. Margaret was now allowed to visit her husband. She was said to be in a 'frenzy of grief' on the day of his execution, 3 January 1946. But Joyce himself was calm, and full of fond reminiscence about his Galway childhood. 'When you have overcome the sickening shock, you will begin to rejoice at all that was good and beautiful in our mortal time together,' he wrote to Margaret. In a letter to Quentin he was unrepentant: 'In death, as in life, I defy the Jews who caused this war and I defy the forces of darkness they represent. I am proud to die for my ideals, and I am sorry for the sons of Britain who have died without knowing why.'

Joyce is said to have smiled as he looked down at his trembling knees before being led by Albert Pierrepoint to the execution chamber at Wandsworth prison, to which he had been moved after his conviction. Three hundred spectators were outside to see nothing more than the usual tiny notice reporting the execution affixed to the prison's gates. One man said he'd come because he had heard one of Haw-Haw's speeches just after identifying his grandchildren's bodies in a morgue during the Blitz. A small group gave Nazi salutes at the moment of his execution before skulking away.

'No man could have had a fairer hearing,' said a Movietone news announcer shortly after the execution. The *Daily Mail* stated that Joyce's execution was 'richly deserved'. The *Daily Telegraph* opined that 'no verdict has ever been more in accordance with the evidence.'

But other newspapers expressed disquiet at the outcome of the proceedings. The *Manchester Guardian* said that on balance Joyce should have been spared the gallows. George Orwell observed that the 'hunting down of petty rats is largely the work of bigger rats'. Even the letters page of the *Daily Telegraph* carried some uneasiness. 'Most lawyers regard this case as a blot on British justice,' it was argued in a letter from N. Long-Brown KC. 'It will be remembered that had Joyce not forgotten to post back his British passport from Germany in 1939 he could not have been convicted.' That Joyce was executed four weeks before the Law Lords gave their full reasons for refusing his appeal was 'a matter for shame', Long-Brown added. J.M. Hall noted in his introduction to the Notable British Trials volume that a majority of lawyers had thought the appeal would succeed and there was a wide feeling that Joyce should not have been convicted. And even Hartley Shawcross, looking back at the trial in his memoirs, written fifty years later, wrote that he was 'not specially proud' to have led Joyce's prosecution.

Two days after her husband's execution Margaret Joyce was quietly transported back to Germany. Given a unique status – 'German but stateless and British-born'– after two years' internment she was allowed to move to Ireland, where she studied philology as her husband once had; she later moved to Hamburg, where she remarried, and then to Shepherd's Bush, where she died in 1972 of septic cirrhosis 'due to chronic alcoholism', an unrepentant Nazi to the end.

In 1944 British troops had found a stash of Rundfunk recordings in Luxemburg labelled 'Frau Joyce', who was soon designated as 'Case Number 9' on MI5's post-war prosecution list. But despite extensive

questioning Margaret was never charged. There has been much speculation that a secret deal was done: in return for keeping silent about his
work for MI5 in the 1930s Joyce was promised that Margaret would be
spared prosecution on compassionate grounds. It is certainly ironic that
Margaret – as 'English as warm beer', noted the historian Nigel Farndale
– was not even prosecuted while her American husband was hanged.

Although a number of English men and women had overtly supported
the German war effort, there was no orgy of reprisals against them. Most
were either allowed to quietly return home or were prosecuted for less
serious offences. Only one other civilian was hanged for treason on
British soil at the end of the Second World War: John Amery, who had
attempted to recruit British prisoners of war to the Legion of St George
(a unit of the Waffen SS), ostensibly to fight Bolshevism. Amery was the
notoriously wayward son of the Secretary of State for India, Leo Amery.
He fought on the Nationalist side in the Spanish civil war, acting as a
liaison officer between Franco's forces and the French Fascist Cagoulards,
before moving to Vichy France and thence to Berlin. On arrival at the
Funkhaus he told Joyce his broadcasts were backfiring and started broadcasting himself, much to Joyce's annoyance. But Amery made a singularly
implausible propagandist and was soon sent out on his hopeless recruitment drive. He ended up in Italy, where in 1945 he was captured by
partisans and handed over to Captain Alan Whicker, later a famous
broadcaster himself. Charged with treason, on 28 November 1945 Amery
found himself in the same Old Bailey dock that Joyce had occupied two
months earlier. Again the representation was the same: Shawcross represented the Crown and Gerald Slade appeared for Amery. Only in this
case the trial in Court Number One lasted just eight minutes. When he
was arraigned, to the shock of those present Amery pleaded guilty to all
charges. The judge, Travers Humphreys (who had just weeks earlier sat
in the Court of Appeal to hear, and dismiss, Joyce's appeal), was so
astonished by this plea – which meant a mandatory death sentence – that
he expressly asked Slade to confirm that Amery knew exactly what he
was doing.

Six months after Joyce was hanged Shawcross was again back in Court
Number One to lead the prosecution of Dr Alan Nunn May, a physics
lecturer at the University of London who had worked on atomic reactor
research in Canada during the war and started passing nuclear secrets to
the Russians. Although Nunn May's treachery, which helped the Soviets
in their development of atomic weapons, was so much more serious than
Joyce's, he received ten years' imprisonment and was free after only six.

(The difference between them was that Britain was not at war with the Soviet Union and so he could only be prosecuted under the Official Secrets Act.) Already the history of English treachery was moving into a new phase.

During the trial both counsel and the judge had wrongly predicted that Joyce would soon be forgotten. Even Slade referred to him as a 'nine-days' wonder', though no doubt it was forensically sensible to diminish his significance in the eyes of the jury. In fact his infamy has endured; if anything it has burgeoned over the decades. There have been many biographies and numerous documentaries and dramatisations about Joyce. As late as 2002 he topped a *Sun* poll of readers' most reviled British villains. The fact that the trial had established beyond doubt that he was not British did not seem to present any hurdle.

PART IV
Gloom

6

'Christie done it'

R v Timothy Evans (1950)

IN APRIL 1948 Sydney Silverman, the Labour MP and 'undisputed leader of the abolitionist campaign in the House of Commons', introduced a clause into the Criminal Justice Bill to suspend the death penalty for a period of five years. The clause was intended as a step on the road towards full abolition and excited one of the most impassioned debates in the Commons in years.

Somebody in the chamber who was not won over was Sir David Maxwell Fyfe KC, a Conservative MP and former Attorney General, who had recently returned from Nuremberg, where he had participated in the prosecution of leading Nazi war criminals. In his contribution to the debate he dismissed one of the main arguments advanced by the abolitionists, the risk of a wrongful conviction.

> As a realist, I do not believe that the chances of error in a murder case, with those various instruments of the State present, constitute a factor which we must consider . . . Of course a jury might go wrong, the Court of Appeal might go wrong, as might the House of Lords, the Home Secretary. They might all be stricken mad and go wrong. But that is not a possibility which anyone can consider likely.

Although the clause was overwhelmingly backed by Labour MPs – who, following the Labour landslide in the 1945 general election, now dominated the House of Commons – Clement Attlee's government, fearful of running ahead of public opinion, was not supportive. The Home Secretary James Chuter Ede told the House that the time was not 'ripe' for the reform, citing a supposed rise in 'armed gangsterism' and the need to protect the police, the usual reasons for maintaining the status quo.

Silverman's motion was nonetheless carried by twenty-three votes, to

much cheering and waving of order papers. The Home Secretary immediately responded by announcing that he would henceforth reprieve as
of right all those sentenced to death until the future of the clause was
resolved. In the months that followed a number of convicted murderers
found themselves the beneficiaries of automatic reprieves, their death
sentence replaced by a term of life imprisonment (in reality 'life' would
prove to be a period of between ten and fifteen years). Some months
later the House of Lords, still consisting almost entirely of hereditary
peers, resoundingly rejected the clause and the status quo was restored
(more surprisingly, the judicial peers were equally opposed to the reform).
The jubilation in the House of Commons had proved short-lived.

Just before teatime on Wednesday, 30 November 1949 a short, dark-haired
young man walked into Merthyr Vale Police Station in South Wales and
asked if there was a sergeant to hand. When Detective Constable
Gwynfryn Evans told him none was available, the man asked to speak
to him alone.

'I want to give myself up. I have disposed of my wife.'

'What do you mean?' asked DC Evans.

'I put her down the drain,' the stranger replied. 'I can't sleep and want
to get it off my chest.'

The man was taken to the larger Merthyr Tydfil Police Station, six
miles away. It was there that he told his story to DC Evans and a detective
sergeant. He was Timothy John Evans, a delivery driver, and he had
until recently lived on the top floor of 10 Rillington Place, in a run-down
terrace in North Kensington in London. His wife Beryl had told him
in October that she was pregnant, and that if she couldn't 'get rid of'
the baby she would kill both herself and Geraldine, their one-year-old
daughter. Although Evans hadn't wanted Beryl to have an abortion, on
Monday, 7 November he gave her a bottle of abortifacient, which a
stranger had handed him at a roadside café. The following morning he
was having second thoughts; he now warned Beryl not to take it. But
Beryl had disregarded his concerns, and that evening Evans returned
from work to a flat in darkness. The gas would not light and he put a
penny in the slot. The glow revealed Beryl lying still on their bed,
Geraldine in her cot nearby. He shook his wife's body; she did not move.
He could tell she was not breathing. He fed the baby and sat down
beside her, smoking. Evans said that in the small hours of Wednesday
– 9 November – he had carried Beryl's body down the stairs and put
her head first into the drain in front of 10 Rillington Place. He had

thrown in his job later that day. He had then sold his furniture and arrived by train in Wales on 15 November. Evans said nothing about Geraldine's whereabouts.

DC Evans moved quickly. Within minutes he had called the Metropolitan Police. The drain was swiftly checked, but no body was found. Evans had insisted he had lifted the heavy cast-iron grating unaided, but it had taken three burly London police officers to raise it.

It was now late in the evening of 30 November. Confronted with these contradictions, Timothy Evans seemed confounded. He now gave a second statement. He said he had concocted his first statement 'to protect a man called Christie', a name not previously mentioned. Evans explained that Christie lived with his wife Ethel on the ground floor at Rillington Place and had offered his services as an abortionist. After Christie had warned there was a chance – 'one out of ten' – that Beryl might die of the 'stuff' he used, Evans said he wasn't interested. But Beryl disagreed, telling her husband on the Monday morning to 'mind his own business' and that Christie would perform the abortion at noon the following day. After Evans returned from a drinking session at the Kensington Park Hotel at about ten in the evening they had another row about it.[1] Nonetheless, Evans told Christie 'everything was all right', as Beryl had instructed, as he left for work early the next morning.

At 6.30 p.m. on the Tuesday – 8 November – Evans had returned home to be confronted by Christie, whose sitting room gave on to the corridor that led from the front door of the house to the staircase. Christie said, 'Go on up. I'll come behind you.' Upstairs, Christie solemnly told Evans, 'It's bad news. It didn't work,' and showed him Beryl's body, which lay covered by an eiderdown. Evans pulled it back; he told the police officers that he saw that Beryl had been bleeding from her mouth, nose and 'the bottom part'.

Christie warned Evans that he would be accused of murder if Beryl's body was found. He said he would dispose of it 'down one of the drains', where it would never be discovered. Evans then helped the 'puffing and blowing' Christie to carry Beryl down to the vacant kitchen of the first-floor tenant, Mr Kitchener, who was fortuitously in hospital for an operation. 'You'd better go to bed and leave the rest to me,' Christie said.

Evans said that he went to work as usual on the Wednesday – 9 November – leaving Geraldine in the care of Christie, who promised to 'slip up and feed the baby' while Evans was away. That evening Christie told him that 'he knew a young couple over in East Acton', unable to have children of their own, who would call at 9 a.m. on Thursday to pick up Geraldine and look after her. Evans quietly acquiesced. Christie urged Evans to 'get out of London somewhere' before Beryl's disappearance was discovered. Evans went to tell his mother, Thomasina Probert, who lived on St Mark's Road nearby, that Beryl and Geraldine had 'gone away on a holiday', before going to the Kensington Park Hotel once more.

Evans then spent most of Friday, Saturday and Sunday at 'the pictures and the pub'. On Monday morning a Ladbroke Grove rag dealer – from whom Evans refused payment – picked up two sacks containing Beryl's clothes and the bloodstained eiderdown her dead body had been found under. At 3 p.m. on the Monday a Portobello Road trader – a Mr Hookway – collected most of Evans's furniture in his van, though Evans left Geraldine's clothing, pram and highchair with Christie, who assured him that he would 'take them over to East Acton' later that week. Evans then made his way to Paddington station for the night train to Cardiff, arriving at the home of an aunt and uncle – the Lynchs – in Merthyr Vale at 6.40 a.m. on Tuesday morning.

In the early hours of 1 December, shortly after Evans had dictated his second statement, London police officers called on Mrs Probert, who told them that her son had 'a very vivid imagination and [was] a terrible liar'. Almost simultaneously, the Glamorgan Constabulary visited the Lynchs and were shown an unpunctuated letter Evans's mother had written to them on 29 November. Its contents did nothing to bolster Evans's credibility. 'Ask Tim what he have done with the Funichter he took from his flat there is some mirstry about him you can tell him from me he don't want to come to me I never want to see him again as long as I live he have put years on my life since last August . . .' she wrote.

Later that morning Evans told the police he'd forgotten to mention a further fact. He had returned to London on 22 or 23 November to ask Christie about Geraldine's welfare. Christie had told Evans that he shouldn't visit his daughter until she had had 'a few weeks to settle down' with the East Acton couple. Evans had then been told by Christie, 'Write to me and I'll let you know when you can see her.' Thus satisfied, Evans went back to Wales.

The Metropolitan Police started searching Rillington Place. The back garden, if the dismal little patch of ragged grass strewn with rubbish was worth the name, showed no signs of any recent disturbance of the earth. Among papers on the floor of Evans's now near-empty rooms they found a press cutting about the recent 'Torso murder' case, alongside a stolen briefcase, giving police – who were still unsure what crime, if any, had been committed – a pretext to charge Evans with theft and bring him to London by train for more questioning. Mr and Mrs Christie assisted the search and willingly gave statements.

The following morning, 2 December, a more thorough search began. While it was taking place Evans was being escorted back to London. At 9.30 p.m. that evening Evans arrived at Paddington station, where he was caught by the flashbulb of a press photographer tipped off by Scotland Yard. It remains the defining image of Evans: frightened, uncomprehending, dwarfed by the two bowler-hatted detectives bundling him on to the platform. He is wearing one of those heavy, shapeless overcoats so characteristic of late 1940s Britain. It seems several sizes too large for his tiny frame.

Evans was taken to Notting Hill Police Station, where he was immediately told by Chief Inspector George Jennings that earlier that day police had made a shocking discovery in 10 Rillington Place's washhouse, a small room only accessible via the back yard, next to the outdoor lavatory. Behind some loose floorboards, the bodies of both Beryl and little Geraldine had been found. Beryl had been tied up in a green tablecloth; the baby lay separately with a man's tie twisted round her neck. 'Later today I was at Kensington Mortuary where it was established that the cause of death was strangulation in both cases,' added Jennings. 'I have reason to believe that you were responsible for their deaths.' The clothing that his wife and daughter had worn when they met their deaths was arranged on the floor of the interview room in two piles, together with the wrapping and cord that had bound Beryl and the tie that had killed Geraldine. Evans started crying and simply replied, 'Yes.'

Evans now gave a third statement, changing his story yet again. His composure seemed to return, his demeanour that of a man relieving himself of a burdensome secret. Evans no longer claimed that Beryl had died at Christie's hands, but rather that, in a fit of anger at her profligate spending habits – 'she was incurring one debt after another, and I could not stand it any longer' – he had strangled her on the evening of 8 November (the day of the supposed botched abortion, according to the earlier statements), with rope kept in his van. He alone had carried her body to Kitchener's rooms below, and then hidden it under the washhouse sink after midnight, without Christie's knowledge or assistance. Evans said he had strangled Geraldine with his tie – citing no motive for doing so – on the evening of Thursday, 10 November, having left her alone in her cot for two days while out at work. That night, after the Christies had gone to bed, he had placed the child's body in the washhouse next to that of his wife. 'It's a great relief to get it off my chest. I feel better already,' Evans apparently said as soon as he had signed the statement.

But Evans was not finished. He immediately launched into a fourth, longer statement: the police later claimed he talked so fast they had to ask him to slow down so their note-taking could keep pace. Evans was now more expansive. He said that he had been frustrated by Beryl's demands that he should work fewer hours, prompting him to quit a full-time job and start working a shorter week for a different employer. The reduction in income came just as Beryl's spending increased. In July 1949 Evans had lost his job and had to make do with part-time work. After discovering that Beryl was badly in debt the couple had argued continually from Sunday (6 November) onwards. On the morning of 7 November Beryl had said that she was taking Geraldine to stay with her father, a railway worker who lived in Brighton. Evans had replied that 'it would be a good job and a load of worry off my mind'. When he found Beryl still there that evening he had said, 'I thought you were going to Brighton.' Beryl had replied, 'What, for you to have a good time?' She had tried to throw a milk bottle at Evans after he had threatened to slap her.

Evans said that after returning from work on 8 November he had strangled Beryl 'in a fit of temper', after slapping her and being slapped back. He had then wrapped her body in a tablecloth, tied up with cord from his kitchen cupboard, before moving it into Kitchener's rooms and then down to the washhouse. On Thursday he hadn't resigned from his job, as he had previously claimed, but rather had been dismissed after 'an argument with the Guv'nor' about missed deliveries and a salary advance, which he said he needed to post to Beryl in Bristol (Evans seemed to refer to both Brighton and Bristol, as the place his wife and child had supposedly left London for, indiscriminately). He had strangled Geraldine that evening before placing her body in the washhouse. No mention was made by Evans of Beryl's pregnancy, of any attempted abortion, or of Christie. Police later said Evans dictated this last statement between 10 p.m. and 11.15 p.m. on 2 December.

On the morning of 3 December Evans was charged by Jennings with the murder of Beryl. 'Yes, that's right,' he replied. On next being charged with Geraldine's murder he remained silent. En route to West London Magistrates Court Evans's confessional mood persisted. He told another police officer, Inspector Black, that he had removed Beryl's wedding ring from her corpse and later sold it to a Merthyr Tydfil jeweller for 6 shillings. At Brixton prison, to where he was then taken, Evans repeated the substance of his final statement to the prison medical officer, Dr Matheson.

On the face of it Timothy Evans's guilt was manifest. He had constantly changed his story before apparently finally confessing to the murder of both his wife and daughter. Even his family condemned him as an extravagant teller of tall tales. Evans had turned up unexpectedly on the Lynchs' doorstep, explaining his arrival in Wales with a story that he had been on a trip 'looking for new branches' with his boss, whose car had unexpectedly broken down in Cardiff. Although Evans bought a toy doll at Woolworths in Merthyr for Geraldine – he described her as an 'absolute smasher' – he then lost his temper when asked exactly where Geraldine was; he told his aunt that Beryl had 'walked out of the flat and left the baby in the cot' and that he had given Geraldine to 'some people from Newport to look after'. Evans seemed to inhabit multiple mental universes in which different versions of reality vied with each other.

The neighbour whom Evans had blamed in his second statement seemed a model of quiet respectability. Born in Yorkshire in 1899, John Reginald Christie, known to all as Reg, had a genteel lower-middle-class upbringing, singing in the church choir, joining the Scouts and winning a scholarship to Halifax Secondary School. During the First World War he joined the army, and was gassed in France in June 1918. Having married Ethel in 1920 Christie found work as a clerk in Yorkshire, before moving down to London. A childless middle-aged couple, the Christies had rented the ground-floor flat at 10 Rillington Place since December 1938. Too old for call-up in 1939, Christie instead enlisted as a special constable in the War Reserve Police, based at Harrow Road. He was dubbed the 'persecuting counsel' locally because of his zealous enforcement of blackout regulations, and twice commended for his 'efficient detection of crime'. After four years' service he was 'released', spending the rest of the war as a van driver.[2] His health had since deteriorated, but despite suffering from fibrositis of the back and enteritis (a form of chronic diarrhoea) – possibly linked to his time on the western front – he still worked intermittently as a ledger clerk.

The Christies' neighbour on the top floor was rather less respectable. Born in 1924, at the age of eight Evans had contracted lupus and tuberculosis, and spent much of his childhood in hospitals and sanatoria. After a couple of years living with his grandmother, at the start of the Second

World War he had joined his mother in London, still unable to read or write. Deemed unfit for military service he drifted in and out of work. On a blind date in summer 1947 Evans met an attractive eighteen-year-old, Beryl Thorley, a telephonist at the Grosvenor House Hotel on Park Lane. That Beryl should be attracted to the diminutive and backward Evans is surprising. Still, they married that September and in late 1948, six months after they moved into Rillington Place, Geraldine was born.

Police enquiries revealed that their marriage had been rocky from the start; Beryl had once thrown a jar at Evans's head, which needed stitches. Whether the fault lay with Evans's drinking or with Beryl's profligacy, they had fallen behind with their rent and hire-purchase payments on their furniture. Tensions grew in their tiny two-roomed flat. Christie, a man 'well used to minding other people's business', was assiduous in informing the police that the Evanses 'got on very badly together' and that Beryl had complained to Ethel that Evans had grabbed her by the throat more than once, and would one day 'do her in'.

The murders of Geraldine and Beryl Evans seemed just another domestic tragedy, undoubtedly harrowing, but all too common in the poorer districts of London. Although the smart garden squares of Holland Park were, tantalisingly, only half a mile away they might as well have been on the other side of the planet. Alan Johnson, a future Labour Home Secretary, grew up in North Kensington in the early 1950s, a now distant world of horse-drawn coal deliveries and buckets of urine in the corners of damp-infested bedrooms: even in the early 1960s most homes only had outside lavatories. In his early teens Johnson worked as a milkman's assistant and once made a delivery to 10 Rillington Place, twelve years after Beryl and Geraldine's deaths. 'There was no natural light on the landings or bulbs in the light fittings,' Johnson recalled in his memoirs fifty years later. 'An awful smell of decay and mould, stale food and detritus seeped from the walls. Each room contained several young West Indian men for whom existing in these conditions was the price they paid for coming to the motherland.'

In 1949, 10 Rillington Place was already only a small step away from being a slum. Owned by an absentee landlord, its flats were not self-contained but simply three sets of gloomy, gaslit rooms, two or three on each floor. There was no telephone or bathroom in the house. A single lavatory in an outbuilding at the back served all three flats. Beside it was the tiny washhouse, just over a yard square, housing a boiler and basin and used by the Christies for 'depositing odds and ends'. Later, the house became the subject of ghoulish fascination (the BBC sent a film crew to record its demolition in 1971). Many photographs taken by the police were subsequently published. The interior they reveal, even if one can put the contorted bodies wrapped in blankets that feature in many of them out of mind, is of a grim and squalid domestic world. The past really is a foreign country. Yet this was post-war London.

'I never done it, Mum, Christie done it,' Evans told his mother after he had been charged. 'Tell Christie I want to see him. He is the only one who can help me now.' Even after he had apparently confessed to her murder, Evans seemed somehow to believe that Geraldine was still alive, being cared for by the mythical couple from Acton. He asked his mother to go to Christie to get his 'baby back'. Dutifully, Mrs Probert went over to Rillington Place to confront Christie. Refusing to speak to her he threatened to summon the police.

Evans, now without a penny to his name, was entitled to legal aid. But it was nearly two weeks before he met with any legal representative. Shortly before the committal on 15 December Baillie Saunders, an octogenarian clerk from the solicitors' firm of Freeborough, Slack and Co, visited him in Brixton. Evans repeated to Saunders what he had told his mother: 'Christie done it.' Geoffrey Freeborough, the firm's principal, attended Evans's committal in the West London Magistrates Court but did not cross-examine any of the prosecution witnesses. What could be put to them? Why would the quietly spoken ex-policeman murder his neighbour's wife and child? It seemed fantastical. Even without any hostile defence cross-examination Ethel Christie nonetheless managed to break down in tears in the witness box. Her demeanour only seemed to bolster the Christies' status as well-meaning, if somewhat nosey, neighbours. Evans's Old Bailey trial was set for early January 1950.

On Wednesday, 4 January 1950, precisely a week before the trial was due to begin in Court Number One, Malcolm Morris received in his chambers at 1 Garden Court in the Temple the brief to defend Evans on the charge of the murder of his daughter.[3] It was barely a month since the discovery of the bodies of Beryl and Geraldine. Had Christmas not intervened the case might have started even sooner than its allotted date of 11 January. The haste towards a trial seemed almost indecent.[4]

Garden Court is a late addition to the buildings of the Middle Temple, built in 1883 just down from Fountain Court and looking out over Middle Temple Hall and Gardens. Tall, patrician and with a fine voice, Morris was then thirty-six years old and a capable and well-regarded junior barrister. But he did not benefit from the view. He and his more junior colleague, Jeremy Hutchinson, shared a room at the back, hard up against the wall of the next-door building. The document Morris received, typed on the traditional 'Brief' paper size (thirteen by sixteen inches, folded over and tied with pink tape), was both perfunctory and contradictory. Notwithstanding Evans's emphatic if inarticulate instructions that 'Christie done it', Morris was asked to consider whether to set up a defence of insanity on behalf of his client. Dark reference was made, without elaboration, to the fact that Dr Teare, the pathologist who had examined Beryl's body, had mentioned in his report that 'there might have been an attempt at sexual penetration after death.' What could Morris do with this information? More than sixty years later Jeremy Hutchinson recalled his discussions with Morris in their cold, gloomy room in chambers, half-heartedly heated by a small gas fire. Morris paced around, despairing of his client. He simply could not see how a cogent defence could be put. Of the suggestion of necrophilia Morris later wrote (when all the facts had become known): 'I ignored it. If Evans was guilty, it only made matters worse. It could not, on the facts as I then knew, possibly assist his defence.'

Morris arrived at the Old Bailey on 11 January 1950 to defend what seemed the undefendable. This was – and is – a not uncommon position for criminal barristers to find themselves in. The prosecuting counsel Morris faced, sitting along the row from him, was Christmas Humphreys, twelve years his senior. The son of Travers Humphreys, perhaps the most famous criminal judge of the century, Humphreys had just been appointed Senior Treasury Counsel, the most prominent prosecutor at the Bailey. Yet Humphreys was the obverse of what one would expect of a man holding such a position. His hinterland was wide and contrary to appearances. Rebecca West described him as a 'passionate joiner of the wilder type'. Since the age of seventeen he had been a Buddhist, founding the first Buddhist lodge in London in 1924, and he had since been a prolific writer on the subject. He was chairman of the Ballet Guild. The *Dictionary of National Biography* would later comment that he 'pursued his interests outside the law with enthusiasm and sometimes with more vigour than sound judgement'. He was a confirmed Oxfordian, believing the courtier Edward de Vere, 17th Earl of Oxford, to have written the plays and poems generally attributed to William Shakespeare.

The courtroom on this January morning was sparsely populated. The public gallery was almost empty. One or two journalists wandered in and out. The case they were waiting for was due to start in the same court on the following Wednesday: the prosecution of Donald Hume for the murder of a Warren Street car dealer and 'spiv', Stanley Setty. Hume, also on remand in Brixton with Evans, was alleged to have stabbed Setty to death before dismembering his body, wrapping the various parts in felt and dropping them from a light aeroplane into the North Sea. The case had dominated the newspapers for weeks and had inevitably acquired its own name – the 'Torso murder'. It was preoccupying Humphreys too: he was due to lead the prosecution. By contrast the Evans case was just another minor domestic tragedy. It presented no particular problems. Humphreys had probably started looking at the papers only the day before.

It was then the practice only to charge a defendant on a single count of murder, even if they were suspected of more than one. The purpose of this rule was to prevent the potential prejudice to the defendant that multiple murder counts might create. To be charged with two murders can create circularity of proof: each charge might be seen by the jury to substantiate the other. Yet Humphreys was now to contend that the fact of Beryl's death, and Evans's confession of responsibility for it, should be admitted in evidence before the jury as probative of guilt of the murder of his daughter. The effect of a ruling against Evans on this issue would be, in practice, to remove from him the protection of the 'one count' rule. As soon as Evans, a tiny figure in the capacious dock, had pleaded 'not guilty', the jury was sent out while this question of admissibility was debated. Humphreys argued that to pretend that Beryl did not exist at all would make a 'limping, lame and altogether impossible story to fit together, and puzzling to the jury', and that it was thus impractical to separate the two killings. After much legal argument the judge, Mr Justice (Wilfred) Lewis, ruled that evidence relating to Beryl was admissible. The two murders constituted 'one transaction', Evans had confessed to both simultaneously, and their bodies had been found together, even though it was the Crown's case that Geraldine had been murdered two days later.

This ruling went a long way to sealing Evans's fate. The prosecution now had the best of both worlds. On the one hand, putting the emotive murder of a tiny child at the centre of the trial obscured questions over how Evans could have concealed the much larger body of a woman in a washhouse just feet away from the Christies' bedroom window. On the other, admitting evidence relating to the Evanses' marital rows and financial troubles – which seemed to provide Evans with a motive for killing Beryl – helped to distract from the lack of any motive for killing baby Geraldine. Perfect circularity of proof had been obtained.

The jury filed back into court to hear Humphreys' opening address. It was easy pickings for him; there it all was in the confessions Evans had made. The narrative that Humphreys unfolded was a simple one. Evans lost his job; he became depressed; he argued with his wife and killed her; and then he killed his daughter. (Nobody seemed to notice that even on Evans's own confession the narrative here was wrong: Evans had only lost his job two days *after* Beryl's death.) Evans's 'terrible accusation' – made in his second confession in Wales – that Christie had killed Beryl during the course of a criminal backstreet abortion, was contradicted by his own confession two days later, said Humphreys. 'You will listen to any defence which the accused may put forward . . . but when you have heard the whole of the evidence you may well think – and indeed, you must be certain in your minds that it is so – that he murdered this baby, and in that case you will find him guilty of wilful murder.'

Police officers testified to the discovery of the bodies. A plan shown to the jury explained the layout of 10 Rillington Place. There on the ground floor was the corridor running alongside the Christies' sitting room and bedroom. It was down that corridor that Evans was supposed to have silently carried the corpses of his wife and child out into the yard. There at the back was the washhouse, overlooked by the Christies' bedroom and kitchen windows. A written statement from Beryl's father, who had had the terrible task of identifying his daughter's and grand-daughter's bodies, was read out.

And then the prosecution's star witness, John Christie, bespectacled and neat, shuffled into court. He passed by the dock, just feet away from where Evans was sitting. The later film of *10 Rillington Place* has Richard Attenborough, as Christie, looking up at John Hurt, as Evans, on his slow journey to the witness box.[5] Whether their eyes actually met is not known. But we can imagine the thoughts of each at that moment. Evans, sitting in the dock on trial for his life, was looking at a man, standing just yards away from him, about to take his oath to tell the truth, the whole truth and nothing but the truth. This was the man who had told Evans he had tried to help out Beryl, to whom Evans had looked up as wise and book-read, who had shepherded Evans into all the successive catastrophic decisions he had made over those days in November. Now he was disclaiming it all, refuting with prim horror the very suggestion that he was an abortionist. Even in Evans's dimly lit mental universe the sense of a world turned upside down, of a sort of anarchic injustice, clothed in the respectable garments of the law, overturning the natural order of things, must have been overwhelming. Was Christie, about to give evidence that would ensure the death of the last member of the Evans family, overborne by the extraordinariness of the occasion?

Very little from the transcripts suggests that Christie was anything other than calm. He had last seen Beryl and Geraldine during the day on Tuesday, 8 November. What had he heard that night? The lies came easily:

> CHRISTIE: Well we were both in bed, my wife and I, and we were startled in the middle of the night by a very loud thud.
>
> HUMPHREYS: A thud do you say?
>
> CHRISTIE: Yes.
>
> HUMPHREYS: Then what did you hear?
>
> CHRISTIE: We listened for a few seconds and didn't hear anything, and I gradually knelt up in bed and looked through the window which overlooks the yard. It was very dark and I couldn't see anything and so I went back and we laid down and shortly after that I heard some movement which appeared to be upstairs.
>
> HUMPHREYS: What sort of movement?
>
> CHRISTIE: As though something was being moved, something heavy was being moved.

So was the image of poor Beryl Evans's body being manhandled by her husband into Kitchener's flat upstairs intruded in the jury's mind. But Christie was careful not to overplay his hand. 'I listened to that for a very short time, I suppose, and I went off to sleep, and I don't remember anything else after that.'

How well Christie performed his role as the respectable, valetudinarian neighbour. He became confused about dates, which only added to the sense that here was a man doing his best to assist the court. When Morris intervened to ask him to speak up, Christie's response was perfect: 'I have a quiet voice; it is the reaction of gas poisoning in the last war.' This was a lie, but it was an unchallengeable one. Christie now explained that in the evening of the Wednesday he had seen Evans, who told him that Beryl had gone with Geraldine to Bristol. On the Thursday – the 10th – Evans had returned from work and told Christie that he had 'packed in' his job. He was going to Bristol to join his family.

'How did he seem in his manner then?'

Christie answered slowly, measured, deadly. 'Well, he seemed extremely angry, upset, really wild, as though he had had a terrific row, I should imagine; he looked that way.'

Late on Friday night Evans had told him he was going to sell his furniture because he could not take it down to Bristol. Of course Evans had in fact decided to sell up and leave London on Christie's advice. Yet now Christie painted himself merely as an onlooker. On the following Monday, after the furniture had been taken away, Evans had shown Christie a roll of £60 in banknotes and then left, supposedly for Bristol, carrying a large suitcase. The next time Christie had seen Evans was when he had returned on 23 November. Evans had in fact come back to enquire after his daughter, believing her to be in the care of the couple from East Acton. Christie's account was now of Evans having returned to tell him that Beryl 'had walked out on me' and that he'd been unable to find work anywhere. Evans told Christie he had spent all but £2 of the money his furniture had fetched before announcing he was returning to Wales. It was a bizarre story: on this account Evans, with no further connection to Rillington Place, had come back simply to report to Christie on his current situation.

Was Christie under medical treatment at the time? Humphreys asked. 'Yes, and still am,' Christie replied.

Then the gratuitous question: 'What were you doing in the last war, Mr Christie?'

'I was a police officer . . . from September 1939 until September 1943.'

'You are rather a sick man now?'

'Yes.'

The judge intervened. 'You said something about your voice and gas?'

'Yes, that was the First War; I was in the 1914 war,' replied Christie, just before the trial was adjourned for the day.

Thus the last thing jurors remembered from the first day was not Christie the supposed backstreet abortionist, but Christie the gassed veteran and wartime police officer.

On day two it was Morris's turn to cross-examine. This was Christie's moment of greatest danger. But Morris was labouring under the handicap of having virtually no material to controvert Christie's evidence. All that Evans could say was that Christie had somehow killed his wife while performing an abortion. His client could offer no explanation why Christie might have gone on to kill Geraldine. Christie had no difficulty answering 'No' when Morris asked whether he knew anyone in East Acton; and he could equally emphatically deny that he had tried to carry out an abortion on Beryl.

Morris asked Christie to look at Exhibit 3, the striped neck-tie that had been used to strangle Geraldine. Christie denied it was his. He was careful not to assert he recognised it as belonging to Evans; he no doubt reckoned that that would have been too definite. Instead he said he had seen Evans wearing a striped tie somewhat similar.

Suddenly the cross-examination turned from neckwear to murder. 'Well, Mr Christie, I have got to suggest to you, and I do not want there to be any misapprehension about it, that you are responsible for the deaths of Mrs Evans and the little girl, or if that is not so, at least that you know very much more about those deaths than you have said,' said Morris.

'That is a lie,' Christie shot back.

Why did Morris choose that particular moment to put to Christie that he was a murderer? Maybe he was trying to catch Christie by surprise. If so, the tactic backfired. Morris's follow-up questions showed that all he had to go on was that Christie had known Beryl was pregnant. But Christie seemed quite happy to confirm that he had advised Beryl, in Ethel's presence, to stop 'taking pills and various things to procure an abortion' as she was looking 'really ill'. He readily admitted that he had shown the Evanses the basic first-aid certificates he had hung on his sitting-room wall, alongside a photo of himself in police uniform. The image of Christie as the avuncular neighbour was still intact.

Christie explained that, on doctor's orders, he had spent 8 November either resting in bed or sitting by the fire in his pyjamas. In the afternoon he had gone to see the doctor and picked up a book for Ethel at a public library on the way home. The only other people he had seen that day were workmen making improvements to the property, only adding, when prompted by Morris and after a long pause, that he had also seen Beryl going out at lunchtime. Scenting blood, Morris asked Christie why, on day one of the trial, he had recalled seeing Beryl that day, only to have forgotten on day two.

Christie was quick to get himself back on track. 'I had to go to the doctor again last night and he prescribed for me and gave me some pills to alleviate the pain, and I have been awake most of the night.'

The solicitous Mr Justice Lewis invited Christie to give the rest of his evidence sitting in a chair. 'Are you still suffering from fibrositis?' asked Lewis.

'Yes, very badly,' Christie replied pitifully.

This was not a man who looked capable of murdering a mother and her baby. Whatever traction Morris had obtained had now been lost.

Morris doggedly took Christie through the events of the next few days, putting to him the version contained in Evans's second statement made in Wales. But all he could do was put Evans's account; there was no independent material that could substantiate it. Effective cross-examination generally needs purchase, some independently verifiable facts to set against the witness's account. Here there were none. Christie easily withstood it, all the while painting himself as the pathetic invalid. At the time when he and Evans were supposedly manhandling Beryl's body downstairs to the first floor Christie said he was in bed waiting for Ethel to bring him some 'milk food'. To the suggestion that he had carried Beryl's body downstairs to Kitchener's rooms Christie answered, 'That is absolutely ridiculous, I had been on a starvation diet, just milk food, because of the enteritis, that I could scarcely bend. I had to crawl out of bed . . . Physically impossible!'

The questioning became more desperate. Christie denied that he had fed Geraldine on the Wednesday and Thursday while Evans was at work ('I don't know how to feed a baby, as a matter of fact. I have no children of my own'). No doubt the jury nodded; the notion of Christie as childminder was a far-fetched one. The elaborate plan Christie had supposedly devised to conceal Beryl's body, which the credulous and trusting Evans had fallen in with, now seemed absurd under the forensic examination of the courtroom and the disgruntled judge frequently intervened. At one point he growled at Morris: 'You are presumably asking these questions on instructions?' The implication was painfully clear, even to the jury: counsel could only properly advance such a case if he had been expressly required to do so by his client. F. Tennyson Jesse, who attended the trial and edited the Notable British Trials volume on the case, later recalled: 'It is difficult to remember, still more difficult to recreate, the atmosphere of antipathy with which the case for the Defence was received. The whole Court despised and rejected it.'

Amid this environment of hostility Morris seemed to become more and more ground down by his task. We are a long way from the fiery histrionics of Marshall Hall or the calculated dominance of Patrick Hastings. Morris put Evans's case to Christie as if it were a matter of distasteful obligation. It was as if he were signalling to the courtroom the tacit words, 'I am sorry to have to put these outrageous suggestions to Mr Christie, but I am professionally obliged to do so.' Morris's final questions relating to Christie's previous criminal convictions (only revealed to him by the prosecution for the first time the day before) were couched in an apologetic tone:

MORRIS: You are not, are you, a man of good character?
CHRISTIE: Well, I have had some trouble.
MORRIS: I apologise for having to ask you these questions, but I am afraid

I must. On four occasions you have been convicted of offences of dishonesty, have you not?

Christie's most serious conviction was for an act of violence. He had hit a young woman about the head with a cricket bat, for which he had been sentenced to six months in prison. But all the jury learned was that in 1929 he had been convicted of 'malicious wounding'. All in all, the jury came away with the impression that the questions had constituted an unworthy attack on a feeble old man. In fact Christie was fifty.

It was now Humphreys' turn to re-examine his witness. He wasted no time in obtaining Christie's eager confirmation that he had spent the Great War 'fighting for his country' in the Duke of Wellington's Regiment. 'I was gassed twice and I was blinded for three months and never spoke for three and a half years,' Christie simpered to an appreciative courtroom. 'Was that all right?' Christie – still perfectly 'in character'– asked a policeman as he left the witness box. For Evans, it had been much too 'all right'.

Ethel Christie – described later as a 'plump, naïve, middle-aged Yorkshirewoman' – was next, faithfully corroborating everything her husband had said. Her near-hysteria in the magistrates court was gone. It subsequently became clear that she was utterly dominated by her husband and for this performance she had been well schooled: she had last seen Beryl and Geraldine on the Monday (the 7th); she told of the 'bump in the night' that woke them on the Tuesday; she refuted the suggestion that her husband had looked after the baby on the Wednesday. Morris asked about Christie's 'wish to be advanced in medical training', but Mrs Christie would only acknowledge that her husband had 'an interest in first aid' and 'one or two' books on the subject. It was flimsy ground on which to build the image of Christie as the local abortionist. Mrs Christie was followed by Mrs Lynch, Evans's aunt. She explained that after his arrival in Wales on 15 November her nephew had told her that Beryl and Geraldine had gone to Brighton. It had of course been a lie, suggested by Christie and now, in the recounting, was leading Evans to the gallows. There was no cross-examination.

DC Evans from Merthyr Vale testified to the two statements Evans had made at the police station in Wales. They were solemnly read out by the clerk of the court. DC Evans was followed by Chief Inspector Jennings, who described the discovery of Beryl's and Geraldine's bodies in the washhouse. He produced Evans's two Notting Hill statements, which were also read out. The full span of Evans's storytelling was thus laid bare. Jennings explained that he had charged Evans with Beryl's murder the following morning. (Morris's objection that Evans's response to being charged – 'Yes, that's right' – was inadmissible, as he was only on trial for murdering his daughter, was brushed aside by Lewis.)

The jury had had each of the police statements made by Evans read out in succession. The last two statements, made in London, made no mention of Christie and flatly identified Evans alone as a double-murderer. In order to explain those later statements away the jury needed to be persuaded that they had been made in conditions that undermined their truth. But nothing was asked of Jennings about this. All that Morris elicited was that, having been shown his wife's and daughter's clothing piled on the floor of the police station, Evans had been 'upset'. Jennings left the box.

Humphreys told the judge: 'That is the case for the prosecution, My Lord,' and sat down.

The only witness for the defence was Timothy Evans himself. None of his relatives were called on his behalf. There were no character witnesses.

His testimony began well enough. He confidently replied, 'No,' when asked by Morris if he was in any way responsible for Beryl and Geraldine's deaths. The narrative that was unfolded coincided precisely with the second statement made in Merthyr Tydfil. So far as one can tell from the transcript Evans spoke well and made no slips. But to read it now is heart-breaking: his discovery under the lambent flame of the gas light of his wife's body lying in bed, half covered by an eiderdown; his credulousness, his pathetic willingness to follow the advice of Christie, the man who had strangled his wife.

MORRIS: What did he tell you?

EVANS: He told me that he had made arrangements for my daughter to go over to East Acton, and the people were coming to collect her on Thursday.

MORRIS: Did he say who the people in East Acton were, or anything about them?

EVANS: No, sir; he just said that the young people could not have any children of their own, sir.

MORRIS: Did he say what he was going to do with your wife's body?

EVANS: He told me he was going to put it down a drain, sir.

MORRIS: What did you say, if anything, to that?

EVANS: Well, I told him he knew what he was doing, sir.

At the time this sounded like nothing but a despicable – and ludicrous – attempt to push the blame on to poor Mr Christie. Worse was to come. Evans explained that he had spent much of the first Sunday and Monday after Beryl's death and the disappearance of his daughter 'at the pictures' and in the pub: no doubt such distractions were the only way Evans could numb the pain of what had happened. But this was not something Evans was able to convey to the jury.

Finally, Morris had to deal with Evans's behaviour at Notting Hill Police Station. Why had he replied 'Yes' when Jennings had said that he had 'reason to believe' that Evans was responsible for the deaths of his family? 'Well, when I found out about my daughter being dead I was upset and did not care what happened to me.'

> MORRIS: Were you very fond of her?
> EVANS: Yes, sir.

What reticence! It is as if the polite language of the 1940s has smothered the expression of feeling. But Evans was a prisoner not only of the register of the period but also of his own inarticulacy. Why had he made the two London statements assuming responsibility for both deaths? This was the crucial question. All he could say was: 'Well, I thought if I did not make a statement the police would take me downstairs and start knocking me about . . . I was upset and I do not think I knew what I was saying.'

This was not good enough. No jury would believe that a man would confess to the murder of his wife and child on the strength of a vague fear that he might otherwise be subjected to violence. There had been no suggestion of any threats made by Jennings.

Christmas Humphreys then rose to cross-examine. The believer in karma set out to destroy Evans. It was not an equal contest.

> HUMPHREYS: Is it a reason for pleading guilty to murder because you are
>   upset because your daughter is dead by some other person's hand?
> EVANS: Yes.

It is excruciating now to read Evans's cross-examination by Humphreys. Much of the time Evans misunderstood the questions being asked, and yet no one intervened to help him. This was an example of cross-examination that occludes rather than illuminates the truth. Through page after page of the transcript Evans convicts himself through his inarticulacy and confusion, through the ghastly ease with which Humphreys, with his thirty years of experience of the criminal courts, baited and effortlessly outwitted him. In this game the better the communicator, the more intelligent the person on trial, the greater his prospect of acquittal.

Humphreys asked Evans if he had still been 'upset' when told that their bodies had been found. 'As I said before, I was upset when Detective Inspector Jennings told me about my daughter's death,' replied Evans.

'You were upset, and therefore you pleaded guilty to their murder?' asked Humphreys.

'I plead not guilty to the murder, sir,' replied Evans, apparently confused by Humphreys' use of the word 'plead' to refer to the confession at the police station. 'I was upset and did not know what I was saying.'

Humphreys' sarcasm now got the better of him. 'Still upset?'

'Yes, sir,' Evans replied.

'Hour after hour, day after day?'

'I did not know my daughter was dead till Detective Inspector Jennings told me about it. I had nothing else to live for,' said Evans.

'Have you anything more to live for now?' asked Humphreys.

'Lots of things,' Evans replied.

'And therefore you make an allegation in terms through your counsel against a perfectly innocent man that he caused the murder?'

Humphreys went through all four statements in turn. Evans had to admit that three of them were untrue. 'Would it not be right to say you are a person who is prepared to lie or tell the truth at your own convenience?' asked Humphreys.

'Why should I tell lies? My life is at stake here,' replied Evans.

'Do answer the question. Was it a relief to you to tell a lot of lies?' Lewis later interjected.[6]

'No, it was not a relief to me at all,' Evans replied.

Humphreys hammered home the lies that Evans had told to everyone. 'You then told half a dozen separate, distinct, deliberate lies to the police, inventing any story that came into your head, is not that right?' asked Humphreys.

'Not any story that came into my head,' replied Evans pathetically. 'I did it all on the advice of Mr Christie.'

And now the finale.

HUMPHREYS: Now, you are the person who alleges that Mr Christie is the murderer in this case; can you suggest why he should have strangled your wife?

EVANS: Well, he was at home all day.

HUMPHREYS: Can you suggest why he should have strangled your wife?

EVANS: No I cannot.

HUMPHREYS: Can you suggest why he should have strangled your daughter two days later?

EVANS: No.

Christie inhabited a hell beyond the imagination of anyone in that courtroom. The very extremity of his derangement was his salvation. The consequence was catastrophic for Timothy Evans. The jury would reject the inconceivable for the seemingly obvious.

'My Lord, that is the case for the defence,' announced Morris. It had been thin indeed.

It was now after half past three in the afternoon of day two. It was for Humphreys to make his closing speech for the prosecution. In the event it would be one of the shortest in a murder trial in Old Bailey history. Humphreys must have known there was no purpose in spending too long with the jury. Evans was surely doomed already. He emphasised just three points, all connected with Christie: his good character as a man who had served in both World Wars; his 'lamentable' state of health ('He is physically incapable of doing half the things which this man [pointing at Evans] says he did'); and the total absence of any motive for him to have committed either murder. Only one of two men could have killed Beryl and Geraldine. It could not be Christie, so it must have been Evans. The final point – that if Christie was indeed an abortionist, then why was Beryl strangled? – no doubt hit home.

> Why, then, should Christie or anybody else strangle Mrs Evans because he has tried to help her commit abortion? It does not make sense. It is bosh! Even if Christie had been responsible for the woman's death, why should he two days later go up to that flat and strangle, unknown to this man, an innocent little baby lying there aged fourteen months? Even this fluent liar [pointing to Evans in the dock], who will lie as and when he pleases, cannot invent an answer to that question.

Nor could anyone in that courtroom. The awful answer lay with Humphreys' beloved Shakespeare (or the Earl of Oxford): 'There are more things in heaven and earth, Horatio, than are dreamt of in your philosophy.'

When Humphreys wound up at a quarter to four, barely ten minutes after he started, Morris was caught off-guard. He had expected Humphreys' speech to last until after four o'clock, the usual adjournment time, so he would not have to start his closing speech until the following morning. All barristers plan out what they are likely to have to do in a court day, and what they can prepare that evening or the next morning. It must have sent a shiver down his spine when Lewis indicated that Morris should start then and there. Every barrister has experienced this; probably none still living in a capital case.

In the circumstances Morris's speech reads very well on the page. Its fluency is remarkable. Gone is the apologetic tone. Instead a number of sensible propositions was placed before the jury, which achieve plausibility, even against the backdrop of the overwhelming edifice of evidence. First Morris denied that the jury was faced with an either/or question. They did not have to choose between Christie and Evans. The only question for them was whether it had been established beyond reasonable doubt that Evans was guilty of his daughter's murder. That did not require a conclusion against Christie. Next, Evans's voluntary attendance at the Welsh police station and the statement that his wife was dead and disposed of in the drain outside Rillington Place. What a thing to do – what a thing to say – if Evans in fact knew that both his wife and child were deposited in the washhouse! And why then (in his second Merthyr statement) had Evans put the blame on Christie for Beryl's death, but not Geraldine's? Third, Evans's evidence in the witness box had been entirely consistent with that second statement, even though it had been made six weeks earlier. Morris turned to the medical handbook in Christie's front room: how would Evans have known it was there unless Christie had shown it to him, and for what reason would he have shown it to the illiterate Evans other than to promote his credentials as an abortionist?

As for the last two statements, made by Evans in the Notting Hill Police Station, there was of course real difficulty. The psychology of false confessions, well known today, was imperfectly understood in the early 1950s. Yet Morris made a valiant attempt to explain them away: here was Evans, still believing that Christie had placed her in the care of the Acton couple, suddenly confronted by the London police with news of his daughter's death and the heart-rending pile of her little clothes there on the floor. He had nothing left to live for. He was frightened and disorientated. He feared violence from the police who believed he was guilty of double murder. He made the confession 'because he has lost interest in the world. He had lost his daughter and the shock of that, hearing that, is enough, temporarily perhaps, to turn his brain.'

Morris concluded on a note of quiet lyricism. 'I ask you when you think about it tomorrow to bring every effort that you conceivably can to bear, every power that you have, and when you have done that, and have been as careful and as fair as I know you will be, Evans will be satisfied, and I, as his advocate, cannot ask for anything more.' A ringing proclamation of Evans's innocence it was not, but Morris had hit the right tone. It has been suggested that had Morris gone 'flat out' for Christie with 'a factual cannonade with rockets . . . like a Patrick Hastings or Marshall Hall' the outcome of the trial might have been different. In fact Evans's best, slender, hope was the modulated suggestion of doubt, not the banging of the drum of innocence.

To this end, there was one point Morris did not make but which might have capsized the prosecution case. Evans was charged with murdering his daughter on the evening of Thursday, 10 November. Christie and his wife had both said that the last time they saw Beryl or Geraldine was on the Tuesday and it was Evans's undisputed evidence that Beryl died that day. This required the jury to believe that a fourteen-month-old baby had been alone in her cot at the top of the doll's-house that was 10 Rillington Place, her mother unaccountably absent, for the whole of Wednesday and Thursday without anyone hearing her frantic cries. There were other oddities in the prosecution case: was it likely that Evans could have carried his wife's and child's bodies past the Christies' rooms undetected? Why would Evans have returned from Wales to Rillington Place on 23 November, knowing that their bodies were wrapped up in its washhouse, in plain sight to anyone who looked in? The later London confessions are couched in language that it is very difficult to ascribe to the illiterate Evans. But it is easy to be wise after the event.

Critics of Mr Justice Lewis's summing-up on the trial's final, third, day have said he was inexcusably biased towards the prosecution (Ludovic Kennedy, who wrote the classic account of the case, called it 'inaccurate and highly prejudiced . . . too long and too untidy'). Lewis did start his summing-up with the usual warning to jurors not to convict Evans unless they were convinced beyond reasonable doubt that he was guilty, but he then proceeded to demolish everything Morris had urged. 'Do not be frightened by the suggestion which was made to you by learned counsel for the Defence of the bogey of sleepless nights if by any chance you should afterwards think you had given a wrong verdict, if your verdict be one of guilty.'

What the jury was left with was the fact that the pathologist Dr Teare had found no evidence of any interference with Beryl's 'private parts', although his original report had actually said the opposite. Beryl had died by strangulation. Yet Christie was, Evans had claimed, an abortionist; his wife had supposedly died during a botched abortion. It made no sense. The senselessness went further: 'Assume for a moment that Christie had a hand in the killing of Mrs Evans; what conceivable reason could there be for his killing that child? Consider it, members of the jury, as I know you will.'

Lewis went out of his way to puff up Christie as a man of rectitude. The inconvenient fact that he had four convictions for dishonesty and one for violence was brushed aside: 'since then he has no stain on his character whatever.' As for Evans, never before convicted of any offence: 'it is a matter for you, you know, you have got to decide this, not me, but you may think that Evans's performance, if I may use that expression, from the beginning of November until today has been one tissue of falsehoods from start to finish . . . that man had lied, and lied, and lied again.'

It came as no surprise to anyone that the jury returned to court in the early afternoon, less than forty minutes after retiring, with a unanimous guilty verdict. The jurors were a mixture of men and women; Kennedy observed that they were 'sensible matter-of-fact people' who could not conceive that Christie might have murdered 'simply for the fun of it'. Like most newspapers the *Manchester Guardian* ignored the trial. But it did report, in its Saturday edition, the verdict, in a short eighty-word column on page five. The anonymous piece recorded one extraordinary fact: 'John Reginald Christie, occupant of a flat in Evans' house, who, said Mr Justice Lewis, the defence alleged had killed the woman and child, was sitting at the back of the court when the verdict was announced.' After sentence of death was passed it was observed that Christie was crying.

Evans looked unmoved as he was led down the steps in the dock. 'Murderer, murderer!' yelled Evans's mother at Christie in the hall outside Court Number One. 'Don't you dare call my husband a murderer. He is a good man,' the loyal Ethel Christie retorted. If only she knew.

By mid-Friday afternoon, with Evans on his way to Pentonville, Christmas Humphreys was back in the collegiate comfort of the Treasury Counsel's room at the Bailey. He had already moved on to his next case. The next Wednesday he was due to prosecute Donald Hume for the 'Torso murder'. On the face of it here was another open and shut prosecution. Unlike Evans's case, it had fascinated the newspapers ever since the discoveries of parts of the dismembered corpse of Stanley Setty in the Essex marshes the previous October. The evidence that Hume, a pilot and business associate of Setty, had dropped the packages from an aeroplane into the North Sea was overwhelming. His London flat had been found copiously besmirched with bloodstains. Whereas Evans had to make do with legal aid, the newsworthy Hume's defence was being paid for by a Sunday newspaper (in return of course for his exclusive story), a common practice in those days, which allowed him the services of a leading criminal silk.

When Hume's trial started Court Number One was packed; even the doyenne of trial-writing, Rebecca West, graced it with her magisterial presence. The trial started before the same Mr Justice Lewis who had donned the black cap the Friday before (he fell ill that evening and died two months later; the trial had to be restarted the next day before a new judge). The case ran for seven sensational days during which Hume mesmerised the court with a story of three fantastical figures, known to him only as 'Greenie', 'Maxie' and 'The Boy', never otherwise identified, who had apparently arrived at his flat with the packages and paid him to deposit them at sea. It sounded even more far-fetched than Evans's story of Christie the abortionist and child-murderer. But it was told with such aplomb and confidence that at least some of the jury bought it. Unable to agree on a verdict on the charge of murder, they instead convicted Hume of the lesser offence of being an 'accessory after the fact'.

Eight years later, after Hume had been released from prison, he sold his story a second time around. Protected from the threat of a further prosecution by the law of double jeopardy,[7] he now admitted the murder, apparently committed after an intense struggle in his flat with an SS-issue dagger he had picked up during the war. Hume proudly boasted that the mysterious trio, bearing monikers that appeared to have escaped from the pages of *Brighton Rock*, were indeed a fiction. In the pages of the *Sunday Pictorial* he revelled in his guilt and in the fact that he had beaten the system. And he had done so because, whereas Evans had been perplexed by Humphreys' subtleties, Hume had repelled them with indignation. 'Absolute boloney,' he had responded to one insinuation; when the judge had intervened to reassure Hume that Humphreys was merely discharging his prosecutorial function in suggesting guilt and that there was nothing personal in those questions, Hume responded with heat: 'But my life is a personal matter to me.' The jury seemed to respect his vigour.

So two injustices were perpetrated in Court Number One in a little over two weeks in that January of 1950. The first was vastly greater than the second, but it is also an injustice when a guilty man walks free. Hume went on to commit another murder within a year of his release.

The main ground of Evans's appeal was the asserted inadmissibility of evidence relating to Beryl's death. It was heard on 20 February 1950 by a court presided over by the Lord Chief Justice Lord Goddard[8] and swiftly disposed of: the appeal judges all agreed that the evidence was admissible as it was 'clearly relevant to the issue of whether he [Evans] had murdered his child'. When told his appeal had failed Evans is said to have called the judges 'bloody old sods' before turning back to the prison officer with whom he was playing patience. 'Let's get on with the game.' Evans carried on playing cards and looking at picture books in Pentonville as he counted down the days to his execution. Although he continued quietly to insist that 'Christie done it' he also bragged of 'dogs and motorbikes, and that he could drink anyone to a standstill'. Evans was a present-dweller, as most people awaiting execution try to be.

No public petition was raised for Evans: merely a last-minute plea to the Home Secretary by his mother, who could only say that her son 'must have had a brainstorm'. She wisely did not try to maintain that Christie was the culprit, but still Chuter Ede refused: what else could he do with a convicted child-murderer? At 9 a.m. on 9 March 1950, having taken communion and received absolution from a Catholic priest, Timothy Evans was hanged by Albert Pierrepoint. The governor of Pentonville wrote that Evans was the only prisoner he had ever met who 'calmly and consistently maintained his innocence until execution'.

Evans's hanging was reported in a single three-line paragraph in *The Times*. The waters closed over him and the world moved on. Nobody remembered him apart from his immediate family and, one assumes, John Christie, who carried on his gloomy existence on the ground floor of Rillington Place. His illnesses became more pronounced, his trips to the doctor more frequent. Notting Hill was changing. Later in 1950 the house was sold to a new landlord, a Jamaican called Charles Brown. Brown's compatriots from Jamaica now arrived to live on the first and second floors (old Mr Kitchener had died). Their arrival was not welcomed by Christie, who claimed that poor Ethel 'was becoming very frightened from these blacks'. Christie went to the local Poor Man's Law Centre and with their help secured exclusive use of the meagre back garden. Well he might.

In March 1952 Christie spent three weeks as an inpatient at St Charles hospital suffering from 'anxiety'. In December he quit his job as a clerk, saying he and his wife were moving to Sheffield, where Ethel's sister lived, so Christie could 'better himself'. Aged fifty-three it was rather late in the day. He told neighbours that Ethel had gone ahead of him. Christie sold most of his furniture to Mr Hookway, the same Portobello Road dealer who had cleared Evans's flat. He stayed on in his rooms, now furnished only with a kitchen table, a deckchair made of string, and a mattress too dirty to sell, for another two months.

When neighbours started complaining of a bad smell and a sanitary inspector was called for, he decided to leave.[9] In March 1953 Christie told a couple called the Reillys that he owned his flat and illegally sublet it to them; by the time the landlord arrived and evicted them Christie had disappeared, taking their rent deposit of £7 13s with him. Three days later an upstairs tenant was given permission by Charles Brown to use Christie's kitchen. Knocking a bracket for his wireless into a wall he found it was a loose partition that could easily be prised open.

Behind the wall the new tenant discovered three female corpses wrapped in dark blankets and crammed into a small cavity. The police hurried to 10 Rillington Place, to carry out a rather more thorough search than the one they had conducted in December 1949. Only now, three years after Timothy Evans had been hanged, did the terrible truth – that Christie was not Evans's kindly neighbour but one of Britain's most prolific serial killers – emerge. The decomposing human remains were identified as those of three missing women – Kathleen Maloney, Rita Nelson and Hectorina MacLennan – all probable prostitutes, and murdered by Christie between January and March 1953. The body of Ethel was found under the living-room floorboards; nearby was a tobacco tin containing four locks of pubic hair. Shortly afterwards, the bodies of two more women, Ruth Fuerst and Muriel Eady, murdered by Christie in 1943 and 1944 – one with a skull in 116 pieces, one without a skull – were found buried in the little garden he had guarded so zealously. Their bodies had both been missed by the desultory police search that Evans's statements had prompted in December 1949.[10]

In 1949 Dr Teare had surmised that someone had tried to sexually penetrate Beryl Evans after her death, a detail that was then ignored as it did not easily fit with her husband murdering her; it now seemed likely that Christie had killed Beryl, having posed as an abortionist, and then attempted to have intercourse with her, and that he had later strangled Geraldine to cover his tracks. When Evans was hanged in 1950 no one knew that two of Christie's victims already lay interred in his garden.

Unlike Evans's, Christie's downfall was a media event. During a well-publicised two-week manhunt, which competed with the death of Queen Mary for press attention, Christie was apparently spotted as far afield as Brindisi, Vancouver and Bognor Regis. In the event he was arrested on 31 March on the Thames Embankment. A press cutting about the Evans case was found in his pocket. It turned out that he had only drifted as far as East Ham before checking into Rowton House, a King's Cross dosshouse at which George Orwell had stayed while writing *Down and Out in Paris and London*. He soon confessed to the killings of all the women whose bodies had been found, including Beryl Evans, though not to baby Geraldine's.

Christie's own trial for the murder of his wife (like Evans, he was only tried on one count) began at the Old Bailey on 22 June 1953, twenty days after the coronation. Christie pleaded not guilty on the basis of insanity and was defended by Derek Curtis-Bennett QC, son of the famous inter-war barrister Sir Henry Curtis-Bennett (see Chapter 3), and a colleague of Malcolm Morris in Garden Court. He told the jury that his client was 'as mad as a March hare'; it was perhaps not the most apt comparison. The Crown had sufficient good taste not to retain its Senior Treasury Counsel Christmas Humphreys to prosecute; instead the Attorney General, Sir Lionel Heald QC MP, stepped in.

Nobody had paid any attention to Evans's trial; Christie's was the sensation of the year. Just as at Robert Wood's trial almost fifty years earlier (see Chapter 1), Court Number One was 'packed with people of fame in the legal, literary, political and social worlds', come to observe at close quarters this prize specimen from the human bestiary. Two famous playwrights – Terence Rattigan and Robert Sherwood, American co-writer of the screenplay for *Rebecca* – were in attendance. Sherwood later wrote that he was impressed by the 'dignity and majesty, the clarity and equity of English justice' and the lack of 'fancy oratory and calculated histrionics'. Had Christie's trial taken place in New York, Chicago or Los Angeles the lawyers 'would be striding up and down, often soaring to the heights of forensic extravagance . . .'

When Christie's counsel informed the court that his client would go into the witness box there was a sensation. Fearful that Christie's low whisper might fool the jury into believing in his alleged madness (it had of course previously been relied upon to establish his standing as an injured war veteran), the prosecution installed a microphone to amplify his voice. Christie acted the part of the March hare well enough, pausing for thirty seconds before taking the oath and affecting all manner of tics.

Christie kept 'pulling at his ear, tugging his collar, stroking his cheek or rubbing his bald head', noted Rattigan, sitting behind counsel's benches in the City Lands rows, and ashamed to meet Christie's gaze. He answered questions about the murders he had committed with the insouciance of a man struggling to recollect whether he had visited his tailor on a Monday, or was it the Tuesday?

CURTIS-BENNETT: Did you strangle her or not?
CHRISTIE: Well, I don't know, but I must have done.
CURTIS-BENNETT: When did you have intercourse with her? It is your recollection that it was before she died, or after, or at the time?
CHRISTIE: It must have been about the time, I should think.

Dr Jack Hobson, Consultant Physician in Psychological Medicine at the Middlesex Hospital, was the only other witness called for Christie, explaining to an unsympathetic court that when he committed the killings the defendant did not know that what he was doing was legally wrong. A more accurate insight into his mental state – and into the banality of evil – would have been obtainable from one of the notes he passed from the dock to his counsel, sitting just feet away: 'I have run out of fags. Can you get me any?'

It suited Curtis-Bennett's purpose to maximise the number of killings his client had committed ('the more the merrier,' Christie said). Yet the courtroom heard from prosecution counsel that there was 'still no doubt' that Evans had killed his wife and daughter. The prosecution was, unusually, downplaying the defendant's own asserted criminality.

On 26 June Christie was – to no one's surprise – found guilty of his wife's murder, after an hour of deliberation by the jury. At the end of Evans's trial the one person who cried had been Christie himself; at the end of Christie's the only tears were shed by the trial judge, Mr Justice Finnemore, who may have been horrified by the dawning realisation that Evans, standing in the very same dock now occupied by Christie, had been sentenced to death for a murder he could not possibly have committed. Christie did not appeal, and was hanged by Pierrepoint at Pentonville on 15 July 1953, three years and four months after one of his victims, Timothy Evans, had dropped through the same trapdoor.

The story did not end there. The extraordinary fact that the chief witness for the prosecution at Evans's trial had, three years later, confessed to the murders, by the same means of strangulation, of seven women including

Beryl Evans, had a stunning effect on the nation. Never had the guilt of a man hanged for murder been more starkly called into question. Yet it took a concerted political effort to force the Home Secretary David Maxwell Fyfe, who had replaced Chuter Ede after the 1951 election, to agree to an official investigation into Evans's conviction.

The enquiry that followed took place in private. John Scott Henderson QC, whom Maxwell Fyfe appointed to conduct it, was given just eleven days in which to arrive at his conclusions, said to be required before Christie's scheduled execution. The most bizarre of the hearings which Scott Henderson convened took place on 9 July 1953 when he led an entourage, including Derek Curtis-Bennett and Malcolm Morris, to interview Christie at Pentonville, where he now occupied the same cell that Evans had before his execution in 1950. Now professing uncertainty whether he had killed anyone at all, but basking in the attention, Christie 'was the enquiry's most interesting and least productive witness'. In the knowledge that he had only days to live, still he conducted himself as if he were as much a part of the enquiry team as his interviewers. Of Beryl and Geraldine he said delphically, as if he had now disowned any form of responsibility for any of his acts, 'If somebody came up to me and told me there is a definite proof that I had something to do with one of them or both of them, I should accept it as being right, that I must have done it, but I want to know the truth about it as much as you do.'

The enquiry concluded that Christie's evidence was worthless, that the conviction of Evans for Geraldine's murder was safe, and that there was 'no ground for thinking there had been a miscarriage of justice'. The fact that these conclusions necessitated the further conclusion that there happened to be two murderers both simultaneously occupying the same dismal house in west London, and both employing the same *modus operandi*, did not appear to deter Scott Henderson from reaching them. The report was immediately seen as 'official whitewashing'. More than twenty MPs signed a motion condemning it; a supplementary report, in which Scott Henderson attempted to rebut his critics, only infuriated them further. Scott Henderson was guilty of 'abominably abusing' the evidence shown to his enquiry, which was 'little short of a shambles', Ludovic Kennedy later wrote. But the result of the enquiry allowed Maxwell Fyfe to sleep easy in his bed, secure in the knowledge that British justice was impervious to the possibility of error. The former Home Secretary James Chuter Ede could find no such comfort. During a further debate in 1955, Chuter Ede made a statement that betrayed his personal disquiet:

If ever there was a clear case when the papers came on to my table, that a man was guilty, it was the case of Evans . . . I was the Home Secretary who wrote on Evans' papers: 'The law must take its course.' I never said in 1948 that a mistake was impossible. I think Evans' case shows, in spite of all that has been done since, that a mistake was possible, and that, in the form in which the verdict was actually given on a particular case, a mistake was made.

Evans's case became the most prominent example of a miscarriage of justice of the post-war period. A sequence of books helped keep it in the spotlight. After the publication of Ludovic Kennedy's 1961 classic *Ten Rillington Place*, the new Conservative Home Secretary Rab Butler flatly refused calls for a new enquiry. Once capital punishment had been effectively abolished in 1965, an event that Evans's execution had done much to bring about (see further Chapter 7), the political and legal consequences of admitting Evans's conviction was unsafe lessened. In late 1965 the Labour Home Secretary Sir Frank Soskice finally gave way and ordered a new enquiry by a High Court judge, Sir Daniel Brabin. Symbolically, at about the same time, Evans's body was exhumed from the grounds of Pentonville, where it had lain unmarked for fifteen years, and reburied in a Roman Catholic cemetery. A change in the law now allowed executed prisoners to be reburied in consecrated ground.

Brabin arrived at the bizarre conclusion that Evans was probably guilty of the murder of Beryl but not of Geraldine, the latter crime of course being the only one for which he had been convicted. Still, on 18 October 1966 Soskice's successor Roy Jenkins finally granted Evans a posthumous free pardon. 'This final, pathetic act of redress owed little to this country's politicians and even less to its lawyers, many of whom behaved shabbily and cravenly throughout,' wrote Kennedy. Many years later, in 2003, a further investigation was carried out by Lord Brennan QC. Brennan concluded what most writers on the case had discovered decades earlier: that Evans was guilty of neither murder.[11]

Few people who knew Evans well thought him capable of murder. One former employer referred to Evans as a 'silly little thing, not at all intelligent, who could not have planned such a thing'. Others said Evans 'hadn't the guts to hurt a fly' and was 'no better and no worse than any of the young men of this district'. Jurors were told Evans was illiterate. But they were not informed that Evans had an IQ of just 68, nowadays considered borderline learning disabled (Christie's IQ, by contrast, was

128, well above average). Kennedy describes a man who could function adequately as a delivery driver, tell the time, write his own name and converse fluently, but who was unable to think analytically, predict consequences, or discern the motives of others. Evans was 'innocent of any crime save that of having a ten-and-a-half-year-old brain', he lamented. With hindsight Evans's artlessness reads like a sign of innocence, but at the time it sounded like proof of guilt.

A Scottish judge, Lord Cooper, noted in 1954 that 'In the eyes of every ordinary citizen the venue [of the police station] is a sinister one. When he stands alone in such a place confronted by several officers, usually some of high rank, the dice are loaded against him.' For a man with learning difficulties the dice were even more heavily stacked than usual. Although Evans may not have been beaten or threatened into making a false confession, he was almost certainly deprived of sleep (he told his mother that he was kept up until five in the morning at Notting Hill Police Station); Kennedy likened his treatment to brainwashing. The aggressive Jennings and the conciliatory Black seem to have played a classic 'good cop, bad cop' routine. Convinced of Evans's guilt, they were anxious to extract a full confession and move on to the five other murders they were investigating at the time. As we have seen that confession, written down by Jennings, is couched in language far removed from Evans's basic register. It would take more than thirty years before the Police and Criminal Evidence Act was enacted, effectively requiring all police interviews to be recorded.

If Evans was arrested today he would immediately be offered access to a solicitor, who would be present during his questioning; if learning difficulties were discerned, an 'appropriate adult' would also be present as a chaperon. Although he would probably be deemed fit to stand trial, most judges would go out of their way to ensure that the prosecution was not deliberately confusing him; in any case the defence would much more readily intervene to provide clarification to the defendant or request a short adjournment. All these safeguards were denied him at Notting Hill Police Station and later at the Old Bailey.

At this period, and for several decades after, it was common for the police to fix upon an early case theory and then stick to it through thick and thin. Here they believed they had their man and were anxious to sew the case up. This meant setting up Christie as a near paragon of virtue. It also meant deliberately suppressing evidence that did not suit that case. During the fatal week of 7 November workmen were on site at Rillington Place. When they were interviewed by Jennings it should have become apparent that Evans could not possibly have placed Beryl's body in the washhouse on 8 November, or Geraldine's on 10 November, as his later confessions had claimed. The workmen said they had been 'constantly in and out of the washhouse' all week, leaving it 'clean and empty' on the Friday (11 November); the floorboards behind which the bodies were concealed weren't ripped up from the hall until that Friday and weren't given to Christie for his use until Saturday or the following Monday.

Incredibly, the defence didn't even know about the workmen until Humphreys said to Morris, on the trial's first morning, 'I have a few workmen's timesheets here, but they don't seem to have any bearing on the case.' Kennedy later discovered that the workmen were recalled for further questioning. Kept waiting for three hours in Notting Hill Police Station, and anxious to get home, the workmen whose earlier statements had holed the police case reluctantly agreed to 'correct' them when told 'what you said yesterday does not quite fit with Inspector Jennings' calculations.' The existence of the earlier statements was never revealed to the defence and the workmen were not called as witnesses.

The back-to-back trials of Timothy Evans and Donald Hume reveal some of the weaknesses of the adversarial system. The respective levels of intelligence of the two defendants and their ability to withstand searching cross-examination, not by taking refuge in the truth but by the quickness (or otherwise) of their wits, undoubtedly affected their fates. The supposed guilt of Timothy Evans was established on a very narrow footing. He was alleged to have killed his daughter for reasons that were never even suggested to the jury. This question surely required an investigation into the course of his life, his relations with his wife, how his family worked as a unit. Yet the jury learned nothing of these matters. The Evans case remains the starkest example in twentieth-century legal history of a case which at face value appears overwhelming but which in fact turns out to be false. This the English trial system failed to discover. Ludovic Kennedy's study of the case left him a convinced advocate of the European inquisitorial system of justice.

7

'It is obvious that when I shot him
I intended to kill him'

R v Ruth Ellis (1955)

A N EARLIER EPOCH may be seen through different lenses. One view of the 1950s is of the Festival of Britain, Ealing comedies and Conservative Party dinner dances: a period of social cohesion and respectability before the dislocations of the 1960s. Get closer up, though, and there are rents in the canvas. We find a decade of anxiety, in which the perceived moral laxity ushered in by the Second World War, and the accelerating decline of British power and prestige, provoked successive Conservative Home Secretaries to fight rearguard actions against the onset of modernity; somehow to engineer a return to a mythical past of 'traditional values' and people behaving themselves.

We have seen in Chapter 6 how in 1953, after the Christie trial, David Maxwell Fyfe papered over doubts about the legitimacy of Timothy Evans's conviction and execution for the murder of his baby daughter with a whitewashing report that strained – in the teeth of the evidence – to uphold his guilt. Six months earlier the Home Secretary had been faced with another challenge to the death penalty as a means of judicial punishment. In December 1952 Derek Bentley and Christopher Craig had been tried at the Old Bailey before Lord Goddard for the murder of a police officer six weeks earlier. The facts of the case are well known: how Bentley, aged nineteen, but with the mind of a child, and Craig, aged sixteen but with the mentality of a hard-bitten adult, had broken into commercial premises in Croydon; how Craig, obsessed with firearms and filled with rage following the conviction of his brother on what he believed were trumped-up charges, had carried a loaded revolver; how Bentley was swiftly apprehended by one of the police officers who had arrived to investigate; how Bentley had shouted out those equivocal words, 'Let him have it, Chris'; how fifteen minutes later Craig, firing his revolver indiscriminately, had shot PC Sidney Miles between the eyes; how both were charged with murder under the doctrine of joint enterprise.

Craig and Bentley were clinically prosecuted by Christmas Humphreys, who had also led the prosecution of Evans nearly three years before, and, after a savage summing-up by the Lord Chief Justice, the jury convicted both of them, although with a recommendation of mercy for Bentley. Craig was too young to be sentenced to death and so the outcome of the trial would be, unless the Home Secretary intervened to grant a reprieve, that the man who fired the gun would live but the man who did not – and who had been in police custody for a full quarter of an hour before the shooting – would die at the hands of the state. Maxwell Fyfe overrode the jury's recommendation, a petition for clemency carrying many thousands of signatures and the expressed views of 200 Members of Parliament. The most eloquent statement made in the House of Commons was by the maverick Labour MP and QC Reginald Paget: 'A three-quarter-witted boy of nineteen is to be hanged for a murder which he did not commit and which was committed fifteen minutes after he was arrested. Can we be made to keep silent when a thing as horrible as this is happening?'

It was to no avail. In January 1953 Derek Bentley was hanged and a second miscarriage of justice scarred the decade. In his memoirs an unrepentant Maxwell Fyfe recalled that when his decision not to exercise the royal prerogative of mercy was announced it 'brought down on my head a storm of vituperation without parallel in my career'. The refusal to reprieve Bentley created a sense of national trauma which the journalist Kenneth Allsop recalled was comparable only to Dunkirk and the death of George VI. That is not to say that Maxwell Fyfe's stance was universally reviled. The killing of a policeman was (and remains) one of the great taboos. The historian David Kynaston records significant contemporary support for Bentley's hanging, quoting one diarist: 'I must say these young thugs scare the life out of me and it needs some drastic measure to make them think twice.'

Maxwell Fyfe had other preoccupations. One was homosexuality. The early 1950s witnessed a Home Office-inspired witch-hunt that counted the mathematician Alan Turing and (albeit with less tragic results) the actor John Gielgud among its more prominent victims. In December 1953 Maxwell Fyfe told the House of Commons: 'Homosexuals in general are exhibitionists and proselytizers and a danger to others, especially the young. So long as I hold the office of Home Secretary I shall give no countenance to the view that they should not be prevented from being such a danger.' A month after this pronouncement the most notorious of the anti-homosexuality prosecutions was brought against Lord Montagu of Beaulieu and two friends, Michael Pitt-Rivers and Peter Wildeblood. Over seven days in March 1954 a High Court judge, Mr Justice Ormerod, three QCs and handfuls of junior barristers and solicitors pondered whether the three defendants had incited two RAF servicemen to commit 'acts of gross indecency' in a beach hut.

The subtext of the prosecution was clear: the three defendants, all of them upper or upper middle class, had to be sacrificed *pour décourager les autres*. A lesson in comportment had to be learned by the governing classes. Wildeblood, convicted and sentenced to eighteen months in prison, would go on to write one of the defining books of the decade, *Against the Law*, which started with the arresting line, 'I am a homo-sexual', one of the first public admissions of homosexuality ever put into print in a mainstream English work. Wildeblood recounted an illegal dawn raid on his Islington house, an indiscriminate search through his private papers, the loss of his job as diplomatic correspondent for the *Daily Mail*, and the nightmare of his trial. The most upsetting moment came when, as he left court, a woman – a 'respectable-looking, middle-aged, tweedy person wearing a sensible felt hat' – spat at him. Counsel for the prosecution, the purple-jowled G.D. 'Khaki' Roberts QC – who had appeared alongside Maxwell Fyfe and Hartley Shawcross as a prosecutor at Nuremberg – went into a supercharged denunciation of metropolitan degeneracy. It is difficult to believe that such words, so heavy with snobbery and sanctimony, could have been spoken in living memory. 'They [the airmen] were willing parties to these unnatural offences, although of course they were committed under the seductive influence of lavish hospitality from these men, who were so infinitely their social superiors.'

Ironically, a few weeks earlier Roberts had acted as defence counsel for a then well-known writer, Rupert Croft-Cooke, being prosecuted on the evidence of two young soldiers claiming to have been enticed down to Croft-Cooke's Kent cottage for an illicit weekend. It was a similar story with the same sad ending: Croft-Cooke was sentenced to nine months and, on his release, retreated to Tangier. Wildeblood found Roberts's volte-face from passionate defender[1] to zealous prosecutor profoundly disconcerting. To discard one part and seamlessly assume another: it is of course a familiar charge against the barrister.

Not all Conservatives were so reactionary. Wildeblood's counsel had been a young barrister named Peter Rawlinson, later Conservative Member of Parliament for Epsom and both Solicitor General and Attorney General during the 1960s and 1970s. Another victim of the witch-hunt, the Labour MP William Field, prosecuted for soliciting in a west London lavatory in 1953, was defended *pro bono* by John Maude QC, himself a former Conservative MP. On his conviction Field, at the time a rising star of the Labour Party, resigned his seat and spent the rest of his life in obscurity. In the 1950s a criminal conviction for homosexual offences could be, in effect, a life sentence.

Another hobby-horse of Maxwell Fyfe was supposedly obscene litera-ture. After a period of comparative liberalisation during the war and under the Labour administration of 1945–51 (as Attorney General Shawcross was criticised in the House of Commons for refusing to pros-ecute Norman Mailer's novel *The Naked and the Dead*), the return of Conservative government in the early 1950s triggered a concerted effort to close down new avenues of thinking and expression. Magistrates across the country banned an extraordinarily eclectic collection of books with Savonarolan fervour: *Madame Bovary*, novels by Zola, Daniel Defoe's *Moll Flanders*, and dozens of trashy American novels. The most notorious case was at Swindon where magistrates – headed by a retired chief engineer of the Great Western Railway – condemned the fourteenth-century Florentine classic, Giovanni Boccaccio's *Decameron*, while inexplicably acquitting a less well-known work, Hank Janson's pseudo-noir *Don't Mourn Me, Toots*. In 1954 even the doyen of end-of-the-pier bawdy, the graphic artist Donald McGill, was hauled into the dock, and had twenty-four of his saucy postcards banned. The nation was to be protected from double entendres about pickled gherkins and the Oddfellows Ball.

Local action was accompanied by a concerted series of prosecutions in the Old Bailey, not – on any modern view – of pornography, but of sensitive novels of human relations, which committed the apparent sin of veering from the received notion of sex as properly occurring exclu-sively behind the closed bedroom door of the more-or-less happily married. Alan Travis, the historian of censorship in the twentieth century, explains that in 1954 there were 132 obscenity prosecutions (with 111 convictions) compared to 39 such prosecutions in 1935; in 1954, 167,000 books were destroyed, compared to 900 in the earlier year. Annually, the Home Office produced a secret 'Blue Book' in which it listed up to 4,000 titles likely to corrupt the morals of the nation for which the constabularies of Britain should keep a watch out. Alongside a series of American pulp novels bearing intriguing titles such as *Angels Bruise Easy* and *Ape-Man's Offering*, were placed in this *Index Librorum Prohibitorum* novels by Guy de Maupassant and Balzac.

Again, in these Old Bailey trials we encounter the foreign language of the past. During the prosecution of Walter Baxter's novel *The Image and the Search* (praised by E.M. Forster as 'a serious and beautiful book'), Mervyn Griffith-Jones, who would go on to find notoriety as moralist-in-chief for his role in the prosecution of *Lady Chatterley's Lover* and Stephen Ward, asked the jury a precursor to his later infamous 'wives and servants' question: 'When Christmas comes, would you go out and buy copies of the book and hand them round as presents to the girls in the office – and if not, why not? The answer is because it is not the type of book they ought to read.'

Fortunately this ludicrous question – a negative answer to which would encompass the bulk of world literature – did not persuade the jury to convict: in the end there were two successive trials which both ended with a jury failing to agree a verdict. Although after the second hung jury the DPP magnanimously decided not to pursue Baxter further, the psychological shock of appearing twice in the dock of the Old Bailey permanently scarred the author. Having published two well-received novels, Baxter wrote no more and went on to adopt the less controversial profession of restaurateur.

Helped along the way by a summing-up of shuddering bile, another Old Bailey jury was however unanimous in its verdict on an equally inoffensive work, *September in Quinze*, by the American author Vivian Connell. After Connell's novel had been found to be obscene in September 1954 the Recorder of London expressed his satisfaction with the result: 'It is a comforting thought that juries from time to time take a very solid stand against this sort of thing, and realise how important it is for the youth of this country to be protected and that the fountain of our national blood should not be polluted at its source.'[2] Well might Gerald Gardiner QC, defending counsel in *The Image and the Search* trial, tell the jury, 'Today no publisher of repute in England knows whether he is standing on his head or his heels and no author, however eminent, can write except in the shadow of the Old Bailey.' It would take the acquittal of Penguin Books in Court Number One in 1960 to bring to an end the attempted proscription of serious literature.

The public morality of the courtroom was not, of course, replicated outside it. One of the attributes of a criminal trial is an intense focus on the minutiae of a person's life, actions and motivations in the lead-up to the alleged crime. The result is often the chance preservation of intimate facts, opening a window on to the way ordinary life was lived, which might otherwise be lost to history. The proceedings of the Old Bailey in the eighteenth century present an extraordinarily vivid record of the demotic life of the period. In a similar way, the private life of Ruth Ellis, exposed to public gaze during her trial for murder at the Old Bailey in June 1955 and the subject of intense scrutiny ever since, shines a bright and unflattering light on the *moeurs* of the mid-fifties.

Although the story of Ruth's life has been told many times, much remains shadowy. She was born Ruth Neilson in 1926 to a Belgian refugee mother and a father who played the cello on transatlantic liners, and then in theatres and cinemas until the arrival of the talkies. Ruth left school – as most did then – at fourteen. The family moved from Basingstoke to wartime London, where her father took a job as a chauffeur. An early account describes the teenage Ruth as having 'the normal vanity of a girl of her age with a good figure and a pretty face'. She took a succession of the sort of jobs available to a young woman with neither qualifications nor connections. Evenings were devoted to dancing in the febrile atmosphere of a wartime London swarming with off-duty servicemen. In 1943 she met a Canadian soldier named Clare, fell in love and, in short order, became pregnant. A son, Andrea, known to all as Andy, was born in 1944. It turned out that Clare was married with three children. After he returned to Canada at the end of the war he was never heard from again. His deception broke the eighteen-year-old Ruth's heart: she would later say, 'Outwardly I was cheerful and gay. Inwardly I was cold and spent.'

But Ruth was not going to let the burdens and social stigma of single parenthood hold her back. While Andy was cared for by her sister Muriel, or by her mother, she started working as a model for a camera club, no doubt featuring in 'artistic' semi-clothed compositions by a succession of middle-aged *amateurs* of the genre. From there Ruth graduated to working as a hostess at the Court Club in Duke Street, off Oxford Street, owned by a then notorious underworld figure called Morris Conley. She was just nineteen and had reached her full height, a petite five feet two inches. She soon became known for her well-coiffed and strikingly made-up appearance, though was yet to acquire her peroxide hair. The Court Club was one of many such establishments that had sprung up in London in the 1940s, where men could while away the afternoon and evening drinking, flirting and, for a price, getting to know the hostesses more intimately at the digs Conley housed them in. But there were far worse places. Ruth could earn up to £20 a week – £5 basic with 10 per cent on all purchases made by 'her' customers, plus tips – simply by looking glamorous and showing interest in the punters. She was good at it.

Ruth's years at the Court Club came to an end when she married, in November 1950, one of its members: an alcoholic, semi-suicidal dentist in his late forties, recently divorced by his wife on grounds of cruelty. Ruth's decision to marry George Ellis – known to all the hostesses as 'the Mad Dentist' – is only partly explicable by his relative wealth and largesse. He might not have been most young women's idea of a catch, romantic or otherwise; but he offered a semblance of normality, stability and a big step up the social ladder to a woman on the furthest margin of even a semi-respectable life. Yet Ruth seems to have genuinely loved him, if only for a time; in lieu of a honeymoon she insisted he enter a mental hospital for treatment. The marriage was the inevitable disaster. Ellis's alcoholism only got worse and led to violent episodes. Ruth experienced her first – and last – taste of provincial married life, playing the part of housewife on the outskirts of Southampton. It was not a role that suited her. At this time she also demonstrated a side to her character that would later prove significant: she became obsessively jealous that her husband was cheating on her, to the point of hiring cars to ferry her to the supposed locations of his illicit rendezvous.

After yet another terrible row, Ruth went back to her parents in London, now four months pregnant and with Andy in tow, while Ellis returned to hospital for treatment for his addiction. The arrival of a daughter, Georgina, in October 1951, did nothing to improve marital relations. Morris Conley gave Ruth her old job back at the Court Club, now renamed Carroll's and with its licence extended from 11 p.m. to 3 a.m. Her life now became a dual existence: the week spent in Mayfair, staying at a flat provided by Conley, and then returning to Brixton to play the role of mother to her two children at the weekend. Conley was sufficiently impressed with Ruth's relearned capacity to fascinate the clientele – it was as if she had buried the debacle of her failed marriage beneath a veneer of forced vivacity – that in the autumn of 1953 he offered her a new job as the manageress of another club he owned, the Little Club, occupying the first floor of a house in the Brompton Road, just by Harrods. Ruth accepted happily – the job came with a flat above, where she could live with her son and daughter. It was now that she bleached her hair for the first time (her peroxided contemporary, Marilyn Monroe, had just achieved global celebrity with her roles in *Niagara* and *Gentlemen Prefer Blondes* earlier that year) and created the look for which she will for ever be remembered.

The Little Club's clientele was predominantly made up of a louche motor-racing crowd, inclined to good-natured rowdiness and hard drinking: a sort of de-sanitised version of the characters in the film *Genevieve*, which was released in the same year. One of its regulars was the twenty-four-year-old David Blakely, a boyish amateur racing driver who came from a prosperous if fractured family background: his father, a general practitioner, and mother had divorced when he was eleven on grounds of Dr Blakely's serial adultery, and his mother had gone on to marry Humphrey Wyndham Cook, a wealthy businessman whose own passion for motor racing was transferred to the young David.

Blakely's face, so familiar from the now iconic photographs of him and Ruth, was weakly handsome; it seemed to betray a complacent sense of upper-middle-class entitlement mixed with chronic idleness. He had proved a dull scholar at Shrewsbury and, despite the best efforts of his well-connected stepfather, was unable – or rather unwilling – to hold down a job that involved any form of serious application. By the time he met Ruth, in late 1953, he was notionally working for an engineering company in Penn – the manicured village in Buckinghamshire where his mother and stepfather now lived – but it was little more than a sinecure. Outside motor racing his principal pleasures were spending money, vacuous horseplay (of the ice-cubes down the back and soda-syphon squirting variety) and sex.

'Who is that pompous little ass?' asked Ruth when she first spotted Blakely in the Little Club. But within days of meeting, Ruth and Blakely became bound up in an intensely sexual relationship: Blakely soon started bragging that Ruth was 'one of the finest fucks in town'. While maintaining a flat at the family home in Penn Blakely would stay during the week at Ruth's flat above the club. He had already burned through the bulk of a £7,000 inheritance from his father, who had died the year before, in building a prototype motor-racing car – the Emperor, as it was grandiloquently styled – which would have its first outing late in 1954 at Brands Hatch.

Blakely's profligate spending meant that he was soon sponging off Ruth. His carelessness was not just financial. Blakely had no conception of sexual continence or emotional loyalty; some weeks after he had started his on-off ménage with Ruth, an engagement to the daughter of a Huddersfield wool manufacturer was announced in *The Times*. And there were other women as well.

It is difficult to comprehend why the older and wiser Ruth, by now well versed in the ways of the world, was so attracted to a spineless wastrel like Blakely. But undoubtedly she fell for him in grand fashion, and for Blakely her maturity and worldliness may well have been a welcome change from the chirruping debutantes he met in Buckinghamshire society. Yet one thing was clear in his mind: Ruth was a nightclub manageress, a *demi-mondaine* far removed from his comfortable social milieu, and he was determined to keep his relations with her separate from his home life. Although Ruth accompanied Blakely to some of his race meetings the social gulf between her and the wives and girlfriends of his associates must have been painfully obvious to her. It was a gulf that Blakely did nothing to hide or cross.

As the relationship continued Blakely's money worries and drinking worsened. He became more and more careless. He would deride her in front of her customers at the Little Club, flaunting his social superiority while treating her as a 'well of free drinks', which she paid for. When Conley learned that Blakely had effectively moved in upstairs he started charging Ruth a rent for her flat; again Blakely made no move to help out. When Ruth organised a party for Blakely's twenty-fifth birthday at the club he did not bother to show up.

The beatings started early on. They may have been prompted by jealousy or Blakely's sense of wretchedness about his financial reliance on Ruth. Whatever it was, Ruth's limbs and shoulders bore the bruises of his blows, which she strove to conceal with make-up. After a bout of violence Blakely would stalk off, only to play the contrition card, tearful and full of promises about the future, the next day. Ruth would forgive him and the familiar cycle would restart. And even in the face of Blakely's brutality her devotion to him only increased. 'Even when other women were there he would smack my face and punch me. When we were alone, it was worse. I took it all because I loved him so much,' she would go on to explain. When George Ellis proposed to take custody of their daughter Ruth accepted; Georgina was later adopted. In a later statement she said: 'It was a measure of my love for David that I was prepared to give up my child.'

Ruth's tenure as manageress of the Little Club had started off a great success. But as 1954 wore on her mood was changing. She had an abortion (illegal, of course) in March, which Blakely neither sought to prevent nor offered to pay for. Their relationship had become destructive and dark and it took its toll on Ruth, not just physically but mentally. She was tense, drinking heavily herself and chain-smoking. Takings were down and Conley was getting restive. Blakely could not bear her interchanges with the Little Club's male clientele and wanted her to quit, though he had no proposals to support her. Whether she was sacked or left of her own accord, Ruth ceased to work as the manageress in December 1954. She moved to a nearby flat owned by another motor-racing crony and Little Club member called Desmond Cussen.

Cussen was a wealthy company director with a pencil moustache that made him look much older than his thirty-three years. In mid-1954, when Ruth was angry with Blakely's prolonged absence on a racing trip to Le Mans, she had allowed Cussen to make love to her. Blakely's return brought an end to their sexual relations without dimming Cussen's ardour or his willingness to help her. Cussen, who had been a bomber pilot during the war, was everything Blakely wasn't: quiet, respectful, financially careful. While Blakely thought nothing of sponging off Ruth, in the autumn of 1954 'Uncle Desmond' stepped forward to pay for Andy to go to a boarding school.

There were moments when the light dawned on Ruth. In a recording she made of a drunken conversation with Cussen on New Year's Day 1955 (Cussen had given her a tape recorder as a Christmas present), she is heard to say, in a surprisingly smart voice: 'I'm still glad it's all over and done with anyway. No, seriously. He's a cheapskate. I think he'd fuck anything, don't you? . . . He's the lowest of the low.' Yet Blakely's pull was unbreakable. Telling Cussen she was going to see Georgina, Ruth would meet Blakely in hotels to carry on their affair. The arguments continued; each would tell others that they wanted to break off; but time and again they would come back together.

In February 1955 Ruth moved from Cussen's flat into a furnished room in a boarding house at 44 Egerton Gardens in Knightsbridge. Ruth now had no job, no income and no permanent home. She rarely saw her family and friends. Obsessive thoughts about Blakely filled the void. 'The tables had been turned,' said Ruth at her trial. 'I was jealous of him whereas he, before, had been jealous of me.' The gnawing jealousy that had consumed her during her marriage to George Ellis returned, this time with full justification, given Blakely's open promiscuity. The docile Cussen would willingly ferry her about in his car as she went in search of Blakely at the addresses of his supposed latest girlfriend. It was a ludicrous, demeaning position for Cussen to be in: chauffeur for the woman *he* was in love with on her quest to discover the whereabouts of the man *she* was in love with; yet he seems to have accepted it without question.

There were inevitable confrontations. 'What about hitting a man instead of a woman?' Cussen once asked Blakely angrily in a pub car park: Blakely just scuttled away. Blakely complained to his friends that he was being hounded by his ex-lover, that although Ruth was still in love with him, he 'hated her guts'. Yet still he kept returning to her and still Ruth had him back. And the violence went on. A French teacher with whom Ruth started a course of lessons at the time – she did not finish them – thought she was on the verge of a nervous breakdown. Ruth explained away the livid bruising on her arm and leg as the consequences of a car accident.

In March 1955 Ruth found that she was pregnant yet again. After Blakely punched her in the stomach, she miscarried. She later reported the following exchange:

'You'll never have any luck, the way you treat me. I'll stand so much from you, David, but you can't go on walking over me for ever.'

'You'll stand it because you love me.'

For several nights at the end of March and the start of April 1955 Blakely stayed at Egerton Gardens. On the face of it their tempestuous relationship had reached a small island of stability. Ruth was now divorced and Blakely was making positive noises about marriage. But things soured when the Emperor broke down before a race at Chester ('You jinxed me!' Blakely shouted at Ruth). Blakely then cadged another £5 from Ruth, money she could now ill afford. She learned that he spent it on drinks at the Steering Wheel Club, while she lay in bed, suffering the after-effects of her miscarriage.

On 8 April, Good Friday, Blakely left in the morning to go to work on the Emperor, promising to call for her later. All seemed well. Come the evening he did not show up: instead he was sitting in a pub in South Hampstead, the Magdala Tavern, with his close friends Carole and Anthony Findlater, who lived in nearby Tanza Road, a quiet street close to the Heath. The Findlaters heartily disliked Ruth, whom they saw as a disaster for their friend. As Ruth waited at Egerton Gardens for Blakely's return, they were persuading him to make a final break with her and offering him a bed in their flat as a refuge for the weekend.

As the minutes ticked by Ruth telephoned the Findlaters' Hampstead number. Eventually Anthony picked up the receiver. No, David was not there, he lied in a voice that made no attempt to conceal laughing contempt for Ruth's situation. Humiliation and anger boiled up inside her. She hailed the ever faithful Desmond Cussen to drive her up to Hampstead that night. Outside the Tanza Road flat Ruth, furious now, made a scene, as Blakely cowered inside, and then stove in the windows of his car, parked in the street. After Findlater had called a police officer she eventually returned to Egerton Gardens. Ruth did not go to bed. She sat in a chair, smoking, waiting for the dawn. 'I just sat and howled. I no longer thought of David as the man I loved, but as someone who was trying to make a fool of me. I felt humiliated and frustrated.'

The next day, the Saturday, Ruth's calls again went unanswered. She returned to Tanza Road and kept a watch on the flat. Ruth had now convinced herself that Blakely was carrying on with the Findlaters' nineteen-year-old nanny. She returned to Egerton Gardens and brooded further. That evening Cussen drove her yet again to the Findlaters' flat. The sounds of laughter and jazz records spilled into the road. Blakely's ebullient voice seemed to provoke female laughter from inside the flat. He came out with the nanny; they drove off, who knew where. The sense of exclusion from his world, and the injustice of that exclusion, was overwhelming.

Ruth spent another sleepless night at Egerton Gardens. Blakely's crimes – the violence, the derision, the carelessness, the rejection and now the cowardly refusal to face her – seemed to demand retribution. 'I had an overwhelming and peculiar desire to kill David,' she later told the Old Bailey. The next day – it was now Easter Sunday – after yet another futile attempt to call the Findlaters, at some point she settled on a plan. She and her son spent the day with Cussen. That evening, having tucked Andy into his camp-bed at Egerton Gardens and kissed him goodnight, fully made-up and wearing a two-piece black suit, she went back again to Tanza Road. This time she carried in her bag a .38 Smith and Wesson revolver loaded with six bullets.

Another impromptu party was in full swing at the Findlaters' flat. Blakely and a racing friend, Clive Gunnell, volunteered to go down to the Magdala for fresh supplies. They drove in Blakely's car, parking just outside the pub, and entered the saloon bar in high spirits. There was time for a quick drink while they were there. It was just after 9 p.m. and the air was warm. An off-duty police constable drinking inside, Alan Thompson, noticed a blonde-haired woman pressing her face to the window, as if trying to find someone, before disappearing into the dusk. Five minutes later the two men left the pub carrying cigarettes and some beer. Ruth was waiting outside, her back to the wall.

As Blakely went to open the car door he saw her. He turned his head away, a final act of indifference. Ruth took out the revolver from her handbag and approached him. He now noticed the gun and started running round the back of the car into the road. She followed and, from a distance of yards, fired. Blakely staggered and continued running. 'Get out of the way, Clive,' Ruth shouted. Further shots rang out. Blakely reached the pavement and fell, face-first. The bottles flew from his grasp and smashed. As he lay on the ground Ruth fired two further shots into him. In all, four bullets had entered or hit his body. Gunnell screamed out, 'Why did you kill him? Why didn't you kill me? What good is he to you dead? You'll both die now.' Ruth raised the gun to her temple as if to shoot herself. She was unable to press the trigger. She turned the gun away and fired randomly. The bullet ricocheted off the pavement, hitting a passer-by, Gladys Yule, in the thumb. Ruth stood passively while Gunnell raised Blakely's head, blood pouring from his mouth, mingling with the spilled beer. 'Will you call the police?' she calmly asked him. PC Thompson, startled by the sound of gunfire, had by now come out of the Magdala, and he gently took the gun from Ruth's hand.

Blakely was dead by the time the ambulance came. Two of the bullets had caused fatal injuries, one puncturing the lung before lodging in his mouth. As they waited for a police car to arrive Thompson did what at the time all English men seemed to do in a moment of crisis: he offered Ruth a cigarette. Later, at Hampstead Police Station Ruth, entirely composed, gave a statement. It started: 'I am guilty. I am rather confused.' But she was also unequivocal: 'When I put the gun in my bag I intended to find David and shoot him.'

She was charged with the murder of David Blakely shortly afterwards. 'Thanks,' she replied.

The fatal shooting by a peroxide blonde of a racing driver wearing his old school tie on a London street was about as good as it could get for Fleet Street. A solicitor, John Bickford, was swiftly appointed, to be paid for by the *Sunday Mirror*, in return for exclusive rights to Ruth's 'life story'. When he managed to reach Ruth, now in Holloway prison, he found a woman who would prove a difficult client. She insisted on her guilt with the implacability of an Old Testament prophet. 'An eye for an eye; a life for a life. I took David's life and I don't ask you to save mine. I don't want to live.' Yet she also insisted on her righteousness. She did not regret what she had done; about this Ruth remained adamant throughout the weeks that followed. David Blakely deserved his fate. But she still loved him and kept a photo of him while in prison. She told Bickford she wanted now to 'be with David'. When a plea of not guilty was registered at the committal hearing in Hampstead Magistrates Court she remonstrated with her counsel afterwards. 'Why do you say I am not guilty when I am? I killed him, and I've got to die for it.'

The principal reason Ruth was eventually persuaded to maintain a plea of not guilty was because she wanted her trial to constitute a record of the reasons why she had shot Blakely. A guilty plea would preclude her from giving her account in a courtroom. 'All I want is that the jury should hear my full story,' she wrote to a friend shortly before her trial. There was also a secondary reason. Ruth had developed a fanatical belief that the Findlaters had poisoned Blakely's mind against her by convincing him of the madness of his association with a nightclub hostess. She wanted their role in taking him from her to be exposed. In a letter she wrote to Blakely's mother just two days after the shooting she explained:

> No doubt you will hear all kinds of stories regarding David and myself. Please do forgive him for deceiving you as regarding myself. David and I have spent many happy times together . . . Friday morning at ten o'clock he left and promised to return at eight o'clock, but never did. The two people I blame for David's death, and my own, are the Findlaters. No doubt you will not understand this but perhaps before I hang you will know what I mean.[3]

As far as the police were concerned the case was a simple one. Having interviewed Cussen and a host of others who had known Ruth and Blakely, the police officer in charge of the case, Detective Chief Inspector Leslie Davies, sent his report to the Director of Public Prosecutions:

> This is clearly a case of jealousy on the part of Ellis, coupled with the fear that Blakely was leaving her . . . The two people concerned, Blakely and Ellis, are of completely different stations in life . . . On meeting Blakely and realising that his class was much above her own, and finding him sufficiently interested in her to live with her and, if we are to believe Cussen, to promise her marriage, it seems she was prepared to go to any lengths to keep him. Finding this impossible, she appears to have decided to wreak her vengeance upon him . . . It is certain that her action was coldly premeditated.

Just as Peter Wildeblood's crime had sprung from his willingness to consort with his inferiors, so the origin of Ruth Ellis's crime was, in the eyes of the police, her aspiration to consort with her superiors – as if social miscegenation led ineluctably to criminality and moral ruin.

Peter Rawlinson had put up a brave defence of Wildeblood in the early spring of 1954. A year later he now found himself instructed as junior counsel for Ruth Ellis. In his memoirs, written almost forty years later, he remembered going to see Ruth in the cells below the Old Bailey after a short hearing in Court Number One in May which had been convened to fix the trial date.

> At that time, to go down to the cells, a barrister, provided that he was in robes, could enter the dock in the court and go down the steps inside the dock which lead to the corridors which run beneath the court. There prisoners in custody are kept to await the start of their trial or the verdict of the jury. The surroundings were grim. The air reflected the tensions and anxieties which were daily experienced in that place.

There Rawlinson met Ruth, to explain what had happened in the court above. She offered him a small, limp hand. He remembered her words: 'You will make certain, won't you, that I shall be hanged. That is the only way I can join him.'

> A little while later I shook her hand and left her with Bickford. I climbed up the steep stairs into the large dock of No 1 Court where a trial was being heard. As I appeared as though from the floor and moved to the door of the dock and was let out by a warder, the judge glanced up and then back to his notes. The traffic of counsel between court and the cells was quite usual. But I felt greatly disturbed.

Ruth's death wish found other expressions. As the weeks went by in Holloway her roots grew out in their natural brown and the peroxide faded. She was desperate that at her trial she should present to the courtroom as she had presented in her former life. She did not wish to be remembered as dishevelled or unkempt. She must exit life's stage proud and radiant. The governor of Holloway gave permission for her hairdressers to send in the materials. A wardress helped to dye and set her hair. It was glorious, but it was not going to help persuade a jury.

In 1955 there were, apart from simple denial, four defences potentially available to a defendant accused of murder. The first was insanity. The then legal definition of insanity for these purposes, as enshrined in the so-called M'Naghten[4] rule, which had been propounded by the judges as long ago as 1843, was so narrow that virtually nobody could get themselves within its boundaries.[5] Although juries had shown a willingness to bend this rule to save defendants from the gallows[6] it surely was not wide enough, even under its most liberal interpretation, to encompass Ruth. More to the point, when Bickford had suggested this to her as a possible defence she had emphatically proclaimed her sanity. 'It's no good. I was sane when I did it, and I meant to do it.' The second defence was accident. Where Ruth had pulled the trigger six times and had later confirmed her intentions to the police, that was implausible. The third was self-defence, which plainly did not arise. The fourth was provocation. As the law stood in 1955, the most authoritative statement of the law on provocation was contained in the recent case of *R v Duffy* in which Mr Justice Devlin had ruled that 'Provocation is some act, or series of acts, done by the dead man to the accused, which would cause in any reasonable person, and actually causes in the accused, a sudden and temporary loss of self-control, rendering the accused so subject to passion as to make him or her for the moment not master of his mind.' If provocation was established the offence of murder was reduced to manslaughter.

By the time of the trial John Bickford had instructed Melford Stevenson QC to lead Ruth Ellis's defence. It was a strange choice. Stevenson was mainly known as a divorce barrister, not a criminal one, and had apparently never appeared at the Old Bailey before. He had stood unsuccessfully as a Conservative candidate against Tom Driberg in the 1945 general election and went on to become a notably harsh judge, known for his acid tongue. Later dubbed by a colleague as 'the worst judge since the war', his obituary in *The Times* noted that his description of a rape case he was trying as 'a rather anaemic affair as rape goes' drew widespread protests.

In the run-up to the trial Bickford prepared very detailed instructions for counsel and a thorough proof of Ruth's evidence (in effect, her witness statement, except that in a criminal trial this is not put before the court but is prepared for counsel's benefit), which delineated in fine detail the history of her relationship with Blakely, upon which Stevenson could cross-examine the Crown witnesses, and question Ruth herself in her examination-in-chief. But as Stevenson swept through the Grand Hall of the Old Bailey to the door of Court Number One on the morning of the trial's first day, 20 June 1955, he saw Bickford and stopped. 'I am not going to cross-examine the witnesses,' he said breezily, as he took his seat in counsel's row. Bickford was horrified. His whole approach to the case depended on saturating the jury with the shocking details of the relationship between Ruth and Blakely. There was no time to remonstrate. Three knocks rapped on the door behind the judge's bench and Mr Justice Cecil Havers came into court.

When Ruth Ellis, peroxided and wearing a white blouse and black suit, was brought up into the dock she was unlike anybody Court Number One had seen for years. The quiet hum of chatter stopped dead in its tracks. As at Christie's trial two years earlier, seats in the public gallery were occupied by what the journalist Robert Hancock, who was present throughout, described as 'direct descendants of the patrons of the Roman Circus'. The press benches were packed with reporters from across Europe and North America as well as Britain. 'Blonde tart!' someone called out, but Ruth showed no reaction. When she said, 'Not guilty,' in a voice that seemed to carry very little conviction, Bickford's only hope was that the jury would accept that Ruth had been goaded, humiliated and abused beyond endurance by Blakely. That hope would be very quickly snuffed out. Duncan Webb, attending the trial for the *People*, recorded that it had been some time since the Old Bailey had witnessed such a 'fashionable' murder trial. If by that he meant a trial of upper-class misdoings, high emotion and rhetorical fireworks – that is, all the ingredients that gave the trials of Madame Fahmy and Elvira Barney such high entertainment value – then in the event there was nothing fashionable about it at all.

The prosecution was led by Senior Treasury Counsel Christmas Humphreys, who opened with a short speech 'laced with enough spice and interest to command the jury's attention and to keep . . . reporters constantly on the telephone to their offices'. Behind him sat two juniors, Mervyn Griffith-Jones – who would replace Humphreys as Senior Treasury Counsel in 1958 – and a young woman barrister, Jean Southworth, later to become a well-known silk and judge.

Humphreys' presentation was as reductive, and as effective, now as it had been five years earlier when he prosecuted Timothy Evans. The right to open in a criminal case has been described as a priceless asset; the first words the jury hears can set a tone that is difficult to dislodge. One eminent barrister's advice was to the point: 'Tell a plain story; put it in language easily understood.' The jury starts (in theory at least) from a position of complete ignorance. It knows nothing about the case apart from what the prosecutor chooses to tell it when they stand up for the first time at the start of a trial. Humphreys had learned this wisdom.

Mrs Ellis is a woman of twenty-eight, divorced and the story which you are going to hear outlined is this; that in 1954 and 1955 she was having simultaneous love affairs with two men, one of whom was the deceased, the other a man called Cussen, who I shall call before you.

It would seem that, lately, Blakely, the deceased man, was trying to break off the connection, and that the accused woman was angry at the thought that he should leave her, even though she had another lover at the time. She therefore took a gun which she knew to be loaded, which she put in her bag. She says in a statement which she signed: 'When I put the gun in my bag, I intended to find David and shoot him.'[7] She found David and she shot him dead by emptying that revolver at him, four bullets going into his body, one hitting a bystander in the hand, and the sixth going we know not where.

That, in a very few words, is the case for the Crown, and nothing else I say to you, in however much detail, will add to the stark simplicity of that story.

These words provide as good an illustration as any of how the complexity of real human relations can be occluded by the language of the courtroom. Simplicity may be a powerful forensic device but it is also one that can obscure and even misrepresent the truth. Humphreys' opening speech lasted no more than twenty-five minutes. Its central theme was of a woman enjoying the benefits of two lovers; it made not one mention of the abuse that Ruth had experienced. The murder seemed an act of caprice. We may praise it as advocacy but deprecate it as a fair account of the events leading to Blakely's death.

As is usual the prosecution evidence started with the uncontentious witnesses. A plan of the area of the shooting was produced. A police officer produced photographs he had taken of Blakely's corpse, placed on a white sheet. The boyishness was gone, replaced by the pallor of death. The jury were surely shocked by the blackness of the wounds cratering the white skin. The landlady of 44 Egerton Gardens mentioned that Blakely, under the assumed name of Mr Ellis (no unmarried couples on her premises), had lived with Ruth from time to time.

Desmond Cussen had been Ruth's most constant and devoted friend. After the shooting he had been a regular visitor to Ruth while she was in Holloway, bringing her flowers, chocolates, cigarettes. It is a shock therefore to find him being called as a witness for the prosecution. He took his oath, perspiring and pale. 'His black hair-line moustache stood out so clearly that it seemed to have been painted on,' noted Hancock. Ruth stared at him. Cussen gave an anaemic account to Humphreys of his friendship with Ruth over the last two years. He wound up by explaining that, after spending Easter Sunday with Ruth and her son, he had dropped her back at Egerton Gardens in the early evening. That was the last time he had seen her before the shooting.

As Cussen was a Crown witness, Stevenson now had the opportunity to cross-examine him widely about the abuse he had witnessed and Ruth's state of mind in the run-up to the shooting. Here is the cross-examination in full.

STEVENSON: You have told the jury that you and this young woman were lovers for a short time in June 1954. Is that right?

CUSSEN: Yes.

STEVENSON: And that was the time when Blakely was away, was it not – at the Le Mans race in France.

CUSSEN: Yes.

STEVENSON: Were you very much in love with this young woman?

CUSSEN: I was terribly fond of her at the time, yes.

STEVENSON: Did she tell you from time to time that she would like to get away from Blakely, but could not, or words to that effect?

CUSSEN: Yes.

STEVENSON: And at that time did she repeatedly go back to him?

CUSSEN: Yes.

STEVENSON: At a time when you were begging her to marry you if she could?

CUSSEN: Yes.

STEVENSON: Have you ever seen any marks or bruises on her?

CUSSEN: Yes.

STEVENSON: How often?

CUSSEN: On several occasions.

STEVENSON: How recently before Easter had you seen marks of that kind?

CUSSEN: On one occasion when I was taking her to a dance . . . on 25 February.

STEVENSON: Did you help to disguise bruises on her shoulders?

CUSSEN: Yes.

STEVENSON: Were they bad bruises?

CUSSEN: Yes and they required quite heavy make-up, too.

STEVENSON: I do not want to press you for details, but how often have you seen that sort of mark on her?

CUSSEN: It must be on half-a-dozen occasions.

STEVENSON: Did you on one occasion take her to the Middlesex Hospital?

CUSSEN: Yes I did.

STEVENSON: Why was that?

CUSSEN: She came back when she was staying at my flat, and when I arrived back I found her in a very bad condition.
STEVENSON: In what respect?
CUSSEN: She had definitely been very badly bruised all over her body.
STEVENSON: Did she receive treatment for that condition at Middlesex Hospital?
CUSSEN: Yes.

And that was it. This was the cross-examination of the tea-table. Stevenson's fastidiousness and distaste for the mire of human relations overcame professional obligation: 'I do not want to press you for details'! It was only through the patient, relentless accretion of precisely such details, the filling in of the canvas with all the dozens of incidents and conversations that Cussen could testify to, that the jury would learn how much Humphreys' opening had failed to depict the truth of the matter. But Cussen was gone.

Next, Anthony Findlater, bearded in the rakish fifties style, stepped into the witness box. Findlater had been Blakely's best friend and racing colleague. The two of them had laboured long hours over the construction of the Emperor, Blakely paying him a weekly wage to work on it. Findlater, married to an ambitious journalist, and the father of a baby daughter at the time of the shooting (to whom Blakely was godfather), had always been mystified by Blakely's on-off infatuation with Ruth. It was Findlater and his wife whom Ruth blamed, with some justification, for trying to prise Blakely from her.

Findlater gave evidence that was suffused with smouldering hatred of the killer of his friend. To build a case based on provocation Stevenson had to establish Ruth's state of mind in the forty-eight hours before the shooting. He asked about the phone calls made by Ruth to the Tanza Road flat on the Good Friday evening.

STEVENSON: Was it quite plain when you spoke to her on the telephone that she was in a desperate state of emotion?
FINDLATER [in a truculent, indifferent voice]: No.
STEVENSON [incredulous]: What?
FINDLATER [pettily proud that he was standing up to Stevenson]: I said no.
STEVENSON: Do you mean she was quite calm? Do you really mean that?
FINDLATER: It was just a telephone conversation. She rang me up, as she had done hundreds of times, and asked if I knew where David was. It was just a telephone conversation.

This flat tone continued for a few minutes before Stevenson gave up. 'Everyone was now waiting for Mr Stevenson to slow down the rapid speed at which the trial was moving,' recalled Hancock. But he didn't. Nothing was asked about Ruth's life with Blakely. Bickford, who had been sitting in front of Stevenson in the well of the court, later explained in a television interview that this failure was 'absolutely horrifying'.

The final pieces in the jigsaw were fitted in. Clive Gunnell recreated the confusion of the last seconds of Blakely's life. Lewis Nickolls, the Metropolitan Police's firearms expert, testified that all the bullets he had found had come from the same gun. One had been fired into Blakely from a distance of three inches. The courtroom seemed to catch its breath; there were 'controlled whistles' from the public gallery. The implication was clear: Ruth had fired on Blakely again as he lay wounded on the pavement, face down. The off-duty police officer, PC Thompson, recalled how he had seen a blonde woman pressing her face against the window of the saloon bar of the Magdala. The gunshots came five minutes later. He left his drink to investigate: there was Blakely lying prostrate, moaning, blood flooding from his mouth.

A pathologist explained the trajectories of the rounds. At least four had hit Blakely. The cause of death? 'Shock and haemorrhage.'

DCI Davies, the officer who led the investigation, spoke of the interview he had had with Ruth later on Sunday night. 'Did you form any impression of her emotional condition at that time?' asked Humphreys.

'I did. I was most impressed by the fact that she seemed very composed.'

The statement she had given and signed was read out. The case for the Crown was closed by lunchtime of the first day. It had taken less than two and a half hours. Whispering to one another, the journalists left the court for their pints of bitter and ham sandwiches at the Magpie and Stump, the affectionately titled 'courtroom number 10' opposite the Bailey.

That afternoon Stevenson stood up to explain Ruth's defence to the jury. Allowing for the fact that at the time barristers' diction seemed to lag about thirty years behind contemporary speech, it now reads rather well:

She is charged with murder, and one of the ingredients in that offence is what lawyers call malice; and the law of England, in its mercy, provides that if a person finding themselves in the position in which this unhappy young woman now is, has been the subject of such emotional disturbance operating upon her mind so as for the time being to unseat her judgment, to inhibit and cut off those sensors which ordinarily control our conduct, then it is open to you, the jury who are charged with the dreadful duty of trying her, to say that the offence of which she is guilty is not the offence of murder, but the offence of manslaughter.

Criminal lawyers generally say that cross-examination is easier than the examination of one's own witnesses. As Richard du Cann QC, a notable post-war criminal lawyer, put it in his celebrated book *The Art of the Advocate*: 'Ideally an examination should be a form of "spontaneous conversation" between examiner and examined . . . He must never forget that the first few minutes in a witness-box can be terrifying. It is the loneliest place on earth. If the examiner does not then appear as a friend, it is unlikely he will ever be able to get everything he wants from the witness or give him the opportunity to appear in the best light.'

Ruth walked from the dock to the witness box with 'high-heeled clicking'. Helena Kennedy has written that whenever a defendant makes that journey 'there is always a strong sense of anticipation; you can almost feel it, especially in a murder trial. For the defending counsel this is the moment to turn the case round and view it from a different perspective.' But Ruth was not in harmony with Stevenson. There was a gulf of misunderstanding between them. Instead of engaging in a 'spontaneous conversation', they seemed to be battling against each other.

Admittedly, Stevenson had a very hard task. He was seeking a verdict of not guilty of murder hampered by a client who seemed to will the opposite. Perhaps the events of the trial's first morning had made Ruth give up hope. Perhaps her residual love for the man she had shot made her shy away from overt criticism of him.

STEVENSON: As time went on, how did he show his feelings for you?
ELLIS: In the December of that year [1953] I had an abortion by him and he was very concerned about my welfare. Although he was engaged to another girl, he offered to marry me, and he said it seemed unnecessary for me to get rid of the child, but I did not want to take advantage of him.
STEVENSON: When he offered to marry you, what did you say to that? How did you take it?
ELLIS: I was not really in love with him at the time and it was quite unnecessary to marry me. I thought I could get out of the mess quite easily.
STEVENSON [perturbed]: What mess?
ELLIS: I decided I could get out of the mess quite easily.

JUDGE: You mean the child?

ELLIS: Yes.

As to the violence inflicted on her:

> STEVENSON: By October 1954, was there a further change in his behaviour towards you? How did he treat you physically?
>
> ELLIS: He was violent on occasions . . . It was always because of jealousy in the bar. At the end of the evening when we got upstairs, it was always about the things he had been seeing me do, and so on and so forth.
>
> STEVENSON: How did this violence manifest itself?
>
> ELLIS: He only used to hit me with his fists and his hands, but I bruise very easily and I was full of bruises on many occasions.
>
> STEVENSON: In February of this year, was there another scene?
>
> ELLIS: Yes, we had been drinking quite a lot.
>
> STEVENSON: And did you sustain injuries?
>
> ELLIS: I sprained an ankle, got lots of bruises and a black eye. But I think David realised he had gone too far, for I was really hurt.
>
> STEVENSON: The next day, did Mr Cussen take you to Middlesex Hospital to have the injuries treated?
>
> ELLIS: Yes.
>
> STEVENSON: After this scene, Blakely sent you carnations?
>
> ELLIS: Yes.
>
> STEVENSON: Was this card enclosed? [handed to Ruth]
>
> ELLIS: Yes.
>
> STEVENSON: Please read it.
>
> ELLIS: 'Sorry, darling, I love you. David.'
>
> STEVENSON: After this you made up your quarrel?
>
> ELLIS: Yes. I took the flat in Egerton Gardens, and David came to live with me.

This was disastrous evidence. Ruth was hardly helping her case with her persistent downplaying of Blakely's violence. It was Stevenson's task to overcome this. But his use of the words 'scene' and 'quarrel' – these were Stevenson's own terms – trivialised what had happened and converted the persistent and endemic into the episodic. References to flowers and cards seemed to imply closure (and redemption) where there was none. The phrase 'you made up your quarrel' suggested two-way fault. Stevenson needed to show Ruth as the victim of sustained mental cruelty and physical violence from a man to whom she was in thrall yet whom, out of love, she was willing to forgive, until she could bear it no longer. Crucially – given the 'reasonable person' test set out in *R v Duffy* – he had to make the jurors empathise with Ruth, and think to themselves, How could she put up with all that? Instead, the picture that he was allowing to be painted was of a desultory, if sometimes hot-blooded, affair punctuated by the occasional lovers' tiff.

The final reference to Blakely's violence occurred a few minutes later.

STEVENSON: In March [1954] did you find that you were pregnant?

ELLIS: Yes.

STEVENSON: At the end of March, did you do anything about that pregnancy? What happened about it?

ELLIS: Well, we had a fight a few days previously – I forget the exact time – and David got very, very violent. I do not know whether that caused the miscarriage or not, but he did thump me in the tummy.

And that was that. Stevenson seemed to find Blakely's violence – which should have been the trial's heart and centre – distasteful.

There was only one moment when the hard surface broke open. On the Wednesday evening before the shooting Blakely had arrived back at Egerton Gardens in good spirits and presented Ruth with a recent photograph of himself, taken in anticipation of a race at Le Mans. The photograph was handed up to her. Written on it were the words: 'To Ruth with all my love, from David'. Looking at it, Ruth began to cry.

STEVENSON: My Lord, I wonder if she could sit down?

JUDGE: Yes, certainly.

ELLIS: No, it is quite all right.

JUDGE: Do, by all means.

ELLIS: I do not want to sit down.

There was something in Ruth's psychology that required that she maintain a kind of poised, almost defiant, composure before the watching world. This is what motivated the re-peroxiding of her hair; it influenced her choice of clothing; it coloured all her answers. She could not show vulnerability or victimhood at the time when that was most demanded.

Stevenson now took Ruth through the events of the Easter weekend. By the end it seemed as if Humphreys' characterisation of the shooting as an act of caprice was not so wide of the mark. Ruth explained that on the Sunday evening she had put her son to bed at Egerton Gardens.

STEVENSON: And what did you do next?

ELLIS: I was very upset and I had a peculiar idea I wanted to kill him.

STEVENSON [in consternation]: You had what?

ELLIS: I had an idea I wanted to kill him.

STEVENSON: Why did you do it?

ELLIS: I do not really know, quite seriously. I was just very upset.

The opportunity had been offered to Ruth to explain her actions to the jury. She indifferently brushed it aside. Never had a defendant so casually thrown away her life.

Humphreys asked Ruth only one question, in what has become notorious as the shortest cross-examination of a person on trial for murder in Old Bailey history.

HUMPHREYS: When you fired that revolver at close range into the body of David Blakely, what did you intend to do?

ELLIS: It is obvious that when I shot him I intended to kill him.

Humphreys thanked her, as well he might, and sat down. 'Defeated and dejected', Stevenson 'had the expression of a man who has been unexpectedly let down by a friend'. Ruth Ellis had appeared, Hancock recalled, at best like a 'blonde, mechanical doll'; at worst a 'cold bitch who never once thought of her children'.

Only one other witness was called by the defence: Dr Duncan Whittaker, who had interviewed Ruth in prison for only a couple of hours. The purpose of his evidence was to try to establish that some women were more susceptible to 'hysterical reactions' than men. He did not start auspiciously:

I agree with the view of Professor Jung[8] that women cannot so easily as men separate their sexual relationship with men from their total personal relationships . . . They are inclined to lose some of their inhibitory capacity and solve their problems on a more primitive level . . . She had drifted into a situation which was for her intolerable, but she could find no way out, and she had not a sufficiently hysterical personality to solve her problems by a complete loss of memory.

This must have sounded like mumbo-jumbo to a London jury.

The evidence was over by four o'clock on the trial's first day. Stevenson had chosen not to ask DCI Davies, Clive Gunnell or Lewis Nickolls any questions; he had also failed to call the doctor who had seen Ruth after her miscarriage, or Dr Rees, who had prescribed Ruth tranquillisers for her anxiety, as witnesses. The judge was looking perplexed. He released the jury, telling them that matters of law needed to be discussed in their absence. Havers was troubled about whether the evidence could properly lead a jury to accept that there was provocation sufficient to reduce their verdict to manslaughter. Stevenson submitted that it was, but also candidly admitted that he could not support his proposition by reference to any legal precedent. In fact the precedents were all against him: the law had not yet come to an adequate understanding of 'slow-burn provocation'. 'But that is new law,' protested Mr Justice Havers, in the time-honoured lawyers' euphemism for 'hopeless'. The next morning, the second and last day of the trial, the judge made his ruling:

> I feel constrained to rule that there is not sufficient material, even on a view of the evidence most favourable to the accused, for a reasonable jury to form the view that a reasonable person so provoked could be driven, through transport of passion and loss of self-control, to the degree and method and continuance of violence which produced the death, and consequently it is my duty as a judge, as a matter of law, to direct the jury that the evidence in this case does not support a verdict of manslaughter on the grounds of provocation.

Stevenson's response was immediate and precise: 'I cannot now with propriety address the jury at all, because it would be impossible to do so without inviting them to disregard Your Lordship's ruling.'

So there would be no closing speech to the jury on behalf of Ruth Ellis. Humphreys responded that in the circumstances he, too, had 'nothing to say' – one of the very rare occasions in recent criminal history when both prosecution and defence counsel waived their right to give closing speeches.

It fell to Havers to sum up the case for the jury. He did so shortly. Really there was very little to say. The law of murder simply required that a person kill another with malice. By 'malice' was meant 'the formation of an intention either to kill or to do grievous bodily harm'.

'If you are satisfied that the accused deliberately fired those shots at Blakely and as a result he died, it is not open to you to find a verdict of not guilty.'

At 11.52 a.m. the jury retired for only twenty-three minutes. While they were out a new jury for Court Number One's next trial was sworn in. Juries had in earlier decades often recommended mercy when delivering their guilty verdict; Ruth received no such recommendation when the jurors returned with an inevitable verdict of guilty. The trial had lasted less than one and a half days. After the dreadful pronouncement of the sentence of death Ruth was heard to mouth the word 'Thanks'. She stood up, smiled at her family, and walked down the stairs to the cells below, the heels of her shoes clipping the steps – 'like a gangster's moll', thought Hancock. Peter Rawlinson remembers her 'looking assured and without regret' as she retreated from view. The court emptied in readiness for the next case. The business of the Old Bailey moved on.

When a person was condemned to hang they were treated with a certain tenderness in prison. A special aura worthy almost of veneration seemed to descend on those marked for death. Ruth was now taken to the special cell at Holloway reserved for the condemned. Separated from the rest of the prisoners, the cell had its own lavatory and bathroom. A wardrobe on castors masked the door to the scaffold, just fifteen feet away from her bed.

There Ruth quietly passed her days, receiving many visitors, reading the Bible, doing jigsaw puzzles, sewing dolls out of scraps provided by her mother. Desmond Cussen had been a regular visitor until her trial; now he came no more. The wardresses, her constant companions night and day, were struck by Ruth's dignity and equanimity. Her desire to die seemed to be undimmed; she refused to appeal and did not press for a reprieve.

But in the world outside there was much agitation about her sentence. A huge correspondence flooded the letters pages of the newspapers, most of it condemning the barbarity that was about to be inflicted. The famous *Mirror* columnist William Connor – who wrote under the name Cassandra – asserted that Ruth's hanging 'would bear the guilt of savagery untainted by mercy'. The outrage extended well beyond Britain. An article in *Le Monde* noted that 'English law does not at the moment recognise any intermediate stage between the rational and balanced being who kills in perfect awareness of what he is doing and the total lunatic who is not conscious of his own acts. As everyone knows, the Englishman is – or believes himself to be – a creature of *sang froid*, and the legal system in force supports this fiction in over-ruling once and for all any emotional troubles or irresistible impulses.'

Notwithstanding her professed indifference to her life, many worked for Ruth's salvation. Family and friends wrote privately to the Home

Office urging a reprieve. Many came forward with concrete examples of Blakely's brutality to Ruth, evidence that had not been given to the court. John Bickford worked indefatigably towards the same end.

On 11 July, two days before the date scheduled for her execution, news came that the Home Secretary, Gwilym Lloyd George, son of the wartime Prime Minister and himself a turncoat Liberal, had decided not to grant a reprieve.[9]

As the moment of execution approached, to the outside world two mysteries remained, neither of which Ruth had attempted to resolve at her trial. The first was where and how had Ruth acquired a fully loaded, well-oiled revolver. She had told the police that it had been given to her a couple of years earlier by a Little Club customer as security for a debt, a story she did not contradict when giving evidence. This was implausible and none of the investigating officers believed it. The other mystery was how Ruth had got to Hampstead that Sunday evening. She claimed that she had taken a taxi but no cab driver had come forward to confirm what would surely have been a memorable fare.

The truth did not fully emerge for over twenty years. It turned out that shortly after her arrest Ruth had told Bickford that the gun in fact belonged to the faithful Desmond Cussen. She explained that on the morning of Easter Sunday, failing to find Blakely's car in Hampstead, Cussen had driven her up to Penn on yet another fruitless quest to try to track him down. On the way back to London they had stopped in some woods and Cussen had shown her how to fire the revolver. That night they had been drinking at Cussen's flat and eventually he had driven Ruth back up to Hampstead and left her there armed with the gun, presumably knowing of her plan. Mindful of the 'Thou shalt not squeal' code of the semi-criminal underworld she inhabited, Ruth had sworn Bickford to secrecy about Cussen's involvement; he had not even told his counsel team.

In 1972 Bickford, by now nearing seventy, and living in retirement in Malta, seems to have suffered a crisis of conscience. He prepared a poignant written statement that disclosed these facts and which he sent to the Metropolitan Police. The solicitor went so far as to question whether he had somehow been complicit in the crime by failing to disclose what he had been told.

In his statement Bickford explained that on 11 July, after the news arrived that the execution would proceed, he had a final meeting with Ruth. He had been convinced that a reprieve would be granted and was very affected by the news from the Home Office. He came to tell Ellis that he would continue the fight but was cut short by his client. Ruth's tone had altered dramatically: she accused Bickford of 'deliberately throwing away her case and of having accepted a bribe from Cussen to ensure that she was hanged and that he got free'. She asked to see a representative from Victor Mishcon & Co, the solicitors who had acted for her in her divorce, and whom she knew and trusted.

This is a difficult conversation to interpret. Ruth had been adamant, ever since her arrest, that she had no fear of death. Was this baseless accusation against her solicitor, who had worked so conscientiously in her interests, a momentary attack of nerves? Was it prompted by Cussen's failure to communicate with her after her conviction? It is unlikely that these questions will ever be answered.

The next day Victor Mishcon, the celebrated solicitor and Labour activist, visited Ruth with his managing clerk, Leon Simmons, in accordance with her wishes. They found her returned to her previous calm. After much coaxing, she confessed to them a version of the narrative that she had previously told Bickford: that she had been sitting in Cussen's flat on the Sunday evening drinking and complaining about Blakely's treatment of her; that at some point, at her request, Cussen had given her a loaded gun; that he had then driven her to Hampstead, leaving her on the corner of Tanza Road. As an afterthought she explained that she had practised firing the gun earlier in the day with Cussen.

'I'll tell you if you promise not to use it to try and save me,' Ellis had told Mishcon and Simmons. But the statement she signed at twelve thirty on 12 July – fewer than twenty-one hours before her scheduled execution – was urgently sent to the Home Office in the hope that it would prompt a review of Lloyd George's decision to refuse a reprieve. There was a flurry of activity. One of the police officers involved in the case was interviewed; the Home Office permanent secretary Sir Frank Newsam was summoned back to London from the races at Ascot; futile attempts were made to track Cussen down, but he had wisely gone to ground.

Years later Lloyd George insisted that the last-minute fuss over the gun Ellis had used 'made no difference'. 'I'd rather have reprieved everyone if I could,' he said dismissively, suggesting that there was nothing extenuating about Ruth's case. 'If anything, if Mrs Ellis' final story was true it made her offence all the greater. Instead of a woman merely acting suddenly on impulse, here you had an actual plot to commit murder, deliberately thought out and conceived with some little care.' At two o'clock in the morning of 13 July a phone call came through to Mishcon. The execution would proceed as planned.

It seems clear that what Ruth initially told Bickford and then, at the eleventh hour, repeated to Mishcon was the truth. Given Ruth's insistence that Cussen should not be implicated, there was no incentive for her to lie. There is no other plausible explanation for the origin of the revolver and for its being in full working order. But the question, now insoluble, remains precisely what Cussen's role was in the killing, and what motivated him. Desmond Cussen is the final enigma of the case. He undoubtedly loved Ruth unconditionally. His role ferrying Ruth around on her jealous expeditions must have been profoundly humiliating for him. He must have grown to hate Blakely, whose misconduct he saw at first hand. To witness Ruth's enduring love for a man who behaved as Blakely did must have been intolerable to Cussen, who offered support and affection and yet received in return only friendship. Did he persuade a drunken Ruth to take his gun; or did she press him insistently until he reluctantly gave way? What did he think would happen? Blakely's death would hardly open the way to his forging a future with the woman he loved. He must have recognised the risk of his own implication in the case, and his prosecution as an accomplice to murder. Even if his role somehow remained hidden, Ruth would inevitably be prosecuted for murder. Did he anticipate that she would be reprieved and, on her eventual release many years later, return to his welcoming arms? If so, it was a long-term, precarious plan. Or had he promised to look after her son Andy after her execution in return for Ruth's silence about his procurement of the gun, as the journalist Duncan Webb would later claim? Perhaps, in the end, the search for a rational explanation of Cussen's part in the killing is futile. Perhaps there was no calculation at all, just a sense of inevitability, an Aeschylean tragedy.

Albert Pierrepoint had been a hangman since 1932 and was the third Pierrepoint to hold such a position in over half a century: his father Henry had been 'Number One' – Britain's top executioner – from 1901 to 1910 (starting his career at the old Newgate prison, on the site of the 'new' Old Bailey), while his Uncle Tom had been a hangman for forty years, from 1906 to 1946, when he finally retired aged seventy-five. After Henry's death in 1922 the seventeen-year-old Albert inherited a pile of papers, including his father's execution book, 'black like a family bible'. Albert had started by assisting his Uncle Tom; he inherited the position of Number One in 1940.

There were only ever a small number of executioners in Britain – at one point just Albert and Tom – and the positions were always freelance. Between executions, for which he would be paid £10 or £15 a time, Albert worked as a grocery delivery driver, and later as the publican of two Lancashire pubs. 'Everything went off champion,' Albert once told his Uncle Tom, after one of his hangings. But contrary to myth he was not a ghoul who took perverse pleasure from his work: the only satisfaction he seemed to derive was from performing his duties as quickly and painlessly as possible. He prided himself on meticulous preparation, and carefully calibrating the length of each drop according to the person's weight so that his 'client' would be killed instantly, by the breaking of the spinal cord between the second and third vertebrae, rather than suffer the slower death from strangulation that often resulted from the standard five-foot drop used in Scottish jails.

As the prison bell started tolling eight or nine o'clock Pierrepoint would enter the cell, quietly murmuring to the condemned man, 'Follow me lad, it'll be all right' before leading him into the adjacent execution chamber. He took infinite care in ensuring that the whole process – reassuring the prisoner, strapping his arms, marching him next door, putting the noose and white hood over his head, removing the trapdoor pin and pulling the lever – was accomplished in a matter of seconds, often before the bell stopped tolling the hour. For Albert Pierrepoint, being executioner was a 'sacred' job that he would never brag about: he claims that his wife, Anne, only learned that he had spent the last eleven years moonlighting as a hangman after their wedding in 1943, not before.

Hangings of women had always been relatively rare. No women at all were executed in Britain between August 1907 and January 1923, when Edith Thompson was hanged by John Ellis, Henry Pierrepoint's successor as Number One. Ellis, who like many executioners found the work profoundly disturbing, committed suicide shortly after his retirement. The Pierrepoints were made of stronger stuff: in 1945 in Germany Albert once hanged twenty-seven war criminals in a single day. He is estimated to have dispatched at least 400 people – including many of Britain's most notorious criminals: John Amery, William Joyce, Neville Heath, John Haigh and John Christie – although he declined to give an exact figure when asked by a Royal Commission in 1949.

In the afternoon of 12 July Albert Pierrepoint arrived quietly at Holloway prison. By execution hour – nine o'clock the following morning – the crowd of 'zombies with their lolly-licking children', as Robert Hancock described them, was a thousand-strong. Some of them were just there for the fun of it, but others were protesters who grimly chanted, 'Evans, Bentley, Ellis,' a trinity of miscarried justice.

At the moment of Ruth's execution her sister Muriel later recalled that she wandered from room to room crying, 'No, no, no'; after a sleepless night at home in Hemel Hempstead, Ruth's mother drank tea while her father played a lament on his cello. John Bickford remembered walking across Blackheath at the time of the hanging, 'feeling quite dreadful'. Later that morning Ruth's brother Granville identified her body, her neck covered with a scarf to conceal the marks left by Pierrepoint's rope. During the inquest the coroner repeatedly referred to his sister as the 'murderess'. 'Isn't there something else you could call her?' Granville shouted.

'No untoward incident' had occurred during the execution, Pierrepoint later insisted in his punctilious language. Ruth was 'as good as gold'; she 'died as brave as any man and never spoke a single word', he wrote to Muriel. Just before the drop she did not cry; instead 'she flicked her eyes and puckered her lips as though she was trying to smile.'

Ruth Ellis was only the tenth woman hanged in Britain since Edith Thompson in 1923. Reprieves were very common: of the twenty women convicted of murder from 1946 to 1955, only four were executed, and Albert estimated that he only hanged twenty women throughout his career, more than half of them guards at Bergen–Belsen and other Nazi concentration and extermination camps. The hanging of women entailed special adjustments (the ankle strap was always adjusted 'for the sake of decency during the drop', his memoirs note, and women were required to wear canvas 'Edith Thompson pants', as they were known, to catch any blood coming from the uterus, which could prolapse). Although women wardresses would escort women to the execution chamber, they would slip out a few seconds before the lever was pulled.

'I have never seen a man braver than a woman,' Albert Pierrepoint later wrote. Most of the women he hanged were 'ordinary . . . rarely beautiful. Square-faced, thin-mouthed, eyes blinking behind National Health spectacles which I have to take off at the last moment, hair scraped thin by curlers, lumpy ankles above homely shoes, in which they have to slop to the gallows because prison regulations demand there are no shoelaces. It is not easy to die like that, but the fortitude of women comes through.' He may well have had Ruth Ellis, who wore glasses and was seen with her hair in pigtails before her execution, in mind.

Attitudes changed quickly after Ruth Ellis's execution. Within a month the National Campaign for the Abolition of Capital Punishment was formed. An array of British establishment figures – the Methodist leader Donald Soper, the editors of the *Lancet*, and many MPs from across Parliament, led by the indefatigable abolitionist Sydney Silverman – lent it their support.

There now seemed to be less and less logic to those who were spared the death penalty and those who weren't. In March 1954 two burglars, Kenneth Gilbert and Ian Grant, tied up a Kensington hotel's night porter, who later banged his head against a bar counter and suffocated on the gag in his mouth. Although Gilbert and Grant had not intended to injure the porter, let alone murder him, they were nevertheless convicted of murder at the Old Bailey and hanged just three months later.[10] But in 1955 a psychopath called Donald Brown escaped the gallows after stabbing a Willesden tobacconist to death; he used the money he had stolen to calmly go to a cinema. These inconsistencies, and the outcry over the hangings of Timothy Evans, Derek Bentley and above all Ruth Ellis, all helped shift political and popular opinion towards abolition. Decades of campaigning by abolitionists like Violet Van der Elst, who would vocally protest outside the prison when any execution took place, and who lived just long enough to see abolition finally enacted, began to pay off.

In February 1956 the House of Commons passed, on a free vote, a motion that the death penalty 'no longer accords with the needs or the true interests of a civilised society', but disagreement in the House of Lords led to another fudge. A further step on the road was the Homicide Act of 1957. Not only did it enact major reforms to the law of murder, including a wider interpretation of the law of provocation[11] and the introduction of the defence of diminished responsibility, it also now confined the death penalty to those found guilty of murders involving theft, shooting, explosion, resisting arrest, escaping from custody, or the murder of police or prison officers. This list was so arbitrary that few abolitionists were satisfied. But in practice most people who committed *crimes passionels* after 1957 were imprisoned, not hanged. In 1958 Christmas Humphreys led for the prosecution at the Old Bailey trial of Ernest Fantle, a Czech-born RAF pilot, who had shot dead his wife's lover in his Piccadilly mansion flat. Humphreys acknowledged the provocation that Fantle had been subjected to, did not press the murder charge hard, and the jury took just thirteen minutes to find Fantle guilty only of the lesser offence of manslaughter. Fantle was sentenced to three years' imprisonment. It would take much longer before the law of provocation adapted itself, albeit imperfectly, to the special position of women who, having been abused over a protracted period, kill their partner. Over all these changes the ghost of Ruth Ellis seems to hover.

After her hanging, another thirty-four executions were carried out in Britain. But none were of women, and Ruth's execution seemed to be a watershed. In 1965 the death penalty was finally suspended for all forms of murder and in 1969 that suspension was made permanent. Yet the mood of policy-makers did not necessarily walk hand in hand with opinion on the street. After Peter Allen and Gwynne Evans were convicted of the sordid murder of John West, a laundry driver, during a botched robbery in Cumberland in April 1964, a petition was raised against the possibility of a reprieve. Executed on 13 August 1964, they were the last people to be hanged in Britain.

But by the time he wrote his memoirs ten years later Albert Pierrepoint had become an unlikely opponent of capital punishment:

> I have come to the conclusion that executions solve nothing, and are only an antiquated relic of a primitive desire for revenge . . . If death were a deterrent I might be expected to know. It is I who have faced them last, young lads and girls, working men, grandmothers. I have been amazed to see the courage with which they take that walk into the unknown. It did not deter them then, and it had not deterred them when they committed what they were convicted for.

*

Very few people reading the full narrative of Ruth Ellis's life would conclude that, even during a time when death by hanging was the prescribed punishment for murder, she deserved to die. In 2003 Ruth's sister Muriel – by now in her eighties, and taking advantage of the same provisions that Derek Bentley's own sister had used in the 1990s to successfully quash his conviction – sought to appeal Ruth's conviction for murder. The case, argued by the well-known barrister Michael Mansfield QC, was that Ellis was a victim of 'battered woman syndrome' and that Havers had misinterpreted the law of provocation as it stood in 1955. The Court of Appeal had no difficulty in disagreeing. Blakely's behaviour over the fatal weekend was, the court ruled, not sufficient to justify a defence of provocation, and the appeal was 'without merit'. It is surprising to find in the court's ruling a tone almost of irritation that its time had been wasted on an old story.

Nonetheless Ruth Ellis's execution, however much she willed it, now seems an atrocity. No death occurs in isolation and Ruth's had terrible repercussions for those around her. Another sister, Betty, died of an asthma attack, aged just eighteen, three months after Ruth's hanging. Her son Andy, who features on the edges of the story, always just outside the frame, last saw his mother on the evening of Easter Sunday 1955, before she made her final journey to Tanza Road. In the three months between her arrest and execution he was permitted neither to meet nor speak to her. Her death left him, at the age of only ten, an orphan. He went on to live a shambolic, hollow existence plagued by mental health problems. He eventually committed suicide in 1982, having weeks earlier desecrated his mother's grave (Ruth had been reinterred in Amersham in 1971, ahead of the rebuilding of Holloway prison). Perhaps this act was motivated by anger at the way his mother had left him; if so that anger was surely justified. Ruth loved Blakely more than she loved her own son and Andy must have realised that. It is said that Christmas Humphreys paid for his funeral.

George Ellis hanged himself with his pyjama cord in a Jersey hotel in 1958. Ruth's mother attempted to gas herself in the late 1960s and spent the rest of her life in a psychiatric hospital. John Bickford felt that his life had been irrevocably changed by the experience of having represented Ruth Ellis. He was haunted by a sense of failure – a not uncommon feeling for lawyers, especially after a client went to the gallows – and ended his life, like so many other characters in this story, a lonely alcoholic. As for Desmond Cussen, he was never prosecuted for his part in Blakely's death and emigrated to Australia a few years after Ruth's execution. He too found solace in alcohol and, after various failed business ventures, died in 1991. He took the truth of what in fact had happened that Easter weekend in 1955 with him to his grave.

PART V
Politics

8

'Equipment for a spy'

R v Giuseppe Martelli (1963)

A CQUITTAL OR CONVICTION in a criminal court can make the difference between subsequent oblivion or notoriety. There is no better example of this statement than the respective fates of the defendants in the two trials that electrified England in the vexed summer of 1963. Over two hot weeks in Court Number One Dr Giuseppe Martelli, an Italian atomic scientist, was tried for espionage under the Official Secrets Act. The trial acquired its own name – 'the Secrets Case' – and in one newspaper this phrase was superimposed on an image of test tubes and Bunsen burners bubbling away in some vaguely scientific, and vaguely disturbing, way.

In the event Martelli was acquitted, a fact broadcast in large letters on the front pages of most of the newspapers. The headlines were accompanied by photographs of an intense-looking man in early middle age embracing a beaming woman and driving off into the night, away from London and into a future which, as it turned out, would be largely untroubled by the curiosity of the press. Days later the trial of another, rather different doctor, Stephen Ward, osteopath, artist and alleged sexual deviant, started in the same court. It ended with Ward's conviction and death in close succession. Over fifty years later Martelli is an almost completely forgotten figure, remembered only by the more assiduous students of the British intelligence services or the history of atomic research. By contrast there was no post-trial life for Ward to seek obscurity in. His conviction for living off immoral earnings, and, three days later, his death by his own hand, assured him a notoriety that only later assumed the more sympathetic garb of martyrdom. Yet notwithstanding the disjunction of their respective fates, it was not fortuitous that the two trials of Dr Martelli and Dr Ward came on back to back. The cases were both born out of an age of paranoia, a fear that alien influences, whether political, national or sexual, were worming themselves into the fabric of British life, intent on its corruption and destruction.

In the early 1960s Britain was besieged by a vast Soviet espionage effort. It has been estimated that some 150 intelligence officers operated out of its London Embassy, engaged on the infiltration of British institutions. Russian attempts to suborn took multiple forms: financial incentives, blackmail and ideological indoctrination had all succeeded in establishing a network of disparate recruits feeding intelligence back to Moscow or one of its Warsaw Pact allies. MI5 attempts to combat this activity had met with some successes, although the publicity generated by the subsequent trials also revealed to an astonished public the scale of the Soviet penetration of Britain's military and its security and civil services. In 1961 the trial in Court Number One of the so-called Portland Spy Ring showed how a couple of rackety clerks employed by the Admiralty Underwater Weapons Establishment had been able to photograph huge quantities of confidential documentation concerned with Britain's development of a nuclear submarine and pass them over to their Soviet handler, a KGB intelligence officer masquerading under the name Gordon Lonsdale, on their monthly jaunts from Dorset to London. The MI6 officer George Blake had been convicted just a few weeks later and sentenced to the longest prison term in legal history, forty-two years. Then, in November 1962, John Vassall, an Admiralty clerk, was sentenced to eighteen years in prison. Vassall had previously worked in the British Embassy in Moscow. In the mid-1950s he had been the victim of a homosexual honey-trap. Photographed in compromising positions (in one picture he was shown lying naked on a divan waving a pair of underpants over his head), he was then lured, by a combination of blackmail and financial sweeteners, to supply, over a five-year period, thousands of illicitly photographed documents revealing developments in radar and anti-submarine weaponry. At the end of 1962 Harold Macmillan could tell the House of Commons, with some justification, that 'I feel it is right to warn the House that hostile intrigue and espionage are being relentlessly maintained on a very large scale.'

This susceptibility of Britain's public servants to Russian entrapment became a metaphor for national enfeeblement. And the sense of a country helplessly in the grip of a relentless external power did not let up in the following year. In January 1963 Kim Philby, long suspected of being a Soviet agent, mysteriously disappeared from Beirut, only to emerge some months later in Moscow. The suggestion was made that he had been tipped off that his arrest was imminent by a Soviet mole who continued to operate in MI5. Then, in June 1963, the Minister of War, John Profumo, resigned, having previously misled Parliament about his liaison with a young model, Christine Keeler. It was through Stephen Ward that Profumo had met Keeler, who had supposedly been simultaneously having an affair with Captain Yevgeny Ivanov, ostensibly the Soviet assistant naval attaché at the Soviet Embassy in London, but in fact a member of the GRU (the Soviet military intelligence organisation). As the storm clouds gathered over Profumo it was being put about that Ivanov, in some mysterious conspiracy with Dr Ward, had sought to use Keeler to extract military secrets from Profumo through unguarded pillow talk. Were not even government ministers immune from Soviet guile?

It was in this febrile atmosphere that it was announced in the spring of 1963 that an Italian atomic scientist, attached to the Atomic Energy Research Establishment (AERE) in Oxfordshire, had been arrested on suspicion of spying offences. There was an inglorious history of atomic espionage associated with the AERE: some years earlier two scientists who had subsequently attained worldwide notoriety, Klaus Fuchs and Bruno Pontecorvo, had both worked there.

Fuchs, a German refugee who found sanctuary in Britain in 1933, had worked on the Manhattan Project to build the atomic bomb before being appointed as head of the Theoretical Physics Division at the AERE in 1946. Over the next few years this outwardly unassuming man had provided his Soviet handler with the principal theoretical outline for creating a hydrogen bomb. His activities were discovered in late 1949 after the so-called Venona Project, a secret American counter-intelligence operation that succeeded in intercepting and decrypting Soviet intelligence communications, had revealed his identity as a spy. When confronted with his crimes Fuchs did not stall or obfuscate: with ingenuous candour he instead set about a prolonged form of written apologia founded on the delusion that sincerity could somehow remove any taint of culpability.[1] The result was a major coup for MI5: the source of the information that had identified Fuchs could never have been made public and so there had been no prospect of Fuchs being prosecuted without a confession.

In March 1950 Fuchs was brought into the dock of Court Number One to be sentenced by the Lord Chief Justice, the irascible Lord Goddard. It was estimated that eighty journalists from across the globe were in court to report the proceedings, many sitting on the floor for lack of bench space. Never have a defendant and a judge confronted each other across a courtroom from such different world-views. Marxist idealism was here pitted against the no-nonsense, perhaps brutish, pragmatism of the English common lawyer. At the Old Bailey, wholly unrepentant, unable to comprehend his guilt – and despite the emollient words of his counsel Derek Curtis-Bennett KC – Fuchs was sentenced to fourteen years in prison, the maximum sentence available for offences under section 1 of the Official Secrets Act 1911.

Rebecca West, who had previously chronicled the Old Bailey trials of Nazi collaborators in 1945 and 1946, was again in court to witness the proceedings. She does nothing to conceal her contempt for Fuchs in her account of his case. She records a 'pale, neat young man . . . with a bulging forehead and glasses, not much of a chin, and a weakly body' who, when asked whether he had anything to say before being sentenced, replied, with 'celestial impudence', by complimenting the court on having given him a fair hearing. With that Goddard pronounced sentence, and his remarks were pregnant with outrage that this man, who had been given asylum at his hour of need and had enjoyed the protection and bounty of his adoptive country, had betrayed it with such seeming insouciance. In all the hearing lasted for some ninety minutes. If the significance of a trial is to be measured by its length then there was a disjunction between the swiftness with which this case was disposed of and the importance of the events that it marked. No doubt the authorities were anxious that Dr Fuchs should be packed away out of the public eye as soon as possible.

It has been said of Fuchs that he is the only physicist to have changed the course of history. Even making allowances for hyperbole it is a fact that in the early 1940s the United States and its allies had a virtual monopoly on knowledge relating to atomic weaponry. Assisted by the revelations of Fuchs and an earlier British atomic spy, Alan Nunn May,[2] that monopoly was destroyed and doors were opened for the Soviet Union towards some measure of equality of arms. So was born, or helped along its way, the Cold War.

The Fuchs case was rightly characterised as a scandal. There was plentiful evidence of his longstanding communist sympathies to which the authorities who employed him blinded themselves. It was followed in short order by a separate crisis involving another AERE scientist. Bruno Pontecorvo was a naturalised Italian and a brilliant nuclear scientist. He was also, like Fuchs, a dedicated communist. He had arrived in

England from Canada in 1949 to work on the British nuclear reactor programme, and then, while on a camping holiday in Italy, disappeared with his family, only to emerge at a press conference in Moscow five years later. Pontecorvo remained working in Russia for the rest of his life. As for Fuchs, unsurprisingly a substantial stretch in an English prison had no impact on his ideological outlook. On his release in 1959 he immediately departed to East Germany, taking with him all his accumulated knowledge and expertise, where he would become the deputy director of the Institute for Nuclear Research.

Both men represented an interesting development in the history of treachery: scientists who did not recognise national allegiance or scientific confidentiality but were actuated by the belief that knowledge should be disseminated across borders and without hindrances to assist the cause of world socialism. There was also something frightening about the subterfuge involved in the double life they led. Outwardly cohering to the conventions and values of their new country, associating warmly with colleagues and friends, inwardly they were providing information to a foreign power whose interests were inimical to those values. It was what Fuchs described as an exercise in 'controlled schizophrenia'.

The scientist who, in spring 1963, had been arrested was Dr Giuseppe Martelli, a thirty-nine-year-old who, like Pontecorvo, was Italian. A member of the resistance in the last years of the war, he graduated in physics at the University of Naples in 1945 before commencing his academic career at the University of Rome. He moved to Birmingham University in 1957 where he was placed in charge of a space research programme. Then, in 1960 he started working for the European Atomic Energy Community, which studied nuclear energy and its peaceful application. By 1962 he had been seconded by Euratom to the AERE laboratory in Culham, Oxfordshire.

Martelli's private life was complex. In 1944 he had married Maria Vicich, who had been born and brought up in the Soviet Union as the daughter of an Italian diplomat in Moscow. Two children followed but the relationship soon came under strain. Martelli moved to England alone. In 1960 his Italian family had come to join him with a view to effecting a reconciliation, but the attempt failed and Martelli started a relationship with an English scientist, Pamela Rothwell. His wife returned to Italy with their children, filled with recrimination, and Susanna, Martelli's daughter with Rothwell, was born in late 1960. Divorce was impossible: Rothwell changed her name by deed poll and Martelli lived unobtrusively with his new family in a quiet street in Abingdon, a short walk from the house Pontecorvo had abandoned ten years earlier, his life taken up by his scientific researches.

In April 1963 Martelli flew into Southend airport after a motoring holiday on the Continent. As he departed the airport he was arrested by Chief Inspector Stratton on suspicion of 'committing acts preparatory to the commission of an offence under section 1 of the Official Secrets Act 1911'. Simultaneously with his arrest, his home in Abingdon, his office in Culham and his car were being searched. An extraordinary and intriguing collection of material – the 'equipment for a spy', as the prosecution later described it – was discovered.

Secreted in Martelli's house was found a packet of Pall Mall in which seven cigarettes had been glued together and cut down to leave a hidden cavity that contained a set of 'one-time' pads. These pads were an undecipherable encryption method[3] much favoured by the KGB. Diaries were found in Martelli's office in which figures and letters were arranged in parallel lines, by which an outgoing message might be enciphered or an incoming message deciphered. Against the date of 12 October 1962 were written the words 'Alpine Blue [a brand of cigarettes at the time]. Twenty packets. Where is Charles Place? Do you mean the art gallery?' Against another date was a sketch of a small park in Wimbledon with the letter 'K' inscribed by it. In another diary was written the name 'Agrafenine' – known to be the name of the Third Secretary at the Soviet Embassy in Brussels; and an address – Flat 6, 16 Airlie Gardens, Kensington – the residence of the former First Secretary at the Soviet Embassy in London, Nikolai Karpekov. A shoe discovered in Martelli's car boot had a hollowed-out cavity that could be revealed by twisting the heel. And secreted in Martelli's desk was a receipt for an Exakta camera – a favourite within the spying fraternity.

The image of Martelli furtively walking through a park in south-west London carrying a prominent packet of Alpine Blue cigarettes, asking some dark-suited passer-by, 'Where is Charles Place?' and receiving the pre-agreed reply, 'Do you mean the art gallery?' was a compelling one. The follow-up thought of him then sitting down on a park bench with his mysterious interlocutor and surreptitiously removing from a cavity in his heel an enciphered message was even more intriguing. Covert meetings in London parks were a commonplace of the Cold War and made their way into the literary imagination of the period. In *The Spy Who Came in from the Cold* Alec Leamas first encounters Ashe, the East German recruiter, in St James's Park. The novel was first published in September

1963 and provides a fictional analogue to the mood that prevailed that summer.

Bedazzled by this Aladdin's cave of incriminating material, Chief Inspector Stratton felt compelled to charge Dr Martelli. But the fact was that there was no evidence that Martelli had ever passed on any classified information to the Russians, nor that he ever had any access to such material. The prosecution theory that emerged to navigate this difficulty was that Martelli was being groomed by the Soviets, learning his craft and awaiting activation once he had moved into a scientific post where he could be useful to his handlers. Hence Martelli was charged with the convoluted offence of 'doing acts preparatory to communicating to another person for a purpose prejudicial to the safety or interests of the state information calculated to be or which might be intended to be useful to an enemy', contrary to section 7 of the Official Secrets Act 1920.

In the early hours of the morning in late April 1963 John Calderan, a young partner in the well-known City law firm Theodore Goddard, was woken by a phone call from a distressed Pamela Rothwell. Born in Italy, Calderan was a fluent Italian speaker and had been recommended to Rothwell by both the Italian Embassy and the *News of the World*. Calderan acted for the newspaper and had recently negotiated on its behalf with Christine Keeler to buy her story for the then astronomical sum of £23,000. For Calderan the next three months would be the most intensive of his career. He in turn instructed as Martelli's counsel Jeremy Hutchinson QC. The left-leaning and cultured Hutchinson was then the most fashionable criminal barrister at the London Bar. Calderan remembers a man who was 'tall, distinguished, with a beautiful languid voice, that made his opponents sound shrill and ill-natured'. He was also a veteran of recent spy cases: in the previous two years he had defended both George Blake and John Vassall.

There followed a succession of consultations in Brixton prison, where Martelli had been remanded. A memory that still haunts Calderan is the thought that their discussions were being bugged. Meetings with Martelli were always conducted in the same interview room at Brixton. It contained a hollow electrical cable fixed to one of the walls that appeared to serve no purpose. Whether or not it was overheard, the story that Martelli told Calderan and Hutchinson was an extraordinary one. For over seven years he had been haunted across Europe by a moon-faced Russian called Nikolai Karpekov. Hutchinson immediately recognised the name: Karpekov had in 1961 become the First Secretary at the Soviet

Embassy in London. But his status as a diplomat was a façade. He was a spymaster who had been the controller of Hutchinson's former client John Vassall, the Admiralty clerk convicted just six months earlier for espionage.

Karpekov had first sought out Martelli as a possible recruit at various European scientific conferences in the 1950s. But he acted very slowly, gradually building up a relationship. 'In his way he was good company, with a fund of stories about life in Russia,' Martelli explained. Then, after Martelli's arrival in England, Karpekov, as if by chance, had appeared as the Italian was walking down the Old Brompton Road.

> He greeted me warmly and said what a pleasant surprise it was to meet me. Then he telephoned me and arranged another meeting outside Baron's Court station. We went to a Chinese restaurant in Earl's Court and Karpekov told me that he knew I had sent certain lecture notes I had made to some professors in Russia. There was something threatening in his voice. He later said he could not understand why I should be working in England. Russian scientists had a much better deal and he mentioned Pontecorvo, who he said was very happy living in Russia.

Martelli explained that then, in about 1960, he had received a letter asking him to meet the writer at Harrow station to 'discuss some matters related to his family affairs'. 'I could not read the signature but there was something distinctive about the letter – it was typed in brown ink, a feature I had noticed in some printed Russian scientific papers. I guessed it had come from a Russian agent. I met the agent in a public house. He called himself Alexander and said he was a friend of Karpekov.'

Hutchinson asked him why he had gone. 'I went because it was something related to my family affairs and at that time they were very important to me.' 'Alexander' had told Martelli that his wife, disconsolately living in Italy with their two children, had been enquiring about obtaining a visa for herself and their children to go to live in Russia. 'I asked him how he could know such a thing. He answered that it was his business to know. "But we know you are a good friend of ours and we will try to help." He went on to tell me that if I wanted to consider changing my job I should get in touch with him – he could assist in improving my status.'

What 'Alexander' told him was eerily consistent with what Martelli's wife had been threatening directly. 'My wife grew up in Russia as the daughter of a diplomat and she still had ideas of the easy life she had had in Russia. I begged her not to but she told me to go to hell. I was horrified at the idea that the children might be brought up in the Soviet Union and Alexander offered to do what he could to help me. But there was a clear though unspoken expectation that I would be expected to do something in return. I began to feel uneasy.'

Later Martelli had met Karpekov again, who repeated Alexander's vaguely comforting words about the denial of Soviet visas for his family. 'But the conversations then turned again to my work – Karpekov suggested I move to America and that he could help me find a job there. A little later, just as Pamela was about to give birth to our daughter, he asked me about the pregnancy. I could not understand how he should know about such a thing. He asked whether my older children knew about the new baby. I had the feeling that someone was exerting pressure on me that they had no right to apply.'

Martelli was offered a job in the United States, but he turned it down. 'When I told Karpekov he was furious. He said I was a fool to turn down such an opportunity. "Why should a man like you want to remain in England?" But one thing was clear to me, I could not touch anything that was classified matter, because as soon as I did, then my trying to gain time would have been finished. At that moment the Russians could apply pressure. I could no longer play the absent-minded scientist.'

But Martelli had waded in even deeper. On a visit to Munich to a scientific conference he was asked to go to Vienna.

Karpekov told me that I was to go to a certain address to meet a certain person. Someone would approach me and we would exchange certain words. That was the first time that the exchanging of code words cropped up. When I met this man he showed me a sheet relating to the transmission of messages in code. He told me how it worked and I copied it into my diary. I asked him what I was meant to do with this information – he told me I would be informed later on. I was later provided with the one-time pads. I asked Karpekov what their purpose was. He answered in this mysterious way: 'Don't worry. They are useful things. I want you to learn useful things for us.' But I never used them for any purpose whatsoever.

Calderan and Hutchinson listened to the story carefully. This was a familiar pattern of blackmail and psychological pressure, similar to that which the Russians had exerted over John Vassall. Martelli insisted that there was no question of going to the police. The clear implication was that if he did not co-operate then Russian visas would be very quickly granted to his

Italian family. Moreover there was the dark suggestion that Karpekov and his associates had infiltrated the English police force. Martelli explained that on one occasion he saw Karpekov studying a typewritten list as they sat in a pub. 'I asked him what he was doing – he explained that he was consulting a list of car registration numbers of members of the Special Branch. "We have friends everywhere, even in Scotland Yard."'[4]

The trial of Dr Martelli started in the Old Bailey on 2 July 1963. Many of the journalists who had crowded into Court Number One at the trial of Fuchs in 1950 were back again to report on a case made even more piquant by the fact that here the defendant was pleading not guilty. The gravity of the prosecution was reflected by the presence in court of Sir Peter Rawlinson QC, the debonair and youthful Solicitor General, leading for the Crown. It was eight years since Rawlinson had appeared in this courtroom to act as Ruth Ellis's junior counsel. He set out a simple case of a man working for the Russian intelligence service caught red-handed with the paraphernalia of spycraft. 'Here was a spy equipped with what was necessary for the exercise of his task. A man who had secret messages and passwords, elaborate codes and ciphers. It might be rejected as the stuff of an inferior film or novel. But no one in these days is unconscious that these things are not the stuff of a novel or film but of everyday life.' In truth the overt facts of the case were largely uncontentious. Martelli accepted that he had indeed in his possession all this paraphernalia, given to him by Karpekov and his henchmen; the only issue was his purpose. Had he been groomed, whether or not by blackmail, into agreeing to act as a Soviet spy, to be activated at the right moment? Or was he merely playing the Soviets along, fencing for time, trying to build a case with which to turn the tables on his sinister associates?

A parade of MI5 witnesses, each known only by a letter – Mr A, Mr B, Mr C and so on, the 'Nameless Ones' as the newspapers described them – stood in the witness box to explain to the jury the significance of all this material. Each entered the witness box by the side door behind it and exited the same way; as if emerging out of and going back to a secret world about which the men and women who walked the streets of London, leading their normal lives, and from whose number the jurors had been chosen, knew nothing. What followed was a fascinating insight into the methodology of modern spying. Here in the heart of London, just a few months after humanity had held its breath during the Cuban missile crisis, the operational realities of the covert intelligence battles of the Cold War were being explained by real spies, men who looked and spoke anonymously, not enacted in inferior – or even superior – films. The Soviet modus operandi was revealed: how potential candidates were located and nurtured; how the Soviet net would then close inexorably around such recruits when made; favoured meeting spots; techniques for photographing documents; how codes worked.

Chief Inspector Stratton, the police officer who had led the investigation, came to give evidence. One of the tenets of cross-examination is to ask questions that, so far as possible, do not allow the witness to elaborate his answer. The question should be directed so as to require a certain answer, allowing no room for digression or expansiveness. There should be no attempt at jousting with the witness. Jeremy Hutchinson, described by Jack Miller of the *News of the World* as 'looking like and talking like your kindly uncle, until his voice flashes with asperity', stood up to cross-examine him.

> HUTCHINSON: Your interrogation of Dr Martelli and all the searches and enquiries which the security service has made since this man's arrest have not produced any evidence at all on which to charge him with actually passing any information prejudicial to the interests of this country?
> STRATTON: That is true.
> HUTCHINSON: All the enquiries of the security service have revealed no evidence to put before this court that Dr Martelli has had access to any classified material, the possession of which would be prejudicial to the interests of the country?
> STRATTON: I am not in a position precisely to say what the security service are in the possession of, but to my knowledge that is true.
> HUTCHINSON: And while Dr Martelli has been in this country your enquiries show that nowhere has he ever worked where he has been asked to give any undertaking as to the non-disclosure of confidential information?
> STRATTON: That is true.
> HUTCHINSON: Your enquiries show that you have no evidence that can be laid before this court that he has received one penny piece from the Russians?
> STRATTON: That is so.

Hutchinson now moved on to Soviet methodology:

> HUTCHINSON: There is no doubt at all, is there, that the Russians spend a vast sum of money on espionage?

STRATTON: No doubt at all, sir.

HUTCHINSON: One of the methods that they use in order to suborn people in the West is blackmail?

STRATTON: Yes, sir.

HUTCHINSON: And it would not surprise you if the job of someone like Karpekov was to try to suborn people to give information?

STRATTON: No, sir.

HUTCHINSON: And to your knowledge there are various ways they use of putting pressure on people, one being to get the person they are interested in into a compromising position?

STRATTON: That is true, sir.

HUTCHINSON: That is what happened in the case of Vassall?

STRATTON: Yes, sir.

HUTCHINSON: And in his case he was taken to a dinner party where he was given an excess of drink and put into a compromising position?

STRATTON: So I have read.

HUTCHINSON: Having done that, would not you agree with me that it is a characteristic Russian method not to ask such people for information for quite a considerable time after they have been compromised?

STRATTON: That is true.

HUTCHINSON: Just meetings with them, not applying pressure, not in fact asking them to do anything?

STRATTON: That is true.

HUTCHINSON: And we know that Russian tactics include threats against a person's family?

STRATTON: Yes.

HUTCHINSON: You were from your enquiries satisfied that Karpekov had other contacts in this country?

STRATTON: I know of no others.

HUTCHINSON: You did not know of them but are you satisfied that he did have other contacts?

STRATTON: It is highly probable.

Here was the conundrum lying at the centre of the case: Martelli had provided no secrets to the Soviets, nor did he have access to any secrets. Unlike so many earlier defendants at the Old Bailey, he had not received any financial inducements. Yet he was not a known communist – indeed when giving evidence he angrily denied any suggestion that he was – so ideological conviction did not appear to provide a possible motive for his acts.

Hutchinson moved on to the suspicious shoes, on which the prosecution placed such weight:

HUTCHINSON: You have given evidence that you found two shoes with
    cavities in their heels?
STRATTON: Yes.
HUTCHINSON: Have you made enquiries with the manufacturers of those
    shoes?
STRATTON: I have.
HUTCHINSON: Did your enquiries reveal that those shoes are manufactured
    with cavity heels?
STRATTON: So I understand. That particular type of shoe occasionally had
    some of the leather cut out of the heels to balance them.
HUTCHINSON: You were in possession of that information when you gave
    your evidence at the magistrates court?[5]
STRATTON: Yes.
HUTCHINSON: And you did not say one word about it?
STRATTON: That is right.
HUTCHINSON: Do you realise that as a result the defence has had to get
    a witness from Italy to prove that fact?
STRATTON: I didn't realise that fact, sir.
HUTCHINSON: There are thousands of people walking about at this moment
    with shoes that have similar cavities. Just tell me, Inspector, what you
    say is sinister about the shoe you found in Dr Martelli's car?

Stratton blustered. It was a palpable hit. A few days later there was seen waiting outside the court a small dark man. He turned out to be Signor Renato Rossetti, a shoe manufacturer from near Milan, the very man who had made Martelli's hollow-heeled shoes. He was duly called by Hutchinson – who was certainly not going to let Stratton's concession be the last word on the matter – and there was passed up to the witness box with proper gravity one of Martelli's now infamous shoes. After due deliberation Signor Rossetti pronounced the shoe entirely unexceptional. ('A cavity is made in the heel of all my lightweight shoes to make them lighter.') John Calderan's memory of this evidence is rather more comic. Years later he recalled: 'this little man, his head barely above the ledge of the witness box, was carrying a sack of his shoes. He kept throwing them in the air mouthing the words "all hollow heels".' Rawlinson did not cross-examine him.

Here was an example of a case being over-egged. The damage done by the realisation that Martelli's shoes were in fact entirely run-of-the-mill was much greater than the benefit they added to the prosecution case in the first place. There would be a further moment of deflating levity when it was revealed that supposedly suspicious references in a notebook that had been seized by the police to numbers prefixed by the letter K were in fact references to a series of Mozart string quartets Martelli had been meaning to buy. The letter K (signifying the musicologist Köchel this time, not the spymaster Karpekøv) was the cataloguing system for Mozart's compositions.

But humour was otherwise in short supply in this trial. The air in the courtroom seemed laden with tension. There was an intensely felt personal element to the proceedings: was this neat man sitting in the dock someone who, like Fuchs and Pontecorvo before him, had betrayed the trust his adoptive country had placed in him? Or was he an innocent pawn in a new iteration of the Great Game? Hutchinson opened the case for the defence by telling the jury that:

> This trial is one of the most remarkable alleged spy cases ever to be tried in this country. It will demand from you the ability to understand the evil, insidious war being waged by the Russians against the West. For two and a half years Dr Martelli — a distinguished and unhappy man — was subjected to the subtle and relentless pressure which the Russian intelligence organisation only knows how to exert, pressure he has managed up to 26 April — the date of his arrest — to resist . . .

Hutchinson set out the story that Martelli would tell in the witness box. 'The Solicitor General has said that things of this kind smelled of a novel. You may think this sounds ridiculous; but is it so ridiculous now you have heard the questions which I have asked?'

Hutchinson explained to the jury that Martelli had been told by Karpekov that he had friends 'everywhere, including Scotland Yard'. Karpekov had been the controller of John Vassall. 'Then, what do we find? On 12 September [1962] Vassall is arrested. On 6 September — six days before — Karpekov disappears and is never seen again. How did Karpekov know that in six days' time his contact, the great spy Vassall, was going to be arrested? Did someone tip him off? It is not so fantastic, is it, that Dr Martelli came to believe what he was told was perhaps true?' The dark picture conjured up was of an establishment penetrated at every level by Russian agents, such that there was no one to whom Martelli could safely turn until he was confident of his position. (Although this was not known at the time, the then current Deputy Director of MI5, Graham Mitchell, had himself been the subject of an internal investigation earlier that year, suspected of having tipped off Philby; some even suspected that the Director General, Roger Hollis, was a Soviet agent.) 'A slow waiting game ensued. Dr Martelli was quite determined that he would go to the authorities: hence the careful preservation of the material found in his desk.'

In the witness box Hutchinson slowly led Martelli's life story out of him. If there is anything in a defendant's case that is potentially damaging it is often better that he gives evidence about it during examination-in-chief, rather than for it to be extracted in hostile cross-examination. So Hutchinson asked Martelli in detail about his wife's communist sympathies, about the meetings with Karpekov, and the receipt of the impedimenta of spycraft. The story Martelli had told to Calderan and Hutchinson many times before the trial slowly unwound itself for the jury: 'Karpekov said words to me to the effect that they were always ready to help friends but if people did not cooperate, or if they let them down, they would have no time to repent themselves and of course their families would suffer.'

The judge intervened:

JUDGE: What do you mean by saying that they would have no time to repent?
MARTELLI: They would be liquidated.
JUDGE: You mean that they would be killed.
MARTELLI: Yes.

Martelli explained to the jury that by 1962 the Russians were losing patience with him.

MARTELLI: At the meeting in Park Astrid in Brussels Agrafenine strongly recommended that I should meet his friends in London and that I should stop being always so late in my meetings and in never trying to get in touch with them. I then met Alexander in London who said that his colleagues were rather fed up with me dodging their request for a meeting. He said they could not go on like that.
HUTCHINSON: What impression did you get of the way things were going and the way they were regarding you?
MARTELLI: I had the impression that they were losing patience with me.
HUTCHINSON: How did you feel about your position?

MARTELLI: I felt as soon as I could lay my hands on something that was really useful, not just the one-time pads, I would be in a position to approach the right people and turn the tables on them.

On to the threats to provide his wife and children with visas:

HUTCHINSON: Do you love those children?

MARTELLI: Of course.

HUTCHINSON: Have you ever had any association or sympathy with communism? Do you believe in any way in the communist ideology? [Martelli gripped the side of the witness box and replied, craning his head to look directly at the jury.]

MARTELLI: No, certainly not.

HUTCHINSON: Do you want to help the Soviet Union as against the West?

MARTELLI: Certainly not.

HUTCHINSON: What is your attitude to England and the English way of life?

MARTELLI: When I first came to England I was fascinated by the many aspects of English life which I liked very much. Then I learned to like England more and more through the eyes of Pamela and when, after the difficult period of 1960 I decided to settle permanently in England I found an extra reason because it was a country where I could search and find peace and where the people are kind and gentle.

It was a very good nod to the jury.

The biggest surprise was when the defence called the recently retired Detective Superintendent George Gordon Smith – then one of the most famous police officers in England. Smith had earned himself the moniker 'the spycatcher' for his work detecting Fuchs, Nunn May, Vassall and the Portland spymaster Gordon Lonsdale. Now he was giving evidence for the defence, explaining to the jury the subtle arts of Russian intelligence: the long cultivation; the playing on weaknesses; the alternate use of threat and enticement.

When he came to make his closing speech Hutchinson addressed the greatest mystery of the case. How was it that the police had got to hear about Martelli's activities? Who had tipped them off? No explanation had been forthcoming from the Crown witnesses. This allowed Hutchinson to put forward his own theory:

Where did the allegations against Dr Martelli come from? We shall never know that for certain. Perhaps, breaking my rule, one would be able to surmise a little about it. Did it come from the Russians themselves? Who knows? It is not liquidation of course, but it is not far short of that so far as Dr Martelli is concerned if he were to be convicted of these offences. This may be supposition but the fact remains that Dr Martelli was, from the Russian point of view, expendable. It has come out during the trial that the Russians were getting fed up with him. If Dr Martelli was telling the truth, he had given no information and had none to give. If Karpekov had other people he was in contact with as well as Vassall – if he had other controlled persons in this country and one of those was known to be a scientist, then of course to turn in the useless Dr Martelli might indeed divert attention from anybody who really was spying in some scientific establishment in this country.

If this were right then the Russians had decided to sacrifice Martelli because he had indeed refused to go along with their demands. But the prosecution declined to offer any counter-explanation.

At 11 a.m. on Monday, 15 July 1963 the jury retired to consider its verdict. After two weeks of evidence what had seemed, when the Solicitor General opened it, such a crystalline case had turned into a finely shaded portrait of Russian intrigue toying with the intricacies of a man's private life. The jurors' task had turned into one of real difficulty. As they filed out of court, Martelli was taken downstairs to a barely furnished room at the bottom of the steps that lead from the dock to the elaborate warren of cells below. Hutchinson and Calderan came to see him as they awaited the jury's decision. Hutchinson later recalled: 'The time waiting for the jury to return their verdict is often excruciating. On this occasion it never seemed to end – in fact it was I think at the time almost the longest deliberation in the history of the Old Bailey. I remember that we spoke little about the trial. Martelli talked of philosophy, travel and music. He chain-smoked throughout.'

During the weeks of his imprisonment on remand in Brixton Martelli had written daily letters to Pamela of utmost tenderness. In the correspondence he reminisces about the past, conjures up carefree images of Italy, and discourses about poetry and music. An ultra-civilised mind is revealed, trying to suppress feelings of optimism or, more usually, foreboding about the future. The last letter is dated 15 July and was written during the long hours immured below Court Number One. It gives a rare insight into the feelings of the defendant during the terrible wait for the verdict.

I am waiting for the verdict, and cannot think of anything but you. Mr Hutchinson has told me that there are very little hopes – the judge has been very bad, but covered himself on all points of law, so there is very little ground for appeal. Let me forget all this for a moment – I want you to be sure that I will not despair, even if the sentence is heavy . . . Amore mio, amore caro – I am desolate, but the pain this is causing you is really breaking my heart.

Until fairly recently jurors were often treated by judges as a necessary evil. To hurry up verdicts court staff were known to lock jurors into their rooms without refreshment, the price of release being a unanimous decision. By the 1960s the juror's lot was a rather more comfortable one. The Martelli jurors, sitting in the Edwardian jury room just off the judge's corridor behind Court Number One, were provided with urns of tea and plates of ham sandwiches to assist them in their deliberations. The newspapers recorded that copious supplies of cigarettes were also shipped in.

Almost ten hours later – at the time, just shy of the longest ever jury retirement in Old Bailey history – at a quarter to nine in the evening the jury returned. Dozens of smouldering cigarettes in many rooms throughout the Old Bailey were extinguished as the court reconvened. Dr Martelli was led back into the dock from his subterranean cell. His solicitor John Calderan, with no time to go back to court the long way, tried to follow his client up the stairs but was stopped by a guard: 'Only defendants allowed in the dock.' Looking strained, Martelli faced the judge as the clerk asked the jury: 'Are you agreed on your verdict?' The foreman answered firmly, 'We are.' To the question, 'Do you find the prisoner guilty or not guilty on the first count?' he answered in a clear voice: 'Not guilty.' Martelli turned sharply towards the jury. These two words were heard eight times more as each count was put to the foreman in turn.

The result was pandemonium. Calderan heard the words standing halfway up the staircase to the dock. Pamela Rothwell started clapping as the usher vainly called for silence. Martelli was seen to shake hands with the warders who had been guarding him. Struggling to make himself heard, the judge informed Martelli that he could be released. He then turned to the jury and excused them from further service for life. Martelli was seen rushing to a telephone to send a telegram to his mother in Pisa. There was no celebratory drink – 'I have had too much tea while waiting for the verdict' – and Martelli and Rothwell were hustled outside by a sea of supporters and well-wishers.

He spoke to a cluster of reporters on the steps of the Bailey. 'Dr Martelli, have you won your one-man war against Russia?'

'Half-won. I don't feel in danger any more.' Running a trembling finger round his collar he spoke of his wait that day as the longest ten hours of his life. 'It has been prophesied by some people in prison that I was due for twenty years. That made a chill run down my spine. That last ten hours have been a torment which only a man on trial who is innocent can understand. I thought it would never end. It was worse than the trial itself. Thank God it is over. All I want now is peace to forget.'

The trial of Dr Martelli only seems visible now through blue clouds of tobacco smoke. Every photograph has him anxiously clutching or hungrily drawing on a cigarette. Cigarette brands punctuate the underlying story. Jeremy Hutchinson later claimed to have given up smoking years earlier; but the press photographs showing him coming to court each morning give the lie to that piece of self-deception. The frantic consumption of tobacco is an apt metaphor for an age of anxiety.

Looking back, Hutchinson mused that there is nothing that a journalist hates more than an acquittal. 'An acquittal shuts a story down; it propels the defendant back into obscurity. I have often seen that irritated shrug of the shoulder and closing of the notebook when the two words "Not guilty" are uttered by the foreman.' But in the aftermath of this verdict the press was rather more benign in its response. The newspapermen who had sat through a long and hot trial, and whose instinct was no doubt that it would end in a guilty verdict, had warmed to the Italian who had chosen to make his life in England with an English family. They had studied Martelli and had discovered not an adamantine ideo-logue in the mould of Fuchs and Pontecorvo, but a man of flesh and blood caught up in an all-too-human predicament, who had – in some obscure way – battled the system and won. They were touched by the love of Pamela Rothwell, the 'tousled-haired' and 'top' woman scientist, as they described her, who had spent every day in a form of vigil at the Old Bailey in his support. They followed Martelli back home and the next day they photographed him outside his modest house in modest Abingdon with little Susanna in his arms. And then they left him alone, to remake his life, and returned to London where the next sensational trial was waiting to be reported.

Dr Martelli's trial had ended on Monday, 15 July. A week later a new jury was empanelled in Court Number One to hear the trial of Dr Stephen Ward. There had been talk that Jeremy Hutchinson would act as his leading counsel. In the end Ward was defended by Hutchinson's Pickwickian colleague, James Burge, who was overwhelmed by the prosecution bulldozer and oversaw a tragedy that ended with Ward, despairing of his fate, taking an overdose of barbiturates. False rumours swirled round the trial, and continued for a long time afterwards, that Ward was himself a Soviet spy. John le Carré, still working in MI6 and then awaiting publication of *The Spy Who Came in from the Cold*, took a West German lawmaker who was on an official visit to England to see English justice in action. He recalls finding himself face to face with Ward in the courtroom during the last days of the case. Looking exhausted, Ward asked them both, in his husky smoker's voice, 'How'm I doing, you reckon?' Le Carré continues: 'You do not expect, as a rule, actors on stage to turn round and chat casually with you in the middle of a drama. Answering for both of us, I assured him that he was doing fine. But I didn't believe myself.'

Martelli's acquittal was a remarkable forensic achievement. Jeremy Hutchinson would later describe it as the case he was most proud of. The judge sent him a personal letter of congratulation, all the more heartfelt because it was possible to detect in his summing-up more than a hint of incredulity at Martelli's story. It says a lot about the camaraderie of the Bar that Peter Rawlinson, magnanimous in defeat, also wrote to Hutchinson: 'A tremendous and thoroughly deserved personal triumph. You did it superbly.' The result was a triumph for John Calderan too. But his memories of the trial itself are not happy ones. He remembers Court Number One as 'a very large court with a heavily baleful atmosphere compounded of past despair, anger, frustration and the pitiless administration of the law'.

MI5 apparently thought that they had a copper-bottomed case against Dr Martelli, and its senior staff were anxious to proceed with the prosecution. The outcome was a significant humiliation. Certainly Peter Rawlinson, writing later in his memoirs, expressed irritation at the way the prosecution had been prepared and a belief that he had not been told the whole truth behind the case. 'I felt at the time that I had not been fully informed by my "clients" about the background and circumstances of this novel prosecution.' In fact Hutchinson's theory, which he expounded in his closing speech, may well have been proved correct. Many years later the truth emerged that Martelli's arrest and prosecution were the direct consequence of information from a Russian operating at the United Nations headquarters in New York, with the code-name FEDORA. After his arrival in New York, Alexei Kulak had made contact with the FBI. Over time he had become highly prized by the Americans as a source. One of his revelations was that there was an ideological agent inside the AERE. But it is now thought that FEDORA was a KGB double agent and his lead was disinformation. Had the KGB concluded that Martelli was useless to them? Had they decided to serve up Martelli to protect a more promising source, one that was never identified by British counter-intelligence? Or to build up the credibility of FEDORA as a source in the eyes of the FBI?

On the steps of the Old Bailey, Giuseppe Martelli was reported as informing journalists: 'I have always believed in British justice and now I shall have a rest. But I like this country and want to stay here.' He made good on his promise, obtaining a position at Sussex University, where he did not return to atomic physics. Instead he began 'a prolonged and public period of research, initially on non-linear electron wave interactions in the auroral plasma', before founding the 'Space and Plasma Physics Group' at Sussex. His relationship with Pamela continued strong until her death in 1991. Dr Martelli himself died in 1994. His life was memorialised in obituaries published in many learned journals which all spoke of his eminence as a scientist. In one obituary, published in the *Quarterly Journal of the Royal Astronomical Society,* it was recorded that in 1992 an asteroid had been named after him.

9

'Trial of the Century'

R v Jeremy Thorpe (1979)

MANY BARRISTERS CAN pinpoint a single case that transformed their professional lives. Edward Marshall Hall was propelled into the public eye, and to later glory, by the successful defence in 1894 of an obscure prostitute called Marie Hermann. More than eighty years later George Carman defended in a trial that would launch him into legal superstardom. Carman would go on to become almost as lauded as Marshall Hall was in his own age, the most recognised lawyer of the last quarter of the twentieth century. The case that made Carman's name was itself labelled the 'Trial of the Century' and its factual backdrop is as extraordinary now as when it was put before a jury forty years ago. Jeremy Thorpe, the former leader of the Liberal Party, and one of the most glamorous politicians in the firmament of the 1960s and 1970s, was alleged to have plotted with an assortment of co-conspirators to murder his former male lover.

It was appropriate that the trial would take place in Court Number One. That courtroom had already been – and would continue to be – the venue for political nemesis. It was here that the extraordinary career of Horatio Bottomley, businessman, newspaper proprietor, swindler and parliamentarian, came to an end in 1922 when he was sentenced to seven years for fraud. Three years before Thorpe's trial the former Postmaster General and Labour MP John Stonehouse, who had faked his own death by leaving his clothes on a Florida beach, received a similar sentence for insurance fraud after a trial lasting sixty-eight days. Later Jonathan Aitken was convicted of perjury here in 1999. Jeffrey Archer, who had earlier written and appeared in a play set in Court Number One and appropriately titled *The Accused*, had to make do with Court Number Eight for his own perjury trial in 2001.

When Carman received the brief from Thorpe's solicitor Sir David Napley, he knew that it would be a case that could transform his life.

At the time he was practising mainly in Manchester and when it became known that he had landed the brief to defend Thorpe the London criminal Bar was not only incredulous, it was scandalised that such a plum had somehow slipped through its collective fingers into the hands of an outsider. It transpired that a few years earlier Carman had acted for the manager of the Big Dipper at the Battersea funfair, who had been charged with manslaughter after several of its cars had left the rails, causing the deaths of five children. Carman's only defence, if it deserved that name, was that the manager was incompetent to perform his tasks: 'My defence is that my client did not know what the job really entailed and should never have been given it to do,' he grimly explained outside court. Napley, the most eminent criminal solicitor of the period, had been in court acting for a co-defendant and, with mounting admiration, watched Carman slowly unfold this non-defence to the jury, who proceeded to acquit. As Napley left court he turned to a colleague and told him that Carman was a man to watch.

Whether Napley would have taken such a gamble on this outsider had he known of Carman's private life, and his modus operandi, is another matter. Shortly after his death in 2000 Carman's son wrote an extraordinary biography of his father.[1] Until then the world at large had known Carman as a man who dominated the courtroom with a voice both mellifluous and stern. Dominic Carman described his father as a man racked by self-doubt, whose three wives all spoke of domestic abuse and emotional complexity; a compulsive drinker and gambler.

The picture presented in the biography was shocking to those who had known Carman; the contrast between the ultra-composed exterior and the interior turmoil seemed unbridgeable. It was not so surprising to some of his contemporaries. Freddy Reynold had acted as Carman's junior in a couple of cases in the early 1970s, including the Big Dipper trial itself. In his memoirs he recalled how

> On one occasion during the trial, my pupil . . . phoned me at about one o'clock in the morning to say she was still with George in a bar and that he was hopelessly drunk. She wanted to know what to do. I did not attempt to conceal my irritation. I told her to leave George where he was and go home; he had, I said rather tartly, a strong instinct for survival, and had remarkable restorative powers. And so it proved.

This was the man whom Napley had retained to defend Jeremy Thorpe in the most eagerly anticipated trial in living memory.

Born in 1929, Jeremy Thorpe was a child of the establishment. Both his father and maternal grandfather had been MPs. He went to Eton and then to Trinity College, Oxford, to study jurisprudence. An undistinguished student, he nonetheless swiftly acquired a reputation as an outstanding public speaker. Thorpe rose rapidly to the top of the university's Liberal Club, its Law Society and then the Oxford Union, whose president he became in 1951. At the Union he got to know a bright young law student called George Carman, who helped Thorpe with essays in return for being allowed a prominent slot at Union debates. Even while at Oxford Thorpe's name was connected with several Liberal seats and by early 1952 he had his heart set on North Devon, whose Liberal association adopted him as their candidate in November of that year.

There had been no Liberal MP in the West Country since the end of the war, and at the 1951 election the Liberals had come third in North Devon. But the region had a long Liberal tradition and Thorpe threw himself into reviving it with the kind of bread-and-butter campaigning that soon became the Liberals' trademark. Although Thorpe had just scraped a third-class degree from Oxford, thanks to his father's legal connections he was able to join Western Circuit Chambers in London. He spent much time in the courts of Devon and Cornwall so he could combine legal work with constituency visits. Thorpe supplemented his meagre legal income with more lucrative work as a TV presenter of a short-lived chat show, *The Scientist Replies*, and the long-running current affairs programme *This Week*. Although he lost in North Devon in 1955, Thorpe ploughed on and in 1959 he won it by 362 votes: the only English seat the Tories lost that year.

Even before he became Liberal leader two of Thorpe's aphorisms had entered the political lexicon. It was Jeremy Thorpe who quipped that the House of Lords was 'proof of life after death'. He also memorably said of Harold Macmillan, after he had carried out the brutal Cabinet reshuffle that became known as the 'Night of the Long Knives', that 'greater love hath no man than to lay down his friends for his life'. He proved to be a remarkable public speaker with a capacity to mix humour, passion and elegant put-downs.[2] Our mental image of Thorpe nowadays is of a stooped, slightly sinister figure, wearing a mask-like frown, an anachronistic double-breasted waistcoat and trilby hat. But although by the time of his trial Thorpe may have appeared prematurely aged, in fact he was a political prodigy who had once exuded vitality and charisma. By the age of thirty-seven, when many people are just embarking on their political careers, he had become leader of his party. In the 1960s and early 1970s Thorpe was a glamorous personality, an attractive amalgam of old-fashioned aristocratic dandyism and energetic modernity who played to the photographers and TV cameras that followed his every move, vaulting over farm gates (indeed gates of all kinds) and enthusiastically greeting constituents with outstretched arms. In North Devon Thorpe could do little wrong. He pulled off stunt after stunt to win favourable press coverage, even taking over a village post office for a week so the postmaster could take his family on a long overdue holiday.

In the 1970 election campaign he toured the country by helicopter; in 1971 he appeared in a party political broadcast alongside Jimmy Savile, then at the height of his fame. Before the October 1974 election Thorpe toured coastal constituencies in a hovercraft, until it broke down. More successfully, he set up a live TV link between London and the Liberal office in Barnstaple, appearing on television as a statesmanlike kingmaker in a book-lined study as Heath and Wilson jostled for position in London.

Despite his rapid rise, Thorpe was never truly an insider. He had joined a party that was on the fringes of contemporary political life. His father had been a Unionist MP and his grandfather a Conservative: he could have used his family connections to seek a safe Tory seat, and might well have found one. Instead he joined a party whose fortunes were at a particularly low ebb. He can hardly be accused of careerism for nailing his colours to the Liberal mast: in 1955 the party only had six MPs and a by-election loss in 1957 meant that the tally fell to just five.

For all his vigour and charm Thorpe was a romantic fantasist with a reputation for vanity and snobbery. He was obsessed with status, titles – and his own innate superiority. At Oxford he would introduce himself as a future Prime Minister without any trace of irony. As Liberal leader he once wore morning dress at the Cenotaph on Remembrance Sunday, not the usual dark suit, and astonished Edward Heath by suggesting that they wear full Privy Counsellors' uniform, with swords, at the signing of the Treaty of Rome by which the UK joined the EEC in 1973.

In the 1950s Thorpe had fantasised about marrying Princess Margaret, and having befriended Antony Armstrong-Jones – who had been in the year below Thorpe at Eton – found himself on the fringes of her social circle. He was said to be furious when the princess's engagement to Armstrong-Jones, later Lord Snowdon, was announced in 1960, although he was later mooted as a possible best man. In the end Thorpe wasn't even invited to the wedding. MI5 made enquiries about his suitability as a royal best man and discovered that while pursuing his meteoric political career, Thorpe was also engaged in a risk-laden double life as a closet homosexual who often cruised the gay pubs and clubs of London.

At the time many politicians – notably Bob Boothby and Tom Driberg – had pursued long parliamentary careers despite being known homosexuals, avoiding public disgrace because the press turned a blind eye to their private lives. But neither Boothby nor Driberg had got anywhere near the leadership of their parties. Paradoxically, just as decriminalisation edged closer in the 1950s and early 1960s it became riskier than ever to be a gay politician. The press's willingness to keep quiet about the sex lives of the political elite was waning, while new publications such as *Private Eye* gleefully reported any gossip they could lay their hands on. At the height of the Cold War the exposure of Guy Burgess and John Vassall – both of them gay – as Russian spies fuelled theories that homosexuals were automatically dangerous, untrustworthy or even treacherous.

Thorpe's affairs typically followed a set pattern: he would form unusually close attachments to men he barely knew, would be flattered into helping them (financially or otherwise), only to be driven to distraction by their demands. Like many politicians Thorpe suffered from a 'Houdini complex', craving risk and the narrow avoidance of disaster. Thorpe's conquests in the early 1950s and 1960s included a Buckingham Palace footman, a Swedish sailor, and a horse trainer who styled himself Norman van de Vater.

It was at Vater's Oxfordshire stables in the summer of 1960 that Thorpe first met one of his grooms – a nineteen-year-old called Norman Josiffe (he soon after changed his name to Norman Scott, by which name he will be referred to in this chapter). Thorpe later described Scott as 'looking simply heaven' and gave him his phone number, urging the young stable-lad to visit him at the House of Commons when next in London. Scott, whose duties apparently included shaving Vater's back while he soaked in the bath, quickly fell out with his employer and descended on Thorpe in London, accompanied by his terrier, Mrs Tish.

Thorpe and Scott soon began an affair, allegedly consummated in a guest bedroom of Stonewalls, Thorpe's mother's house in Surrey. The precise nature of the events that night would later be pored over in detail at the Old Bailey but on Scott's often-repeated account it was at Stonewalls that he had his first experience of gay sex. This involved Thorpe handing him a copy of James Baldwin's recently published novel of homosexual awakening, *Giovanni's Room*, then returning to Scott's bedroom sometime later and, dispensing with preliminary niceties, proceeding to have sex with him. Scott would claim that Thorpe had 'infected' him with what he described as the 'disease' of homosexuality.

Back in London, Thorpe paid Scott's rent and settled his bills. But the politician would soon discover that his younger lover was even more of a fantasist than him. Before changing his surname Scott had styled himself as 'Norman Lianche-Josiffe'; at one stage he boasted of being the illegitimate son of the Earl of Eldon (whose family name is Scott). And although he would later claim to have been an initially unwilling target of Thorpe's advances, even before his seduction he was already talking of his relationship with Thorpe to anyone who would listen. But Scott was also a vulnerable young man. Ever since the start of the 1960s he had been in poor mental health, relying on medication that appeared to do little to prevent him from suicide attempts and self-harm. Scott seemed unable ever to hold down a job and would regularly beg Thorpe, whom he described as his 'guardian', for clothes, money and assistance in finding work. He said his National Insurance card had been stolen by Vater and persuaded Thorpe to help supply him with a new one, which he then accused Thorpe of withholding from him. Thorpe pulled strings to get Scott a short-lived job at Liberal headquarters; Thorpe then found him work with a Major Hambro, a Devon farmer, where Scott lasted only a month. Another family asked Scott to move on after Mrs Tish killed their ducks.

Scott gradually built up a cache of incriminating 'Dear Norman' letters from Thorpe which carried the clear implication that they were lovers (whether the 'Norman' addressed was Scott or Vater was unclear). He later brandished a letter, certainly addressed to Scott, which contained a phrase that has become so infamous that it is now indelibly associated with the Thorpe affair. His enthusiasm for Scott still undimmed, Thorpe told him that 'Bunnies *can* (and *will*) go to France' (where Scott wanted to study dressage), and added the postscript: 'I miss you.' In another letter, Thorpe enthused to his lover, 'My angel, all I want to do is to share a Devon farm with you.' Perhaps fortunately, this letter was later lost by police.

Yet Thorpe's passion soon ebbed. Whenever Scott returned to London they would row: Scott would accuse Thorpe of ruining his life and make vague threats. On one occasion in 1962 a concerned friend, to whom Scott disclosed a half-baked desire to shoot Thorpe and then kill himself, had phoned the police. Scott satisfied two officers that he was an unlikely assassin, but used the opportunity to denounce Thorpe and gave them a cache of love letters. Thorpe would in turn boast that no one would ever believe Scott's story of their affair, given his friendships with people in high places, not the least of whom was the Director of Public Prosecutions.[3] By 1964, Scott would later claim, the affair had fizzled out. Thorpe then procured a passport for Scott and somehow landed him a job in Switzerland; after only a few days Scott reappeared in London, yet again pestering his former lover for money. Thorpe helped track down a suitcase that had gone missing on the trip back to England, but made sure that a stash of his letters was removed before it reached Scott.

In 1967 Jo Grimond, whose son had committed suicide during the 1966 election campaign, resigned as Liberal leader and Thorpe succeeded him. Even before becoming leader Thorpe had exercised an influence on his party disproportionate to his years. In 1965 he had been elected party treasurer and appointed four deputy treasurers, one of whom was a merchant banker called David Holmes. A bisexual Oxford friend and later best man at Thorpe's first wedding, Holmes had hitherto been little known in the Liberal Party. He gradually became a godfather figure, implacably loyal to Thorpe and trusted by him to handle the Liberal Party's – and Thorpe's – finances. After his initial election in 1959 Thorpe had swiftly acquired a reputation as an internationalist, getting to know many African leaders and emerging as a fierce critic of apartheid. He attracted headlines for a speech at the Liberal assembly in 1966 in which he appeared to advocate bombing Rhodesia, lapping up the controversy he caused. He forged cross-party friendships with Tony Benn, and with Tories like Norman St John-Stevas and Christopher Chataway, with whom Thorpe served on the committee of the Homosexual Law Reform Society. Although Thorpe was officially very firmly in the closet (indeed for a gay politician at the time there was nowhere else to be) he was no humbug and campaigned openly for decriminalisation.

But his strongest political friendship was with a fellow Liberal MP, Peter Bessell, who with Thorpe's help had won Bodmin – not far from Thorpe's North Devon constituency – in 1964. Despite serving as a Methodist lay preacher Bessell was, like Thorpe, also a philandering adventurer. At the Old Bailey in 1979 George Carman would describe him as 'a cross between Uriah Heap and James Bond'; to the Liberal MP Russell Johnston he was 'like one of those American pulpit-bashers who's always screwing women'.

Thorpe told Bessell about his entanglement with Scott over lunch at the Ritz in March 1965, just after Scott had written to Thorpe's mother about it. Bessell talked him out of sending a solicitor's letter threatening Scott with a libel action but he nonetheless agreed to communicate with, and give money to, Scott on Thorpe's behalf to keep him quiet. Thorpe's mesmeric charm had caught Bessell in its net. He would prove to be fiercely loyal, willing to do whatever it took to ensure that Scott, and the threat he posed, was contained: sometimes by gentle persuasion, sometimes otherwise.

Bessell offered Scott a move to the US and a job with a chain of hamburger restaurants he was setting up, but Scott instead went to Ireland where, improbably, he ended up living in a Trappist monastery. In the late 1960s he had a bad fall from a horse at the Dublin Horse Show, putting his riding career on hold. Back in London he now pursued a modelling career. But this period of relative success did not last; Scott acquired a reputation for unreliability, and his fortunes turned again. By the time he married Sue Myers in 1969 he was penniless once more and living in a Dorset cottage. It was not a happy marriage and he was loathed by his in-laws from the start. They once presented him with a mug for Christmas with a single word printed on the side: Strychnine.

His marriage soon behind him, Scott then drifted into a new existence at Tal-y-Bont, North Wales, where he ran a dressage business and started an affair with a widow called Gwen Parry-Jones (she would later commit suicide soon after their relationship ended). When Bessell refused to give Scott another handout in 1971 Mrs Parry-Jones wrote on Scott's behalf to Emlyn Hooson, Liberal MP for nearby Montgomeryshire. Parry-Jones and Scott were invited to Westminster where they met the Liberal chief whip, the young David Steel, and then had a meeting with both Steel and Hooson. At first the MPs thought it was Bessell who was the subject of complaint, but they soon realised, to their horror, that it was in fact the Liberal leader who was accused of having conducted an exploitative affair with Scott. Although an internal enquiry exonerated Thorpe of wrongdoing, the incident hardly did his standing at Westminster any good.

In May 1968 Thorpe had somewhat allayed rumblings over his sexuality by marrying Caroline Allpass, a young and vivacious Sotheby's secretary (in a classic display of Thorpian bravado he somehow persuaded the Archbishop of Canterbury to give his blessing to the couple). In April 1969 a son, Rupert, was born and all seemed well in Thorpe's world. Then tragedy struck: a few days after the 1970 election Caroline was killed in a car crash. Thorpe was genuinely devastated by the loss of his wife. However, politically his bereavement did Thorpe no harm: the sympathy he attracted helped to relieve pressure from, on the one hand, Young Liberals who felt he was not radical enough, and on the other the Liberal establishment, for whom he was a flamboyant dandy who had yet to bring them electoral success (at the 1970 election the Liberal tally fell from thirteen to six MPs).

After a period of what, to many, seemed over-ostentatious mourning, Thorpe got married again in March 1973, to the wealthy and well-connected Marion Stein, a pianist and the former wife of the Earl of Harewood. When Thorpe celebrated their marriage with a 'musical evening' attended by nearly 1,000 guests at the Royal Opera House in July 1973 all seemed well: the Liberals were riding high in the polls as the Heath government lurched from crisis to crisis.

But behind the scenes Thorpe was getting increasingly concerned by Scott's continued menacing. Letters can of course be copied, and whenever he and Bessell thought they had intercepted, bought or destroyed all the potentially incriminating correspondence, others cropped up. Thorpe became obsessed with the ongoing threat that Scott posed, and increasingly talked of suicide – or murder. In the summer of 1975 Thorpe suffered some kind of breakdown and went to ground in Devon for six weeks, where he pondered how to silence Scott for good.

Thorpe had hinted at drastic action before. Bessell would later allege that back in December 1968 Thorpe had announced to him and Holmes, 'We've got to get rid of him', followed by the prescient statement, 'It's no worse than killing a sick dog.' At first nothing was done: Bessell continued to buy Scott's silence, even paying Scott's divorce costs after his short-lived marriage ended. Bessell then stepped down as an MP. In 1971 he left his wife and moved to America, where he had a wealthy girlfriend, hoping to shake off his creditors and start anew. Separated by distance, Bessell and Thorpe's friendship cooled. Having relied on Bessell for so long Thorpe threw the blame on to Bessell when a bizarre plan to swindle money out of a wealthy offshore businessman and Liberal donor, named Jack Hayward, fell apart. Nonetheless, Bessell's admiration for the Liberal leader seems to have continued untarnished.

With Bessell in America the more biddable David Holmes had become Thorpe's new Man Friday. In 1975, as Thorpe's obsession with the threat supposedly posed by Scott burgeoned, Holmes finally put Thorpe's demands for drastic action into effect with the help of an odd collection of Welshmen: David Miller, a Cardiff screen printer; a carpet dealer called John le Mesurier; and George Deakin, a one-armed-bandit salesman.

Le Mesurier, who was a client of Holmes's, had introduced Deakin to him for financial advice. Holmes apparently saw in Deakin the kind of man who might know somebody to carry out Thorpe's plan to rid himself of Scott, though he merely told Deakin of the need to put the 'frighteners' on an unnamed blackmailer who was tormenting a friend, adding – falsely – that a woman had committed suicide and a three-year-old's life was somehow in danger as a result of this blackmail. Deakin was sympathetic. In February 1975, at a Showman's Dinner in Blackpool, as they marvelled over the topless girls on display, Deakin asked a friend of his, David Miller, if he knew someone who would do 'anything for a laugh or a giggle'. Miller suggested a twenty-eight-year-old airline pilot called Andrew Newton, who happened to be his guest at the same dinner. Deakin is said to have asked Newton if he was interested in 'a professional frightening job'. 'I'm your man,' the drunken Newton replied. Later that night Newton got into a fight with one of the topless girls and ended up vomiting over Miller's bed.

It may reasonably have been concluded from his conduct that night that Newton was not the ideal choice for any kind of 'job', whether or not it involved murder. Nonetheless when Newton was eventually introduced by Deakin to Holmes, the naïve merchant banker appears to have seen him as the ideal candidate to get rid of Scott. Holmes offered Newton £10,000 up front, a sum that Newton would later claim was the going rate for killing someone, not merely frightening them.

Newton later struck Auberon Waugh, who followed the trial, as 'the voice of the New Age: flippant, cynical, self-righteous, stupid and television-fed into a sort of mindless conceit'. This was not just a manifestation of Waugh's habitual snobbery: Newton himself admitted that his friends called him 'chicken brain'.

Thorpe had arranged the finance for the plot: £20,000 of a £300,000 donation from Jack Hayward would be siphoned off and paid to Holmes for onward transmission to Newton. Although Hayward lived in the Bahamas he was nicknamed 'Union Jack' on account of his patriotism. Though not previously a Liberal, he had come under the Thorpe spell. Hayward was so impressed that he later wrote to Thorpe of 'their joint ambition to see you as Prime Minister in five years' time'. It tells us much about Thorpe's vast reserves of monomania that he repaid Hayward's generosity by using his subsequent donations to the Liberal Party to fund a murder plot.

Meanwhile Norman Scott's life had lurched from one crisis to another. In 1973 he moved yet again, to Thorpe's constituency of North Devon, where he would complain about his erstwhile lover's alleged misdeeds to anyone who cared to listen. Much of the time he was prostrated through drink, drugs or self-pity. The few incriminating letters he still retained (many written by Bessell in the 1960s when he was receiving regular remittances to obtain his silence), his self-styled 'dossier', were somehow procured from him by his new doctor, Ronald Gleadle, at Thorpe's instigation: Gleadle passed on to Scott the £2,500 that David Holmes had paid him. The letters that Scott thought were his lifeline were burned in an Aga the night before the February 1974 election.

On 12 October 1975 Andrew Newton introduced himself to Scott in Barnstaple. Newton claimed to be a journalist called Peter Keene and warned Scott to watch out for a 'man from Canada' sent to assassinate him. He sat down with Scott and won his trust. Twelve days later Scott – this time accompanied by his Great Dane, Rinka – agreed to meet 'Peter Keene' again outside a hotel in Combe Martin, and they then drove off in Newton's car over the Somerset border towards Porlock.

Newton said he felt tired and Scott offered to take over the driving. As they swapped seats at a lay-by on Porlock Hill, Newton suddenly revealed himself as the assassin, producing an antique 1910 Mauser automatic pistol and shooting Rinka in the head at point-blank range. (Newton would later explain that he had a phobia of dogs and that as the enormous Rinka leapt out of the car, fatally misunderstanding the stop-off as the opportunity for a walk, he had instinctively reacted by turning the gun on the wretched hound.) Newton then put the barrel to Scott's head, announcing that 'It's your turn now.' The gun jammed. Mouthing curses, Newton got back into the car and drove off, leaving Scott alone on the moor to mourn his beloved dog.

The hapless gunman was soon tracked down. He was arrested and charged with possessing a firearm 'with intent to endanger life'. But he did not lift the lid on the truth of the matter, instead telling the police a cock-and-bull story that he was being blackmailed by Scott, to whom he claimed he had sent naked photographs of himself, wrongly thinking that Scott was female; and that the shooting had been a warning. Newton calculated that he would be better off if, for the time being, he kept quiet about Holmes's and Thorpe's participation in the plot. Indeed Holmes had promised him a large cash payment once things quietened down. Convicted at Exeter Crown Court in March 1976, Newton was sentenced to two years' imprisonment to run concurrently with a six-month sentence for 'damaging property'.

It is at this stage that the story becomes truly byzantine. In order to substantiate the blackmail claim that Newton was going to make at his trial, Thorpe had dispatched Holmes out to California to enlist Peter Bessell's help. There, Holmes somehow managed to persuade Bessell to write a letter in which he explained that he had originally given money to Scott out of compassion but that Scott had gone on to blackmail him over an affair he was carrying on with his secretary. The Thorpe charm still commanded extraordinary loyalty. Bessell agreed to write what was a patently false, and ludicrous, document.

Having assured Bessell that the letter would never enter the public domain, Thorpe almost immediately broke his word. In March 1976, just before Newton's trial, the *Sunday Times* published an article written by Thorpe himself – headed 'The Lies of Norman Scott' – in which, drawing on Bessell's false blackmail letter, he appeared to claim that Bessell had been blackmailed by Scott over his business affairs as well as his colourful love life. Given that Bessell had only ever contacted Scott to protect Thorpe, this was shabby thanks indeed to an old friend.

Bessell had had enough. From his Californian beach hut he gave an interview to the *Daily Mail* in early May 1976 revealing that he had only written the blackmail letter at Thorpe's request. The headline said it all: 'I Told Lies to Protect Thorpe'. Press interest in the Scott–Thorpe connection had been building throughout the first months of 1976. After years of coyness about the story, the bizarre tale of a dog shot dead on a misty moor was just too intriguing. Notwithstanding the adverse press Thorpe vowed to stay on. Liberal leaders were now elected by the party membership, not just MPs; Thorpe said he would stand for re-election that autumn and was confident he would win. Thorpe was further helped by widespread rumours that the Scott affair had been cooked up by the South African spy agency BOSS to smear him, as a prominent opponent of apartheid. Even Harold Wilson chose to raise the possibility of South African involvement at Prime Minister's Questions on 9 March 1976. Although no evidence has ever emerged of any such involvement in the Scott affair, the theory was sufficiently plausible to buy Thorpe some time. And either by conspiracy or lucky coincidence, Newton's trial in Exeter started on 16 March, the same day as both Wilson's surprise resignation and the announcement by Buckingham Palace that Princess Margaret and Lord Snowdon were to divorce, knocking the case off the front pages.

But Bessell's revelations to the *Daily Mail* changed everything. Suddenly the dam had burst. On 10 May 1976, four days after the Bessell story went into print, Thorpe finally resigned as party leader, furiously denouncing his former friend and colleague as a Judas.

The promise of a further £5,000 had been enough to buy Newton's silence during his imprisonment. But not after. Newton was determined to extract every penny he could from his chance retainer as a hitman. He sold his story, including incriminating recordings of a phone conversation with David Holmes, to the London *Evening News* which splashed with the headline 'I Was Hired to Kill Scott' in October 1977.

From this moment on, Thorpe's prosecution became inevitable. He was invited to report to Minehead Police Station on 4 August 1978 where he was charged, alongside his alleged co-conspirators, Holmes, Le Mesurier and Deakin, with conspiracy to murder Norman Scott. Thorpe alone was also charged with incitement to murder, a charge founded on his alleged conversation with Bessell and Holmes in the House of Commons some years earlier. That evening Thorpe, still a Member of Parliament, attended a 'flower shower' at Bishop's Nympton, a village in his constituency, as if nothing untoward had happened.

Throughout the investigation and subsequent prosecution Thorpe's monomania got the better of him. He tried to persuade Jack Hayward to threaten Bessell with bankruptcy if he returned to England to give evidence. He warned Nadir Dinshaw, a businessman with Liberal sympathies who had unwittingly helped redirect money from Hayward to Holmes, that he could be deported back to his native Pakistan if he did not play ball. Rather than leave Newton well alone, Thorpe and Holmes tried to find him a job with the South African or Rhodesian Air Force.

The first step towards the trial was the committal hearing, which took place at Minehead Magistrates Court. A surreal event to be held in such a small seaside town, the hearing attracted huge media interest. Cameramen climbed trees to get a glimpse of the defendants arriving at the small 1930s courthouse. In the basic courtroom the four defendants sat together, each separately represented. They owed each other no loyalty and certainly Thorpe might have reasonably thought that the faithful Holmes had exhausted the springs of fealty that had motivated his behaviour for so long. They made up an odd assortment. Thorpe had never met Deakin or Le Mesurier until the criminal proceedings began – any dealings with them had only ever been via Holmes, who himself was hardly on intimate terms with either – and he must have found the notion of joining them in a single dock almost as extraordinary as the charges themselves.

Deakin's counsel was an unpredictable and brilliant young Welshman called Gareth Williams QC (later a highly regarded Labour Attorney General and Leader of the House of Lords). Le Mesurier's advocate was a steady old hand with a walrus moustache called Dennis Cowley QC, a Midland Circuit silk who had none of the glamour of the other defence counsel. Holmes had the impressive John Mathew QC, who had the unnerving habit of contemptuously looking over the shoulder of witnesses while cross-examining them. Mathew had been David Napley's first choice to represent Thorpe had Holmes not bagged him first. Instead, remembering the Big Dipper trial, he had settled for Carman.

Nonetheless, while the other defendants' silks all made their way down to Minehead, George Carman stayed in his chambers. Napley had a high opinion of his own advocacy skills and insisted on leading for the defence at the committal proceedings, much to Carman's fury. One of the myths that has grown up about the Thorpe case is that somehow Napley mishandled his cross-examination of the main prosecution witnesses at the committal hearing. This is a story which of course suits barristers anxious to preserve a monopoly on a reputation for good advocacy. George Carman would in later life give some support to the myth, citing the fact that Napley had asked Scott in cross-examination whether there was anything unusual about Thorpe's body: to which Scott replied that Thorpe had three nodules in his armpit. This was later said to be one of the key reasons Thorpe would later not testify at the Old Bailey, fearful that he might be asked to unbutton his shirt. In fact Napley succeeded in exposing several weaknesses in the prosecution case. In particular it emerged that Bessell had signed a contract with the *Sunday Telegraph* to tell his story after the trial had ended: in effect £50,000 if Thorpe was convicted but only £25,000 if he was acquitted.

As was perhaps inevitable, the Minehead magistrates decided that the prosecution evidence disclosed a case to answer and on 10 January 1979 the case was committed to be heard at the Old Bailey four months later.

The interrelationship between each of the defendants was complex. There was the constant fear that one or other would try to mount a 'cutthroat defence'. Newton's evidence was hostile to Deakin, but not to Le Mesurier; conversely another witness, David Miller, was far more favourable to Deakin than to Le Mesurier. Thorpe and Holmes had been close friends but there was always the danger that Thorpe would point the finger at his erstwhile best man and suggest that the whole plan was dreamed up by Holmes in a misguided attempt to protect him from the political damage that the rampant Scott could inflict. After all, there was clear evidence of contact between Holmes, Deakin and Newton, while Thorpe had wisely kept himself well removed from the execution of the plot. Before the trial started John Mathew had said Holmes would be willing to plead guilty to a charge of 'conspiracy to frighten', a deal the prosecution refused; Thorpe always denied everything.

And what evidence would the four defendants give? The right to remain silent in the face of a criminal charge is a cornerstone of English law. It is for the prosecution to make out its case to the required standard of proof. At the time the decision by a defendant not to give evidence in their own defence was not a matter from which the prosecution or the judge were entitled to invite the jury to draw adverse inferences. Nonetheless, in reality a jury might well treat a failure by a defendant to explain themselves as strange and suggestive of a desire to hide something.

A defendant can do more harm than good to their defence in the witness box. Cross-examination can destroy a defendant's credibility and carry home a verdict of guilty even when at the close of the prosecution case the evidence looked thin. So the decision to advise a client to give evidence or not is often one of the most delicate and finely balanced any criminal barrister has to take: most barristers will seek a written confirmation from a client that they have been advised of the risks of not giving evidence and have nonetheless chosen not to do so.

Thorpe, whose twenty-five years in politics had given him undoubted skills as a public speaker, was apparently keen to use the witness box as an opportunity for further speechifying. By contrast George Carman was equally desperate to keep Thorpe out. He feared, with good reason, that Thorpe, who went as far as to deny any form of sexual relationship with Scott at all, would say too much – or be asked about his three nodules. Moreover, there was prosecution evidence to which Thorpe simply had no answer. Carman's junior Graham Boal, later an Old Bailey judge, recalls an 'all-counsel' meeting one evening at the Old Bailey, with no solicitors or clients present, at which Mathew said he did not want Holmes to give evidence, but wanted to know whether Thorpe would appear in the witness box and stab Holmes in the back. They eventually agreed that neither of their clients would give evidence. Dennis Cowley, who had been snoozing in a leather armchair in the corner of the room, woke to announce that they had made it impossible for Le Mesurier to give evidence either. But Gareth Williams was keen to make his mark and said he wanted Deakin to give evidence, despite Mathew's and Carman's protestations that this could ruin everything.

Napley's memoirs recall that Thorpe only decided at the last possible moment not to give evidence; Boal's recollection is that it had been agreed a lot earlier. Either way, Carman did well to keep Thorpe out of the witness box that the exhibitionist in him longed to enter. When Thorpe arrived at his first consultation with Carman he brought with him an out-of-date copy of *Archbold* (then the criminal lawyer's bible), intent on directing his own defence: Carman somehow managed to tell him to do as he was told. By the time of the trial Thorpe was compliant to Carman's plans for the conduct of the defence.

The Minehead proceedings had been reported in detail. All the Crown witnesses had given evidence in Minehead and unfolded the extraordinary story that reached its climax with a dead dog and a man pleading for his life on a windswept moor in Somerset. Many feared its 'West End transfer' to the Old Bailey a few months later would be an anticlimax. It wasn't. It lived up to its billing as the 'Trial of the Century'.

It is a testament to Thorpe's delusional level of self-belief that he genuinely thought that he could hang on to his seat in Parliament with a charge of conspiracy to murder louring over him. He even managed to have the start of the trial delayed until after the general election, set to take place on 3 May 1979, so that he could concentrate on campaigning. Thorpe duly lost the seat he had held for twenty years by more than 8,000 votes.[4]

On 8 May 1979, just five days after Margaret Thatcher's election victory and Thorpe's unceremonious exit from Parliament, the trial began. According to Jean Rook, writing for the *Daily Express*, Court Number One looked like 'a scene from Madame Tussaud's: the carved wooden room, the lawyers in starched linen and stone-grey wigs, the dummy-silent figures in the dock'. Thorpe had arrived earlier at the Bailey as if – so it was wryly recorded – he were some visiting dignitary, and was ushered into rooms normally reserved for defence lawyers, not defendants. Tickets for the public gallery had had to be allocated by the Old Bailey staff: sixty-nine journalists managed to get seats in the courtroom itself (one of them going to Auberon Waugh, and another to Sybille Bedford, who had a good nose for a classic trial), with a further eighty applications rejected. Peter Chippindale, who followed the case for the *Guardian*, echoed a complaint made by many journalists over the years: 'Most of the reporters will be unable to see very much. Court One in the original part of the Old Bailey building in Central London bears all the hallmarks of the severe Victorian [*sic*] legal system for which it was designed – yards of dark oak panelling, a gloomy half-light from the high-up windows, and a deep well across which the defendants and the judge face each other.'[5]

Leading for the Crown was the dignified and universally respected Peter Taylor QC ('a handsome, blunt man with a fine Roman profile', one journalist described him). 'He would have been happier as a judge,' wrote Auberon Waugh, and indeed he did become a High Court judge soon after the Thorpe trial, and later a well-regarded Lord Chief Justice.

The judge chosen for the trial was the sixty-eight-year-old Mr Justice Joseph Cantley. Until the age of fifty-six a bachelor, Cantley had been the Presiding Judge of the Northern Circuit in the early 1970s; Simon Freeman, who later wrote a book about the affair, has suggested he was chosen because he was 'untainted by metropolitan prejudice'. He was certainly unworldly: in 1970 he had tried a case about a young man who had been injured in an accident in a bulldozer. Informed that his injuries had affected his sex life Cantley had asked whether the man was married. When the answer came that he was not, the judge had remarked, 'Well, I can't see how it affects his sex life.' But while Cantley appeared doddery – Bessell later described him as a 'sozzled old eunuch' in a letter to Auberon Waugh – his summing-up would later show he knew exactly what he was doing.

Thorpe sat in the corner of the dock supported by three velvet cushions, never once casting a glance at any of his co-defendants; a symbolic distancing to indicate to the jury – placed just yards away and able to study his every expression – the absurdity of the notion that he would conspire with such people. 'Stiff as his dapper little waistcoat, as unmoved as wax. Under the neon lighting his tan is yellow as candle-grease and his round, brown, glass marble eyes are fixed on Norman Scott,' Rook noted with razor-sharp accuracy. Thorpe's mother looked on grimly, as did his wife, the formidable Marion. They were both constant presences in Court Number One. Auberon Waugh would later record the 'steady, depressing influence' that Marion exercised over the press benches throughout the trial. It was, after all, largely down to the investigative efforts of inquisitive journalists that the case had been brought at all. She would later bark out, 'Stop that woman talking to the witness,' in an Old Bailey corridor when she saw Scott approach his own mother during a break in his testimony.

Sitting next to Thorpe, Holmes looked surprisingly nonchalant whereas Deakin and Le Mesurier appeared rather nervous. Here they were in the dock at the most eagerly anticipated trial in decades, accused of plotting with one of the most famous politicians in the land to kill a man about whom they knew nothing, and from which, had it occurred, they stood to gain nothing. As the trial proceeded they started to relax.

Judges at criminal trials have in the past usually been notable – if they were noted at all – for their more or less overt attempts to ensure a conviction. Cantley would buck that judicial trend. He showed himself almost always hostile to the prosecution and the assembled media. One of his first utterances was to remind the journalists present that they should never ask any of the jurors questions, or try to interview them. 'If I find anyone who has in any way interfered with a member of the jury I'll bring him back here and punish him. Better bring a toothbrush if you are going to do that.' It was a bizarre outburst, which the press corps had done nothing to prompt.

Carman then persuaded Cantley to have Barrie Penrose and Roger Courtiour, two journalists whose investigations, published under the sobriquet 'Pencourt' as *The Pencourt File*, had done much to uncover the existence of the conspiracy between Thorpe and Holmes, excluded from the courtroom on the erroneous grounds that they might be called as witnesses (they weren't); he even argued that the Crown's main witnesses – Scott, Bessell and Newton – shouldn't be permitted to testify at all as all three had sold, or promised, their stories to the press. For once the normally calm Taylor was furious.

At the start of the second day Carman raised a report on the previous evening's *Tonight* programme during which Bessell had been referred to as a 'key witness'. Carman argued that this prejudged Cantley's forth-coming ruling on whether or not Bessell should be a witness at all. Although Cantley said he could see nothing important in the programme, he was more sympathetic to Carman's second point: a story in the previous day's *Evening News*, which said that 'the walnut-faced Mr Peter Bessell held the floor' outside court. All that Bessell (apparently well-known for his prodigious tea consumption) had told the press was that he was still drinking as many cups as he had done at Minehead, but this did not stop Cantley from hauling him into the well of the courtroom and fiercely warning him never to speak to reporters again during the trial. Taylor then managed to persuade Cantley that Bessell, Scott and Newton should be allowed to give evidence. In doing so he made an important revelation: Bessell had been threatened with bankruptcy in a bid to stop him coming to testify (as a bankrupt he would have had great difficulty returning to his beloved Diane in the US).

Legal arguments now over, Taylor could finally begin setting out what Waugh described as a 'brilliantly summarised thumbnail sketch of the prosecution case'. But, to some at least, it seemed that Taylor then spoke for much too long. Taylor's monologue continued for the rest of day two, all of day three and much of day four of the trial. Some in court reported later that they had found the financial details of the case 'baffling' and by the time Taylor sat down still did not understand a crucial pillar of the prosecution case: how the £20,000 to be used for the conspiracy had reached David Holmes.

It was lunchtime on Friday – hardly a good time to pull a rabbit out of a hat – when Taylor called Peter Bessell. Suntanned and with dyed hair that appeared luminous orange under Court Number One's lighting, Bessell had a 'strange croaky voice, slight figure and unusual colouring', Waugh observed. He looked unwell, like 'a creature from outer space going bravely to its execution'. Bessell himself would later recall how the witness box 'could have been designed by a keen disciple of the Marquis de Sade – it is just too wide to enable the occupant to support himself by resting his hands on the side-rails, while the ledge in front is just too low for him to lean on'.

Bessell was undermined as soon as he had taken his oath. Cantley immediately – and wholly unnecessarily – reminded him that the general immunity from prosecution that he had been granted by the Director of Public Prosecutions in return for his agreement to return to England to give evidence against Thorpe did not extend to perjury while giving evidence now. So was planted in the jury's mind the general suspicion that Bessell was likely to lie to them. 'The kindest interpretation of the judge's behaviour is that he was simply being gratuitously offensive,' Waugh later remarked.

In response to Taylor's examination-in-chief Bessell explained his friendship with Thorpe, his function as a go-between with Scott, the pay-offs, and how Thorpe had warned he would have to 'blow his brains out' if his affair ever came to public light. He explained that Thorpe had first raised the possibility of murder with him and Holmes in 1968. On that tantalising note the court adjourned to the next Monday, 14 May, when Bessell resumed his narrative. He recounted how Scott had continued to pester Thorpe in the late 1960s and that the Liberal leader now started to talk of an 'ultimate solution' to what he called the 'Scottish problem'. One suggestion was that Holmes might kill Scott and throw him down a Cornish tin-mine (at this evidence Thorpe 'gave an incredulous smile and gazed at the ceiling as if he had just discovered a keen interest in plaster moulding', Bessell later recalled). From the witness box Bessell explained another one of Thorpe's demented plans: that Scott's body be dumped in the Florida Everglades to be eaten by crocodiles. 'It sounds crazy,' Cantley interjected: Bessell could only agree.

Bessell's account then jumped forward to a meeting with Holmes in California in 1976. Holmes had told Bessell that Lord Goodman – at that time both Thorpe's solicitor and chairman of the Press Council, so well placed to scare newspapers – had suggested that Bessell write the letter that accused Scott of trying to blackmail him. Assured by Holmes that he would never have to testify that it was true in court (at the time, as we have seen, the trial of Newton was pending), Bessell had reluctantly written it but later had second thoughts and asked Holmes to destroy it. But instead it was, to Bessell's fury, leaked to the *Daily Mail*. Bessell wanted to make a statement refuting its contents: a desperate Thorpe wrote to Bessell from London to talk him out of it and assure him that he had the backing of the Prime Minister. 'The press are still being bloody and trying to destroy me,' he complained. 'Harold [Wilson] on the other hand is being quite superb.'

But for once Thorpe's powers of persuasion had failed him. Bessell had heard that Scott was now suing the Commissioner of the Metropolitan Police for the return of letters he had given the police back in 1962. Fearful that he would be publicly exposed as Thorpe's fall guy, in May 1976 Bessell told Douglas Thompson, the *Daily Mail*'s man in California, that the letter was untrue, and that he had only ever paid Scott on Thorpe's behalf. Holmes had made two tense phone calls to Bessell to beg him not to 'spill the beans', but Bessell's mind had been made up.

By the start of day six of the trial the prosecution was riding high. Bessell had got through two days of testimony without any errors or unhelpful interruptions from Cantley. And then his cross-examination began. To the English criminal lawyer cross-examination is an art form which, if done well, can entirely change the course of a case. A witness who gives his testimony guided by the gentle prodding of examination-in-chief may seem to build up an impregnable wall of evidence. But a carefully constructed cross-examination can succeed in entirely dismantling that edifice. This right of sustained challenge – the hallmark of the adversarial system – constitutes one of the most valuable bulwarks of the fairness of the criminal trial. It has been described by a prominent jurist 'as the greatest . . . engine ever invented for the discovery of truth'. Yet it can also serve to occlude the truth. A sustained attack on a witness's credibility can overwhelm and exhaust him, leading to confused answers and a willingness to reply in the affirmative, simply to try to please the questioner. There are certainly parallels to be drawn between a cross-examination and an interrogation; in both cases the person questioned can become so desperate to escape the onslaught that they will eventually depart from their own memory if they sense that to do so will ease their predicament and lead to gentler handling. But a jury is not trained in the art of divination of truth. It relies primarily on impression. In this sense cross-examination is as much to do with presentation as substance. The tone of the questioning can convey as much as the answers that it procures; a countenance of ironic incredulity or righteous indignation, if carried off well by the cross-examining advocate, can speak directly to the jury as if the advocate and the individual members have entered into some form of secret compact to hunt down and expose a witness's lies. It is then that the advocate becomes the actor, indeed the dissembler, because he intends to convey a mood and a message irrespective of his private beliefs.

John Mathew QC, Holmes's counsel, went first, immediately focusing on Bessell's *Sunday Telegraph* deal, his extensive contact with Pencourt, and his own 60,000-word aide-memoire: clearly a means of making even more money out of the trial, Mathew suggested. Unwisely, Bessell confessed he had sometimes exaggerated. Mathew then claimed that many of Bessell's less credible claims were exaggerations as well. Bessell held firm, and insisted that Thorpe had ordered him and Holmes to kill Scott, not just frighten him. But Mathew had successfully planted a seed of doubt about Bessell's credibility.

Carman stood up next. Most advocates rely on meticulous preparation. A good cross-examination has nothing to do with the indiscriminate application of the bludgeon. It concerns itself with the particular and the concrete rather than the general. It is most successful when it proceeds by minute accretions, forcing admissions of small facts so that ground is taken from the enemy by degrees. At its deadliest cross-examination is the product of careful thought, not casual inspiration. Yet the night before Carman started his examination of Bessell he was not going over his notes in the privacy of his room; rather he was sitting at the kitchen table of his junior Graham Boal, drinking a great deal of whisky and ruminating aimlessly on the best way to deal with Bessell. By about 2 a.m. it was agreed that the *Sunday Telegraph* contract was the only real Achilles heel Bessell had. Carman and Boal called it a night and the QC headed off unsteadily to his own bed for an uncertain rest in advance of the most significant day of his professional career. 'I remember seeing George shambolically packing up his papers into a plastic bag and thinking what a horrific hangover he would have the following morning,' recalls Boal.

In fact Carman's constitution had remarkable powers of recovery. Years of late-night drinking had created iron resilience. The next morning Carman arrived at court, at his customary time of a minute before the judge came in, looking as if the night before had been spent in monastic contemplation. He started slowly, asking soft-ball questions that preyed on Bessell's residual respect for Thorpe. Yes, Bessell did think Thorpe was a dedicated MP, a distinguished and successful Liberal leader, and, yes, the two had once been loyal friends.

Carman then proceeded down a path that used Thorpe's own alleged guilt as a means to traduce Bessell's character. It was an odd, but strangely effective, tactic. Had Bessell been a lay preacher when Thorpe first raised the idea of murdering Scott? Yes, he had.

CARMAN: Did that trouble your conscience?

BESSELL: No, sir, it did not.

CARMAN: Did you not feel it was your duty to tell the party that its leader was a man intent on murder?

BESSELL: My first loyalty was to Thorpe. I thought it could be prevented. I saw no purpose in seeking to damage his career in that way.

CARMAN: Didn't you think Mr Thorpe must have needed to see a psychiatrist?

BESSELL: Yes, I suppose that is true.

Carman turned to a matter not previously aired at Minehead and which had not featured in Taylor's opening. This was Bessell's uncorroborated claim, mentioned in *The Pencourt File*, that Thorpe had asked him to 'deal with' a blackmailer called Hetherington, who had threatened to hand out pamphlets detailing Thorpe's affair with Scott just before the 1970 election. Bessell seemed surprised that Hetherington's name was mentioned and his self-assurance took a further knock.

CARMAN: If your evidence has a vestige of truth, the leader of the Liberal Party had proposed the death not only of Norman Scott but of another person . . . this time it was not the unfortunate Mr Holmes but you who were to be the assassin? [One might pause to note what a beautifully constructed question this was; its studied formality of language conveying sotto voce incredulity.]

BESSELL: That is correct.

CARMAN: What steps did you take to acquaint the Liberal Party, police, doctors, Mrs Thorpe, with the fact that the leader of the Liberal Party was insane?

BESSELL: None, sir.

CARMAN: Yet when he got his vote of confidence in 1976 you were delighted. [Thorpe had survived a challenge to his leadership early in that year.]

BESSELL: Yes, sir.

CARMAN: Does this make you a thoroughly immoral person?

BESSELL: I think it does.

CARMAN: If you were publicly preaching Christianity, one might add hypocrite too?

BESSELL: Yes.

This exchange captures the extent of the dominion that Carman, a still, small, compact figure in counsel's row, attained over the witness. Bessell was a genuinely conflicted figure; he had a residual admiration, even adoration, for Thorpe. He found the role of giving testimony against his former friend a mortifying one. As if to expiate his treachery he treated the witness box like a confessional; if he was forced to condemn Thorpe then he would not spare himself either. Forty years on his evidence comes across as touchingly sincere but at the time the jury must have been simply bemused. A courtroom is rarely a suitable place for the unpicking of psychological complexity. Certainly Carman was not going to play the role of confessor. 'You have now told us there were two people Thorpe wanted murdered. Is that all? Or will there be some others to tell us about tomorrow morning?' The judge was now falling in line behind Carman's remorseless juggernaut. He eagerly joined in the game, asking Bessell excitedly, 'Did *you* kill Hetherington, Mr Bessell?'

Carman's cross-examination of Bessell lasted a full three court days, a slow character-assassination that roved over Bessell's personal, political and business life. Rarely has an advocate found a witness so willing to participate in his own destruction. The penitential mood was fortified by a sort of grim delight in self-abasement. Of one particular business scheme, allegedly aimed at defrauding Jack Hayward, Carman asked him: 'So you deserved to be put behind bars, did you, in January 1974?' Bessell's answer must have surprised even Carman: 'Yes, what I had done in respect of Mr Hayward was in my view totally unforgivable, inexcusable, and therefore deserving punishment.'

Carman started taking liberties. An advocate's responsibility when cross-examining is of course to promote his client's case and identify weaknesses in the witness's testimony. If his client's instructions are that the witness is lying then the advocate can properly set out to demonstrate that witness's mendacity. What is always impermissible is rudeness or gratuitous abuse. And yet when an advocate attains mastery over the court then rules somehow become more flexible and the power of the judge to dictate the course of the proceedings seems to wither. Carman was now the master of this court, the judge his meek vassal. At the end of one long day of badgering and sanctimony, Carman wrapped up:

CARMAN: Have you told any whoppers since 1976?
BESSELL: Not to my knowledge.
CARMAN: You have told quite a few in this case, haven't you?
BESSELL: No.

It was now a quarter past four, the normal time for a criminal court to adjourn. Carman used the time-honoured phrase by which counsel seek to bring the proceedings to a close for the day by asking the judge whether that was 'a convenient moment'. 'Oh no, Mr Carman,' retorted Cantley. 'We've got time for one more whopper if you like.' Peter Bessell, a former Member of Parliament and one of the chief prosecution witnesses, was now being treated with unconcealed contempt by the judge, whose duty it was to maintain impartiality and ensure the fairness of the trial. This moment did not go unnoticed by the journalists present. What seemed an impregnable prosecution was beginning to look very shaky.

The next day Carman returned to a wound that Mathew had already opened, and rubbed salt into it. 'It's what you might call a "double your money" contract: half on acquittal and double on conviction,' Carman said of the *Sunday Telegraph* deal. The wretched Bessell could only agree. Bessell was a 'good Janus' to boot, Carman said, 'facing both ways' during the 1967 Liberal leadership contest and approaching both Conservative and Labour whips about defecting a year later. 'It is the oscillation that interests me,' quipped Cantley, who now seemed to delight in his own starring role in the case, to much simpering laughter in court.

After Carman had caught out Bessell in some minor inconsistency he delivered the withering *coup de grâce*: 'It takes a long time to nail down your lies. At last we have nailed one.' Bessell was forced to admit he had once been addicted to the sleeping drug Mandrax and that this might have muddled his moral values at the time of the attempted fraud on Hayward. But even more humiliation was to follow: Carman got Bessell to admit he had contemplated suicide over his money worries, and then accused him of attempted insurance fraud (Bessell had, at one low moment, hoped that if he drove off the road into a tree his suicide would look like an accident and his children would get a payout). After Carman's last volley ('May I suggest to you that you have reached the stage of being incapable of belief by anyone else?') even Cantley felt that Carman had gone too far. 'You can't expect him to agree to that,' said the judge.

At this Bessell managed to regain some tiny vestige of his dignity. 'If I believed I was no longer capable of being believed I would not be here at the Old Bailey,' said Bessell. 'I would be at Oceanside, California.' The torture was over.

Norman Scott came next. He entered the witness box, Waugh thought, like a frightened rabbit, as if he had heard of the treatment meted out to Bessell. In the event he had reason to be nervous: he would be in the box for almost three whole days, from Friday, 18 May until Tuesday, 22 May. The prosecution had a dilemma with Scott. To establish a motive for a murder plot Taylor had to demonstrate that Scott's behaviour had been sufficiently manipulative and dangerous for the leader of the Liberal Party to seriously contemplate and then orchestrate his demise. Yet he also had to avoid making Scott seem so unattractive that the jury would entirely discount his evidence.

Taylor took Scott gently through the story of his seduction by Thorpe, his move to London, how Thorpe had paid his rent and bought him clothes, and the 'Bunnies' letter. Scott described his first sexual encounter with Thorpe at his mother's house in lurid detail. As Scott gave this evidence Thorpe looked on from the dock, entirely impassive. Thorpe's mother and wife had to endure it from the public gallery.

Scott managed to stay calm throughout the Friday and the Monday, as Taylor took him through the long chain of events culminating in the shooting on Exmoor. In 1975 strange things had started happening: one day at the Imperial Hotel in Barnstaple Scott was called to the phone to speak to a German reporter – apparently called Steiner – about his story, only to find documents missing when he returned to his table. Soon afterwards he received calls from a man styling himself Wright (who claimed to be from an Italian fashion house and invited Scott to London for a photoshoot) and from a journalist called Masterson (who invited him to a hotel in Bristol); Scott declined both invitations. (Andrew Newton would later claim that he had posed as Wright and that Holmes had masqueraded as Masterson.)

Scott recounted the now familiar story of how he had been approached by a man who introduced himself as Peter Keene one day in October 1975. Andrew Newton had not been good at aliases ('It's Andy – sorry, Peter,' he'd said on the phone) but Scott had agreed to get in to Newton's Mazda and drive to Porlock on 24 October as long as Rinka could come too. 'I will not have that bloody dog,' Newton had said at first, but relented. Later that evening, after Scott had been left at the Castle Hotel for several hours while Newton attended a mysterious 'meeting', they began the drive back to Combe Martin. Newton started driving erratically, weaving the car from side to side on the narrow road. (Newton would later claim he was peering through the fog to spot a cardboard box he'd left at the roadside earlier to mark a suitable spot to bury Scott's body once he had been shot.)

Scott offered to take over the driving even though he had never passed his test. As they swapped places in a lay-by Newton suddenly said, 'Oh no, this is it,' produced his Mauser and shot Rinka dead, before pointing the gun at Scott and then shaking it vigorously and swearing. Newton jumped in the car, shouted, 'I'll get you,' and turned the car around to drive back to Porlock, leaving Scott by the roadside, vainly giving Rinka the kiss of life until an off-duty AA patrolman happened to pass by ten minutes later.

In answer to Taylor's questions Scott had given his evidence quietly; at times his voice was punctured by emotion. He was baring his soul in the most talked-about trial in decades, in a cavernous courtroom thronged with bewigged lawyers and journalists, all studying his every word. The stress of the occasion must have been overwhelming.

Almost all Scott's evidence was of course directed at Thorpe. Still, barristers generally do not like to be silent for too long and Mathew, Williams and Cowley all availed themselves of their right to put questions to Scott. But this trial was fast becoming a showcase for George Carman's forensic skills and it was his cross-examination that everyone was waiting for. Scott's evidence had provided a detailed account of his sexual relationship with Thorpe; it was that relationship, and Scott's exploitation of it, that provided a motive to kill. Yet it was Thorpe's case that while he had been a fond friend to Scott, the notion that they had been lovers was fantastical. If this was right, then it meant that Scott's minute accounts of their sexual encounters were all a fabrication. But, for all his faults, Scott did not present as a scheming perjurer.

Carman adopted a radically different approach to the one that had worked so well with Bessell. While Bessell had been painted as a fiendish master of manipulation, Scott would be portrayed, at least to begin with, as a sad delusional case. Carman started gently, deploying the tone of a 'friendly doctor with a hopeless psychiatric problem on his hands', noted the admiring Waugh. Carman, exuding *faux* kindness, started by enquiring about Scott's mental health. He took Scott back to his spell at a clinic in Oxford in 1961 after his first brief meeting with Thorpe at Norman Van de Vater's house.

SCOTT: I was very drugged at the time and some details of the incident [i.e. the stay at the clinic] might have gone out of my mind.

CARMAN: You don't remember telling them [i.e. other patients] that you knew Jeremy Thorpe?

SCOTT: I still had a bundle of love letters of Jeremy Thorpe that he had written to Van de Vater. [Scott had taken them from Van de Vater.]

CARMAN: Never mind what you say are love letters between Mr Thorpe and Mr Van de Vater, answer the question.

JUDGE: You are not giving a proper answer. That was just a bit of dirt thrown in. Listen to the question and answer and behave yourself. [It soon became apparent that Cantley's loathing for Scott was, if anything, even greater than for Bessell.]

CARMAN: You met Mr Thorpe and talked to him for five minutes or less. He hadn't written you a single letter before you went to the House of Commons, neither had you written a single letter to Mr Thorpe before that. Why did you say Mr Thorpe was a friend of yours when all you had done was to speak to him for less than five minutes?

SCOTT: Because when I had had the therapy at the hospital I was going through a delusion and I had these letters. I was using these letters to say that I had had a relationship with him already.

CARMAN: You were saying you had a sexual relationship with Mr Thorpe before you went to the House of Commons?

SCOTT: Yes.

CARMAN: Quite obviously that was not true?

SCOTT: No, it wasn't.

CARMAN: In fairness to you, were you saying it because you were suffering from a delusion?

SCOTT: Yes.

Carman had planted another very large seed of doubt in the jury's mind. He now turned to the heart of the matter: sex. In his police statement of December 1962, Carman recounted, Scott had said of his first sexual experience with Thorpe: 'I am almost certain his penis did not go into my anus. I am not sure whether he ejaculated, but he seemed satisfied,' which implied that no penetrative sex had taken place. But in the Old Bailey witness box Scott had claimed, Carman added, that he had been 'buggered' twice and had to bite the pillow to stop himself crying out in pain. Scott said he had lied to the police as he was 'trying to make myself out a cleaner person than I was'.

After lunch Carman started to turn the screw, provoking a hysterical outburst from Scott. 'Jeremy Thorpe lives on a knife-edge of danger,' he shouted, having been asked about testimony that he had been fondled by Thorpe in his Westminster office moments before police arrived to interview Scott about a raincoat a flatmate had accused him of stealing.

'What about you?' asked Carman quietly.

'I don't at all. I have certainly lived in danger of my life for many years because of your client,' Scott ricocheted back.

'Do you think I enjoy saying these terrible things or talking about it?' Scott raged a little later, as he was probed again about the now infamous night at Mrs Thorpe's house.

'If only you'd spoken up like that when you began your evidence, we could have heard everything you said,' was Cantley's extraordinary interjection ('rather as one might approach a lunatic waving a knife in the street and give him a prod with one's umbrella – uncertain of what will happen next, but sure that it will be interesting,' was Waugh's depiction).

Goaded by Carman's deliberate provocations, Scott refused to cooperate further:

SCOTT: Sir, I am in contempt of court. I will not answer any more questions.

JUDGE: You may find that an uncomfortable place to be.

SCOTT: I have gone on enough over the years with this story. I will not say any more.

JUDGE: Do you want to go home now?

SCOTT: I don't mind where I go. I won't have myself destroyed in this way when he [Carman] knows very well his client is lying. I have had enough.

Like a recalcitrant child being gently persuaded to eat his greens, the overwrought Scott was cajoled into staying in the witness box.

Amid his volley of questions Carman slipped in a vital admission. Towards the end of the day he asked, 'You knew Mr Thorpe to be a man of homosexual tendencies in 1961?' – to which Scott answered, predictably, 'Yes.' Taylor had warned Carman before the trial that, if Thorpe were to deny his sexuality, the prosecution would adduce evidence, including a sexually explicit letter to an American boyfriend known only as 'Bruno', to make it abundantly clear that Thorpe was a homosexual. After long discussions with Carman, and occasional consultations with Thorpe and his wife, it was eventually agreed between counsel that an admission of Thorpe's 'homosexual tendencies' – though not that he'd had a homosexual relationship with Scott of course – was enough to forestall the prosecution from calling various former lovers to the witness box, which understandably did not appeal to Carman. Many observers would later suggest that Carman had managed to drive a favourable bargain for his client: the only words of admission ever made by Thorpe as to his sexuality was the veiled reference to 'homosexual tendencies' made by his counsel in the course of a question. A parade of witnesses testifying to Thorpe's vigorous promiscuity while serving as the Member of Parliament for North Devon might well have made a rather different impression on the jury. And Carman even managed to bury the admission in a wider attack on Scott's motives. The follow-up question suggested that the explanation for Scott's years of persecution lay in the thirst for revenge of a scorned would-be lover: 'You were flattered that for a short time he introduced you into a different social world. I suggest you were upset and annoyed because he did not want to have a sexual relationship with you.'

Carman had only gone at Scott for less than a day. Although Jean Rook remained enthralled, using her *Express* column to report that the trial was 'the greatest show on earth', still there was a feeling of slight anticlimax among the journalistic cohort, who were hoping for a more prolonged duel between the fiery Scott and the deadly Carman. But Carman knew when to stop. The art of advocacy lies as much in things unsaid as in things said. For all his histrionics Scott posed a real danger to Thorpe. A more thorough confrontation with his story could surely only lead the jury to the conclusion that it was true. Better to paint in broad outline the image of a man who was in turn delusional and bent on revenge, and avoid the detail. The more time the jury had to ponder that final suggestion made by Carman – that Scott was determined to bring about Thorpe's destruction because more than fifteen years earlier the politician had rebuffed his advances – the more ludicrous it would surely appear.

It was now the prosecution's turn to re-examine. Taylor tried to ask Scott about the letters between Thorpe and Van de Vater that he had taken in 1960, but Cantley stopped him. This was a shame for the many people looking to the trial for fresh sensation or hilarity. It was later revealed that the correspondence included a postcard sent by Thorpe to Van de Vater at the time of Princess Margaret's engagement to Antony Armstrong-Jones that contained the immortal words: 'What a pity about HRH. I rather hoped to marry one and seduce the other.'

The trial was now in its twelfth day. The tension temporarily eased as evidence was heard from a number of minor witnesses, none of whom

Haw-Haw: William Joyce goes for a walk round the Brandenburg Gate, Berlin, c. 1942.

British soldiers pose with the recently captured William Joyce, June 1945.

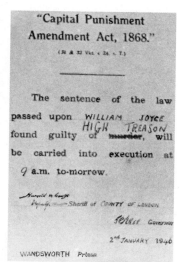

"Capital Punishment Amendment Act, 1868."

(31 & 32 Vict. c. 26, s. 7.)

The sentence of the law passed upon WILLIAM JOYCE found guilty of ~~murder~~ HIGH TREASON, will be carried into execution at 9 a.m. to-morrow.

Harold n Geoff
Deputy Sheriff of COUNTY OF LONDON

Rees Governor

2nd JANUARY 1946

WANDSWORTH Prison

'I am proud to die for my ideals.' Notice of William Joyce's execution is posted outside Wandsworth prison, January 1946.

Prelude to tragedy: Timothy and Beryl Evans with baby Geraldine in the garden of 10 Rillington Place, 1949.

Frightened and uncomprehending: Timothy Evans arrives at Paddington Station, accompanied by police officers, December 1949.

Timothy Evans, as played by John Hurt, in the dock: a still from the 1971 film *10 Rillington Place*.

Derek Curtis-Bennett QC goes for lunch during the Christie trial, June 1953.

Described by his counsel as 'mad as a March hare', John Reginald Christie arrives at court, June 1953.

Children playing outside 10 Rillington Place, 1966. The terrace would be demolished in the early 1970s.

Albert Pierrepoint's busy hanging diary, 1945–6. Traitors are interspersed with Nazis.

Date	Name	AGE.	HEIGHT	WEIGHT	DROP	Town	EXECUTIONER
DEC. 13 1945	WILHELM DORR.	24	6·2	176	6·5	BELSEN. HAMELN GERMANY.	A.P.
DEC. 13 1945	SANDROCK.	42	5-10	145	7·8	HAMELN GERMANY.	A.P.
DEC. 13 1945	SCHEINBERGER.	39	5-5½	141	7·10	HAMELN GERMANY	A.P.
DEC. 19 1945	JOHN AMERY	33	5-7½	140	7·8	LONDON.TREASON WANDSWORTH	H.CRITCHELL A.P
DEC. 21 1945	JOHN. RILEY YOUNG	40	5-7½	163	6·10	PENTONVILLE	S.WADE A.P.
DEC. 21 1945	JAMES MC NICHOL	30	5-4½	141	7·9	PENTONVILLE	H.MORRIS
DEC. 29 1945	ROBERT BLAINE	24	5-10	160	6·11	WANDSWORTH	H.KIRK A.P
JAN. 3 1946	WILLIAM JOYCE. LORD. HAW. HAW	39	5-5½	151	7·4	WANDSWORTH	H.RILEY A.P
JAN. 4 1946	THEODORE. WILLIAM SCHURCH.	28	5-9	144	7·8	PENTONVILLE	H.RILEY A.P
JAN. 31 1946	MICHAEL NEISCIOR	29	5-8	150	7·4	WANDSWORTH	S.WADE A.P
MARCH. 8 1946	HANS RENOTH	49	5-7½	154	7·3	HAMELN	A.P
MARCH. 8 1946	AUGUST. BUHNING	50	5-8½	154	7·3		A.P
MARCH. 8 1946	FREDRICK KONIG	51	5-6½	154	7·3	GERMANY	A.P
MARCH. 8 1946	OTTO FRANKE.	32	5-8½	164	6·10		A.P

112

Crowds surge outside Wandsworth prison on the morning of the execution of Derek Bentley, 28 January 1953.

'He's the lowest of the low': Ruth Ellis with David Blakely, *c.*1954.

The Home Secretary stands firm: no reprieve for Ruth Ellis, 12 July 1955.

The 'Secrets Case':
Jeremy Hutchinson
QC strides towards
court with his legal
team, summer 1963.

'That last ten hours have
been a torment which
only a man on trial who is
innocent can understand.'
Giuseppe Martelli and
Pamela Rothwell leave
court immediately after
his acquittal, 15 July 1963.

Norman Scott arrives at Minehead
Magistrates Court to give evidence about
Jeremy Thorpe's physiognomy, 1978.

'A creature from outer space going
bravely to its execution': Peter Bessell
arrives at the Old Bailey, 11 June 1979.

Jeremy Thorpe hails the crowds
after his acquittal, 22 June 1979.
George Carman QC looks on,
contemplating a glorious future.

The Blake escape: a belated parking ban is imposed around the perimeter walls of Wormwood Scrubs, December 1966.

Michael Randle and Pat Pottle explain themselves at a press conference, 1989.

The art of the court-room: Ian Huntley is cross-examined by Richard Latham QC as Mr Justice Moses looks on, November 2003.

said anything of much consequence (though one wonders whether the jury was in any way perplexed to hear from one that Thorpe had paid Scott's divorce costs in 1973). Then it was the turn of the third of the three central – if rather shaky – pillars of the prosecution case. Andrew Newton arrived at the Bailey, studiously ignored by Scott as they bumped into each other in the Gents.

Newton seemed, at least to begin with, more subdued than the cocky jack-the-lad who'd roared up to the courthouse in Minehead in a blacked-out sports car, clad in a balaclava apparently to avoid being identified by photographers. But he soon showed himself to be the last person on earth anyone in their right mind would hire as an assassin. 'Did you ask any questions?' Taylor enquired. 'Yes, only the sort of questions you would expect a hitman to ask . . . from what I have seen in films,' replied Newton. He explained that he had enquired of Holmes, with some degree of prescience, as it turned out, whether Scott had a dog: 'It bothered me. If I had to approach Mr Scott I would not want a dog to attack me.' Waugh reports that this answer elicited 'laughter in court'. Cantley now appeared to take the view, not uncommon among the judiciary, that the only person allowed to tell jokes in his courtroom was himself. 'This is certainly not funny,' he barked, to the tacit disagreement of everyone else in court.

The following day Newton explained that although he had been at the outset hired to kill Scott, in the end he had bottled out. For all his big talk, by the time he had met Scott in Barnstaple in October 1975 he had made up his mind merely to frighten, not murder him. He only shot Rinka because he feared the dog would attack him. When he had levelled the gun at Scott he had deliberately not pulled the trigger. The trouble was that Newton had told a completely different story – that he was being blackmailed by Scott and had set out to warn him off – at his own trial in Exeter in 1976. His evidence also rather undermined the Crown's case that he, along with the defendants in the dock, was party to a conspiracy to murder. Under cross-examination by John Mathew, Holmes's counsel, Newton admitted to having told a 'pack of lies' when he had been on trial a few years earlier. Was he doing so again at the Old Bailey?

MATHEW: You find it difficult to remember what is fact and fiction?
NEWTON: I think you are falling into the realms of sorcery with words.
MATHEW: I was quoting what you said on a previous occasion.
NEWTON: I am being taken out of context.
MATHEW: I will put it in context. Did you answer, in reply to the very

first question which was put to you in cross-examination at Minehead:
'I do sometimes find it difficult to distinguish between fact and fantasy
regarding this case'?

NEWTON: Oh yes, I do remember saying that.

MATHEW: It accurately described your state of mind at Minehead?

NEWTON: Yes.

MATHEW: But not now?

NEWTON: Not now.

But Newton started to give as good as he got. 'It comes to this: in order
to protect yourself you were prepared falsely to accuse someone [i.e.
Scott] of a very serious crime – blackmail?' asked Mathew.

'Yes, with the help of your client [Holmes],' was Newton's astute reply.

And when Mathew asked Newton about an initial plan to lure Scott
to a hotel and bludgeon him to death with a poker hidden in a bunch
of flowers, the judge intervened to try to make Newton look foolish –
yet only succeeded in making himself look the fool. 'But you were going
to meet a man. Why was it necessary to have flowers?' Cantley asked.

Nonetheless Mathew did inflict some real damage when he forced
Newton to admit that he'd been offered more money by the newspapers
for his story if he testified that the conspiracy had been to murder Scott,
not merely to frighten him. Newton even blurted out that he had been
offered £200,000 if Thorpe was convicted of conspiracy to murder.
Cantley could not resist intervening.

JUDGE: You are resolved to milk this case as hard as you can?

NEWTON: Yes, sir.

JUDGE: I see.

The withering Mathew decided to pursue the point. 'It is going to be
a very much easier case to milk and you are going to obtain a great deal
more milk if these defendants are convicted on this charge – correct?'

'That is absolutely correct,' was 'chicken-brain's' candid answer.

Now it was Gareth Williams's turn to cross-examine on behalf of
Deakin, whom Newton claimed had promised him £10,000 to murder
Scott. The cross-examination got off to a bad start.

WILLIAMS: Do you know what a buffoon is, Mr Newton?

NEWTON: Yes, I would think so.

WILLIAMS: A buffoon would be someone who lacked moral sense?

Waugh reports that Newton looked uncertain at this point, noting that in fact Williams had alighted upon an entirely erroneous definition.

WILLIAMS: Why did you wear that absurd hat at Minehead? [This was a reference to the balaclava.]

NEWTON: I didn't want to make the press's job any easier.

WILLIAMS: Do you agree that it was the action of a buffoon?

NEWTON: No. One is entitled to wear what one wants. After all, I mean to say, you wear what is on your head.

One begins to warm to Newton after an answer like that.

It turned out that, just like Bessell and Scott, Newton was proposing to write his own book about his involvement with Thorpe. Williams read extracts from a synopsis which had been hawked round to publishers. 'It begins with his own graphic account of the shooting . . . Switches back to Andrew Newton's life as a well-paid airline pilot leading a glamorous bachelor existence,' said Williams, with relish. 'Meetings with amazing characters . . . After the shooting the conspirators tried to murder him . . . his arrest, his trial and the beginning of the cover-up. His attempts to protect names of leading politicians . . . Highly placed people in another attempt on his life.' But the only 'attempt' on his life that Newton could now recall was a red Mini that he claimed had tried to run him over in Chiswick. Williams was able to deploy that most favoured barristerial question: 'You are just making it up as you go along, aren't you?'

Mathew and Williams had succeeded in portraying Newton as an incompetent fantasist whose lust for money seemed to infuse every aspect of his testimony. Nonetheless they had had a difficult line to walk. Both Holmes and Deakin admitted, through their counsel, that they had successively approached Newton about a 'frightening job' – to put the 'fear of God' into Scott, but go no further. So any displays of righteous indignation by counsel had to be tempered by the fact that their clients were not exactly innocents abroad. As for Carman, he of course was entitled to cross-examine Newton if he wished. But Thorpe had wisely kept his distance from his hit-man. The two had never spoken nor met; several degrees of separation intervened. Carman stayed in his seat.

So, day after day, prosecution witnesses came and went. The jury was belaboured with information as Taylor constructed his vast, if unstable, edifice. A high point for the increasing band of students of Mr Justice Cantley's judicial idiosyncrasies was the evidence of David Miller. We have seen that Miller had introduced his business associate George Deakin to his friend Andrew Newton. It was at Miller's premises that Newton cleaned his car of Rinka's blood after the shooting. He had been involved in the byzantine dealings between Deakin, Newton, Holmes and Le Mesurier after the shooting. At one stage the evidence turned to his and Newton's predilection for 'wife-swapping' parties, advertised in various 'adult contact' magazines. This exchange allowed Cantley to engage in a studied display of judicial obtuseness:

> JUDGE: Is *Contact* magazine a respectable publication? I don't know. I get the impression that there is something wrong with it.
>
> WILLIAMS: The reference to 'contact' magazines means a number of magazines. They are for people who wish to contact other people about sexual deviation.
>
> MILLER: I would not put it like that. I would put it as a friendship club . . . a lonely hearts club.

The prosecution case was nearing its end. Two of the final witnesses, Jack Hayward and the Liberal sympathiser Nadir Dinshaw, were treated with kid gloves by the defence. 'I want to make it perfectly clear . . . that there is no suggestion you have been guilty of any kind of financial or commercial impropriety,' Carman told Hayward, as if he were administering a papal benediction on behalf of Thorpe. His caution was well-advised: both witnesses had cast-iron proof that £20,000 generously intended for Liberal coffers by 'Union Jack' had, on Thorpe's instructions, passed from Hayward via Dinshaw to Holmes's personal account. And then? Neither Mathew nor Carman was in the mood to enlighten the court. Dinshaw recounted a particularly damaging conversation with Thorpe over lunch at Boulestin's in 1977, as the police investigations were beginning to intensify:

> THORPE: That money of Jack Hayward's – what did you do with it?
>
> DINSHAW: I gave it to David Holmes, of course.
>
> THORPE: Why?
>
> DINSHAW: Because you told me to.
>
> THORPE: You could say that you'd given it him yourself.
>
> DINSHAW: How can I say I've given it him myself – I haven't given it him. My accounts will show it in any case.
>
> THORPE: They won't look at your accounts.

Carman did not challenge this evidence. He simply repeated the fatuous Thorpe benediction.

The prosecution closed its case. A submission of no case to answer by each of the defendants failed. But the judge's decision to allow the case to continue had what some thought to be a sugar coating: 'Remember, I have the last word,' he told the court.

The moment that the squads of journalists had all been waiting for had come: the defendants' account, out of their own mouths, of what had happened. But instead the defence dropped its first bombshell. 'My Lord, on behalf of Mr Holmes I call no evidence,' announced Mathew first thing the next morning with supreme composure. Disappointment on the press benches was temporarily staunched when Gareth Williams called his own client, George Deakin. 'Red-haired and pasty-faced, Deakin was not the most beautiful of the four defendants,' commented the laconic Waugh. He explained that he was a Tory voter, he was not a homosexual and he had no connections to the Liberal Party. All he had done was give Newton Holmes's phone number to talk about 'a frightening job' against a blackmailer where a three-year-old child was at risk. Taylor's cross-examination, based, as it had to be, on the braggadocio of Newton, made few inroads.

Two more bombshells then followed in quick succession. 'I call no evidence,' said Cowley, for Le Mesurier, before subsiding back onto his seat. 'My Lord, on behalf of Mr Jeremy Thorpe I call no evidence,' said Carman portentously, every word carefully orchestrated. After four weeks of prosecution testimony the evidence for the defence, confined as it was to George Deakin, had taken less than a day.

It was now Thursday, 7 June. The judge granted Peter Taylor's request for an adjournment to the next Monday to allow him to prepare his closing speech. Taylor had presumably been counting on several days, even weeks, of defence evidence and had no doubt prepared elaborate cross-examinations of each of the defendants. That morning, before the three defence bombshells had been dropped, the task of closing speeches had seemed a distant prospect. Now Taylor had to get to work, collating all twenty-one days' evidence into a single narrative for digestion by the jury. Carman, back home in Cheshire, spent the long weekend chain-smoking and scribbling notes.

The next Monday, 11 June, Peter Taylor commenced his two-day peroration. It is remembered now for his lofty declaration that Thorpe's story was 'a tragedy of truly Greek or Shakespearean proportions – the slow but inevitable destruction of a man by the stamp of one defect'. The image of Thorpe as a hero brought low by a tragic flaw was oddly discordant with the evidence that had been adduced over four weeks in the Old Bailey. Whether or not it demonstrated beyond reasonable doubt that Thorpe was guilty of conspiracy to murder, that evidence vividly depicted a character of unbridled egotism, ruthlessness and indifference to truth.

Sitting in the press gallery Auberon Waugh was especially struck by Taylor's tone. Waugh heartily wished for Thorpe's conviction and he was puzzled throughout the trial by what he saw as Taylor's over-punctiliousness, his refusal to go in for the kill. Unlike defending counsel, a prosecutor must be a guardian of justice; he must not seek a conviction at all costs. He presents the evidence and explains why that evidence might lead the jury to convict. And yet there have been suggestions since the trial that Taylor perhaps showed too much respect for Thorpe's position. Although Waugh was wary of criticising Taylor overtly, the subtext of his account of the trial is that Thorpe got off lightly. He was less restrained in his view that Taylor's closing speech went on too long and confused the jury. The prosecutor listed sixty incriminating facts that had gone undisputed by the defence. As a result he may have muddled them with too much information, and by the time he concluded with an attack on Thorpe's lies about the £20,000 given to Holmes, many jurors seemed to have lost interest.

The defence's closing speeches were more succinct. Their predominant theme was indignation rather than engagement with the actual evidence. John Mathew worked himself up into a frenzy of agitation at the so-called lies of Peter Bessell and Andrew Newton. 'I wonder whether the scales of justice held by that figure on the dome of this court are still trembling having heard the startling admissions from the witness Mr Peter Bessell.' It was obvious that Mathew was concerned that Holmes's silence at the trial would be held against him by the jury. The point had to be met head-on: 'Through me, what Mr Holmes is saying to you is this: "I am not guilty of this offence. You have not proved through the evidence that I am, because the evidence you have brought defies belief. Therefore, there is no need, because there is no evidence, for me to deny the charge."'

This logic is a staple of the defendant who elects to exercise his right not to give evidence in his own defence. It is perhaps surprising that it sometimes works. One might have thought that Holmes, who throughout all his police interviews before he was charged had given 'no comment' replies, had quite a lot to answer: not least what had happened to the £20,000 the unsuspecting Nadir Dinshaw had channelled to him. Mathew suggested that it had gone on Thorpe's secret election expenses: 'If these monies were, in fact, for some illicit under-counter election expenses, that could explain a great deal of this part of the evidence.' The only problem with that was that there was not one shred of evidence that it was true, and Holmes had never even suggested it.

Gareth Williams, with the air of a moralising Methodist minister, set up Deakin as an everyman wrongly implicated in the machinations of the well-connected and the powerful. 'You will recall Mr Peter Taylor's analogy of this trial as a Greek or Shakespearean tragedy. They have their tragedies also in humbler places, and if on this evidence you were minded to convict Mr Deakin, it would be wrong. It would be a tragedy in a small town . . . Mr Deakin does not have powerful friends in high places. Mr Deakin does not write letters to the Home Secretary starting "Dear Reggie" so far as we know' (a reference to solicitous letters that Thorpe had written to Reginald Maudling, Conservative Home Secretary in the early 1970s). As for Newton, Williams added to the lexicon of inventive sanctimony by describing him as 'a sort of moral amputee . . . not just a man from whom you would hesitate to buy a second-hand car, you would not even sell him one.' The sermon was rounded off with a rousing finale: 'There is a hymn which people sometimes sing in Wales: "*Rwyn gweld o bell y dydd yn dod*" which may be translated into English: "I see from afar off the day which is coming". Mr Deakin has waited a long time since 1977 and his day will come with your verdict of not guilty.'

Dennis Cowley QC had throughout the trial borne the air of a man who had through some inexplicable mistake found himself in the wrong courtroom in the wrong case. He seemed so disconnected from the proceedings in Court Number One that he even managed to get Gareth Williams's name wrong in his own closing speech. By this stage Cowley had spent twenty-four days sitting hugger-mugger with Williams on counsel's row. Either this was insufficient time to make his acquaintance or Cowley was intruding into the jury's mind a subtle sense of Le Mesurier's own ignorance of whatever plot his co-defendants may have come up with. As with everything else he said throughout the trial, his speech was inconsequential.

Again, it was Carman's closing on behalf of Thorpe that everyone was waiting for. Carman had by now imprinted his own personality on the case. He, almost as much as Thorpe, had become its star turn. But Carman had one advantage over Thorpe: he opened his mouth. He did not content himself with the short bursts of fire and brimstone that

Mathew and Williams had settled on. Instead he donned the garb of martyrdom on his client's behalf. Whatever Thorpe had done he had been punished already, brought low by harrying furies. Tacitly recognising that, for all its internal contradictions, the evidence deployed by the prosecution was in large part unanswered, and unanswerable, Carman sought a verdict founded on pity and admiration. Just as Williams had played the small man card so Carman would unashamedly play the great man card. One of Carman's outstanding qualities as an advocate was the capacity to cleanse his clients of their supposed wrongdoing through the astringent of his own voice. His slow, calm, authoritative delivery converted Thorpe into a latter-day St Sebastian. Some of the phrases he deployed, worked on with his junior Graham Boal day after day, demonstrate Carman's verbal mastery:

> Privately he is a man with a life that has had more than its fair share of grief and agony. Nature so fashioned him that at the time he had the misfortune to meet Norman Scott he was a man with homosexual tendencies . . .
>
> Mr Jeremy Thorpe does not wish any advantage or disadvantage. He is now in your sole charge and he is content with that position. But inevitably because of the prominence he has achieved in the public life of this country, the case has centred to an extent on the life and times of Jeremy Thorpe – his frailties, his weaknesses have been exposed remorselessly to the public gaze . . .
>
> He is a man with a sense of humour, capable of real wit, and certainly a man to whom comedy was never absent for very long in his life. But tragedy has replaced it in large measure . . .
>
> At his age, if your conscience and oath permit you to say not guilty, there may still be a place somewhere in the public life and public service of this country for a man of his talents.

As for Scott, he was 'sad, mad or bad, or a combination of all three, I care not'. Of Bessell: he 'may go down at the end of this case as the Judas Iscariot of British politics of the twentieth century because he has three things in common: one, he seeks to betray a friend; two, he seeks to betray him for money; and three, he seeks to betray a man who, I submit, is innocent of the charges laid against him. If, by your verdict you say not guilty, that may be the final epitaph of Mr Bessell.'

Maintaining a countenance of utmost gravity, Carman even managed to suggest that Thorpe's refusal to give evidence sprang from a desire not to create sensationalised material for disreputable newspapers: 'We are not here to entertain the public or provide journalists with further copy. We are here for a much more serious purpose, to determine whether these charges are made out.' As for the missing £20,000 which Thorpe had never explained and which surely made it obvious that he was the instigator of the plot: 'I'm not going to solve for you the mystery of this money. You can spend a long time trying to work it out, and come up with six different answers. The Crown has to prove it is referable to guilt. That is one possibility, but there are many others the prosecution has not explored.' This must rank as one of the most brazen submissions ever made in a courtroom. A lesser, or more self-aware, man might have baulked at it, but Carman carried it off, concluding with a rhetorical flourish:

> You have the right as citizens to vote in elections. But you have a much more important right and a much greater responsibility to vote guilty or not guilty. Mr Thorpe has spent twenty years in British politics and obtained thousands and thousands of votes in his favour. Now the most important twelve votes of all come from you. And you. And you . . . [Carman pointed theatrically at each juror in turn]. I say to you, on behalf of Jeremy Thorpe, this prosecution has not been made out. Let this prosecution fold their tents and silently steal away.

Some advocates might have found this showmanship risible. But George Carman was a man who never laughed at himself. Portentousness was his default tone, whether in private or public. No one laughed. The jury looked impressed.

After counsel have made their submissions it is left to the judge to sum up for the jury. On Monday, 18 June, the twenty-seventh day of the trial, Cantley started his summing-up in Court Number One. Judges have in the past often been criticised for a pro-prosecution bias. Cantley was to provide a corrective: what followed has become notorious as one of the most unashamedly anti-prosecution summing-ups in legal history. For the trial's last two days the judge could luxuriate in the sound of his own uninterrupted monologue as he schooled the jury in the inadequacies of the prosecution evidence and case. Each of the main prosecution witnesses was denounced. Bessell was a 'humbug', his conduct 'deplorable'. The jury could not convict on his word alone. Given that much of the case against Thorpe rested on Bessell's testimony the prosecution was probably doomed from that point on. Once Cantley had described the evidence against Thorpe as 'almost entirely circumstantial', the acquittal of Thorpe – if not the others – seemed a foregone conclusion.

It was in relation to Scott that the judge dug most deeply into his reserves of revulsion. 'You will remember him well – a hysterical, warped personality, accomplished sponger and very skilful at exciting and exploiting sympathy . . . He is a crook. He is a fraud. He is a sponger. He is a whiner. He is a parasite.' Then this extraordinary statement: 'But of course, he could still be telling the truth. It is a question of belief.' Even then the judge had not finished with Scott. The man who stood in fear of his life on Porlock Moor, the bloodied corpse of his beloved dog at his feet, was 'a spineless neurotic character, addicted to hysteria and self-advertisement'.

Auberon Waugh listened in astonishment to this performance. His habitual pose of ironical detachment was being overtaken by a far from detached sense of outrage at the travesty of justice that was unfolding from the bench. As his summing-up wore on Waugh noted that the judge's sentences were punctuated by 'private chuckles' and 'wheezing noises'. At one stage in his verbal wanderings through the byways of the evidence, Cantley appeared to concede that there may well have been a conspiracy to murder. But he then 'suddenly noticed his rambling discourse was heading in the wrong direction' and reminded the jury of the 'conceited bungler', Newton. 'But what a chump the man is. To frighten or to murder – that is no way to go about it.' Finally the judge came to the last witness, George Deakin. Cantley noted, bizarrely, that he was 'the type of man whose taste ran to a cocktail bar in his living room'. But whatever crimes against interior design Deakin may have committed, he and his co-defendants were held up by the judge as men of 'hitherto unblemished reputation'. The admitted conspiracy to frighten, the unchallenged pyramid of lies told by Thorpe, the threats to have Dinshaw deported, were all ignored.

What was perhaps most offensive about the judge's performance was his unconcealed revelling in the comic aspects of the case. Undoubtedly the trial had been marked by hilarity. A bestiary of bizarre characters had paraded into the witness box for the judge to have his fun with. Yet the core fact at the heart of the case was that a man's life had been threatened because he posed a risk to the reputation of a senior politician. But because the victim was supposedly a 'parasite' and the would-be perpetrator a 'chump', that fact was reduced to another absurd episode in a human comedy.

On Wednesday morning, 19 June, the judge finished his survey of the evidence. He now sent the jury off to commence its deliberations. 'You may go now. Take as long as you like. There is no hurry. We shall wait for you.'

It was then customary for the defendants' bail to be revoked while the jury considered its verdict. As the hours wore on the news arrived that the jury would not conclude its deliberations that day and was to be sequestered in a hotel for the night. Arrangements were made for the defendants' own overnight accommodation. They were taken away by van to Brixton prison, Thorpe handcuffed to Deakin and all four of them prostrate on the floor to avoid being photographed through the windows. Pleading a highly convenient upset stomach Thorpe was allowed to sleep in the comfort of the prison hospital. The next morning, the Thursday, they were carted back to the Bailey for a second day of waiting. After five weeks of keeping their distance, the defendants seemed to come together. They whiled away the hours playing cards. Le Mesurier taught them 'liar dice', which Thorpe played enthusiastically.

Still the jury had not reached their verdict. Another night in Brixton beckoned, and the Friday, 22 June, saw them back at court, continuing their daytime vigil. Thorpe's upset stomach healed itself miraculously and the four enjoyed a lunch of rare beef and smoked salmon, with wine, brought in by the sympathetic Liberal MP and *bon viveur* Clement Freud.

The jury returned into Court Number One at 2.30 p.m. A fifty-two-hour wait was over. The forewoman delivered 'not guilty' verdicts on all counts. Le Mesurier seemed to steady himself on Thorpe's arm; Deakin grinned and leaned forward with tears in his eyes; Holmes looked stunned and swayed from side to side. Thorpe was motionless, 'staring at infinity', as if that which he had always expected had come to pass. He casually threw his three red cushions out of the dock and into the well of the court. He bent forward to kiss the faithful Marion, before – ever the politician – thanking the policemen and ushers who surrounded him. It had been an expensive business for Thorpe but no application to have his legal costs paid by the Crown was made on his behalf.

Emerging into the warm afternoon sunlight, Thorpe looked states-manlike and held his arms aloft, drinking in adulation from the crowd. As he returned home in triumph to drink champagne and tell TV interviewers about his 'complete vindication', Fleet Street had to rapidly rewrite its front pages. Despite the judge's near exhortation to acquit, editors had expected a guilty verdict for Thorpe. Newton was left to give his own verdict to the press pack outside the Bailey. 'I'm not too wrapped up in that judge,' he grumbled in his trademark argot. David

Steel said he hoped that 'after a suitable period of rest and recuperation Jeremy may find many avenues where his great talents may be used' – but not, he implied, in the Liberal Party.

Thorpe soon reverted to type. He had promised to invite all his co-defendants for a celebratory lunch after their acquittal; the invitations never arrived. In fact he never saw any of them again. Deakin and Le Mesurier returned to welcome obscurity in Wales. Holmes, loyal to the end, was now a hindrance to Thorpe's planned return to public life. Having mouthed congratulations to Carman across the courtroom ('Well rowed, Balliol!'), Thorpe did not write to thank him until prompted to do so by David Napley three months later. A few weeks after the trial Thorpe attended a 'Thanksgiving service', conducted by a maverick Devon vicar called John Hornby. 'Rise up and call him blessed!' exhorted Hornby. 'We have the opportunity to give thanks to God for the ministry of his servant Jeremy in North Devon,' he added, after the local Liberal chairman had read the 'Let us now praise famous men' passage from Ecclesiastes.

Others apart from Mr Justice Cantley had noted the comedic potential of the case. Rex Barker and the Ricochets, a group hastily formed for the occasion, released a single named 'Jeremy is Innocent'. It involved the repeated incantation of the words 'Jeremy, Jeremy' to the accompaniment of a barking dog and the sound of gunfire. *Private Eye* made the best of the outcome by issuing a 'Souvenir Acquittal Issue'. And the days that Auberon Waugh had spent in court were not wasted. He had presumably been planning a book in which the finale was a conviction. But he turned the unexpected to his advantage. *The Last Word*, his account of the case published early the next year, is a minor classic of trial writing. It is also a triumph of sustained irony. Waugh succeeded in creating a narrative of over 200 pages of sotto voce insistence that Thorpe was patently guilty, the judge half-mad, and the jury entirely bamboozled by the wiles of defence counsel, all behind a façade of outward respect for the verdict. But the greatest comic memorial to the trial was Peter Cook's superb (and very hastily prepared) parody of Cantley's summing-up at *The Secret Policeman's Ball* which had fortuitously been fixed for a four-night run in late June, starting just days after the verdict: 'We have been forced to listen to the testimony of Mr Norma St John Scott. A scrounger, parasite, pervert. A worm. A self-confessed player of the pink oboe. A man, or woman, who by his or her own admission chews pillows for kicks . . .'

★

Jeremy Thorpe's brief affair with Scott haunted him for more than fifty years. While he was acquitted in Court Number One of the Old Bailey he was convicted in the equally important court of public opinion. Apart from his liberty and his marriage – which endured until Marion's death just eight months before Thorpe's own – Thorpe lost everything else: his seat in Parliament, his reputation, a good deal of money, his dignity, the well-remunerated retirement he'd expected, and his health. Although only fifty when he had stood trial, one journalist described him as a 'walking cadaver' with the 'lumbering gait of an 80-year-old arthritic'. Parkinson's disease was diagnosed in the same year.

Although the Liberals in North Devon went through the motions of congratulating Thorpe on his acquittal, and Thorpe rashly vowed to stand again at the next election, he soon discovered that his political career was over. Carman himself had told the jurors that a verdict of not guilty was not a certificate of innocence. So it proved. Most people who studied the evidence carefully thought that Thorpe was probably guilty of the offences with which he had been charged. On any view it revealed an unscrupulous liar. Now that the case has moved beyond the realm of burdens of proof and reasonable doubts into the embrace of history, it can be concluded with a degree of certainty that Thorpe and Holmes were both guilty of conspiracy to murder. By contrast the not guilty verdicts on Deakin and Le Mesurier seem entirely justified and it was probably a mistake to prosecute men who had no possible motive to participate in a murder plot.

Former party leaders are invariably offered directorships and public appointments – as well as a peerage, or at the very least a knighthood. Thorpe had no honours in retirement. Attempts to find work were rebuffed. In 1982 Thorpe was appointed as head of the UK section of Amnesty International – a charity he had helped set up in 1961 – only to be forced to turn down the post after a public outcry led by the former *Observer* editor David Astor. At a memorial service in the 1980s several members of the congregation turned their backs on Thorpe. One by one, most of Thorpe's admirers deserted him. Even Sybille Bedford, who had sat alongside Auberon Waugh through the trial with the intention of writing a sympathetic book, was so disillusioned by what she heard at the Old Bailey that she abandoned the project. Thorpe tried to revive his television career as a chat show host, but after a pilot interview with Peter Ustinov the series was scrapped once it became clear that many celebrities would refuse to appear alongside him. Thorpe's memoirs, *In My Own Time*, were finally published by Politico's in 1999. Even by the standards of political autobiography the book was thin gruel. Self-awareness or honesty were entirely absent. The trial was dismissed as a ridiculous charade. His former lover was referred to as 'one Norman Scott'.

After his acquittal Thorpe would live on for another thirty-five years, increasingly racked with Parkinson's disease; in the end he was only able to communicate with his hands. He died on 4 December 2014, aged eighty-five. His funeral at St Margaret's Westminster was attended by all five Liberal leaders who had followed him. The obituarists were kind – 'He could have been one of the greatest post-war politicians,' Anthony Howard lamented in the *Guardian* – but Thorpe had rarely read such generous verdicts during his lifetime.

Despite the verdict David Holmes was left desolate. For him the greatest shock of the trial was hearing Carman, in his closing submissions, suggesting to the jury that they might well conclude that Holmes had orchestrated a murder plot behind Thorpe's back: the so-called Thomas Becket defence. (Waugh noted that the objection to this point was that 'Henry II did not send large sums of money to the four knights after Becket's murder to reimburse them for any incidental expenses.') Such a submission – an invitation to convict Holmes but save Thorpe – can only have been made with Thorpe's approval. 'I realized that the whole nightmare had not been worthwhile,' Holmes told the *News of the World* in 1981. The same year he was fined for 'importuning' an undercover policeman on the Old Brompton Road. Unable to find another job in finance Holmes ended up managing a roller disco in Camden Town and died, possibly of an AIDS-related illness, in 1990.

Peter Bessell had not stayed for the verdict. He went back to California, never to return, three days after his testimony at the Old Bailey ended (his son later recalled that one of the last things Bessell had seen on British soil was a newspaper board displaying the words 'Bessell – Drug Addict'). His contract with the *Sunday Telegraph* was cancelled, although they let him keep his initial £25,000. He never found a publisher for *Cover-up*, his memoir of the Thorpe affair, which had to be published privately. Hundreds of unsold copies were found in his garage after his death, from emphysema, in 1985.

Nearly forty years on, what does the Thorpe trial tell us about the Britain of the 1970s? Most obviously, it highlights how much homophobia, stigma and hypocrisy still infected human attitudes, even though homosexuality had been decriminalised several years before. Thorpe was part of the last generation of politicians who had to keep their sexuality a closely guarded secret. (The first MP to choose to come out as gay was Chris Smith in 1984.) The extraordinary events that led to his trial were surely caused by the terror of exposure and the certainty of the personal ruin it would bring. In this sense Thorpe, whatever his personal failings, was a victim of his times. At Newton's trial at Exeter in 1976 his counsel Patrick Back QC had told the jury that homosexuals 'have a terrifying propensity for malice' and mocked Scott's 'soft effeminate voice'. The BBC reporter Keith Graves was told it was 'improper and indecent' of him to ask Thorpe if he was gay at a press conference in 1977; Marion Thorpe had demanded he stand up and repeat his allegation. 'To ask a man if he has ever been a homosexual is as indefensible as to ask him if he has ever committed adultery,' The Times pontificated. 'It scrapes the barrel of journalistic slime.' Auberon Waugh wrote that, while campaigning in Devon against Thorpe for the so-called 'Dog Lovers' Party', he was asked by a reporter from Gay News about his attitude to gay dogs: Waugh assured him of his 'compassionate attitude to homosexuality among dogs, while secretly feeling they ought to be whipped'.

Although Carman had constantly criticised the press for throwing unsubstantiated mud at Thorpe, if anything the media had shown extraordinary reticence before the trial. And here lies the irony of the case. Although Thorpe's actions were prompted by fear of exposure, he was in fact the beneficiary of a culture of journalistic restraint towards the powerful. Hardly a word about the Scott affair had appeared in the press until the shooting incident in 1975: in 1971 Scott had tried to give his story to the Daily Mirror but they ducked it. In November 1974 builders renovating Bessell's office found a briefcase of material on Thorpe, including nude photographs; the Sunday Mirror refused to buy it from them. In late 1972 or early 1973 a similar dossier had reached Private Eye but even they decided not to publish out of deference to Thorpe. As Auberon Waugh explained, 'Thorpe had married, fathered a child and been widowed in the meantime.' It was not until 1974 that Waugh – who had heard local rumours about Thorpe – used his Eye column to say that Thorpe was 'already conceited enough and now threatens to become one of the great embarrassments of politics. Soon I may have to reveal some of the things in my file on this revolting man.' But no revelations did follow, even after the Sunday Express in November 1975 reported that Scott knew Thorpe, and speculated why a dog shooting was being investigated by the deputy head of Avon and Somerset CID. 'My only hope is that sorrow over his friend's dog will not cause Mr Thorpe's premature retirement from public life,' added Waugh in the Eye in December 1975: facetious, but hardly explosive. Nonetheless, once the story finally broke the newspapers fell over themselves to buy up Bessell, Newton, Scott and even Miller. The contracts each had entered proved, as we have seen, a very happy hunting ground for John Mathew and George Carman.

The case also led to a significant change in the law. After the trial journalists approached members of the jury to find out how they had arrived at their verdict, with Peter Chippindale and David Leigh writing a detailed account of their deliberations in the *New Statesman*. When the Attorney General applied to commit the publishers for contempt of court the Divisional Court held, to the consternation of some, that under the existing law there was no blanket prohibition on disclosure of the so-called 'secrets of the jury-room'. The swift legislative response was section 8 of the Contempt of Court Act 1981, which slammed the door to that room firmly shut. It expressly provided that 'it is a contempt of court to obtain, disclose or solicit any particulars of statements made, opinions expressed, arguments advanced or votes cast by members of a jury in the course of their deliberations in any legal proceedings.'

Although Auberon Waugh had admired George Carman's conduct of Thorpe's defence he thought John Mathew the more persuasive advocate. It is interesting that while Mathew remained a highly respected criminal silk until his retirement, it was Carman who became, on the back of the case, a legal star. The next twenty years saw him become a household name. Attracted by the intellectual stimulation of the civil courts, and perhaps also following the money, he moved from crime into the defamation field at a time when juries still sat on libel trials and habitually doled out stratospheric damages awards to defamed politicians, businessmen and celebrities. Carman's roll-call of clients was an illustrious one: Richard Branson, Imran Khan and Tom Cruise all came knocking at his chambers' door. The apogee of his glory came in two landmark libel cases of the 1990s. In 1997 he saw off Jonathan Aitken's claim against the *Guardian*; and then in 1999 he successfully defended Mohamed Al Fayed against Neil Hamilton in the so-called 'cash for questions' affair.

Carman's manner in court suggested a man of supreme self-confidence and it was his unruffled gravitas that drew clients to him. As his fame and fortune burgeoned there was little personal satisfaction. His appearance on *Desert Island Discs* in 1990 was excruciating. His stonewall answers to Sue Lawley's gentle probing suggested that somehow he was fearful of the inner turmoil being exposed. In the end he could ask the questions but not answer them.

IO

'No apologies and no regrets'

R v Michael Randle and Pat Pottle (1991)

IT WAS 22 October 1966, just another Saturday at Wormwood Scrubs, the grim Victorian prison in west London. Most of its high-security prisoners spent their 'free association' period watching television in a compound off D Hall. At about five forty-five in the afternoon inmate 455 told a prison officer that 'the wrestling was a farce' and that he was returning to his cell to read. Instead, upstairs on a second-floor landing, he squeezed through a hole that had been cut in the hall's huge windows and shinned down into the exercise yard. On Artillery Road, just the other side of the prison's twenty-foot walls, an accomplice was waiting.

'Strong walls do not a prison make, nor iron bars a cage. Over,' said the accomplice into his walkie-talkie.

'Minds innocent and quiet would take this for a hermitage. Over,' replied inmate 455 into his.[1]

After an agonising wait – and unnervingly close encounters with a patrolman's Alsatian dog and a courting couple – Artillery Road was finally clear. Inmate 455 had had to endure minutes that seemed like years in the prison yard waiting for a rope ladder to come over the top of the wall before the internal security patrol, which performed its regular rounds of the prison perimeter, reached him. Then it came. Within seconds, inmate 455 had clambered up and jumped down on to the pavement the other side. Landing heavily – damaging his wrist and grazing his forehead – he was bundled into the back of a parked Humber Hawk saloon. The accomplice jumped into the driver's seat and giddily took off. The Humber pranged another car at a zebra crossing before disappearing into the early evening traffic.

Within an hour, prison officers discovered that inmate 455's cell was empty. Shortly afterwards the governor of Wormwood Scrubs telephoned a PC Frankling at Shepherd's Bush Police Station to report that 'one of our chaps has gone over the wall.'

Inmate 455 was not just 'one of our chaps'. His name was George Blake, an MI6 officer who had been unmasked as a Soviet spy in 1961 and was widely considered one of the most dangerous traitors of modern British history. Many of the British spies of his generation were public-school English men recruited by a tap on the shoulder in an Oxbridge quadrangle. George Blake was different. Born George Behar in 1922 in Rotterdam, to a Dutch mother and a Sephardic Jewish father, the young Blake visited Britain only once before the Second World War. After joining the Dutch resistance he managed to escape to Britain where he served briefly in the Royal Naval Reserve before his recruitment to MI6 in autumn 1943.

Blake had been sent to Seoul in 1950 where, disillusioned with Korea's extremes of wealth and poverty and the corrupt US-backed government, he began to correlate communism with his latent Christian faith. Three years of captivity in North Korea, after the Chinese invasion in June 1950, did not dent his newly found ideals. Flattered by the attentions of two Russian agents, Blake agreed to become a Soviet spy. Between his return from Korea in 1953 and his unmasking eight years later Blake would meet a handler in London or Berlin, and hand over a sheaf of documents or microfilm, every few weeks.[2] Respectably married to an MI6 secretary, with whom he had three children, Blake had the perfect cover, and until a tip-off from a Russian defector, no one had suspected him as a double agent.

In March 1961 Blake was summoned to London from Beirut, where he was then stationed, and after three days of questioning he suddenly confessed all. News of his treachery came midway through a string of incidents, from Suez to Profumo, that shook the Conservative government, and the British establishment, to its foundations. There was also shock and disbelief within the security services. At an MI6 training centre an instructor broke down and wept after telling recruits about Blake's treachery.

Blake's trial took place in Court Number One of the Old Bailey on 3 May 1961 where he pleaded guilty to all five charges against him. Held mostly in camera Blake's employer was not mentioned once. The Attorney General, Sir Reginald Manningham-Buller,[3] merely referred to Blake as a 'government official . . . employed in the government service, both in this country and abroad' in his eight-minute speech outlining the prosecution case; Blake's counsel, Jeremy Hutchinson QC's hour-long plea in mitigation was not reported at the time and its contents were only printed when he gave a copy to Blake's biographer Roger Hermiston fifty years later. Emphasising Blake's wartime service and his incarceration in North Korea, Hutchinson sought the court's 'patience and understanding'.

Hutchinson knew that obtaining a lenient sentence for Blake – who remained wholly unrepentant – would be difficult, but he expected a sentence of no more than the fourteen years that had been handed to the atomic scientist Klaus Fuchs in 1950. Instead – to audible gasps of surprise – the Lord Chief Justice, Lord Parker of Waddington, sentenced Blake to forty-two years: three of his five fourteen-year sentences would run consecutively, not concurrently (Blake had been charged with five separate counts under section 1 of the Official Secrets Act, for which a maximum term of fourteen years of imprisonment was prescribed). 'Your conduct in many other countries would undoubtedly carry the death sentence,' Parker told him.

Blake did not collapse in the dock, as was widely reported. In fact Hutchinson later recalled his extraordinary serenity in the face of this catastrophe. But he did later sink into depression and wasn't well enough to attend his unsuccessful appeal a few weeks later. Blake knew that his infamy meant he was unlikely ever to be exchanged in a swap with the Russians, who would anyway have little use for his services: the only way to get out of prison would be to organise his own escape. But after the initial shock of the sentence Blake became stoical. He proved a surprisingly popular and congenial prisoner, participating enthusiastically in music appreciation classes, studying Russian and Arabic, and helping less literate prisoners compose letters to the Home Office.

Although it had to compete for attention with the Aberfan landslide, which had killed 144 people, mostly schoolchildren, the day before, Blake's escape still dominated the front pages for weeks. A full-throated British press eagerly peddled competing rumours. Blake had been smuggled out of Britain in a Czech orchestra's cello case; had flown incognito to Sydney; had driven up the M1 in a hearse, en route to who knew where; he had even rowed out in a rubber dinghy to a waiting Russian ship in the English Channel. Blake seemed to have emerged from the pages of a John le Carré novel: le Carré himself was convinced that his escape was a KGB operation. Others speculated that the KGB had subcontracted it to the IRA.

The truth was only slightly more prosaic. Within hours of the escape a former Scrubs inmate called Seán Bourke was identified by prison officers, and by Blake's mother, as the likely mastermind. Born in Limerick in 1934, Bourke was a serial trouble-maker who in 1961 had been sentenced to seven years at the Sussex Assizes for attempted murder. Bourke claimed that his target, a police officer, had spread false rumours about his sexuality, which had cost him his job at a youth centre in Crawley. (Bourke had posted a bomb in a biscuit tin to his putative victim's home address. It might have proved fatal had the suspicious officer not opened it at arm's length.) In Wormwood Scrubs he had met and befriended Blake before his release in the mid-1960s, after which he had sunk from view. Bourke's photograph was belatedly issued by the police to the press in January 1967, but all enquiries led nowhere. Blake, and the man who had supposedly sprung him, had disappeared.

For months Blake's whereabouts, and the circumstances of his escape, remained entirely opaque. Almost two years went by; then it was reported that Bourke was in Moscow and had approached the British Embassy to obtain a passport with which to return to Britain. This seemed an unlikely plan; and in fact Bourke returned instead to Ireland in 1968 amid a ferment of speculation. Extradition proceedings instituted by the British government before the Irish High Court failed to procure his return to England for prosecution and the triumphant Bourke, a man of charm and loquacity, became a minor celebrity in the public houses of Dublin. The full truth – or at least a version of it – did not emerge until 1970, when Bourke published a tell-all memoir, *The Springing of George Blake*, revealing, or rather trumpeting, his part in the escape.

Bourke explained how, towards the end of his time in prison, Blake had raised the question of escape. Bourke's sympathy for his friend's terrible predicament had led him to readily agree to assist. A vague plan had been discussed, but nothing concrete had been resolved by the time of Bourke's release in 1966. Rootless and lacking purpose out of prison, Bourke now latched on to the notion of springing Blake as a project to give him direction and his life significance. With remarkable ease he had managed to smuggle a walkie-talkie and tools into Wormwood Scrubs. His reconnaissance established that the best wall for an escape was one that ran along Artillery Road, between the prison's eastern perimeter and Hammersmith hospital, where a waiting getaway car would not arouse suspicion.

Blake's behaviour in prison was exemplary, and by 1966 he had been moved to a prime cell – with excellent walkie-talkie reception. On Sunday mornings this cell became a sort of literary salon, with Blake serving coffee to other members of the prison's 'intellectual mafia' as they listened to arts reviews on the BBC Third Programme. It was never searched. After the Scrubs literati had returned to their cells Blake would take out his concealed two-way radio and discuss with Bourke the next step in the plan.

Bourke made the escape ladder from a clothes line bought at Woolworths; its rungs were thirty size 13 knitting needles bought at a nearby haberdashery. Under an assumed name he then rented a bedsit on Highlever Road, half a mile from the prison, to receive and hide his friend. Blake escaped over the very same wall that six violent prisoners had scaled four months before. Security was supposedly tightened further after the unrelated murder of three police officers on a street nearby in August 1966 (by a gang led by the notorious Harry Roberts, tried in Court Number One in December of that year). But at the time of Blake's escape the windows of D Hall had yet to be fitted with the new security mesh recently installed over those of the prison's other three halls.

Bourke had tried, and failed, to persuade Blake's family to help fund the escape. They feared, with good reason in view of Bourke's antecedents, that its failure was assured and the result would be an extension to Blake's sentence, as well as a transfer to a harsher prison ('I hate to think of poor George being sent to that dreadful Durham prison with all those train robbers,' Blake's mother protested). Bourke had instead turned for help to 'Pat Porter', a small business owner who lived in Hampstead, and 'Michael and Anne Reynolds', two graduates living in Camden Town. 'Michael was a thinker while Pat was impetuous and a little excitable,' Bourke wrote.

Bourke explained that, once assured that the Russians were not involved in the escape plan, these young recruits readily agreed to help. Bourke's most pressing need was money and the man he referred to as 'Reynolds' was able to pass on funds from a young woman who had just received a large inheritance and was keen to distribute it for good causes. But after the escape their involvement deepened to an extent neither 'Porter' nor 'Mr and Mrs Reynolds' had anticipated. When Bourke arrived with Blake back at the room in Highlever Road that he had rented it became apparent that Blake's wrist was broken and required urgent medical attention. 'Reynolds' was able to call upon a friendly doctor who asked no questions. The next crisis was the discovery that the landlady came to clean the flat once a week on a Wednesday. Blake had to be moved before then. He and Bourke moved to a series of 'safe houses' offered up by friends of 'Porter' and 'Reynolds' before it was decided that they would both move more permanently into Porter's flat in Hampstead. The remainder of the year was spent pondering how to get Blake – and Bourke – out of the country.

Just before Christmas 1966 Reynolds, pretending to take a continental holiday with his wife and two young sons, drove to Berlin in a second-hand Commer camper van, with Blake concealed in a secret compartment. Blake was duly deposited and handed himself over to East German guards. After initial scepticism Blake's identity was confirmed; by 7 January 1967 he was being fêted by the KGB in Moscow. As for Bourke, he had been named in the press as a suspect shortly after the breakout. This meant that his original plan to return to Ireland had been scrapped. It was decided that the only solution was for him to follow Blake eastwards. On New Year's Eve, using a false passport that Porter had created, he took the boat-train to France. From Paris he flew to West Berlin, crossed into East Berlin via Checkpoint Charlie and arrived in Moscow at around the same time as his friend.

Bourke had run huge risks. But he had gone further than that: it was as if he had positively courted discovery. On the morning of the escape he had chatted to a prison officer he recognised outside the jail. While in hiding Bourke had accosted a boy on a Hampstead street and asked him to write 'Bourke, 28 Highlever Road' on the back of a photo portrait, which he posted to a Fleet Street newspaper. He had even made tape recordings of his walkie-talkie conversations with Blake, which he later sold to the *News of the World*. The Blake escape had been the most significant event in Seán Bourke's chaotic life and he wanted to ensure that his part in it was documented for posterity.

Now in Moscow, Bourke's account of life in the Soviet Union was like a Cold War sitcom. Despite being given a generous allowance, VIP tours and a string of young women to entertain him, Bourke found it a depressing place. He soon fell out with Blake, the man for whom he had risked so much. The two shared a flat, but Bourke now found him 'sullen, intolerant, arrogant and pompous'.

Bourke's criticisms of Blake meant that his book caused only mild irritation in British intelligence. But peace campaigners Michael Randle and Pat Pottle – the real 'Michael Reynolds' and 'Pat Porter' – were furious that Bourke had been so reckless in the way he had gone about so thinly masking their true identities. It was as if Bourke's desire to publicise his own involvement had led him to wish to do so by proxy for the other members of the Blake 'escape committee'.

In February 1962 Pottle, Randle and four other young members of the Committee of 100 anti-nuclear campaign had been convicted at Court Number One for trying to stage a sit-down protest to prevent US Air Force tactical fighters capable of carrying nuclear bombs from using the runway at RAF Wethersfield in Essex.[4] Five of the six (bar Pottle, who defended himself) were defended by Jeremy Hutchinson, who had nine months earlier represented George Blake in the same courtroom; again the prosecution was led by the Attorney General, Reginald Manningham-Buller. Both Randle and Pottle were sentenced to eighteen months by Mr Justice Havers, the judge who had sentenced Ruth Ellis to death seven years earlier.

Arriving at Wormwood Scrubs, Pottle soon struck up a friendship with Blake at the weekly music appreciation class and in the tailor's shop where they both stitched mailbags. Pottle saw Blake as a fellow political prisoner whose sentence was 'vicious'; Blake in turn told Pottle he admired his anti-nuclear cause. 'Do you ever think of escaping?' he asked Blake as they stood side by side at a prison urinal in May 1962, 'I never think of anything else.' Pottle was transferred to Ford open prison before he could discuss questions of escape further with Blake. But Randle – who had been caught sending letters to *Peace News* advocating a new public civil disobedience campaign and criticising the quality of prison food – stayed longer in the Scrubs, where he continued his own one-man campaign of civil disobedience against the prison authorities. By the time Michael Randle was released in 1963 he knew both Blake and Bourke well. He continued to correspond with both and made no secret of his friendship: soon after his release Randle wrote a story in *Peace News* saying that Blake was 'looking forward to a holiday in Moscow'. It was in May 1966 that Seán Bourke telephoned Randle with his plan.

After Bourke had been waved off at Victoria station, en route to Moscow, in 1967, both Pat Pottle and Michael Randle had hoped that they could put the last nerve-shattering months behind them. Several times in the previous weeks Bourke had seemed to invite exposure; while hiding out in Pottle's flat he had regularly wandered around Hampstead Village and drawn attention to himself. Their wayward Irish friend's antics in Moscow and then Dublin had made Randle and Pottle even more anxious. And once Bourke's book was published in 1970 they expected the police to come knocking at any moment. Incredibly, that knock never came.

During the 1970s Randle went to Ireland several times to meet Bourke, whose short-lived literary celebrity was now dwindling into an alcoholic twilight. 'It goes to show that I'm not the simple, uncomplicated Irishman people sometimes take me for,' Bourke replied delphically when Randle chastised him for using such poor pseudonyms for his erstwhile comrades. At their second meeting Bourke was morose and quarrelsome, accusing

Randle of 'betraying his country' before drunkenly passing out on a hotel bed. But between his inebriated rants Bourke claimed that a Special Branch detective inspector, one Rollo Watts, had told him that the police had long known about Pottle and Randle's involvement, but had decided not to prosecute because they 'were now living useful lives in the community'.

Their radicalism undimmed, Michael Randle and Pat Pottle carried on to the full those useful lives over the next fifteen years. Then in 1987 they had another rude awakening. The veteran espionage and crime writer H. Montgomery Hyde added to the already substantial literature on Blake by publishing *George Blake: Superspy*, which dropped very heavy hints about the identity of Bourke's accomplices. He revealed for the first time that 'Reynolds' and 'Porter' were Committee of 100 members who had been imprisoned at Wormwood Scrubs in the early 1960s following the Wethersfield protest. Short of giving their full names and addresses, Hyde could not have done more to identify Randle and Pottle.

The press had now become very interested. The *Sunday Times* ran a series of articles written by Barrie Penrose, which first positively identified Pottle and Randle by their real names on 4 October 1987. Photographers started camping outside their homes. All this placed them in a dilemma. For twenty years they had tried to keep their involvement in the escape secret; neither wanted another spell in prison. But their loyalty to the peace movement was so great that incriminating themselves seemed more palatable than seeing that movement tainted by false accusations that it had collaborated with the KGB in freeing Blake.

Rather than lie low they decided to go public in the most overt way possible. They outed themselves in a book of their own, *The Blake Escape*, published in April 1989. Pottle had favoured an 'ambiguously worded' title but in the end they decided on a policy of total transparency – and self-incrimination. The book's subtitle, *How we Freed George Blake – and Why*, laid bare its authors' unapologetic stance. The book sometimes descended into over-detailed accounts of the frugal fish-pie suppers they had shared with Bourke and Blake and the technicalities of passport forgery. But it was otherwise a riveting read, giving an extraordinary account of how haphazard Blake's escape had been, and how incompetent the authorities had been to allow Blake to slip through their fingers.

Having settled on a principle of full disclosure Randle and Pottle could now tell the unvarnished truth. It emerged that much of Bourke's earlier account was a self-aggrandising fiction. More than twenty years later Pottle and Randle's annoyance with him was still palpable. They revealed that after Blake's breakout Bourke had himself called the police from a Paddington station phone box to let them know the escape car's whereabouts on a street in Kensal Green. Bourke's Highlever Road landlady had apparently called the police to raise concerns about her dubious tenant, only to be told, 'Yes, ma'am, keep on taking the pills.' Eventually the police had searched the flat on Christmas Day 1966, supposedly 'looking for a deserter'. But no watch was put on it, and just days later Pottle and Randle were able to clear the flat of all the incriminating evidence that Bourke had left behind.

In the book they also candidly explained the amateurishness of the whole escapade. Dozens of people had got to know of the plot: Randle had approached numerous friends for assistance. Dr Alex Comfort, a Committee of 100 member (and later bestselling author of *The Joy of Sex*), had told him 'what we were contemplating was madness' and refused to help. On the other hand, as we have seen, a doctor friend had willingly agreed to set Blake's broken wrist, using plaster supplied by another friend who worked at the BBC make-up department at Lime Grove. Until they bought the Commer van the Randles did not own a vehicle and had to beg yet another friend to ferry Blake around from one hideout to another. A 'priest-hole' under the Randles' staircase had been mooted but abandoned. Instead Randle initially moved Blake and Bourke from Highlever Road to the Earl's Court home of the environmentalist John Papworth,[5] whose oblivious mother served them a meagre meal of boiled cauliflower. Papworth had assumed the fugitives were US Army deserters but, when he learned the truth, nonetheless continued to provide them sanctuary. It was when he told an aghast Blake that his wife Marcelle revealed all to her psychoanalyst ('The course of analysis requires her to be absolutely frank . . . there is no point in it if she isn't'), the duo realised it was time to move on.

If it hadn't been for the Commer van idea Blake would probably never have got out of Britain. During this phase of the escape plan the Ealing-comedy quality of the operation reached new heights. The first leg of the journey to Berlin had Blake lying prone in a specially created secret compartment beneath the Randles' sleeping children, peeing into a hot-water bottle when the need arose. Once their ferry had reached Ostend without incident Blake left his cubby-hole and (as the only Flemish speaker in the vehicle) had to ask a pedestrian for directions when they got lost in the suburbs of Brussels. After dropping Blake off near an East German checkpoint in Berlin, the Randles continued their 'holiday'. Their only trouble with the authorities came when a Christmas tree they had chopped down in the Harz Mountains was confiscated by customs at Dover. Somehow a hard-drinking Irishman burdened by a perverse desire to be found out, and two idealistic peace campaigners, had managed not only to spring Blake from prison but smuggle the most wanted man in Britain out of the country.

In September 1988 – almost twenty-two years after Blake's escape – the police first made contact with Michael Randle and Pat Pottle and requested that the pair attend at Holborn Police Station for questioning. Randle and Pottle enlisted the help of two prominent civil rights solicitors, John Wadham and Benedict Birnberg. On advice they gave 'no comment' interviews, which were short, formal and very polite.

But the two had broken an unspoken bargain ('Keep your mouths shut and we won't prosecute,' as Randle saw it). They had signed the contract with their publisher Harrap in 1988; the anticipated date of publication of *The Blake Escape* was June 1989, although in the event it was brought forward to April to try to forestall any legal action that might be brought to suppress it. Once this became known the political floodgates opened. In November 1988 the chairman of the Conservative backbench 1922 Committee, Sir Marcus Fox MP, protested about the forthcoming book; a *Sun* editorial said, 'It would be poetic justice if this nasty pair could be locked away for the remaining 40 years' of Blake's sentence. Just before Christmas another Conservative MP, Graham Riddick, put forward an Early Day Motion, signed by 111 Tory backbenchers, calling for Pottle and Randle to be prosecuted and for steps to be taken to stop them profiting from their 'illegal and treacherous' book.

The Director of Public Prosecutions then announced that he had ordered a reopening of the enquiry into the Blake escape. Detective Inspector Richard Bird of Special Branch phoned Harrap to ask for a copy of the book as soon as it was available.[6] At 1 p.m. on 3 May 1989, just after they had returned from a promotional tour in Ireland, Pottle and Randle were arrested, cautioned and interviewed (a perfunctory affair as they again refused to answer any questions); Anne Randle was also questioned but not arrested. The police investigation was at first a good-natured affair. A Sergeant Lloyd later testified that while being driven home Pottle admitted that book sales would surely increase following their arrest. Michael Randle offered to make cups of tea for police officers searching his Bradford home. Bird himself offered to go shopping for them if they did not want to run the gauntlet of the press. As they had not yet been charged, the two friends, still as close as they had been in the mid-1960s, gave a number of TV and radio interviews in the weeks that followed. Superintendent Eileen Eggington, now in charge of the case, once told them laughingly, 'I think you are enjoying it. It's your wives I feel sorry for.'

On 10 July 1989 Randle and Pottle were both charged with three offences: aiding the escape of a convicted prisoner; conspiring to harbour him; and conspiring to prevent, hinder or interfere with his arrest. They shortly afterwards made their first appearance before Stipendiary Magistrate Ronald Bartle at Bow Street ('after a number of cases involving prostitutes, vagrants, drunks, and two men whom a policeman had spotted engaged in mutual masturbation in a park', Randle recalls). Suddenly things looked more serious: if convicted and given consecutive maximum sentences, as Blake had been, they could each go down for nine years.

At their committal hearing on 7 August, again at Bow Street, the defendants revealed their novel defence. They would plead not guilty on grounds of 'necessity of conscience': in short they had been obliged to act to prevent the psychological harm Blake's long sentence would cause him, and that aiding his escape was therefore justified. It will be unsurprising to learn that this was not a defence then known to the law; Michael Randle privately wondered whether 'the judge could succeed in totally blocking' its presentation.

As the two pondered their impending trial they toyed with zany ideas: perhaps they should call as witnesses Jim Callaghan (Home Secretary in 1970); and even Harold Wilson (who as Prime Minister had told the Commons in 1966 that Blake's escape had 'in no way endangered national security')? Suspecting the police had known all along about their involvement, they also wanted to track down Detective Inspector Watts, who in 1984 had apparently told an Irish journalist, Kevin O'Connor of RTE, that a decision had been taken 'from above' not to prosecute because they were 'perfectly law-abiding citizens in every other respect', confirming what Bourke had himself told Randle during one of his momentary periods of lucidity more than fifteen years before.

Pottle engaged the leading human rights silk Geoffrey Robertson, whose CV already read like a lexicon of the causes célèbres of the 1970s and 1980s. 'Refreshingly informal', Robertson discussed the case with Pottle over a bottle of wine in his chambers. He suggested an appearance by Blake by video to guarantee maximum publicity; his junior, Tom Mackinnon, went to Russia and obtained Blake's ready agreement. Randle retained Anthony Scrivener QC, with Edward Fitzgerald as his junior.[7] 'I love your book,' Scrivener told him, 'I must get you to sign my copy before you leave.' But he urged Randle to reconsider his not guilty plea, warning him that if convicted (as he thought inevitable) he would probably get three or four years plus a hefty fine, a much heavier sentence than if he pleaded guilty now. He suggested approaching the prosecuting counsel Julian Bevan ('a reasonable sort of chap') with a plea bargain.[8] Neither defendant was keen. Randle also feared that having pleaded guilty 'the drama would go out of the trial . . . no one was likely to be interested in what we had to say, since nothing depended on it.'

Still, there remained several other avenues to explore. Robertson proposed trying to get the prosecution dismissed as an 'abuse of process', on the basis that, despite knowing of their involvement in the escape since at least 1970, the police had taken no action against them. But he was less optimistic at the suggestion that Blake's sentence amounted to 'cruel, inhuman and degrading treatment' contrary to the European Convention on Human Rights. If the charges weren't thrown out before the trial, he echoed Scrivener's advice. If Randle pleaded guilty he could still make his moral and political points in mitigation. There was even worse news: Pottle and Randle were told that if they ended up pursuing their 'necessity' defence at a trial they were on their own. In accordance with their professional obligation, the barristers could not properly advance a defence not recognised by the law. Scrivener and Robertson could only represent them at preliminary hearings.

The lawyers said they had never met such cheerful clients; in reality Pottle and Randle had little to be cheerful about. Undeterred, in February 1990 they went to Moscow to record Blake's statement on a video camera loaned by Thames TV. After twenty-four years it was an emotional reunion. Blake arrived at the vast Brezhnev-era Hotel Cosmos in a chauffeur-driven Volga. In the new Russia Blake was only allowed to enter as the guest of a foreigner. Back at Blake's flat, on whose wall was hung a commemorative plate celebrating the wedding of Prince Charles and Lady Diana, the Pottles gave him presents of tea and soap, the Randles stoneware goblets; in return, Blake offered them political asylum. They politely declined.

Back in England the focus was now firmly on seeking disclosure of the transcript of Blake's trial and appeal in 1961 (because most of the proceedings were heard in camera they had not been reported at the time), and all the Special Branch and MI5 files on Blake's escape, the publication of Bourke's book in 1970 and the Irishman's attempted extradition. A year of legal wrangling followed. Arguing that in 1970 the police 'had details which even Inspector Clouseau could not avoid connecting with these defendants', Geoffrey Robertson persuaded Mr Justice Auld to order the release of some documents to assist in the abuse of process argument. Crucially, a statement emerged from Detective Inspector Bird indicating that Randle and Pottle had been under suspicion as early as 1966, but had not been investigated further. It was also revealed that in 1970 Detective Inspector Watts had written a file note, dubbed the 'Watts report', which had been sent to the Home Office, and reviewed the case against Randle and Pottle. The suspicion was that the Watts report provided the real reason for the failure to prosecute them back in the 1960s or after the publication of Bourke's book: the British state simply did not want to admit that one of its most high-security prisoners had been sprung from the Scrubs by a bunch of amateurs.

A number of setbacks for the defence then followed. They heard that the trial judge would be Mr Justice Macpherson of Cluny, a robust honorary colonel in the SAS ('You won't get much change out of him,' said Scrivener).[9] Then, days before the trial was due to start yet another judge made orders confiscating the payments they had received from their publishers. Everyone pitched up at the Old Bailey on 25 April 1990 to argue, as a preliminary point, before the trial started, the abuse of process issue. Macpherson refused Scrivener's application to release the Watts report, or to allow Bird, the senior officer in charge of the prosecution, to be called as a witness and cross-examined. As expected, he gave short shrift to the application. But on the day the trial was due to start, an application for permission to judicially review Macpherson's decision to refuse to stop the prosecution as an abuse was made – the irrepressible Robertson even managed to complete his submissions in time to make his wedding to the author Kathy Lette – and granted. The trial was postponed pending a full hearing before the Divisional Court. This was a legal first: never before had the High Court assumed jurisdiction to stop a criminal trial.

By July 1990 the lawyers were all back in court; this time the battle had moved from the Bailey to the Royal Courts of Justice in the Strand. The judicial review was heard by Sir Tasker Watkins, an old-school judge who had won a VC in 1944 for single-handedly flushing out a German machine-gun nest in Normandy, and the milder Mr Justice Hutchison. Watkins was, as predicted, unsympathetic ('Their confession is scandalous. Why should they now complain?' he asked). But even though the Home Secretary David Waddington had claimed public interest immunity on the Watts report and related documents, to everyone's surprise Watkins announced he wanted to read it, and then released the report to the defence forthwith 'because he could not say for sure that it would be of no assistance to them'. The cantankerous judge had swept aside prosecution assurances that the report had no relevance. To even more surprise Watkins then ordered Watts to testify, along with two retired Special Branch commanders, Arthur Cunningham and Jock Wilson. Meanwhile Bevan said the Crown 'would drop the case at once' if there had been evidence in 1970 of Pottle and Randle's involvement: words he would later regret.

Newly released correspondence showed that in 1969 MI5 had obtained a pre-publication copy of Bourke's book from a source at his publisher Cassell, and that Watts's report had been sent not only to MI5 but to the Permanent Secretary at the Home Office, the Foreign Office and MI6, bolstering the theory that a political decision had been taken not to prosecute. Disappointingly, Watts – a shortish, red-faced man with long sideburns, who refused Watkins's offer of a seat – denied ever telling the journalist Kevin O'Connor that the proposed prosecution had been stopped for political reasons. But just after Watts left the witness box there was a moment of drama. Two men (MI5 officers, Pottle and Randle assumed) came into court and handed a note to Philip Havers, acting as an *amicus curiae*, who passed it to the judge. Another relevant document had just been unearthed: a memo, written on 29 April 1970 by an MI5 officer, 'Miss A', recording Watts as saying that Special Branch had decided 'to take no steps to interview or attempt to prosecute the Randles [or] Pottle' because 'to do so might be persecution – a big fish had got away so they were taking it out on the little fish'.

The so-called 'Big fish' minute all but confirmed that the decision not to prosecute in 1970 was taken not on evidential grounds but policy ones, raising ominous questions about why it was being revived twenty years later. Watkins at once ordered Watts to be recalled. In the corridor outside court Pottle overheard Eggington ask Bevan, 'This means we've lost, doesn't it?'

Next morning Bevan announced that Watts, who had suffered a stroke three years before and had angina, had been taken ill with renal spasms and was in hospital; he had apparently collapsed when told he was being recalled to court. The release of the 'Big fish' minute – possibly down to the longstanding feud between MI5 and Special Branch, Randle suspected – had done as much damage to Watts's fragile health as it had to the prosecution, which now seemed on the verge of collapse.

But Watts's collapse bought Bevan vital time. The hearing of the judicial review had been listed hard up against the end of the summer legal term. The court resumed more than two months later at the start of the new term in October. Unhelpfully, in September a TV interview with George Blake, in which he said he may have betrayed as many as 400 agents, was broadcast. And the prosecution had been able to regroup. Watts had been allowed to see the 'Big fish' minute and the prosecution had new statements from Watts, Cunningham and 'Miss A'.

In cross-examination Robertson teased Watts unsparingly: 'The big fish, the great white shark in the form of Blake, and the rather plump Irish salmon had got away . . . and you are left with a couple of little CND sardines.' Scrivener asked why elementary enquiries – such as checking whether Pottle or Randle owned a camper van, whether their passports contained evidence of travel to Germany, or talking to neighbours – had not taken place.

Kevin O'Connor then outlined his 1984 meeting with Watts at the Sloane Street offices of Saladin, a security company Watts worked for after retiring from the police. O'Connor recalled Watts saying, 'Poor old Seán. He died sadly,' before adding that the other accomplices weren't 'real-life effing and blinding villains' and implying that a decision not to prosecute Randle and Pottle had been taken on high. Although O'Connor had no audio recording of the interview – only indecipherable notes – and couldn't remember its date, the damage was done.

Speaking in a clipped, educated voice from behind a curtain, 'Miss A' maintained that the relationship between MI5 and Special Branch had been 'harmonious' and that her minute didn't mean what it appeared to. The sole reason for the decision not to prosecute was lack of evidence, she insisted. The trouble was that Watts had already admitted that no steps had been taken to find that evidence. Cunningham then argued that he did not 'feel that we could obtain useful evidence' as Pottle and Randle were 'shrewd political activists, well versed in legal procedures'. All in all, the defendants' counsel argued, it seemed a dilatory way of pursuing what Cunningham agreed was one of the most important manhunts in British history. The police hadn't even taken the 'elementary steps that would be followed in a common burglary', Scrivener said.

Yet the year of legal wrangling ended in failure for the defence. On 15 November 1990 Watkins and Hutchison issued a lengthy judgement that dismissed the 'abuse of process' argument. It is an extraordinary document, entirely divorced from what seemed the obvious reality that emerged from the documents, the disclosure of which the court itself had ordered. 'In the light of the contents of the book the plea of fading memory could simply not be advanced. Memories of events are seemingly all too clear,' their judgement said acidly.

The trial finally began on 17 June 1991, 9,004 days after Blake's escape and in the same court in which Blake, Pottle and Randle had each been sentenced for the offences that had brought them together at Wormwood Scrubs thirty years before. The twenty-five-year interval between alleged offence and trial was thought at the time to be the longest in English legal history. Michael Randle noted that the delay caused by their application to the High Court had meant that the trial wouldn't have to compete with the Gulf War for media attention. Unlike most defendants in criminal trials he wanted to attract rather than repel publicity, not for hope of personal gain or any pleasure in being in the limelight, but to promote the motives that had impelled him and Pat Pottle to act as they did.

Since their first appearance at the Old Bailey in February 1962 its main entrance had been moved to the 1970s South Block extension, with its toughened glass and airport-style security. In those long-gone innocent days one had entered through the High Edwardian ceremonial gateway, under its time-worn, soot-blackened allegorical figures, and into the huge lobby, as if one were visiting an art gallery or a grand hotel. Now the defendants' wives had to compete for spaces in the public gallery, a far cry from 1962 when relatives were allowed as of right to sit in the well of the court. Nearby Julia Quenzler, the doyenne of court artists (and still very active today), sat watching, sketching in her mind the demeanour of the defendants (to have lifted her pen in court would have been a contempt). A piece of good news for the defendants was that the seemingly unsympathetic Macpherson was no longer available. A newly appointed judge – Mr Justice (John) Alliott – was taking his place.

Pat Pottle had experience of representing himself. At the Wethersfield Six trial, he had stood apart from his co-defendants by not availing himself of the services of Jeremy Hutchinson as counsel. His intention was transparent: to allow himself the latitude to pose questions a barrister could not properly ask (the trick had worked: he had been able to ask an air commodore, 'Would you press the button that you know is going to annihilate millions of people?'; 'If the circumstances so demanded it I would,' came the answer, reported round the world, before the judge could intervene). This time both Randle and Pottle were forced to defend themselves (though with continuing assistance behind the scenes from

Ben Birnberg and John Wadham) because their 'defence', being unknown to law, was not one that could properly be advanced by counsel.

Unlike the privilege granted to Noel Pemberton Billing seventy years earlier, Alliott would not allow the defendants to sit in the well of the court during the trial and so on the first day they passed through security checks in the cells beneath before being walked up the white-tiled stairs into the dock. Alliott, a well-built man in his late forties, strode in, slapping his silk gloves down on the bench. There was something proprietorial about the gesture, as if the new judge was determined to make it clear to the defendants who was in charge.

Some chance! Veterans of several trials, Randle and Pottle seemed unbowed by the grandeur of the occasion. Straight away they stood up and declared – politely but firmly – that the trial was an 'abuse of process'. Despite Alliott's reminders that they had failed to persuade the Divisional Court on that point, and his insistence that he was not going to allow the trial to become a political platform, they persisted. Alliott answered that this point was best made later, if the defendants were convicted, in mitigation. The judge's stance was that 'the only issue I am to have debated in the trial is whether or not it is proved by the Crown that the defendants did the acts constituting the three counts in the indictment . . . In the light of what I have read, you have no defence.' The heavy implication was that he wanted the defendants to reconsider their plea of not guilty. 'It's clear what Alliott's line is going to be,' Birnberg said during the adjournment the judge had allowed them for that purpose. 'He's determined to shut you up completely.' But no one in their ad hoc legal team suggested any change of approach: all knew that Randle and Pottle were not for budging. 'I take it you are not changing your plea?' Bevan asked laconically as they returned to court.

Bevan – 'slim, affable, anxious almost to the point of self-deprecation that we should not see him as a demon figure bent on exacting retribution', Randle recalls – took up most of the afternoon opening the prosecution case. He explained to a poker-faced jury how Randle and Pottle had freely admitted their role in Blake's escape: 'There is no need to doubt their word.'

Throughout the trial the defendants strayed back to their 'necessity' defence and reiterated their 'abuse of process' argument. Like a patient teacher trying to shepherd recalcitrant pupils, Alliott would repeatedly – and unsuccessfully – try to steer them back to the charges they faced. The judge soon realised the task was hopeless. Rather than find the defendants in contempt of court – 'a sledgehammer to crack a nut', he said – he softened. Randle recalls how a smile 'flickered across his face' when the judge turned down Pottle's suggestion that jurors should be asked if they had ever been members of MI5, MI6, the CIA or the KGB. Alliott accepted assurances that the defendants would make no contact with jurors, thereby allowing Randle and Pottle to spend the 'short adjournment' – i.e. their lunchbreaks – as free men. Throughout the trial – even while the jury was deliberating – Randle and Pottle would regularly have a lunchtime pint at the Magpie and Stump, often joined by the journalist Richard Norton-Taylor, who did double duty by covering the trial for the *Guardian* while putting up Randle in his flat for its duration.

But Alliott's patience had its limits. 'We have all been so pleasant with one another, but do not let us overlook the fact, you are on trial on a number of very serious offences,' he once said. Pottle asked if they could take it in turns to cross-examine, which Alliott readily agreed to, while reminding him that 'I would prefer you to refer to your co-defendant as Mr Randle [not Michael] when you are speaking publicly,' a ruling he did not later enforce. From the beginning it was 'Michael' and 'Pat' and the gravity of the prosecution seemed imperceptibly to lift. The defendants had learned an important lesson: a criminal trial is all about atmosphere. Their good-natured amateurism, coupled with the obvious sincerity of their position, suffused the court. The notion that these two idealists should be convicted of a criminal offence seemed to become more and more nonsensical.

At the end of day one the trial was adjourned to allow jurors time to read *The Blake Escape* in the jury room, not at home as suggested by the defendants. (Similarly the judge in the *Lady Chatterley's Lover* trial thirty years earlier had declined a defence request that the jury be permitted to read Lawrence's novel in the comfort and solitude of their own sitting rooms.) The impromptu book group over, at two o'clock on day two the trial resumed with a showing of the drama-documentary *The Blake Escape* – which had been aired on ITV a year earlier – on three monitors ('I thought they cast Mr Pottle splendidly,' said Alliott good-naturedly; 'Mr Randle not quite so well').

Then Alliott apologetically asked the jury to withdraw while he ruled on whether the defence of 'necessity' was one that could properly be put before the jury (although he said he was 'a great exponent of Glasnost' he saw no need to detain them during a procedural discussion). Randle immediately challenged his decision to ask the jurors to absent themselves, citing a 1930 precedent, 'the case of *Anderson*, which is quoted in that very fat book whose title has slipped my mind' ('It's *Archbold*,' interposed Pottle – what was then the criminal lawyers' bible). Bevan 'pulled a succession of wry faces'; Alliott responded, playfully: '1930! That was before I was born!' But still, Alliott allowed the jury to stay.

The defence of necessity had been defined in a textbook as requiring the person accused to show that the alleged crime was committed only in order to prevent consequences that could not otherwise be avoided, and which, if they had followed, would have 'inflicted upon him or upon others whom he was bound to protect inevitable and irreparable evil'. The book added: 'It does not extend to the case of shipwrecked sailors who kill a boy, one of their number, in order to eat his body' – a reference to the famous case of *Dudley and Stephens*.[10] It will be obvious that this concept was a long way from the case before the court. But this was not something to deter Michael Randle. Having spent days in public libraries, he stood in the dock with a mass of legal texts before him. His legal odyssey involved citing cases of ever more dubious relevance.

'I sometimes wonder, from the direction you face, whether you are addressing me,' said Alliott drily as Randle – who had looked straight at the jury throughout – wound up his address. 'My Lord, every time I look up, you have your head buried in your papers,' Randle replied good-naturedly.

'I am not going to stop you, Mr Randle, but you have strayed a long way from the theme that you set yourself,' returned Alliott. Few could disagree. Of course Michael Randle knew exactly what he was doing: he had been speaking not to the judge, but the jury. Pottle followed up, speaking rather more plainly than the loquacious Randle: 'If you or the jury think it's a load of codswallop, then you can say so. You can say I think what they have just said is a load of rubbish, on your bike! . . . But at least give us the chance of being able to say it.'

Bevan responded that these arguments, if correct, would give *carte blanche* for anyone to aid the escape of a prisoner whose sentence they felt was excessive. 'The consequences of that, Your Lordship will appreciate, would be anarchy.' Bevan didn't need to strive too hard. Under the law as it stood, the 'necessity' defence was unarguable.

Alliott ruled, as he had to, 'without any hesitation, that it is not open, on the apparently admitted facts of this case, for defendants to raise the defence of necessity'.[11] Alliott urged Randle and Pottle 'to discuss the state of affairs that now presents itself to you with Mr Birnberg and Mr Wadham', hinting that further attempted pursuit of a 'necessity' defence before the jury could lead to contempt charges. But the defendants were buoyant: they had at least got to make their points in front of those jurors.

Somehow Pottle and Randle's unconventional, scatter-gun approach won them friends. Peter Clark, a former prison officer, testified that they had been on the same landing as Blake at Wormwood Scrubs. As he left the witness box he gave them a thumbs-up sign in full view of the jury and exited the court with the words 'Good luck, lads'.

The following Monday Detective Superintendent Eggington took the stand. She dismissed Watts and 'Miss A' as 'junior officers' and, a savvy witness, frequently asked Alliott to rule on the relevance of Pottle's questions. Then came Bird, who confirmed that Dr Alex Comfort and John Papworth, who had been named in the press as possible accomplices, had refused to answer his questions. Pottle then asked why fourteen other people suspected of involvement hadn't also been interviewed, to which Bird gave the non-answer: 'At that stage the enquiries that I was conducting required the questions to be asked to the people that I had asked,' before admitting that he had only interviewed Nicolas Walter, another former Committee of 100 member, two weeks earlier. 'So for the last three and a half years this man had been portrayed as somebody who had information that could probably be of help to your enquiries and you ring him two weeks ago and you speak to him on the telephone?' asked Pottle rhetorically. The scatter-gun had hit a target at last.

The prosecution case was now over. It was simplicity itself. The facts making out the offences were admitted and the only defence put forward had been ruled inadmissible by the judge. Nonetheless it is a principle of English criminal law that the judge can never direct a jury to convict. The question of guilty or not guilty remains inviolably within the domain of the jurors, regardless of the facts. Into that province the judge can never trespass. The defendants knew this. They understood that their prospects of success rested on persuading the jury to put aside the law and embrace wider, perhaps higher, considerations.

Looking unwaveringly at the jurors, Pottle opened his own defence unrepentantly. 'I believe that anyone who was involved in the escape of George Blake should have no guilt or shame for what they did. I consider breaking George Blake out of prison to be a decent humanitarian act.' Bizarrely, he was then cross-examined by Randle ('You'll get used to this double act,' Alliott told the jury). As he recounted his activist career he recalled being arrested in China for inciting the overthrow of the state and being branded 'a running-dog lickspittle of the American imperialists'. 'Are you in fact a running-dog lickspittle of the American imperialists?' Randle asked. For the first time, several jurors laughed.

Pottle explained how his co-authorship of *The Blake Escape*, and the prosecution that followed, had forced him to sell his antiques business and give up his home. Still, he said, 'I don't care what the verdict of this court is now. I don't care what anybody says . . . I refuse to believe that George Blake would have been better off rotting in some English jail than living a semiordinary life back in Moscow.' Birnberg and Wadham had warned that discussing out-of-court negotiations for a plea bargain in open court was 'never done' and that both prosecution and judge would be furious. 'We could forget about the relatively relaxed atmosphere that had prevailed up to then; the gloves would be off,' Randle recalls. But such warnings only egged him on. 'One final question, Pat. Did our solicitors inform you that Mr Bevan had told them that he would recommend that the main charge against us would be dropped if we pleaded guilty to one of the lesser charges of harbouring and preventing re-arrest?'

'Yes, we've been offered that deal four times in the course of this trial,' Pottle replied. Bevan 'pulled a succession of grimaces'. Twisting the knife, Pottle said he'd refused as 'we don't like the idea of deals being done behind anyone's back.'

In his own cross-examination Bevan retaliated by reminding Pottle that it was Scrivener who had first proposed the plea bargain, to which Pottle disarmingly agreed. Moving on, Bevan could only pointlessly ask Pottle to confirm that he did not deny committing the acts alleged; naturally Pottle did so.

Pottle announced his next witness: George Blake, by video. 'Mr Blake, for very obvious reasons, can't be with us,' the judge quipped, adding to the relaxation of the atmosphere. 'As a film it would win no Oscars,' Randle later wrote. 'Blake sat centre picture throughout, dressed in a blazer and muffler, reading his statement. Occasionally he would look up from the text, but mostly his head was bent forward . . . Yet a Hitchcock thriller could not have been more riveting for everyone in the courtroom.' Although Blake said little that was genuinely newsworthy – merely explaining that Pottle and Randle had acted 'out of purely humanitarian concern', had had no contact with the KGB, and hadn't been paid – his testimony was enough to turn the trial into a major news story the next day. As Randle went into the witness box afterwards, the press benches emptied. 'It seems, Mr Randle,' said Alliott, more

playful than ever, 'that the press are more interested in Mr Blake's statement than in what you have to say.'

Randle's evidence carried less bravado than Pottle's. He again tried to
reintroduce his 'necessity' defence until Alliott stopped him: 'I am afraid
not, because I have ruled that the defence of necessity does not arise in
your case.' David Calvert-Smith, Bevan's junior (and later a distinguished
judge), then cross-examined, concentrating on admissions in *The Blake
Escape* that Blake had 'blood on his hands'. But the jury had heard all this
before, and allowed Randle the opportunity to launch another series of
salvos about the CIA's involvement in the overthrow of the Chilean President
Salvador Allende in 1973 and a failed plot to assassinate the Egyptian President
Gamal Abdel Nasser, and, for good measure, MI6's role in the toppling of
the Iranian Prime Minister Mohammad Mossadegh in 1953.

Then came a character witness: the former Czech dissident Jan Kavan.[12]
Randle questioned him in such laborious detail that Bevan soon dropped
a hint that he wanted Randle to get on with it ('Mr Kavan is a highly
respected and honest individual and I would have no questions of this
witness so Mr Randle could take it as shortly as he wished'). But Randle
didn't listen; in fact he had no intention of listening. A lengthy dialogue
ensued about how Randle had smuggled books and Gestetner duplicators
into Czechoslovakia in the early 1970s, using the same camper-van compartment that had temporarily housed George Blake. 'I am sure all this is an
immense contribution to the much happier state of affairs that prevails
in Czechoslovakia today,' said an impatient Alliott, who reminded Randle
that Kavan was a 'character witness to say what a good chap you are, not
to give us a lecture on the recent political history of Czechoslovakia'. So
ended the defence evidence.

Bevan then went to the opposite extreme. He told Alliott that 'no
useful purpose would be served addressing the jury', given that the
defendants had admitted their involvement in Blake's escape, and that
their necessity defence had been ruled invalid. It was an honourable
position, but from the point of view of obtaining a conviction might
have been a misjudgement. The judge adjourned: the next day would
be the occasion for the defendants to make their final address to the jury.
That evening optimism was in short supply. Both defendants still feared
that by the following night they 'would almost certainly be behind bars'.
Randle stayed up into the early hours that night re-working his final
speech. Wadham had urged both defendants to address the jury for no
more than ten minutes each, but Randle realised the speech he had
crafted was nearer two hours' worth. Fearing that he would make himself

ill, Anne ordered him to call it a night at 2 a.m. In the courtroom fatigue is the enemy of eloquence.

On the trial's final day, 26 June 1991, Pottle was first to make his closing address. 'He stood tall and spoke with confidence, using plain down-to-earth language,' recalls Michael Randle, but behind the dock's wooden walls Pat Pottle's legs were shaking with fear. 'Sitting in the jury box must be boring and frustrating. If it's any consolation to you, I can assure you it beats sitting in the dock. Let's open the windows, let the fresh air in, and blow away the cobwebs,' Pottle began. 'The judge and Mr Bevan have told you that the issue you have to decide is simple. I disagree . . . This prosecution is taking place today not because of what we did twenty-five years ago, but because 110 MPs signed a motion.'

Pottle explained that he and Randle had written their book simply because they felt they had to quell rumours that they had worked with MI6, MI5 or the KGB. He continued: 'It is a case of politics, a case of how governments lie, cheat and manipulate, and then cover their tracks in a smokescreen of official secrecy . . . In 1970 it had been too embarrassing to prosecute us . . . It was better that the world continued to believe that the whole thing was organised by the KGB rather than the Lavender Hill Mob.'[13] He urged the jury to 'look at the whole case, not just the legal mumbo-jumbo . . . Unlike most judges you exist in the ordinary world of everyday life.'

Disarmingly, Pottle then said he could understand the 'moral indignation' that Blake's espionage had prompted. 'But moral outrage is only genuine if it is applied to both sides.' Spies were 'international pawns in a game, some to be swopped, some to be given immunity, and the unlucky ones left to rot in prison'. Blake's sentence 'ain't justice', Pottle argued, and had been imposed simply because he was 'not of the old school, not "one of us". Deep down he was a foreigner and half-Jewish to boot . . . Not like dear old Kim [Philby], who was offered immunity, or dear old Anthony [Blunt] who was not only given immunity but allowed to continue his work as Surveyor of the Queen's Pictures.'

When Pottle urged Bevan to abandon the prosecution then and there, Alliott reminded him, 'There is no place in a final address to the jury for an appeal of that kind.' But Pottle pressed on regardless. 'If you or I walked into a local police station tomorrow and confessed to doing something twenty-five years ago which carried a maximum sentence of five years – hit someone perhaps – they would not listen.' Walking solemnly to the back of the dock and gesturing to the steps down to the cells, Pottle said, 'Every building has a sewer running underneath it.

These steps lead to the sewer underneath this court. Forty-two years down in that sewer means death. You are twelve individuals with minds of your own . . . We think that what we did was right. If you think the same, then obviously you will find us not guilty . . . I will finish by quoting Bertrand Russell: "Remember your humanity and forget the rest".'

However shaky Pottle's grasp of the law, he had wowed the courtroom. This was advocacy that hit you in the pit of the stomach. During the lunchtime adjournment that followed he was congratulated by several barristers who had come to the trial's final day out of curiosity.

It was now the turn of Michael Randle. He started hesitantly with a self-deprecating joke ('Pat and I are as anxious to get back home as you are – perhaps slightly more so') before becoming very serious. 'There has been a suggestion . . . that we are seeking martyrdom and do not mind the prospect of being sent to prison,' said Randle. 'Nothing could be further from the truth.' He reminded the jurors that he had spent his honeymoon in 1962 on bail and his first year of marriage, during which his eldest son was born, in Wormwood Scrubs. 'The last thing I want is to go back to prison now. Nevertheless this is something Pat and I and our families are prepared to face if that is what it takes to put the record straight.' He went on to explain for one final time his motives back in 1966. Blake's sentence 'reflected the obsessions of the Cold War, not considerations of justice . . . If this is not a cruel and unusual punishment, what is?'

As a spy Blake had been expected to carry out 'blackmail . . . theft, deception, lies, mutilation and even murder'. Randle added, 'George Blake does bear a moral responsibility for the fate of the agents he named to the Soviet Union. But it is clear that his hands would not have been clean if he had continued working faithfully for the British Intelligence Service.' Randle contrasted Blake with the KGB officer Oleg Gordievsky, whom MI6 had smuggled out of the Soviet Union in 1985 hidden in a secret compartment of a Ford van, 'a copy-cat crime' if ever there was one. It was a powerful point. 'What is sauce for the security goose is sauce for the citizen gander. If it is right, in exceptional circumstances, for members of the security service to break the letter of the law, the same must apply to every other citizen,' Randle continued, citing the apartheid laws in South Africa, the Clive Ponting case – tried in Court Number Two in 1983 – and the 1670 trial of the preachers William Penn and William Mead, who were found not guilty of 'an unlawful and tumultuous assembly' even after a judge had directed the jury to convict and had fined the jurors when they refused. 'Now I am not suggesting that if you bring in a not guilty verdict His Lordship is going to lock you up,' said Randle: for the first time in the trial, he saw all the jurors laughing. 'I appeal to you today to keep the lamp of freedom burnished and shining and to allow considerations of humanity and common sense to guide your judgement.'[14]

Randle had expected Alliott to intervene whenever he said he disagreed with his rulings. But the judge had remained silent. He started his summing-up by referring to Randle and Pottle's defiant opening statements, in which they had 'both readily admitted their guilt'. Whether or not prosecuting them after all these years was an 'abuse of process', was a 'matter which you are not concerned with in any way', Alliott reminded the jurors. The evidence they'd heard was 'Wide-ranging, partly because of an indulgence shown by counsel for the Crown and myself to those appearing for themselves'.

As in the Ponting case, the judge came very close to directing the jury to convict. This was understandable given that a series of offences had been admitted where no defence recognised by the law was disclosed. The judge could hardly tell the jury that they should simply proceed according to their own consciences. But he could not order a conviction. And yet by highlighting the defendants' constant refusal to abandon their 'necessity' defence, Alliott inadvertently bolstered it. His request that jurors 'must loyally honour my ruling on the law, whatever view you have formed of the defendants' rang hollow, given that the defendants had so blatantly ignored his other rulings throughout the trial. Alliott had by now given up trying to get them to play by his rules; when Randle interrupted his summing-up with the words, 'Remember the Ponting case!' he just ignored him.

Randle thought that it was 'an entirely fair summing-up'; five minutes into it Pottle scribbled a note saying, 'This isn't too bad!' Once the jury retired, just before noon, Randle and Pottle went back to the canteen to await their verdict. When the jury still hadn't returned by 1 p.m., they went to the pub as usual for what they feared would be a final drink and sandwich before prison. 'No rounds on Pat and myself that day: others could pay for the last square meal of the condemned,' recalls Randle.

Back in the Old Bailey cafeteria they drank endless cups of coffee and 'laughed too loudly at our own quips'. Randle gave everything he had on him to Anne except for his glasses, a book and a toothbrush. 'It saved time to be carrying very little when the screws were listing your possessions.' At 3 p.m. Randle was anxiously filing his nails in the Gents when the announcement, 'Will all those concerned with the case of Pottle and Randle please report to Court Number One,' came over the tannoy. 'If you can cope, so can I,' Anne Randle whispered in her husband's ear. 'The jury have got a verdict,' Birnberg said quietly.

Back in the packed courtroom, two prison officers were in the dock for the first time since the trial's first day. As the jury returned Randle tried to catch the eye of two women jurors who'd smiled briefly at him on the second day, but neither glanced at him: not a good sign. A juror in his mid-thirties and dressed in an open-necked shirt and light anorak had been elected foreman.

Three knocks on the door behind the bench announced Alliott's arrival. 'Be upstanding in court!' an usher commanded. Alliott laid down his silk gloves nonchalantly; perhaps there was a hint of hesitation where previously the gesture had been assured. As Pat Pottle and Michael Randle stood the two prison officers inched closer. 'Members of the jury, in respect of count one, aiding a prisoner in escaping from a prison, do you find the defendant Pottle guilty or not guilty?' asked the clerk.

Pottle and Randle had first stood side by side in the same dock almost thirty years before. Then they had been taken down to the cells, firmly gripped by the elbow, straight after being found guilty. This time was different. 'Not guilty,' said the foreman in a determined, clear voice. A shout like a football supporter's victory whoop came from somewhere (Pottle's younger son Julian was a keen Spurs supporter). Randle's sons, who as young children had been unwitting accomplices in the flight of George Blake, burst into tears. Others, both in the well of the court and the public gallery, shouted and clapped as the foreman announced not guilty verdicts on all five other counts. 'If there is any further disturbance I will order the court to be cleared,' Alliott announced futilely, in the time-honoured fashion of scores of judges before him.

'Members of the jury, you find the defendant Patrick Pottle and the defendant Michael Randle each not guilty on the counts of this indictment and that is the verdict of you all?' asked the clerk, as if he needed confirmation of the words he had just heard – or thought he heard. 'It is,' the foreman replied, nonchalant.

'Let the defendants be discharged,' said Alliott, his voice all resignation now. The two friends spontaneously embraced each other. 'Members of the jury, will you please vacate those benches. We have another case to hear,' the judge added, his voice now testy, the usual words of thanks for the jurors' attention to their task dispensed with. 'Please leave now!' said an usher to Pottle and Randle, opening the side door of the dock, as if they were dinner guests who had outstayed their welcome.

In the Old Bailey's Grand Hall there is a plaque to the Penn and Mead case which serves as a commemoration of the judicial decision that finally upheld the independence of jurors to deliver their verdict free from scrutiny or risk of punishment. In freeing the jurors who had been locked up for their impertinence in refusing to obey the trial judge's direction to convict, Lord Chief Justice Vaughan had established, in the words of the plaque, 'the right of jurors to give their verdicts in accordance with their convictions'. It was near this plaque that the jurors in their trial hugged or shook hands with Pottle and Randle. They later regretted not inviting them to a victory party then and there. 'Thank God for the jury system, and the independence of jurors,' said Randle amid a throng of reporters and supporters outside.

That night ITV re-ran *The Blake Escape*, which the defendants, their families, lawyers and friendly journalists half watched during a euphoric party at the Pottles' house. George Blake phoned from Moscow with congratulations; Edward Fitzgerald, Randle's erstwhile junior counsel, sent a magnum of champagne and a note commending the 'little fish' for their victory over the Leviathan.

The next day, Pottle and Randle received spontaneous congratulations on the street and in the Underground before being driven to Birmingham for a live broadcast of *After Dark* with Norris McWhirter and the barrister and Conservative MP Ivan Lawrence. Back in Bradford a few days later Randle held his own victory party with a traditional Irish band. A death threat did not detract from his jubilation. 'Well done, lad! You beat the buggers – that's the main thing,' said an elderly neighbour.

Not everyone was so jubilant. Graham Riddick MP said that the jury had 'collectively gone soft in the head'; Sir Marcus Fox was 'absolutely astounded'. The *Daily Telegraph* said it was a 'Bad Day for British Justice'; the *Sun* ran an editorial headed 'Stinkers of the Old Bailey', expressing the hope that 'Pottle and Randle now crawl back under the stone from which they should never have emerged'. The *Spectator* even called for the reinstatement of educational and property qualifications for jurors 'because property owners have an automatic stake in the preservation of law and order'. But support also came from an unexpected quarter: Auberon Waugh said the 110 backbenchers who had called for the prosecution were 'punishment freaks' who had 'miscalculated the mood of the nation'.

★

Having gone into print to parade the fact that they had helped in the escape of a traitor who had been given the longest sentence in modern British history, it is legitimate to ask why Michael Randle and Pat Pottle were acquitted. Luck undoubtedly played a big part: aside from his slight show of petulance at the verdict, Alliott proved a remarkably indulgent and patient judge. 'With courtesy and charm you pay not a blind bit of notice to the ruling I have made,' he once told the defendants. But the courtesy and charm were reciprocated, and despite ruling that abuse of process was no longer available as a defence, Alliott had both the 'Big fish' minute and the unexpurgated Watts report shown to the jury ('You have not jumped up and objected, Mr Bevan'). In fact one of the hall-marks of the trial was the conspicuous fairness with which Bevan and Calvert-Smith conducted the prosecution.

Any barrister attempting Pottle and Randle's tactics would have soon been thrown out of court, but Alliott was tolerant of the 'brilliant exploitations by those unrepresented of judicial leeway', as he put it. It was a surprisingly good-humoured trial; Calvert-Smith once exchanged a Monty Python joke with Pottle about the 'ex-Passport' he'd modified for Bourke's use; Alliott, apparently joining in Randle and Pottle's attempts to ridicule prison officers, made a quip about the TV sitcom *Porridge*. Timing also helped. When Randle and Pottle were first arrested in connection with the Blake affair the Berlin Wall had not yet fallen. By the time the jury retired in June 1991 the Cold War was over, and it was even harder to convince a jury that George Blake's escape twenty-five years before was not ancient history.

Finally, a sympathetic jury was obviously vital. Like everyone else, the jurors probably had a wide range of views about George Blake. Although the defendants constantly quoted Jeremy Hutchinson's description of Blake's sentence as 'inhuman', some may have felt that if anything forty-two years was too lenient. But even if his treachery had led to the execution of agents working for MI6, few could argue that he had more blood on his hands than the MI6 or CIA operatives who had planned to assassinate Nasser and Castro, aided the murderous Sandinista forces in Nicaragua, or brought about the overthrow and killing of Salvador Allende in Chile. Blake had not sought material gain from his treachery, and his escape had been enabled by extraordinary lapses of security, not by violence.

Unlike Blake, Pottle and Randle were neither spies nor communists: instead they were part of a much older British nonconformist tradition. Although later condemned by some as products of the self-indulgent

1960s, for them that decade had begun not in 1963 with Profumo and the Beatles but with the anti-Suez demonstrations seven years earlier. The Committee of 100's first pamphlet was entitled 'Act or Perish'. Randle and Pottle genuinely believed that civil disobedience was the only way to avert nuclear Armageddon and that Air Commodore Graham Magill's statement at the Wethersfield Six trial that he would 'if circumstances demanded it' press the nuclear button 'was the most important statement ever to have been made in an English court of law'. If springing Blake might somehow help to make Washington and Moscow realise the futility of Cold War espionage and the arms race, then it was the right thing to do in making the world a safer place. That such idealism was mere chaff in the wind of geopolitical reality made it no less admirable, and perhaps more so.

Randle and Pottle's logic could easily be questioned, but not their sincerity. Their principled stand attracted respect even from those who viewed it as quixotically futile or misconceived, and venomous attacks in the right-wing press only seemed to make them more likeable. Elsewhere much of the coverage was surprisingly sympathetic: after their first appearance at Bow Street the *Daily Mirror* carried a picture of them drinking beer outside a pub, captioned 'Men of Peace'.

Above all they were underdogs. Two weeks after the verdict Richard Norton-Taylor wrote in the *Guardian* that Pottle and Randle were 'ideal defendants-in-person: they were convinced that what they had done was right; they could easily master the evidence; they were articulate; and they were palpably, almost suicidally, honest.' They somehow emerged from the collision of Cold War realpolitik and the *bien-pensant* peace movement not as humbugs, but as saints. Far from making them money, their book had brought hardship. Anne Randle had to resign as a nurse at Bradford Royal Infirmary. Michael Randle felt obliged to quit his job as a lecturer in Peace Studies at the University of Bradford, and was warned that if convicted he would probably never work at a British university again; in summer 1990 he collapsed with a bleeding duodenal ulcer and was hospitalised for two weeks during which time, he later recalled, 'it was apparently touch and go at one point whether I would pull through.' Although Randle fully recovered and remains very active, living in Bradford, Pat Pottle died in 2000 aged sixty-two; he had spent more than half his life in the shadow of George Blake.

Perhaps the biggest heroine of the case was English justice itself, and its traditions of independent juries and equality before the law. Even if the prosecution of Randle and Pottle was a political one, still, they were given a latitude unthinkable in countries where there is no system of trial by jury. Many years later, one of the judges involved in the early stages of the prosecution, Sir Robin Auld, by now a Court of Appeal judge, was asked by the government to conduct a wide-ranging *Review of the Criminal Courts of England and Wales*. When addressing the issue of 'perverse juries' Auld noted that when the jury in *R v Randle and Pottle* brought in a verdict of not guilty they had acted contrary to the oath they had to swear, 'faithfully [to] try the defendant and give a true verdict according to the evidence'. He proposed that the law should 'be declared, by statute if need be, that juries have no right to acquit defendants in defiance of the law or in disregard of the evidence, and that judges and advocates should conduct criminal cases accordingly'.

This view was quickly denounced by Michael Zander QC, Emeritus Professor of Law at the LSE, in resounding terms: 'I regard this proposal as wholly unacceptable – a serious misreading of the function of the jury. The right to return a perverse verdict in defiance of the law or the evidence is an important safeguard against unjust laws, oppressive prosecutions or harsh sentences.' Auld's proposal has never been brought into effect.

PART VI
Grief

II

'There is no greater task for the criminal justice system than to protect the vulnerable'

R v Ian Huntley and Maxine Carr (2003)

B Y THE START of the new millennium Court Number One's status as the nation's foremost criminal courtroom was diminished. A court building programme in the 1980s and 1990s meant that many provincial towns now had crown courts with the high security, and strict segregation of jurors, witnesses and defendants, that prominent trials demanded. With the increasing dominance of television and the internet, and of national newspapers over regional ones, the argument that defendants in high-profile cases could only get a fair trial outside their localities had less force.

While some of Britain's notorious murderers of the 1980s – the 'Yorkshire Ripper', Peter Sutcliffe, and Dennis Nilsen among them – were tried in Court Number One, its automatic pre-eminence was ceding ground to questions of practicality and security. Judges increasingly favoured the greater amenity provided by the new courts that had been added to the Old Bailey by the extension built in the early 1970s. The narrow benches of the four original courts, designed in a pre-photocopier age, did not easily accommodate paper-heavy trials. And in that decade, with the emergence of terrorism trials as a seemingly permanent fact of national life, Court Number Two had had its dock altered so that high reinforced Perspex screens were installed to impede prisoner escapes and provide protection to the judge and lawyers. So, it was in Court Number Two that many of the IRA trials of the 1970s and 1980s took place.

But the historic courtroom still continued to hear nationally significant cases. In 1996 it was the location for the trial of a sixteen-year-old, Learco Chindamo, found guilty of murdering west London headteacher Philip Lawrence outside his school in December 1995, and the private prosecution of five men for the 1993 murder of Stephen Lawrence in south-east London. In 1999 the first (and only) conviction under the War Crimes Act 1991 was secured in Court Number One when Anthony Sawoniuk was found guilty of the murder of Jews in Belarus during the Second World War. In 2000 it was the setting for the trial and the conviction of David Copeland, a neo-Nazi whose nail-bombing of the Admiral Duncan pub in Soho had claimed three lives the previous year; and in July 2001 it saw the conviction of Barry George for the 1999 murder of TV presenter Jill Dando.[1]

After Dando the next sensational trial to be held in Court Number One was not a murder case but a tale of tabloid titillation: the prosecution of former royal butler Paul Burrell for allegedly stealing valuables belonging to the late Diana, Princess of Wales. The case collapsed in November 2002 when it became clear that Burrell had told the Queen he was taking some of Diana's possessions into 'safekeeping'. Court Number One had gone from being a venue of tragedy to one of farce.

A year after Burrell's acquittal a six-week-long, double child murder trial was heard at Court Number One that alternately horrified and fascinated the public and restored the court's status as a truly national crucible. The trial led to a murder conviction carrying an unusually long forty-year tariff; a rare 'Mary Bell' anonymity order being given to a co-defendant; and a change in the law that has had a profound effect on British police forces, employers and jobseekers ever since.[2] It was also the culmination of a tragedy that had provoked an outpouring of national grief on a scale that has never since been surpassed.

The case was in many ways very modern, involving detailed analysis of mobile phone signals, concerns about the prejudicial impact of tabloid newspaper reporting, rolling TV news, and the dangers of children being 'groomed' by paedophiles in online chat rooms, as well as a host of forensic techniques unheard of a generation earlier. Both the investigation and the trial were accompanied by wall-to-wall media coverage. All the case papers were electronically scanned so they could be viewed on the laptop computers that the judge, the jury and the respective legal teams had open in front of them throughout the trial, still a relatively novel concept in Court Number One. But in other respects the case tapped age-old feelings of anger and retribution. Frenzied mobs, egged on by elements of the media which drew comparisons between the defendants and the Moors Murderers, Ian Brady and Myra Hindley, sought out the accused and pelted them as they arrived in provincial courthouses for committal hearings. Such was the concern that they could not receive a fair trial in the locale where the alleged crimes had been committed that the prosecution was moved to the Old Bailey.

Soham, where the murders took place, has been described as an 'ordinary, slightly run-down town, where nothing much happened'. It is situated on the southern edge of the Cambridgeshire Fens just off the A142 between Ely and Newmarket. As the crow flies Cambridge is only twelve miles away. In 2002 Soham was a close-knit place. Two families – the Chapmans and the Wells – were typical inhabitants of this typical town. Leslie Chapman, a fifty-one-year-old engineer, and his forty-three-year-old wife Sharon lived in a 1930s semi on Brook Street with their three daughters. Nearby on Red House Gardens, a modern cul-de-sac, lived a thirty-something couple, Kevin and Nicola Wells, with their twelve-year-old son Oliver and ten-year-old daughter Holly.

Both families had always lived in or near Soham. Sharon Chapman worked as a learning support assistant at the town's primary school, St Andrew's, which her youngest daughter Jessica, aged ten, attended. Nicola Wells had been born three miles away in Isleham, whose village cricket and football teams Kevin later captained. Kevin had worked for five years in Soham as a postman. Directly opposite the Wells' family home lived Kevin's sister Lesley, her husband Graham and their daughter Emily, who doted on her cousin Holly. The Wells were hardworking: by 2002 Kevin's window-cleaning business was doing well, Nicola was working as a legal secretary, and the couple had a 'five-year business plan' so they could afford to send Holly to the fee-paying King's School in Ely.

On Sunday, 4 August 2002 a barbecue was under way at the Wells'. Kevin and Nicola were entertaining friends, Rob and Trudie Wright. The barbecue had to sit under the garage door to escape intermittent drizzle. 'All is well in a small town in middle England,' Kevin Wells later recalled. Earlier that day Holly's friend Jessica Chapman – whom she had known since nursery – had come over to give Holly a necklace she'd bought on a recent holiday. Holly was blonde and more 'girly' than the dark-haired Jessica, but they both loved football and idolised David Beckham. Both were confident, streetwise girls who knew about the dangers that strangers can pose, and knew what parts of Soham they could explore alone and what parts they couldn't.

Just before five the girls were called downstairs to have tea; a last photo of them, smiling and wearing identical Manchester United football shirts beneath a wall clock giving the time as 5.04 p.m., was taken. They soon returned upstairs to carry on playing on Holly's computer, which was logged on to the internet from 5.11 to 5.32 p.m. No one could later remember whether they had then asked for permission to go out, but they must have left the house at about six. CCTV footage later revealed that they had wandered the streets of Soham aimlessly, as ten-year-olds do, going into the foyer of the sports centre to buy sweets from a vending machine at quarter past six before walking down Gidney Lane towards the grounds of Soham Village College, the town's 1,300-pupil comprehensive school, adjacent to St Andrew's primary.

By 8.20 p.m. the Wrights were ready to go home. Nicola Wells called the two friends downstairs to say goodbye. There was no reply: the girls were nowhere to be seen. When Jessica's mobile phone was called there was no answer; Holly had left hers at home. 'The journey from being irritated that your daughter has broken the rules, to starting to worry, to feeling real fear takes about an hour,' Kevin Wells later wrote. At 9 p.m. the Wells called the Chapmans, who reported that there was no sign of the girls at their house. Les Chapman started driving round the streets of Soham. Kevin Wells – increasingly worried, but aware that he might be over the alcohol limit – started cycling around, and was later driven around by his business partner Scott Day.

By 10 p.m. the police had been called and by midnight the extended Wells and Chapman families, many of their friends, and dozens of police officers were searching all over the town and the fields nearby. After 11 p.m. Kevin Wells and Scott Day made a second visit to the college grounds, where they saw the college's twenty-eight-year-old caretaker Ian Huntley walking his dog away from a rubbish skip in the corner of a car park. At about the same time Huntley told Sharon Chapman that the college had already been searched by police.

After several more hours of frantic searching Kevin Wells visited the college a third time, just before 4.30 a.m., and spotted a light on. Huntley came to the door and explained that he was there to write a note to a colleague to say he would be absent that morning, having helped search for the girls overnight. Huntley again said that there was no need to search the college grounds as the police had already been round.

By dawn on Monday, 5 August a major police operation was under way. A press notice was issued, which to the families' annoyance suggested that Holly and Jessica had run away. On the Tuesday, David Beckham issued a statement reassuring the girls that they weren't in any trouble, and urging them to come home. At three thirty that afternoon, at council offices in Ely, the first of several press conferences, at which the parents made an anguished appeal for their daughters' safe return, was held. But subsequent press conferences were held at the Village College, where Huntley laid out seating, directed reporters to power sockets and set up the video equipment on which CCTV footage of the girls' final walk was screened; at the end of one Huntley approached Kevin Wells to comfort him with the words, 'Kev, I just wanted to say I did not realise it was your daughter.'

A mobile police station was soon opened on the college's grounds. Local employers gave staff time off to help look for the girls. On the Monday evening some 600 people turned up and Huntley was seen helping to organise the search. At eleven that evening the Wells' home was searched from top to bottom, and the computer that Holly and Jessica had played on was taken away. By the Tuesday the police thought that Holly and Jessica had probably been abducted but still had some hope they could be found alive. The search became one of the biggest manhunts in British history, with police leave cancelled and 700 officers scouring hedgerows and ditches for miles around, many of them working sixteen-hour shifts. Cambridgeshire officers voluntarily curtailed their summer holidays to assist and others were drafted in from other forces.

Scores of journalists from across Britain, and beyond, soon started descending on Soham. On Tuesday, 6 August the *Daily Mail* splashed the headline 'How Did They Just Vanish?' TV news programmes weren't just dominated by the girls' disappearance for the next two weeks; many were actually anchored from the town. Within days, £1.25 million of reward money had been offered by businesspeople and tabloid newspapers for any information that led to the girls' safe return. On 8 August a reconstruction of the girls' last known movements was filmed; on 9 August roadblocks were set up around the town, at which police questioned everyone driving in or out. Later that day – less than a week after the girls' disappearance – the four parents were interviewed for a *Tonight with Trevor McDonald* programme.

The media soon started speculating that the girls had gone to meet someone they'd befriended on an internet chat room ('Did Weirdo Lure Girls?' ran one headline). Many locals avoided the media and Kevin Wells felt that those who did speak to TV cameras came over as 'moronic rustics'. But two apparently credible people who were eager to talk were Huntley and his twenty-five-year-old fiancée, Maxine Carr. For two weeks Huntley 'campaigned for his innocence like a politician in an election race', the *Daily Mirror* reporter Nathan Yates later wrote. Huntley told several reporters – including Jeremy Thompson, a well-known Sky News anchor and later a trial witness – that he might have been the last person to see the girls before they vanished. Huntley claimed that at about 6.15 p.m. he had been washing his Alsatian, Sadie, in his front garden at 5 College Close when two girls in red shirts walked over to pet it, and asked him how Carr – apparently upstairs having a bath at the time – was. The girls both knew Maxine Carr well as she had been a teaching assistant in their class at St Andrew's, though she hadn't been kept on beyond the end of the summer term. Huntley said he'd told them, 'She's not very good, she didn't get the job.' The girls had apparently replied, 'Tell her we're really sorry,' before walking off in the direction of Soham's public library, never to be seen again.

On Monday, 12 August Acting Detective Superintendent David Beck issued a stark 'Stop this now' message to whoever had kidnapped the girls, urging him or her to read text messages sent to Jessica's mobile phone (a ruse to get it switched on so police could track its location). An *Evening Standard* reporter, Harriet Arkell, later knocked on the front door of Huntley and Carr's house, to ask if she could watch a tape of Beckham's appeal on a VHS player, as she was in a hurry to file a story. They gladly obliged, telling Arkell she was lucky as they were about to upgrade to a DVD player. 'It beggars belief,' said Huntley of the girls' disappearance when the video ended. On the morning of 16 August he told GMTV that the community was 'coping very well' with their ordeal and that there was a 'glimmer of hope' that the girls were still alive. He had placed an *Ely Standard* 'Missing' poster, with photos of the girls, in a window of his house.

Carr also seemed willing to talk to the reporters and camera crews. She struck Nathan Yates as 'flustered and exceptionally worried' about the girls' safety, telling him disarmingly that the press were 'really pushy nasty people [who] won't leave us alone' before gladly granting him an interview in which she said the girls would have 'screamed out' and 'kicked up a right stink' if anybody had tried to abduct them. Carr, a 'TV natural', later told Jeremy Thompson that Holly 'was lovely, really lovely'.

The 14,000 phone calls received by police inevitably brought many false sightings, and as many false leads: a mystery cyclist seen near the sports centre; a white van (linked to a nearby travellers' site) seen 'cruising' around town on Sunday and which two local girls claimed had tried to 'pick them up'; a 'wide-eyed' woman spotted staring at children outside Saucy Megs, a Soham café. On 6 August the police homed in on Little Thetford, a village five miles away, where the girls had apparently been spotted by a 'local character' who was later found to be unreliable.

Rumours circulated that Terence Pocock, jailed for life in 1985 for raping and stabbing two thirteen-year-olds not far from Soham, had just been released (he hadn't). A taxi driver claimed to have seen a green car being driven erratically down the A142 at the time of the girls' disappearance; its driver, of Mediterranean appearance, 'thrashing out' at two child passengers before turning into the Studlands Park estate in Newmarket, where many US servicemen and women from nearby airbases lived. Only when the clock in the driver's car was found to be an hour fast did the police realise that the children could not have been Holly and Jessica. On 13 August a jogger came forward claiming to have heard screams at Warren Hill Gallops near Newmarket at 10.40 p.m. on the night of the disappearance: two mounds of fresh earth found nearby were at first thought to be shallow graves but, after extensive excavation, turned out to be badger setts.

Many stories that began circulating were much more malicious. As the parents visited the police incident room in Huntingdon several calls alleging 'The dads did it' flashed up on screen. In Scotland a *Sunday Herald* columnist was sacked for suggesting they were to blame for having not 'kept the Lord's day' by letting Holly and Jessica go out on the Sabbath.

By the end of the first week, friends' questions had changed from 'Is there any news?' to 'How are you coping?' Frustrated by the lack of news, Kevin Wells almost started his own private investigation: two plumber friends of his planned to search twenty-five homes in Soham whose occupants had aroused suspicion on the pretext of investigating a gas leak. They only abandoned the plan when the police agreed to search the homes themselves. As early as 7 August Kevin Wells was using the services of psychic mediums, most of whose 'visions' – 'a dark-haired person standing outside an Italian restaurant' and 'the name of Muggsy, Muttley or Muggly' – were entirely useless.

But the media were becoming more and more suspicious of Huntley and Carr. 'Have they found the girls' clothes?' Huntley once asked BBC reporter Debbie Tubby, who immediately passed her suspicions on to the police. Veteran *Mirror* reporter Harry Arnold was soon convinced that Huntley was guilty, as was the Press Association's East Anglia reporter Brian Farmer, who told police, 'He's your man.' Press photographers began taking surreptitious shots of Huntley, including one of him sitting alone in his Fiesta, anxiously biting his nails.

The police had believed from the start that the answer to the case 'lies in Soham' and gradually came to the conclusion that their most likely suspect had been under their noses all along. Huntley's odd behaviour had aroused their suspicions early on. At 1 a.m. on 5 August – barely seven hours after the girls' disappearance – Huntley helped PC Anna Burton search the college grounds but denied having keys to a storage shed on site known as the Hangar. A few hours later, and only at the suggestion of a teacher to whom he had mentioned it, Huntley told Sergeant Pauline Nelson that he had seen the girls briefly at about 6.50 p.m. the previous evening; Nelson found him 'vague and evasive' (Huntley later changed his story and said he'd seen the girls at least twenty minutes earlier than 6.50). Later that morning Huntley was questioned by two detective constables, who noticed that he seemed nervous, with sweaty palms, and that there was washing on the line in his garden even though it was raining heavily; Huntley asked them if he needed to make a formal statement and whether he was a suspect. When a policeman asked to search Huntley's house a few days later, Huntley told him, 'You think I have done it,' and started to cry, only to be reassured that there had been other possible sightings.

When asked to provide a DNA sample – routine procedure for anyone who had contact with a missing person – Huntley asked, 'How long does DNA last for?' and hesitated when told that it could survive for thousands of years. At the end of the search's second week Huntley – by now with an 'ashen tinge' to his face, suggesting he was washing infrequently – asked DCI Andy Hebb (another senior officer involved in the investigation) how an abductor could access a message police had left on Jessica's phone.

'Nothing,' Carr told police jokingly when asked what she had been wearing when the girls had spoken to Huntley as they passed their house in the early evening of 4 August. 'I was upstairs having a bath,' which she said had helped relieve heavy period pains. But it wasn't long before the police started receiving calls from people who said that they had seen Carr being interviewed on the television, and that she had in fact been staying with her mother in Grimsby, almost 100 miles north of Soham, that Sunday night.

Huntley had no alibi. On the afternoon of 4 August he had rented a video and then walked his dog. Apparently paranoid that Carr was being unfaithful to him in Grimsby, he tried to arrange a meeting with a woman in Soham for that evening, but failed. Phone records showed that Carr had called him at 6.24 that evening; they clearly had a row, as she texted him at 6.30 to say, 'Don't make me feel bad I'm with my family.' Jessica's phone was turned off at 6.46. It emerged that it had last picked up a signal in a small part of Soham, centred on College Close.

Other callers began to tell police about Huntley's murky past in Grimsby, where he and Carr had lived until moving south in 2001: Cambridgeshire Constabulary then learned from Humberside Police that they had had nine 'contacts' with Huntley in the late 1990s: these included allegations of sex with underage girls in 1995 and 1996, two separate rape allegations in 1998, an allegation of indecent assault on a twelve-year-old girl living on the same street as Huntley in 1998, and two more allegations of raping seventeen-year-olds in 1999. All these records had been routinely 'weeded' from the force's criminal intelligence system by the time Huntley had moved to Soham. He had no criminal record: although he had been charged with burglary in 1995 and rape in 1998, both charges had been dropped before they came to trial. The Village College had requested a police check on Huntley when they gave him the caretaker's job; in fact he had given his name as Ian Nixon on his application form, and the search had been carried out on that name – but it had made no difference, because the name Ian Huntley would also have drawn a blank. Within days of the girls' disappearance the police had tracked down 700 known sex offenders in the nearest three counties. Huntley's name was not on the list.

By 15 August the police were under enormous pressure either to find the girls or make arrests. Cambridgeshire's newly appointed chief constable Tom Lloyd was criticised for not returning from a family holiday in France until 14 August; Beck for not visiting Soham until well into the second week of the manhunt; the force as a whole for closing Soham's police station in the 1990s and (it was suggested) dragging their feet over a comprehensive CCTV system for the town.

Police psychologists had profiled the likely abductor as 'a local man aged twenty-five to forty' who 'might be susceptible to emotive appeals', and they began to study Huntley's and Carr's body language in their TV appearances. Officers were by this stage regularly having 'friendly chats' with them, trying to tease out information without revealing that they were under suspicion. The police deliberately moved their apparent focus away from the Village College, holding their 15 August press conference in Huntingdon instead, hoping that Huntley would relax and start making errors. Later the same day, during the close, thundery evening, the police held a public meeting in Soham, ostensibly to re-assure the public and allow them to vent frustrations, but in reality to pile psychological pressure on Huntley. The following morning the media were asked to leave the college site as it was being cordoned off, and the pressure began to tell: the previously chirpy Huntley 'mumbled something inaudible and walked off' when the reporter Nathan Yates approached him.

At a quarter to four that afternoon – it was now 16 August, twelve days since Holly and Jessica had gone missing – Huntley and Carr were driven away from College Close in unmarked cars, to Ely and Peterborough police stations respectively, to be 'cognitively interviewed' as 'significant witnesses'. Huntley confidently assured police he knew nothing about the girls' disappearance, and Carr still persisted in her claim that she had been in Soham on 4 August. At nine thirty that evening they were allowed to meet in a secretly bugged room at a Holiday Inn near Cambridge, from where Huntley was later driven to his parents' house in nearby Littleport.

Then came two sudden breakthroughs. While Huntley was in Ely the police searched 5 College Close again. They found that Huntley did after all have a key to the Hangar – the shed on the college grounds – and immediately opened it. Inside PC Tim Wade found burned fragments of the girls' trainers and Manchester United football shirts in a dustbin, under a black bin-liner later found to bear Huntley's fingerprints. The police finally had the evidence they needed to justify their suspects' arrests. Just over an hour after they had dropped Huntley off at Littleport, the police returned to arrest him at four twenty in the morning of 17 August; Carr was arrested at the Holiday Inn five minutes later.

Events were now speeding up. At just after noon that same day a gamekeeper, Keith Pryer, was walking along a track by the perimeter fence of RAF Lakenheath near Wangford, a Suffolk hamlet fifteen miles north-east of Soham. An unpleasant smell led Pryer to an overgrown ditch where he discovered two small bodies, unclothed, arm-in-arm and badly burned. Although Jessica still wore her Love necklace, a free gift from a magazine, and Holly the dolphin necklace Jessica had given her on the day of their disappearance, the condition of the bodies meant that formal identification took some time. The absence of broken bones seemed to rule out stabbing, shooting or bludgeoning. The pathologists' initial view was that the two girls had probably both been strangled.

It was Maxine Carr – who, after her arrest, was cooperative and even waived her right to a solicitor at first – who provided the further break-through police needed. The admission that she had been in Grimsby, not Soham, on the day of the girls' disappearance, swiftly tumbled out.

She said she had been persuaded into giving a false alibi for Huntley's sake; he had told her that the girls had entered the house but sworn that he hadn't killed them, and feared that he might be 'fitted up', just as he claimed he had been on his 1998 rape charge.

But Huntley, who had been both engaged and lucid when talking to the media and during his first police interviews, started to play the madman, 'dribbling constantly, foaming at the mouth, mumbling gibberish' and 'crying incessantly' now that he was under arrest. On 20 August he was precautionarily sectioned under the Mental Health Act and taken to Rampton Secure Hospital in Nottinghamshire. There he was charged with the two girls' murders. When told that her partner had been charged with murder, Carr was incredulous and started crying. Reading the transcript of the police interview that day, one gets the impression that she was not play-acting any more, that she had clung to the totem of her partner's innocence. Later that night Carr was charged with the crime of perverting the course of justice. The following day she appeared before Peterborough magistrates, to be remanded in custody at Holloway prison: the van that took her between the court and the nearby police station was screamed at − 'murdering bitch', 'rot in hell', 'scum' − and pelted by a large mob.

The families were initially astonished by Huntley's arrest. Kevin Wells had a contract to clean the college's windows; although they weren't friends, Wells felt he 'sort of knew him'. During the hunt for the girls the college's vice-principal, Margaret Bryden, had offered the families access to the school buildings if they ever wanted privacy, telling Huntley to expect them any time of day or night. At the start of term in September two doves were released at the college; the local vicar, Tim Alban Jones, blessed its buildings as if to exorcise demons.

Even if Huntley had been involved in the girls' disappearance, the parents could not at first believe that they would have entered his house voluntarily, and could not understand how he could have forced them inside without one of them running away and raising the alarm. But Maxine Carr was well known to Holly and Jessica. At the end of the previous term Holly had given her an affectionate card, which Carr would go on to show proudly to several reporters; Carr even suggested that Holly had asked to be a bridesmaid at her wedding to Huntley. He could easily have tricked them into the house by telling them that 'Miss Carr' was inside.

★

Huntley did not look like most people's idea of a murderer. Nicci Gerrard, who attended every day of the trial for the *Observer*, described him as a man with a 'heavy-browed shyness', a 'tight, vigilant smile' and 'anxious eyes'. Some thought him good-looking, albeit in a bland way, resembling a 'tense-shouldered' version of the actor Russell Crowe.

Both he and Carr had had miserable childhoods in Grimsby. Maxine's father had left her mother Shirley when she was just two and a half and she had rarely seen him since; as a teenager she changed her name from Carr to Capp, her mother's maiden name, and developed serious eating disorders. Huntley had been badly bullied at school and attempted suicide at least twice during his teens. At thirteen he had apparently been beaten by his father Kevin, whom, he said, he had discovered in bed with a babysitter. Kevin Huntley later ran off with another woman; his mother entered a relationship with a woman and Ian started occasionally using her surname, Nixon, as well as Huntley.

Both Huntley and Carr had left school at sixteen. Between 1995 and 1999 Huntley moved between no fewer than eight addresses in and around Grimsby. Both of them drifted in and out of dead-end jobs in fish processing factories and care homes before meeting each other, through mutual friends, on a pub crawl in 1999. Huntley by then had a white-collar job as an insurance company supervisor. It is unlikely he told Carr of his many brushes with the police. They later estimated that he may have had sex with sixty underage girls, some of them plied with alcopops and held captive in his flat. He fathered a child by one of his rape victims. Another had a miscarriage after he kicked her in the stomach. No fewer than twenty-eight of Huntley's former 'girlfriends' would later be interviewed by the police.

Huntley may also not have told Maxine Carr about his brief marriage in 1995 to Claire Evans, who, having endured frequent beatings at his hands, left him after two weeks for his younger brother Wayne, an RAF engineer. Huntley seems to have started physically abusing Maxine soon after they moved in together within a few weeks of meeting: as in many abusive relationships she both feared and doted on him. In 2000 they moved to Lincolnshire, where Huntley briefly worked as a security guard. But he had difficulty repaying a £4,000 loan he'd taken out to buy Maxine's engagement ring. Pursued by debt collectors, he needed a fresh start. Huntley's parents – now reunited – had moved to Cambridgeshire, where Kevin Huntley worked as a school caretaker in Littleport. In 2001 Huntley and Carr moved in with them. After a short spell as a barman, with his father's help Huntley landed the job at Soham Village College in November 2001.

At last Huntley had a good job in a new place where he could put down roots: he even became reconciled with Wayne, now working at RAF Mildenhall nearby. According to Nathan Yates, Soham was an unremarkable town but compared to the 'overwhelmingly depressing' Grimsby it was a place of 'charm and beauty'. Huntley seemed 'a very presentable young man on his way up in the world' and was given 5 College Close, a newly refurbished house on the edge of the college grounds, at a subsidised rent. Carr soon started working as an interim classroom assistant at St Andrew's primary, at first voluntarily. Although she was not kept on beyond July 2002 this was simply because a better qualified candidate came along, not because of concerns about her working with children; teachers later said that Carr had been 'like an older sister' to Holly and Jessica.

Huntley was not a model employee. He was slow to get the hang of his duties – which included managing four staff, and supervising pupils during detentions – and strangely tearful whenever the quality of his work was criticised; Carr seemed very protective of her boyfriend and would often accompany him to meetings as a kind of advocate on his behalf. But the college's principal Geoff Fisher had no real complaints. There was never any suggestion he was a danger to children. Huntley seemed popular with pupils. At interview Huntley had been asked how he would react if a female student developed a crush on him, and when one did in July 2002 he had properly reported it to management. According to Carr, they once discussed what should happen to paedophiles. They had agreed they should be 'castrated and shot'.

After six weeks of observation at Rampton, Huntley was found to be sane: his apparent insanity had been feigned. In October 2002 he was transferred to Woodhill prison, a high-security jail near Milton Keynes, where he was held in isolation for his own safety. At a hearing at Norwich Crown Court on 15 November it was announced that the trial would take place at the Old Bailey. In bygone decades it would have started soon thereafter: we have seen how quickly the trials of Timothy Evans and Ruth Ellis came on fifty years before. But the world had changed: after a series of miscarriages of justice in the 1970s and 1980s, new legislation had ushered in a culture where the fairness of the trial process for defendants, however ghastly the charge, was given considerably more emphasis than before. It was a culture that Kevin Wells, who chronicled the agonisingly slow road to the trial in his later published account of the murder of his daughter and the pursuit of her murderer, frequently found himself baffled and frustrated by. The case was so high-profile, and the evidence so complex, that it was almost a year before the trial began.

On 15 January 2003 the charges against Huntley and Carr were finally set out, again at Norwich: two counts of murder against Huntley, a joint count of perverting the course of justice, and against Carr alone two new counts of 'assisting an offender', in circumstances where that offender was an alleged murderer, a much more serious offence than perversion of the course of justice. It was now alleged against Carr that 'knowing or believing Ian Kevin Huntley had committed the said offence or some other arrestable offence – [she had] provided false accounts of her own whereabouts and the activities and whereabouts of Ian Kevin Huntley.' This was very different to lying to protect a man she believed to be innocent. To Kevin Wells, it seemed that Huntley's defence team were constantly playing for time, filing documents at the last minute, or late. In reality it is likely that his lawyers had a near-impossible task in obtaining coherent instructions from their erratic client, caught in a labyrinth where the chances of escape were steadily diminishing as the evidence against him mounted up.

The fourteen-month news vacuum between arrest and trial had been filled by prejudicial newspaper stories that came close to derailing the entire prosecution. As early as 22 August 2002 the Attorney General, Lord Goldsmith, wrote to editors to warn them that their stories and cash offers to potential witnesses, both in Soham and Grimsby, risked breaching the Contempt of Court Act. But elements of the media remained uncooperative: some stories falsely claimed that items of the girls' clothing had been found inside Huntley's house, not the Hangar. When police asked TV companies to hand over footage of Huntley and Carr only one did so voluntarily: the others had to be compelled by court orders.

It was a time of paranoia and wild rumours. The central question of what had happened to the two girls in Huntley's house, and all the horrific speculation that could crowd into that question, was in everyone's minds. The prosecution feared that adverse publicity might lead the defence to apply to stay the prosecution because the defendants could not, as a result of it, obtain a fair trial; that an unexpected 'hijack defence' might be produced at trial; that Huntley might be deemed unfit to stand trial at all. In April 2003 both the Crown's lead counsel, Richard Latham QC, and Detective Inspector Gary Goose – in charge of the families' liaison officers – were seriously assaulted (Latham in London and Goose in Peterborough, where he was stabbed in the head with a screwdriver). Although the police soon concluded that the attacks were coincidence, some thought – bizarrely – that Huntley might have ordered them from his prison cell.

In Soham tensions were rising. Local people stopped introducing themselves as being from Soham, which had become a 'byword for evil'; a place that had, for centuries, been known for nothing at all, and was now known by millions for the most terrible thing they could imagine. The Reverend Alban Jones caused some upset by allowing photographs to be taken at a vigil service. On New Year's Day 2003 he was awarded an MBE, which some considered in poor taste given that the trial was still months away. The families soon became involuntary celebrities. Ten days after the discovery of the girls' bodies the Wells were invited to Old Trafford to watch a match and be introduced to David Beckham and Sir Alex Ferguson. The girls' memorial service on 30 August was seen as a national event: at first the police suggested St Paul's Cathedral – only a stone's throw from the Old Bailey – as its venue. The families preferred Soham's church but it was deemed much too small; as a compromise Ely Cathedral was chosen. Up and down the country, bank holiday weekend crowds observed impromptu two-minute silences. Some collective instinct for ritual, an upwelling of vicarious emotion, gripped large parts of the nation, much as it had done following the death of Princess Diana five years before. In December 2002 both of the girls' families took tea with Prince Charles at Sandringham. A new variety of pale pink rose was later named the 'Soham rose' in the girls' memory. Channel 4 television even invited Kevin Wells to deliver its Christmas message for 2002, but the CPS vetoed the idea.

Yet for both families this was not a 'community disaster' but a personal one. Although there was much kindness in Soham – local florists refused payment for memorial wreaths – some neighbours at first gave the Wells and Chapman families the cold shoulder, uncertain of what to say, only to overwhelm them with condolences when they viewed the piles of flowers in the town's churchyard, which had become a magnet for 'grief tourism'. Amid thousands of letters of sympathy there also came a lot of vile abuse: one abusive caller, a Mr Westgate, only desisted when served with an Anti-Social Behaviour Order.

'Egos are ballooning,' wrote Kevin Wells in his diary as the first anniversary of the girls' disappearance approached; he thought that a consultative 'Gold group', formed of members of the local community, had given some in Soham an over-inflated view of their own importance.

Wells was irritated by an overlong anniversary statement by the town's Methodist minister, and the emphasis it placed on 'forgiveness'. 'Kick him in the bollocks next time I see him,' was his pithy response. The Wells chose to spend the anniversary in the Lake District, with their friends the Wrights, rather than in Soham.

On remand in Holloway, Carr exercised compulsively and refused to eat properly, falling from eight to six stones in weight and being put on a saline drip at Whittington hospital in October 2002. At first she wrote repeatedly to Huntley, perhaps continuing to believe in her boyfriend's innocence and the possibility of the resumption of their life together. She had nursed a craving for stability and a future where 'normal' things would happen – marriage, children, home ownership. Ian Huntley had seemed to hold out the promise of that longed-for future. It was in order to protect that dream that Maxine Carr had been willing to lie for the man she loved. But in December she presumably woke up to the reality, or was at least advised of it by her lawyers: Huntley was probably guilty and a continuing connection with him would not do her any good at the trial. The letters stopped and Huntley was told she no longer wanted to hear from him – a titbit leaked to, and gleefully reported by, the press.

The pre-trial hearing was fixed to take place in Court Number One on 16 April 2003. The Wells and the Chapmans were invited to view the Bailey and its historic courtroom in advance, to accustom themselves to the venue where Huntley would be tried. Kevin Wells found the main hall impressive but also oppressive. Court Number One was smaller than he had expected. He noted that the dock was not completely screened off and fantasised about vaulting over the low glass screen to administer a beating to Huntley. When the day arrived, the first time the families would see their daughters' murderer since his arrest, there was no sign of him. Was there to be a sudden change of plea? Had Huntley attempted suicide, fallen ill, or sacked his legal team? In fact one of his lawyers had merely been delayed by a train cancellation; after twenty minutes of anxiety Huntley was taken up the stairs into the dock only to be sent down again as Mr Justice Moses, who had been designated the trial judge, had not yet entered court. Kevin Wells recorded how he was shaking throughout the hearing; he sat with his wife, behind counsel, a few yards from Huntley in the dock, staring at him. Huntley avoided eye contact, unable to face the girls' parents.

Reading out the charges on the indictment for the formal entry of a plea by the defendants the court clerk's voice broke with emotion. A moment of drama followed: while Huntley pleaded – almost inaudibly – not guilty to murder (in his defence statement,[3] served the day before, he still persisted in his story that he had not killed the girls and had last seen them outside 5 College Close), he nonetheless registered a guilty plea to the charge of perverting the course of justice. Carr pleaded not guilty to all charges. This was the first time that Maxine Carr had seen her former partner since the night of 16 August 2002. Now, in the same dock as him, sitting just feet away, she did not cast a single look or word at him. The breach between them was final.

Despite being on twenty-four-hour 'suicide watch' at Woodhill, in June 2003 Huntley overdosed on medication that he had stored up and doctors initially feared he might survive only in a vegetative state; when he came round a day later he was reported as telling the doctors, 'Why didn't you bastards let me die?' Kevin Wells recorded how unbearable it would have been had Huntley cheated the legal process. For the families the trial was the moment when Huntley would finally be held to account and it could not come soon enough. It would be the time for a reckoning and an expiation. They were stunned when Huntley's lawyers applied to delay the trial from autumn 2003 to early 2004. It was a request that Mr Justice Moses refused.

At a further hearing in October, just a week before the trial was to begin, back in Court Number One Huntley's and Carr's legal teams tried to get all charges against them stayed on the grounds that so prejudicial had been the press coverage that a fair trial was now impossible. Latham reminded Moses that the most prejudicial reporting had been more than a year earlier and subject to 'fade factor' since, and that it was hypocritical of Huntley to argue against press coverage as he had thrust himself into the media spotlight. Inevitably, the application was dismissed, though the Wells passed an excruciating night of anxiety before Mr Justice Moses delivered his judgement the next morning.

There was now nothing standing between Huntley and the rigour of a criminal trial. It was at this moment that Stephen Coward QC, Huntley's counsel, stood up to make a startling declaration. Huntley's stated position had throughout been that, although he had seen them pass his house that Sunday evening, he had had no involvement in the deaths of Holly and Jessica. But Coward now listed to the judge fourteen 'admissions' that his client made, revealing, for the first time, the central plank of the defence. (This was necessary because of the requirement for a defence statement. Now that Huntley had changed his instructions his statement had to be amended. Until 1996 the defence did not need to provide any indication of its position, which would only become apparent during the trial itself.) Huntley would admit that the two girls had died at 5 College Close shortly after 6.30 p.m.: Holly in the upstairs bathroom, accidentally falling into a bath that had been half-filled with water by Huntley to wash his dog; and Jessica on the bathroom's threshold, as Huntley tried to stop her screams. Huntley denied that he intended to kill or seriously injure either of the girls (hence he maintained his plea of not guilty to murder). But he would also admit, Coward explained, that that evening he had driven their bodies to 'the deposition site' wrapped in an old carpet, had removed their clothing, and set fire to their bodies with petrol from a can kept to fill the college lawn mower. The court was stunned. The Wells and the Chapmans heard this revelation in court for the first time, without forewarning, stared at by the journalists and public, searching out a reaction. Kevin Wells recalled his wife's dignity, silent tears flowing down her face.

These admissions made, Coward now argued that the planned site visit of the jurors, first to 5 College Close and then to the deposition site, had become unnecessary. It hardly suited Huntley for the jury to be confronted with the physical reality of the girls' last moments and later resting place. Again Moses gave the application short shrift. But, in response to another of Huntley's counsel's requests, the judge did rule that the girls' families should not be able to have any eye contact with jurors. The Wells and the Chapmans would have to watch the trial from the very back of the courtroom, marooned behind the dock.

On that Sunday evening in August, in the minutes after the girls' deaths, the desperate Huntley had thought fast. He had driven their bodies fifteen miles from Soham to dispose of them: far enough for them not to be easily found, but not so far as to require a long drive on the evening of their disappearance, which might prove difficult to explain later. Huntley had been seen visiting his father's house at Littleport, and his eighty-year-old grandmother's home nearby – both within a few miles of Wangford – giving him a plausible reason for being in the area. But he had also made mistakes. On the Monday he had his car's tyres changed at a garage in Ely, bribing the mechanic £10 to put a false registration number on the receipt. He had later been seen washing the car from top to bottom, which struck some as insensitive – and suspicious – given the search that was then gathering pace.

Although Huntley had done his best at cleansing the Fiesta of incriminating evidence, a forensic botanist, Professor Patricia Wiltshire, later found traces of pollen and soil on its underside that could only have come from the track down which he had driven the girls' bodies. Huntley's bizarre, and ghoulish, decision to remove the girls' clothes with scissors while they lay in the ditch, take them back to the Village College and then set them alight with a cigarette lighter in a dustbin, had filled the Hangar with acrid smoke; he had been forced to extinguish the fire with water before the clothes were destroyed. Once the college became the focus of the search he had apparently calculated that it was less risky to leave the clothes where they were rather than move them elsewhere or try again to destroy them by fire.

'The long, meticulous trial' finally began on the morning of Wednesday, 5 November 2003 with 'painstaking slowness', wrote Nicci Gerrard. Bouquets of flowers, crosses and poignant messages had been placed against the outer wall of the Bailey, as if the building itself, through the processes of justice that it administered within, was now going to expiate the terrible wrong that had occurred the year before. The press interest was so great that another courtroom served as an overflow for journalists – a first for the Old Bailey. Seventy reporters packed into Court Nineteen, immediately below Court Number One, to watch the proceedings via three giant plasma screens. The process of empanelling the jury, usually fairly mechanical, was itself treated with almost reverential care. Mr Justice Moses took the unusual step of informing prospective jurors of the identity of the case that they might be trying. He impressed upon them that 'serving on a jury is probably the most important obligation any citizen has to undertake.'

The three key barristers – Richard Latham for the prosecution; Stephen Coward for Huntley, and Michael Hubbard for Carr – were all experienced QCs in their fifties or sixties, highly competent but unflashy; none was particularly well-known or a regular at the Old Bailey. Paradoxically, the magnitude of the crime of which Huntley was accused put a dampener on their rhetoric, as if it would be somehow disrespectful to Holly and Jessica to give barnstorming speeches. The trial's 'extraordinary psychological climax' would be the result of words spoken by Huntley and Carr themselves, not the advocates.

Latham set out the prosecution case by pointing to a large map of Soham, red dots showing the girls' final movements. Early on he dropped a bombshell for the jurors. 'It is unlikely to be disputed that the two girls went into Huntley's house shortly after 6.30 p.m., and that they died within a short time.' Latham explained that despite Huntley's strenuous efforts to clean up in the days after their deaths, forty-nine microscopic fibres from their Manchester United shirts had been found in the house. Methodically and unhurriedly, he took the jury through the forensic evidence which inextricably trapped Huntley: there it was in the house, in the car, at the deposition site, at the Hangar – human traces everywhere, which no amount of scrubbing or ingenuity could expunge. By burning the girls' bodies Huntley had, however, succeeded in obscuring the cause of their deaths. This corner of uncertainty gave him his one faint chance. Yet, by the time Latham finished his meticulous recitation of the facts, at 3 p.m. on 7 November, there seemed to be little doubt about Huntley's guilt.

After the jury visited the caretaker's house – now stripped bare of all its furniture, doors and bathroom fittings – on 10 November, and the deposition site at Wangford on 11 November (a police helicopter hovered overhead, to ward off aerial photographers), the prosecution started calling its many witnesses. The first was Benjamin Hickling, managing director of a glazing company, who said that Huntley had told him five months before the girls' disappearance about the site where their bodies were later found, recommending it as a good place to view the military aircraft taking off and landing at Lakenheath, which Huntley and his father – both keen plane spotters – had often visited.

The defence did their best to undermine the evidence of these witnesses. Although the vast majority of the facts that the witnesses spoke to were uncontested, Huntley's counsel's strategy was to present his actions in the days following the girls' deaths as those of a semi-innocent man flailing around in panic after a tragic series of accidents, rather than those of a murderer engaged in a calculated set of steps to cover up his guilt. On 14 November Mark Abbott, an employee at the sports centre where Holly and Jessica had bought sweets, was accused by Coward of embellishing his account of the first night's search, during which Abbott claimed that Huntley had denied having seen the girls. Abbott was later seen leaving the Old Bailey in tears. 'I despise him [Coward] for his skills,' Kevin Wells wrote in his diary. It is a reminder of the impact of criminal proceedings on witnesses not directly involved in the crime. Even if you are not on trial yourself, the witness box can be a frightening place. And to have your word challenged, even if on a peripheral matter, can be devastating. Hubbard, who Wells thought 'aggressively queries notes and statements', later asked a Grimsby bus driver, Paul Walmsley, why he had not written contemporaneous notes of a conversation with Carr on

4 August, prompting an irritated Moses to tell him, 'I'm sorry you've been dragged all the way down here.'

But this was barrel-scraping. When Coward opened his case he now made a further seven admissions on behalf of his client. Huntley, who was the only witness in his own defence, spent two and a half days in the witness box, wearing a new grey suit and a neat haircut in a futile play for respectability. Defendants on trial for serious offences often try to signal to the jury that they and the jurors inhabit the same world of normality and decency, to prevent their being defined by the enormity of the accusation. He seemed superficially sane and normal, reassuringly deploying terms like 'coping mechanisms' and 'closure', as if fluent in the comforting jargon of counselling.

Huntley was anachronistically formal, addressing Latham throughout as 'sir'. But he could not help revealing his narcissism, telling the court he had changed out of his Brushers – smart indoor shoes he did not want to get dirty – before driving the bodies to Wangford as if, wrote Nicci Gerrard, 'there was nothing odd about personal vanity in the middle of brutal double murder'. When he was described as the school caretaker, he bridled, as if his true status – his technical job title was 'residential senior site manager' – had not been properly recognised. He still referred to Kevin Wells as 'Kev', as if it were inconceivable that such matiness was consistent with having murdered the man's daughter. And he spoke of his domestic life with Maxine Carr in the present tense, as if being on trial for a double murder were merely an inconvenient interruption to quotidian life. In fact normality was now far beyond his reach. At one point he told the court that he had promised his mother 'to make it through the trial' in order to tell 'the truth' to the girls' parents, as if they should feel grateful that his suicide attempt had failed. Not once in the course of the trial did he turn round in the dock to look them in the face.

Only now did Huntley's complete story, in all its absurdity, come out, carefully woven round the various incontestable pillars of evidence that the prosecution had erected. The girls' deaths had been a 'terrible accident', he claimed. Holly had a nosebleed that wouldn't stop; Huntley had taken both girls upstairs, where he had tried to staunch the bleeding with paper towels. Holly had sat on the edge of the bath; she had been accidentally knocked into the bath by Huntley slipping on a bath mat. Rather than help lift her out of it, Huntley 'panicked and froze'. Jessica had then cried out, 'You pushed her, you pushed her,' and Huntley, now frantic, had muffled her cries with his hands. Huntley claimed to have no memory of the moment of death: he'd suddenly realised Jessica's body was limp and then turned to Holly, only to find her lifeless in the bath: she had spontaneously drowned in eighteen inches of water, in which Huntley had been about to wash his dog. He had then vomited in the hallway and 'huddled, semi-conscious' in a corner before washing the bodies and driving them to Wangford that same evening.

'I wish I could turn back the clock,' said Huntley, fighting back tears. 'I'm sorry for what happened and I'm ashamed of what I did.' 'One died as a result of my inability to act and the other died as a direct result of my actions,' he later added. His words were heard in appalled silence. No one could believe that Huntley had told the truth about how, and why, Holly and Jessica had died. 'We never got there, to the dark heart, the convulsed mind, the actual moment, the still point when time stopped for Jessica Chapman and Holly Wells,' Nicci Gerrard, sitting in court, later wrote.

On 28 November, in less than half an hour of examination by Latham, the Home Office pathologist Nat Carey had already pre-emptively demolished Huntley's account. There was no secondary transfer of blood through water on to Holly's clothing, meaning that either she had fallen into the bath naked or not at all. This seemed to explode the nosebleed story and it would become apparent that the defence could offer no expert evidence in rebuttal of this point. For Kevin Wells, Carey's evidence was a 'joy to behold'. On the morning of Tuesday, 2 December, Richard Latham QC's cross-examination of Huntley began.

Latham rubbished the notion that the girls had gone into the house that evening because of a nosebleed. He painted the picture of an inwardly raging man into whose orbit the girls, by terrible chance, came. 'It was just too tempting, wasn't it, two girls of ten?' Huntley's demolition was swift. He had to admit that the bath had not had eighteen inches of water in it – the overflow was only eleven inches above its bottom – making his drowning story even more implausible. He was forced to concede that he had originally claimed that it was the 'dark-haired girl' – Jessica – who had had the nosebleed, only changing his story when he later heard that Holly had herself occasionally suffered from nosebleeds. 'You were inventing a defence to fit the facts, weren't you?' asked Latham.

The cross-examination was devastating in its starkness:

LATHAM: The only way Holly could have drowned in the bath is if you were holding her under the water.
HUNTLEY: I wasn't holding her.

LATHAM: If Jessica was screaming it was because you were murdering Holly. That's the truth, isn't it?

HUNTLEY: No.

LATHAM: You watched Holly drown.

HUNTLEY: I just froze, sir.

LATHAM: Jessica would have pulled her friend's head out of the water. Effectively, the two of you stood within touching distance of this child and watched her drown?

HUNTLEY: I didn't watch her drown. I comprehended that she was in the bath and she wasn't breathing. In these circumstances, it's easy to be rational. [Shouting] Believe me, I know.

LATHAM: You can be perfectly assertive when you want to, can't you?

HUNTLEY: Yes.

LATHAM: You can get angry, can't you, Mr Huntley?

HUNTLEY: Yes.

LATHAM: You have just lost your temper with me, haven't you?

HUNTLEY: Yes.

LATHAM: Did you lose your temper with one of those girls? Did you become the assertive individual you became two minutes ago?

HUNTLEY: No. I didn't.

Everyone in the courtroom felt that there had been a decisive turning point in the trial. Latham turned to the circumstances of Jessica's death.

LATHAM: If you had given that girl the slightest chance she would have lived, wouldn't she?

HUNTLEY: Yes.

LATHAM: You had killed her, hadn't you?

HUNTLEY [in a whisper]: Yes.

LATHAM: You advanced towards her?

HUNTLEY: Yes.

LATHAM: Putting up your hand towards her mouth?

HUNTLEY: Yes.

LATHAM: If you block the mouth and nose, what starts to happen to someone?

HUNTLEY: You starve them of oxygen.

LATHAM: They start, in effect, to die?

HUNTLEY: Yes.

LATHAM: It doesn't happen in a moment.

HUNTLEY: No.

Latham took Huntley through the terrible events of that evening. 'How did it feel, Mr Huntley?' he asked as each step was accomplished: taking the girls' bodies downstairs; placing them in the car; depositing them in the ditch; setting them on fire. 'Not good,' was Huntley's only response, a sort of whimpering inarticulacy in the face of the enormity of his crime. Yet he bolstered Carr's own defence by insisting that she had not heard the full story of the girls' deaths until now, in the grim silence of the Old Bailey. He explained that he had been unable to 'get the words out' when talking to Carr on her return from Grimsby. He had told her instead that the girls had walked out of the house alive, happy and laughing.

The favour was not returned when Carr entered the witness box the following day. Throughout all the pre-trial hearings, and during the trial itself, Huntley often stared at Carr, as if to try to reconnect with his partner of three years, the person with whom he had been planning to spend the rest of his life. She never even glanced back at him.

Maxine Carr used her examination by Hubbard – a 'slick performance', Kevin Wells conceded; 'brilliant' others have privately agreed – to turn on Huntley, explaining that when she had returned home to find the washing machine full and the house spotlessly clean she had suspected that he'd been entertaining another woman. Hubbard himself strove to demonstrate that Carr had 'done nothing wrong'; she had only claimed to have been at 5 College Close that Sunday because she loved and trusted Huntley.

Carr's vulnerability lay in the fact that, on her arrival back at Soham, she had noticed that her partner had been engaged in an out-of-character clean-up operation. It was one she seemed to have then participated in. Under cross-examination she was asked why, given that she described Huntley as a 'slob' who had previously never done any housework, she had not told police about the incriminating details she had found in the house on her return: the strong smell of lemon-scented cleaner; the freshly cleaned Fiesta with a new carpet in its boot; the quilt, sheets and bathmat in the washing machine; a small chip on the rim of the bath.

Carr's response was a long way from these domestic details. 'I'm trying to make it clear the kind of person Ian Huntley is towards me,' she said, adding that Huntley was 'an abusive person who controls you . . . I was scared of him.' This was potentially hugely damaging for Huntley, and, once it was out, Stephen Coward had no choice but to try to neutralise it. If the option of leaving well alone had existed before, now it was gone. Coward, as he had to, accused Carr directly of embellishing her story, of denigrating her ex-boyfriend now that it suited her. Carr snapped. Having earlier giggled nervously in the witness box, she now became deadly serious. Her devastating reply – 'I know what I have done, sir. I have come in this witness box and I am not going to be blamed for what that *thing* has done to me or those children' – left Court Number One stunned. A man fainted in the public gallery and had to be carried out. Huntley seemed to be crushed. It was not just the utter loathing with which she called him 'that thing'. He must have known too that, in those thirty-three blunt, plain words, Carr had just destroyed any hope of acquittal to which he might still have clung. Eyewitnesses described Carr as 'owning' the court, so overwhelming was her outburst.

Late that afternoon, Moses sent the jury out and suggested to Hubbard that his client should now plead guilty to the lesser charge of conspiring with Huntley to pervert the course of justice. But she made no change to her plea, and Latham's cross-examination swiftly destroyed what was left of her defence at least to that lesser charge. When read a transcript of one of her many TV interviews, Carr admitted that she had lied repeatedly about having been in Soham, not Grimsby, on 4 August. But she was insistent that she had continued the cleaning that Huntley had started not in order to erase any forensic evidence, but because she was 'obsessive about tidiness'.

Hubbard then re-examined his client. He asked whether she and Huntley had slept in the same bed after her return from Grimsby: Carr said she had, and added that she wouldn't even be in the same house as him if she'd known that Huntley had 'unlawfully killed' the children.

On Friday, 5 December, a day of legal argument, Coward persuaded Moses to allow three possible verdicts for Huntley: guilty of murder, guilty of manslaughter (through 'gross negligence' in Holly's case), or not guilty. In his short speech Latham reminded jurors that Carr and Huntley were both 'accomplished liars'. He argued that Huntley had been 'motivated by something sexual' when he lured the girls into his house, but that whatever he had planned 'plainly went wrong' and the girls had paid with their lives: 'Each was a witness, a potential complainant, and he was quite merciless.' But Latham spoke of Carr more in sorrow than in anger: 'She had the prospect of marriage, a baby, a nice home and a new start. She preferred to do what she could to make the best of the position she was in. That involved at all costs protecting Ian Huntley.'

Coward followed, trying to bolster Huntley's defence by referring to multiple cot deaths, 'rare events' that were nonetheless not unheard of. But Jessica Chapman and Holly Wells were not babies: they were both almost eleven years old, fit and well. (Holly had been a keen Fenlander Majorette and Jessica a champion swimmer.) Even if their deaths had been accidental, Coward accepted that Huntley should have immediately called an ambulance, although he urged jurors only to convict Huntley of manslaughter as there was no evidence of premeditation or a sexual motive. 'Let's be blunt. On the evidence you have heard, we are not going to argue on behalf of Mr Huntley in the case of either girl that what he did makes him innocent and unworthy of punishment. He is worthy of punishment.' This was, in the circumstances, the best that Coward could do: rather than alienate the jury, to invite them to punish Huntley for criminal responsibility for the girls' deaths, but in a way that fell short of a verdict of murder.

The next day Hubbard ignored Moses' warning that 'Hasn't she suffered enough?' was not a valid defence for Carr. Her counsel relied heavily on the thank-you card that Holly had given to Carr, a copy of which he waved around 'like a prop'. Appealing to the jury's pity, he said coyly that Carr had 'let herself be stroked' by Huntley after her return to Soham. 'Would she ever allow the hand that had drowned Holly and killed Jessica . . . to wander over her body? It's against every female instinct, isn't it?' Yet Hubbard had done a good job: the jury seemed to have warmed to his understated demeanour and by refusing to accede to Moses' suggestion that his client should plead guilty to perversion of the course of justice he had allowed the jury a route to signalling their repugnance without having to convict of the more serious offence.

The families had been warned that an Old Bailey murder conviction had recently been quashed because of a flawed summing-up by the trial judge. The following morning, Mr Justice Moses' summing-up was short, and carefully worded. He reminded jurors that Huntley's lies after Holly and Jessica died did not prove that he murdered them. But, he added, 'You are left with the sudden deaths of two healthy girls without a credible explanation as to how the deaths came about from the one person who could have explained them to you.' He then told them to consider Huntley first and Carr second, and to convict her of the more serious of the two charges she faced (of assisting an offender) only if they were sure that she'd known Huntley had killed the girls: 'The mere fact that you conclude that she was suspicious or even very suspicious or ought to have been suspicious is not enough.' It was a model of fairness.

At 11 a.m. on Thursday, 11 December the jury retired, with a warning from Moses that he expected absolute silence in court when they returned:

if there were any interruptions, the public gallery would be cleared and the verdicts heard in closed court. Kevin Wells, who had found the legal system so incomprehensible in its capacity for needless complexity, had taken comfort in the judge's headmasterly manner during the proceedings. From the start of the trial Moses had stamped his authority on the courtroom. Wells recorded appreciatively the judge's 'extraordinarily dismissive tone of voice'.

Despite the overwhelming case against Huntley it still took several days for the jury to find him guilty of murder, by a majority of eleven to one (Moses had wanted a unanimous verdict and only gave a majority direction three days into the deliberations). Carr was found guilty of perverting the course of justice but not the more serious charge of 'assisting an offender'. Valerie Grove reported that the guilty verdicts were met with quiet exhilaration in the courtroom; and 'the silence beforehand' had been 'almost electric with a heart-thumping tension and anticipation that filled Court Number 1 of the Old Bailey'. Nicola Wells burst into tears; Kevin Wells, who had developed a visceral hatred of the 'do-gooders brigade' who seemed to bend over backwards to ensure Huntley got a fair trial, just smiled: Huntley was a 'sick, pathetic, wretched bastard' he was pleased to see the back of.

Moses immediately moved into his sentencing; despite having been found guilty of double murder Huntley showed 'not a flicker of feeling'. A trial that had hitherto lacked memorable speeches concluded with one of the most moving sentencing statements that Court Number One had ever heard.

Ian Kevin Huntley, on August 4th, 2002, you enticed two ten-year-old girls, Holly Wells and Jessica Chapman, into your house. They were happy, intelligent and loyal. They were much loved by their families and all who knew them. You murdered them both. You are the one person who knows how you murdered them. You are the one person who knows why.

You destroyed the evidence but you showed no mercy and you show no regret. It is plain that once you killed one, you had to kill the other in your attempt to avoid detection. On August 10th, but six days later, you told the BBC that you thought you might be the last friendly face that these two girls had to speak to. That was a lie which serves to under-line the persistent cruelty of your actions. On the contrary, one of those girls died knowing her friend had been attacked or killed by you.

After you had murdered them both, you pushed their bodies into a ditch, stripped them and burned them, while their families searched for them in increasing despair.

And, as Kevin Wells called out their names, you pretended to join in the search. Three days later you demonstrated the extent of your merciless cynicism by offering that father some words of regret. Your tears have never been for them, only for yourself.

In your attempts to escape responsibility in your lies, and your manipulation up to this day, you have increased the suffering you have caused two families. But it is not just those two families whose lives you have sought to destroy. Your crimes are those for which the community suffer. The children you murdered were children whose lives brought joy to the community and whose deaths brought grief.

There is no greater task for the criminal justice system than to protect the vulnerable. There are few worse crimes than your murder of those two young girls.

Huntley was given two life sentences; Carr three and a half years, considerably less than the six years the prosecution had expected. Moses had not allowed public sentiment to get in the way of justice. Angela Rafferty had been part of Maxine Carr's counsel team. Then a very junior barrister (and now herself an Old Bailey judge), the case dominated her professional life for months and proved to be a watershed in her career. She recalls the trial, taking place under an unprecedented spotlight of publicity, as unique in its drama and horror. She was not alone; even the more seasoned lawyers involved in the case were said to be marked by it.

On 5 April 2004, 5 College Close and the Hangar were demolished in just thirty-eight minutes by mechanical diggers, whose operators were contractually obliged to ensure all its bricks were ground into dust and then disposed of in secret locations to thwart any ghoulish souvenir-hunters. It had taken twenty years for 10 Rillington Place to be demolished, and then it was for reasons of slum-clearance.

But the trial has had a very long afterlife: far from disappearing from view, Huntley has regularly hit the headlines ever since. In 2005 he was attacked by another prisoner with boiling water in HMP Wakefield; in 2006 he attempted suicide by overdosing on pills; in 2007 he was reported to be on hunger strike. In 2010 his throat was slashed at HMP Frankland, to which he'd been moved two years before. In early 2018 the *Sun* obtained a recorded confession in which he maintained that Holly's death was a 'genuine accident' but admitted that he had killed Jessica to stop her raising the alarm. But this was just the latest in a string of supposed 'confessions': in an earlier one he had claimed, without evidence, that it was Carr who had ordered him to 'brazen out the manhunt' and return to Wangford to burn the bodies, rather than give himself up immediately.

But the media's hatred of Huntley was if anything surpassed by its horror of Carr, the girlfriend with a 'nearly pretty face', 'pale and crooked' under a mop of reddish-brown hair. It was conveniently forgotten that she was acquitted of the most serious charges she was tried for. Being tried alongside a murderer meant Carr was made a 'primitive scapegoat'. She was even dubbed 'the new Myra Hindley'. No one ever denied that Carr had been devoted to Holly and Jessica, and was horrified that they had gone missing. Her decision to provide Huntley with a false alibi was motivated either by misplaced loyalty, or fear. Many sanctimonious media commentators chastised Carr for not coming forward earlier to lessen the families' ordeal. But although Carr was clearly gullible and naive, it is implausible that she knew that the girls had been killed by her boyfriend. He only himself accepted any form of responsibility for their deaths just before the trial started. When told Huntley had been charged, Carr cried, 'I knew him!', as if the man she loved could not possibly be accused of murder.

According to Nicci Gerrard, Carr was 'quick rather than clever, eager rather than bright' and no better or worse than a 'foolish, glib young woman who looked the other way'; the feminist writer Beatrix Campbell argued that Carr shouldn't be punished at all as she was 'in thrall' to Huntley. Even the families realised that she had, at worst, been only a secondary culprit. 'So long as Huntley goes down we don't give a damn about Carr,' noted Kevin Wells in his diary during the trial.

There was a 'prison revolt' at Foston Hall near Derby when Carr was transferred there from Holloway towards the end of her sentence. In May 2004 placards saying 'child killer' were held up outside Nottingham Crown Court, where Carr was convicted of benefit fraud. Although Carr's appeal against her sentence had been unsuccessful she was nonetheless released a few days later, five months after her Old Bailey trial had ended. The same newspapers that had hounded Carr in jail then complained about the reported £15 million cost of her new identity, and the 'Mary Bell' order imposed after her release. Such an order had only been necessary because of the witch-hunt that the newspapers themselves had unleashed. Maxine Carr has now spent the last fifteen years living under an assumed name, in fear of exposure and its consequences.

★

More than fifteen years on, why is the Soham case still so seared into the national consciousness?

Although the trial took place three years into the new millennium it is located exactly on the emotional cusp between the buttoned-up twentieth century and the demonstrative twenty-first. After the Aberfan disaster of 1966, in which 116 children were killed, no counselling was offered, their school reopened just two weeks later and the community healed itself remarkably well. In Soham in 2002 counsellors were on hand for all the police officers involved, the children who had gone to school with Holly and Jessica, and even to reporters who covered the story. For Gerrard, emotion 'is our new religion . . . filled with its own rapidly evolving rites, everyday liturgies and a Medieval irrationality'. If so, the Soham murders were one of the new religion's inaugural conclaves.

The case reveals generational differences. Kevin Wells' father never even mentioned Holly's name between her death and his own in June 2004. But Kevin and Nicola Wells, born in the 1960s, preferred to share their grief: within hours of the girls' disappearance they had 'lost control of the house' amid a constant stream of visitors. Before the trial began Kevin met with the literary agent Sonia Land to discuss a book he wanted to write about their ordeal. *Goodbye, Dearest Holly*, published in 2005, carried harrowing details such as the family's decisions not to place Holly's favourite soft toy, Snoozums, inside her coffin as Kevin could still smell Holly on its fabric, and to burn Holly's 2002 class photo because Carr appeared in it. Contrary to what its title might suggest, the book that Wells wrote is a remarkable and insightful account, shorn of cliché or self-pity, of the experience of the criminal justice system, all the way through to trial, from the point of view of the victim (and Kevin Wells was undoubtedly one of Huntley's victims); a perspective not often articulated.

While their story contains examples of official insensitivity the families were also the recipients of many acts of kindness, even tenderness, which showed how much the treatment of victims' families had improved. The Wells' tale is full of sleepless nights and grown men in tears. Family liaison officers are a constant and welcome presence. Sir Ronnie Flanagan, the tough former Royal Ulster Constabulary Chief Constable, greeted Kevin Wells with a hug, not a handshake, when they met to discuss Flanagan's post-trial review. The prosecution is described as 'our legal team'.

The case attracted media hysteria from the very start. Holly and Jessica were murdered in what journalists call the 'silly season' of August, when newspapers struggle to fill their pages; and the inescapable fact that the girls were white, photogenic and from respectable families in 'Middle England' was not lost on hard-nosed tabloid editors. And there were political consequences. Amid the usual calls, from the usual quarters, for the restoration of the death penalty, in April 2003 – six months before Huntley's trial began – the Home Secretary David Blunkett announced plans to extend whole-life tariffs to those found guilty of murdering a child; although the new rules came too late to apply to Huntley it was obvious what case he had in mind. In 2005 Moses imposed a minimum forty-year tariff on Huntley, as stringent as the law allowed given that the murders had not been premeditated. But in 2007 the Lord Chancellor asserted that Huntley should never be freed. Interviewed for a TV documentary to mark the fifteenth anniversary of the murders, Blunkett said he had 'nothing to say about Ian Huntley' before adding, a moment later, 'I hope he rots in hell.'

Blunkett's decision to order two post-trial enquiries – one by Sir Ronnie Flanagan, an HM Inspector of Constabulary, into the police investigation; another by Sir Michael Bichard (a former permanent secretary at the Department for Education and Employment) into child protection and vetting procedures – led to heads rolling. Bichard was damning. Both Cambridgeshire and Humberside forces had shown 'errors, omissions, failures and shortcomings . . . so extensive that I cannot be confident that it was Huntley alone who "slipped through the net"', he concluded in June 2004. While Cambridgeshire Constabulary could possibly have done more in the 'golden hours' immediately after the girls were reported missing, it would have made no difference to the fate of Holly and Jessica. The murders had probably been carried out by 6.45 p.m., well before the parents realised the girls were even missing; their bodies were probably already lying in a ditch by the time they started to worry. Richard Latham had told the Wells that no police force had ever worked harder in a murder case.

It is said that the Soham murders had a tangible impact on parents' willingness to allow their children out to play or roam about unsupervised. It was as if the bogeyman had become real. And to this day, British people are reminded of the Soham case whenever they apply for a job or voluntary position that involves any contact with children or vulnerable adults. Bichard's thirty-one recommendations led directly to a new national police intelligence database, and much more stringent checks by the newly formed Criminal Record Bureau (since renamed the Disclosure and Barring Service). From now on police forces passed on information about arrests and charges, not just convictions. But the real problem in

Soham hadn't been that existing procedures were wrong but that they weren't followed properly: a fax from Humberside had gone missing, and the Village College hadn't taken up Huntley's references before offering him a job as its caretaker. At first the new checks led to paralysis in the education system, and they have been subject to complaints about civil liberties and onerous bureaucracy ever since.

One aspect of the case escaped criticism: the trial itself. Moses deserves credit for presiding so fairly and firmly under such a bright spotlight: as well as dozens of reporters, the newly appointed Director of Public Prosecutions, Ken Macdonald, was often in court. The judge's rolling basso voice seemed to embody a conception of justice that infused the courtroom and made the trial a fitting riposte to the enormity of the crime. Everyone went away feeling that justice had been done. A High Court judge since 1996, Moses was experienced – he had presided over the trial of the former MI5 officer David Shayler in the Old Bailey's Court Number Two a year before – but he nevertheless had a sense of humour. Sitting in the administrative court in summer 2003, he delivered a written judgement on a case involving mobile phone companies, in which he thanked counsel in textspeak: 'To them I hope it is not inappropriate 2 xpress thnx 4 all thr gr8 wrk.'

During the trial the 'whiny self-pity' of Huntley and the frequent presence of psychologists in court grated with Kevin Wells, who was annoyed that Moses granted Carr and the 'visibly agitated' Huntley the frequent adjournments that their counsel asked for because their clients 'felt unwell'. Yet Moses knew that the integrity of the conviction would be the greater if he gave no inch of room for complaint on the part of the defendants. Moses urged the media to 'dampen down emotions' to ensure that Huntley and Carr received a fair trial, at one point ordering the media not to report Huntley's supposed facial responses to the evidence. But he also forewarned the families of evidence they might find unduly distressing and refused to allow Huntley's histrionics to derail the momentum of the trial. After his retirement as a Lord Justice of Appeal in 2014 Moses became chairman of the Independent Press Standards Organisation, for which the Soham trial was good preparation.

And for Kevin Wells, enduring the long weeks of an excruciating trial, Court Number One was at least an island of order and discipline in a sea of media hysteria and rumours. When the longed-for verdict came in he wrote: 'It has finally happened. Justice has been done. Nothing else matters now.' Court Number One had done its job.

Appendix I

The Old Bailey: A Brief History from 1907

THE PRESENT OLD Bailey stands on the site of a prison – the notorious Newgate – that had, in various incarnations, held prisoners since the Middle Ages. In the late eighteenth century the prison and an adjacent criminal court were rebuilt. It was this Sessions House – universally known as the Old Bailey – which was designated the Central Criminal Court in 1834. But by the start of the twentieth century the Old Bailey was no longer fit for purpose, unable to cope with the volume of business it had to deal with. It was therefore decided to demolish both the existing court and the neighbouring Newgate prison and build a new, larger, courthouse on its site. The new Central Criminal Court building, designed by Edward William Mountford, was opened by Edward VII on 27 February 1907. It was a state occasion in all but name, with over 200 dignitaries rammed into Court Number One. More than 110 years on it is extraordinary how liberal and pioneering the words spoken at the opening still sound. The Recorder of London Sir Forrest Fulton gave a loyal address at which he promised the King that the court would 'temper justice with mercy'. In his response, the King referred to the 'barbarous legal code' of a century before. To much applause, he highlighted the 'mercy shown to first offenders which is, I am well assured, often the means of reshaping their lives'.

The new court was seen as a break with, not a continuation of, the past; despite its ongoing rituals it was much more businesslike than its predecessor. Nowadays these rituals are pared back: the Lord Mayor processes in to Court Number One in full regalia only twice a year, at the start of the legal terms in January and October. Yet to this day the City of London Corporation owns and maintains the Old Bailey, the only courthouse in England not owned by the Ministry of Justice. The Lord Mayor technically still has the right to preside in court (although in practice never does so). The central seat on the bench in Court

Number One, reserved for the Lord Mayor's ceremonial visits, still stands empty at other times; the presiding judge invariably sits to its side.

A building that may to twenty-first-century eyes seem designed to intimidate and awe was in fact designed to reassure and heal. On top of its dome was erected, and still stands, a twelve-foot gold leaf statue of 'Lady Justice', by the sculptor F.W. Pomeroy, holding a sword aloft in one hand and the scales of justice in the other. Many such statues preside over courthouses across the world but most are depicted blindfolded, as a metaphor of impartiality. However here Lady Justice's eyes are not bound: justice in this new building was to be circumspect, not blind. Over the main entrance were (and remain) stone figures representing Fortitude, the Recording Angel and Truth, along with the carved admonition: 'Defend the Children of the Poor and Punish the Wrongdoer', a rebuke to previous judicial practices and Newgate's parlous record as a place where the children of the poor had been habitually punished, not defended.

When completed the Old Bailey was said to be the most 'spacious and elaborate' criminal court in the world. Although the English would never use such a continental phrase, the new Old Bailey was intended as a Palace of Justice, a public statement of belief in the values of fairness and open justice. As we have seen in the preceding chapters, it was an aspiration that would often be blunted by reality.

Like so many courthouses of the period, the architectural style of the 'New Bailey', as it was sometimes known at first, is Edwardian Baroque, a muscular and confident mode that reflected Britain's might and civilising mission at the highpoint of Empire. Its rusticated face to Newgate Street and Old Bailey, mostly Portland stone but with granite at lower levels, recalls the blank walls of the old prison (indeed many of its stones were reused). Inside, a monumental staircase leads from the lobby up to a vast first-floor Grand Hall with Sicilian marble floors and allegorical mosaics and murals representing Labour, Art, Wisdom and Truth.

The Grand Hall is a marked contrast to the four main courtrooms that lead off it – foremost of which is Court Number One – which have no marble and are panelled in Austrian oak. Originally these four courts each had a designated judge: the Lord Chief Justice or a High Court judge of the King's (since 1952 the Queen's) Bench Division would typically sit in Court Number One, and the Recorder of London (the senior resident judge of the Bailey), the Common Sergeant and an additional judge, known as the Commissioner, in Courts Two to Four respectively.

In contrast to the cramped courtrooms of the old 'Old Bailey' the new courts had much more space for solicitors, counsel, journalists and the public, though they had the same adversarial configuration (discussed in the introductory chapter) as the courtrooms of the previous Sessions House. The gloom of the past was at least partially banished: each of the new courtrooms had glass skylights, with natural illumination being assisted by electricity. There were centrally heated jury rooms off the long corridor running behind the courts, in which jurors could consider their verdict in relative comfort.

Each courtroom's capacious dock was linked by stairs to the holding cells beneath (previously defendants had to be marched from adjoining Newgate through the well of the court into the dock). Barristers' accommodation, in contrast to the single room in the old courthouse, included a mess room lined with judicial portraits, a separate robing room, and rooms where lawyers could consult privately with their clients. There were separate waiting rooms for male and female witnesses, and – in a sign that modernisation could only go so far – another for witnesses of 'the better class'. Finally, a 'refreshment bar', now sadly closed, was positioned in the ground-floor lobby. Witnesses could seek a cup of tea, or perhaps a fortifying glass of ale, while waiting to be called.

At the first trial in the new Court Number One, the Lord Chief Justice Lord Alverstone complained about the acoustics of the courtroom (a complaint echoed many times since) and its coldness. Despite the lengthy design process there was also some controversy over the grandeur of the new building's architecture and interior murals. Even the author of the official subscription volume marking the court's opening later sniffed that 'There are many who think that artistic decoration has been carried too far for a court of criminal justice.' Nonetheless Lady Justice soon became a potent symbol of the English judicial system as a whole rather than just of the Bailey itself. The Old Bailey had been transformed from a Hogarthian den of chaos and misery to 'The Bar of the greatest Assize Court in the Empire', wrote one historian.

Up to a point. The opening of the new Central Criminal Court did coincide with the passing of a long-lived Victorian generation of unlamented judges. Yet the early years of the twentieth century did not witness an entirely new dawn in judicial appointments. The practice of appointing High Court judges as repayment for political favours (many judges had previously been Conservative Members of Parliament), rather than on merit, continued well into the new century. The court's opening also coincided with another legal sea-change. Various miscarriages of justice, most notably the two wrongful convictions of Adolf Beck, who had the misfortune to be the doppelgänger of a swindler, had generated a clamour for an appeal court to review convictions and sentences. In 1907 the Criminal Court of Appeal was instituted and almost immediately had a substantial impact. Of twenty-nine appeals heard in its first nine months, eighteen were allowed. Other legislative reforms followed. In 1908 the Children Act abolished the death penalty for under-sixteens, and the imprisonment of under-fourteens in adult jails (it took more than another twenty years, until 1933, for hanging to be restricted to over-eighteens). Legal aid – often assumed to be a creation of the post-war Labour government – in fact began in 1930.

Standards had certainly improved, but both the Bar and bench of the Old Bailey remained a tight-knit circle. In 1908 the modern Treasury Counsel system was instituted, under which a group of barristers appointed by the Director of Public Prosecutions, in private practice but permanently based in rooms at the Bailey, would prosecute the vast bulk of the 'heavy' work. In the past, some have considered the system a cabal, and appointment to it is much coveted: the ultimate goal being the position of Senior Treasury Counsel, in years gone by usually a stepping stone to the judiciary. Bar Mess dinners were said to be more closely 'tiled' than those of a Masonic lodge. Many Old Bailey judges and barristers were – and still are – members of the Garrick Club, where they rub shoulders with actors, writers and journalists. Numerous barristers and judges have also been actors and writers themselves: Patrick Hastings was an accomplished playwright in the 1920s and John Mortimer's own career as a playwright and novelist started in the 1950s.

In accounts of Old Bailey trials of the first decades of the twentieth century, perhaps the golden age of English criminal law, the same names constantly recur: for the defence Edward Marshall Hall, and later Henry Curtis-Bennett, Patrick Hastings and Norman Birkett; for the prosecution Charles Mathews, Archibald Bodkin, Travers Humphreys and Richard Muir. The new twentieth-century generation of barristers were often quieter and subtler than their Victorian counterparts, and arguably more effective. Many came from the usual public school and Oxbridge backgrounds: Rayner Goddard and Travers Humphreys were both sons of wealthy solicitors; Curtis-Bennett was the son of a Bow Street magistrate. But many others came from more humble origins. Richard Muir, a workaholic known as the 'master watchmaker', was a Scotsman from Greenock who had paid his way through training as a parliamentary reporter for *The Times*. He would become a formidable Senior Treasury Counsel between the 1900s and 1920s, and prosecuted Crippen. Patrick Hastings had to leave Charterhouse at the age of sixteen when his father was no longer able to afford its fees; as a Bar student he would walk to and from the Temple rather than catch the bus, and like Muir he relied on freelance journalism to pay his Call fee. Both Norman Birkett and Gordon Hewart were the sons of Lancashire drapers; Henry McCardie, one of the great judges of the twenties, was an orphan who had left school in Birmingham at the age of sixteen.

The law was often also a family business. Percival Clarke, who prosecuted both Madame Fahmy and Elvira Barney (see Chapters 3 and 4), and was later chairman of the London sessions in the 1930s, was the son of Sir Edward Clarke KC. When Clarke junior died suddenly in 1936 he was succeeded by Eustace Fulton, whose father was Sir Forrest Fulton. Humphreys was an omnipresent name at the Bailey for almost a century: Travers Humphreys appeared regularly at the Bailey from his Call in 1889 and sat as a High Court judge, at the Bailey and elsewhere, from 1928 until 1951. His son Christmas Humphreys was also a renowned Bailey Treasury Counsel, who prosecuted Timothy Evans, Derek Bentley and Ruth Ellis (see Chapters 6 and 7) and later sat as a judge at the Bailey until 1976. Henry Curtis-Bennett's son Derek followed his father to the top of the criminal Bar, trying unsuccessfully to persuade an Old Bailey jury that John Christie was insane in 1953 (see Chapter 6).

Alongside these barristers came a new generation of more humane and thoughtful judges. Bad judges were now generally political appointments, such as Lord Hewart, appointed as Lord Chief Justice by Lloyd George in 1922. Hewart, described by Henry Cecil as 'by common consent the worst Lord Chief Justice we have had this century and for a long time before that', used to write fulminating articles for the *News of the World* for £100 a go. Although now remembered for his famous dictum that 'Not only must Justice be done; it must also be seen to be done', in his eighteen years as Lord Chief Justice Hewart rarely followed it himself.

Nowadays the Attorney General and Solicitor General are political appointees who do not often appear in court, but in the twentieth century they frequently acted as prosecution counsel at the Bailey and other courts (one of the last occasions was in 1981, when Attorney General Sir Michael Havers led for the Crown in Court Number One at the trial of Peter Sutcliffe, the so-called 'Yorkshire Ripper'). There was, and to some extent still is, a revolving door between politics and the Old

Bailey Bar: Edward Carson QC, who acted for the Marquess of Queensberry during the Wilde case, later became an MP and leader of the Ulster Unionist Party before finishing his career as a Lord of Appeal. The most famous barrister of them all, the 'Great Defender' Edward Marshall Hall, sat in Parliament twice. Patrick Hastings was a Labour MP and became Attorney General in the first Labour government of 1923–4. John Simon MP regularly appeared as a King's Counsel at the Bailey until the 1930s before and between stints as Home Secretary, Foreign Secretary and Lord Chancellor. Peter Rawlinson MP acted both as Solicitor General and Attorney General in the 1960s and '70s. A noted Old Bailey defender, Geoffrey Cox, was made Attorney General in 2018.

The Second World War had a profound effect on the business of the Old Bailey, discussed in Chapter 5. Despite heavy bombing, prosecutions continued for espionage, treason and grisly murders – most notably the sexual sadist Neville Heath – providing sensational copy for the newspapers. The year 1944 even saw the last witchcraft trial, that of Helen Duncan, convicted for carrying on séances in which fake ectoplasm (in fact cheesecloth) emerged from her mouth.

The 1957 film *Witness for the Prosecution*, adapted from the Agatha Christie short story and directed by Billy Wilder, is a highly entertaining portrayal of the post-war Old Bailey. But the business of the real Old Bailey was rather less glamorous during the years of austerity and beyond. The key figure on the post-war bench was Rayner Goddard, appointed by Attlee as Lord Chief Justice in 1946 but very far from a Labour stooge (he had stood as an Independent Conservative at the 1929 election). He was the first ever non-political appointment as Lord Chief Justice and there would be no return to the old system of patronage. Like most judges of the time Goddard fiercely opposed the experimental five-year suspension of the death penalty proposed in the 1948 Criminal Justice Bill, discussed in Chapter 6.

The 1950s are remembered for the trials of Timothy Evans, Derek Bentley and Ruth Ellis and they are sometimes assumed to be the last three people hanged on British soil (see Chapters 6 and 7). In fact there were many more hangings in the late 1950s and early 1960s that are now much less well-remembered. Ronald Marwood was convicted at the Bailey of murdering a policeman and hanged in May 1959, as was the German-born Guenther Podola, who went to the gallows in November 1959 despite claiming to have no memory of his crime, the shooting of another policeman. Hubert Parker, who had succeeded Lord Goddard as Lord Chief Justice in 1958, dismissed his appeal. As discussed in Chapter 7 the last hanging in Britain took place in August 1964.

Abolition of the death penalty meant less prurient interest in the Old Bailey's murder trials. It also diminished their excitement: the stakes were reduced, the momentousness of the occasion diluted. The paradox was that the end of hanging coincided with an increased judicial willingness to hand down much longer prison sentences: in April 1964 the ringleaders of the Great Train Robbers were given sentences of thirty years each, even though no one had been killed in the robbery. Despite his treatment of Podola, and the forty-two-year sentence he handed down to the spy George Blake in 1961 (see Chapter 10), Parker turned out to be a more liberal and well-rounded Lord Chief Justice than Goddard had been, quashing many convictions while sitting in the Court of Appeal and reducing many sentences.

Aside from the usual fare of murder, in the 1950s the Old Bailey witnessed a number of obscenity and homosexuality prosecutions (see Chapter 7). The social and political upheavals of the 1960s also left their mark on the Old Bailey. As well as the excitement of the Profumo scandal and the prosecutions of Aloysius 'Lucky' Gordon, Stephen Ward and Christine Keeler that it generated, the Bailey presided over the extraordinary *Lady Chatterley's Lover* case and the trials of a succession of Soviet spies or alleged spies, Gordon Lonsdale, George Blake, John Vassall and Giuseppe Martelli being the most prominent (see Chapters 8 and 10). The decade also saw a new wave of criminal gangs that prompted many to regret the abolition of the death penalty. In 1966 George Witney, Harry Roberts and John Duddy were each sentenced in Court Number One to a minimum of thirty years for shooting three policemen dead near Wormwood Scrubs. The case so shocked the nation that a memorial service for the officers was held in Westminster Abbey with Prime Minister Harold Wilson in attendance. In 1967 the south London gangster Charlie Richardson was found guilty of fraud, extortion, assault and grievous bodily harm and sentenced to twenty-five years in prison. Court Number Two heard that the Richardson gang had tortured victims by pulling teeth using pliers, cutting off toes with bolt cutters and even nailing victims to the floor. In early 1969 the Kray brothers were both sentenced to a minimum of thirty years by Mr Justice Melford Stevenson, who had defended Ruth Ellis fourteen years earlier. A new, hardened world had emerged.

Repairs to the Bailey's wartime bomb damage had finally started in 1950 and were completed in 1953 at a cost of some £500,000. The number of courts was increased from four to six, and Court Number Two was completely rebuilt. A children's nursery – in effect a modern crèche – was opened, a new cafeteria installed, and more care was taken to ensure that witnesses and jurors could not be tampered with. Despite its 1950s renovation the Bailey struggled to cope with its ever-growing workload. It was clear that it needed extending and its cadre of serving judges increased, and in 1962 the City Corporation agreed to finance a new southern extension. More land was acquired and a new Portland stone extension, much larger than first envisaged and designed by the architectural practice McMorran and Whitby, was opened by Lord Chancellor Hailsham in November 1972.

Although some architectural critics were scathing about its conservative style the extension was immediately popular with judges, juries and counsel. At a stroke the number of courtrooms was increased from six to eighteen; the new courtrooms were well-lit, simple, wood-panelled and well-ventilated, with a roof terrace for jurors to use. The need to allow judges, jurors, barristers, witnesses, defendants and the general public to use the building while remaining separate 'demanded an astonishing plan, which exists as a legacy of an exceptional talent', the architectural historian Edward Denison has written.

On 8 March 1973 – the day of an independence referendum in Northern Ireland – a huge IRA car bomb exploded directly outside the Bailey. Only one person was killed, as the Bailey's gates had been closed as soon as a bomb warning was received and the area had been partly evacuated. But 174 others were injured, including the charismatic barrister and wit James Crespi, who was memorably photographed, shirtless and bloodied, minutes after the bomb exploded. Twenty years later Crespi's obituarist recorded that he would have been killed by the bomb had he not been so fat: 'surgeons told him that pieces of the bomb were still inside him, but that it would require a major archaeological expedition to find them and they were better left alone.' The Old Bailey's crèche was wrecked and all its courtrooms made unusable because of broken glass, one shard of which was left in situ, embedded and still visible in an interior wall above the main entrance. A temporary courtroom had to be set up in a downstairs committee room, though repair work was swift and all the courts were back in use by the following Monday. In November 1973 two sisters, Dolours and Marian Price, were sentenced to life imprisonment at Winchester Crown Court for planning the bombings.

A longer-term consequence of the bomb was, naturally enough, enhanced security at the Bailey: sniffer dogs became a common sight. The grand entrance to Mountford's building was henceforth reserved for ceremonial use only: all other visitors had to pass through X-ray machines in McMorran and Whitby's extension, whose low entrance arches have served as a backdrop to thousands of TV reports over the last forty-five years. The 1970s and 1980s saw a huge number of terrorism trials, including those of the 'Guildford Four' and 'Maguire Seven'. The bulk of these cases took place in Court Number Two, its dock adapted for defendants perceived as especially dangerous. Mr Justice Cantley was given an armed guard at home while he tried the Balcombe Street Gang – four IRA terrorists who had conducted a number of bombings on the mainland in 1974–5 – at the Old Bailey in 1977. The terrorism cases also extended to other forms of direct political action. The prosecution of the Angry Brigade in 1972 was then the longest trial ever heard in Court Number One.

At the same time obscenity trials continued in the Old Bailey, though for rather less decorous material than *Lady Chatterley's Lover*. In the decade from 1967 prosecutions were brought against the novel *Last Exit to Brooklyn*, the magazine *Oz* and the cultural/scientific history *The Mouth and Oral Sex*. Trials involving the written word came to a virtual end when the publisher of *Inside Linda Lovelace* was acquitted in 1976.

Other big changes were afoot in the early 1970s. In January 1972 the Old Bailey welcomed the first woman to sit on its bench, Rose Heilbron QC. In 1971 the new Lord Chief Justice Lord Widgery – now best known for his flawed enquiry into the Bloody Sunday killings the following year – had succeeded Parker. Widgery was no soft touch – at his first Old Bailey trial as Lord Chief Justice he sentenced a youth to five years' imprisonment for robbing the choirmaster of Westminster Cathedral at knifepoint – but almost immediately he oversaw the biggest shake-up of the criminal courts for a century, abolishing the old assize courts and renaming them as crown courts.

Like many other institutions the Old Bailey had to grapple with the complex ethical and legal questions raised by an increasingly diverse Britain. In 1972 three youths were convicted at the Old Bailey of the murder of a twenty-six-year-old man called Maxwell Confait, a mixed-race transvestite and homosexual prostitute, whose murder had not been a high priority for the police. They had their convictions quashed in 1975. A number of IRA terror convictions were later found to be equally unsafe. In 1977 six defendants, on trial for a robbery and six-day siege at the Spaghetti House restaurant in Knightsbridge, unfurled a 'Black Power' banner in the Old Bailey dock: when asked to plead one shouted, 'We have been pleading for 500 years,' while another later shouted, 'This is not a trial . . . this is a lynching party.' Heavy sentences were imposed. But the mid-1970s also saw an outcry about excessively lenient sentences: in 1975, just before he retired, Judge Christmas Humphreys gave a suspended sentence of just six months to a youth who had committed two rapes at knifepoint. Nowadays the Attorney General has the right to ask the Court of Appeal to review sentences that seem unduly lenient.

The Old Bailey's judges certainly became younger in the 1970s – James Miskin was only fifty when appointed as Recorder of London in 1975 – but not all were moving with the times. In the *Gay News* trial of 1977 (the first blasphemy trial in over fifty years) Judge King-Hamilton gave its editor Denis Lemon a fine of £500, and a suspended nine months' imprisonment, for publishing a sexually explicit poem about a Roman centurion's longings over the body of the dead Christ: it had been 'touch and go', said the judge, whether he would send Lemon to jail. In the 1982 trial of the director of the play *The Romans in Britain*, the judge tried to stop the prosecutor abandoning the case.

Steadily rising levels of violent crime and a wave of inner-city riots in the 1980s, accompanied by the punitive rhetoric of Thatcher's government, ensured that judges were under constant pressure to hand down ever more severe sentences. And if judges did not impose them, politicians were ready to step in. In 1983 the serial killer Dennis Nilsen was tried in Court Number One and given a life sentence with a twenty-five-year minimum term. Again there were calls for the return of the death penalty, and in 1994 Home Secretary Michael Howard replaced his twenty-five-year sentence with a 'whole life' tariff, meaning that Nilsen would never be released. He died in prison in 2018.

Increasingly, the complexity of the law means that trials, retrials and appeals relating to the same case – such as the 1993 murder of Stephen Lawrence – are played out over many years, or even decades. Barry George was tried twice for the murder of Jill Dando. Initially convicted in 2001, it took a number of appeals before a fresh trial, heard in the same Court Number One where he was earlier convicted, saw him acquitted. The abolition of the double jeopardy rule in 2003 allowed, in exceptional circumstances, a person originally acquitted to be tried again.

In the last two decades many of the Bailey's most prominent trials have been of public figures accused of perjury and deception. In 1999 the former Conservative minister Jonathan Aitken was jailed for eighteen months at the Bailey after admitting perjury and perverting the course of justice; similarly Jeffrey Archer, the millionaire author and aspiring Conservative candidate for Mayor of London, was sentenced to four years in 2000 when it emerged he had lied about his contact with a prostitute, Monica Coghlan, in a libel action against the *Daily Star* fourteen years earlier.

Since the turn of the millennium the Bailey has seen the prosecution of ex-MI5 officer David Shayler for offences under the Official Secrets Act, and more recently the trials of Rebekah Brooks, Andy Coulson and a number of other News International journalists on charges of phone hacking. Sometimes the impact of such trials depends not so much on the verdict at their end but the revelations made during their course: although many phone-hacking trials ended in acquittal in 2014, their impact on the reputation of the tabloid press was immense.

There was a flurry of renewed interest in the Old Bailey's architecture at the time of its centenary in 2007, and its modern extension is now seen as favourably as the majestic, if rather unfashionable, Edwardian building it adjoins. While most American courthouses and French Palais de Justice are surrounded by forecourts, gatehouses and huge flights of steps, at the Old Bailey there is no space for such pretensions: the court-house is right on the corner of the two streets, its two façades curved to follow their course. It remains a security headache. Nonetheless, alongside murder cases (now mainly gang-related), terrorist cases remain the most important work of the Bailey; except that most terror defendants are no longer inspired by Irish nationalism but by Islamist and right-wing fundamentalism. It was at the Old Bailey that both Michael Adebolajo and Michael Adebowale were convicted of the murder of Fusilier Lee Rigby and Thomas Mair of the murder of Jo Cox MP.

Today, the eighteen courts of the Bailey are in near constant use. There are thirteen permanent judges, headed until 2019 by His Honour Judge Nicholas Hilliard QC the Recorder of London and His Honour Judge Richard Marks QC the Common Serjeant, one or two High Court judges of the Queen's Bench Division and Recorders, part-time judges drawn mainly from the Criminal Bar. Thanks to McMorran and Whitby's extension, the Old Bailey has proved surprisingly adaptable to twenty-first-century demands. It now ponders human rights conventions, internet crimes and anti-terrorist legislation that would make little sense to the judges or barristers of 1907. It also often handles high-profile sex cases, such as the Oxford grooming case tried by Judge Peter Rook QC in 2013, and much has been done to make the daunting task of giving evidence in such cases easier.

The Old Bailey remains a working courthouse, not a shiny museum. The judges who sit now are a far cry from some of the martinets of the past: conscientious and hardworking, they deliver a criminal justice system which, for all the huge pressures it faces, can claim to be the best in the world in terms of fairness, transparency and efficiency. The Sword of Justice – presented to the City of London by the cutler Richard Mathew in 1563 – still hangs on the wall behind the bench in Court Number One whenever the most senior judge in the Old Bailey sits there and it looks set to hang there for some time yet.

Appendix II

The Criminal Trial

His Honour Judge Edward Bindloss

O N THE FIRST page of Franz Kafka's novel *The Trial* (1924) a bank clerk, Josef K., is unexpectedly arrested in his own bed for an unspecified crime. On the last page of the novel he is executed in a quarry by court officials. During the course of the novel K. never discovers the reason he was arrested, nor who accused him, nor what law he was alleged to have contravened. Nor does he ever learn what the evidence is against him (if there is any). He is never told on whose authority the court officials he encounters act, the identity of his judge, how the verdict has been reached and on what basis and who reached it. This is a legal world in which the charge is secret, the rules are unknown and the authority of the court is unspecified. K. is swallowed up by an unseen and incomprehensible machine of domination. By the final scene K. is broken; a willing participant in his own extinction, waiting quietly for his executioners.

The common law of England and Wales,[1] over the last few hundred years, has established an alternative method of discharging criminal justice. It is called trial by jury, once referred to as 'the lamp that shows that freedom lives'.[2] Had Josef K. been suspected of committing a crime in this jurisdiction there are a series of conditions and steps, from arrest to appeal, that could have provided him with some sanctuary from unfairness.

Arrest

The criminal process usually commences with an arrest. The arrest of a person is only lawful if there are proper grounds for it. A police constable can arrest any person the constable has reasonable grounds for suspecting is (i) *about* to commit an offence, or is (ii) *in the act of* committing an offence, or (iii) *has* committed an offence. An arrested person in this country must be told as soon as practicable that they are under arrest, and why they have been arrested, and should be taken to a police station and handed over to the custody of the custody sergeant.

Police Custody

There is one ground for police detention prior to charge: that the custody sergeant reasonably believes detention is necessary either to secure or preserve evidence relating to the offence for which the detainee is under arrest, or for the purpose of obtaining evidence by interview. All detainees must be held free of police oppression. In 1975 an eleven-year-old girl called Lesley Molseed left her home in Rochdale and was abducted and murdered. A man with learning difficulties called Stefan Kiszko was arrested and a false confession was extracted from him through oppressive questioning. Within the hour Kiszko had tried to retract the statement. At trial he denied all knowledge of the incident, repudiated the confession and called sound alibi evidence. The jury believed the false confession over the alibi evidence and convicted him. He was sent to prison for life and only released, when the miscarriage of justice was recognised by the Court of Appeal in 1992, after he had served sixteen years. He died eighteen months after his release from custody. Years later another man, Ronald Castree, was convicted.

The evil of false confessions is that those who are brought before a court are saddled with a de facto presumption of guilt rather than a presumption of innocence. The defence has to prove the falsity of the confession evidence. This poisons the whole process. The trial of Kizsko had *seemed* fair, but the hidden reversal of the burden of proof, unknown to all but the police and the defendant, led to what an MP described as the 'worst miscarriage of justice of all time'.

In 1984 Parliament passed the Police and Criminal Evidence Act. The Act significantly reduced the risk of miscarriages of justice. Among its provisions are: the welfare of the accused is the responsibility of the custody sergeant who is separate and independent of the investigating officers and ensures the detained person is treated in accordance with the Act and its codes; the detainee is entitled to free independent legal advice; a custody record must be kept (a document available at trial) and must record the times of the detainee's sleep, the food given, any medicine received, any times of police interviews etc.; the police interview is recorded and a copy made available to the defence to keep afterwards.

The recording of questions and answers in a police interview on tape or electronically (which if necessary can be played to the jury in court) protects straight police officers, deters unscrupulous ones and gives defendants who *have* confessed nowhere to hide. Prior to 1984 what were called the 'verballing' provisions were a mainstay of many criminal trials. Police officers in the witness box displayed a prodigious memory in recounting verbatim chunks of lengthy conversations they remembered from many months before. In other cases unscrupulous defendants accused straight police officers of inventing bona fide confessions. Jurors could believe the wrong side and justice was not served.

At the end of the detention period the detainee must be either released, bailed or charged.

Charge

A person can be charged if a two-stage test is satisfied. For more serious offences the decision whether to charge will be made by a prosecutor at the Crown Prosecution Service. First, prosecutors must be satisfied that there is sufficient evidence to provide a realistic prospect of conviction. Second, the prosecutor must be satisfied that a prosecution is in the public interest. People who are particularly young, old, ill or vulnerable in some other way may be better dealt with by out-of-court resolutions (cautions, restorative justice schemes etc.) or by no action being taken at all, even if there is a realistic prospect of conviction on the evidence.

Once charged with a serious offence the accused must be brought before a crown court.

Indictment

In the crown court the written charge is called the indictment. This must contain an allegation of an offence known to law. It is read out in the presence of the accused at the outset. The accused then pleads either guilty or not guilty. The cornerstone of the criminal law is that if an accused pleads not guilty in a crown court they *must* be tried by a jury.

The Judge

The judge who sits in the crown court, like those who sit in other courts, must be independent, impartial and free of bias. The key to a judge's role is fairness. The judicial oath or affirmation contains the following words: 'I will do right to all manner of people after the laws and usages of this realm, without fear or favour, affection or ill will.' Judges are servants of the public. They must exclude personal feelings and must suspend judgement until all the evidence has been heard. They must do what is just irrespective of public opinion. They must not hear a case in which they have any form of personal interest. They must receive no private representations concerning a pending case. If judges are asked to try a case in which any of these compromises occur they must recuse themselves.

Members of the Nazi High Command were tried at a court without a jury at the Nuremberg Trials in 1945. Two of the eight judges, General Nikitchenko and Lieutenant Colonel A.F. Volchkov, were from the USSR. They seemed to entertain significant differences of outlook from the judges from the United States, France and Great Britain in relation to their conception of judicial process, procedure and what constituted a fair trial. General Nikitchenko had been head of the Soviet delegation to the London conference that had set up the Nuremberg Tribunal and established its general approach and parameters. He even had a hand in preparing the charges against the accused and suggested a way of dividing the prosecution case against them so it could more conveniently be presented. Volchkov did not seem to understand legal concepts at all and it was universally assumed that he was Nikitchenko's keeper as he smacked more of the KGB than the bench. Nikitchenko seemed to regard the trial as a mere formality: its purpose, he stated, was not to determine guilt (or otherwise) but only to decide the punishment for the accused. 'The fact that the Nazi leaders are criminals has already been established. The task of the Tribunal is only to determine the measure of guilt of each particular person and to mete out the necessary punishment,' he said. Nikitchenko did not accept the proposition, which is central to the British idea of justice, that judges must be independent and impartial and have no prior involvement in a case. He asserted that 'there is . . . no necessity to create a sort of fiction that the judge is a disinterested person. If such procedure is adopted that the judge is supposed to be impartial, it would only lead to unnecessary delays.' At a party held for all the judges during the early days of the trial, and long before most of the evidence had been heard or any verdicts given, one Soviet guest raised a toast to the embarrassed assembly in the following terms: 'To the speedy conviction and execution of the defendants.' Preordained justice is not justice.

The Jury

Twelve independent citizens are chosen to sit on a jury. Jurors are selected at random by open ballot in open court and can only sit on a case once they have sworn the oath or affirmation to give a true verdict according to the evidence. Those eligible for jury service are persons aged between eighteen and seventy-five on the electoral register. Before 1919 only men could sit on a jury.[3] Just as the voting franchise was determined by property ownership in the past, so was the entitlement to sit on a jury. That meant that most jurors were male, middle class and middle-aged. That restriction was removed in 1974, with the result that the average age of jurors has fallen, numbers of women have increased, and juries have become more representative. The defence used to have the right to challenge seven jurors (that is have them de-selected from the trial about to commence for no reason). In 1989 that right was abolished.

Burden and Standard of Proof

Every person tried in a criminal court is regarded as innocent until proven guilty. The prosecution must prove guilt, whereas (except in very narrow circumstances) the defendant need not prove anything. The law is now clear that a jury can only convict if the prosecution has made them *sure*[4] of the defendant's guilt based on all the evidence. It is therefore a key feature of a fair trial that the jury must be directed correctly on the burden and standard of proof. In the notorious murder trial of Derek Bentley in 1952 Lord Goddard, Lord Chief Justice, directed the jury in the following terms in relation to the burden of proof:

> It is for the prosecution to prove their case, and it is said correctly that it is not for the prisoners to prove their innocence. In this case the prosecution have given abundant evidence for a case calling for an answer, and although the prisoners do not have to prove their innocence, when once a case is established against them they can give evidence, and they

can call witnesses, and then you have to take their evidence as part of the sum of the case. The effect of a prisoner's evidence may be to satisfy you that he is innocent, it may be it causes you to have such doubt that you feel the case is not proved, and it may, and very often does, have a third effect: it may strengthen the evidence for the prosecution.

In relation to the standard of proof the judge continued: 'And if you find good ground for convicting them, it is your duty to do it if you are satisfied with the evidence for the prosecution.' Bentley was convicted and hanged.

In 1995 the Criminal Cases Review Commission was created to investigate suspected miscarriages of justice in England and Wales. The commission has the power to remit a case back to the Court of Appeal even if it was tried many years before and even where the defendant has died. Bentley's case eventually came back before the Court of Appeal in 2001, via this method, after years of campaigning. Lord Bingham, Lord Chief Justice, giving judgement in the Court of Appeal,[5] set aside the conviction in part on the grounds of Lord Goddard's inadequate directions. The court came to the view that the directions were dangerously close to reversing the burden of proof and that the required standard that the prosecution had to reach was not sufficiently articulated.

Commentators occasionally lament the propensity of juries to acquit defendants. In 2014, written in the wake of a high-profile acquittal, a *Daily Telegraph* article posed the question: why are legal systems weighted in favour of those standing trial? The author's suggestion was to lower the standard of proof in a criminal trial to 'the balance of probabilities'. This would undoubtedly lead to the conviction of more guilty people, but it would also lead to the conviction of more innocent people.

William Blackstone's *Commentaries on the Laws of England*, published in 1766, contains the classic justification of the higher standard of proof in criminal trials: 'It is better that ten guilty persons escape than one innocent suffer.' The point is that if there is to be any slant in the system it should be on the side of acquittal, even if that means that guilty persons go unconvicted.

The Adversarial System and the Trial

Over many years the English and Welsh common law evolved an adversarial system of trial. The trial, in simple terms, commences with an opening address to the jury by prosecuting counsel who then adduces by examination-in-chief the relevant evidence from witnesses. The witness's evidence is then tested by cross-examination by defence counsel. After the prosecution calls all its evidence it is the turn of the defence (if it chooses to do so). Counsel then each make a closing speech to the jury. The judge then directs the jury as to the law and summarises the relevant evidence and the jury retires to consider its verdict.

It has been said that cross-examination is at the heart of the criminal trial. A great cross-examination can entirely change the direction of a case and turn what seemed to be impregnable evidence into a shambles.

During the Nuremberg trials the relentless cross-examination of Hermann Göring by David Maxwell Fyfe, the former Attorney General, elicited much admiration from the Russian lawyers, who had no tradition of cross-examination. Göring was articulate and evasive, but Maxwell Fyfe, deploying original documents with skill, demonstrated by cross-examination, for example, that it was impossible for Göring not to have known about the shooting of fifty airmen who had been recaptured after escaping from Stalag Luft III, nor that he was unaware of the extermination of Hungarian Jews. But apparently the French lawyers thought the technique unfair because it caught the defendant by surprise. The French system requires all questions to be put through the judge.

The Prosecution

While prosecution counsel presents the Crown's case, they are under a duty to act as a minister of justice in the fullest sense. The prosecutor must make sure that all relevant and reliable evidence that goes to the issue in the case is put before the court even if it undermines the prosecution case. If a proposed witness for the prosecution has given an inconsistent previous statement, or is of bad character, or there is material that undermines their reliability the prosecutor must disclose it to the defence so that the witness can, if necessary, be cross-examined upon it. The prosecutor must present the case against the defendant with scrupulous fairness; they must prosecute not persecute.

The accused is entitled to be present when the evidence is heard and, if necessary, have the benefit of an interpreter. No court should consider material in secret that a defendant has no sight of or cannot answer. In one case Lord Mustill said that 'a first principle of fairness is that each party to a judicial process should have an opportunity to answer by evidence and argument any adverse material which the tribunal may take into account when forming its opinion.'[6]

At the close of the prosecution evidence the judge has a duty to withdraw the case from the jury and order an acquittal if the prosecution case, taken at its highest, is insufficient for a jury to safely convict. Defence counsel will sometimes make a 'submission of no case to answer'. If there is some evidence upon which a properly directed jury could safely convict, the judge must reject that submission and let the trial continue.

The Defence

Since 1836 defendants have had a general right to legal representation. But it was only in 1898 with the passing of the Criminal Evidence Act that a defendant was given the right (not the obligation) to enter the witness box and give sworn evidence. The defendant still retained – and retains now – the right to silence. This means that they can refuse to answer questions put to them by police officers after arrest and refuse to go into the witness box to be cross-examined. This has now been tempered by the Criminal Justice and Public Order Act 1994,[7] which permits the jury to draw such inferences as are appropriate when an accused fails to testify at their trial, although the accused still retains an entitlement to silence.

Defence lawyers famously get a bad press. Jonathan Swift wrote in *Gulliver's Travels* that advocates at the Bar were 'a Society of Men among us, bred up from their Youth in the Art of proving by Words multiplied for the Purpose, that *White* is *Black* and *Black* is *White*, according as they are paid'. The most commonly asked question of a criminal barrister is: how can you defend someone you know to be guilty? They never seem to be asked: how can you prosecute someone you know to be innocent? This suggests an unhealthy presumption of guilt of all those charged. But what is the answer? If the accused admits guilt to a defence advocate the accused is told to plead guilty and if he or she refuses then the advocate must withdraw from the case rather than present a knowingly false defence. An advocate is not permitted to put forward a positive defence of someone they *know* to be guilty.

The accused is entitled to have their version of the case put before the court. It is no part of the advocate's role to judge the case (which is the exclusive province of the jury). In the words of Dr Johnson: 'you do not know the cause to be good or bad until the [court] determines it.' An advocate is not present in court to act as themselves but solely to represent the accused and put forward *their* case to the best advantage. What the lawyer thinks is irrelevant. The eminent barrister Thomas Erskine once said to a jury, 'I will now lay aside the role of the advocate and address you as a man,' whereupon the judge rightly intervened: 'You will do nothing of the sort. The only right and licence you have to appear in this court is as an advocate.'

Counsel is not entitled to refuse a brief purely because of personal distaste for the defendant, incredulity at their story, or pessimism as to their chances of an acquittal. The defence barrister Edward Marshall Hall represented a man charged with running prostitutes and when publicly criticised for having done so replied, 'Barristers are public servants and may be called on just as a doctor may be called on to operate on a man suffering with a loathsome complaint.' The cab-rank rule (like a taxi driver who collects the next passenger off the rank, a barrister cannot pick and choose clients) protects barristers from unfair criticism for taking unpopular clients.

The Legal Aid Act 1950 made the services of both solicitor and barrister available to most and was the single greatest step towards equality before the criminal courts. It was, like health, a national legal service and remains a crucial element of a fair society. It is because a defence lawyer cannot refuse a brief on the grounds that the accused is loathsome, or the charge against him is heinous, or that the lawyer suspects he may be guilty, combined with the existence of the system of payment under the legal aid scheme, that *anyone* charged with a crime in this country can obtain first-rate representation. That is a strength of the system, not a weakness.

Summing-up and Verdict

At the end of the evidence, after the advocates have given their closing speeches, the judge is required to explain the law to the jury in open court and summarise the evidence relevant to the issues it has to decide. The jury must take the law from the judge and apply it to the facts as it determines them, and so reach a verdict. The judge should not influence the jury as to the facts and the jury must not apply any law other than that the judge directs. The jury deliberates in private but delivers the verdict in open court. For over 600 years no majority verdict was allowed. It was long ago said that 'If there be eleven agreed, and but one dissenting who says he will die in prison, yet the verdict shall not be taken by eleven.' Since 1966 a majority verdict of at least ten out of the twelve has been permitted in some circumstances. This prevents a perverse juror creating injustice.

Lord Chief Justice Mansfield said in 1784, when he recognised the sovereignty of the jury, that a judge could tell a jury how to do right but that the jury had it 'in their power to do wrong, which is entirely a matter between God and their own consciences'. Chapter 10 above considers the trial of Randle and Pottle in 1991, a classic example of the stubborn determination of a jury to retain its independence. The other famous modern instance is when a jury refused to convict Clive Ponting in 1985, notwithstanding that the acts he admitted doing were criminal. This independence is a safeguard against oppressive prosecutions, politically motivated charges, unpopular laws and unruly judges. Those jurors who place conscience above the law and return what has come to be known, pejoratively, as *perverse* verdicts, may defy legal reasoning but their actions are a guarantee of freedom. These are verdicts that accord with what the *jury* thinks is fair and just.

Some judges in the past have been notorious for summing up the facts in a partial way that invited conviction while adding the weasel words, 'but of course, members of the jury, it is all a matter entirely for you.' The Court of Appeal will not permit this. In one case Lord Justice Lloyd said that 'a judge . . . is not entitled to comment in such a way as to make the summing-up as a whole unbalanced . . . It cannot be said too often or too strongly that a summing-up which is fundamentally unbalanced is not saved by the continued repetition of the phrase that it is a matter for the jury.'[8]

Sometimes Parliament responds to the behaviour of juries. In the eighteenth century jurors often refused to convict in trivial theft cases because of the death penalty; the punishment was changed. In 1922 the law of infanticide was introduced as a lesser charge than murder for women who had killed their babies because juries had stopped convicting them.

The jury gives no reasons for the verdict it returns and cannot be questioned afterwards about its deliberations. This provides the jury with an immunity that protects its independence. Since 1981 section 8 of the Contempt of Court Act 1981 prohibits jurors revealing to anyone what passed between them in the privacy of their deliberating room.

Sentence

In the absence of a plea of guilty no one can be punished unless a jury has determined guilt on the evidence to the required standard.

Sentence is a matter not for the jury but for the judge. In the past judges had considerable leeway to impose what sentence they thought fit. This led to disparities between harsh and lenient judges and public criticism. Sentence is at the discretion of the judge, but that discretion is not unfettered. The maximum (or minimum term) must be respected. Since 2003 sentencing guidelines have been published to help identify those factors that aggravate or mitigate culpability and harm and that must be considered and applied by the sentencing judge. The defendant can appeal to the Court of Appeal if it is thought that the sentence is manifestly excessive or wrong in law. The Attorney General can refer the case to the Court of Appeal if the judge's sentence is considered unduly lenient.

The responsibility for passing a correct sentence is, these days, a heavy one. There are so many guidelines and statutes and ancillary applications to consider that it is not a straightforward task. The judge must declare the sentence, and the reasons for arriving at it, and the effects of it on the defendant, so that it is simultaneously understood by the defendant, their lawyers, the Court of Appeal Criminal Division and members of the public. Twenty years ago a sentence after a three- or four-day trial would last no more than two minutes. A sentence in a case involving sexual offending now takes at least half an hour to deliver. The judge is required to explain his or her assessment of the level of culpability and level of harm, assessment of the risk the defendant poses, find the appropriate guideline for the case, calculate the effect of any plea, consider the victim's personal statement, approve or amend the draft of the terms of the sexual harm prevention order (if the conditions are met), assess whether the offender is dangerous or not (according to the statute), calculate the level of compensation (if any), order the victim surcharge, explain the effect and length of the licence period and the effect and length of the notification requirements of the sexual offenders register, and decide whether or not the case is to be regarded as of particular concern (within the meaning of the statute) and so on. It is a different world from that of the judge in Leeds who some years ago said, 'Stand up, I am going to show you as much mercy as you showed that poor woman. Fourteen years. Take him down.'

Once sentence has been passed (and the appeal process exhausted) no other person can increase the sentence.

Appeal

An accused may appeal a conviction, if unsafe, and a sentence, if manifestly excessive. The real test of a country's justice 'is not the blunders that are sometimes made but the zeal with which they are put right'.[9] No human system is infallible, and so every system of justice is fallible.

Prior to the Criminal Appeal Act 1907 there was no appeal available from any sentence or conviction made in a criminal court.[10] After 1907 the Court of Criminal Appeal (the predecessor of the current Court of Appeal Criminal Division) provided a remedy for both miscarriages of justice in the factual sense and failures of due process. But before 1964 the appeal court had no power to order a retrial and therefore setting aside a conviction meant setting the appellant free. Since 1964 the appeal court has been permitted to order retrials if a conviction was overturned because fresh evidence came to light. Since 1988 the appeal court has been permitted to order a retrial when overturning a conviction for any reason, if it was in the interests of justice. The current test for the court in conviction appeals is set out in section 2 of the Criminal Appeals Act 1995: 'The Court of Appeal shall allow an appeal against conviction if they think the conviction is unsafe, and shall dismiss such an appeal in any other case.' The prosecution has no power to appeal an acquittal.

Successful conviction appeals can occur when the original trial judge has misstated the law or misrepresented unfairly the facts in his or her summing-up, or for some significant technical irregularity such as the admission of evidence ruled by the Court of Appeal to be in fact inadmissible. The key question is would the legal error have made a difference to the result: is it an *unsafe* conviction? There is a steady flow of applications for appeals against conviction where fresh evidence is placed before the Court of Appeal. Fresh scientific evidence can be very powerful in the correct case and lead to the overturning of convictions.

It has been said that judges at first instance spend the first half of their judicial careers in fear of being overturned on appeal, and the second half convinced that appeal judges are always spectacularly in the wrong.

Coda

The great English political philosopher John Locke wrote: 'Wherever law ends, tyranny begins.'

Where criminal law holds criminals to account, trial by jury holds the state to account. The crown court process allows these twin goals to be achieved simultaneously. The governed have only an indirect voice in the making of the laws of the land, through the ballot box, but jury service allows the application of criminal laws directly by them. In what other area of public life does this occur? Jurors have been described by one noted jurist as a 'microcosm of democratic society'. Laws that are placed on the statute book in the name of the citizen are applied by the citizen in the jury retirement room. In this sense jurors serve a political function: they are lay people who administer the law as a direct act of citizen engagement. The duty jurors undertake every day in courts up and down the country is civic public virtue. In these days of computer algorithms, data analysis and quantitative assessments it seems anachronistic to oblige twelve individuals, chosen at random, and given no legal training, and required to deliberate in secret, to give a verdict without reasons. But jurors, in the case they are trying, not only apply the law but have a chance to consider the fairness and relevance of that law, the probity of the police and the prosecution and the trial process. When the jury decides, 'the conscience of the community speaks.'

To the old vexed questions in political philosophy – Who will guard the guardians? Who will police the police? Who will judge the judge? – trial by jury is a living answer. In Patrick Devlin's words: 'a jury cannot fight tyranny outside the law, but it ensures that within the law liberty cannot be crushed.' With jurors' independence may come unpredictability but also a real safeguard against oppressive behaviour. The retention of juries is a way of securing confidence in the law.[11]

In a sensational case, when the papers are in uproar and politicians are agitating for easy justice, trial by jury goes about its methodical and undemonstrative business. When the stakes are at their highest, and when they are not, what stands between the citizen and the all-powerful state is the jury system. Criminal laws are necessary because human beings are imperfect, and a justice system is operated by human beings and therefore is fallible. Thomas Grant's chapters include examples of significant failings. There are inevitable problems: with understaffed prosecutors' offices, underpaid legal aid lawyers, overworked judges, overstretched court staff, increasing caseloads, the system comes under pressure.[12] But there is not a clamour from judges or criminal lawyers to abolish trial by jury. None of these rules, customs and conventions are embedded in a written constitution. So, it is up to prosecutors, defence advocates, judges, academic lawyers and legal journalists to venture out and fight for these principles and for fairness afresh each day. It falls to us to uphold at all times the principles of justice and the rule of law.

Georg Lukács, the Hungarian literary theorist and Marxist philosopher, disliked Kafka's novels, preferring the literary style known as realism. In an essay called 'Franz Kafka or Thomas Mann', Lukács asserted Mann's superiority as an artist over Kafka because Mann wrote in realist prose whereas Kafka's work consisted of bizarre fables. After the suppression of the Hungarian uprising by the Soviet authorities in 1956 Lukács was arrested and imprisoned in a Romanian fortress, with no indication of what the charge against him was, what if any evidence there was to support the charge, under whose authority he was being held, nor when or if he would ever be released. He is said to have remarked in the fortress courtyard while taking some air, 'So, Kafka was a realist after all.'

Edward Bindloss
Newcastle Crown Court
March 2019

Acknowledgements

I have benefited from a vast amount of generosity of time and spirit from a large array of people. I wish to give each of them my heartfelt thanks: Jonathan Aitken, Anthony Arlidge QC, His Honour Judge Philip Bartle QC, His Honour Graham Boal QC, Liz Bull, John Calderan, Naomi Cooper, Dr Martin Crossley-Evans, Mark Davies Jones, Sophie Davies Jones, David Etherington QC, Francis Fitzgibbon QC, David Gottlieb, Tara Grant, Mark Heywood QC, His Honour Judge Nicholas Hilliard QC, the Recorder of London, Jonathan Hough QC, Charles Howard QC, David Jeffreys QC, Sir Ivan Lawrence QC, John le Carré, John Mathew QC, Tim Moloney QC, Sir Alan Moses, Juliet Nicolson, Her Honour Judge Angela Rafferty QC, Michael and Anne Randle, Freddy Reynold QC, Geoffrey Robertson QC, His Honour Peter Rook QC, Susanna Thompson, Hugh Tomlinson QC and Alex Winter.

I wish to single out in particular my friends His Honour Judge Edward Bindloss and Peter Zombory-Moldovan for their very helpful suggestions and close reading of the book; and to Judge Bindloss for writing Appendix II.

I also thank my agent Caroline Dawnay, Martin Millard for his wonderful pictures and Douglas Matthews for another super index.

Roland Philipps launched this project before deciding to become a successful writer. Joe Zigmond and Caroline Westmore have seen it through with enthusiasm and charm. Juliet Brightmore found an array of superb photographs and images, and Sara Marafini designed two wonderful covers – I thank them both.

My wife Hester has been steadfast in her support and tolerance.

Finally, and most heartily of all, I thank my brother Alex, whose knowledge and understanding of the social and political history of the twentieth century is unrivalled by anyone I have ever met, and who has been a constant support and inspiration.

Illustration Credits

Alamy: 4 below/The Picture Art Collection, 9 above right/Atomic and below right/Mirrorpix, 12 centre/Andrew Hasson, 13 above/Mirrorpix, 15 above right/Keystone. Associated Newspapers/REX/Shutterstock: 5 below right, 14 below/Leopald Joseph, 15 above left/James Gray. Associated Newspapers/Shutterstock: 16 above left/Charles Davis. Nicolas Clerihew Bentley, *Sir Patrick Hastings* 1948 © reserved, collection National Portrait Gallery, London: 7 below right. © Jane Bown/Observer/eyevine: 15 below. Priscilla Coleman/MB Media: 16 below. *'Curtis': The Life of Sir Henry Curtis-Bennett KC* by Roland Wild and Derek Curtis-Bennett (Cassell, 1937): 6 above left. Mary Evans Picture Library: 5 above right. Getty Images: 1/Oli Scarff, 2, 3 above, 7 above left, centre right and below left, 8 above, 9 below left, 10 above right, 11 above left and below/ Terry Fincher, 12 above right and below, 14 above/Dennis Oulds. Granger/Shutterstock: 6 below left. © Illustrated London News Ltd/ Mary Evans Picture Library: 3 below. ITN/Getty Images: 16 centre. Mirrorpix: 4 centre right, 6 below right, 13 below. PA Images: 10 below. TopFoto: 4 above left, 6 above right, 8 below, 10 above left, 11 above right.

Illustration of Court Number One reproduced courtesy of His Honour Judge Nicholas Hilliard QC, the former Recorder of London, and the City of London Corporation.

Illustrations by Martin Millard

Part I: The original main entrance to the Old Bailey, now used only for ceremonial occasions.

Part II: The doorway on Newgate Street to the public galleries of Courts One to Four.

Part III: The main door into Court Number One from the Grand Hall.

Part IV: The dock of Court Number One.

Part V: The bench of Court Number One. The judge sits to the left.
Part VI: The witness box of Court Number One. The jury box is just
   visible to the left.

Martin Millard is a professional artist who was born in London. He studied
Fine Art at the School of Visual Arts in New York, where he lived for
five years, after which he returned to London to read for the Bar. He is
a member of Middle Temple and practised at the Bar for several years
before deciding to return to painting full time.

Notes

Court Number One, The Old Bailey

1. The Sword of Justice is placed in whichever court the senior judge happens to be sitting. That used almost always to be Court Number One; sadly no longer. See generally Appendix I.
2. When I use the words English and England I am intending to encompass Welsh and Wales. England and Wales have a common legal system. The Northern Irish and the Scottish have separate courts which apply somewhat different rules of procedure. The Scottish have a different law.
3. In 1969 the Hosein brothers kidnapped the wife of Alick McKay, Rupert Murdoch's deputy chairman at News International, mistaking her for Murdoch's own wife. After making ransom demands they killed her, though her body was never found. They were convicted of murder in October 1970.
4. Clarence Hatry was an infamous fraudster who was sentenced in Court Number One in 1929 to fourteen years' imprisonment. The collapse of his companies is said to have partly caused the Wall Street Crash.
5. Horatio Bottomley, Member of Parliament, demagogue, swindler, newspaper proprietor and serial litigant, eventually sentenced to seven years' imprisonment in 1922 for promoting a fraudulent investment scheme.
6. See Duncan Campbell's interesting article in the *New Statesman* on the decline of court reporting: https://www.newstatesman.com/lifestyle/2013/11/decline-british-trial.

Chapter 1: The Camden Town Murder

1. So recent was the Bailey's rebuilding that it is called 'the New Bailey' in several press reports of the Camden Town murder trial.
2. A more measured, but fascinating, account is *Marshall Hall: A Law unto Himself* by Sally Smith QC. This is required reading for anyone with an interest in the man or his period.
3. See Appendix I below.

4. Literally 'the thing speaks for itself'; an evidential principle whereby the very circumstances of the event causing damage can be presumed to have occurred as a result of a legal wrong.

5. As he is described by Smith, op. cit.

6. Marshall Hall was under no illusions about at least some of his clients, however. He once secured the acquittal of a Nonconformist minister on a 'terrible charge of immorality'. When the minister offered to shake his hand afterwards Marshall Hall refused to touch it with the words, 'No, that is not included in the etiquette of the Bar, or in the brief-fee.'

7. Camden Town railway station has since been renamed Camden Road to distinguish it from the Tube station of the same name.

8. Many press reports claimed that Ruby gave Wood a 'Judas kiss' just before Neil apprehended him, but Neil denied it.

9. In those days pubs stayed open very late: licensing hours weren't restricted until the First World War.

10. A driver of a van or cart.

11. In 1907 coroner's juries had the power to identify the person they thought responsible for someone's death, a power they no longer have.

12. The law was changed by section 41 of the Criminal Justice Act 1925, by which taking a photograph or drawing any form of sketch in court was criminalised.

13. The statue is actually by the sculptor F.W. Pomeroy, not George Frampton.

14. Recent research by David Barrat has established that Crabtree's criminal career was even longer, and more colourful, than Marshall Hall knew: see David Barrat, *The Camden Town Murder Mystery*, pp. 60–75 and 309–14. Barrat's meticulously researched book is the most detailed account of the case.

15. Wellesley Orr. A devil was a young barrister who, in his early years of practice, would act as a form of assistant to more senior counsel in his chambers. He would be paid by counsel.

16. This convention was only changed in 1964 to give the final word to the defence in all cases.

17. In fact Grantham often acted contrary to type. In the 1911 trial of the Latvian revolutionaries charged with murder after the Sidney Street Siege, which also took place in Court Number One, Grantham withdrew most of the charges from the jury because of insufficiency of evidence.

18. Of course the figure of Justice that rises above the Old Bailey wears no blindfold: see Appendix I.

19. I should say 'transcripts'. The transcript of the evidence that was published contemporaneously in the *Proceedings of the Old Bailey* (now digitised at www.oldbaileyonline.org) shows that the version in the Notable British Trials volume is highly selective and misses out vital parts of the evidence. *The Times* also produced an extremely detailed account of each day of the trial. The case can only be understood by reference to all three sources.

Chapter 2: 'The Cult of the Clitoris'

1. Douglas's own memoir of Wilde, *Oscar Wilde and Myself* (ghost-written by Crosland) had its publication delayed by an injunction from Ross, until 4 August 1914 – the day the war began.

2. The aircraft company he founded, Pemberton-Billing Ltd, was (under different ownership) renamed Supermarine Aviation Works Ltd and built the seaplanes that dominated the Schneider Trophy in the 1920s. Acquired by Vickers in 1928, the company went on to design the Spitfire.

3. The diplomat Duff Cooper wrote to his sweetheart Lady Diana Manners that his main amusements on the western front in June 1918 were censoring his men's letters and following the 'notorious Pemberton Billing trial' at home. Cooper found the trial a 'source of never-flagging amusement' precisely because the supposed 47,000 included many of his friends – indeed, he was disappointed not to feature on it himself: see John Charmley, *Duff Cooper*, pp. 22–3.

4. The actual Lord Chief Justice, Lord Reading, had been appointed to be the British ambassador in Washington earlier in the year.

5. For Douglas's role in the case see further Douglas Murray, *Bosie*, pp. 217–24.

6. The phrase used by Robbie Ross in a letter to Charles Ricketts at the time of the trial. Quoted in Margery Ross, *Robert Ross*, pp. 333–4. Ross died of a heart attack on 5 October 1918, aged forty-nine; some say his demise was hastened by the outcome of the Allan trial.

Chapter 3: Unnatural Practices

1. For a full account of Marguerite's early life see Andrew Rose's classic study, *The Prince, the Princess and the Perfect Murder*, which provides the most detailed account of the case.

2. Marshall Hall's clerk A.E. Bowker records that he was suffering from severe phlebitis – inflammation of the veins – during the trial: see Bowker, *Behind the Bar*, p. 115.

3. These Norman French words, meaning 'hear' and 'determine', denoted a judge's authority to try cases in courts of assize, which were replaced in 1972 by crown courts.

4. The Sex Disqualification (Removal) Act 1919. However there was an important caveat by section 1(b) which allowed the judge a discretion to exclude women from the jury 'in respect of any case by reason of the nature of the evidence to be given or of the issues to be tried'.

5. The *Manchester Guardian* omitted these last words from its report.

6. Many years later the law would be extended so that imputations against the character of the deceased victim of the alleged crime also exposed the defendant to bad character cross-examination.

7. It was described in 1939 as having 'long since passed into legal tradition as one of the greatest forensic orations of modern times': E.S. Fay, *The Life of Mr Justice Swift*, p. 122.

8. Bowker, Marshall Hall's clerk, recalled a conversation immediately after the trial: '"You certainly made an impression dropping that pistol," I said. "It's one of the best things you've done." He loved a compliment. "Yes – it was a bit dramatic," he agreed, "but in fact the actual dropping was an accident. It slipped from my hands."' See Bowker, op. cit., p. 115.

9. Sir Edward Clarke had defended Adelaide Bartlett on a charge of murder by poisoning in 1886. She was acquitted.

Chapter 4: Poor Little Rich Girl

1. See Chapter 2 above.
2. It was subsequently destroyed in a German air raid in 1944.
3. The play, *Scotch Mist*, was a huge success, despite poor reviews, apparently 'due to the belief that Tallulah Bankhead had only escaped being raped by Godfrey Tearle [who played the male lead] in full view of the audience by the fortunate intervention of the curtain at the end of the second act'.
4. See Chapter 3.
5. See Chapter 3.

Chapter 5: Haw-Haw

1. On Udham Singh, see Anita Anand, *The Patient Assassin: A True Tale of Massacre, Revenge and the Raj* (Simon & Schuster, 2019).
2. The new breed of callous criminal gangs was memorably depicted in Graham Greene's 1938 novel *Brighton Rock*, which was inspired by a gang fight at Lewes racecourse in 1936.
3. A practice that has long since ceased.
4. For a detailed account of his life and his interactions with Joyce, see Henry Hemming, *M*.
5. The ill-feeling was mutual: Mosley would later describe Joyce as 'that horrid little man', and 'intensely vain: a common foible in very small men'.
6. Haw-Haw was often associated with Hamburg as that is where the signals that carried his broadcasts were often transmitted from, although he only ever broadcast from the city at the very end of the war.
7. They were referring to conditions at the recently liberated Belsen concentration camp, where inmates had had to drink water similarly infected.
8. Quisling faced justice even faster than Joyce: he was executed by firing squad on 24 October 1945.

9. Until Ireland's departure from the Commonwealth in 1949 anyone born in Ireland, even after the declaration of the Irish Free State in 1922, was automatically a British subject.

10. Until the passing of the Treason Act 1945 – which effectively brought the procedure for the prosecution of treason trials in line with modern criminal trials – three judges had had to sit on treason cases and the punishment was technically hanging, drawing and quartering, not just hanging.

11. Oddly, leave to appeal to the Lords was granted by Shawcross: as Attorney General he had the power both to prosecute and to decide if appeals should proceed.

Chapter 6: 'Christie done it'

1. Despite its grand name, the 'KPH' was, and still is, an ordinary pub on Ladbroke Grove, then frequented by the local Irish community. In his memoirs Alan Johnson recalls that the KPH was nicknamed 'Keep Paddy Happy' and was notorious for fights.

2. Christie may have resigned after being beaten up by another officer, with whose wife Christie had an affair and who later cited Christie as co-respondent in his divorce.

3. As explained below, at the time the practice was to charge a defendant with only one murder, even if suspected of more than one.

4. A modern criminal judge described the timetable to trial as 'staggering'.

5. Directed by the American Richard Fleischer in 1971, the film also starred Geoffrey Chater as Humphreys and Robert Hardy as Morris; the hangman Albert Pierrepoint was an uncredited technical adviser.

6. According to Kennedy, Lewis was more caustic than the transcript suggests, telling Evans, 'I wish you would listen to the questions you are asked,' like a schoolmaster to a child.

7. The law has now been amended such that in certain circumstances a defendant can be prosecuted twice: see sections 75–80 of the Criminal Justice Act 2003.

8. Mr Justice Travers Humphreys, father of Christmas, was a member of the court. He did not think it necessary to recuse himself from a case prosecuted by his own son.

9. In November 1949 – the start of an unusually harsh winter – no smells were detected from the bodies of Beryl and Geraldine as they lay for three weeks in the unheated outside washhouse; the cold weather refrigerated them. The spring of 1953 was considerably milder.

10. Christie claimed that he had killed many of his victims in self-defence, sometimes while fending off their unwanted sexual advances, or that they had died accidentally; he claimed that the strangling of Ethel in December

1952 was a mercy killing after she had woken up choking, having overdosed on sleeping pills. In fact, in most cases Christie seems to have met his victims in pubs or cafés and offered to 'treat' their ailments with medicinal 'vapours' from a bizarre gas mask contraption; they were then rendered unconscious after Christie removed a bulldog clip from a piece of rubber tubing running from the mask to the gas mains. They were then strangled as Christie raped them, or attempted to do so.

11. Brennan's report, which was produced in his capacity as independent assessor for miscarriages of justice compensation, has never been published. A FOI request was refused. It is referred to in the Divisional Court decision in *Westlake v Criminal Cases Review Commission* [2004] EWHC 2779 (Admin), in which it was decided that because Evans had been pardoned, it was inappropriate to remit the case back to the Court of Appeal to consider whether the conviction should be quashed.

Chapter 7: 'It is obvious that when I shot him I intended to kill him'

1. In his own account of his trial, *The Verdict of You All*, Croft-Cooke described Roberts's performance as 'a very powerful speech, charged with sincere indignation at what I had undergone already at the hands of the police and at the prosecution's methods in general. He spoke, I thought, so brilliantly, he thundered in righteous ire . . . wholly in earnest . . . a passionate honest speech.'

2. An anonymous piece in the *Spectator* of 22 October 1954 lamented: 'In some quarters indeed there is a feeling almost of panic. If this feeling were confined to the handful of disreputable fly-by-nights there would be no occasion for anything but approval. But it is not. It is the directors of old-established firms of unimpeachable reputation who are anxiously thumbing through the manuscripts of established writers in the fear that some delineation of lust (described perhaps, only to illustrate its evil consequences), some unguarded reference to the facts of life, some touches of Rabelaisian humour, will involve a prosecution.'

3. The spelling and syntax have been regularised.

4. They are so named after Daniel M'Naghten, who had been prosecuted for the murder of the Prime Minister's secretary, whom he believed to be Peel himself.

5. 'Every man is to be presumed to be sane, and . . . to establish a defence on the ground of insanity, it must be clearly proved that, at the time of the committing of the act, the party accused was labouring under such a defect of reason, from disease of the mind, as not to know the nature and quality of the act he was doing; or if he did know it, that he did not know he was doing what was wrong.'

6. In the decade 1940–9 more than 50 per cent of those not acquitted of murder were found by juries to be either 'insane on arraignment' (i.e. unfit to plead at all) or 'guilty but insane', in the old, illogical, phrasing.

7. The first statement she gave at Hampstead Police Station on the night of Easter Sunday.

8. Jung was very fashionable in Britain at the time, appearing as an interviewee on John Freeman's *Face to Face* in 1959.

9. Often referred to as Major Lloyd George – the army rank he had attained during the First World War – the Home Secretary was a cricket enthusiast who had controversially accompanied his father to visit Hitler at Berchtesgaden in 1936; in 1957 Harold Macmillan forced him to retire to 'make way for younger men'. Later ennobled as Lord Tenby, he explained that a significant factor behind his decision not to reprieve Ellis was the injury inflicted on Mrs Yule, the bystander. 'We cannot have people shooting off firearms in the street! This was a public thoroughfare where Ruth Ellis stalked and shot her quarry . . . As Home Secretary I was determined to ensure that people could use the streets without fear of a bullet.'

10. Gilbert and Grant were hanged by Albert Pierrepoint side by side in Pentonville on 17 June 1954: the last double hanging ever in Britain.

11. In particular section 3 of the 1957 Act: (i) made it clear that 'things said' alone may be sufficient provocation, if the jury should be of the opinion that they would have provoked a reasonable (wo)man; (ii) took away the power of the judge to withdraw the defence from the jury, as Mr Justice Havers had done, on the ground that there was no evidence on which the jury could find that a reasonable (wo)man would have been provoked to do as the defendant did; (iii) took away the power of the judge to dictate to the jury what were the characteristics of the reasonable (wo)man.

Chapter 8: 'Equipment for a spy'

1. The author's father, who was born in 1938 and at the time lived in Abingdon, close to Fuchs, recalls carol-singing at Fuchs's door in the Christmas of 1949 and being testily sent on his way by a man who appeared troubled and who certainly was not charmed by boyish renditions of 'Oh Come All Ye Faithful'. At almost exactly the same time Fuchs was having regular meetings with Jim Skardon, MI5's chief interrogator.

2. See Chapter 6.

3. For its efficacy the code requires the deployment of a one-time randomly created key pre-shared as between sender and recipient.

4. This evidence later inspired a Giles cartoon in the *Daily Express*. Grandma drives the wrong way down a one-way street. She is stopped by a policeman.

As she remonstrates with him he retorts: 'No, Lady, I don't know how you're to know I'm not a spy – you'll just have to take my word for it.'

5.   At this time there was a committal stage at which the prosecution would adduce evidence to show that the case should be committed to the crown court. See Appendix II.

Chapter 9: 'Trial of the Century'

1.   Dominic Carman, *No Ordinary Man* (Hodder & Stoughton, 2002).
2.   An excellent example of his oratory towards the end of his political career is the 1975 Oxford Union debate on the EC referendum in which he spoke with Edward Heath against Barbara Castle and Peter Shore. It can be seen in full on YouTube.
3.   The DPP at the time was Sir Theobald Mathew, whose son John Mathew QC represented David Holmes at the Old Bailey fifteen years later.
4.   The *Private Eye* journalist Auberon Waugh – who loathed Thorpe – stood as a Dog Lovers' Party candidate in North Devon in 1979 (Lord Denning, who had once been engaged to Thorpe's aunt, granted an injunction stopping Waugh from distributing a scurrilous election address, which called Thorpe's candidacy 'disgusting' and proclaimed: 'Rinka is NOT forgotten').
5.   Fifteen years earlier Ludovic Kennedy had been irritated that, sitting at the back of the court behind the dock, he had found it very difficult to follow the Stephen Ward trial: see *The Trial of Stephen Ward* (Gollancz, 1964), p. 17.

Chapter 10: 'No apologies and no regrets'

1.   The lines were from 'To Althea, from Prison' by Richard Lovelace, a seventeenth-century cavalier and metaphysical poet.
2.   In total Blake is estimated to have handed over 5,000 pages of secret documents over eight years. 'I don't know what I handed over,' he admitted to the journalist Tom Bower in 1990, 'because it was so much.'
3.   Dubbed 'Bullying-Manner' by *Private Eye*, Manningham-Buller was later made Lord Dilhorne ('Lord Stillborn' in the *Eye*) and served as Lord Chancellor 1962–4.
4.   For a full account of the attempted blockade, and the Wethersfield Six's trial, see Thomas Grant, *Jeremy Hutchinson's Case Histories*, pp. 237–65.
5.   Identified as 'Will and Mary' in Pottle and Randle, *The Blake Escape*; their true identity was only revealed later.
6.   Reluctantly Harrap agreed, knowing that the police could get a search warrant, but only sent them a copy on the very eve of publication, Thursday, 27 April.

7. Scrivener was a leading criminal silk whose diverse range of defence clients included Tony Martin, a farmer convicted of shooting a burglar; Jack Lyons in the Guinness case; the paratrooper Lee Clegg, sentenced to life imprisonment for his part in the shooting of two joyriders in Belfast; former Westminster Council leader Dame Shirley Porter; Gerry Conlon of the Guildford Four; and Winston Silcott, convicted of murdering PC Keith Blakelock in 1985, at his successful appeal.

8. Bevan, then a Senior Treasury Counsel, also often acted for the defence, representing Lester Piggott at his tax evasion trial, and Mohamed Al Fayed in the Harrods deposit box case. Before retiring he led the prosecution at the courts martial of several British soldiers accused of abusing Iraqi prisoners.

9. Belying his conservative reputation, in 1997 Macpherson was appointed head of the enquiry into the racist murder of Stephen Lawrence in 1993. The enquiry's report, which made over seventy recommendations about institutional racism in the criminal justice system, was widely acclaimed.

10. This was a famous Victorian case which established the principle that necessity is not a defence to a murder charge. Shipwrecked with two others, one of them a cabin boy called Richard Parker who had fallen into a coma, Dudley and Stephens decided to kill Parker and cannibalise him. They were later convicted and sentenced to death, but the jury's recommendation of clemency meant their sentence was commuted to just six months in prison.

11. A few days later, with the jury again out, Alliott read out his reasons: for a defence of necessity to be valid 'the threat of death or serious injury [to Blake] must be reasonably imminent which is not so in the present case. In any event, the defendants cannot be said, from an objective standpoint, to have been acting reasonably and proportionately in assisting the escape of a prisoner lawfully convicted on his own confession and lawfully sentenced.'

12. Kavan, a deputy in the Czech parliament, had run into controversy in the run-up to the trial, being named as one of ten deputies who had allegedly collaborated with the StB, the former communist regime's secret police, by unwittingly passing information to a Czech diplomat when he was a member of the Czechoslovak Students Union in London in 1969–70. Kavan said the charge was absurd but later lost his seat in the Czech elections of 1992. See the *Guardian*, 23 March 1991.

13. Pottle was shrewd to liken the escape to an Ealing comedy rather than a spy thriller. Although Blake's escape did partly inspire *The Mackintosh Man*, a serious 1973 film directed by John Huston, its most famous retelling is indeed a farce: Simon Gray's 1995 play *Cell Mates*. *Cell Mates* is today best remembered for its off-stage dramatics: Stephen Fry, playing George Blake, had a nervous collapse and walked out of the production three days after its West End opening in February 1995.

14. Randle's reference to keeping a lamp 'burnished and shining' was a reference to Lord Devlin's famous description of trial by jury as 'the lamp that shows that freedom lives'.

Chapter 11: 'There is no greater task for the criminal justice system than to protect the vulnerable'

1. After two unsuccessful appeals, George's third appeal led to his conviction being quashed and a retrial, again in Court Number One, at which he was acquitted in August 2008.
2. First granted to Mary Bell (who as an eleven-year-old strangled to death two young boys in Newcastle in 1968) in 2003 – the judgement is reported under neutral citation [2003] EWHC 1101 (QB). A 'Mary Bell' order makes it a contempt of court to disclose the new identity given to the subject of the order, almost inevitably a former defendant in criminal proceedings.
3. Since 1996 a defence statement has been effectively mandatory, requiring the defendant to state his defence.

Appendix II: The Criminal Trial

1. There are different systems in Scotland and Northern Ireland. This essay is limited to considering the crown courts of England and Wales. Many cases, of a less serious kind, are tried in magistrates courts without a jury.
2. Patrick Devlin, *Trial by Jury*, Chapter 6.
3. See The Sex Disqualification (Removal) Act 1919.
4. The phrase 'beyond all reasonable doubt' is no longer used.
5. *R v Derek Bentley* (deceased) [2001] 1 Cr.App.R. 21.
6. *In Re D* (Minors) (Adoption Reports: Confidentiality) [1990] AC 593, 603.
7. Sections 34 to 37.
8. *R v Gilbey* (26 January 1990, unreported).
9. Cyril Connolly, *The Times*, 15 January 1961.
10. Unless, in a capital case, the Home Secretary exercised the power of reprieve.
11. In a MORI poll in 2002, 85 per cent of those surveyed said that they trusted juries to come to the right decision.
12. The Secret Barrister in *The Law and How It's Broken: Stories of Crime and Punishment* (Picador, 2018) expresses the view that the criminal justice system is currently on its knees.

Select Bibliography

General

Ackroyd, Peter, *London: The Biography* (Vintage, 2001)

Aitken, Jonathan, *Officially Secret* (Weidenfeld & Nicolson, 1971)

——, *Porridge and Passion* (Continuum, 2006)

Bedford, Sybille, *The Best We Can Do: An Account of the Trial of John Bodkin Adams* (Collins, 1958)

——, *The Trial of Lady Chatterley's Lover* (Daunt Books, 2016)

Crew, Albert, *The Old Bailey: History, Constitution, Functions, Notable Trials* (Ivor Nicholson & Watson, 1933)

Devlin, Patrick, *Trial by Jury* (Stevens & Sons, 1956)

——, *The Judge* (Oxford University Press, 1979)

Du Cann, Richard, QC, *The Art of the Advocate* (Penguin, 1993)

Furneaux, Rupert, *Guenther Podola* (Stevens & Sons, 1960)

Grant, Thomas, *Jeremy Hutchinson's Case Histories* (John Murray, 2015)

Hetherington, Sir Thomas, *Prosecution and the Public Interest* (Waterlow, 1989)

Hooper, W. Eden, *The History of Newgate and the Old Bailey: And a Survey of the Fleet and Other Old London Jails* (Underwood Press, 1935)

Jackson, Stanley, *The Old Bailey* (W.H. Allen, 1978)

Kafka, Franz, *The Trial* (trans. Willa and Edwin Muir) (Vintage Classics, 2001)

Lustgarten, Edgar, *Defender's Triumph* (Pan, 1957)

Murphy, Theresa, *The Old Bailey: Eight Centuries of Crime, Cruelty and Corruption* (Mainstream, 1999)

O'Connor, Sean, *Handsome Brute: The True Story of a Ladykiller* (Simon & Schuster, 2013)

Playfair, Giles, *Six Studies in Hypocrisy* (Secker & Warburg, 1969)

Porter, Roy, *London: A Social History* (Hamish Hamilton, 1994)

Robertson, Geoffrey, *The Justice Game: Tales from the Bar* (Chatto & Windus, 1998)

——, *Rather His Own Man: In Court with Tyrants, Tarts and Troublemakers* (Biteback, 2018)

Rolph, C.H., *The Trial of Lady Chatterley* (Penguin, 1961)

——, *Living Twice: An Autobiography* (Gollancz, 1974)

Williams, Glanville, *The Proof of Guilt: A Study of the English Criminal Trial* (Stevens & Sons, 1958)

Chapter 1: The Camden Town Murder

Barber, John, *The Camden Town Murder: The Life and Death of Emily Dimmock* (Mandrake of Oxford, 2007)

Barrat, David, *The Camden Town Murder Mystery* (Orsam Books, 2014)

Hamilton, Patrick, *Twenty Thousand Streets Under the Sky* (Constable, 1935)

Hicks, Seymour, *Not Guilty, M'Lord* (Cassell, 1939)

Hogarth, Basil (ed.), *The Trial of Robert Wood: The Camden Town Case* (William Hodge, 1936)

Marjoribanks, Edward, *The Life of Sir Edward Marshall Hall* (Victor Gollancz, 1929)

Napley, Sir David, *The Camden Town Murder* (Weidenfeld & Nicolson, 1987)

Neil, Arthur, *Forty Years of Man-Hunting* (Jarrolds, 1932)

Smith, Sally, *Marshall Hall: A Law unto Himself* (Wildy, Simmonds & Hill, 2016)

Young, Filson (ed.), *Trial of The Seddons* (William Hodge, 1912)

Chapter 2: 'The Cult of the Clitoris'

Charmley, John, *Duff Cooper: The Authorized Biography* (Weidenfeld & Nicolson, 1986)

Cherniavsky, Felix, 'Maud Allan, Part V: The Years of Decline, 1915–1956', *Dance Chronicle*, vol. 9, no. 2, 1986

Graham, Evelyn, *Lord Darling and His Famous Trials: An Authentic Biography* (Hutchinson, 1929)

Hoare, Philip, *Wilde's Last Stand: Scandal, Decadence and Conspiracy During the Great War* (Duckworth, 1997)

Hume-Williams, Ellis, *The World, the House and the Bar* (John Murray, 1930)

Humphreys, Travers, *Criminal Days* (Hodder & Stoughton, 1946)

——, *Book of Trials* (Pan, 1956)

Jenkins, Roy, *Asquith* (Collins, 1964)

Kettle, Michael, *Salome's Last Veil: The Libel Case of the Century* (Granada, 1977)

Murray, Douglas, *Bosie: A Biography of Lord Alfred Douglas* (Hodder & Stoughton, 2000)

Rowbotham, Sheila, *Friends of Alice Wheeldon* (Pluto Press, 2015)

Smith, Derek Walter, *The Life of Charles Darling* (Cassell, 1938)

Stoney, Barbara, *Twentieth-Century Maverick: The Life of Noel Pemberton Billing* (Bank House Books, 2004)

Chapter 3: Unnatural Practices

Bland, Lucy, *Modern Women on Trial: Sexual Transgression in the Age of the Flapper* (Manchester University Press, 2013)

Bowker, A.E., *Behind the Bar* (Staples Press, 1951)

Broad, Lewis, *The Innocence of Edith Thompson: A Study in Old Bailey Justice* (Hutchinson, 1952)

Fay, E.S., *The Life of Mr Justice Swift* (Methuen, 1939)

Hastings, MacDonald, *The Other Mr Churchill: A Lifetime of Shooting and Murder* (Harrap, 1963)

Hichens, Robert, *Bella Donna* (Heinemann, 1909)

Marjoribanks, Edward, *The Life of Sir Edward Marshall Hall* (Victor Gollancz, 1929)

Rose, Andrew, *Scandal at the Savoy: The Infamous 1920s Murder Case* (Bloomsbury, 1991)

——, *The Prince, the Princess and the Perfect Murder* (Coronet, 2013)

Thompson, Laura, *Rex v Edith Thompson: A Tale of Two Murders* (Head of Zeus, 2018)

Weis, René, *Criminal Justice: The True Story of Edith Thompson* (Hamish Hamilton, 1988)

Wild, Roland, and Curtis-Bennett, Derek, *'Curtis': The Life of Sir Henry Curtis-Bennett KC* (Cassell, 1937)

Young, Filson (ed.), *Trial of Frederick Bywaters and Edith Thompson* (William Hodge, 1923)

Chapter 4: Poor Little Rich Girl

Cotes, Peter, *The Trial of Elvira Barney* (David & Charles, 1976)

Hastings, Patricia, *The Life of Patrick Hastings* (Cresset Press, 1959)

Hastings, Sir Patrick, *Cases in Court* (Heinemann, 1950)

Hyde, H. Montgomery, *Sir Patrick Hastings: His Life and Cases* (Heinemann, 1960)

Lustgarten, Edgar, *Defender's Triumph* (Pan, 1957)

Montgomery, John, *The Twenties: An Informal Social History* (Allen & Unwin, 1957)

Rolph, C.H., *Living Twice: An Autobiography* (Victor Gollancz, 1974)

Taylor, D.J., *Bright Young People: The Rise and Fall of a Generation* (Chatto & Windus, 2007)

Waugh, Alec, *A Year to Remember: A Reminiscence of 1931* (W.H. Allen, 1975)

Chapter 5: Haw-Haw

Bechhofer Roberts, C.E. (ed.), *The Trial of Jones and Hulten* (Old Bailey Trial Series) (Jarrolds, 1945)

Casswell, J.D., QC, *A Lance for Liberty* (Harrap, 1961)

Farndale, Nigel, *Haw-Haw: The Tragedy of William and Margaret Joyce* (Macmillan, 2005)

Hall, J.W. (ed.), *The Trial of William Joyce* (Notable British Trial Series), (William Hodge, 1946)

Hemming, Henry, *M: Maxwell Knight, MI5's Greatest Spymaster* (Preface, 2017)

Joyce, William, *Twilight Over England* (Blurb, 2017)

Kenny, Mary, *Germany Calling: A Personal Biography of William Joyce, Lord Haw-Haw* (New Island, 2003)

Mosley, Oswald, *My Life* (Arlington House, 1968)

Orwell, George, 'Decline of the English Murder', *Collected Essays, Journalism and Letters of George Orwell*, vol. 4 (Secker & Warburg, 1968)

Raymond, R. Alwyn, *The Cleft Chin Murder* (Condor, 1946)

Report of the Royal Commission on Capital Punishment 1949–1953, Cmd.8932 (National Archives, 1953)

Shawcross, Hartley, *Life Sentence: The Memoirs of Hartley Shawcross* (Constable, 1995)

Taylor, A.J.P., *Beaverbrook* (Hamish Hamilton, 1972)

Thomas, Donald, *An Underworld at War: Spivs, Deserters, Racketeers and Civilians in the Second World War* (John Murray, 2003)

West, Rebecca, *The New Meaning of Treason* (Viking, 1964)

Chapter 6: 'Christie done it'

Altrincham, Lord, and Gilmour, Ian, *The Case of Timothy Evans: An Appeal to Reason* (*Spectator*, 1956)

Baker, Rob, *Beautiful Idiots and Brilliant Lunatics: A Sideways Look at Twentieth-Century London* (Amberley, 2015)

Eddowes, John, *The Two Killers of Rillington Place* (Little, Brown, 1994)

Eddowes, Michael, *The Man on Your Conscience: An Investigation of the Evans Murder Trial* (Cassell, 1955)

Furneaux, Rupert, *The Two Stranglers of Rillington Place* (Panther Books, 1961)

Johnson, Alan, *This Boy: A Memoir of Childhood* (Bantam Press, 2013)

Kennedy, Ludovic, *Ten Rillington Place* (Victor Gollancz, 1961)

Knowles, Julian B., *The Abolition of the Death Penalty in the United Kingdom: How it Happened and Why it Still Matters* (The Death Penalty Project, 2015, https://www.deathpenaltyproject.org/wp-content/uploads/2017/12/DPP-50-Years-on-pp1-68-1.pdf)

Paget, Reginald, and Silverman, Sydney, *Hanged – and Innocent?* (Victor Gollancz, 1953)

Rillington Place, 1949: A Report of an Inquiry by the Hon. Mr Justice Brabin into the Case of Timothy John Evans (Uncovered Editions, 1999)

Tennyson Jesse, F. (ed.), *Trials of Timothy John Evans and John Reginald Halliday Christie* (William Hodge, 1957)

West, Rebecca, 'Mr Setty and Mr Hume', in *A Train of Powder* (Virago, 1984)

Williams, John, *Hume: Portrait of a Double Murderer* (Heinemann, 1960)

Chapter 7: 'It is obvious that when I shot him I intended to kill him'

Blake, Victoria, *Ruth Ellis* (National Archives, 2008)

Bresler, Fenton, *Reprieve: A Study of a System* (Harrap, 1965)

Brown, Craig, *Ma'am Darling: 99 Glimpses of Princess Margaret* (Fourth Estate, 2017)

Croft-Cooke, Rupert, *The Verdict of You All* (Secker & Warburg, 1955)

Goodman, Jonathan, and Pringle, Patrick, *The Trial of Ruth Ellis* (David & Charles, 1974)

Hancock, Robert, *Ruth Ellis: The Last Woman to be Hanged* (Barker, 1963)

Jakubait, Muriel, and Weller, Monica, *Ruth Ellis: My Sister's Secret Life* (Robinson, 2005)

Kennedy, Helena, *Eve Was Framed: Women and British Justice* (Vintage, 2005)

Kynaston, David, *Family Britain: 1951–1957* (Bloomsbury, 2009)

Lee, Carol Ann, *A Fine Day for a Hanging: The Real Ruth Ellis Story* (Mainstream, 2013)

Marks, Laurence, and Van den Bergh, Tony, *Ruth Ellis: A Case of Diminished Responsibility?* (Penguin, 1990)

Maxwell Fyfe, David, *Political Adventure: The Memoirs of the Earl of Kilmuir* (Weidenfeld & Nicolson, 1964)

Parris, John, *Most of My Murders* (Frederick Muller, 1960)

Pierrepoint, Albert, *Executioner: Pierrepoint* (Harrap, 1974)

Rawlinson, Peter, *A Price Too High: An Autobiography* (Weidenfeld & Nicolson, 1989)

Roberts, G.D., *Law and Life: The Memoirs of G.D. Roberts QC* (W.H. Allen, 1964)

Robertson, Geoffrey, *Obscenity* (Weidenfeld & Nicolson, 1979)

Travis, Alan, *Bound and Gagged: A Secret History of Obscenity in Britain* (Profile, 2000)

Webb, Duncan, *Line-Up for Crime* (Frederick Muller, 1956)

Wildeblood, Peter, *Against the Law* (Weidenfeld & Nicolson, 1955)

Chapter 8: 'Equipment for a spy'

Bulloch, John, and Miller, Henry, *Spy Ring: The Full Story of the Naval Secrets Case* (Secker & Warburg, 1961)

Close, Frank, *Half-Life: The Divided Life of Bruno Pontecorvo, Physicist or Spy* (Oneworld, 2015)

Kennedy, Ludovic, *The Trial of Stephen Ward* (Victor Gollancz, 1964)

le Carré, John, *The Spy Who Came in from the Cold* (Victor Gollancz, 1963)

——, *The Pigeon Tunnel: Stories from My Life* (Viking, 2016)

Macintyre, Ben, *A Spy Among Friends: Philby and the Great Betrayal* (Bloomsbury, 2014)

Robertson, Geoffrey, *Stephen Ward Was Innocent, OK: The Case for Overturning His Conviction* (Biteback, 2013)

Vassall, John, *The Autobiography of a Spy* (Sidgwick & Jackson, 1975)

West, Nigel, *A Matter of Trust: MI5 1945–72* (Weidenfeld & Nicolson, 1982)

Chapter 9: 'Trial of the Century'

Bloch, Michael, *Jeremy Thorpe* (Abacus, 2016)

Carman, Dominic, *No Ordinary Man: A Life of George Carman* (Hodder & Stoughton, 2002)

Chester, Lewis, Linklater, Magnus, and May, David, *Jeremy Thorpe: A Secret Life* (André Deutsch, 1979)

Chippindale, Peter, and Leigh, David, *The Thorpe Committal* (Arrow, 1979)

Courtiour, Roger, and Penrose, Barrie, *The Pencourt File* (Secker & Warburg, 1978)

Freeman, Simon, and Penrose, Barrie, *Rinkagate: The Rise and Fall of Jeremy Thorpe* (Bloomsbury, 1996)

King-Hamilton, Alan, *And Nothing But the Truth: An Autobiography* (Weidenfeld & Nicolson, 1983)

Preston, John, *A Very English Scandal: Sex, Lies and a Murder Plot at the Heart of the Establishment* (Viking, 2016)

Reynold, Frederic, *Chance, Cheek and Some Heroics* (Wildy, Simmonds & Hill, 2018)

Sandbrook, Dominic, *Seasons in the Sun: The Battle for Britain, 1974–1979* (Allen Lane, 2012)

Thorpe, Jeremy, *In my Own Time: Reminiscences of a Liberal Leader* (Politico's, 1999)

Waugh, Auberon, *The Last Word: An Eye-Witness Account of the Thorpe Trial* (Michael Joseph, 1980)

Chapter 10: 'No apologies and no regrets'

Blake, George, *No Other Choice: An Autobiography* (Jonathan Cape, 1990)

Bourke, Seán, *The Springing of George Blake* (Cassell, 1970)

Hermiston, Roger, *The Greatest Traitor: The Secret Lives of Agent George Blake* (Aurum, 2013)

Hyde, H. Montgomery, *George Blake Superspy* (Futura, 1988)

Knightley, Phillip, *Philby: The Life and Views of the KGB Masterspy* (André Deutsch, 1988)

Pottle, Pat, and Randle, Michael, *The Blake Escape: How We Freed George Blake – and Why* (Harrap, 1989)

Randle, Michael, 'Rebel Verdict' (Unpublished memoir)

Sisman, Adam, *John le Carré: The Biography* (Bloomsbury, 2015)

West, Nigel, *The Friends: Britain's Post-War Secret Intelligence Operations* (Coronet, 1990)

Chapter 11: 'There is no greater task for the criminal justice system than to protect the vulnerable'

Gerrard, Nicci, *Soham: A Story of Our Times* (Short Books, 2004)
Wells, Kevin, *Goodbye, Dearest Holly* (Hodder & Stoughton, 2005)
Yates, Nathan, *Beyond Evil: Inside the Twisted Mind of Ian Huntley* (John Blake, 2005)

Index

NOTE: Titles and ranks are generally the highest mentioned in the text

Abbott, Mark, 364
Ableman, Paul: *The Mouth and Oral Sex*, 385
'A, Miss' (of MI5), 326–7
Adams, Dr John Bodkin, 2, 19, 332
Adebolajo, Michael, 387
Adebowale, Michael, 387
Admiral Duncan public house, Soho, 346
Admiralty Underwater Weapons Establishment, 248
After Dark (broadcast), 339
Agrafenine (Soviet Embassy official), 252, 261
Aitken, Jonathan, 2–4, 9, 13–14, 268, 312, 386; *Porridge and Passion*, 14
Albemarle, Arnold Keppel, 8th Earl of, 69
Alexander (Russian agent), 252, 254–6, 261
Alexander, George, 33
Alexandra, Queen of Edward VII, 62
Al Fayed, Mohamed, 312
Allan, Maud: and *Salome* criminal libel case, 61–3, 68–70, 81, 83, 87, 89, 123; Billing questions in court, 74–7; post-trial decline, 92; and Jeffress's 'Red and White' party, 123; *My Life and Dancing*, 76
Allan, Theodore, 61, 75
Allen, Peter, 243
Allende, Salvador, 334
Alliott, Sir John (Mr Justice): tries Randle–Pottle case, 328–35, 337–8, 340; summing-up, 337
Allpass, Caroline *see* Thorpe, Caroline
Allsop, Kenneth, 211
Alverstone, Richard Everard Webster, Viscount (Lord Chief Justice), 379
Amery, John, 173, 240
Amnesty International, 309
Angry Brigade, 2, 385

anti-Semitism, 66, 151
Apen, Germany, 156
Appeal, Court of, 394, 398–400
Archer, Jeffrey, Baron, 268, 387
Arkell, Harriet, 350
Arnold, Harry, 331
arrest: procedure, 389–400
Askey, Arthur, 154
Asquith, Herbert Henry, 63, 79
Asquith, Margot, 62–3, 68, 76, 79
Astor, David, 309
Atomic Energy Research Establishment, Oxfordshire, 249
atomic weapons, 249–51
Attenborough, Richard, 188
Attlee, Clement, 177, 382
Attorney General, 381
Auld, Sir Robin (Lord Justice), 325, 342

Back, Patrick, QC, 311
Balcombe Street Gang and siege, 19, 385
Baldwin, James: *Giovanni's Room*, 272
Barker, Rex and the Ricochets, 308
Barney, Elvira: at Jeffress's 'Red and White' party, 124; relations with Michael Scott Stephen, 124; and shooting of Stephen, 125–6; throws party, 125; appearance, 126–7, 129; trial, 126; charged with murder, 127; public interest in trial, 128, 226; gives evidence, 135–6; acquitted, 137–8; social effects of trial, 138–9; subsequent life and behaviour, 138; death, 140; prosecuted by Percival Clarke, 381
Barrington, Jonah, 149, 154
Bartle, Ronald, 323
Baxter, Walter: *The Image and the Search*, 214

425

Beattie, John Paul: witnesses Fahmy quarrel and shooting, 96–7, 110–11; testimony in court, 105

Beck, Adolf, 380

Beck, Detective Superintendent David, 350, 353

Beckett, John, 152

Beckham, David, 347–8, 350, 359

Bedford, Sybille, 2–4, 6, 283, 309; *The Best We Can Do*, 14; *The Trial of Lady Chatterley's Lover*, 15

Benn, Tony, 274

Bentley, Derek, 210–11, 242–3, 381–2, 394

Berlin: William Joyce in, 153–6; Blake reaches, 318, 321

Beron, Leon, 73

Bessell, Peter: and Thorpe case, 274, 278–81, 285; leaves parliament and moves to USA, 276; on Cantley, 284; testifies in court, 286–92, 302; Carman on, 304; Cantley denounces, 305; book (*Cover-up*) published privately, 310; return to California and death, 310; material on Thorpe found in briefcase, 311; press interest in, 312

Bevan, Aneurin, 150

Bevan, Julian, QC: prosecutes Randle–Pottle case, 324, 326, 328–9, 331, 333, 335, 340

Bichard, Sir Michael, 375

Bickford, John, 222, 225–6, 237–9, 241, 244

Billing, Noel Pemberton: trial, 60, 73; life and career, 65–6; denounces homosexuality, 66–7; charged with criminal libel, 68–70, 123; and staging of *Salome*, 68; defends self in trial, 70, 74–7, 80, 329; Repington invites to join anti-Lloyd George conspiracy, 71; Eileen Villiers-Stuart attempts to seduce, 72; enters plea of justification, 72; objects to Darling's presence, 74; behaviour in court, 78, 88; cross-examines Grein, 85–6; closing speech, 87; acquitted, 88–9; press and popular reaction to, 89, 91; suspended from Commons, 90; subsequent life and interests, 91–2; wife's German ancestry, 91; death, 92; *High Treason* (play), 91

Bindloss, Edward (His Honour Judge), 20, 402

Bingham, Thomas Henry, Baron (Lord Chief Justice), 394

Bird, Detective Inspector Richard, 322, 325, 332

Birkenhead, F.E. Smith, 1st Earl of, 25

Birkett, Norman, QC, 9, 118, 380–1

Birnberg, Benedict, 322, 329, 331, 333, 338

'Black Book': Billing exposes, 67; Eileen Villiers-Stuart claims to have seen, 77; Spencer claims to have seen, 79, 81; cited in court, 87

Black, Inspector, 182

Blackstone, William: *Commentaries on the Laws of England*, 394

Blake, George: tried in Court No. One, 9; falls out with Bourke in Moscow, 33; confesses to spying and sentenced to 42 years, 248, 314–15, 324, 383; Hutchinson defends, 253, 314–15, 319; escapes from Wormwood Scrubs, 313–17, 332, 340; background and career, 314; behaviour in prison, 315–17, 319; reaches Berlin and Moscow, 318, 321; friendship with Pottle, 319; Randle and Pottle tell of escape, 320–1, 335–6; agrees to testify by video in Randle–Pottle case, 323–4, 333–4; confesses to multiple betrayals in TV interview, 327; congratulates Randle and Pottle on acquittal, 339

Blake Escape, The (TV programme), 330, 339

Blakely, David: relations with Ruth Ellis, 217–20, 243; Ruth Ellis turns against, 220–1; Ruth Ellis shoots, 221–3, 230; and Ruth Ellis trial, 227

Blunkett, David, 375

Blunt, Anthony, 335

Boal, Graham, 282, 288, 304

Boccaccio, Giovanni: *Decameron*, 213

Bodkin, Archibald, 380

Boothby, Robert, 272

Bottomley, Horatio, 9, 268

Bourke, Seán: engineers Blake's escape from Wormwood Scrubs, 315–17, 321–3; refuge in Moscow, 318; friendship with Michael Randle, 319; Randle and Pottle on, 320–1; death, 327; *The Springing of George Blake*, 316, 320

Bow Street Magistrates Court, 69

Brabin, Sir Daniel (Mr Justice), 207

Brady, Ian, 346

Branson, Richard, 312

Bray, Percival, 72, 90; Albert Pierrepoint hangs, 240

Brennan, Daniel, QC, Baron, 207

Brenton, Howard: *The Romans in Britain* (play), 10, 19, 386

Brest-Litovsk, Treaty of (1918), 64
Bright Young people ('BYP'), 123, 139
Britain: arms deficiency in First World War, 65–6
British South-African Motor Car (magazine), 65
British Union of Fascists (BUF), 150–2
Brooks, Rebekah, 387
Brown, Charles, 202
Brown, Donald, 242
Bryden, Margaret, 355
Burge, James, 147, 266
Burgess, Guy, 272
Burrell, Paul, 346
Burton, PC Anna, 352
Butler, R.A. (Rab), 207
Byrne, Dorothy, Lady, 6
Byrne, Sir Lawrence (Mr Justice), 6, 147
Bywaters, Frederick, 5, 8–9, 100, 119

Cable Street: battle of (1936), 151
Caine, Sir Hall: *The Christian*, 33; 'The Law and the Man' (essay), 58–9
Calderan, John: and Martelli trial, 253, 255, 259, 261, 263–4, 266
Callaghan, James, 323
Calvert-Smith, David, 328, 334, 340
Camden Town murder case, 15
Campbell, Beatrix, 373
Campbell-Bannerman, Sir Henry, 25
Canaris, Admiral Wilhelm, 153
Cantley, Sir Joseph (Mr Justice): as judge in Thorpe trial, 284–5, 296–7, 299–300, 308; and Bessell's testimony, 286–7, 290–2; antipathy to Scott, 294–5, 306; summing-up, 305–7; given armed guard, 385
Capaldi, Peter, 58
capital punishment *see* death penalty
Carey, Nat, 366
Carleton, Billie, 118
Carman, Dominic, 269
Carman, George, QC: defends Jeremy Thorpe, 268–9, 281, 285, 299, 301; private and inner life, 269, 312; at Oxford with Thorpe, 270; on Bessell, 274; persuades Thorpe not to give evidence, 282–3; cross-examines Bessell, 288–91; drinking, 288; questions Scott, 293–6; obscures Thorpe's homosexuality, 295–6; caution with Hayward, 300; closing speech in Thorpe case, 303–5; criticises press, 311; and press contacts with defendants, 312; reputation, 312

Carnarvon, George Edward Stanhope Molyneux Herbert, 5th Earl of, 98
Carr, Maxine: tried in Court No. One, 2; and disappearance of Holly Wells and Jessica Chapman, 349–51; gives false alibi, 352, 354–5; suspected, 353; interviewed by police and arrested, 354; charged, 355, 358; background, 356; relations with Huntley, 356, 360, 365, 368; works in St Andrew's primary school, Soham, 357; loses weight, 360; not guilty plea, 361; conduct in trial, 363–4, 376; Hubbard defends, 363–4, 368–70; questioned in court, 368–9; found guilty of perverting course of justice, 371; sentenced, 372; demonised and given new identity, 373
Carson, Edward, QC, 382
Carten, Audrey and Kenneth, 139
Carter, Howard, 98
Casement, Sir Roger, 73, 147–8, 169
Cassel, Sir Ernest, 64
Castree, Ronald, 390
Caulfield, Sir Bernard (Mr Justice), 4
Cecil, Henry, 381
Celebrated Trials series, 15
Chamberlain, Neville, 152
Chaplin, Charlie, 73
Chapman, Jessica: disappears, 347–9; rumoured sightings, 350–1; phone signals, 352; body found, 354; memorial service, 359; Huntley's account of death, 365–6; *see also* Huntley, Ian
Chapman, Leslie and Sharon, 347–8
charges (prosecution), 390
Charles, Prince of Wales, 359
Charles, Sir Ernest (Mr Justice), 159
Chataway, Christopher, 274
Children Act (1908), 380
Chindamo, Learco, 345
Chippindale, Peter, 283, 312
Christian Scientists: support Billing, 72
Christie, Agatha, 145
Christie, Ethel, 179, 181, 185, 193, 200, 203
Christie, John Reginald Halliday: tried in Court No. One, 2, 9; literature on, 15; Derek Curtis-Bennett defends, 147; and disposal of Beryl Evans's body, 179; Evans protects, 179; gives statements to police, 181; background, 183; denigrates Evans to police, 184; Evans accuses of murders, 185, 196–7; testifies against Evans, 188–93; cross-examined by Morris, 191–2; previous conviction

Christie, John Reginald Halliday (*cont.*)
for violence, 193; judge's prejudice in
favour in Evans case, 200; ill-health,
202; and discovery of bodies at home,
203; confesses to killings, 204; pleads
not guilty on basis of insanity at trial,
204, 381; pursued and arrested, 204;
behaviour at trial, 205; found guilty and
hanged, 205; and enquiry into Evans's
conviction, 206
Churchill, Randolph, 150
Churchill, Robert, 105–6, 134–5
Chuter Ede, James, 177, 202, 206
Clark, Peter, 332
Clarke, Sir Edward, QC, 381
Clarke, Frank, 29
Clarke, Sir Percival, KC: prosecutes
Marguerite Fahmy, 100, 108; opening
speech, 100–3; questions Marguerite,
111–12; manner in court, 115; pros-
ecutes Elvira Barney, 129–30, 136, 137;
family background, 381
Clerk of Arraigns, 101
clitoris: word used in Billing case, 68–9,
74, 80
Coghlan, Monica, 387
Cold War, 150
Comfort, Dr Alex, 321, 332
Committee of 100, 318, 320, 341
Confait, Maxwell, 385
confessions, false, 390
Conley, Morris, 215–16, 218
Connell, Vivian: *September in Quinze*, 214
Connor, William ('Cassandra'), 25
Contempt of Court Act (1981), 398
Cook, Humphrey Wyndham, 217
Cook, Peter, 308
Cooke, Dr Serrell, 81
Cooper, Thomas Mackay, Baron, 208
Copeland, David, 346
Corelli, Marie, 68
Corporation of London: City Lands
Committee, 5
Coulson, Andrew, 387
Court Club (*later* Carroll's), London, 215
Court Number One (Old Bailey): setting,
1–8, 14; criminal trials in, 2, 15–16,
18–20; arrival of judge, 6; public
admitted, 8; status, 10–12; as film
setting, 10; early photographs, 11; press
presence, 12; *Trial and Error* performed
in, 13; writings on, 14–15; in Second
World War, 146; status diminished,
345; *see also* Old Bailey

Court Number Two (Old Bailey), 345
Courtiour, Roger, 285; *see also* Penrose,
Barrie
Coward, Stephen, QC: defends Huntley,
361–5, 368–70
Cowley, Dennis, QC, 280, 282, 293, 301,
303
Cox, Geoffrey, QC (Attorney General),
382
Cox, Jo, 387
Crabtree, John William, 29, 31, 45–6
Craig, Christopher, 210
Criminal Appeal Act (1907), 400
Criminal Appeals Act (1995), 400
Criminal Cases Review Commission (1995),
394
Criminal Court of Appeal, 380
Criminal Evidence Act (1898), 47, 108, 396
Criminal Justice Bill (1948), 177, 382
Criminal Justice and Public Order Act
(1994), 396
criminal libel, 68–9
Criminal Record Bureau (renamed
Disclosure and Barring Service), 375–6
criminal trials *see* trials
Crippen, Dr Hawley Harvey, 2, 9–11,
17–18, 73, 381
Croft-Cooke, Rupert, 212
Crosland, T.W.H., 62
cross-examinations, 17–18, 231, 287–8, 395
crown courts, 385, 391, 401
Crown Prosecution Service, 390
Cruise, Tom, 312
Cummins, Gordon, 144
Cunningham, Arthur, 326–7
Curtis-Bennett, Derek, QC: defends
William Joyce, 147; defends Christie,
204–5, 381; and enquiry into Evans
conviction, 206; defends Klaus Fuchs,
250; family background, 381
Curtis-Bennett, Sir Henry, KC: defends
Marguerite Fahmy, 100, 119; defends
Edith Thompson, 119–20; regrets Edith
Thompson's conviction, 121; as defence
lawyer, 380
Cussen, Desmond: relations with Ruth Ellis,
219–21, 223, 226–7, 232; provides gun to
Ruth Ellis, 237–9; emigration to
Australia and death, 244
custody *see* police custody

Daily Express, 121
Daily Herald, 139
Daily Mail, 58, 89, 150, 279, 287, 349

Daily Mirror, 75, 101, 311, 341
Daily Sketch, 121
Daily Star, 387
Daily Telegraph, 339, 394
Dando, Jill, 346, 386
Darling, Charles John, 1st Baron: tries Douglas–Ross libel case, 62; tries Billing case, 73, 75, 78–9, 82–5, 88
Davies, Detective Chief Inspector Leslie, 223, 230
Day, Scott, 348
Deakin, George: and Thorpe, 276–7; charged with conspiracy to murder, 280; and Newton's evidence, 281; in Thorpe trial, 282, 284, 301, 303; Cantley on, 306; acquitted, 307–8
death penalty: abolished (1965), 12, 138, 207, 242, 383; right of condemned to speak after guilty verdict, 169; Silverman's proposed suspension rejected (1948), 177–8, 382; late victims, 243, 381–2
Debussy, Claude, 62
defence: in criminal trials, 396–7
defendants: give sworn evidence, 47, 108; right to remain silent, 282, 302, 397
Denison, Edward, 384
Devlin, Sir Patrick (Mr Justice), 225, 401
Diana, Princess of Wales, 346
Dimmock, Emily: life as prostitute, 26–8, 30; meets Wood, 27–8, 31, 43; body discovered, 29, 32, 37; and trial of Wood, 34, 43; speaks well of Wood, 42–3; posthumous anonymity, 58
Dimmock, Henry (Emily's brother), 57
Dinshaw, Nadir, 280, 300, 302
divorce laws: liberalisation, 12
Douglas, Lord Alfred: libel case against Ransome, 62, 73; vendetta against Robbie Ross, 62–3; testifies in Billing libel case, 82; ejected from court, 88
Driberg, Tom, 225, 272
drugs, 118, 123
du Cann, Richard, QC: *The Art of the Advocate*, 231
Duddy, John, 383
Dudley and Stephens case, 331
Duncan, Helen, 19, 382

Eady, Muriel, 203
Edward VII, King, 62, 377
Edward, Prince of Wales (*later* King Edward VIII), 96, 151

Eggington, Superintendent Eileen, 323, 326, 332
Ellis, Clare Andrea ('Andy'; Ruth Ellis's son), 215–16, 219, 239, 244
Ellis, George, 216, 218, 244
Ellis, Georgina, 216, 218
Ellis, John, 122, 240, 299
Ellis, Ruth: tried in Court No. One, 2; effect of trial and execution, 10, 243–4; appearance and demeanour in court, 121, 226, 233; background and career, 215–17; illegitimate child, 215; works at Court Club, 215–16; marriage to George, 216; relations with Blakeley, 217–20; relations with Cussen, 219–21, 223, 226–7, 232; divorce, 220; miscarriage, 220; turns against Blakeley, 220–1; shoots Blakeley, 221–2, 230; not guilty plea, 222–3, 226; letter to Blakeley's mother, 223; Rawlinson defends, 223–4; death wish, 224, 236; defence, 225, 383; conduct of trial, 226–30, 357; testimony in court, 231–4; in condemned cell at Holloway Prison, 236; guilty verdict with no recommendation for mercy, 236; public reaction to death sentence, 236–7, 242; acquires gun from Cussen, 237–9; executed, 241–3; prosecuted by Christmas Humphreys, 381; trial remembered, 382
Ely Standard, 350
Enani, Said: stays in Savoy Hotel, 95; and shooting of Fahmy, 97; questioned in Fahmy trial, 102–5, 108; Hall disparages, 113
Erskine, Thomas, 397
espionage cases (Second World War), 145–6; *see also* spies
Evans, Beryl (*née* Thorley): murdered, 178–82, 184, 199; apparent post-mortem penetration, 186, 200, 203; in Christie's testimony at Evans trial, 190–1; Christie confesses to killing, 204, 206
Evans, Claire, 356
Evans, Geraldine, 178–84, 199, 204
Evans, Detective Constable Gwynfryn, 178–9, 193
Evans, Gwynne, 243
Evans, Timothy John: trial in Court No. One, 2, 9, 185–94, 209, 357, 382; literature on, 15; condemned, 18; confesses to murder of wife and child, 19, 178, 181–3, 188, 198–9; outcry over hanging, 142; arrested, 180–1; charged, 182;

Evans, Timothy John (*cont.*)
background, 183–4; marriage to Beryl, 184; accuses Christie of murders, 185, 196–7; Morris defends, 185–6; pleads not guilty, 187; Christie testifies against, 189–90; testimony in court, 194–6; appeal, 202; hanged, 202; enquiry into conviction, 206, 210; backwardness and limitations, 207–8; body exhumed and reinterred, 207; granted posthumous free pardon, 207; Christmas Humphreys prosecutes, 381
Evening News, 285
Evening Standard, 109
evidence and proof, 393–4

Fahmy Bey, 'Prince' Ali: stays in Savoy Hotel, 95–7; marriage to Marguerite, 96; shot and killed, 97; press comments on, 98–9; Marguerite accuses of sodomy, 99; sexual demands, 106–7; Marguerite traduces during trial, 109–10; Hall casts as oriental monster seducer, 117–18
Fahmy, Marguerite: background, 95; Hall defends, 95, 97, 100, 116–18; stays in Savoy Hotel, 95; marriage to Ali, 96; charged with murder, 97–8, 102, 128; and shooting of Ali, 97, 105–6, 110–11, 120; accuses Ali of sodomy, 99; haemorrhoids, 99–100; appears in court, 101; testifies in court, 108–11, 120; questioned by Clarke, 111–12, 381; found not guilty, 116, 119; posthumous image, 121; popular interest in, 226
Fantle, Ernest, 242–3
Farmer, Brian, 351
Farndale, Nigel, 173
Field, Jack, 55
Field, William, 213
Findlater, Anthony, 220–1, 223, 229
Findlater, Carole, 220–1, 223
Finnemore, Sir Donald (Mr Justice), 205
First World War (1914–18): German bombings and bombardments of Britain, 63–4; German spring offensive (1918), 64, 72, 83; sexual liberation, 64; and German impending defeat, 89
Fisher, Geoff, 357
Fitzgerald, Edward, 323, 339
Flanagan, Sir Ronnie, 374, 375
Forster, E.M., 214
Fox, Sir Marcus, 322, 339
Frankling, PC, 314

Freeborough, Geoffrey, 185
Freeman, Simon, 284
Freud, Clement, 307
Fripp, Sir Alfred, 82
Fuchs, Klaus, 147, 157, 249–51, 260, 262, 315
Fuerst, Ruth, 203
Fulton, Eustace, 100, 381
Fulton, Sir Forrest, 377, 381
Fyfe, Sir David Maxwell, QC, 177, 206, 210–11, 213, 395

Gamble, Gertrude, 139
gangs (criminal), 383
Garden Court, Middle Temple, 185
Gardiner, Gerald, QC, 214
Garrick Club, 380
Gathorne-Hardy, Eddie, 125
Gay News blasphemy case, 19–20, 311, 386
George, Barry, 2, 346, 386
Germany: image in First World War, 63–4; spring offensive (1918), 64, 72, 83; Billing's hostility to, 65–6; offensive halted, 89
Germany Calling (wartime broadcasts), 154
Gerrard, Nicci, 356, 363, 365–6, 373–4
Gielgud, John, 211
Gilbert, Kenneth, 242
Glasgow, Oliver, QC, 13
Gleadle, Ronald, 278
Goddard, Rayner, Baron (Lord Chief Justice): hears Evans appeal, 202; tries Bentley and Craig, 210, 393–4; sentences Fuchs, 249–50; background, 380; appointed LCJ by Attlee, 382
Goddard, Theodore, 253
Goebbels, Joseph, 153, 156
Goldsmith, Peter, Baron, QC (Attorney General), 358
Goodman, Arnold, Baron, 286
Goodman, Jonathan, 15
Goose, Detective Inspector Gary: assaulted, 358
Gordievsky, Oleg, 336
Gordon, Aloysius ('Lucky'), 383
Gordon, Dr Edward, 97, 99–100, 106
Göring, Hermann, 395
Graham, Evelyn: *Lord Darling and his Famous Trials: An Authentic Biography* (with Darling), 89
Grant, Ian, 242
Grantham, Sir William (Mr Justice), 33–4, 42, 52–3, 58
Graves, Keith, 311

Gray, William, 55
Great Train Robbers, 383
Greenwood, Harold, 55
Grein, Jack Thomas, 68–9, 74, 85–6, 92
Griffith-Jones, Mervyn, 7, 214, 226
Grimond, Jo, 274
Grove, Valerie, 371
Guardian (newspaper) see Manchester Guardian
Gunnell, Clive, 221–2, 230
Gwynne, H.A., 70

Haig, Field Marshal Douglas, 70
Haigh, John, 9, 240
Hailsham, Quintin McGarel Hogg, Baron (Lord Chancellor), 383
Haldane, Richard Burdon, Viscount, 79, 116
Hall, Dorothy, 127, 129–32
Hall, Sir Edward Marshall, KC: in Court No. One, 9; defends Seddon, 10; appearance and character, 24; defends Wood in Camden Town murder case, 24–6, 32–3, 37, 41–2, 56–7; manner in court, 24–5, 38, 40, 41, 114–15, 118; loses seat in Parliament (1907), 26; challenges jurors, 35; rebukes Grantham, 34; questions Bertram Shaw, 36–7; examines Roberts, 38–9; and Alice Lancaster's testimony, 40; questions Ruby Young, 43–4; aggressive questioning, 44–5; interrogates Emily Lawrence, 44–5; opening speech for the defence, 45–6; calls witnesses, 46; and Wood's giving evidence, 47–9; closing speech in Camden Town murder case, 50–2; reputation, 55; 'scales of justice' peroration, 55; and Wood's acquittal, 55; defends Marguerite Fahmy, 95, 97–100, 102, 107–9, 116–17; questions Enani in Fahmy trial, 102–5, 108; on Marguerite Fahmy's handling and firing of gun, 106, 110; closing speech in Fahmy case, 112–17; depicts orientals as sexual monsters, 117–18; death, 118; gains fame through Marie Hermann, 268; as defence counsel, 380; as MP, 382; on defending distasteful clients, 397
Hall, J.W., 148
Hall, Admiral Sir William Reginald, 86
Hambro, Major (Devon farmer), 273
Hamilton, Neil, 312
Hamilton, Patrick: Twenty Thousand Streets Under the Sky, 58
Hancock, Robert, 226, 230, 234–5, 241

Handley, Tommy, 154
Harrap (publishing house), 322
Hastings, Sir Patrick, KC: Kennedy invokes, 9; on public interest in trials, 9; memoirs, 12; on awaiting jury verdicts, 16–17; courtroom manner, 118, 128, 131, 136; character and interests, 127–8; as playwright, 127, 380; defends Elvira Barney, 127–8, 130, 133, 137; and 'Hooded Man' case, 128, 134; questions Dorothy Hall, 131–2; questions Robert Churchill, 134–5; closing speech in Barney trial, 136–7; gives account of Barney case in memoirs, 140; near accident with motor car driven by Elvira Barney, 140; defends William Joyce and Mosley, 151; background, 381; as MP, 382; Cases in Court, 118
Hatry, Clarence, 9
Havers, Sir Cecil (Mr Justice): tries Ruth Ellis, 225, 235, 243
Havers, Sir Michael, QC (Attorney General), 381
'Haw-Haw, Lord' see Joyce, William
Haystack, May, 69
Hayward, Jack, 276–7, 280, 290–1, 300
Head, C.B.V., 159
Heald, Sir Lionel, QC (Attorney General), 204
Heath, Edward, 271, 276
Heath, Neville, 2, 19, 240, 382
Hebb, Detective Chief Inspector Andy, 352
Heilbron, Dame Rose (Mrs Justice), 385
Hermann, Marie, 24, 33, 268
Hermiston, Roger, 315
Hetherington (blackmailer), 289–90
Hewart, Gordon, 1st Viscount (Lord Chief Justice), 381
Hichens, Robert: Bella Donna, 115, 117, 120
Hickling, Benjamin, 364
Hilliard, Nicholas, QC (His Honour Judge, Recorder of London), 13, 387
Himmler, Heinrich, 156
Hindley, Myra, 346
Hitler, Adolf, 150–1, 153
Hogarth, Basil, 15, 21, 32
Hoggart, Richard, 10
Hollis, Roger, 261
Holmes, David: relations with Thorpe, 274, 276–8; and assassination attempt on Scott, 278, 286, 299; charged with conspiracy to murder, 280; offer to Dinshaw, 280, 300; in Thorpe trial, 281–2, 284, 286, 297, 301–3; and Bessell, 286–7;

Holmes, David (cont.)
acquitted, 307; and Thorpe's acquittal,
308; later career and death, 310
Home Office: 'Blue Book' (listing obscene
literature), 213
Homicide Act (1957), 242
Homosexual Law Reform Society, 274
homosexuality: as criminal offence, 62, 383;
Billing denounces, 66–7; Lord Alfred
Douglas on, 82–3; suppressed in 1950s,
211–13; among politicians, 272; and
Jeremy Thorpe, 272, 310; public atti-
tude to, 311
'Hooded Man' case, 128, 133
Hookway (Portobello Road dealer), 180
Hooson, Emlyn, QC, 275
Hoover, J. Edgar, 159
Hore-Belisha, Leslie, 155
Hornby, Revd John, 308
Hoseins, the, 9
Hough, Jonathan, QC, 1
Howard, Brian, 125
Howard, Gerald, 147
Howard, Michael, 386
Hubbard, Michael, QC, 363–4, 368–70
Hull, E.M.: The Sheikh, 117
Hulten, Karl, 145, 147
Hume, Donald, 187, 200–2, 209
Hume-Williams, Ellis, KC: prosecutes in
Billing case, 73–5, 78–82; Mrs Villiers-
Stuart accuses, 84–5; cross-examines
Grein, 86; closing speech, 87–8; reads
out Bywaters' letters to Edith
Thompson, 119; The World, the House
and the Bar, 89
Humphreys, Christmas, QC (later His
Honour Judge): prosecutes Evans,
186–9, 194, 209; prosecutes in 'Torso
murder', 187–8, 200; cross-examines
Christie in Evans trial, 193; cross-
examines Evans, 195–6; closing speech in
Evans trial, 197; prosecutes Craig and
Bentley, 211; prosecutes in Ruth Ellis
case, 226, 234; brief cross-examination of
Ruth Ellis, 234; prosecutes Fantle, 242;
pays for funeral of Ruth Ellis's son, 244;
family background, 381; gives lenient
sentences as judge, 386
Humphreys, Sir Travers (Mr Justice): prosecutes in Salome libel case, 69–70, 73, 88;
cross-examines Mrs Villiers-Stuart, 84;
sympathy for Maud Allan, 89; tries Elvira
Barney case, 137; tries John Amery case,
173; as prosecuting lawyer, 380

Hunt, Detective Inspector Albert, 160,
163–5, 167
Huntley, Ian: in Old Bailey dock, 2; and
disappearance of Holly Wells and Jessica
Chapman, 348–9, 351; suspected,
arrested and charged with murder,
351–5; earlier Humberside police
contacts involving underage girls, 353;
feigns insanity, 355, 357; appearance and
background, 356; earlier promiscuity
and marriage, 356; employment at
Soham Village College, 356–7; relations
with Maxine Carr, 356, 365; preliminary hearing and trial, 360–1;
admission statements, 361–2, 365;
Coward defends, 361–5, 368–70; not
guilty plea, 361; overdoses, 361; movements and actions after murder, 362–3;
conduct of trial, 363–4, 366; jury visits
Huntley's house, 364; behaviour in
court, 365, 368, 376; gives account of
girls' deaths, 365; cross-examined,
366–8; Maxine Carr denounces in court,
368–9; found guilty, 371; given two life
sentences, 372; prison life, 372–3
Huntley, Kevin, 356
Huntley, Wayne, 356–7
Hurt, John, 188
Hutchinson, Jeremy, QC: at Lady Chatterley's
Lover trial, 6; and Romans in Britain trial,
10; shares room with Morris, 186; questions and defends Martelli, 253–4, 260–3,
266; cross-examines Chief Inspector
Stratton, 257–9; surmise over source of
allegations against Martelli, 263; on journalists' dislike of acquittals, 265; smoking,
265; defends George Blake, 314–15, 319;
defends anti-nuclear protesters, 319; and
Pottle's self-representation, 328; criticises
length of Blake's sentence, 340
Hutchison, Sir Michael (Mr Justice), 325, 327
Hyde, Harford Montgomery: George Blake:
Superspy, 320
Hyde, Jonathan, 58

Ibsen, Henrik: The Lady from the Sea, 69
Imperialist (magazine) see Vigilante
indictment, 391
infanticide, 398
insanity: defined in law, 224
IRA (Irish Republican Army), 384–5
It's That Man Again (ITMA; radio
programme), 154
Ivanov, Captain Yevgeny, 249

Jack the Ripper murders, 32
Janson, Hank: *Don't Mourn Me, Toots*, 213
Jeffress, Arthur, 123, 125
Jennings, Chief Inspector George, 181–2, 193–6, 208
Jesse, F. Tennyson, 192
Jews: Billing's hostility to, 66
Johnson, Alan, 184
Johnson, Samuel, 396–7
Johnston, Russell, 274
Jones, Elizabeth, 145, 147
Jones, Revd Tim Alban, 355, 359
Jowitt, William Allen, Earl (Lord Chancellor), 170–1
Joyce, James: *Finnegans Wake*, 122
Joyce, Margaret (*née* White): marriage to William Joyce, 151–3, 155, 157–8, 166; life after William's execution, 172; never charged, 173
Joyce, Quentin, 158, 165, 169, 171
Joyce, William ('Lord Haw-Haw'): trial in Court No. One, 2, 10, 146–8, 168; literature on, 15; wartime broadcasts from Germany, 147, 153–5, 164; voice, 148–9; appearance, 149; background, 149; nicknamed, 149, 154; political ideas, 149–50; marriages, 150, 152, 155; in British Union of Fascists, 151; character, 153; moves to Germany, 153–6; evacuated from Berlin, 156; wounded and captured, 157; returned to England, 157–8; in Brixton prison, 158; nationality and allegiance question, 159–61, 164–7; gives no evidence in trial, 160–1; pleads not guilty, 160–1; treason charge, 160–2; conduct of trial, 161–3; found guilty, 168; silence after guilty verdict, 169; appeals, 170–1; execution, 172; public unease at conviction, 172
judges: appointment to High Court, 379; backgrounds, 380–1; sentencing policy, 386, 399; fairness and impartiality, 392
jury: advocacy to, 16; Marshall Hall addresses, 35; women serve on, 101; numbers reduced to seven in Second World War, 144; treatment in court, 264; and defendants' right to remain silent, 282, 397; and effect of cross-examinations, 288; findings protected by law, 312; exclusive right to verdict, 332; granted independence to deliver verdict freely, 339; eligibility and selection, 393; sovereignty, 398; as democratic institution, 401; *see also* trials

justice: status, 8–9; adversarial system, 9, 16, 209, 395; miscarriages, 390

Kafka, Franz: Lukács on, 402; *The Trial*, 389
Karpekov, Nikolai, 252–4, 256, 258, 260, 263
Kavan, Jan, 334
Keeler, Christine, 7–9, 249, 253, 383
'Keene, Peter' *see* Newton, Andrew
Kennedy, Helena, QC (Baroness), 231
Kennedy, Ludovic: at Stephen Ward trial, 7–9; on public at Ward trial, 8; criticises judge in Evans case, 199; on jury in Evans case, 200; and enquiry into Evans conviction, 206; on treatment of Evans, 208; favours inquisitorial system of justice, 209; *10 Rillington Place*, 15, 207; *The Trial of Stephen Ward*, 15
Keppel, Alice, 79
Khan, Imran, 312
King-Hamilton, Alan, QC (His Honour Judge), 386
Kiszko, Stefan, 389
Kitchener (resident of 10 Rillington Place), 179, 181, 202
knife and gang crime, 13
Knight, Maxwell, 150, 153
Krafft-Ebing, Richard von: *Psychopathia Sexualis*, 81
Kray Twins, 2, 9, 383
Kulak, Alexei, 266–7
Kynaston, David, 211

Lambert, Joseph, 28, 31, 42–3
Lancaster, Alice, 28, 40
Lancaster, Osbert, 139
Land, Sonia, 374
Laski, Harold, 148
Latham, Richard, QC: assaulted, 358; prosecutes in Huntley trial, 361, 363–4, 366–8; on Maxine Carr, 369; on hardworking police investigation, 375
Lawley, Sue, 312
Lawrence, D.H.: *Lady Chatterley's Lover*, 2–3, 19, 330, 383
Lawrence, Emily, 31, 44–5, 49
Lawrence, Sir Ivan, QC, 339
Lawrence, Philip, 345
Lawrence, Stephen, 345, 386
le Carré, John: on George Blake's escape, 315; *The Spy Who Came in from the Cold*, 252, 266
legal aid, 380

Legal Aid Act (1950), 397
Lehár, Franz: *The Merry Widow*, 99
Leigh, David, 312
le Mesurier, John, 276, 280–2, 284, 301, 303, 307–8
Lemon, Denis, 386
Lewis, Sir Wilfred (Mr Justice), 187, 191, 194, 199, 201
Liberal party: under Thorpe, 274–6
Lickorish, Captain, 164
Little Club, London, 216–18
Lloyd, Anthony, Baron (Lord of Appeal), 398
Lloyd, Sergeant, 322
Lloyd, Tom (Cambridgeshire Chief Constable), 353
Lloyd George, David: in First World War, 64, 70–1; and British Union of Fascists, 150; appoints Hewart Lord Chief Justice, 381
Lloyd George, Gwilym, 237–8
Locke, John, 401
London, City of: Corporation owns and maintains Old Bailey, 377–8, 384
Long-Brown, N., 172
Lonsdale, Gordon, 248, 262, 383
Lord Chamberlain: bans performance of *Salome*, 61, 69
Lords, House of: hears William Joyce's appeal, 170–1; rejects proposed suspension of death penalty (1948), 178
Lovelace, Linda: *Inside Linda Lovelace*, 385
Lucraft, Mark, QC (His Honour Judge, Chief Coroner), 1
Lukács, Georg: 'Franz Kafka or Thomas Mann?' (essay), 402
Lynch, Mr (Timothy Evans's uncle), 180, 183
Lynch, Mrs (Timothy Evans's aunt), 180, 183, 193

McCardie, Sir Henry (Mr Justice), 381
MacCowan, Robert, 31, 35, 40–1, 43, 45–6, 51, 56
Macdonald, Ken, QC, 376
MacDonald, Ramsay, 123
McGill, Donald, 213
Mackinnon, Tom, 23
MacLennan, Hectorina, 203
Macmillan, Harold, 248, 270
McMorran and Whitby (architects), 384–5, 387
MacNab, Angus, 152, 169, 171
M'Naghten rule (on insanity), 224
Macpherson of Cluny, Sir William (Mr Justice), 325

McWhirter, Norris, 339
Magdala Tavern, Hampstead, 220–1, 230
Magill, Air Commodore Graham, 341
Magpie and Stump (pub), 230, 330
Mailer, Norman: *The Naked and the Dead*, 213
Mair, Thomas, 387
Maloney, Kathleen, 203
Manchester Guardian, 106, 109, 111, 172, 200
Mann, Thomas, 402
Manners, Lady Diana (*later* Cooper), 63
Manningham-Buller, Sir Reginald, QC (Attorney General), 314, 319
Mansfield, Michael, QC, 243
Margaret, Princess, 271, 279, 296
Marjoribanks, Edward: *Life of Sir Edward Marshall Hall*, 24–5, 44, 50, 52, 56, 114
Marks, Richard (His Honour Judge, Common Sergeant), 387
Marshall Hall *see* Hall, Sir Edward Marshall
Martelli, Dr Giuseppe: tried for espionage and acquitted, 247, 256–60, 264–6, 383; background and career, 251; marriage relations, 251, 254–5, 261; charged, 253; Hutchinson defends, 253–4, 257–8, 260–3; and Karpekov, 254; shoes with hollow heels, 259–60; testifies in court, 261; lengthy jury deliberation, 263–5; liked by journalists, 265; and agent FEDORA, 266–7; later career and death, 267
Martelli, Susanna (Giuseppe's daughter), 251, 265
Marwood, Ronald, 382
Mason, A.E.W., 33
Masood, Khalid, 1
Masters, Brian, 11
Mathew, John, QC: defends Holmes in Thorpe trial, 280–2, 288, 291, 300, 312; questions Scott, 293; questions Newton, 297–9; calls no evidence on Holmes's behalf, 301; closing speech, 302
Mathew, Richard, 388
Mathew, Sir Theobald: favours treason charge against Joyce, 158
Mathews, Charles, KC: prosecutes Wood in Camden Town murder trial, 33, 35–7, 39–40, 46; questions Crabtree, 45; concedes account of Wood's gait, 46; cross-examines Wood, 49–50, 56; closing speech, 52; Hall Caine on, 58; as defence counsel, 380

Maude, John, QC, 213
Maudling, Reginald, 303
May, Alan Nunn, 173, 250, 262
Mead, William, 336
Merthyr Tydfil, 178
MI5: counters Soviet espionage, 248–9; and Martelli case, 256, 266; investigates Thorpe, 272; and Pottle–Randle case, 326
Miles, PC Sidney, 211
Miller, David, 276–7, 281, 299–300, 312
Miller, Jack, 257
Miller, Max, 154
Minehead, Somerset, 280
Mishcon, Victor, 238–9
Miskin, Sir James (His Honour Judge, Recorder of London), 386
Mitchell, Graham, 261
Molseed, Lesley, 390
Monde, Le (French newspaper), 236
Monroe, Marilyn, 216
Montagu of Beaulieu, Edward John Barrington Douglas-Scott-Montagu, 3rd Baron, 212
Morgan, Professor J.H., 164
Morning Post, 70–1
Morris, Malcolm: defends Evans, 185–6, 189, 193, 197, 209; cross-examines Christie, 190–2; questions Evans in court, 194–5; closing speech in Evans case, 198–9; and enquiry into Evans conviction, 206
Morrison, Steinie, 73
Mortimer, Sir John, QC, 8, 147
Moses, Sir Alan (Lord Justice): imposes minimum 40-year tariff on Huntley, 75; tries Huntley and Carr, 360, 371, 376; refuses postponement of Huntley trial, 361; rules out eye contact between parents and jurors in Huntley trial, 362; prepares jury for trial, 363; and possible verdicts for Huntley, 369; suggests Maxine Carr change plea, 369–70; declines Hubbard's defending Carr as having suffered enough, 370; summing-up, 370; sentencing statement, 371–3
Mosley, Sir Oswald, 150–3
Moss, William, 42
Mossadegh, Mohammad, 334
Mountford, Edward William, 377
Muir, Richard, KC, 10, 17–18, 380–1
Mullens, Evelyn Maude, Lady, 139
Mullens, Sir John, 124

Mussolini, Benito, 149, 152
Mustill, Michael, Baron (Lord of Appeal), 395–6
Myers, Sue, 275

Napley, Sir David: and Thorpe case, 268, 282; recommends Carman, 269; and John Mathew, 281
Nasser, Gamal Abdel, 334
National Campaign for the Abolition of Capital Punishment, 242
National Socialist League, 152
Neil, Detective Inspector Arthur, 31, 41–2, 46
Neilson, Betty (Ruth Ellis's sister), 244
Neilson, Elisaberta (née Goethals; Ruth Ellis's mother), 244
Neilson, Granville (Ruth Ellis's brother), 241
Neilson, Muriel (Ruth Ellis's sister), 241, 243
Nelson, Sergeant Pauline, 352
Nelson, Rita, 203
New Statesman, 312
New Yorker, 146
Newark Advertiser, 148
Newgate prison, 377
News of the World, 53, 145, 253, 381
Newsam, Sir Frank, 238
Newton, Andrew ('Peter Keene'): in assassination attempt on Scott, 277–81, 300; in Thorpe trial, 285; trial, 287, 311; in Scott's testimony, 292–3; testifies in court, 297–9, 302; drafts book on involvement with Thorpe, 299; Cantley denounces, 306; press interest in, 312
Newton, Arthur, 32, 53–4
Nickolls, Lewis, 230
Nicolson, Harold, 151
Nikitchenko, Major General Iona, 392
Nilsen, Dennis, 2, 11, 19, 345, 386
North Devon (parliamentary constituency), 270–1
Norton-Taylor, Richard, 330, 341
Notable British Trials series, 15, 23, 121, 192
Nuremberg Trials, 392–3, 395

obscene literature, 213–14
obscenity trials, 383, 385
O'Connor, Kevin, 323, 326–7
O'Dwyer, Sir Michael, 143–4
Official Secrets Act (1920), 247, 253

Old Bailey (Central Criminal Court): building and architecture, 1, 377–9, 387; character, 12–13; the cage, 14; bombed in Second World War and repaired, 144, 146, 383–4; espionage cases (Second World War), 145; owned by City of London Corporation, 377; site, 377; 'Lady Justice' statue, 378–9; IRA car bomb attack on, 384; security precautions, 385; adapted to modern cases, 387–8; Sword of Justice, 388; see also Court Number One

Old Bailey Trials series, 15

Oliver, Roland, 100–1

orgasm: word questioned in Billing libel case, 80–2

Ormerod, Sir Benjamin (Mr Justice), 212

Orwell, George: on conviction of William Joyce, 172; 'Decline of the English Murder', 8, 145; Down and Out in London and Paris, 204

Oxford, Edward de Vere, 17th Earl of, 186

Oz trial, 19

Paget, Reginald, 210

Palmer, Frederick Freke, 97

Palmer, PC Keith, 1

Pan Intercultural Arts, 13

Papworth, John, 321, 332

Papworth, Marcelle, 321

Parker, Hubert, Baron (Lord Chief Justice), 3, 315, 382–3

Parry-Jones, Gwen, 275

Paul, Brendan Dean, 123

Penguin Books: in Lady Chatterley trial, 10, 214; Famous Trials series, 15

Penn, William, 336

Penrose, Barrie, 285, 320; The Pencourt File (with Roger Courtiour), 285, 289

Philby, Kim, 248, 261, 335

phone-hacking, 387

Pierrepoint, Albert: as public hangman, 145–6, 172, 202, 239–41; opposes capital punishment, 243

Pierrepoint, Anne, 240

Pierrepoint, Henry, 239

Pierrepoint, Tom, 239–40

Pinero, Sir Arthur Wing, 33

Pitt-Rivers, Michael, 212

Plath, Sylvia, 3

Pocock, Terence, 350–1

Podola, Guenther, 382–3

Police and Criminal Evidence Act (1984), 208, 390

police custody, 390–1

Pomeroy, F.W., 378

Pontecorvo, Bruno, 249–52, 254, 260

Ponting, Clive, 20, 336–7, 398

'Porter, Pat' see Pottle, Pat

Porter, Samuel Lowry, Baron (Lord of Appeal), 171

Portland Spy Ring, 248

Pottle, Pat ('Pat Porter'): behaviour in court, 74; assists Blake in escape, 317–18, 320–2; convicted of anti-nuclear protest, 318–19; friendship in prison with Blake, 319; shelters Bourke, 319; activities known to police, 320; Montgomery Hyde on, 320; self-disclosure, 320; questioned by police, arrested and charged, 322–3; meets Blake in Moscow to record statement, 324; trial postponed, 325; official decision not to prosecute in 1970, 326; conducts own defence in court, 328–32; trial, 328; closing address, 335–6; found not guilty, 338–40; actions justified, 340–2; death, 341; and jury's independence, 398; The Blake Escape (with Randle), 320, 322, 330, 333

Price, Dolours and Marian, 384

Priestley, J.B., 154

Primrose, Neil, 72, 77, 83

Private Eye (magazine), 272, 308, 311

Probert, Thomasina (Timothy Evans's mother), 180, 185, 202

Profumo, John, 249

proof: burden and standard of, 393–4

prosecution, 395–6

Pryer, Keith, 354

Public Order Act (1937), 151

Queensberry, John Sholto Douglas, 8th Marquess of, 63, 70, 100, 382

Quenzler, Julia, 328

Quisling, Vidkun, 158

Rafferty, Angela, 372

Randle, Anne, 322, 335, 337–8, 341

Randle, Michael ('Michael Reynolds'): behaviour in court, 74; assists Blake in escape, 317–18, 320–2; conviction for anti-nuclear protest, 318–19; drives to Berlin with Blake, 318; friendship with Bourke, 319; activities known to police, 320; Montgomery Hyde on, 320; self-disclosure, 320; questioned by police, arrested and charged, 322–3;

meets Blake in Moscow to record statement, 324; trial postponed, 325; official decision not to prosecute in 1970, 326; trial, 328; conducts own defence in court, 328–31, 333–4; cross-examines Pottle, 332–3; closing address, 334, 336–7; questions Kavan, 334; found not guilty, 338–40; celebrates acquittal, 339; actions justified, 340–2; quits job as lecturer, 341; survives bleeding duodenal ulcer, 341; and jury's independence, 398; *The Blake Escape* (with Pottle), 320, 322, 330, 333–4

Ransome, Arthur, 62, 73, 82

Rattigan, Terence, 204, 205

Raven, Lillian, 28, 43

Rawlinson, Sir Peter, QC (Solicitor and Attorney General): defends Wildeblood, 213, 223; as junior counsel for defence of Ruth Ellis, 224; prosecutes Martelli, 256, 259; congratulates Hutchinson on Martelli verdict, 266; as MP, 382

Raymond, Ernest: *For Them That Trespass*, 58

Rees, Dr: prescribes tranquillisers for Ruth Ellis, 235

Reilly family, 203

Repington, Lieutenant Colonel Charles A'Court, 70–1

Reynold, Frederic, QC, 269

'Reynolds, Michael' *see* Randle, Michael

Rice-Davies, Mandy, 7, 9

Richardson, Charlie, 383

Richter, Karel, 145–6

Riddick, Graham, 322, 339

Rigby, Fusilier Lee, 387

Rillington Place, North Kensington (No. 10), 178, 180, 184, 188, 202–3, 208–9

Rinka (Scott's Great Dane): shot, 278–9, 292–3, 297, 300

Roberts, C.E. Bechhofer, 15

Roberts, G.F., QC ('Khaki'), 212

Roberts, Harry, 317, 383

Roberts, Robert, 28–9, 37–40, 49

Robertson, Geoffrey, QC, 324–6

Rogers, Joseph, 46, 51

Rolph, C.H., 137–8

Rook, Jean, 283, 296

Rook, Peter, QC (His Honour Judge), 13, 387

Ross, Robbie: Lord Alfred Douglas's vendetta against, 62–3; and Wilde's *Salome*, 63, 68

Rossetti, Renato, 259

Rothermere, Harold Harmsworth, 1st Viscount, 150

Rothschild, Major Evelyn, 77, 84

Rothwell, Pamela, 251, 253, 263–5, 267

Royal Court Theatre, Sloane Square, 69, 92

Russell, Bertrand, 336

Russia: revolutions (1917), 64; *see also* Soviet Union

St John-Stevas, Norman, 274

Salome (Biblical figure), 60–1

Sassoon, Siegfried, 91

Saunders, Baillie, 185

Savile, Jimmy, 271

Savoy Hotel, London: Fahmy killing in, 95, 97; Billie Carleton dies of cocaine overdose in, 118

Sawoniuk, Anthony, 346

Scientist Replies, The (TV programme), 270

Scott Henderson, John, QC, 206

Scott, Norman (*formerly* Josiffe): Thorpe's affair with, 272–3, 294; instability, 273, 275; quarrels with Thorpe, 273–4; as threat to Thorpe, 274–5; marriage to Sue Myers, 275; Thorpe pays divorce costs, 276, 297; Thorpe plans elimination, 276–7; incriminating letters burnt, 277–8; moves to North Devon, 277; Great Dane ('Rinka'), 278, 292, 297, 300; Newton meets and attempts to shoot, 278; Bessell's letter making blackmail claim against, 279; in Thorpe trial, 284–5; in Bessell's testimony, 286; sues Metropolitan Police over letters, 287; testifies in court, 292–6; Cantley denounces, 306; in Thorpe's autobiography, 310; homosexuality mocked, 311; proposes giving story to *Daily Mirror*, 311

Scott, Captain Robert Falcon, 64

Scrivener, Anthony, QC, 323–5, 327, 333

Second World War (1939–45): crime increases, 143–4; effect on Old Bailey, 382

Secret Policeman's Ball, The (stage show), 308

Seddon, Frederick, 2, 10–11, 55, 169

Selby, Hubert: *Last Exit to Brooklyn*, 19, 385

sentence, 399–400

Setty, Stanley, 187, 201

Shadow of the Noose, The (TV series), 58

Shaw, Bertram: liaison with Emily Dimmock, 26–7, 29; discovers Wood's postcard, 30; alibi, 36; Marshall Hall questions, 36

Shaw, George Bernard, 150

Shawcross, Sir Hartley, QC: prosecutes Joyce, 147, 160–2, 164–5, 167, 170, 172; prosecutes Amery, 173; declines to prosecute *The Naked and the Dead*, 213

Shayler, David, 376, 387

Shearman, Sir Montague (Mr Justice), 120

Shepton Mallet Prison, Somerset, 144–5

Sheriffs' and Recorders' Fund, 13

Sherwood, Robert, 204

Sickert, Walter, 57

Silverman, Sidney, 177, 242

Simmons, Leon, 238

Simon, John, KC, 382

Singh, Udham, 143–4

Skardon, Captain William (Jim), 157, 159, 164

Slade, Gerald, KC: defends Joyce, 147, 160, 163–8, 170; character, 148; defends Amery, 173; on Joyce's posthumous reputation, 174

Smith, Chris, 311

Smith, Florence, 44

Smith, George ('Brides in the Bath'), 2, 47, 55

Smith, Detective Superintendent George Gordon, 262

Snowdon, Antony Armstrong-Jones, 1st Earl of, 271, 279, 296

Soham, Cambridgeshire: Holly Wells/Jessica Chapman murdered in, 347–9, 357, 359; buildings demolished, 372; effect and resonance of case, 374–6; *see also* Huntley, Ian

Solicitor General, 381

Somervell, Sir Donald, KC, 158

Soper, Donald, 242

Soskice, Sir Frank, QC, 207

Southworth, Jean, 226

Soviet Union: espionage in Britain, 248, 257; acquires nuclear weapons, 250

Spaghetti House restaurant, Knightsbridge, 386

Spectator (journal), 138–9, 339

Spencer, Harold Sherwood, 67–9, 74, 78–81, 86, 88–90

Speyer, Sir Edgar, 64

spies, 248–52, 256, 272, 383; *see also* espionage cases (Second World War)

Spilsbury, Sir Bernard, 105, 120, 133–4

Stagg, Colin, 2

Steel, David, 275, 307–8

Stephen, Michael Scott: relations with Elvira Barney, 124–5; shot dead, 125–7

Stevenson, Sir Melford (Mr Justice): leads defence of Ruth Ellis, 225, 228–31, 235; questions Cussen, 228–9; questions Ruth Ellis, 231–4; makes no closing speech at Ruth Ellis trial, 235; sentences Kray brothers, 383

Stocks, Mr (Emily Dimmock's landlord), 26–7

Stocks, Mrs (landlady), 26–9, 37

Stonehouse, John, 2, 268

Stopes, Marie: *Married Love*, 69

Strachey, John, 150

Stratton, Chief Inspector David, 252–3, 257–9

Strauss, Richard: *Salome* (opera), 61

Sullivan, Serjeant Alexander Martin, 148 summing-up, 397–8

Sun (newspaper), 339

Sunday Dispatch, 138–9

Sunday Express, 98, 311

Sunday Mirror, 223, 311

Sunday Pictorial, 201

Sunday Telegraph, 3, 9, 281, 288, 291

Sunday Times, 279, 320

Sutcliffe, Peter, 2, 19, 345, 381

Swaffer, Hannen, 139

Swift, Jonathan: *Gulliver's Travels*, 396

Swift, Sir Rigby (Mr Justice), 101, 108

Taylor, Peter, QC: prosecutes in Thorpe trial, 31, 283, 285, 301; calls Bessell in court, 286; questions Scott in court, 292–3, 296; questions Newton, 297; closing speech, 301–3

Teare, Dr Donald (pathologist), 186, 199, 203

10 Rillington Place (film), 188

terrorism cases: tried in Court No. Two, 4, 385; Islamist and right-wing fundamentalist, 387

Thatcher, Margaret, 283

This Week (TV programme), 270

Thompson, Douglas, 287

Thompson, Edith: tried in Court No. One, 2, 5, 9; effect of trial and execution, 8; public at trial, 8; screams innocence in court, 11; charged with Bywaters for murder of husband, 100, 119–21; affair with Bywaters, 119; Curtis-Bennett defends, 119; fantasises about poisoning husband in letters, 120; insists on giving

evidence in court, 120; found guilty and executed, 121–2, 138, 240
Thompson, Jeremy, 349
Thompson, Dr John, 29, 37, 44
Thompson, Percy, 119
Thompson, PC, 222, 230
Thorpe, Caroline (née Allpass; Jeremy's first wife), 275
Thorpe, Jeremy: tried in Court No. One, 2; acquitted, 10, 307; Sybille Bedford fails to write on, 15; quarrels with Scott, 173–4; Carman defends, 268–9, 281, 285, 299, 301–3; in 'Trial of the Century', 268, 281, 283, 302; background and career, 270–1; character and personality, 270–1; as Liberal MP, 270–1; homosexuality, 272, 295–6; meets Norman Scott and begins affair, 272–3; political activities and friendships, 274; succeeds Jo Grimond as Party leader, 274; first marriage (to Caroline), 275; breakdown, 276; pays Scott's divorce costs, 276, 297; plans elimination of Scott, 276; Scott threatens, 276; second marriage (to Marion Stein), 276; and assassination attempt on Scott, 278; betrays Bessell over blackmail letter, 279; resigns as party leader, 279; charged with incitement to murder, 280; persuaded not to give evidence in trial, 282–3; loses parliamentary seat (1979), 283; behaviour in court, 284; and Dinshaw's passing money to Holmes, 300; prosecution closes case, 301; Carman on, 304; taken to Brixton prison awaiting verdict, 307; post-trial behaviour, 308; retirement, Parkinson's disease and death, 309–10; effect of trial, 310–11; press attitude to, 311; In My Own Time, 309–10
Thorpe, Marion (earlier Stein; Jeremy's second wife): marriage to Jeremy, 276; present at Jeremy's trial, 284, 295; at Jeremy's acquittal, 307; denies Jeremy's homosexuality, 311
Thorpe, Rupert (Jeremy's son), 275
Thorpe, Ursula (née Norton-Griffiths; Jeremy's mother), 284, 292, 295
Times, The, 57, 72, 78, 121, 139, 202, 311
Tonight with Trevor Macdonald (TV programme), 349
'Torso murders', 186–7, 200
Travis, Alan, 213
Treasury Counsel system, 380

Tree, Helen Maude (Mrs Beerbohm Tree), 54
Trial and Error: performed in Court No. One, 13
trials: adversarial system, 8, 16, 209, 394–5; public interest in, 9; by jury, 389, 401
Tubby, Debbie, 351
Tucker, Sir Frederick (Mr Justice): tries Joyce case, 148, 164, 166, 168–9
Turing, Alan, 211
Tutankhamun: tomb discovered, 98

United States of America: servicemen in Britain in Second World War, 144
Ustinov, Peter, 309

Valentino, Rudolph, 117
Van de Vater, Norman, 272–3, 293–4, 296
Van der Elst, Violet, 242
Van Druten, John: Somebody Knows (play), 58
Variety (magazine), 70
Vassall, John, 3, 248, 253–5, 258, 260, 262, 272, 383
Vaughan, Sir John (Lord Chief Justice), 339
verdicts, 397–8
Verona Project, 248
Vigilante (magazine; earlier Imperialist), 66–9, 71
Vigilantes Society, 66, 89–90
Villiers-Stuart, Eileen (née Graves): and Billing libel case, 71–2, 74, 77–8, 83–5, 89; convicted of bigamy, 90
Villiers-Stuart, Captain Percival, 72
Vision of Salome, The (dance version of Wilde's play), 61
Volchkov, Lieutenant Colonel Alexander, 392

Waddington, David, 325
Wade, Hugh, 123, 125
Wade, PC Tim, 354
Wadham, John, 322, 329, 331–4
Walmsley, Paul, 364
Walter, Nicolas, 332
War Crimes Act (1991), 345–6
Ward, Stephen: trial in Court No. One, 2–4, 7, 266, 383; public at trial, 8; Sybille Bedford fails to publish account of, 15; literature on, 19; Burge defends, 147, 266; Griffith-Jones prosecutes, 214; conviction and death, 247; and Christine Keeler, 249
Warren, Gladys, 31

Watkins, Sir Tasker, VC (Lord Justice), 325–7

Watts, Detective Inspector Rollo, 320, 323, 325–7, 332, 340

Waugh, Auberon: reports on Thorpe case, 277, 283–6, 292–3, 299, 301, 310; on Cantley's summing-up, 306; on gay dogs, 311; promises revelations on Thorpe, 311; praises Mathew's advocacy, 312; on acquittal of Randle and Pottle, 339; *The Last Word*, 15, 302, 308

Webb, Duncan, 226, 239

Wells family, 347

Wells, Holly: disappears, 347–9; rumoured sightings, 350–1; body found, 354; memorial service, 359; Huntley's account of death, 365–6; *see also* Huntley, Ian

Wells, Kevin (Holly's father), 347–9, 351, 355, 357–61, 364, 366, 368, 371–4, 376; *Goodbye, Dearest Holly*, 374

Wells, Nicola (Holly's mother), 347–8, 362, 371, 374

West, John, 243

West, Rebecca: account of Joyce trial, 14, 146, 148–9, 153, 166; on Quentin Joyce, 165; on Joyce's interest in trial proceedings, 168; on Joyce's appeal to Lords, 170; on Christmas Humphreys, 186; attends trial of Donald Hume, 201; condemns Fuchs, 250; *The Meaning of Treason*, 147

Western Brothers (entertainers), 154

Westgate (abusive caller in Soham case), 359

Wethersfield Six trial, 341

Whicker, Alan, 173

'White Slave Murders', 144

Whittaker, Dr Duncan, 234

Widgery, John Passmore, Baron (Lord Chief Justice), 385

Wilde, Oscar: libel action against Queensberry, 63, 70; Lord Alfred Douglas denounces, 82; conviction and public reaction to, 91; posthumous reputation, 92; defended by Sir Edward Clarke, 100; effect of trial, 126; *De Profundis* (letter), 62; *Salome* (play), 60–1, 68, 76, 87

Wildeblood, Peter, 212, 223; *Against the Law*, 212

Wilder, Billy, 10, 382

Williams, Gareth, QC: defends Deakin in Thorpe trial, 280, 282, 293, 298–91, 303

Wilson, Harold, 279, 287, 323, 383

Wilson, Jock, 326

Wiltshire, Professor Patricia, 363

witchcraft trial, 382

Witness for the Prosecution (film), 10, 382

Witness Service, 13

witnesses: coaching forbidden, 130

Witney, George, 383

women: as Old Bailey judges, 6; jurors, 101; attend Edith Thompson–Bywaters trial, 121; hanged, 240

Wood, George (Robert's father), 46

Wood, Robert: photograph of, 1; tried for Camden Town murder, 23, 45, 204; defended by Marshall Hall, 24–6, 56–7; appearance and character, 27, 34, 56; meets Emily Dimmock, 27–8, 31, 43; postcard to Emily found, 30; relations with Ruby Young, 30; arrested, 31–2; given financial support, 32; prosecution case against, 32, 35; supposed unusual gait, 32, 35, 40–2, 46, 48, 51; pleads not guilty, 34; and Roberts' testimony, 38; alibi, 46; gives evidence, 47–50; denies murder, 48; and judge's summing-up, 52–3; sketching during trial, 53; composure in court, 54; found not guilty, 54, 58; changes name after acquittal, 55; popular support for, 56; Hall Caine on, 59

Woolf, Virginia, 122

World (newspaper), 69

Wormwood Scrubs prison, London, 313, 317

Wright, Rob and Trudie, 347

Yarmouth murder case (1901), 47

Yates, Nathan, 349–50, 354, 357

Young, Filson, 121

Young, Ruby, 30–2, 35, 43–4, 50–1, 56

Yule, Gladys, 222

Zander, Michael, 342